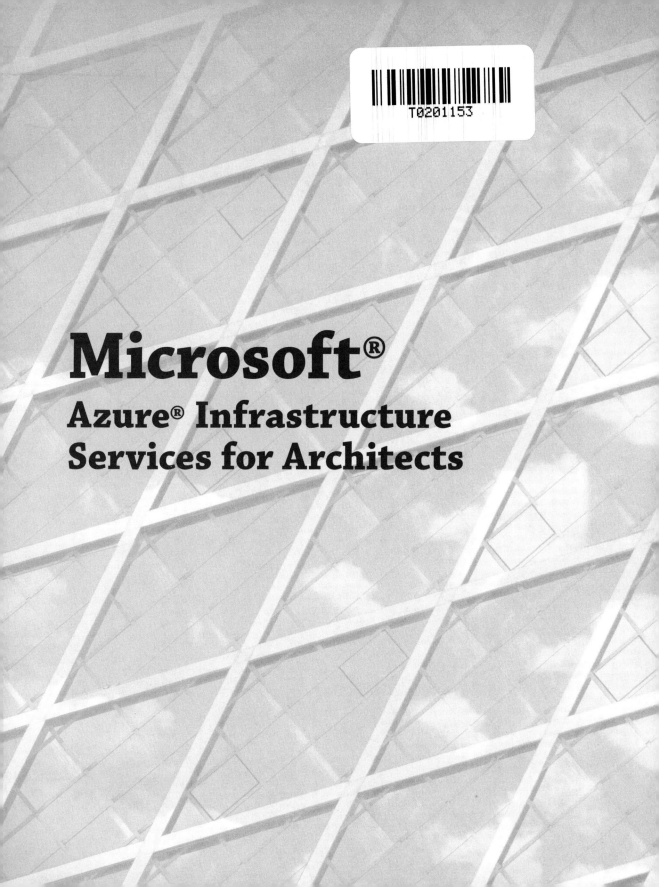

Microsoft®
Azure® Infrastructure
Services for Architects

Microsoft®
Azure® Infrastructure Services for Architects Designing Cloud Solutions

John Savill

SYBEX®
A Wiley Brand

For my wife, Julie, and my children, Abby, Ben, and Kevin

Acknowledgments

I could not have written this book without the help and support of many people. First, I need to thank my wife, Julie, for putting up with me for the last 6 months being busier than usual and for picking up the slack and for always supporting the crazy things I want to do! My children, Abby, Ben, and Kevin always make all the work worthwhile and can always make me see what is truly important with a smile.

Of course, the book wouldn't be possible at all without the Wiley team: Kenyon Brown, the acquisitions editor; Janet Wehner, the project editor; Christine O'Connor, the production editor; John Sleeva, the copyeditor; and Nancy Carrasco, the proofreader.

Many people have helped me over the years with encouragement and technical knowledge, and this book is the sum of that. The following people helped with specific aspects of this book, and I want to call them out for helping make this book as good as possible: Alex Shteynberg, Alexander Frankel, Ali Mazaheri, Anavi Nahar, Andrew Mason, Anuj Chaudhary, Ashish Jain, Bala Natarajan, Brian Tirch, Charles Joy, Christina Compy, Cosmos Darwin, Daniel Savage, David Berg, David Browne, David Powell, Derek Martin, Doug Lora, Elisabeth Olson, Gunjan Jain, Jason Hendrickson, Jeff Cohen, Jeff Peterson, Jim Benton, Jose Rojas, Kiran Madnani, Klaas Langhout, Larry Claman, Marc Kean, Maria Lai, Markus Hain, Mark Russinovich, Mike Stephens, Mutlu Kurtoglu, Rajat Luthra, Ramiro Calderon, Randy Haagens, Raphael Chacko, Reed Rector, Rena Shah, Rich Thorn, Rimma Nehme, Rochak Mittal, Sadie Henry, Satya Vel, Simon Gurevich, Sibonay Koo, Steve Espinosa, Steve Linehan, Sujay Talasila, Thomas Weiss, Trinadh Kotturu, Tyler Fox, Varun Shandilya, Yugang Wang, Yunus Emre Alpozen, Yves Pitsch, and Zif Rafalovich. If I've missed anyone, I'm truly sorry.

About the Author

John Savill is a technical specialist who focuses on Microsoft core infrastructure technologies, including Microsoft Azure, Windows, Hyper-V, and anything that does something cool. He has been working with Microsoft technologies for over 20 years and was the creator of the highly popular NT FAQ website. He has written eight previous books, covering Azure, Hyper-V, Windows, and advanced Active Directory architecture. When he is not writing books, he regularly writes magazine articles and whitepapers, creates a large number of technology videos, which are available on his YouTube channel, https://www.youtube.com/ntfaqguy, and regularly presents online and at industry-leading events. John has a large library of technical learning materials available via Pluralsight (https://www.pluralsight.com/authors/john-savill), including entire tracks focused on identity, infrastructure, data, and more in the Microsoft cloud.

Outside of technology, John enjoys fitness training, including weightlifting and cardio to help prepare for his full IRONMAN triathlon events. John has completed 12 full IRONMAN events and while writing this book is busy training for IRONMAN Texas, Canada, and Maryland, for which he has signed up to complete in 2019 (hopefully).

John tries to update his blog at https://savilltech.com/ with the latest news of what he is working on and tweets at https://twitter.com/NTFAQGuy.

Contents at a Glance

Contents

Introduction

The book you are holding is the result of my 25 years of experience in the IT world, including 20 years of virtualization experience, which started with VMware, Virtual PC, and now Hyper-V, and many years focusing on public cloud solutions, especially Microsoft Azure. My goal for this book is simple: to make you knowledgeable and effective architecting an Azure-based infrastructure. If you look at the scope of Microsoft Azure functionality, a single book would be the size of the *Encyclopedia Britannia* to cover it, so my focus for this book is the infrastructure-related services, including VMs in Azure, storage, networking, and some complementary technologies. Additionally, the focus is on architecting a solution. I will also show how to automate processes using technologies such as templates and PowerShell/CLI, how to integrate Azure with your on-premises infrastructure to create a hybrid solution, and even how to use Azure as a disaster recovery solution.

There is a huge amount of documentation for each feature of Azure. The documentation walks through each feature's basic functionality and provides step-by-step instructions for the basic deployment. When performed through the GUI, these steps often change, as interfaces continue to evolve. Additionally, as this book will show, while the portal is great for learning about the options, you won't be using it for production deployments, preferring instead to use prescriptive technologies like templates. Therefore, the goal of this book is to help you understand the options, to understand how to use them as part of a solution to meet requirements, to enable architectures to be created using the right components, with best practices developed over years of working with many Fortune 500 organizations. Yes, this book will expose you to all the important Azure infrastructure services, but it will focus on providing real value to enable the most complete and optimal utilization of Azure. It will focus on walkthroughs only for more involved or complex scenarios where they really provide value. But don't worry—the basic step-by-steps will still be referenced so that you can easily find them.

Microsoft is one of only three vendors with a solution in the public cloud IaaS Gartner Magic Quadrant as a leader in addition to being used by many of the largest companies in the world and I will cover this in more detail in Chapter 12.

I am a strong believer that doing an action is the best way to learn something, so I encourage you to try out all the technologies and principles I cover in this book. Because Azure is a public cloud solution, you don't need any local resources except for a machine to connect to Azure. You can even run command-line interfaces (CLIs) directly within the Azure portal environment. Ideally, you will also have an on-premises lab environment to test the networking to Azure and hybrid scenarios. However, you don't need a huge lab environment; for most of the items, you could use a single machine with Windows Server installed on it and with 8 GB of memory to enable a few virtual machines to run concurrently. As previously mentioned, sometimes

I provide step-by-step instructions to guide you through a process; sometimes I link to an external source that already has a good step-by-step guide; and sometimes I link to videos I have posted to ensure maximum understanding.

This book was one of the most challenging I've written. Because Azure is updated so frequently, it was necessary to update the book while writing, as capabilities would change. The Microsoft product group teams helped greatly, giving me early access to information and even environments to enable the book to be as current as possible. To keep the content relevant, I will be releasing a digital supplement and updating it as required. This will be available, along with any sample code, video links, and other assets, on the books GitHub page at:

```
https://github.com/johnthebrit/MasterIaaS2019
```

As you read each chapter, look at the GitHub repository for videos and other information that will help your understanding, as I do not specifically call these references out in the text of the book. The main page shows how to get a local copy of the repository, which has the benefit of making it easy to get updates as they occur.

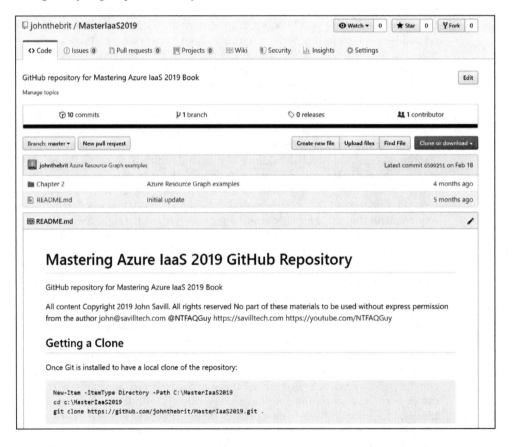

Who Should Read This Book

I am making certain assumptions regarding the reader:

◆   You have basic knowledge about and can install Windows Server.

◆   You have basic knowledge of what PowerShell is.

◆   You have access to the Internet and can sign up for a trial Azure subscription.

This book is intended for anyone who wants to learn Azure Infrastructure services, but it is really focused on exposing the options and offering guidance on architecting solutions. If you have basic knowledge of Azure, that will help, but it is not a requirement. I start off with a foundational understanding of each technology and then build on that to cover more advanced topics and configurations. If you are an architect, a consultant, an administrator, or really anyone who just wants a better knowledge of Azure Infrastructure, this book is for you.

There are many times I go into advanced topics that may seem over your head, in which case don't worry. Focus on the preceding elements you understand, implement and test them, and solidify your understanding. Then, when you feel comfortable, come back to the more advanced topics, which will seem far simpler.

There are various Azure exams. The most relevant to this book are AZ-100 and AZ-101 (replacing the old 70-533 exam), which, when passed, give the participant the Azure Administrator Associate certification:

```
https://www.microsoft.com/en-us/learning/azure-administrator.aspx
```

Additionally, exams AZ-300 and AZ-301 (replacing the old 70-534 exam), when passed, give the Azure Solutions Architect Expert certification:

```
https://www.microsoft.com/en-us/learning/azure-solutions-architect.aspx
```

Will this book help you pass the exams? Yes, it will help. I took the exams for both certifications cold, without knowing what was in the exams and without any study, and I passed. Since most of my Azure brain is in this book, it will help. However, I advise you to look at the areas covered in the exams and use this book as one resource to help, but also use other resources that Microsoft references on the exam site. This is especially true of the architect certification, which includes a significant amount of content of application and database concepts, which I cover in this book only at a very high level.

What's Inside

Here is a glance at what's in each chapter.

Chapter 1, "The Cloud and Microsoft Azure Fundamentals," provides an introduction to all types of cloud services and then dives into specifics about Microsoft's Azure-based offerings. After an overview of how Azure is acquired and used, the Infrastructure as a Service (IaaS) will be introduced, with a focus on what is really the difference between a best-effort and a reliable service and why best-effort may be better!

Chapter 2, "Governance," focuses on the first item companies must consider and address before using any service, including the public cloud and Azure. This chapter focuses on key concepts around Azure Resource Manager, understanding core governance around structure, role-based access control, naming, policy, cost and more.

Chapter 3, "Identity," addresses the next consideration for service usage, understanding identity. This chapter walks through the importance of identity in the public cloud and how it becomes the key security perimeter for many services. Azure AD will be introduced, along with its population and authentication options.

Chapter 4, "Identity Security and Extended Identity Services," builds on the previous chapter by looking at key security capabilities with Azure AD and how AD can be extended into the public cloud in a secure manner. Other identity services for custom applications will be explored.

Chapter 5, "Networking," explores offering services running in Azure out to Internet-based consumers. It looks at key concepts such as endpoints to offer services and also providing load balanced services for greater service availability. Virtual Networks provide a construct to enable customizable IP space configurations that are used by many services in Azure. This chapter dives into architecting, configuring, and managing virtual networks. Finally, various types of connectivity between virtual networks and on premises are explored.

Chapter 6, "Storage," examines the core capabilities of storage accounts in Azure and then walks through the storage capabilities used by infrastructure services in Azure, including managed disks. Services for large-scale data import and export are introduced.

Chapter 7, "Azure Compute," starts by introducing virtual machines, the building block of nearly every Azure service, including their key capabilities, before moving on to more advanced concepts around availability and placement. An introduction to some of the Platform as a Service offerings is provided to provide a complete knowledge for architects for the key available options.

Chapter 8, "Azure Stack," explores the on-premises Azure capability through partner appliances, including key scenarios and architecture considerations. Key concepts such as plans and offers will be covered, including how to manage the marketplace.

Chapter 9, "Backup, High Availability, Disaster Recovery, and Migration," starts by looking at key requirements for disaster recovery and some of the key considerations to architect a successful disaster recovery plan. A number of technologies commonly used for disaster recovery will be explored, including types of replication and service provisioning. The orchestration of a failover is explored using recovery plans. Finally, the chapter examines the same technologies used for replication that can also be used in combination with other capabilities for migration purposes. Finally, the chapter introduces backup capabilities and discusses best practices for their usage.

Chapter 10, "Monitoring and Security," dives into Azure services related to monitoring, enabling complete insight into the entire Azure-based solution. Key security services that are not covered elsewhere in the book are also covered.

Chapter 11, "Managing Azure," looks at the right way to manage Azure. This includes command-line interfaces, scripting and automation, and using templates for resource provisioning. A number of management services to enhance the overall solution are covered, including some seamless options to connect to Azure-based virtual machines.

Chapter 12, "What to Do Next," brings everything together and looks at how to get started with Azure, how to plan next steps, how to stay up-to-date in the rapidly changing world of Azure, and the importance of overall integration.

How to Contact the Author

I welcome your feedback about this book or about books you'd like to see from me in the future. You can reach me by writing to john@savilltech.com. For more information about my work, visit my website at https://savilltech.com.

Sybex strives to keep you supplied with the latest tools and information you need for your work. Please check their website at www.wiley.com/go/sybextestprep, where we'll post additional content and updates that supplement this book, should the need arise.

Chapter 1

The Cloud and Microsoft Azure Fundamentals

This chapter focuses on changes that are impacting every organization's thinking regarding infrastructure, datacenters, and ways to offer services. "As a Service" offerings—both on premises and hosted by partners, and accessed over the Internet in the form of the public cloud—present new opportunities for organizations.

Microsoft's solution for many public cloud services is its Azure service, which offers hundreds of capabilities that are constantly being updated. This chapter will provide an overview of the Microsoft Azure solution stack before examining various types of Infrastructure as a Service (IaaS) and how Azure services can be procured.

In this chapter, you will learn to:

♦ Articulate the different types of "as a Service."

♦ Identify key scenarios where the public cloud provides the most optimal service.

♦ Understand how to get started consuming Microsoft Azure services.

The Evolution of the Datacenter

When I talk to people about Azure or even the public cloud in general, where possible, I start the conversation by talking about their on-premises deployments and the requirements that drove the existing architecture. For most companies, needs have changed radically over recent years to meet both customer and employee requirements. Employees expect to be able to work anywhere, from anything, using a large number of cloud-based services. Customers are similar, wanting engaging digital experiences across devices that use existing social identities where practical. Organizations are looking to digitally transform and focus on creating only what helps differentiate themselves in the market through accelerated innovation. For organizations, this means more agility and the capability to Elastically scale, potentially globally. Additionally, these drivers often mean getting out of the datacenter business in favor of cloud service utilization, which enables a greater focus on the application and optimized IT spend, all while dealing with new security implications. As organizations embrace cloud services, a complete rethinking is required, as the network can no longer be a trusted boundary since many services will live outside the corporate network. Instead of thinking of the corporate network as this completely trusted area that is impenetrable at the network edge, the focus shifts to identity as the new security perimeter, while a zero-trust model is increasingly common for the network.

But I am getting ahead of myself, and I like to start off with an interesting use case of the cloud that pre-cloud would have been very difficult.

Video gaming is a hugely popular industry. Many games today host massive, multiplayer environments that need additional resources, such as storage and compute, to deliver the best experience. These resources will have huge spikes in demand that vary around the world, and to enhance rather than degrade the user experience, they need to be close to the player to reduce latency. A great example of this is Halo, which I've been playing since its first version on the original Xbox. Gaming resource requirements are opposite to many other industries. Most services start out and grow over time, requiring more resources (that the cloud is great for); however, games are the opposite. When a game releases, it tends to require huge amounts of resources for the first few weeks and then sees a significant ramp down. Before the cloud, game services would have to build huge datacenters with a lot of resources that would sit largely idle after the first few weeks. With the cloud, 1000s of cores can be used for services then scale down to 100s. Halo game services use Azure for several services, including statistics, which are a huge part of gaming that track every activity the player performs, providing end of game summaries and overall player history. The elasticity of the cloud enables Halo to access the resources as required to provide an amazing player and community experience while optimizing their costs to only pay for what they need, when they need it.

Introducing the Cloud

Every organization has some kind of IT infrastructure. It could be a server sitting under someone's desk, geographically distributed datacenters the size of multiple football fields, or something in between. Within that infrastructure are a number of key fabric (physical infrastructure) elements:

Compute Capacity   Compute capacity can be thought of in terms of the various servers in the datacenter, which consist of processors, memory, storage controllers, network adapters, and other hardware (such as the motherboard, power supply, and so on). These resources provide a server with a finite amount of resources, which includes computation, memory capacity, network bandwidth, and storage throughput (in addition to other characteristics). I will use the term *compute* throughout this book when referring to server capacity.

Storage   A persistent method of storage for data—from the operating system (OS) and applications to pure data, such as files and databases—must be provided. Storage can exist within a server or in external devices, such as a storage area network (SAN). SANs provide enterprise-level performance and capabilities, although newer storage architectures that leverage local storage, known as *hyper-converged*, which in turn replicate data, are becoming more prevalent in datacenters. Additionally, non-persistent, aka ephemeral, storage is available for most resources.

Network   These components connect the various elements of the datacenter and enable client devices to communicate with hosted services. Connectivity to other datacenters may also be part of the network design. Options such as dedicated fiber connections, Multiprotocol Label Switching (MPLS), and Internet connectivity via a DMZ are typical. Other types of resources, such as firewalls, load balancers, and gateways, are likely used in addition to technologies to segment and isolate parts of the network—for example, VLANs.

Datacenter Infrastructure   An often overlooked but critical component of datacenters is the supporting infrastructure. Items such as uninterruptable power supplies (UPSs), air conditioning, the physical building, and even generators all have to be considered. Each consumes energy and impacts the efficiency of the datacenter as well as its power usage effectiveness (PUE), which provides a measure of how much energy a datacenter uses for computer equipment compared to the other aspects. The lower the PUE, the more efficient the datacenter—or at least the more power going to the actual computing, reducing overall power consumption. An interesting point is that although power efficiency is important, there are other metrics starting to be discussed, such as water efficiency, which start to become more important when considering all the types of resources impacted by datacenters.

Once you have the physical infrastructure in place, you then add the actual software elements (the OS, applications, and services), and finally the management infrastructure, which enables deployment, patching, backup, automation, and monitoring. The IT team for an organization is responsible for all of these datacenter elements. The rise in the size and complexity of IT infrastructure is a huge challenge for nearly every organization. Despite the fact that most IT departments see budget cuts year after year, they are expected to deliver more and more as IT becomes increasingly critical. With digital transformation, the business expects more agility for IT resources, enabling new offerings to be created and deployed quickly with potentially highly elastic compute needs throughout the world.

Not only is the amount of IT infrastructure increasing but that infrastructure needs to be resilient. This typically means implementing disaster recovery (DR) solutions to provide protection from a complete site failure, such as one caused by a large-scale natural disaster. If you ignore the public cloud, your organization will need to lease space from a co-location facility or set up a new datacenter. When I talk to CIOs, one of the things at the top of the *don't-want-to-do* list is write out more checks for datacenters—in fact, write out *any* checks for datacenters is on that list.

In the face of increased cost pressure and the desire to be more energy and water responsible (green), datacenter design becomes ever more complex, especially in a world with virtualization. If the three critical axes of a datacenter (shown in Figure 1.1) are not properly thought out, your organization's datacenters will never be efficient. You must consider the square footage of the actual datacenter, the kilowatts that can be consumed per square foot, and the amount of heat that can be dissipated, expressed in BTU per hour.

FIGURE 1.1
The three axes of
datacenter planning

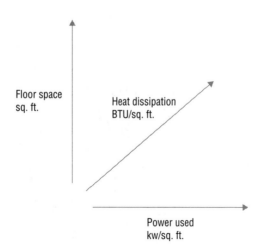

If you get any of these calculations wrong, you end up with a datacenter you cannot fully use because you can't get enough power to it, can't keep it cool enough, or simply can't fit enough equipment in it. As the compute resources become denser and consume more power, it's critical that datacenters supply enough power and have enough cooling to keep servers operating within their environmental limits. I know of a number of datacenters that are only 50 percent full because they cannot provide enough power to fully utilize available space. It's also critical to plan for the power resiliency as if you want resilient power, and then that may double the overall power requirements of a facility and if that is neglected, then once again you can only half fill the datacenter if you want to meet the power redundancy requirements. Not a good day!

The Private Cloud and Virtualization

In the early 2000s, as organizations looked to better use their available servers and enjoy other benefits, such as faster provisioning, virtualization became a key technology in every datacenter. When I look back to my early days as a consultant, I remember going through sizing exercises for a new Microsoft Exchange server deployment. When sizing the servers required that I consider the busiest possible time and also the expected increase in utilization of the lifetime of the server (for example, five years), the server was heavily overprovisioned, which meant it was also highly underutilized. Underutilization was a common situation for most servers in a datacenter, and it was typical to see servers running at 5 percent. It was also common to see provisioning times of up to 6 weeks for a new server, which made it hard for IT to react dynamically to changes in business requirements.

Virtualization enables a single physical server to be divided into one or more virtual machines through the use of a *hypervisor*. The virtual machines are completely abstracted from the physical hardware; each virtual machine is allocated resources such as memory and processor in addition to virtualized storage and networking. Each of the virtual machines then can have an operating system installed, which enables multiple operating systems to run on a single piece of hardware. The operating systems may be completely unaware of the virtual nature of the environment they are running on. However, most modern operating systems are enlightened; they are aware of the virtual environment and actually optimize operations based on the presence of a hypervisor. Figure 1.2 shows a Hyper-V example leveraging the VHDX virtual hard disk format.

FIGURE 1.2
A high-level view of a virtualization host and resources assigned to virtual machines

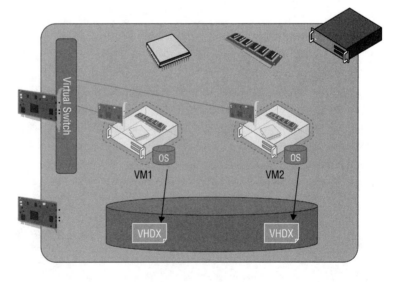

Virtualization has revolutionized the way datacenters operate and brought huge benefits, including the following:

High Utilization of Resources   Complementary workloads are hosted on a single physical environment.

Mobility of OS Instances Between Completely Different Hardware   A single hypervisor allows the abstraction of the physical hardware from the OS.

Potentially Faster Provisioning   Faster provisioning is dependent on processes in place, but the need to physically rack hardware for new environments can be removed with proper planning.

High Availability Through the Virtualization Solution   This ability is most useful when high availability is not natively available to the application.

Simplicity of Licensing for Some Products and OSs   For some products and OSs, the physical hardware is allowed to be licensed based on the number of processor sockets, and then an unlimited number of virtual machines on that hardware can use the OS/application. Windows Server Datacenter is an example of this kind of product. There is also an opposite situation for some products that are based on physical core licensing, which do not equate well in most virtualized environments.

There are other benefits. At a high level, if it were to be summed up in five words, I think "more bang for the buck" would work.

The potential of the datacenter capabilities can be better realized. The huge benefits of virtualization on their own do not completely revolutionize the datacenter. Many organizations have adopted virtualization but have then operated the datacenter as though each OS is still on dedicated hardware. New OS instances are provisioned with dedicated virtualization hosts and even dedicated storage for different projects, which has resulted in isolated islands of resources within the datacenter. Once again, resources were wasted and more complex to manage.

In this book, I'm going to talk a lot about "the cloud." But, for on-premises environments, I would be remiss if I didn't also talk about another big change—the private cloud. Some people will tell you that the private cloud was made up by hypervisor vendors to compete against and stay relevant in the face of the public cloud. Others say it's a revolutionary concept. I think I fall somewhere in the middle. The important point is that a private cloud solution has key characteristics and, when those are implemented, benefits are gained. This is an important point. You must have a solution that has these key characteristics, or at least some of them. Many customers tell me they have a private cloud when really, they just have a virtual environment—i.e., they use a hypervisor.

A customer once told me, "Ask five people what the private cloud is, and you will get seven different answers." While I think that is a true statement, the U.S. National Institute of Standards and Technology (NIST) lists what it considers to be the five critical characteristics that must be present to be a cloud. This applies to both private clouds and public clouds.

On-Demand Self-Service   The ability to provision services, such as a virtual machine, as needed without human interaction must be provided. Some organizations may add approval workflow for certain conditions.

Broad Network Access   Access to services over many types of networks, mobile phones, desktops, and so on must be provided.

Resource Pooling   Resources are organized in a multitenant model with isolation provided via software. This removes the islands of resources that are common when each business group has its own resources. Resource islands lead to inefficiency in utilization.

Rapid Elasticity   *Rapid elasticity* is the ability to scale rapidly outward and inward as demands on services change. The ability to achieve large-scale elasticity is tied to pooling all resources together to achieve a larger potential pool.

Measured Service   Clouds provide resources based on defined quotas, but they also enable reporting based on usage and potentially even billing.
The full document can be found here:

```
http://csrc.nist.gov/publications/nistpubs/800-145/SP800-145.pdf
```

People often say there is no difference between virtualization and the private cloud. That is not true. The difference is the management infrastructure for a private cloud enables the characteristics listed here. To implement a private cloud, you don't need to change your hardware, storage, or networking. The private cloud is enabled through software, which in turn enables processes. You may decide that you don't want to enable all capabilities initially. For example, many organizations are afraid of end-user self-service; they have visions of users running amok and creating thousands of virtual machines. Once they understand quotas and workflows, and approvals, they understand that they have far more control and accountability than manual provisioning provided.

ENTER THE PUBLIC CLOUD

The private cloud, through enhanced management processes and virtualization, brings a highly optimized on-premises solution. Ultimately, it still consists of resources that the organization owns and must house the resources year-round in a finite number of locations. As I mentioned earlier, CIOs don't like writing checks for datacenters, no matter how optimal. All the optimization in the world cannot counter the fact that there are some scenarios where hosting on premises is not efficient or even logical.

The public cloud represents services offered by an external party that can be accessed over the Internet. The services are not limited and can be purchased as you consume the service. This is a key difference from an on-premises infrastructure. With the public cloud, you pay only for the amount of service you consume when you use it. For example, I pay only for the amount of storage I am using at any moment in time; the charge does not include the potential amount of storage I may need in a few years' time. I pay only for the virtual machines I need turned on right now; I can increase the number of virtual machines when I need them and pay only for those extra virtual machines while they are running.

TURN IT OFF!

In Azure, virtual machines are billed on a per-second basis. If I run an 8-vCPU virtual machine for 12 hours each month, then I pay only the cost for 12 hours of runtime. Note that for the majority of VM types, it does not matter how busy the VM is (the exception being the B-series, which I'll cover later). You pay the same price whether the vCPUs in the VM are running at 100 percent or 1 percent processor utilization. It's important to shut down and deprovision from the Azure fabric any virtual machines that are not required to avoid paying for resources you don't need. (*Deprovision* just means the virtual machine no longer has compute resources reserved in the Azure fabric.) The virtual machine can be restarted when you need it again. No state would be lost as the storage is kept; only the VM is re-created. At that point, resources are allocated in the fabric automatically; the VM will start as expected. It is also for this reason a lot of small VMs are preferred over a few large VMs, more granular control of services provisioned. Note that if you only shut down an OS from within the guest, you are not deprovisioning the VM—the resources are still reserved on the fabric. To deprovision, you need to shut down from the portal, PowerShell, CLI, or the REST API.

In addition to the essentially limitless capacity, this pay-as-you-go model is what sets the public cloud apart from on-premises solutions. Think back to organizations needing DR services. Using the public cloud ensures there are minimal costs for providing disaster recovery. During normal operations, you only pay for the storage used by the workload and replication licensing used for the replication of state and possible virtual environments like virtual networks. Only in the case of an actual disaster would you start the virtual machines in the public cloud. You stop paying for them when you can fail back to on premises.

There are other types of charges associated with the public cloud. For example, Azure does not charge for ingress bandwidth (data sent into Azure—Microsoft is fully invested in letting you get as much data into Azure as possible), but there are charges for egress (outbound) data. There are different tiers of storage, some of which are geo-replicated, so your data in Azure is stored at two datacenters that may be hundreds of miles apart. I will cover the pricing in more detail later in the book, but the common theme is you pay only for what you use.

If most organizations' IT requirements were analyzed, you would find many instances where resource requirements for a particular service are not flat. In fact, they vary greatly at different times of the day, week, month, or year. There are systems that perform end-of-month batch processing. These are idle all month, and then consume huge amounts of resources for one day at the end of the month. There are companies (think tax accountants) that are idle for most of the year but that are very busy for 2 months. There may be services that need huge amounts of resources for a few weeks every four years, like those that stream the Olympics. The list of possible examples is endless.

 **Real World Scenario**

SUPER BOWL SUNDAY AND THE AMERICAN LOVE OF PIZZA

I'll be up front; I'm English and I don't understand the American football game. I watched the 2006 Super Bowl. After 5 hours of 2 minutes of action, a 5-minute advertising break, and a different set of players moving a couple of yards, it'll be hard to get me to watch it again. Nonetheless, it's popular in America. As Americans watch the Super Bowl, they like to eat pizza, and what's interesting is the Super Bowl represents a perfect storm for pizza-ordering peaks. During the Super Bowl halftime and quarter breaks, across the entire United States, with all four time zones in sync, people order pizza. These three spikes require 50 percent more compute power for ordering and processing than a typical Friday dinnertime, the normal high point for pizza ordering.

Most systems are built to handle the busiest time, so our pizza company would have to provision compute capacity of 50 percent more than would ever normally be needed just for Super Bowl Sunday. Remember that this is 50 percent more than the Friday dinnertime requirement, which itself is much higher than is needed any other time of the week. This would be a hugely expensive and wasteful exercise. Instead Azure is used.

During normal times, there could be 10 web instances and 10 application instances handling the website and processing. On Friday nights between 2 p.m. and midnight, this increases to 20 instances of each role. On Super Bowl Sunday between noon and 5 p.m., this increases to 30 instances of each role. Granted, I'm making up the numbers, but the key here is the additional instances only exist when needed, and therefore the customer is charged extra only when the additional resources are needed. This elasticity is key to public cloud services.

To be clear, I totally understand the eating pizza part!

The pizza scenario is a case of predictable bursting, where there is a known period of increased utilization. It is one of the scenarios that is perfect for cloud computing. Figure 1.3 shows the four main scenarios in which cloud computing is the clear right choice. Many other scenarios work great in the cloud, but these four are uniquely solved in an efficient way through the cloud. I know many companies that have moved or are moving many of their services to the public cloud. It's cheaper than other solutions and offers great resiliency.

FIGURE 1.3
The key types of highly variable workloads that are a great fit for consumption-based pricing

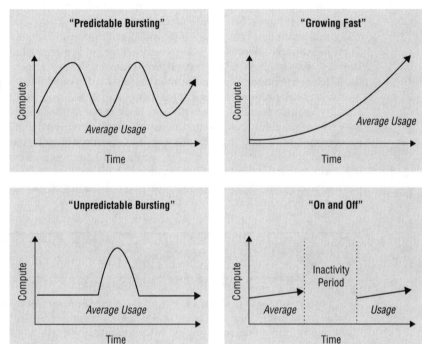

In a fast-growing scenario, a particular service's utilization is increasing rapidly. In this scenario, a traditional on-premises infrastructure may not be able to scale fast enough to keep up with demand. Leveraging the "infinite" scale of the public cloud removes the danger of not being able to keep up with demand.

Unpredictable bursting occurs when the exact timing of high usage cannot be planned. "On and Off" scenarios describe services that are needed at certain times but that are completely turned off at other times. This could be in the form of monthly batch processes where the processing runs for only 8 hours a month, or this could be a company such as a tax return accounting service that runs for 3 months out of the year.

Although these four scenarios are great for the public cloud, some are also a good fit for hybrid scenarios, where the complete solution has a mix of on premises and the public cloud. The baseline requirements could be handled on premises, but the bursts expand out to use the public cloud capacity.

For startup organizations, there is a saying: "fail fast." It's not that the goal of the startup is to fail, but rather, if it is going to fail, it's better to fail fast. Less money is wasted when compared to a long, drawn-out failure. The public cloud is a great option for startups because it means very little up-front capital spent buying servers and datacenter space. Instead, the startup just has operating expenditures for services it actually uses. This is why startups like services such as Microsoft Office 365 for their messaging and collaboration. Not only do they not need infrastructure, they don't need messaging administrators to maintain it. Public cloud IaaS is a great solution for virtual machines. Once again, no up-front infrastructure is required, and companies pay only for what they use. As the company grows and its utilization goes up, so does its operating expenditure, but the expenditure is proportional to the business. This type of pay-as-you-go solution is also attractive to potential financers, because there is less initial outlay and thus reduced risk.

Additionally, as you shall see, while VMs in the cloud are attractive, the reality is that there are vast numbers of different types of service available in the cloud that will enable companies to light up new capabilities faster and really focus on what they care about, without reinventing any wheels or maintaining layers of technology they don't care about. Because of the concentration of resources, and thereby economies of scale in cloud providers, a level of cost optimization and quality of service is possible that is hard to match for ordinary organizations. In early industrialization, the factories would have their own power generators; however, these were hard to maintain and of varying quality. Instead, power generation moved to utilities (starting with Edison's Pearl Street), which factories would leverage for a more reliable, better quality, and cheaper service. It is inevitable that compute for most companies will go the same way and that hosting services in their own datacenters, which is not the focus of their business, will fall to the side as services move to the cloud.

I see the public cloud used in many different ways today, and that adoption will continue to grow as organizations become more comfortable with using the public cloud and, ultimately, trust it. Key use cases today include but are not limited to the following:

Test and Development   Test and development is seen by many companies as "low-hanging fruit." It is less risky than production workloads and typically has a high amount of churn, meaning environments are created and deleted frequently. This translates to a lot of work for the IT teams unless the private cloud has been implemented.

Disaster Recovery   As discussed, for most companies a DR action should never be required. However, DR capability is required in that extremely rare event when it's needed. By using the public cloud, the cost to implement DR is minimal, especially when compared to costs of a second datacenter.

International DMZ   I have a number of companies that would like to offer services globally. This can be challenging—having datacenters in many countries is hugely expensive and can even be politically difficult. By using a public cloud that is geographically distributed, it's easy to offer services around the world with minimal latencies for the end users.

Special Projects and Highly Elastic Workloads   Imagine that you have a campaign or special analytics project that requires large amounts of infrastructure for a short period of time. The public cloud is perfect for this, especially when certain types of licensing (for example, SQL Server licensing) can be purchased as consumed and other resources are paid for only as required. Likewise, a workload that is highly elastic in resource requirements is a perfect fit for the consumption, pay-for-what-you-use, cloud model.

A Desire to Get Out of the Datacenter Business   I'm seeing more companies that just don't want to maintain datacenters anymore. These organizations will move as much as possible to the public cloud and maintain minimal on-premises infrastructure needed for certain services, such as domain controllers and file and print servers.

Moving to Platform as a Service and Beyond   If you only care about VMs, you have a choice. You can host them on premises, or you can host them in the cloud; however, as organizations want to focus just on the applications and not the underlying infrastructure and even to server-less technologies, that may be something that is not possible on premises but where the cloud and in this case Azure, really delivers.

Types of Service in the Cloud

Throughout this chapter, I have talked about making services available on premises with a private cloud and off-premises in the public cloud, but what exactly are these services? There are three primary types of service: Infrastructure as a Service (IaaS), Platform as a Service (PaaS), and Software as a Service (SaaS). For each type, the responsibilities of the nine major layers of management vary between the vendor of the service and the client (you). Figure 1.4 shows the three types of service and also a complete on-premises solution. There are many other types of "as a Service," but most of the other types of services use one of these three primary types. For example, Desktop as a Service really has IaaS as a foundation.

FIGURE 1.4
The responsibility levels for different types of "as a Service"

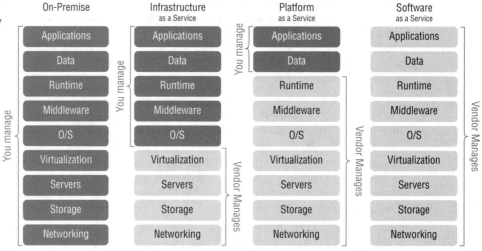

Note while this helps you to understand the basic differences of responsibility for the various types of as a Service, it is not absolute. For example, Azure SQL Database is known as a platform service; however, you are not patching SQL Server nor worrying about backing up its data, which means technically it should be thought of as SaaS. However, the truest definition of the types of service takes a different approach. The reality is that, depending on how something is being used, it could be PaaS or SaaS.

The NIST definitions of SaaS, PaaS, and IaaS are as follows:

Software as a Service (SaaS)   The capability provided to the consumer is to use the provider's applications running on a cloud infrastructure. The applications are accessible from various client devices through either a thin client interface, such as a web browser (e.g., web-based email), or a program interface. The consumer does not manage or control the underlying cloud infrastructure, including network, servers, operating systems, storage, or even individual application capabilities, with the possible exception of limited user-specific application configuration settings.

Platform as a Service (PaaS) The capability provided to the consumer is to deploy onto the cloud infrastructure consumer-created or acquired applications created using programming languages, libraries, services, and tools supported by the provider. The consumer does not manage or control the underlying cloud infrastructure, including network, servers, operating systems, or storage, but has control over the deployed applications and possibly configuration settings for the application-hosting environment.

Infrastructure as a Service (IaaS) The capability provided to the consumer is to provision processing, storage, networks, and other fundamental computing resources where the consumer is able to deploy and run arbitrary software, which can include operating systems and applications. The consumer does not manage or control the underlying cloud infrastructure but has control over operating systems, storage, and deployed applications; and possibly limited control of select networking components (e.g., host firewalls).

The official NIST document related to cloud definitions can be found at:

`https://nvlpubs.nist.gov/nistpubs/Legacy/SP/nistspecialpublication800-145.pdf`

As you can see from this definition, something like Azure SQL Database would be more of a platform service when used as part of a solution, as the author does have control over the deployed solution and configurations. Another way to think about it is SaaS delivers a complete business function without requiring other software that leverages it, whereas PaaS provides technology functions that have to be utilized by other software running on top to provide business value. A user that opens a session to a database is unlikely to get much business function; we need applications on top.

IaaS can be thought of as a virtual machine in the cloud. The provider has a virtual environment, and you purchase virtual machine instances. You then manage the operating system, the patching, the data, and the applications within. Examples of IaaS include Amazon Elastic Compute Cloud (Amazon EC2) and Azure IaaS, which offer organizations the ability to run operating systems inside cloud-based virtual environments.

PaaS provides a framework where custom applications can be run. Organizations only need to focus on writing the very best application within the guidelines of the platform capabilities, and everything else is taken care of. There are no worries about patching operating systems, updating frameworks, backing up SQL databases, or configuring high availability. The organization just writes the application and pays for the resource used. Azure is the classic example of a PaaS solution that has numerous offerings, including web apps, containers, server-less offerings, data offerings, and much more.

SaaS is the ultimate in low maintenance. The complete solution is provided by the vendor. The organization has nothing to write or maintain other than configuring who should be allowed to use the software. `Outlook.com`, a messaging service, is an example of commercial SaaS. Office 365, which provides cloud-hosted Exchange, SharePoint, Skype, and many more services accessed over the Internet with no application or operating system management for the organization, is an enterprise example.

Ideally, for the lowest management overhead, SaaS should be used, and then PaaS where SaaS is not available. IaaS would be used only if PaaS is not an option. SaaS is gaining a great deal of traction with services such as Office 365. PaaS adoption, however, is fairly slow. The primary obstacle for PaaS is that applications have to be written within certain guidelines in order to operate in PaaS environments, although this varies greatly based on the type of PaaS service being used and in many cases there may not actually be any changes to code required. While we say PaaS with the very defined levels of responsibility, I actually think of more gradients based on the type of PaaS service utilized, which I want to briefly cover here.

Figure 1.5 gives some insight into how not every PaaS service falls into the very neat solid blue band of application and data only. For example, you can run containers in an Azure IaaS VM where you are still managing VMs but get certain optimization through containers and container images. You can move up the stack with Azure Kubernetes Service with aspects managed of the container orchestration solution; however, you still have certain responsibilities for the nodes, such as rebooting them after patching (the patches being applied as part of the solution). Then, with Azure Container Instances, you're not managing actual infrastructure but still have some decisions and possible involvement with the images used for the container, until moving into Application Services, where you truly start to focus only on the application. The only involvement with VMs is that you pick the scale and performance SKUs (which is what is paid for). Finally, at the top is server-less, where there is no concept of a VM for the service. Yes, they exist behind the scenes, but they are invisible to your usage, and you can pay only for the resources you actually consume. All of these are PaaS, but specific responsibilities do vary.

FIGURE 1.5
A more detailed view of responsibilities for different PaaS offerings

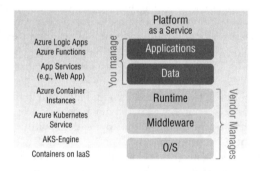

Many organizations have custom applications that cannot be modified. Others don't have the budget to change their applications, which is why IaaS is so popular. With IaaS, an existing virtual machine on premises can be moved to the IaaS solution fairly painlessly. In the long term, I think PaaS will become the standard for custom applications, especially with containers, but it will take a while. And although some thought containers would kill off the VM, I think in reality there is a place for both.

IaaS can help serve as the ramp to adopting PaaS. Consider a multitiered service that includes a web tier, an application tier, and a SQL database tier. Initially, all these tiers could run as IaaS virtual machines. The organization may then be able to convert the web tier from Internet Information Services (IIS) running in an IaaS VM and use the Azure web role, which is part of PaaS. Next, the organization may be able to move from SQL running in an IaaS VM to using SQL Azure. Finally, the organization could rewrite the application tier to directly leverage Azure PaaS. It's a gradual process, but the reduced overhead and increased functionality and resiliency at the end state are worth it.

I saw an interesting analogy using the various types of service put in the context of pizza services. (Yes, it's a second pizza example in one chapter; I like pizza.) Take a look at Figure 1.6. No matter where you plan to eat the pizza or how you plan to have it prepared, the actual pizza ingredients are the foundation. Other services and facilities, such as assembling the pizza, having an oven, cooking the pizza, having a table, and serving drinks, are also required. But as we move up the levels of service, we do less and less. At the highest level of service, pizza at a restaurant, we just eat and don't even have to wash up.

FIGURE 1.6
Various types of
Pizza as a Service

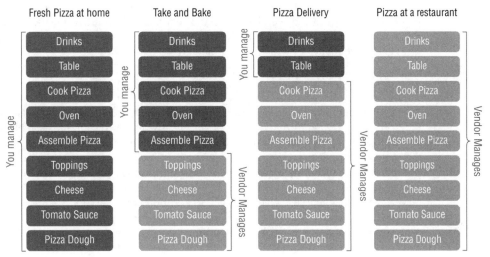

There is a key area in which the pizza analogy is not perfect. In the pizza world, as you progress up the service levels, the service gets better, but the total cost increases. When I make a pizza from scratch at home, it's cheaper than eating out at a restaurant. In the IT service space, this is likely not the case. From a total cost of ownership (TCO) for the solution, if I can buy a service like Office 365 as SaaS, that solution is likely cheaper than operating my own Exchange, SharePoint, and Skype solution on premises when you consider the server infrastructure, licenses, IT admin, and so on—plus, I get only a subset of what is possible with the Office 365 offering.

Microsoft Azure 101

Microsoft has many solutions in the public cloud that are actually enabled through a number of different cloud services, of which Microsoft Azure is just one. There are others, such as Office 365 and Dynamics 365, and then sovereign Azure clouds, such as U.S. Government, China, and Germany. The focus of this book is the Azure-related clouds, but all these different clouds are physically hosted on a core set of capacity (think compute) and network resources.

Microsoft Datacenters and Regions

While "the cloud" seems mysterious and magical and that things can just run there, the reality is that workloads have to run on servers, data has to be stored on storage, and networks need to connect resources. This can all be thought of as capacity. Microsoft has a Cloud Operations + Innovation team that architects and operates the Microsoft datacenters that the various cloud services, including Azure, run on.

THE SERVERS

It all starts with the servers themselves, and while Azure in its early days used fairly standard hardware that you would find in any datacenter, but as the scale has increased and the requirements around performance, power, and optimization advanced, Microsoft actually designs their own servers. The Open Compute Project is utilized to document the server architecture required and then various vendors can build servers that meet that specification, which are then utilized in Azure datacenters. The current specification for server hardware (the nodes and the rack) is Project Olympus, which is documented at:

```
https://azure.microsoft.com/en-us/blog/
microsoft-reimagines-open-source-cloud-hardware/
```

If you look at racks of servers in an Azure datacenter, there are no fancy vendor bezels on the front; there are a minimal number of very neatly deployed cables to each blade at the front. Anything not required for a purpose is removed. The goal is to easily be able to replace blades in the event of a problem, so simple cabling with minimal interference is key. Additionally, when you think about reducing latencies, placing components close to the cable points actually starts to matter. So, in the new designs, most of the boards and components are at the front of the server, which is where the cables connect. In addition to the servers, Microsoft uses components such as FPGAs (Field-Programmable Gate Array) which enable coding at the hardware level to perform certain functions, such as offloading aspects of the networking flow to improve performance—but that's just the start. Microsoft has projects underway to use these types of hardware for new types of service, such as AI, which you can read about at:

```
https://docs.microsoft.com/en-us/azure/machine-learning/service/
concept-accelerate-with-fpgas
```

We will explore specific types of hardware later in the book when looking at compute services. However, to give some idea of the change we have seen in hardware, the original Azure compute nodes nearly 10 years ago had 32 GB of RAM with 12 cores, whereas today there are nodes with 12 TB of memory and 224 cores, and the numbers keep increasing.

Although the nodes power the underlying services, they are actually delivered to datacenters pre-racked. A fully loaded, pre-tested rack is unloaded at the datacenter, wheeled into a server room, where it is connected to power and network, and put to work. All the nodes in a rack share a number of common single points of failure—for example, a top-of-rack router or the power distribution unit (PDU). If either of those components in the rack fails, all the nodes in that rack become unavailable. A rack can therefore be considered a Fault Domain (FD).

But even that unit is too small. New capacity is deployed in units of clusters (also known as *stamps* or *scale units*). This is typically between one and three thousand nodes spread over many of these pre-populated racks. All the nodes in a cluster are identical and of a certain type and are managed by a common fabric controller instance. There are storage clusters and compute clusters, and within those broad categories are specific generations and types. Each cluster has a number of management components that communicate to management agents on the nodes. For example, each cluster has a tenant manager responsible for compute operations and placement, a network state manager, software load balancer components, and directory service components that enable all the capabilities of the software-defined datacenter that powers Azure. Each cluster has these components to minimize the blast radius of any failure.

DATACENTERS

The clusters reside in datacenters, and this is the first of these layers where you really have visibility as a unit of resiliency, which I will cover later in this chapter. In most cases, these datacenters are huge—the size of multiple football fields. Datacenters are grouped into regions, and a region may consist of one datacenter or dozens of datacenters. A region is defined as an area where all the datacenters live within a 2-ms roundtrip latency envelope, which means they could be several miles apart. Each datacenter commonly has hundreds of thousands of servers.

There are some nice video resources available about the Azure datacenters:

◆ https://cloud-platform-assets.azurewebsites.net/datacenter/

◆ https://azure.microsoft.com/en-us/global-infrastructure/ (which links to a good video: "Take a video tour inside one of the newest Microsoft datacenters")

Microsoft makes a huge investment in its datacenter footprint and continually looks at new ways to evolve the datacenter to optimize its cost and reduce its environmental footprint. Most datacenter facilities are owned and operated by Microsoft. You will often hear Microsoft talk about generations of datacenter and also years of design. These generations reflect shifts in datacenter architecture—for example, a move from traditional raised floor datacenters with traditional AC to concrete floors with different types of air-handling technology. The goal is to optimize energy efficiency, with as much power going to actually powering the servers and less on surrounding components like air conditioning and power conversion. Power usage effectiveness (PUE) aims to express the efficiency of power in a datacenter with the following formula:

$$PUE = Total\ Facility\ Power/IT\ Equipment\ Power$$

The lower the PUE, the better. Whereas a traditional datacenter may run at a PUE of 2 or 3, the latest Microsoft datacenters are hovering around 1.1, which means that only around 10 percent of the power is not going to the actual IT load. The exact PUE varies by location. In colder locations, AC may not be required, and the outside air can be used to cool, reducing power overhead and enabling a better PUE. Microsoft is experimenting with placing datacenters in the sea and using the ocean to cool the facility. If you are interested, have a look at the Project Natick website at https://natick.azurewebsites.net/. There is even a live camera where you can look at the unit under the sea; however, it's normally biofouled (fish poop!), so you can't see very much, but the site has some good information. Remember that energy is just one dimension of efficiency. Many are also starting to look at water efficiency and other environment impact measures, which Microsoft is also investing in as ways to be more efficient.

I recommend watching the aforementioned videos. They give great insight to the attention to detail and resiliency of the datacenters. Battery backup, diesel generators, and days' worth of diesel on-site with contracts to multiple suppliers are all standard to help minimize any chance of an outage to services even in the event of significant regional problems.

REGIONS AND CLOUDS

As previously mentioned, the datacenters are deployed in regions which is a 2-ms round-trip latency envelope. A region is typically the locale construct used when deploying a resource— i.e., I deploy a VM to a specific region, such as East U.S. There are regions throughout the world, and new regions are being added constantly. A good map of the current regions is provided at:

```
https://azure.microsoft.com/en-us/global-infrastructure/regions/
```

At the time of this writing, there are 54 regions worldwide, which can be accessed from 140 countries. Regions are selected based on a number of criteria and as a customer it is likely multiple regions are highly desirable for a number of reasons.

♦ Regions are typically deployed hundreds of miles apart and in different fault and flood zones. They utilize different electrical grids and avoid areas that are prone to natural disasters as much as possible. The goal is to select parcels of land that have good supplies of power, water, and communications with low risks of natural disasters or civil unrest events.

♦ Typically at least two regions are deployed to any geo-political boundary with typically hundreds of miles between them—for example, two in Canada, many in the United States, multiple in Europe, multiple in Germany specifically, multiple in Asia, and so on. This is to meet potential data sovereignty requirements while still allowing data to be replicated between regions to meet resiliency and availability requirements. The only exception to this is Brazil, which only has a single region and typically services replicate to regions in the United States. Azure regions are actually paired for some of the native replication capabilities—for example, storage account replication. Additionally, the paired regions have updates deployed sequentially, which minimizes the chance of an update impacting the paired regions at the same time. The pairings can be seen at:

```
https://docs.microsoft.com/en-us/azure/
best-practices-availability-paired-regions
```

♦ Azure customers may need to make services available throughout the world, and while a single large deployment may technically work, albeit prone to an outage if any kind of region incident occurred, the user experience may be very poor if the user were a significant distance, as latency would be significant. For example, a user in Asia accessing a service in the United States may see a latency of 200 ms, which could be reduced to maybe 50 ms for a local instance of the service. Additionally, because of the consumption nature of the cloud, the cost of one large deployment in a single region would be roughly the same as having 6 smaller deployments globally distributed, which enables a great user experience and exponentially improves the resiliency of the service.

The location of each region can be found at:

```
https://azure.microsoft.com/en-us/global-infrastructure/locations/
```

which is generally as much detail as needed to identify the correct region based on desired location. Remember that a region is typically made up of datacenters spread over potentially a number of miles, so there may not be a single physical location for any given region.

I previously mentioned that Microsoft owns and operates most of the Azure regions, but there are exceptions, typically because of certain regulations. Two major ones are China and Germany. For China, the Azure regions are actually operated by 21Vianet to meet China's regulatory requirements. For Germany, T-Systems International acts as the data trustee to meet German law; see:

https://docs.microsoft.com/en-us/azure/germany/germany-overview-data-trustee

It is becoming increasingly common to see Microsoft create country-specific deployments of Azure to better meet specific country regulations and to keep data within a country. For example, originally there were European regions, but now there are pairs of regions being deployed to each of France, the UK, Switzerland, and Norway.

For the most part, any customer can use any region, but there are exceptions. Some regions are ring fenced, and you must have a company in that location to use the region. For example, you must have a company in China to use Azure China. For Germany, you must be part of the European Free Trade Association (although additional Germany regions are planned that will be part of standard Azure global cloud for use by anyone). To use Azure US Government, you must be part of the government or one of its partners. These conditions are all documented at:

https://azure.microsoft.com/en-us/global-infrastructure/geographies/

Not every service is available at every region. There is a model where there are classifications of regions where some regions will receive new services as a priority, and then those services may propagate out to other regions. However, for some specialized types of service (e.g., a VM SKU with highly specialized hardware), it may never be present in every region. The goal typically is to try to have services available in at least one region in every geographic area (i.e., the United States, Europe, APAC, etc.).

To check service availability for regions using a web browser, you can navigate to:

https://azure.microsoft.com/en-us/global-infrastructure/services/

You can filter down to specific products and regions. You can also check using PowerShell/CLI. The following example lists the resource providers, gets the details of the `Microsoft.Compute` resource provider, and then looks at the locations the `virtualMachines` resource type is available at. The final command then looks at specific VMs available at a location.

```
Get-AzResourceProvider
$resources = Get-AzResourceProvider -ProviderNamespace Microsoft.Compute
$resources.ResourceTypes.Where{($_.ResourceTypeName -eq
'virtualMachines')}.Locations
Get-AzVmSize -Location "East US"
```

In fact, although I am talking about Azure as a single cloud, that is not entirely accurate. Most regions belong to the Azure commercial cloud, which pretty much anyone can use. There are also sovereign clouds with limited access. These clouds can be seen in the following:

```
PS C:\> Get-AzureRmEnvironment

Name                   Resource Manager Url                          ActiveDirectory
Authority
----                   -------------------                           ---------------
----------
AzureChinaCloud    https://management.chinacloudapi.cn/
https://login.chinacloudapi.cn/
```

```
AzureStackDallas https://management.dallas.savilltech.com/
https://login.microsoftonline.com/
AzureCloud        https://management.azure.com/
https://login.microsoftonline.com/
AzureGermanCloud  https://management.microsoftazure.de/
https://login.microsoftonline.de/
AzureUSGovernment https://management.usgovcloudapi.net/
https://login.microsoftonline.us/
```

Notice that there is a separate China cloud (codename Mooncake), a separate Germany cloud (codename Blackforest), and a separate U.S. Government cloud (codename FairFax). If you look at the Azure regions map, it also describes two Azure Government Secret regions whose locations are not disclosed, and we can assume make up another sovereign cloud that does not even show (because it's secret). These sovereign clouds are completely separate physical and logical environments that have a different cadence for service availability—i.e., they typically lag behind in new service availability and are operated by different groups to meet the sovereign requirements. They also use separate Azure AD for identity services.

If you looked carefully, you may have spotted AzureStackDallas in there. Azure has regions throughout the globe, but if there is not a region where you need it, or if you have very specific requirements for on-premises services, then you can deploy an appliance that brings certain Azure services to your location. This Azure Stack deployment shows like any other Azure cloud! I will cover this in detail in Chapter 8, "Azure Stack."

Also realize that I am focused on types of Azure cloud, but other cloud services are offered out of the Microsoft datacenter footprint. Consider that services such as Bing, Office 365, and Dynamics 365 are just some of the other cloud services that Microsoft provides, many of which are actually built on Azure.

A WORD ON RESILIENCY

The topic of resiliency will be recurring in this book, but I would be remiss if I did not mention it here while talking about datacenters and regions, as these form the core building blocks for resiliency in Azure. Often people think that once they deploy something to the cloud, it can never go down and their job is done. For some SaaS services, that may be the case, but it's likely not the case for PaaS and IaaS services. While Microsoft architects their datacenters with great resiliency in mind, things can happen, and we always need to think about the desired resiliency of our services and architect accordingly from the start.

In Azure, as services need to scale, the preference is to scale out (aka scale horizontally), as opposed to scaling up (aka scale vertically). On premises, when workloads run on hypervisors, it is common to scale up by making the VM bigger, thus allocating more resources. However, this motion, while increasing the scalability, does nothing to increase the resiliency of the service. You have one large instance that could crash or must be taken down as part of planned maintenance, rendering the service unavailable. Additionally, there is a limit to how much resource a single instance of a service may be able to effectively utilize, and so just adding more resource may not improve the scalability of a service at a certain point.

If you scale out by adding more, smaller instances, you not only increase the scalability but also increase the reliability, as there are now more instances giving resiliency for the service if an instance crashed or had to be taken down for planned maintenance. Remember that in the cloud we pay for the amount of resource, so one large VM with 16 cores and 32 GB of RAM would cost the same as four VMs with 4 cores and 8 GB of RAM. Also remember that because we pay for when something is running, when we scale out, we can also scale in by deallocating instances, thereby reducing cost, and then start them again when needed. Because the instances are added and removed to the existing instances, there is no interruption to the service availability during the scaling motion. To change the scale of a single instance deployment when scaling up, you typically would need to shut it down to modify its resources. The one negative of the scale-out approach is that the service must be written to support multiple instances, but this is very common in today's application architectures. This is summarized in Figure 1.7.

FIGURE 1.7

Scale out vs. scale up

We are talking about scale, as hopefully you have guessed the cornerstone of resiliency services is when they are built on multiple instances that can then be distributed across various blast zones. (Think of a blast zone as the radius of impact of some kind of incident.) This does not mean there is no service-level agreement (SLA) for single-instance services, which may be the case for some workloads, especially older applications that have been lifted and shifted from on premises. If you have a VM that cannot have more than one instance, then, provided that you utilize premium Azure storage, the instance is covered by a 99.9 percent SLA. However, it is susceptible to failures at a node, rack, datacenter, and region level. Note that even with a single-instance VM, if a component did fail in the Azure datacenter, such as the node or rack the VM was running on, the fabric would essentially "heal" itself by reinstantiating the VM to a new node/rack, which would be an operation in the order of minutes, but it would be unavailable during that time. Additionally, during planned maintenance of hosts, there would be a brief interruption to the service availability as it is paused, although these pauses are getting shorter (some sub second) and less frequent as new technologies are employed to minimize customer impact. Also, just because a service supports only a single instance running does not preclude another instance from being available that can be replicated to and started in the event the primary instance is unavailable—something we will explore in Chapter 9, "Backup, Disaster Recovery, and Migration."

The preceding paragraph may give you a warm, glowing feeling that a single instance meets your requirements; however, the aim is for no downtime, and for any service that has variable load, we want the ability to dynamically scale without impacting access to the service—i.e., scale out. Things get far more interesting when we can have multiple instances of a service in terms of service resiliency. Let's be clear what we mean by a multi-instance service:

◆ Domain controllers (I can have multiple domain controllers.)

◆ SQL server cluster (Multiple SQL servers can operate to provide a SQL service.)

◆ Farm of IIS services offering a web page

◆ An application tier providing service to some other tier

As you can see, multiple instances are very common today. For some of these multi-instance services they just work. For example, clients can use one of a number of domain controllers through records returned by DNS. For some, it may have a native component to accept requests and distribute, such as the availability group listener for a SQL cluster; for others, there may need to be some networking component to distribute requests between the multiple instances, such as load balancer in front of a web farm. Azure has multiple options where load balancing is required, so don't worry about that—I'll cover them in detail in Chapter 5, "Networking." For now, let's just think about the options when we can have multiple instances.

The most obvious type of failure and the most common is to protect against a node or rack failure—i.e., the blast radius of a Fault Domain. If a service has multiple instances, at minimum, we want to ensure that those instances are spread over multiple Fault Domains. This is achieved using availability sets. When workloads are added to an availability set, they are distributed over a maximum (and default) of three Fault Domains within the same cluster. (Three is a common number in resiliency, as it enables various types of quorum by enabling a majority (i.e., two out of three), something not possible if you had distribution only over two units). This is shown in Figure 1.8 and demonstrates that the service is now protected from a node or rack failure. If a Fault Domain were to have an incident, only a third of the instances would be impacted, and requests to the service would be distributed to the remaining two thirds while the fabric healed itself and redeployed the now missing instances to another Fault Domain. This means there would be a drop in scale during the outage, since a third of the instances are missing, which potentially could impact the performance of the service until the redeployment completes. When using an availability set, the workloads deployed are just deployed in a round-robin fashion between the three Fault Domains—e.g., if you add six VMs to an availability set, you would have two deployed to each Fault Domain. The placement of the VMs in the availability set has no consideration to what is actually running inside the workload—i.e., the fabric has no clue if a VM is a SQL box, an IIS web server, etc. If you mixed workloads in a single availability set, then through bad luck you could end up with all the IIS boxes on one Fault Domain, all the SQL on another Fault Domain, and all the domain controllers on another Fault Domain, leaving any service still susceptible to a Fault Domain failure. For this reason, as Figure 1.8 shows, each unique workload is deployed to its own availability set to ensure that each workload is distributed over three Fault Domains, removing a single point of failure for each service. IIS App1 is deployed to its own availability set, SQL cluster 1 to its own, and so on. If I had another IIS application even though it's also IIS, if it was separate servers it would be in its own availability, a second SQL cluster in its own availability set. You get the idea. Using availability sets gives the service deployed an SLA of 99.95 percent, which is documented at:

https://azure.microsoft.com/en-us/support/legal/sla/virtual-machines/v1_8/

FIGURE 1.8
Example availability set deployment

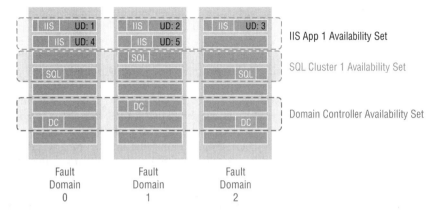

A QUICK WORD ON RELIABLE VS. BEST EFFORT

For most datacenter virtual environments, on premises means that the infrastructure is implemented as a reliable infrastructure. Virtualization hosts are grouped into clusters, and storage is provided by enterprise-level SANs. A stand-alone virtual machine is made reliable through the use of clustering. For planned maintenance operations such as patching, virtual machines move between nodes with no downtime through the use of technologies like Live Migration. The result is minimal downtime to a virtual machine.

This type of reliable infrastructure makes sense for on premises, but it does not work for public cloud solutions that have to operate at mega-scale. Instead, the public cloud operates in a best-effort model. Despite the name, best effort does not mean it's worse—in reality, it often is better. Instead of relying on the infrastructure to provide reliability, the emphasis is on the application. This means always having at least two instances of a service and organizing those services in such a way as to assure that those two instances do not run on the same Fault Domain.

The reality is with a multiple-application instances model, the level of application availability is higher than when using a reliable infrastructure model. Although the reliable infrastructure provides zero downtime from planned maintenance operations (as does the best-effort infrastructure with multiple instances of the application on different Fault Domains), a reliable infrastructure cannot protect from downtime in an unplanned failure. If a host fails, the cluster infrastructure in the reliable model will restart the VM on another node. That restart takes time, and the OS and/or application may need integrity checks and possibly recovery actions because essentially the OS inside the VM was just powered off. In the best-effort infrastructure using multiple instances of the application, unplanned failure is covered without risk of corruption, as the other instance would still be running. Additionally, though the reliable infrastructure protects against host failure, it cannot provide protection if the OS inside a VM hangs or errors in some way that is not seen as a problem for the host environment. In such a case, no corrective action is taken, and the service is left unavailable. Using an application-aware approach, any issues in the application could be detected, and clients would be sent to the other instance until any problems were resolved.

It should be noted that Azure does live migrate VMs in certain scenarios between nodes to reduce any impact to customer workloads, such as when diagnostics indicates an impending hardware failure or BIOS updates are required, as documented at the following site:

```
https://azure.microsoft.com/en-us/blog/
improving-azure-virtual-machine-resiliency-with-predictive-ml-and-live-migration/
```

There is another aspect to availability sets: update domains (UDs). While the Fault Domains provide protection from hardware failure, the other aspect is planned maintenance, such as updates to the underlying Azure node. An availability set can be made up of up to 20 update domains (5 is the default), which are each updated separately. In the Figure 1.8 example, my IIS App 1 may be using 5 update domains, so during planned maintenance operations in Azure, only a fifth of the instances would be impacted at any one time. These are shown for the IIS App 1 only but would apply to every availability set. Note that while update domains impact the Azure host updates for IaaS when using PaaS, they are also utilized for updates to the applications themselves. A final word on availability sets is that as a side effect of the three Fault Domains being placed on different racks in the same stamp, it does ensure that the workloads are all very close to each other from a proximity and latency perspective, which can be a requirement for certain types of workload. Although there is no guaranteed latency envelope around an availability set, it should be very low.

Because workloads in an availability set deploy within a cluster (which is of a single hardware type and supports a certain set of VM series), there are limits on which types of VMs can be within the same availability set. These conditions are documented at:

```
https://docs.microsoft.com/en-us/azure/virtual-machines/
virtual-machines-availability-set-supportability
```

For example, an availability set could contain a mix of A and D series VMs but could not also include an M series VM (which runs on its own clusters).

Availability sets protect against the most common type of failure, i.e. a server failing (which if you consider the millions of servers that are deployed across the global Azure footprint happens daily) but a datacenter-level incident would impact the entire availability set. I previously mentioned that a region is made up of multiple datacenters. Some regions expose a feature called an *availability zone (AZ)*. To check which regions support this capability, see:

```
https://docs.microsoft.com/en-us/azure/availability-zones/az-overview
```

An availability zone is made up of one or more datacenters that have independent power, cooling, and networking from those in other availability zones in the region. When deploying resources to a region that has been enabled for availability zones, the option to select which availability zone will be present, 1, 2, or 3 (once again, three). Note that this differs from availability sets, where you just deploy to the set and the fabric distributes the resources over the three Fault Domains. With availability zones, you specify which specific AZ to deploy to, as shown in Figure 1.9 (although many higher-level services will perform this distribution for you).

It is important to realize that within a subscription, the availability zones are unique to that specific subscription. There is no specific physical datacenter called "AZ1" that will always map to AZ1 within every subscription. Instead, the AZs within a subscription are guaranteed to be separate physical locations from each other; there is no correlation with another subscription's AZs, which could map completely differently, as shown in Figure 1.9.

With availability zones, the blast radius moves up to an entire datacenter and the SLA increases to 99.99 percent. There is no official latency envelope for workloads within an availability zone, but, from my own observations, I've never seen it above 1 ms. If your service is distributed over the three exposed AZs, then a datacenter-level incident would impact only a third of the service (provided that all aspects of the service are using AZs—for example, the standard load balancer, etc.).

FIGURE 1.9
Availability zone
architecture

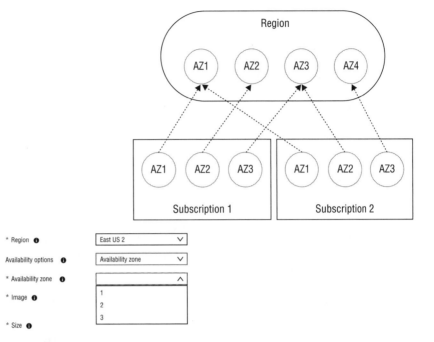

The final level of resiliency is to protect against a region-level incident, which, while extremely unlikely, should still be architected for. The solution here is to deploy services across multiple regions. For most on-premises deployments, there is a primary location and then a disaster recovery location (possibly a shared co-location facility) that is used only if the primary location is not available. In the cloud, it is more common to simply have multiple active deployments and distribute the capacity across those regions without really increasing the cost compared to one single large region deployment. The only additional component is a global-level entry point for requests, which then distribute to the various regional deployments. Azure has a number of solutions, such as Azure Traffic Manager and Azure Front Door Service, depending on the exact type of service being offered.

There are other aspects to multiple deployments that are globally distributed. One is the operational process, but once again as organizations move to DevOps workflows, the deployment across many regions is the same work as the deployment to one. Another one that can be challenging is if there is some kind of database involved that needs to be written to locally for each instance. A relational database like Azure SQL Satabase is really a single master solution, with one region being writable while replicas in other regions are read-only. There are solutions such as Cosmos DB, but this may require some re-architecture of the application.

All these considerations will be covered throughout the book, but I wanted to touch on them here to get you thinking about them from the start. As you design services, think about the various blast zones and the resiliency you want for your service. In most cases, you will use availability sets or availability zones within a region for any specific deployment and have that deployment duplicated to at least one region with some kind of balancing of requests between the regions. Figure 1.10 shows an example of this type of architecture using some VMs running a web service spread across AZs in each region talking to Cosmos DB that has replicas in both regions. The zone-aware standard load balancer is used and the Azure Front Door Service provides a single, global entry point for the HTTPS requests.

FIGURE 1.10
Resilient service
using multiple
constructs

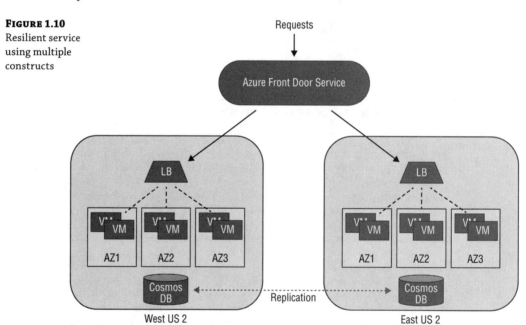

Microsoft Network

Having capacity across the world is not useful unless there is also an abundance of connectivity—i.e., the network. Often when using the cloud, a concern is the performance and responsiveness, as servers are no longer "down the hall" and may be hundreds of miles away. Microsoft operates one of the largest global data networks, making it (strangely) one of the largest telcos in the world. Not only does Microsoft have its own capacity, it also leases a significant amount of connectivity, which, when combined together provide massive connectivity and enable thousands of peering points around the world that enable customers to connect.

The Microsoft global wide area network (WAN) connects all of its datacenters across regions using highly available connections that have very high capacity. When data moves between Azure regions, it is not sent out over the Internet but rather stays on the Microsoft dark fiber network. To give some idea of the scale of the Microsoft network, here are some interesting figures that are current at time of writing (January 2019):

- 2 million miles of intra-datacenter fiber

- 72 Tbps backbone

- 1.6 Pbps regional network

Microsoft has also invested in connectivity across continents and, in partnership with Facebook, recently developed and deployed a new cross-Atlantic, 160 Tbps, 4,000 mile long subsea cable. The MAREA (`https://news.microsoft.com/marea/`) cable runs from Virginia Beach, Virginia to Bilbao, Spain. These unique locations were chosen to provide resilient connectivity that is geographically separated from the more common New York to North-West Europe connections that were impacted during events such as hurricane Sandy. If you are interested, you can see all the subsea cables that exist at `https://www.submarinecablemap.com/`.

Microsoft offers customers numerous ways to connect to services via this network, including connectivity via the Internet via thousands of Internet partners through private connectivity up to 100 Gbps using ExpressRoute via a large number of peering partners. In fact, some new offerings enable customers to connect their own facilities via this network, but I'll save the details on that for Chapter 5. More information on the Microsoft network can be found at:

```
https://azure.microsoft.com/en-us/blog/
how-microsoft-builds-its-fast-and-reliable-global-network/
```

From the global WAN, each region then uses a resilient but efficient architecture. Instead of creating a mesh of connections, where every datacenter in a region connects to every other datacenter, which would get very messy and complex where there could potentially be tens of datacenters in a region, a pair of regional network gateways (RNGs) are deployed that each have connections to each datacenter and combine network gateways with main distribution frames. The RNGs are physically and logically separated. The RNGs are deployed in a number of sizes—small, medium, and large—that reflect the number of datacenters planned for the region. The deployments are currently architected to support 1.6 Pbps of inter-datacenter switching and utilize Microsoft-created technology that reduces the amount of hardware and power required. Figure 1.11 shows the architecture utilized for the regional network connectivity.

FIGURE 1.11
Regional network
gateway architecture

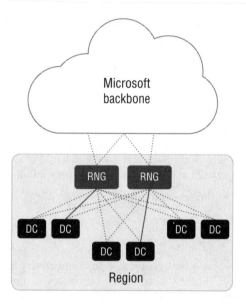

Like all aspects of Azure, the actual network connectivity for Azure is software-defined, removing the need for a lot of complex, inflexible single-purpose network equipment. Instead, by using software-defined networking (SDN), a large amount of the network work can be distributed among hosts (and to local host special hardware such as the FPGAs), which are enabled by a three-plane architecture:

◆ **Management**—The Azure Resource Manager API that accepts the configuration requests

◆ **Control**—Azure network controllers that take the configuration requests and make the changes required to apply the desired configuration

◆ **Data**—The switches in the hosts that perform the communications, including the virtual filtering platform, which is a key component of the virtual switch on each node

The three-plane model enables each plane to scale independently of the others and also makes it highly resilient to any kind of failure. I will explore the depth of the Azure network capabilities enabled by the SDN in Chapter 5.

Azure Resource Providers

Today's Azure environment is built on the Azure Resource Manager (ARM), which provides the management and deployment service for Azure. This replaces the legacy Azure Service Manager. ARM utilizes declarative, prescriptive JSON templates, which should be used for deployments to Azure, with resources being deployed to Resource Groups, which support granular delegation.

Many years ago, I would use the image shown in Figure 1.12 to show the scope of the Azure services, but it doesn't really work today. There are just too many services. However, it does demonstrate some of the Azure structure that is still present today. You can tell how old it is by the fact that it says there are only 30 regions! If you want to see the complete list of services, take a look at `https://azure.microsoft.com/en-us/services/`. Be warned, however. It's a long list!

FIGURE 1.12
An old view of available Azure services

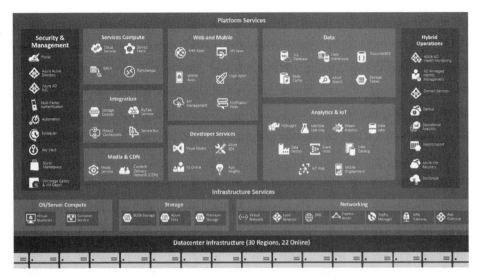

The picture shows that at the foundation are the actual datacenters, and then there are core services around compute, storage, and networking, which then have various platform services built on top. There are actually a few missing layers in that picture. Just above the datacenters sits a few other things, as shown in Figure 1.13. Note that there are other components involved such as insights and role-based access control (RBAC) which would sit in that space to the left of the components above the Azure Fabric Controller, but they are not the focus here.

FIGURE 1.13
How resource providers fit in the Azure Resource Manager architecture

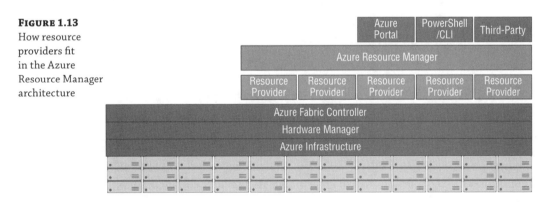

You might wonder what enables all these different types of service. It's the resource providers. There are a huge number of resource providers, and those resource providers offer a set of resources and the operations supported by them. Some key ones would be `Microsoft` `.Compute`, which contains VMs, VM scale sets, disks (because a disk is an abstraction of Azure

Storage used by VMs), and more. `Microsoft.Network` contains virtual networks, public IPs, load balancers, and more. `Microsoft.Storage` contains storage accounts (and not much else). If I quickly count all the default resource providers for a subscription, I see there are currently 36:

```
PS C:\> Get-AzResourceProvider | measure
```

```
Count           : 36
```

If I look at how many are available, I see there are currently 156. So those default resource providers containing common services are not even scratching the full breadth of what is available. Note that some resource providers are available only in certain locations; this is an attribute of the resource provider. In the following code, you can see the Locations attribute, which, when expanded, shows all locations it is available at:

```
PS C:\> Get-AzResourceProvider -ListAvailable | measure
```

```
Count           : 158

PS C:\> Get-AzResourceProvider -listavailable | ? ProviderNamespace -eq
Microsoft.PowerBI


ProviderNamespace : Microsoft.PowerBI
RegistrationState : NotRegistered
ResourceTypes     : {workspaceCollections, locations, locations/
checkNameAvailability}
Locations         : {South Central US, North Central US, East US 2, West US...}

PS C:\> Get-AzResourceProvider -ProviderNamespace Microsoft.PowerBI | select
-ExpandProperty locations
South Central US
North Central US
East US 2
West US
West Europe
North Europe
Brazil South
Southeast Asia
Australia Southeast
Canada Central
Japan East
UK South
West India
```

If you want to graphically look at the various resource providers, open the Azure portal (or do it when you have access to Azure) and in All Services, select Resource Explorer. You can then see all the resource providers, as shown in Figure 1.14. To see those registered for your Azure subscription, open Subscriptions and select Resource Providers. From here, you can register for those not currently registered. (Of course, you can do this via the command line as well!)

FIGURE 1.14
Viewing the
resource providers
via the Resource
Explorer

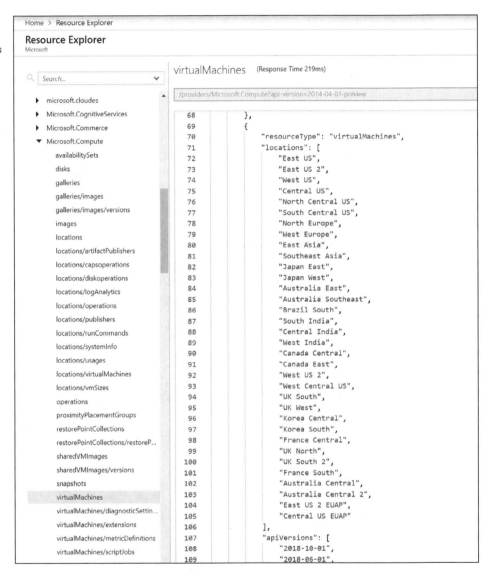

As you look at Figure 1.14, you will also see apiVersions. Resource providers are updated as capabilities are enhanced and added. By specifying an API version, you can ensure that your interactions will continue to function as expected. Some resource providers are restricted as new features are in private preview, which means limited to specific customers who have been selected to participate. Once features go into public preview, you may need to enable the resource provider before seeing the new feature.

Within a resource provider are often microservices, which focus on a specific aspect of the functionality. For example, the Compute resource provider has microservices for the VM manager, for the disk manager, for the orchestrator, and more. These microservices work together to enable the complete solution to function. For example, a virtual machine in Azure seems like just a VM, but that VM requires a network adapter, it requires a disk; the network adapter may be part of a load balancer. Different microservices all work together to orchestrate the various operations in sequence to successfully provision the required resources.

Most of the time, you don't need to worry about the resource providers, but it's good to understand how resources are provided in Azure. You will interact with them when planning granular access controls, which will require selecting available operations for specific resource types that all live in those resource groups. You will interact with them if you need to enable a new resource provider for a subscription. The key point is that they are very logically structured and are all accessed in a common fashion via ARM. The huge breadth of services in Azure is built on some core capabilities around compute, storage, and networking, and continues to evolve and grow.

Getting Access to Microsoft Azure

For a typical on-premises solution, there are many hurdles to the access and adoption of a new technology. You need hardware to run the solution and somewhere to store that hardware, and you have to obtain and deploy the various operating system requirements and applications. With public cloud solutions, the services are sitting out there, just waiting for you to start using them. Primarily, that means a way to pay for the services. If, however, you want to just try Azure, you don't even need that.

THE IMPORTANCE OF PLANNING FOR SERVICES

Azure services (like most public cloud services) are easy to access and can be used with almost no barriers. This does not mean an organization should instigate the use of public cloud services with any less consideration and planning than would be given to solutions implemented on premises. In fact, because the services are hosted externally, additional planning is likely required to ensure integration with on-premises solutions and adherence with security and compliance requirements.

Many organizations (or more specifically, parts of organizations) have not done this planning and adopted public cloud services without central governance or planning, which causes problems in the long run. It is common to hear about a particular business unit in a company using the public cloud because their own internal IT department takes too long to deliver a service. Essentially, that business unit makes a decision to host the solution themselves without the required skill sets to ensure the solution is secure and adheres to requirements. The public cloud offers huge benefits, but ensure that its adoption is well thought out with a strong governance model in place.

Free Azure Trials and Pay-as-You-Go

The first way to gain access to Azure (and the best way for most people who want to get an idea of what it's like to use Azure) is to sign up for a free trial. The trial includes a $200 Azure credit that can be used for any Azure services over 30 days, in addition to a number of other free services for 12 months (such as a certain number of compute hours and storage), and then some that are always free! The free trial offer is available at `https://azure .microsoft.com/en-us/free/`.

To sign up, you will need a Microsoft Account (formerly known as a Windows Live ID), a phone number, and a credit card. Nothing is charged to the credit card, nor will anything be charged to the credit card—by default, once you hit the $200 Azure spend, the paid services will stop. You have to agree to pay for services beyond the included $200 and change the default configuration to a Pay-as-You-Go subscription before any expense is incurred. A credit card is required for identity verification only. Of course, you can always simply buy Azure services on a Pay-as-You-Go basis and be billed for the service used at the end of each billing cycle.

As you can imagine, any kind of public cloud service where VMs can be run for free is attractive to people with dubious intentions, such as running botnet services and even mining cryptocurrencies. Microsoft, like all public cloud services, tries to ensure that trial services are used in the spirit they are intended: to try out Azure.

A BUCKET OF AZURE MONEY

Unlike many other types of purchasing in the IT world, with Azure you essentially have a bucket of money to use for Azure services. You can use that bucket for any of the types of service (virtual machines, storage, media services, backup, databases—it doesn't matter). You don't purchase $10,000 of VM quota and $5,000 of storage. You purchase $15,000 of Azure service and then spend it however you want. This is a much better option for organizations that, over time, may change the type of Azure service they want. You may begin by running SQL Server in Azure IaaS VMs with a lot of storage but eventually move to using Azure SQL Database. You can make that change easily, since Azure money is not service-specific.

Azure Benefits from Visual Studio Subscriptions

Another great way to experiment with Azure (and even use it on an ongoing basis as part of development and testing) is to leverage the Azure benefits that are part of Visual Studio and MSDN subscriptions. Visual Studio subscriptions are paid services that enable access to pretty much all Microsoft software. They are intended to be used as part of development and testing efforts. Also included with subscriptions is a monthly Azure credit, which varies depending on the level and type of the subscription, as shown in Table 1.1. (The credits are accurate as of this writing, but they could change over time.) Additionally, the Azure credits go further than regular Azure spending since the OS licenses are part of the subscription, which means you don't have to pay for them again in Azure since these credits are for dev/test only. Windows virtual machines are billed at base Linux rates (you don't pay for the Windows license), as are some other services. Full details on the dev/test pricing can be found at:

`https://azure.microsoft.com/en-us/pricing/dev-test/`

TABLE 1.1:   Visual Studio Azure benefits

SUBSCRIPTION LEVEL	VISUAL STUDIO PROFESSIONAL	VIRTUAL STUDIO TEST PROFESSIONAL	MSDN PLATFORMS	VISUAL STUDIO ENTERPRISE
Azure Credits per month	$50	$50	$100	$150

http://azure.microsoft.com/en-us/pricing/member-offers/msdn-benefits-details

Like the Azure trial accounts, by default the Azure benefit accounts will not allow you to exceed the Azure credits associated with your subscription. When your monthly limit is reached, your services will be stopped until the start of the next billing month. You need to manually disable the spending limit and specify a credit card if you wish to use more than the Azure benefit credits each month. With the highest-level subscription (Visual Studio Enterprise), it's possible to run three standard-service single-core virtual machines with just under 2 GB of memory all month, which is a pretty nice testing environment. However, you likely won't be running them all month; instead, you will start them when you want to use them and deprovision them when not using them, to stretch that credit even further and get even more use. Remember it's consumption-based billing—you pay only for what you are using. So, if you are not using it, shut it down. It is important to note and stress that the Azure benefit is for development and testing only and cannot be used to run production services. Microsoft can shut down your services if it finds they are being used for production purposes.

Most Microsoft-focused developers already have Visual Studio/MSDN subscriptions, so this is a great way to get Azure services to continue that development into the cloud. When I talk to customers about the various subscription benefits, a common question I hear is: "We have a lot of subscriptions. Can we pool all the Azure credits together to use as an organizational credit pool?" The answer is no; there is no way to pool Azure credits together—they are designed to be used by the individual subscriber for their test and development efforts.

As Figure 1.15 shows, it's easy to check on the current credit status of your subscription; by default, the Cost Management + Billing is pinned as a favorite to the navigation. If you select the item, more details related to the billing appear (for example, the amount of credit left and the forecast spend based on usage trend). You can also dive into Cost Analysis for deeper insight into how you are spending and where, and even set budgets with actions—but we will cover that in the next chapter.

If you want to remove the spending limit and pay for Azure services beyond the subscription, perform the following steps:

1. Navigate in a browser to https://account.windowsazure.com/Subscriptions/.

2. Select the Azure subscription that has a spending limit enabled. Click the subscription name.

3. In the Subscription Status section, click the Remove Spending Limit link.

4. When the Remove Spending Limit dialog box opens, change the selection to Yes, remove the spending limit, and then select if this is being removed for the current billing period or indefinitely.

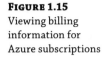

FIGURE 1.15
Viewing billing information for Azure subscriptions

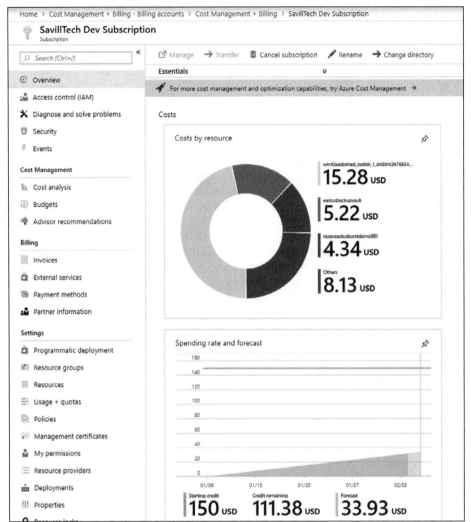

It's important that you understand the ramifications of removing the spending limit. If you accidentally start a lot of virtual machines and leave them running, you may end up with a large bill at the end of the month. So, if you do remove the spending limit, ensure that you keep a close eye on your Azure spend.

Enterprise Enrollments for Azure

For larger organizations wanting to adopt Azure, the idea of using a credit card to pay for monthly services is not ideal. Although it is possible to be invoiced by Microsoft, enterprises typically want more granular control of their expenditures. For example, they may wish to have high-level enterprise administrators who administer the entire Azure service for the organization. Those enterprise administrators can then create separate accounts and delegate account owners, who can group like services or groups together into subscriptions. The subscriptions can be used by service administrators and co-administrators. Azure enterprise enrollment allows exactly that. Organizations can add Azure services as part of their Microsoft Enterprise Agreements or their Server and Cloud Enrollment (they work the same for Azure service addition) based on a certain amount of Azure spend. For example, an organization might make a commitment to spend a million dollars a year, and with that agreement comes possible incentives (where it is a large commit), such as specific discounts, credits, and investment funds, and then all size commits can utilize special management capabilities, cost control, and other benefits.

A key benefit for enterprise enrollment is the account and subscription flexibility and control. Typically, when an individual or small organization purchases Azure services, that user receives an individual Azure subscription with a specific subscription ID. That user is the service administrator for that subscription. An unlimited number of additional people can be made co-administrators who have full access and rights to everything in the subscription, or more granular access can be given using built-in or custom roles.

An enterprise enrollment via an Enterprise Agreement enables more flexibility in the administration and separation of services by providing a number of layers, as shown in Figure 1.16. Within the enterprise's enrollment, one or more departments, accounts, and subscriptions can be authorized.

FIGURE 1.16
The hierarchy when using an enterprise enrollment

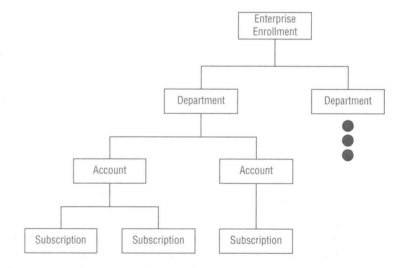

At the top of the enterprise enrollment is the enterprise administrator for the entire enterprise Azure enrollment. Nominate someone from your organization to receive an email. While these accounts can be Microsoft accounts (which may be required additionally), the long-term identity should be an Azure AD account from your organization's Azure AD tenant. (This will be covered in detail in Chapter 3, "Identity.") If you are an existing user of Office 365 or Dynamics 365, you already have this Azure AD. If you are brand new to the Microsoft cloud world, you will create an ID very shortly! The work email address associated with the Microsoft account must be someone who will be able to activate the service. Once the service is activated, additional people from the organization can be made enterprise administrators. The enterprise administrators can, in turn, create separate departments, which have department administrators. Departments can also have a soft spending limit set, which means an alert is generated if this threshold is breached (but no action taken). The department administrators can then create accounts within the enrollment. Note that accounts don't have to be created under departments. The department construct is optional. An account can be directly part of the EA and not part of a department.

Each account can have one or more account administrators assigned although typically an account is for an individual. Once again, each administrator needs an account—Azure AD or Microsoft. The organizational account owners can create one or more subscriptions within the account. An account can be enabled for dev/test, which means they have Visual Studio/MSDN subscription and can therefore create dev/test subscriptions, which get billed the same way as those Visual Studio/MSDN subscriptions. The account owners can view the usage across all subscriptions under the account. Each subscription has a single service administrator who manages the subscription and can add additional co-administrators who can also perform full management of the subscription and the resources within it, in addition to more granular role-based assignments.

A key benefit is that the enterprise administrators at the top of the hierarchy have visibility into Azure usage across all accounts, whereas account owners have visibility into Azure usage for all subscriptions within the account. Billing reports are broken down at a subscription, department, and account level for easy accounting, although there are continued advances in billing options and visibility.

I want to bring up an alternate approach to billing that has been gaining traction with many organizations and I believe really is the future model. Departments were added to provide a way to see accumulation of costs for multiple accounts and to set a spending alert at that accumulation level. There are better approaches for the alerting, as now there are subscription-level budgets with actions groups (which I'll cover in the next chapter). Azure Resource Manager enables you to "tag" resources. A tag is a name/value pair—for example, "cost center" or "department." A single resource can have up to 15 tags (and there are advanced methods to use JSON in a value to hold even more info as part of a CI/CD pipeline). The tags show up in the monthly Excel CSV export, in addition to Power BI, which means instead of focusing accounting through departments, etc., you can just tag the resources, which actually gives more flexibility. Azure Policy can be used to enforce the presence of the tag and/or just apply tags to a resource group (the container for resources with a common lifecycle/type) and, through automation, copy to the resources (as they are not inherited as part of ARM). I will be covering this in more detail in the next chapter but definitely wanted to bring this up now, as historically people used the departments for billing purposes, and with the tags it's just not necessary anymore. You still need accounts for the delegated ability to create subscriptions and aspects of organization of the subscriptions, but departments, meh! As we look at some hierarchical models using the EA constructs, keep these in mind as in the next chapter we will look at management groups. Management groups replace a lot of the functionality of the EA construct. Management groups are focused, as the name suggests, around how resources are managed such as access control and policy assignment which is more applicable to how resources would be structured and the hierarchies we talk about. This is likely not something that applies to the same extent as the EA structure.

The above being said, the hierarchical nature of an enterprise enrollment opens a number of methodologies for setting up departments (remember, completely optional), accounts, and subscriptions, some of which are shown in Figure 1.17. Due to space limitations, each department has one account, but commonly there would be many. Notice that in a functional methodology, the departments are based on the functions of different groups. When using a geographical methodology, the departments are based on physical locations. Business group methodologies often give each group their own department, and accounts become projects. Your organization may need a hybrid methodology. Ultimately, the right methodology depends on how you want to delegate the creation of subscriptions and how billing information and even chargebacks will be used within the organization. Once the methodology is decided, how subscriptions are used must also be decided. This can be broken down by group, task, location, deployment lifecycle stage (such as a subscription for development and one for testing), and so on, ideally complementing the methodology picked for the accounts. (Again, I cover the cost options in detail in the next chapter.) Although you can implement this structure with departments and accounts, my guidance would be to likely ignore departments and instead use the tags and other cost and management structure capabilities.

FIGURE 1.17
Possible methodologies for enterprise enrollment account setup

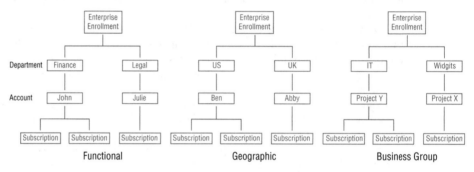

With the introduction of role-based access control (RBAC) and resource groups, some of the reasons for separate subscriptions and accounts no longer apply, since granular permissions, and even spend reporting are now possible based on specific resources. However, the concept of separating departments, accounts, and subscriptions can still be very useful. Additionally, more focus is shifting to management groups (covered in the next chapter), which allows subscriptions to be part of a hierarchy for policy and RBAC purposes.

Note that when paying by credit card or via invoice, you pay the list price for Azure services. However, when you purchase via an Enterprise Agreement, you may potentially get certain incentives, credits, and SKU discounts (but only on very large commits). The exact terms vary, but it is important to realize the Azure purchase on an EA is pre-purchased on an annual basis and is "use it or lose it." Suppose that as part of an EA you purchase $100,000 of Azure for Year 1. This gets you a certain level of benefit. However, if at the end of the year you have used only $80,000 worth of Azure service, that other $20,000 is lost. There is a slight silver lining. At the end of each year, you can true up or true down. At the time of writing, Microsoft allows you to "carry over" any remaining balance. This means for Year 2, you can true down to $60,000 (and add the $20,000 carried over), getting you back to $80,000, and you've not lost any actual usage.

The risk of losing Azure dollars may encourage customers to commit to a lower up-front Azure spend and then true up, but the amount of commit will influence the benefits offered.

Numerous calculators and tools are available to help you estimate the Azure spend and reach to as accurate a number as possible for the coming year. This is another benefit of the commit: It can help an organization budget and plan for the spend instead of getting a big invoice at the end of the year. In general, I would err a little on the low side, as you don't want to waste money. Be aware that erring on the low side could impact possible incentives. Also, remember that there are many services available in Azure that can be used to consume your bucket of Azure money. If you are not using as much IaaS as you planned, maybe you can use more storage or media services.

For information about Enterprise Agreements, head over to:

https://www.microsoft.com/en-us/licensing/licensing-programs/enterprise

To summarize, Azure can be obtained in a number of ways, including:

◆ Trial subscription

◆ Pay-as-You-Go subscription

◆ Visual Studio/MSDN Azure benefits

◆ Enterprise Azure enrollment

Reserved Instances and Azure Hybrid Benefit

There are two major vehicles for reducing cost and optimizing your Azure spend for infrastructure services.

Reserved Instances

Reserved Instances (RIs) enable a customer to guarantee that they will use a certain amount of a certain series of vCPU over a 1-year or 3-year period for a significant cost saving. A 3-year RI offers a bigger discount than a 1-year RI and is not available on all SKUs of VMs. Details on RIs, including a FAQ section, can be found at:

https://azure.microsoft.com/en-us/pricing/reserved-vm-instances/

So, why do this? Well, it helps Microsoft plan capacity. If a customer has an RI for a series of vCPU in a region with a 3-year commit, that's 3 years worth of capacity they know will be used. As the customer, you get a good discount. It is important to buy the right amount, as any you are *not* using 24/7 will still be billed. As an organization, you would work out the minimum of a certain vCPU series that will ever be running and make that your RI baseline. When you add an RI, the interface will actually recommend numbers based on the previous 30 days of activity.

The actual RI you are purchasing has become more flexible. Initially, you were buying an exact SKU—for example, 40 D2v2s that could only be used on D2v2 SKU. However, it evolved to now be based on the RI VM group—e.g., based on a number of Dv2 cores that could be used on single core, 2-core, 4-core, 8-core, and even 16-core Dv2 VMs. This is known as *instance size flexibility*. The exact groups can be found at:

https://docs.microsoft.com/en-us/azure/virtual-machines/windows/
reserved-vm-instance-size-flexibility

Now you buy a number of RIs of a certain RI VM group and use them across sizes within that group and region.

You are not assigning an RI to a specific VM instance. An RI is not a new SKU but rather a billing engine that wakes up hourly, for each RI per VM group core looks to see if it's attached. If it is attached, it rerates the VM accordingly; if it's not attached, it finds a VM to attach to and rerates. The cores will auto-fit based on the number available and the VMs currently not attached to RIs to fill as best it can. Note that if on the hour there are unattached RIs and no VMs that need them, they are still billed. It's like a hotel room. You pay for the room for 24 hours. If you are in the room for 18 hours, you still pay the 24 hours.

Figure 1.18 shows a very simple example applying to the same VM size and assuming you only have two cores of RI for the Dv2. Initially, a Windows VM is running using the RI for the first 5 hours. Note that a second VM starts in the fourth hour, but no RIs are available at that time. When VM1 is stopped, the RIs move over to VM2. There is no VM running in hour 14, so you've just lost that money's worth of RI (though the overall discount would still justify this). Then it gets applied to VM3, when it starts, before moving to VM4, when VM3 stops. Easy! You're pre-buying reduced rate compute that will auto-size based on workloads running within the family.

FIGURE 1.18

A simple RI example

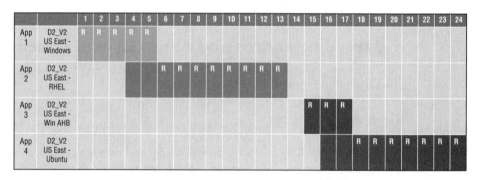

Figure 1.19 shows a more complex example. In this example, two D5_v2 VMs are purchased for RI (which gives 16 cores each, for a total of 32 cores). The top two lines are these primary VMs, which, even though not running 24 hours with the 3-year discount, still saved money. With the instance flexibility in times when one is not running, those cores of RI can now be auto-sized to fit other VMs in the same family, providing reduced costs there as well.

FIGURE 1.19

A more complex
RI example using
instance size
flexibility

	Instance/DC	1	2	3	4	5	6	7	8	9	10	11	12	13	14	15	16	17	18	19	20	21	22	23	24
App 1	D5_v2 US East																								
App 2	D5_v2 US East																								
App 3	D4_v2 US East																								
App 4	D3_v2 US East																								
App 5	D2_v2 US East																								
App 6	D3_v2 US East																								
App 7	D3_v2 US East																								
VMs in service by hour																									
VMs covered by RI with instance size flexibility		2	2	2	3	3	3	2	2	2	2	2	2	2	2	2	2	2	2	3	3	4	4	3	3
VMs - On Demand		1	1	1	2	2	2	2	2	2	2	2	1	1	1	1	1	1	2	2	2	3	3	2	2

In the example, you see that in times when both the main VMs are not running (the first 6 hours and the last 7 hours), there are sufficient spare cores of RI available to cover the various other on-demand VMs (the VMs covered by RI with instance size flexibility rows), providing additional savings that would not have been the case prior to the instance size flexibility. The D4_V2 has 8 cores; the D3_V2 has 4 cores; and the D2_V2 has 2 cores. If you walk through the various VMs running, you can see that the spare 8 cores when any one of the main VMs not running are redistributed to cover the other smaller combination VMs. You should consider this flexibility when planning RI purchases.

TIP   You can convert between families without penalty and even early terminate via a cancellation. However, cancellations will incur an early termination fee based on a percent of remaining credit.

Azure Hybrid Benefit

Many organizations that adopt Azure have on premises existing infrastructure and licensing that includes Windows Server and SQL Server. Azure Hybrid Benefit enables organizations to use their existing Windows Server and/or SQL Server licenses in Azure. This means those resources will no longer incur the OS/SQL part of the billing. For example, a Windows Server VM would bill at the same rate as a Linux VM (the base compute rate), in the same manner as test/dev billing for VMs.

The on-premises licenses must be covered by software assurance or Windows Server subscriptions. For Windows Server, the following applies:

◆ Standard licenses can be used on premises *or* in the cloud, but not both.

◆ Datacenter licenses can be used simultaneously covering deployments on premises and in Azure.

◆ For Standard and Datacenter licenses, each 2-processor license or 16-core license covers two instances up to 8 cores or one instance of 16 cores.

Azure Hybrid Benefit for Windows Server can be applied as new VMs are created as well as be applied to existing VMs via the Configuration option and selecting to use the Azure Hybrid Benefit, as shown in Figure 1.20.

FIGURE 1.20
Enabling Azure
Hybrid Benefit for
an existing VM

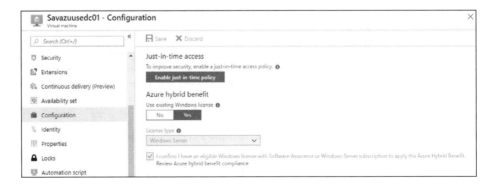

The Azure Hybrid Benefit for SQL Server enables existing SQL licenses to be used over a number of Azure SQL servers instead of on premises—i.e., they cannot be used simultaneously outside of a 180-day grace period designed to cover migration efforts. Each core of SQL Enterprise edition maps to four vCores of SQL Database General Purpose at the reduced rate. This is supported for the following:

◆ vCore-based tiers of Azure SQL Database (single database, elastic pool, and managed instance)

◆ SQL Server running in Azure IaaS VM

◆ SQL Server Integration Services (SSIS)

Full information on the Azure Hybrid Benefit can be found at:

`https://azure.microsoft.com/en-us/pricing/hybrid-benefit/`

I recommend that you read this information, as the preceding list could change. It also has calculators, to help identify how much you can save, and next steps to use.

Also note that you can combine Azure Hybrid Benefit with Reserved Instances. When you do, it's common to see discounts up to 70 percent applied to Windows-based VMs.

Increasing Azure Limits

By default, new Azure subscriptions are initially configured with very low limits. The default limits are in place to stop new Azure customers from initially over-consuming services. The limits can (and should) be increased for serious Azure usage. Most limits have a default value and a maximum value. Although it may be tempting to try to raise limits to the maximum, remember that the limits are there to help protect your own usage. I advise increasing to a realistic value that meets your needs. It's also critical to have proper processes in place to ensure that services are running only as needed, and monitoring is in place to ensure that you have the required levels of insight to your environment. (I will cover those throughout this book.)

The Azure default limits and maximums are outlined here:

`https://docs.microsoft.com/en-us/azure/azure-subscription-service-limits`

ASM vs. ARM

The limits web page talks about Azure Service Manager and Azure Resource Manager. Azure Service Manager (ASM) was the v1 of Azure, where PaaS was the initial offering with IaaS bolted on top. It had many limitations in terms of capability, communications, management, parallel execution, and more. Azure Resource Manager (ARM) is the current management structure, which should always be used today. It is where all the investment from engineering is performed; it solves connectivity challenges; it has rich RBAC, massive parallel capabilities, template-based deployments, rich consistent APIs, and a lot more. When you see ASM or classic, run the other way. Always use ARM!

The key limits you will want to change include the following:

VM Total Cores per Subscription Twenty cores per subscription per region is the default, which is a very low number and should be increased.

VM per Series Cores per Subscription   Like the previous entry, 20 cores per subscription per region is the default. An additional limit is the number of each series of VM and can be increased per-series. Increase the ones you know you will be using.

To raise a limit, navigate to the Azure subscription in the Azure portal, and then open Usage + Quotas. Click the Request Increase button and complete the required fields to request the increase. The full process is outlined at:

```
https://docs.microsoft.com/en-us/azure/azure-supportability/
resource-manager-core-quotas-request
```

The Azure Portal

I want to quickly introduce the Azure portal. I'm not going to cover it in great detail, for a number of reasons:

- It frequently evolves. (It may have changed as I type this sentence.)

- It is highly intuitive. The best way to learn it is to actually navigate to it and look around all the different areas.

- Microsoft has its own help for the portal, including a nice walkthrough.

- Most importantly, you won't use it in production.

That last item might seem odd, and I may be exaggerating, a little. To be more precise, I should say that you wouldn't use it to create resources. The Azure portal is great. As you are learning, it is nice to use it because of its intuitiveness; it makes it easy to see what is available and what the options are. It's easy to see current state and to interact with components such as logging and monitoring—but not for resource creation.

You can create a VM through the portal with about 10 clicks and by typing a few things—not really a big deal. You could probably rush through it in about a minute. Now create 10 VMs. Well, you may click something wrong or deploy something slightly inconsistently, which then introduces supportability issues. Now deploy 100 VMs. Now deploy to a dev environment, and then copy that deployment to a user acceptance environment, and then deploy to production. The documentation of the exact options that were clicked would have to be very detailed, with no way to really audit if it were indeed deployed the same way. Likewise, there is no way to see if anything has changed since deployment.

Therefore, when deploying resources in non-learning environments, you use JSON-based templates (which I cover in Chapter 11, "Managing Azure."). You can have a declarative, idempotent template file that you can deploy between environments with no changes. You simply modify a separate parameter file for anything environment-specific—for example, naming or connections. You can check that file into source control; you can deploy via a DevOps pipeline; you can compare what is deployed to the template to detect drift and resolve.

Hopefully, you start to get the idea. I'll be stressing this throughout the book: For the most part, you won't use the portal for operational tasks. Resources are created via templates, and actions are required via scripts, like PowerShell/CLI, so that they can be scheduled in a hands-off fashion. You use the portal for certain types of insight into service status, to see dashboards for a service, to run queries against logs and metrics, and, while you are learning, you'll definitely use it to create things—and that's okay.

Portal Basics

The portal is available at `https://portal.azure.com`. There is a legacy portal that only supports classic (ASM) resources, but you don't want to use that, so I won't include its URL. You will authenticate to the portal using an identity, which will be a Microsoft account or an organizational (work or school) account that is housed in Azure AD. Note that you may not get prompted for an identity but just seamlessly access the site. If this happens, it means your organization has enabled single or seamless sign-on between your regular Active Directory account and Azure AD. That identity you use has to be granted access to one or more subscriptions (or resources within subscriptions). Even if you don't have access to subscriptions, you will be able to log in. You just won't be able to create any paid resource (for example, a VM); instead, the portal will try to help you by suggesting that you create a free account, as shown in Figure 1.21.

FIGURE 1.21
The prompt to create a free account when your identity has no access to Azure subscriptions

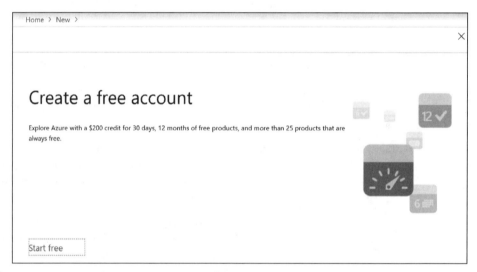

Once logged in, you should see something like Figure 1.22. On the left side is a navigation element, known as the *resource pane*. From the resource pane are links to the home page (the content in the main pane of the portal), links to dashboards (which contain tiles showing information), a link to view all services, and a list of your favorite resources (which you configure via the All Services view and by clicking the star next to its name). At the top of the portal is the status bar, which enables easy searching and access to recent resources, along with a number of other elements I will cover shortly. The main body of the portal is the main panel, the content of which changes based on the active content. By default, it contains the home page, which shows common services, key services to help you use Azure, your most recent resources, and some helpful information.

FIGURE 1.22
The Azure portal structure

When you select All Services, you will see a long list of all the different services available in Azure. Note the star next to each one. The services that show in Favorites have a gold star instead of the default black. This means service has been selected. You can click any star to toggle its favorite status. If you select Subscriptions and then select a subscription, the Subscriptions page (a panel of content focused on a type of resource or activity) opens. When you select a subscription, that subscription's page opens with a new set of menu items on the left side, which, when selected, open that contents page—for example, Access Control. The top items in the menu items on a resource-landing page are consistent across resources and are core elements, such as Overview, Access control, Diagnose and Solve Problems, Security, and Events. The rest of the menu items are contextual based on the topic of the page. At the top of the page is also a command bar featuring key actions. Notice at the top of the main panel is a navigation tree that you can click on to move back various levels, as shown in Figure 1.23. For example, if you clicked Subscriptions, you would move back to the Subscriptions blade.

FIGURE 1.23
Using the navigation tree in the portal

At the top of the Azure portal is the command bar, as shown in Figure 1.24. Moving from left to right, you first see the search bar, which is actually more than just search. By default, it shows the most recent used resources; then, as you type, it can find deployed resources, resource groups, and available services that you can deploy or use, in addition to documentation links. This makes the search far more than just a search bar but rather part of your navigation toolset, especially when moving between recently used resources.

FIGURE 1.24
The Azure portal command bar

Continuing to move from left to write, there are a number of other icons:

◆ **Cloud Shell**—Opens an Azure-hosted shell enabling PowerShell or the CLI via Bash. The cloud shell includes a storage area for assets housed in a storage account. This is the same container-based shell that is available via `https://shell.azure.com`. This will be covered in detail later in the book.

◆ **Directory + Subscription Filter**—A single identity (i.e., your account) can have access to multiple subscriptions, which may be linked to different Azure AD tenants. The filter enables you to select which subscription(s) you wish to act upon and from which linked directories (Azure AD tenants).

SUBSCRIPTIONS AND TENANTS

While I will talk more about this later in the book, it's useful to cover the basic relationship between subscriptions and tenants here. A tenant is an Azure AD instance which contains identities—typically, the users in the organization. Azure AD instances live outside of Azure subscriptions. An Azure subscription is linked to an Azure AD instance, which is the Azure AD it will use for authentication and authorization of resources. A single Azure AD can be linked to from multiple subscriptions, but a subscription can only link to one Azure AD. This is how a single user may have access to multiple subscriptions. Additionally, a user from one Azure AD can be invited as a guest to another partner Azure AD. This is known as a B2B (business to business) guest. The guest user may be given access to resources in subscriptions that use that partner's Azure AD instance. Now a single user can have access to resources that are tied to different tenants. A user in this situation needs to select the appropriate tenant to see the resources they have access to that use that tenant. This is why in the filter you can select directories (tenants) and then the subscriptions tied to that directory the user has access to.

- ◆ **Notifications**—Will show a number over the bell with the number of unread notifications. Often the notification will link to more detail.

- ◆ **Portal Settings**—Enables configuration around the theme of the portal in addition to other customizations related to the portal experience

- ◆ **Help**—Provides links to help resources

- ◆ **Feedback**—Gives positive and negative feedback to Microsoft

- ◆ **Account (your login name/directory)**—Shows the current logged in account and the current focus tenant. Enables sign-in as a different account, in addition to other accounts recently used

Azure Portal Dashboards

Until 2019, the landing page for the Azure portal was not the home page but rather a default dashboard that had basic service status for Azure. This dashboard could and can (it's still there by selecting Dashboard in the navigation menu) be modified by pinning tiles to it from various resources that were of most interest. You can also change the size of tiles to increase or decrease the amount of information shown. Tiles don't have to just show things; an ARM Actions tile type enables you to configure a command that will trigger when clicked—for example, to stop a VM. While you can manually modify the dashboard, as shown in Figure 1.25, you can also browse resources, select a tile of interest, and click the pin icon, which will add it to the currently selected dashboard. Behind the scenes, the dashboard is defined at JSON, which can be downloaded and even uploaded to restore a previously saved dashboard (although there is a different option to share dashboards).

You can also create multiple dashboards that have different focus areas. For example, you could create a database dashboard showing the status of your database services; you could have an identity dashboard; and so forth. You can also share your dashboards, making them available to other users within your subscription. (Because the focus would be resources within a subscription, using dashboards between subscriptions would likely not be very useful.) To share a dashboard, click the Share button (the circle icon with three smaller circles next to the Edit icon), enter a name, and check the Publish to the "Dashboards" resource group, which is a default collection. You can also deploy to a specific resource group—for example, the resource group that contains the actual resources the dashboard is focused on. The shared dashboard will now be visible to anyone with the right permissions when selecting the dashboard drop-down menu and selecting Browse all dashboards and then selecting Shared dashboards. Dashboards can be searched as shown in Figure 1.26 and added to your list of dashboards, in this case the Monitoring

Dashboard has been shared and is available to be added. Only dashboards you have permissions to will be shown. Figure 1.26 also highlights the icon to share the current dashboard.

FIGURE 1.25
Customizing a
dashboard

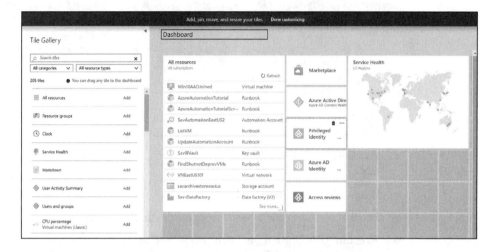

FIGURE 1.26
Viewing shared
dashboards

The Dashboards resource group is the default resource group and is used to contain the shared dashboards you want to make generically available. If you publish a dashboard to a specific resource group, you have the option to Manage users' access, and normal RBAC applies. For example, a user with Read access can use the dashboard but can't make changes to the master shared dashboard, whereas someone with Contributor access could modify it.

Microsoft has great walkthroughs of sharing and granular access to dashboards:

- Creating and sharing dashboards:

  `https://docs.microsoft.com/en-us/azure/azure-portal/azure-portal-dashboards`

- Customizing dashboard permissions:

  `https://docs.microsoft.com/en-us/azure/azure-portal/`
  `azure-portal-dashboard-share-access`

Chapter 2

Governance

This chapter focuses on the considerations and technologies to assist when applying governance to Azure services. While often initially overlooked, governance is critical to ensure that deployments meet company and regulatory requirements and also enable a more consistent and supportable environment. Governance should be one of the first work items when looking at using the cloud and will ultimately provide a securer and auditable deployment with some upfront effort.

In this chapter, you will learn to:

- ◆ Understand the key constructs of Azure Resource Manager and their application to governance.

- ◆ Explore governance technologies available in Azure.

- ◆ Manage costs in Azure.

What Is Governance?

I'm going to answer that question eventually, but not right away. Instead, I want to explore how things have evolved so that we now need a whole chapter on governance in a book that is all about infrastructure in Azure. The best way is to go back to creating services on premises.

Many eons ago (well, a few years at least), the only way to host applications was to run them in your datacenter. This required significant investment, as facilities were required to hold large, expensive servers and their supporting infrastructure components, such as storage and networking. As applications moved from running on dedicated hardware to virtual machines, a problem manifested, as it now became easier to create resources, which resulted in virtual machine sprawl. Without the right guardrails, VMs would be created. There was little control or stewardship of VMs, and there was no way to track if VMs were still needed or even being used. On the business side, there was often no downside or cost to requesting VM after VM. The only restriction on an explosion of VMs was often the process to actually create a VM. A request had to be made which would manually be actioned by an IT admin. The IT admin would create the VM matching the requested requirements (if you were lucky). The IT admins could also give themselves access to audit what was happening inside the workload giving IT/compliance visibility. The delay in many organizations was measured in weeks, during which time the progress on the application or service stopped. True private cloud implementations attempted to address some of the problems in terms of self-service, quotas, and pooling resources, but true private cloud implementations were in reality few and far between. However, the IT admin in the middle provided the control for the organization and would enforce naming standards, the types of resource allowed and enabled control at the expense of speed.

Today, most businesses are moving to the cloud for a variety of reasons, but one of the biggest is digital transformation to enable the organization to stay relevant and complete in the market. No one is moving to the cloud because it's fun to do or that it's the new thing; there are legitimate business justifications. With this digital transformation comes a need to modernize processes, deliver services faster, and improve your agility, which the cloud promises through its various attributes. This agility is achieved, as the organization can focus on what they care about, which is not managing infrastructure nor maintaining datacenters; it is the service that is created by the software engineers within the organization that results in a great customer experience. This is an enormous time pressure for the organization, and the software engineers need services instantly. They need new types of services, and with DevOps methodology you can't have an IT admin in the middle of deployments manually creating and deploying things that would traditionally be the control gate. Sacrificing speed for control is not an option in the cloud and for organizations embracing digital transformation. Instead, the engineers will be deploying services directly through various types of pipelines. This can lead to a challenge for cloud engineers (those responsible, the custodians for the cloud services): cloud sprawl. If the engineers of the applications now directly create the resources, the complexity of trying to maintain standards of compliance and architecture, to ensure accountability and compliance, to control cost, grows exponentially. Also consider that engineers deploying services directly on premises, while painful, was still within the guardrails of the datacenter, where public-facing services and storage were still within your control. In the cloud, creating a public-facing service is easy. In the cloud, adding a replica of data to another country is easy. These are just a few of the nightmare scenarios that haunt many cloud architects and cloud engineers.

The solution is governance. Controls can be implemented through policies that are part of the Azure platform. These policies can address requirements around configuration of resources, permissions, and costs. Policies provide the guardrails you need without impacting the speed the engineers want to work at. Policies can also enforce standards such as the naming of resources and the use of tags. Another important aspect is the various roles assigned and really getting visibility to the resources deployed. There are then a number of ways to use and manage the policies along with the other discussed aspects that we will explore in this chapter. The end result, however, is that an organization gets speed and control, with the software engineers having full self-service and speed while functioning with the guardrails defined by the cloud engineers. No sacrifices are required! Cloud governance is one of if not the top customer requirement for most organizations.

This chapter focuses on the following key aspects of cloud governance:

◆ Compliance and understanding requirements

◆ Resource structure

◆ Role-based access control

- Subscriptions and management groups

- Naming standards

- Tags

- Policies

- Templates

- Blueprints, which bring together many of the previous bullet items

- Visibility into resources

- Cost management

Something I do want to point out before I discuss the technologies is that they are all free. There is no cost to use policies, no cost for role-based access control, and no cost to use templates or all of the items put together to create blueprints. These are really core functions that have to be available and that shouldn't have a pay gate. You also don't have to "install" them. They are there, waiting to be used. There is no special resource provider to enable or marketplace item to install. There is no barrier to utilization other than the configuration to make them meet your requirements. This requires some upfront work but also means you need to know to a level you can actually prescriptively document what your requirements actually are.

The Microsoft starting page for all things governance is a great resource. You can find it at `http://aka.ms/governancedocs`.

Understanding Governance Requirements in Your Organization

This is often one of the biggest challenges for a large organization. What exactly are the governance requirements that need to be adhered to. A large, multi-national may have to adhere to country-specific regulatory requirements, industry-specific regulatory requirements, and then their own internal requirements. To understand the documentation exercise of requirements may be a company-wide effort involving legal teams, business units, security, and IT, and often will be broken down by business unit and application, since certain applications may fall under different types of requirements that you don't want to apply to other applications if not required.

Once you understand the requirements, you need to ensure that your organization is compliant with them, which is achieved through governance—or at least partly. For your areas of responsibility, capabilities such as Azure Policy, Management Groups, and more will be critical, and significant work may be required to either create or identify policies that can control and also show compliance of environments as required. But this is only half the story.

As you saw in Chapter 1, when you leverage the cloud, you are not responsible for all layers. Depending on the type of service used, you will be looking for the provider (in this case, Azure) to certify that the elements they are responsible for are compliant and meet the various requirements. That the Azure component may meet the criteria to achieve certain compliance certifications does not mean your complete solution will be compliant. The application you create and the way you use resources will also have to meet the requirements to ensure that the holistic offering consisting of the Azure solutions and your solution meets the requirements and is therefore compliant. Microsoft has a whitepaper that walks through this shared responsibility. It is available for download at:

```
http://download.microsoft.com/download/0/D/6/0D68AE95-6414-4074-B4B8-34039831E2BF/
Microsoft-Cloud-Security-for-Legal-and-Compliance-Professionals.pdf
```

Microsoft holds more compliance certifications than any other cloud provider and has numerous resources you can use to understand the compliance position and how some of the responsibilities are divided. The compliance overview site is:

```
https://www.microsoft.com/en-us/trustcenter/compliance/compliance-overview
```

A detailed list is available at:

```
https://www.microsoft.com/en-us/trustcenter/compliance/complianceofferings
```

This site breaks the offerings down by region, industry and/or Microsoft service. You can select a specific offering, which will link to more detail, including a large PDF file that covers many of them. Audit reports, which are performed by independent third parties, are also available at:

```
https://servicetrust.microsoft.com/ViewPage/MSComplianceGuide
```

Other resources that can help you on your compliance journey can be accessed via `https://servicetrust.microsoft.com/`. The Service Trust Portal brings together many resources, including some of the previous materials, such as the reports, deep GDPR compliance information, and the Compliance Manager tool. Compliance Manager (`https://servicetrust.microsoft.com/ComplianceManager`) helps to identify the shared responsibilities related to a number of key standards and regulations. The Compliance Manager identifies the areas Microsoft is responsible for and their compliance posture and the areas the customer is responsible for, with the ability to essentially check off in the tool where you have met those requirements and can therefore track overall compliance via a number of built-in assessments. When using the assessments, you can drill into every associated control. The testing that was performed where it is a Microsoft responsibility is shown and recommended actions where it is a customer owned responsibility with the ability to assign actions to a member of your organization and detail evidence of your compliance, including testing performed and the results. All of this comes together to give an overall compliance score. The results can be exported to Excel for reporting purposes. Figure 2.1 shows an example dashboard where the organization has not yet started to tackle their actions. Figure 2.2 shows some of the detail and options when selecting the customer-managed controls and highlights the ability to assign actions to a user and track the compliance status.

FIGURE 2.1
Basic Compliance
Manager
dashboard

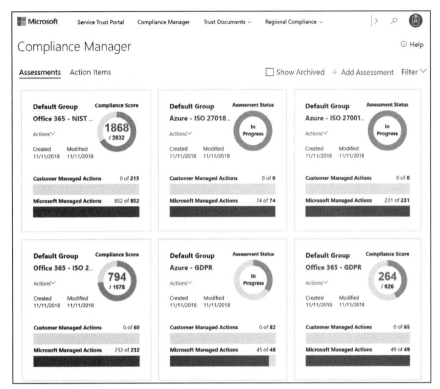

If you are unsure how best to tackle your responsibilities related to compliance, want to see details about Microsoft service compliance, or simply need a tool for tracking, check out Compliance Manager. It is a great free asset that at a minimum can help to give a starting point and help your organization start making progress related to compliance adherence. Microsoft has some high-level governance journeys that you can review to also get some steps and ideas. You can find them at:

https://docs.microsoft.com/en-us/azure/architecture/cloud-adoption/governance/
journeys/overview

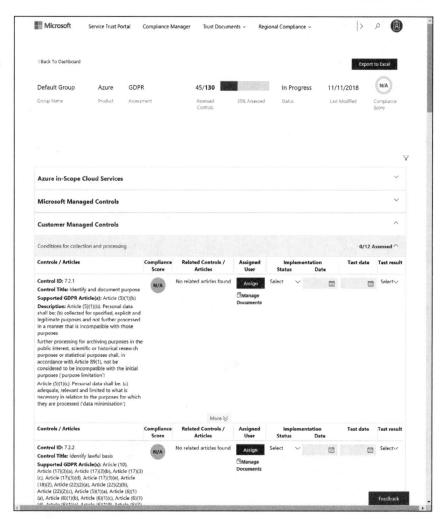

FIGURE 2.2
Tracking
customer-
managed controls

Azure Subscriptions and Management Groups

Organizations will often have multiple subscriptions for various reasons. Deciding on the right criteria to create new subscriptions is critical. As the number of subscriptions increases, the governance can become complex, which is where management groups can greatly assist.

Subscriptions

A subscription is a primary building block of your Azure environment. All Azure resources live within a subscription. A subscription provides one level where role-based access control can be configured, which is then inherited by everything that lives within that subscription. Subscriptions can also have policy assigned that is enforced on everything within that subscription. Subscriptions are also a granularity unit within Azure billing, enabling easy ascertainment of cost per subscription. By default, an Azure subscription is also a unit of isolation between certain types of resources. However, where desired, it is becoming far easier to enable cross-subscription communication and integration. For example, virtual networks (which are contained within a subscription and region) can be easily connected to other networks in other subscriptions using VNet peering.

An Azure subscription trusts a specific Azure AD instance (a tenant) for its authentication and authorization. This does not mean users from outside that Azure AD cannot be part of role assignment within the subscription; those non-native Azure AD users would be guests within your tenant through B2B (business to business), which provides the benefit of enabling resource access without your tenant having to maintain identities for them. (I will cover this in detail in the Chapter 3.)

It is possible to move a subscription between Azure AD tenants. If this is a requirement, you should do it early in the subscription's lifecycle, as any existing role assignments to the subscription (including co-admins) or to resources within the subscription will be lost and will have to be re-created. Figure 2.3 shows the option to move a subscription. Selecting Change Directory will bring up a warning about the loss of role assignments, before allowing you to select a new directory instance to trust. You can also transfer the ownership of a subscription (i.e., the person who gets the bill), which is a separate operation from changing the trusted Azure AD tenant. For instructions on changing the ownership, see:

https://docs.microsoft.com/en-us/azure/billing/billing-subscription-transfer

FIGURE 2.3
Moving a
subscription to
a new Azure AD
tenant

As the primary container for resources, the subscription has many limits/quotas and are documented at:

https://docs.microsoft.com/en-us/azure/azure-subscription-service-limits

It's important to understand the limits, as they may impact your subscription model. Also confirm whether a subscription is a hard limit or a default limit that can be increased to a higher level, if required. For example, by default, a subscription has a very low number of vCPUs, but this can be increased greatly. The absolute limit for a subscription likely will become a reason to require multiple subscriptions, as a scale unit.

Note that in an EA environment, it is possible for people with credit cards to add pay-as-you-go subscriptions added by developers. These will still be tied to your Azure AD tenant. You can contact support, and they can "flip a bit" that would block non-EA subscriptions from being associated with your Azure AD tenant. Furthermore, at the time of writing, a customer-usable PowerShell command is also in development to perform the same change.

When thinking about creating subscriptions under an EA, note that although they can be created manually, another approach is to create them via the subscription-creation API, which can then be hooked into service catalogs and other processes. By default, the API can create 50 subscriptions per account. This can be raised to 200 subscriptions, if required.

The limits per subscription—coupled with the fact that it's a unit where RBAC and policy can be assigned and that it acts as a billing aggregation point—lead to a number of different subscription models that organizations use. As you plan your model, remember that for billing, the tag capability gives a lot of granularity. My guidance is typically *not* to focus on the billing as part of subscription-decision criteria, especially when you consider there is some additional management for each subscription you create.

There are three primary patterns used for subscriptions:

Application/Service   In this model, a unique subscription is used for each application or function within the organization. For example, there may be a core services subscription that contains IT-managed elements (such as ExpressRoute gateways, hub virtual networks, domain controller VMs, and Log Analytics workspaces) that does not contain any application workloads. Then, each application has its own subscription. This enables the application owners to have subscription-level permissions, and means each application can fully utilize resources up to subscription limits without impacting other applications and can still tie into core services through VNet peering (if applicable) and other cross-subscription capabilities. Another benefit of this approach is that some services need permissions at the subscription level (i.e., an owner) and/or require resource providers to be registered, which provides a sandbox for each application without risk of impacting another application. Many times developers need to be owners of the subscriptions they use. Note that this model will result in a *lot* of subscriptions. Outside of the subscription limits, the granular control is also available with resource groups for most things. A slight variation on this model is to have a subscription for each category of application. This approach meets many of the same goals but results in fewer subscriptions.

Lifecycle   In this model, a subscription represents the point of a service's lifecycle—for example, a development subscription, a user acceptance subscription, a production subscription, and so on. Applications would share a subscription based on its lifecycle point, likely with each application running in its own resource group. This enables specific policies to be enabled at a subscription level that are appropriate for the lifecycle point. For example, in development, higher SKU (and therefore higher-priced) services may be blocked; public IPs may be blocked. In production subscriptions only globally redundant storage is allowed, diagnostics must be enabled with logs sent to a central log analytics workspace and so on. Challenges may be the subscription limits and whether any service requires subscription-level permissions or modifications.

Department   In this model, each department is given its own subscription where its applications co-habitat. This is not commonly used, as it does not bring many benefits and likely would not meet requirements since it ignores the lifecycle of the application.

There may, and most likely will, also be hybrids. For example, it is very common to see a separate subscription for core services and then other subscriptions that house multiple applications each. For example, there could be a development subscription where each application has its own resource group, and then a separate subscription for user acceptance testing, and then another subscription for production. Some will also have a subscription per business unit per lifecycle phase that contains applications for that business unit. There is no right or wrong model. Use the model that works to most optimally meet your requirements. My preference is to minimize the number of subscriptions, especially when you consider it is a boundary for virtual networks. I try to use a production and test/dev subscription only. The separate test/dev is required, as many previews are enabled at the subscription level via resource providers, and this should not impact production. Separate subscriptions may be required if you sell Azure services as part of a bill of goods, or in multinational scenarios where you buy in different countries.

If you are not sure where to start, at minimum think about a production subscription and a non-production subscription. Individual applications can be deployed to their own resource groups as can core services. This enables subscription-level policies that can target core governance that is appropriate.

Management Groups

A major challenge for subscriptions is the work involved in trying to apply consistent RBAC and policy where environments have many subscriptions that use a hybrid model. How do you know which should get a development policy, which should be allowed to use this SKU, and how this team can get a role assignment across their specific subscriptions? Before management groups, the option was to use automation/scripting or to perform assignment of RBAC and policy manually. As scale increases, however, performing assignment manually ceases to be an option. Even automation hits challenges. One option is to have some automation task that checks a tag at the subscription level and applies policies and RBAC as required, but that's pretty ugly and would apply at some time-delayed point after creation. Additionally, in an environment with a lot of subscriptions all at a single, flat level with no hierarchy, it's very difficult to understand what organization is in place.

MANAGEMENT GROUP BASICS

Management groups provide a layer that sits on top of subscriptions and more precisely, layers since it is possible to create a hierarchy of management groups that fits your organization. At the time of writing, the management group hierarchy can be up to six levels deep, which opens a lot of flexibility to create a structure that meets requirements. The six levels do not include the root management group or the contained subscriptions, which are placed within a management group. A subscription can only be within a single management group. However, because a hierarchy can be created, the settings further up the hierarchy will also apply (as we will see shortly). Figure 2.4 shows an example management group hierarchy. As you can see, subscriptions of different types can exist within the same management group structure—in this case, EA subscriptions, trial subscriptions, and even dev/test subscriptions. In this example, there is a core IT management group under which environments for dev and production live, with production further broken down into regions. Specific departments also have their own management group with their subscriptions.

There are two primary types of settings that can be applied to management groups:

- ◆ RBAC

- ◆ Policy

These are key and will drive the management group structure. You can apply roles and policy that will be inherited down the structure. In my sample hierarchy, for example, I had production and development. The policies for production and development would likely be very different, as would the roles assigned. Development would have an emphasis on optimizing spend, restricting Internet-facing services while enabling flexibility for the developers, whereas production would be far more locked down, with an emphasis on resiliency and protecting data.

FIGURE 2.4
An example
management group
hierarchy

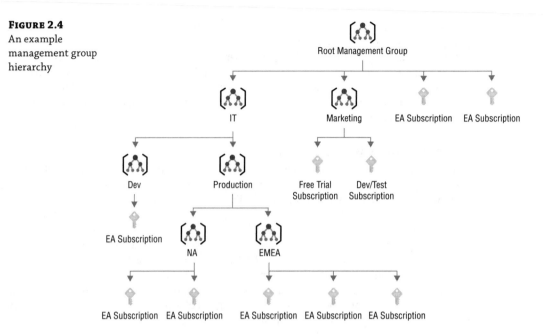

Management groups also surface when it comes to cost reporting via the analytics and aggregation. This is why it is common to see a department/business group as part of a management group structure. This, along with tags, really does kill using the department construct that is available as part of Enterprise Agreements. Typically, management groups are used in one of the following two models:

◆ **Organizational-Based**—Top-level management groups reflect core businesses, and then child management groups are departments within the core business unit, which then have subscriptions.

◆ **Environment-Based**—This is gaining more traction and is built around top-level management groups reflecting R&D, development, and production. Then application-specific management groups are created as children, which then have subscriptions within.

While care should be taken to identify the right hierarchical model to use in your organization, they are very flexible. Apart from the root management group, it is possible, with very little work, to move management groups around the hierarchy (prune and graft), move subscriptions (you need to be a subscription owner to move it to another management group), delete management groups, and create new ones.

Management groups support inheritance, which makes the hierarchical nature of management groups especially powerful. Settings applied higher up the hierarchy are inherited by child management groups and the contained subscriptions. This enables organizations to apply settings that should apply everywhere at the top of the hierarchy that are broader in scope and universally applicable, and then more specific settings can be applied at the appropriate management group level. For example, a central security team would apply policies or permissions required for the entire organization at the top of the hierarchy. A setting applied at the top of the hierarchy would get inherited all the way down to subscriptions at the bottom of the tree. As new subscriptions are added, they would be placed into the right location in the management group hierarchy, which would cause the right combination of settings to be applied based on that placement. If a role is required for a certain group across many subscriptions, apply it at the appropriate management group, and every management group and subscription under that level will inherit that role assignment. For example, giving the network admins group the Network Contributor role across every subscription would enable them to manage network resources in any subscription.

In the previous section, I mentioned in the model where each application has its own subscription that commonly the developers are made the owners of the subscription. Ordinarily, however, a challenge with this is that any guardrails you applied could be removed by them. This is not the case when policies and RBAC are applied via a management group and inherited by the subscription. Settings applied at parent levels cannot be overridden by settings in a child management group or a subscription. This ensures all adherence to the governance configured for every resource that falls under the level the settings are applied. This also means care should be taken when applying roles and policies near the top of the hierarchy, as the effect will be far-reaching. You don't want to accidently apply a policy that blocks resources for the entire organization. When starting with a new policy, consider testing its application in a management group with only a test subscription child to ensure that it behaves as expected, and then apply it further up the chain once you have confidence in its impact.

You will notice in Figure 2.4 a root management group. The root management group is Azure AD tenant-wide (i.e., there is a single root management group under which every subscription that trusts the tenant will reside within the hierarchy). You cannot have more than one root management group. You cannot delete it, but you can change its display name, which by default will be Tenant Root Group. Its ID will be the same as the Azure AD ID, as shown in Figure 2.5. Any subscription that trusts the Azure AD tenant will by default be a child of the root management group, until it is moved elsewhere within the management group hierarchy. A subscription that trusts a different Azure AD tenant cannot reside in a different tenant's management group structure.

A few facts about management groups:

- 10,000 management groups are supported in a single tenant (spread over those 6 levels).

- A management group or subscription can only have one parent—i.e., belong to one management group.

- A management group can have many children, which can be a combination of management groups and subscriptions.

Even if you have a fairly small environment, I would recommend identifying how you will structure management groups. You should have a skeleton structure and place subscriptions accordingly, and then grow and evolve as required. With the flexibility they bring and the ability to apply settings and gain insight, management groups are invaluable to organizations both big and small.

FIGURE 2.5
Common ID
between the root
management
group and the
Azure AD tenant

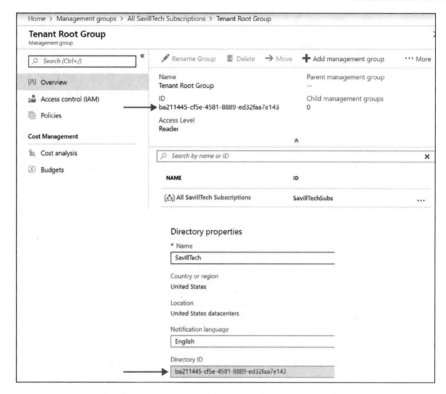

GETTING STARTED WITH MANAGEMENT GROUPS

You don't have to "enable" management groups in the traditional sense. As soon as you start using management groups, a process triggers in Azure that will create the root management group for the Azure AD tenant, and every subscription associated with that tenant will automatically roll up under it, as will the first management group created that triggered the process. All new management groups and subscriptions will be made children of the root management group. Subscriptions can then be moved, provided that the user has the proper RBAC. This ensures that a tenant-wide policy or role assignment won't be skipped by any subscriptions. Note that because of this initial creation and subscription rollup, there can be up to a 15-minute delay the first time a management group is created in an Azure AD tenant (although a delay of this magnitude is unlikely and is very much a worse case).

There is, however, a step required to manage the Root Management Group. By default, even global administrators of the Azure AD will have no permissions (like everyone else) on the Root Management Group and will need to give themselves permission to perform actions against the Root Management Group. This will give the user a new role, User Access Admin, which will apply to every management group and subscription under the tenant, since it is applied at the root and then inherited. This role enables modifications to role assignments to anything. To give this permission to yourself, you must be a global administrator of the Azure AD tenant (either permanently or via Privileged Identity Management):

1. Open Azure Active Directory in the portal.

2. Open the Properties navigation item under the Manage group.

3. At the bottom of the Properties page, select Yes for Access Management for Azure Resources, as shown in Figure 2.6, and then click Save.

FIGURE 2.6
Enabling access for all subscriptions and management groups under the Azure AD tenant

This can also be done from the command line or PowerShell. The process is documented at:

```
https://docs.microsoft.com/en-us/azure/role-based-access-control/
elevate-access-global-admin/
```

If you now look at any resource's access control role assignments, you will see you have the User Access Administrator role, which has been inherited from the Root (i.e., the tenant). This is the same permission you would give yourself if permissions were somehow lost to a management group or subscription and is generally considered a "break glass" permission. So once you have done what you need under normal circumstances, you should un-elevate yourself by repeating the previous process and setting the Access Management for Azure Resources option to No.

Note that in many environments, you will not need permissions on the root management group, as RBAC and policies are often applied at child management groups; however, the capability is available if you want to apply certain policies to every subscription that trusts the tenant.

Creating a management group is very easy. It can be done through all the normal means, such as the portal, PowerShell, and the CLI. In the following example, I create a new management group using PowerShell with a different display name from the actual group name (which cannot contain spaces) and make it a child of an existing management group:

```
PS C:\> New-AzManagementGroup -GroupName ProductionMG `
-DisplayName "Production MG" -ParentId (Get-AzManagementGroup `
-GroupName SavilltechSubs).Id


Id        : /providers/Microsoft.Management/managementGroups/ProductionMG
Type      : /providers/Microsoft.Management/managementGroups
Name      : ProductionMG
TenantId  : ba211445-cf5e-4581-8889-ed32faa7e143
```

```
DisplayName       : Production MG
UpdatedTime       : 2/11/2019 10:56:03 PM
UpdatedBy         : ed17220d-a6d8-45d0-a7bd-2aadc44c39e7
ParentId          :
/providers/Microsoft.Management/managementGroups/SavillTechSubs
ParentName        : SavillTechSubs
ParentDisplayName : All SavillTech Subscriptions
```

Notice that in the command to create I need to pass the ID of the parent. Rather than manually entering that full ID, I use member enumeration and embed another command in parentheses to get the object for the parent, and then use the Id attribute via the dereference (dot) operator. Also notice in the output of the creation that I get a lot of detail, including the parent name and ID. This is the same information that is available when using `Get-AzManagementGroup -GroupName`.

NOTE   In my examples, I am using the Az modules, which replace the AzureRM modules and have the benefit of being PowerShell core-compatible and therefore available through the Azure cloud shell. By the time you read this, you should be shifting from AzureRM to Az. However, if you are still using AzureRM, most of the Az commands are available via AzureRM. Just replace Az with AzureRM. For example, in this case, you could use `Get-AzureRMManagementGroup`.

Anyone in a tenant can create a management group, which becomes a child of the Root automatically. From there, you can build out a hierarchy branch with management groups and subscriptions. A user can move management groups and subscriptions from the Root to be under-targeted management groups.

The design of management groups is to allow anyone to start using management groups for easier adoption but establishes controls on who can move subscriptions and other management groups around. This creates strict rules on who can move objects. In order to move a management group or subscription:

◆   The user needs to have write access on the targeted parent Management Group and the existing parent management group.

  ◆   Write access is given with roles Owner, Contributor, and Management Group Contributor. (More on this soon.)

  ◆   If the Target or Source Parent management group is the Root MG, there is no check on the users' access on that Root. This is to allow users to move management groups/subscriptions to and from the Root, as it is the default area.

◆   The user needs to have Owner access on the child item being moved. This can be a subscription or management group.

  ◆   This is to ensure the user has access on that item and is authorized to move it.

  ◆   Owner is required, since when you move a child object, you could be changing who has access to it via inheritance.

For an example of all the different methods for management group creation, have a look at:

`https://docs.microsoft.com/en-us/azure/governance/management-groups/manage`

Note there are two management group-specific roles: MG Contributor and MG Reader. These roles give the Contributor and Reader rights, respectively, but only for management groups. These rights do not apply to any other type of resource.

Once you have management groups, you can inspect them and perform various actions, including assigning roles and policies, as shown in Figure 2.7. The standard cmdlets, etc., will also work (for example, `New-AzureRmRoleAssignment`), but you must use the full providers URI for the management group—for example:

```
New-AzureRmRoleAssignment `
-Scope "/providers/Microsoft.Management/managementgroups/{mgID}"
```

FIGURE 2.7
The wonderous things you can do with your new management group

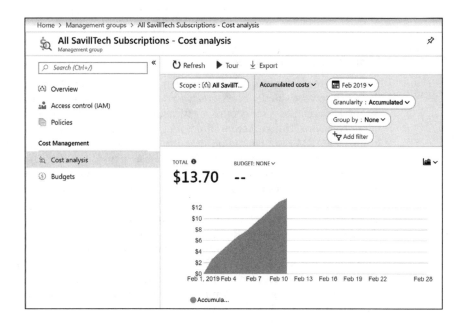

You can also view the cost analysis for all subscriptions under the management group hierarchy (including subscriptions that belong to its child management groups) or apply a budget to trigger alerts at certain thresholds. This detail is accessed by clicking the Details link next to the name of the management group, as shown in Figure 2.8.

FIGURE 2.8
Accessing the
properties of a
management
group

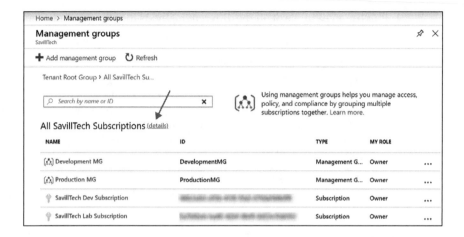

Resource Groups

Resource groups are probably one of the most powerful objects in Azure Resource Manager—and are also very simple. Every created resource lives in a subscription, and it also lives in a resource group. Resource groups, as the name suggests, group resources together into a container construct. Unlike Active Directory groups, where a user can be a member of multiple groups, an ARM resource can only be in a single resource group and indeed must be in a single resource group. Resource groups cannot be nested, making them a flat structure that lives within a subscription. This means a resource group cannot span subscriptions. Each subscription will have its own set of resource groups and, at time of writing, supports 980 resource groups (per subscription).

A resource group is very simple. It has a name (which should be made up of alphanumeric characters, periods, underscores, hyphens, and parentheses, but no spaces) and a region it is deployed to. Note that while a resource group is deployed to a region, it can contain resources from any region, not just those in the same region as the resource group. The actual region of the resource group does very little; it is just where the metadata of the resource group lives (which may be important for compliance reasons). You will often use the region of the resource group to automatically create resources in the same region as the resource group, to simplify deployments.

As with any other resource, you can apply tags to a resource group. Note they are *not* natively inherited by the resources within the resource group, but there are ways to achieve this either through automation tasks that scan the resource group then apply to all the resources within (an example of this can be found at:

```
https://marckean.com/2018/12/17/
easy-tagging-of-resources-in-azure-for-billing-and-charge-back/
```

or apply a policy at the resource group that applies the tag automatically. Tags only at the resource group can still be useful for tracking of type of content, cost centers, etc.

Additionally, RBAC can be applied at a resource group, which *is* inherited by the resources within it. The application of RBAC is a huge reason to use resource groups. You can also apply policies to a resource group and even assign budgets and track costs. This makes the resource group a very logical administrative scope that will drive the resource group design.

So how do you decide which resources to group together? The primary driver for grouping resources is resources that share a common lifecycle. They are created together, run together, and ultimately will get decommissioned together. When you delete a resource group, everything within it is also deleted. This will typically mean the resources that make up a certain application, which may include web services, storage services, VMs, load balancers, and more. When you are deploying an Azure JSON template, those resources must all be deployed to the same resource group, which drives the idea of grouping a service into a resource group. When you consider that RBAC can be applied to a resource group, this makes a lot of sense where the group of people working on a product can easily be granted roles on the components that make up that product by applying at the resource group level that are then inherited. It is therefore very common for resource groups to be heterogeneous resources of different types. There may also be homogeneous resource groups where the resources are of the same type. It is very common to see a networking resource group that contains all the virtual networks that the network teams have permissions to. You may also see a resource group with the Azure database instances that the DBAs manage. This is possible because resource groups are not an isolation boundary. Resources can use other resources in different resource groups. For example, a VM in one resource group can connect to a virtual network in a different resource group. An application can connect to a database in a different resource group. You create the resource groups and place resources based on your requirements around logical grouping, RBAC, policy, and even cost management. It is possible to move resources between resource groups and often even between subscriptions with minimal impact.

Many organizations will have "core services" resource groups that are more rigid and controlled by traditional IT and contain core resources, such as the previously mentioned virtual networks, gateways, core VMs such as DCs, Key Vaults, etc. Then there will be more agile resource groups that each contain a certain service. If resources will update separately from other resources in the same resource group, then it may be more logical to separate them into separate resource groups.

Note that it is possible to lock resources via a resource lock. This can be at a subscription, resource group, or individual resource. When a resource is locked, it cannot be accidently deleted or modified. A lock can be ReadOnly, stopping it being deleted or modified, or be CanNotDelete, allowing it to be modified but not deleted. Only Owners of resources/resource groups/subscriptions can lock/unlock (and the User Access Administrator role).

Role-Based Access Control

It was a dark and hostile time as little as five years ago in the Azure cloud when it came to granular access control. Azure Service Manager ruled, and there were essentially two types of people in a subscription: those that could do management actions (i.e., the service administrator and co-administrators) and those that could not (i.e., everyone who was not in the previously mentioned roles). These were subscription-level assignments, which meant it was common to have to separate resources and projects into separate subscriptions to enable separate security containers. Even then, however, often groups of people would have to be given permissions above what they actually needed, which breaks a fundamental security principal, least privilege—to only give what is required. This should guide you as you look at your RBAC design.

Introduced in 2014 and really becoming mainstream late 2015 was the Azure Resource Manager (ARM), which is what everything we know about Azure today is built on. ARM completely changed the way Azure was architected, with its JSON-based nature, resource groups, and a true RBAC solution than enabled granular built-in and custom roles to be assigned at subscription, resource group, and even individual resource levels, and, as the service has continued to evolve, at management groups as well. These permissions are then inherited down to any children of the assigned level. A role assigned all the way at the top of a management group would be inherited all the way down to all the resources beneath it—its great-grandchildren! This gives us the following levels of assignment:

- Management group

- Subscription

- Resource group

- Resource

We generally stay away from assigning roles at the resource level. This is very hard to manage, hard to troubleshoot, and generally not required if the resource groups have been correctly architected. Most assignments will be at the resource group level, as they relate to roles around specific teams and applications, but there will also be some at the management group and subscription level. Additionally, we are not living in 2014, so we don't have binary permissions. That is, regardless of whether or not we have management, ARM enables specific actions for specific resource types to be granted at a defined scope—i.e., a resource group, subscription, or management group. There are a large number of built-in roles that can be assigned, or you can create custom roles (which I will cover later).

AZURE ROLES ≠ AZURE AD ROLES

There are a large number of Azure roles, which are those roles applying to Azure resources. There are also roles in Azure AD that relate to Azure AD identity functionality and also some used by services such as Office 365, Dynamics 365, etc. They do not overlap. Permissions assigned in Azure AD do not grant permissions on resources in Azure that trust the Azure AD tenant, with one exception. When managing the root management group, we elevated ourselves and gave the Global admin the can manage Azure Subscriptions and Management Groups right. When this is activated, the user gains the User Access Administrator role at the root management group and, therefore, every resource that trusts the Azure AD instance. This enables them to manage access to resources and essentially take ownership or grant whatever permissions they wish. They can read anything except secrets in a key vault (unless they gave themselves specific permissions).

The following three roles can be applied to anything in Azure:

- **Owner**—Has full access to all resources and can modify access control

- **Contributor**—Can create and manage all Azure resource types but cannot modify the access control

- **Reader**—Can view resources

I would give the Owner role to someone who will be managing a container (for example, a resource group) and will be giving others access. I would give the Contributor role to people who need to manage all the resources in that container but don't need to change the access control. I would give more granular access via the other types of roles based on specific user group need.

This is a key point: I don't want to grant permissions to users. This gets messy. Permissions are hard to track and hard to remove. Roles should be granted to groups that are well named and help identify the type of user and access. Then add and remove users to groups as required. There are even features like Access Reviews that enable membership of groups to be validated on a periodic basis or even via self-review.

There are a large number of built-in roles for Azure. You can view them all at:

```
https://docs.microsoft.com/en-us/azure/role-based-access-control/built-in-roles
```

Whatever type of access you want to grant, there is probably a built-in role that meets that requirement. The roles are built around the actions available for each resource type contained in the various resource providers. Figure 2.9 walks through looking at this via the portal. You can see that initially I view the access control for a resource group, which shows every role. I select the Virtual Machine Contributor role, and then click Permissions. From here, I select a specific resource provider (in this case, Compute), and then I see the actions enabled for each type of resource and its components, with basic read, write, and delete visible, and then drill down to the other actions. Note that some organizations may struggle with some built-in roles, as they may have more privilege than actually required for the specific person. If that is the case, don't worry—there are other options.

FIGURE 2.9
Viewing the roles available for assignment at a resource group level, and then the permissions for a specific role

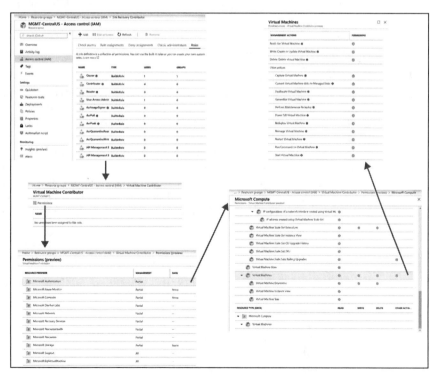

The roles available will vary depending on the scope you are applying at. For example, applying at a management group, subscription, or resource group will expose all roles, since any type of resource may be contained within that construct. If you manage access control to a specific type of resource, you will only see roles that have some action for that resource type. In this example, I use PowerShell and the Az module to examine the roles available, look at some details, and then look at roles for a virtual machine. (Note that I show those directly operating on virtual machines and those on anything compute or on anything.)

```
Get-AzRoleDefinition | FT Name, Description
Get-AzRoleDefinition | measure
Get-AzRoleDefinition Contributor | FL Actions, NotActions
(Get-AzRoleDefinition "Virtual Machine Contributor").Actions

$roles = Get-AzRoleDefinition
foreach ($roledef in $roles) {
    if ($roledef.Actions -match "^Microsoft.Compute/virtualMachines/" -or
$roledef.Actions -match "^Microsoft.Compute/\*" -or $roledef.Actions -match
"^\*/")
    {
        Write-Output "Role: $($roledef.Name)"
    }
}
```

Microsoft has full documentation on all the commands to view, grant, and revoke permissions at:

```
https://docs.microsoft.com/en-us/azure/role-based-access-control/
role-assignments-powershell
```

Although a large number of roles are built-in, you can also create your own roles by assigning specific actions for resources to a custom role. The role can then be applied at the subscription, resource group, or resource level. (Remember, however that you generally don't apply permissions at resource levels). The easiest way to create a new role is to find a role that is close to what you want and modify its actions by adding and removing provider operations. Following is an example of fetching the Virtual Machine Contributor role, giving it a new name, looking at the current actions, removing some actions, and then adding specific actions to enable start and restart. Finally, the scope is set to the subscription and then added. When you view the roles in the portal, the custom role will show with an orange cube instead of blue in the portal. Basic view shown in Figure 2.10. You can also export roles to JSON, modify the JSON, and then import the roles back in.

```
PS C:\> Get-AzProviderOperation "Microsoft.Compute/virtualMachines/*" |
FT OperationName, Operation, Description -AutoSize
PS C:\> $sub = Get-AzSubscription -SubscriptionName "SavillTech Dev Subscription"
PS C:\> $role = Get-AzRoleDefinition "Virtual Machine Contributor"
PS C:\> $role.actions
Microsoft.Authorization/*/read
Microsoft.Compute/availabilitySets/*
Microsoft.Compute/locations/*
Microsoft.Compute/virtualMachines/*
```

```
Microsoft.Compute/virtualMachineScaleSets/*
Microsoft.DevTestLab/schedules/*
Microsoft.Insights/alertRules/*
Microsoft.Network/applicationGateways/backendAddressPools/join/action
Microsoft.Network/loadBalancers/backendAddressPools/join/action
Microsoft.Network/loadBalancers/inboundNatPools/join/action
Microsoft.Network/loadBalancers/inboundNatRules/join/action
Microsoft.Network/loadBalancers/probes/join/action
Microsoft.Network/loadBalancers/read
Microsoft.Network/locations/*
Microsoft.Network/networkInterfaces/*
Microsoft.Network/networkSecurityGroups/join/action
Microsoft.Network/networkSecurityGroups/read
Microsoft.Network/publicIPAddresses/join/action
Microsoft.Network/publicIPAddresses/read
Microsoft.Network/virtualNetworks/read
Microsoft.Network/virtualNetworks/subnets/join/action
Microsoft.RecoveryServices/locations/*
Microsoft.RecoveryServices/Vaults/backupFabrics/backupProtectionIntent/write
Microsoft.RecoveryServices/Vaults/backupFabrics/protectionContainers/protectedI
tems/*/read
Microsoft.RecoveryServices/Vaults/backupFabrics/protectionContainers/protectedI
tems/read
Microsoft.RecoveryServices/Vaults/backupFabrics/protectionContainers/protectedI
tems/write
Microsoft.RecoveryServices/Vaults/backupPolicies/read
Microsoft.RecoveryServices/Vaults/backupPolicies/write
Microsoft.RecoveryServices/Vaults/read
Microsoft.RecoveryServices/Vaults/usages/read
Microsoft.RecoveryServices/Vaults/write
Microsoft.ResourceHealth/availabilityStatuses/read
Microsoft.Resources/deployments/*
Microsoft.Resources/subscriptions/resourceGroups/read
Microsoft.SqlVirtualMachine/*
Microsoft.Storage/storageAccounts/listKeys/action
Microsoft.Storage/storageAccounts/read
Microsoft.Support/*$role.Id = $null
PS C:\> $role.Name = "Virtual Machine Operator"
PS C:\> $role.Description = "Can monitor and restart virtual machines."
PS C:\> $role.Actions.Remove("Microsoft.Compute/virtualMachines/*")
PS C:\> $role.Actions.Remove("Microsoft.Compute/virtualMachineScaleSets/*")
PS C:\> $role.Actions.Add("Microsoft.Compute/virtualMachines/read")
PS C:\> $role.Actions.Add("Microsoft.Compute/virtualMachines/start/action")
PS C:\> $role.Actions.Add("Microsoft.Compute/virtualMachines/restart/action")
PS C:\> $role.AssignableScopes.Clear()
PS C:\> $role.AssignableScopes.Add("/subscriptions/$($sub.id)")
PS C:\> New-AzRoleDefinition -Role $role
```

FIGURE 2.10
A slightly modified icon
for a custom role

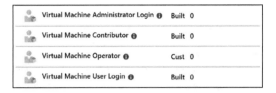

Ordinarily, when a role is applied to a group, that role is an enduring assignment that is in effect until the user is removed from the applied group. Best practices in security today are just-enough-administration (JEA) and just-in-time administration (JIT). The idea is that users ordinarily have basic privileges, and then, when a more privileged action needs to be executed, the user can elevate up to a higher set of permissions that are just enough to get the job done for a limited period of time. Privileged Identity Management (PIM) is an Azure AD Premium 2 capability that initially applied to Azure AD roles. For example, a user could elevate up to Global Administrator for a period of time after performing MFA. (Additional authentication is used when gaining additional privilege.) The same capability is available for Azure Resource Manager: to elevate up to an ARM role only when required for a limited time.

To use PIM with ARM resources at a subscription level, you need to switch to using PIM for role management. This can be done via Azure AD Privileged Identity Management - Azure Resources and by performing a discovery of subscriptions. (This can also be done at a management group level). A list of unmanaged subscriptions will be displayed, as shown in Figure 2.11. Select Manage Resource to enable the switch. (PIM will be covered in detail in Chapter 3.) Once enabled, PIM can be used to grant roles on the level enabled and any child objects. For example, if you enable PIM on a subscription, then PIM for Azure roles can be applied at the subscription, resource group, or resource level. When enabling a user (or group) for a role, change the drop-down shown in Figure 2.12 to your desired scope for PIM Azure role assignment. Note that even after enabling PIM, you can still use the traditional access control for resources. Any changes via the standard access control will be reflected in the PIM (and vice versa).

FIGURE 2.11
Switching to PIM-
based role resource
management.

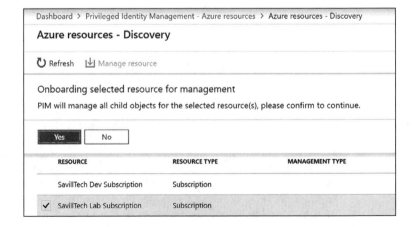

FIGURE 2.12
Changing the scope
for Azure PIM role
assignment.

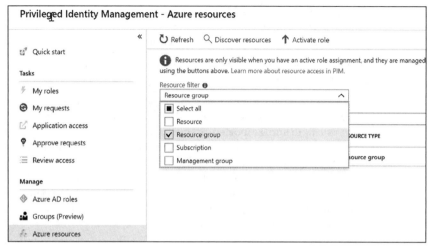

If you have a service provider that manages your resources, historically you would add users from that organization to your Azure AD instance using B2B, and then place those users in groups and give those groups various permissions via RBAC. That is a significant amount of work for the customer and also very cumbersome for the service provider, which has to constantly switch Azure AD instances to manage resources across their customers. The Azure Delegated Resource Management feature, which is part of the Azure Service Provider Management Toolkit, addresses this by enabling resources to be projected from customer environments into the service provider's environment with specific rights assigned as part of the projection. This can be via a managed services offer the service provider creates in the Azure Marketplace that includes the required rights or through the deployment of an ARM template in the customer's tenant. This enables the service provider to view all their various customers through a single portal and management interface (with resources grouped by customer). This functionality could also be used within an organization that uses multiple Azure AD tenants.

Naming Conventions

Most organizations have some kind of naming convention for their operating system instances. These typically include some kind of location identifier, perhaps a company identifier (to protect against future organizational mergers), a service type identifier, and then some kind of instance number. For example, I might use the following for the first (01) domain controller (DC) in Dallas (DAL) for my SavillTech (SAV) organization:

SAVDALDC01

Naming is even more important when leveraging Azure resources, which can be in many regions and of many different types. Also remember that some resources have different requirements about what is supported as part of the name. In the cloud, the resources may include the type of resource in addition to the environment plus the types of information previously covered. The organization should pick a standard set of codes for the various Azure regions. Microsoft has detailed guidance on possible naming approaches to be used at:

```
https://docs.microsoft.com/en-us/azure/architecture/best-practices/
naming-conventions
```

This is worth reviewing and either following or getting input to help with your own standards. The article also walks through a number of the limits for different types of resources, such as length and supported character sets.

While the name of a resource is important, to potentially quickly see its type, location, and purpose, additional metadata can be added to every Azure resource. The metadata can contain additional detail that is not only viewable but also fully searchable. This does not take away from having a naming standard, but realize that not everything has to be in a name. For example, use tags. Many organizations chose to enforce the use of tags and, potentially, naming conventions through Azure Policy.

Using Tags

Often, naming conventions are used to help identify attributes of a resource, but Azure has a more direct and preferred option: tags. Tags are available for nearly every type of Azure resource at:

```
https://docs.microsoft.com/en-us/azure/azure-resource-manager/tag-support
```

Tags are name/value pairs with no built-in fixed set of names, meaning you can use any tags you want.

In most environments, a standard set of tags will be defined and required (policies can help enforce) that provide the data required in the organization for identification, tracking, operational tasks, billing (remember, this is a big use for granular cost accumulation), indexing (you can search and filter based on tags), and more. Think of a tag as a method to add metadata to your resources. The exact tags required will be driven by governance requirements. In addition to defining a standard set of tags that should be present on all resources, it is important to have a standard set of values to be used for each tag. For example, if Environment were a required tag, there should be possible values, such as Prod, QA, UAT, DEV, and so on. The benefit of tags is lessened if the values are not consistent. For example, some people put a value of Production, some put Live, some put Prod, etc. The same would apply to department abbreviations, countries, projects, and so on. Therefore, before even starting the technology implementation of tags, work on the information you want exposed via the tags and the taxonomy details.

The following are some key limitations related to tags that you should consider when designing your implementation:

◆ Each resource can have up to 15 tags. (This includes resource groups.)

◆ Tag names can be up to 512 characters (128 for storage accounts).

◆ Tag values can be up to 256 characters.

- The total number of characters for tag names and values for virtual machines is 2048 characters.

- Tag names cannot contain the following characters:

    - < > % & \ / ?

For most organizations, 15 tags is plenty, and the character limits are a non-issue. Following are some of the core tags I have seen working with a number of organizations. This is not an exhaustive list, and tags can be added and removed. As mentioned previously, however, it is good to sit down with all the stakeholders in the organization and whiteboard out what tags will be useful and get that taxonomy identifier. You would need the security, application, governance, IT, network teams, and pretty much anyone who uses resources involved in the tags' taxonomy design.

- `ApplicationID`
- `ApplicationOwner`
- `ProjectID`
- `ProjectTask`
- `Role`
- `Description`
- `CostCenter`
- `Dept`
- `Company` (This is useful if a split of the organization may occur after mergers, etc.)
- `Region`
- `Cloud` (This can be useful in a multi-cloud organization where resources are aggregated to a single inventory store.)
- `ExpirationDate`
- `UpdateMgmt`
- `AVAgent`
- `ExclusionGroup`
- `MaintenanceWindow`

Note that the last four tags are all operational tags used to identify how a resource is being patched, whether it's protected with anti-virus, and whether it's part of any exclusions against standard policy. Figure 2.13 shows a whiteboard that was the output of a working session with a customer to define the goals for tags.

FIGURE 2.13
Whiteboarding output of tags taxonomy discussion

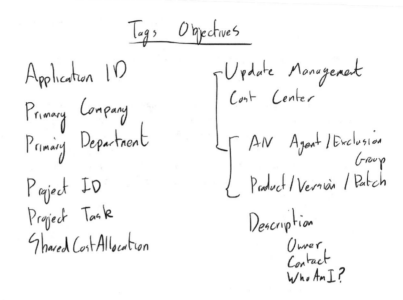

TAGS AND GDPR

Remember that there are numerous regulations today about storing personal data and an individual's right to be forgotten. These may impact your tags and processes to update, so keep possible regulatory impact in mind when designing your tags and maintaining tag-related processes.

It may be the case that you need more than 15 tags. At this point, it is unlikely that you are expecting anyone to manually enter the details; instead, you probably have some CI/CD pipeline that is adding/updating/using the tags. A common approach is to store JSON, which itself can contain its own data or other sets of name/value pairs, in a tag. For example, consider operational details. A single `OpsDetail` tag could be used that contains JSON. The content of the JSON would be maintained by the operational processes that could store details such as last patch date, AV version, exclusion, and so on. Again, you cannot expect users to manually maintain JSON values and the content of the tag would have to be used as part of a CI/CD pipeline or other process. In the following PowerShell, I walk through some basic tag management on a resource, just to show a number of the key processes (note that I had already set the tags on another VM in the environment), and then set a tag with some JSON content and modify the tag content.

```
#Using tags
PS C:\> $VMName = 'Savazuusscdc01'
PS C:\> $RGName = 'RG-Infra-SCUS'
PS C:\> $VM = Get-AzVM $RGName $VMName
#Currently empty
PS C:\> $VM.Tags
```

```
#Adding two tags to a VM (uses hash table in PowerShell)
PS C:\> Set-AzResource -ResourceId $VM.Id `
-Tag @{ Dept = "CoreServices"; Role = "DC"; Region = "EUS"} -Force
#Add another tag for the owner
PS C:\> $Res = Get-AzResource -ResourceGroupName $RGName -Name $VMName
PS C:\> $Res.Tags
Key     Value
---     -----
Dept    CoreServices
Region  SCUS
Role    DC
PS C:\> $Res.Tags.Add("Owner", "John Savill")
PS C:\> Set-AzResource -Tag $Res.Tags -ResourceId $Res.Id -Force
#Find all DCs by searching for any resource with Role of DC in the tags
PS C:\> Get-AzResource -Tag @{Role = "DC"} |
Format-Table Name, ResourceGroupName -AutoSize
Name             ResourceGroupName
----             -----------------
Savazuusedc01    RG-Infra-EUS
savazuusscdc01   RG-Infra-SCUS
#Create a JSON document in a variable
PS C:\> $OpersHash = @{AVAgent = "Defender";PatchSystem = "MU";MaintWindow =
"1:00-4:00"}
PS C:\> $OpersJson = $OpersHash | ConvertTo-Json
#Add to tags of VM
PS C:\> $res.Tags.Add("Operations",$OpersJson)
PS C:\> Set-AzResource -Tag $Res.Tags -ResourceId $Res.Id -Force
PS C:\> $res.tags.Operations
{
  "AVAgent": "Defender",
  "PatchSystem": "MU",
  "MaintWindow": "1:00-4:00"
}
#Fetch the updated object
PS C:\> $Res = Get-AzResource -ResourceGroupName $RGName -Name $VMName
PS C:\> $OpersObj = $res.tags.Operations | ConvertFrom-Json
#Update maintenance window and add a patch day of today
PS C:\> $OpersObj.MaintWindow = "1:00-3:00"
PS C:\> $OpersObj | Add-Member -Name "PatchDate" -Value (Get-Date -UFormat
"%Y/%m/%d") -MemberType NoteProperty
PS C:\> $OpersJson = $OpersObj | ConvertTo-Json
PS C:\> $res.Tags.Operations = $OpersJson
PS C:\> Set-AzResource -Tag $Res.Tags -ResourceId $Res.Id -Force
```

Detailed examples of many tag usage scenarios can be found at:

https://docs.microsoft.com/en-us/azure/azure-resource-manager/
resource-group-using-tags

A special consideration around tags is the resource group. Every resource lives within a resource group, and inheritance is a property of Azure that we use extensively with resource groups. For example, access control applied at the resource group is inherited by the contained resources; however, inheritance does *not* apply to tags. Therefore, if you assign tags to a resource group, the resources will not also have those tags. This also means if you view costs based on tags or search based on tags, you won't see the resources in the resource group. Often, you do want tags on the resource group to be applied to resources. There are two primary approaches to achieve this.

The first approach is to write an automation that copies the tags from the resource group to the child resources either if missing or overwritten. This automation can be run on a schedule or even triggered via alerts via Azure Monitor to call the automation via an action group. This would not stop extra tags from being specified on the resources themselves. You can find an example of a script that copies tags for a specific resource group at:

```
https://docs.microsoft.com/en-us/azure/azure-resource-manager/
resource-group-using-tags
```

In the following code, I have modified that script slightly to perform the process for every resource group in a subscription, instead of just one:

```
$groups = Get-AzResourceGroup
foreach($group in $groups)
{
    if ($null -ne $group.Tags) {
        $resources = Get-AzResource -ResourceGroupName $group.ResourceGroupName
        foreach ($r in $resources)
        {
            $resourcetags = (Get-AzResource -ResourceId $r.ResourceId).Tags
            if ($resourcetags)
            {
                foreach ($key in $group.Tags.Keys)
                {
                    if (-not($resourcetags.ContainsKey($key)))
                    {
                        $resourcetags.Add($key, $group.Tags[$key])
                    }
                }
                Set-AzResource -Tag $resourcetags -ResourceId $r.ResourceId `
                    -Force
            }
            else
            {
                Set-AzResource -Tag $group.Tags -ResourceId $r.ResourceId -Force
            }
        }
    }
}
```

Another approach would be to use policies. An append policy could be used to apply tags from the resource group and to the resources. The following is an example policy file that does this for a `costCode` tag:

```
{
    "mode": "indexed",
    "policyRule": {
        "if": {
            "field": "tags.costCode",
            "exists": "false"
        },
        "then": {
            "effect": "append",
            "details": [
                {
                    "field": "tags.costCode",
                    "value": "[resourcegroup().tags.costCode]"
                }
            ]
        }
    }
}
```

When it comes to enforcing the use of tags, Azure Policy is the best option. However, be careful of using the Deny action if tags are not specified, as I have run across a number of third-party solutions and marketplace items that do *not* support the specification of tags and would therefore fail to deploy. A good option is to require tags on the resource group, as most solutions allow the resource group to be pre-created, and then use Azure Policy to append (fix) the resources in the resource group to match those of the resource group. If additional tags should be present on resources, then use Azure Policy with an effect of audit to enable actions to be taken to fix post-creation or even set a default, if one is not specified. (Azure Policy templates are available for all these options.)

Another approach would be to have exception options in your policies to ignore certain resource groups and ordinarily apply the deny action. In this case, the deployment would fail. The person trying to deploy would see that the policy was rejected and could contact operations, where the exception could be added.

Azure Policy

In previous sections, I talked about some aspects of governance around compliance requirements, naming standards, and tags, but how do you ensure that users adhere to your requirements? Azure policies provide the guardrails: structured, declarative definitions of the cloud engineer's intent that is codified that can then become a core element of the environment, enforced by the platform and in real time.

In the previous chapter, in Figure 1.13, I drew out the basics of the Azure Resource Manager and how it relates to key components. I noted some "stuff" to the left of the various components. Some key aspects of that "stuff" related to governance. Figure 2.14 shows a different view of the layers related to the Azure Resource Manager—this time with a focus on governance. You'll also notice Azure Blueprints, which bring together multiple governance artifacts for pre-active applications, and Azure Resource Graph, which brings a native query capability across every resource you have in Azure.

FIGURE 2.14
How governance and policy fits into the core of Azure Resource Manager

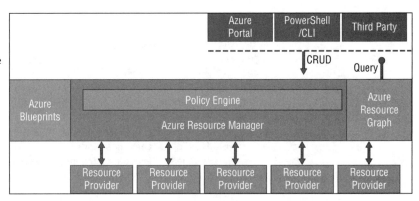

As you can see, the policy engine that Azure Policy uses sits in the control plane (ARM) layer of Azure, built natively into the platform, and is the gate through which all requests must pass, be it via the portal, PowerShell, CLI, REST API, or third parties. The policy engine is not called on a schedule to check what has been deployed already but rather at the time of any request via ARM. Before any request is actioned, it is first evaluated against Azure Policy. This enables a number of Azure Policy effect types, which most importantly can include Deny, i.e., don't allow this request to be completed because it would violate the policy. A good example would be a policy that blocks a non-globally resilient storage account. If a request via any means came to ARM to create a locally resilient storage account, the request would be evaluated by the policy; it would match the Deny policy that had been created; and the request would be denied. Not only would the request be denied, but the message back would explain why it was denied, with a reference to the enforcing policy, which would then enable the requesting user to further research and understand what happened and either correct the request or contact the owner of the policy for further guidance or to request an exception. This would surface even in CI/CD tools such as Azure DevOps, so as the developer is testing a pipeline, if they violate a policy, it would surface as they test, and they could take corrective actions.

Before going further, I want to stress something that may be obvious (and likely will become so as we look at policy in more detail): The enforcement of settings is a huge capability and will be widely used; however, the ability to also audit environments against policy and show compliance is as useful—and potentially more useful, as this can be used to access compliance state for your environment and as part of audit processes. Don't think of it only to lock things down.

There are a number of primary types of effects when applying policy:

◆ Audit—Creates a warning in the activity log when a non-compliance resource is evaluated but will not stop the request. There is a variation called `auditIfNotExists` that can be used to generate the warning if components listed are not present. For example, it could audit if the antimalware extension were missing.

- Deny—Prevents a resource request that would result in non-compliance by failing the request. In the failure message, the policy would be noted as the reason for the failure as part of the 403 (forbidden) result.

- Append—Adds fields to the request (for example, adding tags)

- DeployIfNotExists—Similar to auditIfNotExists, but this action will run an ARM template if the condition is not met—for example, turning on encryption if encryption is not enabled. This can be very useful to remediate existing resources that are out of compliance. When using this type of effect, note that resources are being deployed, which means they must deploy as some identity with certain roles. A managed identity will be created and assigned required roles—for example, Contributor.

- Disabled—Used mainly for testing purposes and does not evaluate the definition

When you are starting with policy, the best option is to start with Audit and use the compliance reporting to ascertain the compliance percentage of the environment, and then use this as a guide of when to move to Deny. For example, if I had a policy that currently had a compliance of 10 percent and I moved to Deny, I would probably severely impact the environment, resulting in lost productivity and angry users. It would be better to wait until my compliance was around 90 percent (after notifying users via warnings to educate them to help them change behavior) and at that point enforce (using the Deny or DeployIfNotExists effects) the policy. When performing remediation (DeployIfNotExists), start off small (i.e., at a resource group) and ensure that it works as expected, before impacting large amounts of resources by applying at subscriptions or management groups. The Overview page of policies can quickly show the compliance state of the environment, as shown in Figure 2.15. This view can be useful to quickly gain insight.

FIGURE 2.15
Overview page of Policy

Policy can be applied to any ARM resource and has certain capabilities in-guest for the OS running inside VMs through PowerShell DSC integration via a guest configuration extension. Policy can be applied at the following three levels:

- Management group (which itself has a hierarchy)
- Subscription
- Resource group

Policies are inherited down the tree, which means more general policies should be assigned high in the hierarchy, such as at a top management group, which would then be inherited and evaluated for any child management groups, subscriptions, resource groups, and the actual resources. More specific policies would be applied lower down. Care should be taken when applying policies high in the hierarchy, as their impact will be vast. The compliance status is rolled back up to the assignment point, which means if an assignment is made at a management group, the compliance state for all child objects would be shown at that point. Figure 2.16 shows an example assignment that allows me to select the management group for assignment (which could be any of the management group levels) and, optionally, a more specific assignment at a subscription or resource group (within that subscription). It is also possible to separately select exclusions from the policy.

FIGURE 2.16
Assigning a policy

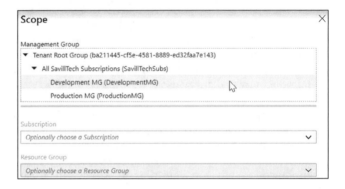

More than 200 built-in policies are available. Others are available via GitHub, or you can create your own custom policies. Some common policies used are:

- Restrict type of VM SKUs used in development (avoid expensive VM types).

- Restrict regions where services can be created (to meet regulatory data sovereignty requirements).

- Require certain tags to be present.

- Restrict public IP addresses to only a specific subnet (eg., the DMZ).

- Require the use of managed disks.

Policies are simple JSON files with an if-then statement. The following is the template to limit resource creation to certain regions. As you can see, it has an if block that is checking all of the conditions that the location specified is not in the list of allowed locations, is not global, and is not a B2C directory. If all these are true, then they are denied.

```
{
  "if": {
    "allOf": [
      {
        "field": "location",
        "notIn": "[parameters('listOfAllowedLocations')]"
      },
```

```
      {
        "field": "location",
        "notEquals": "global"
      },
      {
        "field": "type",
        "notEquals": "Microsoft.AzureActiveDirectory/b2cDirectories"
      }
    ]
  },
  "then": {
    "effect": "deny"
  }
}
```

The array for the list of allowed locations is specified when the policy is assigned to a scope (management group, subscription, or resource group), which is common for any policy that requires some configuration element. To view all the built-in definitions, navigate to Policy within the portal and select Definitions. It is fully searchable, and I recommend taking a look at some of them to get a better understanding of how they work. If you click the +Policy definition button, you can paste in your own JSON or import policies from GitHub, where a large repository is broken down into various areas, such as networking, key vault, storage, SQL, and more. You can browse this directly at `https://github.com/Azure/azure-policy`. One of the really nice policies is the `samples/Network/no-public-ip-exccept-for-one-subnet` policy, which, as the name suggests, blocks public IP addresses except for a single subnet (e.g., your DMZ subnet). You can find it at:

```
https://github.com/Azure/azure-policy/tree/master/samples/Network/
no-public-ip-except-for-one-subnet
```

GitHub also shows using the `New-AzPolicyDefinition` and `New-AzPolicyAssignment` cmdlets to create and assign policy from PowerShell instead of using the portal (and also shows the CLI commands). In the `chapter2.ps1` file in the GitHub repository for this book, I include code to quickly list the subnet IDs for all subnets in all networks in a subscription.

While individual policies can be assigned, it is often the case where your requirements necessitate multiple policies, but they collectively meet a certain set of requirements or, more specifically, a certain initiative. For this reason, policies can be grouped into initiatives and the initiative (and all its policies) assigned. A number of initiatives are already included in Azure Policy. A major one is the Azure Security Center (ASC), which, at the time of writing, includes 82 policies that audit the state of a large number of configurations to help ASC report on resource compliance state. When creating your own initiative, you simply specify a name for the new initiative and then add the definitions. If the definition had values (for example, allowed SKUs), you could either specify the values as part of the initiative configuration or let the values be specified when the initiative is assigned—i.e., the values would vary based on the assignment target. If the initiative were around GDPR, then likely values related to location would be configured within the actual initiative rather than at assignment time. Figure 2.17 shows an example of the two options. The list of allowed storage SKUs has been configured as part of the initiative, whereas the allowed VM SKUs will be chosen at assignment time via an automatically created parameter for the initiative. You can also see that for the available definitions, I filtered those returned to definitions containing SKUs.

FIGURE 2.17
Definition configuration as part of initiative

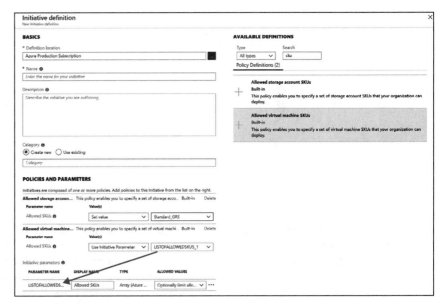

Policies are amazingly powerful and are a primary weapon for your governance battles. Take time to understand requirements and then craft definitions and initiatives and roll out in a phased approach to gain insight and compliance for your environment.

Azure Templates

Azure Resource Manager is built on JSON (JavaScript Object Notation). All of the metadata about ARM resources is stored as JSON and while we talk about the portal for resource creation, as we will learn, all of the REST APIs ultimately result in resources defined via JSON, even when provisioning using PowerShell or the CLI. If you navigate to https://resources.azure.com, you can directly view the JSON for all your resources. As you may expect, you can deploy resources by creating a JSON file and deploying that directly to Azure. In fact, this is the preferred way to create resources, as using a template brings a number of key benefits:

◆ The deployment is prescriptive, in that it will always deploy the same way.

◆ It is declarative, meaning the end desired state is documented rather than the actual steps to perform the deployment (which would be imperative—e.g., PowerShell deployments are imperative).

◆ The deployment is idempotent, which means the template can be run multiple times without damaging existing resources already deployed that match those in the template nor result in errors, something that rerunning a PowerShell script to create resources would not exhibit and multiple errors about existing resources would be returned.

◆ Templates can be stored in source control systems with parameters as separate files, enabling a single template to be deployed across environments without modification, and only the parameter file would differ—for example, a parameter file for development and a different parameter file for production.

JSON templates, which should be used for all deployments, enable organizations to embrace infrastructure as code (IaC), which is a common goal for many organizations today to optimize operations and enable easier, automated processes for deployment and compliance checking. Leveraging templates makes it easy to integrate with CI/CD pipelines of deployment. For example, resources can be deployed as part of the testing pipeline, code compiled and deployed to the deployed resources, tests performed, and then the whole environment destroyed. This is very efficient and optimizes costs, as resources exist only while needed.

I cover templates in detail in Chapter 12. For now, think of them as the preferred way to deploy resources in Azure. Following is a very simple template that deploys a storage account. Notice that it uses a certain schema and then has parameters, which are values that can be passed—in this case, the type of storage account, which can be one of the allowed values, and a location, which by default will use the location of the resource group. There are then variables that can be used in the template. In this case, it generates a storage account name based on the lowercase of the resource group name (removing any - characters) and adding a static string. Then it creates resources—in this case, a storage account—and outputs the name of the storage account.

```
{
  "$schema": "https://schema.management.azure.com/schemas/2015-01-
01/deploymentTemplate.json#",
  "contentVersion": "1.0.0.0",
  "parameters": {
    "storageAccountType": {
      "type": "string",
      "defaultValue": "Standard_LRS",
      "allowedValues": [
        "Standard_LRS",
        "Standard_GRS",
        "Standard_ZRS",
        "Premium_LRS"
      ],
      "metadata": {
        "description": "Storage Account type"
      }
    },
    "location": {
      "type": "string",
      "defaultValue": "[resourceGroup().location]",
      "metadata": {
        "description": "Location for all resources."
      }
    }
  },
  "variables": {
    "storageAccountName": "[concat(replace(toLower(resourceGroup().name),'-
','') , 'standardsa')]"
  },
  "resources": [
```

```
      {
        "type": "Microsoft.Storage/storageAccounts",
        "name": "[variables('storageAccountName')]",
        "location": "[parameters('location')]",
        "apiVersion": "2018-07-01",
        "sku": {
          "name": "[parameters('storageAccountType')]"
        },
        "kind": "StorageV2",
        "properties": {}
      }
    ],
    "outputs": {
      "storageAccountName": {
        "type": "string",
        "value": "[variables('storageAccountName')]"
      }
    }
  }
}
```

The parameters can be passed live or a parameters' file can be used. Leveraging a parameters' file is useful as part of the source control and automation. The following is an example parameter file for the previous JSON file:

```
{
  "$schema": "https://schema.management.azure.com/schemas/2015-01-
01/deploymentParameters.json#",
  "contentVersion": "1.0.0.0",
  "parameters": {
    "storageAccountType": {
      "value": "Standard_LRS"
    }
  }
}
```

Notice the parameter file only has the parameters value. By executing the JSON template and the parameter file, the resource would be required. This is a very simple template file. Often template files will deploy multi-tier services, which could be in one large template file or through nesting smaller template files, each of which defines one aspect of the application. Separating tiers into separate templates enables a library of templates that are purpose-specific to be created and reused as required across different applications.

Every resource in a template file is deployed to the same resource group—i.e., a template cannot span resource groups. This fits with the idea that a template file will likely contain an application, and an application would exist in a single resource group, as the application resources share a common lifecycle. When deploying templates, there are two modes of deployment:

◆ **Complete**—The target resource group after deployment will exactly match the template. Resources that already exist and match the template will not be modified; missing resources will be created; and resources that exist in the resource group that are not in the template will be removed. Care should be taken when using this mode, for obvious reasons.

◆ **Incremental**—Resources that already exist in the resource group that match the template will not be modified; missing resources will be created, but resources in the resource group that are not in the template will be left unchanged and not deleted.

This was just an introduction to templates so that you understand what they do, as we will be using them in the next governance construct. As mentioned, I will go into greater detail about templates and IaC in Chapter 12.

Azure Blueprints

I have talked about a lot about resources and the settings available to help manage your environment and ensure governance. Attempting to manually assign all these different resources in the right combinations based on the type of subscription would be very difficult, prone to error, and hard to assess actual compliance.

Azure blueprints bring together several key governance artifacts and combine them into a declarative, pro-active resource that can be applied to cloud environments—i.e., a subscription. Think of it as a foundational scaffold of (potentially) minimum governance that meets the organization's requirements and which can be expanded and built on as required. Using a blueprint quickly brings a subscription into a governed state. The goal would be to define blueprints for your various sets of governance requirements, perhaps based on type of environment (i.e., development and production), and then apply the appropriate blueprint as new subscriptions are created, effectively stamping it with the required governance. This means new subscriptions can be provisioned very quickly, and embrace the agility required in today's digitally transformed organizations. While this can be thought of as a benefit to IT and governance, it helps the application developers as well. The developers care about their applications. They don't want to be experts in networking or databases, but they need those elements to be in place. With blueprints, their new environment can quickly be stamped, with the required resources configured to best practices, and meet the organization's governance needs. Blueprints still allow the developers to add additional resources they require with full configuration, but those core resources deployed via the blueprint can be locked down, stopping any modification.

A blueprint can consist of the following governance resource types:

◆ Resource groups

◆ RBAC

◆ ARM JSON templates (which would result in the resources in the template being deployed when assigned)

◆ Policy

◆ Custom script artifacts

Blueprints are stored in management groups, allowing them to be available to any child resource (i.e., subscriptions), or they can be stored directly in a subscription. However, the best practice for maximum reusability would be to store blueprints in a management group. In order to store a blueprint, the author must have Contributor rights.

When a new blueprint is created, a name and description is given, along with the definition location—e.g., a management group. Then artifacts are added to the blueprint, which can be any of those previously discussed. When certain types of artifacts are added, certain values can be configured to be specified when the blueprint is assigned. The specification of the value during assignment is useful when the value will vary depending on its target. For example, a role assignment may vary between development and production, or a different policy may be used. Figure 2.18 shows a very simple blueprint that applies a tag policy to the subscription and then creates a new resource group that has a Contributor role assignment to the networking group and deploys an ARM template that creates the core networking.

FIGURE 2.18

A simple blueprint

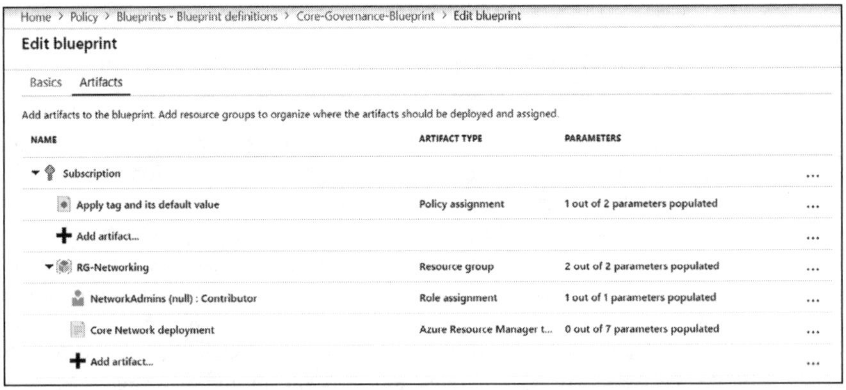

After saving a template as a draft, the next step is to publish it, which requires setting a version number and populating the change notes. Once the blueprint is published, it can be assigned to a subscription. Multiple blueprints can be assigned to a single subscription, which is useful when each blueprint holds the scaffolding for one aspect of governance or configuration, and as each blueprint is assigned, a certain layer of governance is built on the subscription.

When assigning the blueprint, you specify the target subscription, a location, which is used for the managed identity that is leveraged, and the version of the blueprint that has been published. You will need to specify values for any parameters not configured for any of the artifacts and configure the lock assignment and managed identity, as shown in Figure 2.19.

The lock assignment governs how the artifacts deployed are protected in the deployed subscription—i.e., can users remove or modify the artifacts post blueprint deployment? This will really depend on your goals with the blueprint. If your goal is to just get a starting point in the subscription for the users, then you may not need to lock any aspect. However, if your goal is to enforce a set of core resources, permissions, and policies, then you would definitely not want them removed or modified, which means they need to be locked. The lock options are as follows:

◆ **Don't Lock**—The resources deployed are not protected by Blueprints, and users with appropriate permissions will be able to modify or remove deployed artifacts.

◆ **Read Only**—No changes can be made to deployed resources, which includes deleting them.

◆ **Do Not Delete**—The resources can be altered but cannot be deleted.

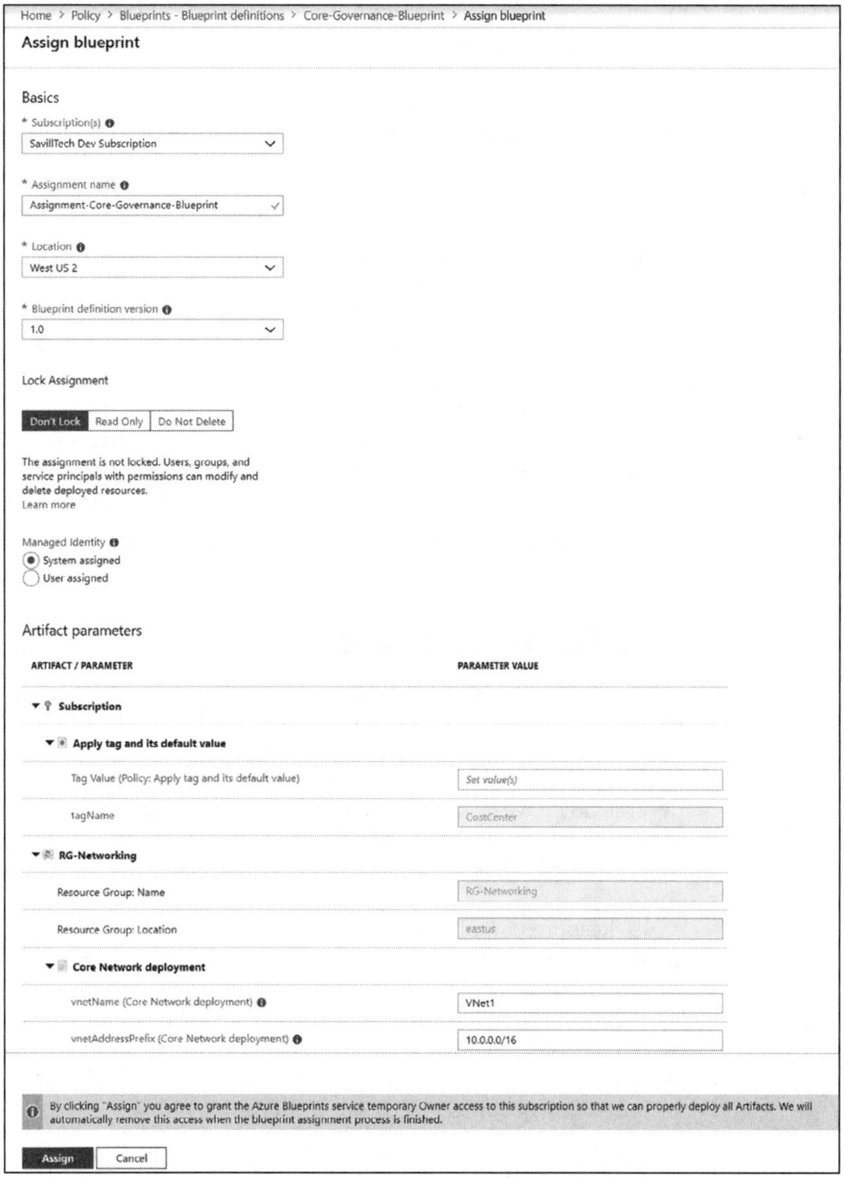

FIGURE 2.19
Assigning a
blueprint to a
subscription

Home > Policy > Blueprints - Blueprint definitions > Core-Governance-Blueprint > Assign blueprint

Assign blueprint

Basics

* Subscription(s) ❶

| SavillTech Dev Subscription | ⌄ |

* Assignment name ❶

| Assignment-Core-Governance-Blueprint | ✓ |

* Location ❶

| West US 2 | ⌄ |

* Blueprint definition version ❶

| 1.0 | ⌄ |

Lock Assignment

| Don't Lock | Read Only | Do Not Delete |

The assignment is not locked. Users, groups, and
service principals with permissions can modify and
delete deployed resources.
Learn more

Managed Identity ❶
● System assigned
○ User assigned

Artifact parameters

ARTIFACT / PARAMETER	PARAMETER VALUE
▼ 💡 **Subscription**	
▼ ⚙ **Apply tag and its default value**	
Tag Value (Policy: Apply tag and its default value)	Set value(s)
tagName	CostCenter
▼ ⚙ **RG-Networking**	
Resource Group: Name	RG-Networking
Resource Group: Location	eastus
▼ ⚙ **Core Network deployment**	
vnetName (Core Network deployment) ❶	VNet1
vnetAddressPrefix (Core Network deployment) ❶	10.0.0.0/16

ⓘ By clicking "Assign" you agree to grant the Azure Blueprints service temporary Owner access to this subscription so that we can properly deploy all Artifacts. We will
automatically remove this access when the blueprint assignment process is finished.

| Assign | Cancel |

For the managed identity, the option is to use System- or User- Assigned. The System-Assigned will be created automatically and have a scope to the local subscription. A User-Assigned managed identity can be useful if you need to use resources cross-subscription—for example, to perform network peering.

Once assigned, the defined artifacts will be deployed to the subscription. Blueprints can be edited, creating new drafts, which can then be published to create new versions. Assignments can be updated to use a newer published version, change values of parameters, or modify the resource locking options. Assignments can also be removed, if required.

Following are some of the common blueprint uses I have seen, although you can really use blueprints for what makes sense within your organization:

◆   ExpressRoute connectivity

◆   Types of environment (production, pre-production)

◆   Hub and spoke (library of spoke "types")

When using blueprints, think about building them out incrementally and not starting with too much. Focus on a certain artifact and test to a limited scope. For example, I typically will test deployments to a resource group that I can easily clean up between tests.

At the time of writing, blueprints are in preview, and their exact functionality will likely rapidly evolve over time. Be sure to view the following site frequently to see the latest updates and functionality—for example, starter packs for standards like ISO 27001:

```
https://docs.microsoft.com/en-us/azure/governance/blueprints/
```

Azure Resource Graph

Over time, you will have a lot of resources deployed in Azure that will likely be spread over many subscriptions. Using REST APIs, PowerShell, and the CLI, there are ways to query and filter resources. However, these can be fairly expensive (in terms of ARM processing) and not always the fastest (in terms of response times). You may think of something simple, like "how many VMs do I have across all my subscriptions," which in reality is very difficult to do in large environments. Azure Resource Graph addresses this by bringing a query capability that can operate across all environments and includes rich capabilities to filter, group, and sort resources.

Azure Resource Graph uses the same query language as Log Analytics, which is at the heart of Azure Monitor: Kusto. You only need Read access to the objects that you wish to query. (If you don't have Read access, you simply won't see those results.)

You can call Azure Resource Graph from PowerShell or the CLI, both of which can be accessed via the Azure Cloud Shell (available via the Azure portal or via `https://shell.azure.com`). The easiest way to understand Azure Resource Graph is to walk through some queries. A large number of starter and advanced queries is available at:

```
https://docs.microsoft.com/en-us/azure/governance/resource-graph/samples/starter
```

In my examples, I am going to call the query via PowerShell, but the exact same query strings would work via the CLI by using `az graph query -q` instead of `Search-AzGraph -Query`. I will explore the Kusto language later in the book. The good news is the language is fairly intuitive and these starter queries basic, which should make tracking what they are doing possible even without a good knowledge of Kusto. One item to note is the language is case sensitive, which is unusual for those of us used to Windows!

```
PS C:\> Search-AzGraph -Query "summarize count ()"

count_
------
   534


PS C:\> Search-AzGraph -Query "summarize count () by subscriptionId" |
Format-Table

subscriptionId                        count_
--------------                        ------
414XXXXX-XXXX-XXXX-XXXX-XXXXXXXXa207      56
412XXXXX-XXXX-XXXX-XXXX-XXXXXXXXb502     478

PS C:\> Search-AzGraph -Query "project name, location, type|
        where type =~ 'Microsoft.Compute/virtualMachines' | order by name desc"

name            location        type
----            --------        ----
savazuussclnx01 southcentralus  microsoft.compute/virtualmachines
savazuusscds01  southcentralus  microsoft.compute/virtualmachines
savazuusscdc01  southcentralus  microsoft.compute/virtualmachines
Savazuusscwin10 southcentralus  microsoft.compute/virtualmachines
Savazuusedc01   eastus          microsoft.compute/virtualmachines


PS C:\> Search-AzGraph -Query "where type =~ 'Microsoft.Compute/virtualMachines' |
        project name, properties.storageProfile.osDisk.osType | top 3 by name desc"

name            properties_storageProfile_osDisk_osType
----            ----------------------------------------
savazuussclnx01 Linux
savazuusscds01  Windows
savazuusscdc01  Windows


PS C:\> Search-AzGraph -Query "where tags.Role=~'DC' | project name, tags"

name            tags
----            ----
savazuusscdc01  @{Owner=John Savill; Role=DC; Region=EUS; Dept=CoreServices;
Operations={...
```

```
Savazuusedc01   @{Role=DC; Dept=CoreServices; Region=EUS}


PS C:\> Search-AzGraph -Query "project tags | summarize buildschema(tags)"

schema_tags
-----------
@{Role=string; defaultExperience=string; ms-resource-usage=string; Dept=string;
Region=string; Opera...
```

You can do some really advanced things with the queries. For example, searching for all VMs that are not using managed disks is easy with Azure Resource Graph—and very fast. (Most queries respond in less than 2 ms.) That's good news in my environment. No VMs not using managed disks!

```
PS C:\> Search-AzGraph -Query "where type =~ 'Microsoft.Compute/virtualMachines' |
where isempty(aliases['Microsoft.Compute/virtualMachines/storageProfile.osDisk
.managedDisk.id']) |
summarize count()"

count_
------
     0
```

Cost Management

The goal of cost management is to optimize costs without sacrificing capability and agility. There is a continual cycle of cost optimization that consists of Visibility ➤ Accountability ➤ Optimization, which then feeds back into Visibility as the cycle continues, as shown in Figure 2.20. Azure Cost Management (ACM) focuses on all three of these areas. Different teams will be part of this process: the various management teams, the organization's finance teams, and then the application teams themselves.

FIGURE 2.20
The cost optimization
cycle

In the cloud, the spending behavior needs to greatly change compared to on premises, and the responsibility is also shared. On-premises developers will demand the biggest box to ensure the application performs, and that box is sized for the next 5 years of projects growth plus a cushion of 30 percent. We don't need to do that in the cloud. We can add/remove instances. We can resize. We don't need to provision resources weeks before the project so they are already wasting money. Resources can be deployed as part of deployment pipelines and created as needed (and then deleted or stopped when not needed). Cost becomes a shared responsibility between the developers, business, and IT.

Historically, there were two key places for enterprises to go for cost management: the EA portal and the purchased Cloudyn solution. Each had their specific strengths (and weaknesses). Today, the capabilities have merged into a new Azure Cost Management (ACM) experience. The long-term direction will be for all the capabilities to be part of Azure Cost Management, which is what I will focus on. At the time of writing, Cloudyn uniquely supports aspects of cross-cloud cost management (for example, budgets in AWS), but that will change long term. ACM has full capabilities for Azure, has a lower data latency than Cloudyn, and is available by default. You don't need to do anything to start using it; it is already turned on. It is also completely free for Azure resource cost management, while having a 1 percent cost for AWS cost management. (That's right—it works for AWS as well.)

With Azure Cost Management being a core part of Azure and tightly integrated with both the portal and ARM, it enables utilization of all the key levels of Azure resources for visibility: management groups, subscriptions, resource groups, and tags. Costs and other optimization mechanisms work at all these different levels, which is a key reason the EA portal and its department construct are deprecated.

Visibility

For the visibility aspect, Azure Cost Management provides the platform to perform analysis of spend and an intuitive user experience to see overviews and detailed analysis. Azure Cost Management is available from the Cost Management + Billing area of the Azure portal. Selecting Cost Analysis enables you to see information about the costs of the current scope, which can be changed by selecting Scope and selecting anything from a top-level management group down to a specific resource group. The viewed data can be modified in terms of date range, granularity, and how the output is grouped (I have changed to by resource type), as shown in Figure 2.21. All the pie charts at the bottom of the screen can be changed to different types of grouping by selecting the drop-down.

You can also add additional filters, as shown in Figure 2.22, which includes the ability to filter based on certain tag values. For many of the data areas, you can click them to drill into that portion of the graph or pie chart, which will update the filters to the data selected. This is very intuitive to use and enables you to quickly drill down into the source of costs.

FIGURE 2.21
Basic cost analysis with resources grouped by type

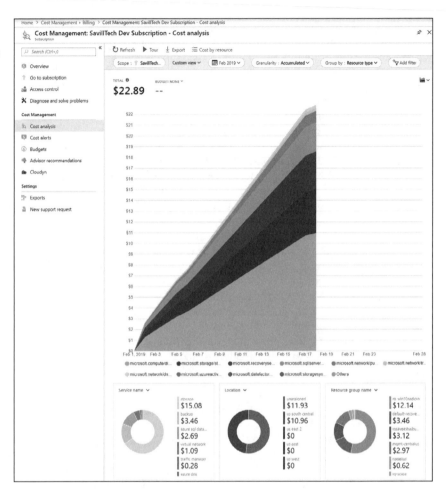

FIGURE 2.22
Adding a new filter

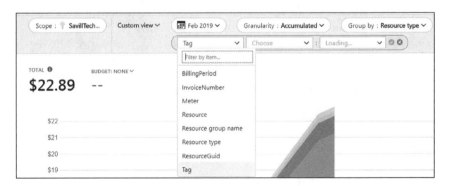

You can also change the main chart to a new type of view by clicking the Chart drop-down button, as shown in Figure 2.23. Changing the chart type may enable better identification of cost sources.

FIGURE 2.23
Changing the type
of chart

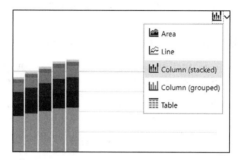

You can also export data to a CSV or even schedule a recurring export to a storage account, to be used by other processes.

Note that while Azure Cost Management provides a huge amount of capability via the portal, you can also use the Power BI Microsoft Azure Consumption Insights application, to create custom reports, or even the Azure APIs, for cost management:

```
https://docs.microsoft.com/en-us/rest/api/consumption/
```

This gives you flexibility to use cost management in the way that works best for your purposes.

Normal Azure roles apply to cost management. For example, Reader can view all data but cannot make changes. There are also two specific cost management roles:

◆ **Cost Management Reader**—Has read access to all cost management data features but cannot make changes. This could be useful for executives to see summary data, service owners, and finance analysts.

◆ **Cost Management Contributor**—Same as the Reader role but can also create budgets and alerts

Accountability

Azure Cost Management also has the ability to create alerts based on various levels of budget thresholds. Like the granularity of the visibility, the accountability can also focus budgets at management groups, subscriptions, and resource groups. When using the API instead of the portal, you can also apply budgets to resources and by tag.

When creating an alert at a particular scope, a name is given as well as an amount, which by default will reset monthly but can be changed to quarterly or annually, along with an expiration date (with an optional started date). The real power comes with the alert conditions and alert recipients. By default, any budget alerts will surface under the Cost Alerts, but being able to trigger actions in addition to communications at various thresholds of the budget enables completely new types of automated behavior.

Budgets leverage the same action groups that are defined in Azure Monitor and are used as the action used on alerts created. These action groups can perform many types and combinations of actions:

- **Email/SMS/Push/Voice**—Numerous types of communication across mediums

- **Azure Function**—Triggers a server-less compute function, which is a piece of code across many types of language that can integrate with many other types of Azure service

- **LogicApp**—Triggers the other main type of server-less compute in Azure that is designed around flows across many types of service

- **Webhook**—Runs a RESTful API

- **ITSM**—Integrates with a service management solution—for example, creating a ticket

- **Automation Runbook**—Triggers an Azure Automation PowerShell (normally) runbook that can do anything PowerShell can do

My guidance is to manage these action groups via Azure Monitor and then leverage them across Azure, including budgets. Figure 2.24 shows an example budget creation at a subscription level. I have an email action group at 80 percent of the budget, and then I run an Azure Automation at 100 percent to shut down VMs. This is just a development subscription, so I'm okay stopping resources. In a production environment, however, this is likely not a good idea and would have significant business impact. Another example use may be when you are devoting resources to a certain workload, but once you hit a certain threshold, you may want to stop processing or reduce the SKU to reduce further spending. All of these would be possible using the action groups and configured thresholds.

Most likely, your thresholds for production workloads would result in communications moving up the management chain and integration with service management systems to ensure people are aware of the budget impact and steps can be manually taken. Remember, Azure is consumption-based. If you are using more resources, your service could be extra busy, which means business is doing well. You likely would not want to impact this.

Note that at the time of writing, the portal is focused on dollars—i.e., the cost. If you use the API, however, it's possible to create budgets based around the usage of various meters. You can see by looking at the Create REST API at:

```
https://docs.microsoft.com/en-us/rest/api/consumption/budgets/createorupdate
```

This would allow the same action group usage at thresholds of various types of resource use, not just dollar cost.

In addition to the actions budgets can take, the current percentage of the budget utilized is displayed, making it easy to quickly see the budget status across your environment. Create budgets where you need to, focus on the accountability, and ensure that the thresholds and actions will have the desired results—i.e., inform the right people.

FIGURE 2.24
Creating a budget

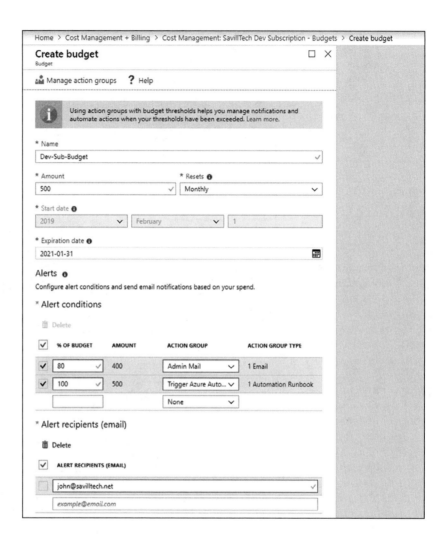

Optimization

On-premises servers tend to have a history of heavy under-utilization, which was partly by design, as servers were purchased based on potentially future growth plus a certain cushion extra. In the cloud, we have greater flexibility and can continually re-scale by changing instance sizes or changing their number. Capabilities like auto-scale can help when services scale horizontally, but changing the size of instances can also be critical. Azure Cost Management integrates directly with Azure Advisor, which examines workloads and gives guidance on how to size them correctly to optimize your Azure spend. Figure 2.25 shows two groups of recommendations: recommendations related to underutilized virtual machines that should be resized to a smaller SKU or shutdown and SQL databases that can be resized to a smaller SKU. Selecting either of the recommendations will open a details screen that gives the option to perform the recommended actions (which for VMs will be a reboot if resizing, so ensure that you perform this out-of-hours) or to postpone or dismiss the recommendation, as shown in Figure 2.26.

FIGURE 2.25
Viewing
advisor cost
recommendations

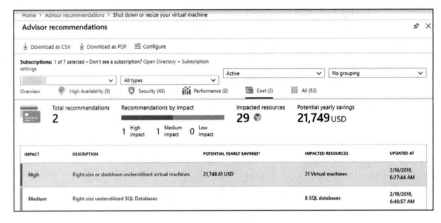

FIGURE 2.26
VM recommenda-
tion options

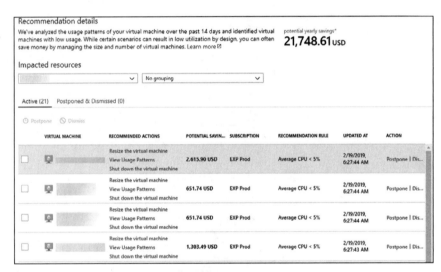

Azure Advisor is a very useful tool when you are optimizing costs. However, also ensure that you use Reserved Instances and Azure Hybrid Benefit, which can result in huge discounts for your Azure spend. Proper architecture of services will also help to optimize your spend, for example, not just using auto-scale but where you can leverage serverless compute offerings like Azure Functions and Azure LogicApps in your architecture. Serverless compute usage will result in savings and for storage consider all the different options for data storage and data tiering where applicable.

Chapter 3

Identity

This chapter focuses on two key elements of the cloud that are critical to every organization, and while they initially may seem an odd combination, they are two sides of the same coin in the cloud. As you will see throughout this book, many organizations leverage cloud services and applications. This means the old security mindset of a big firewall at the edge of the network to provide security for the enterprise no longer works, as many of the most important assets now live outside the corporate perimeter. This means the identity becomes the new primary security perimeter instead of the network (but still keep that firewall!), especially as many organizations adopt a zero-trust network position.

In this chapter, you will learn to:

◆   Architect an identity solution that enables your organization to use on-premises and cloud services across vendors.

◆   Secure both on-premises and cloud identities.

◆   Use key Azure security services.

The Importance of Identity

The use of identity has changed radically over the past 10 years. Twenty-five years ago, as I started my first job as a (trainee) VAX/VMS systems administrator at Logica in their financial group as a fresh-faced 18-year-old, I had visions of amazing computers and systems that only Star Trek had seen, I was saddened as I sat in front of my VT220 and its green glow. My PC at home was better than this! I would discover better machines down in the basement (where I went frequently to change backup tapes and fetch printouts for developers) that were the systems I would connect to via my VT. I was given an account that worked for all the servers in the basement and for the mail application that ran on the environment as well for local team type communications. A few years later, we started to get Windows machines, a separate logon for the corporate email system, and, eventually, a domain. Therefore, I had a few different logons for the systems within Logica but over time most focused around the domain account that all systems would trust and leverage; because the systems were all on premises, the network security was the primary protection.

This has changed. Today, many organizations leverage SaaS applications in the cloud. Where do you book corporate travel? Where is your timecard hosted? Where is your email hosted? Where is your corporate intranet? The list goes on. As I will cover shortly, the SaaS applications can't natively use Active Directory domains, so organizations are faced with choices for the identity. The cloud services also are not on your network, so no matter how good your network perimeter security is, it won't help that much. When thinking of identity in the cloud, either users will give a separate identity in the cloud service or, if possible, extending the AD identity to the cloud service. Now imagine that your company uses 10, 20, or 30 different cloud SaaS applications! Having separate identities is a huge challenge:

◆ Users are not good at remembering passwords, which means they will likely use the same password across all SaaS applications. If one SaaS app is hacked and credentials stolen, the attackers now have credentials that will work across the other cloud services and your home AD.

◆ If users do use different passwords, they are likely to forget them, resulting in helpdesk tickets and lost productivity.

◆ Corporate IT has no view into activities being performed using the separate identities.

◆ The onboarding and offboarding to many different systems is slow. It can be very difficult for an organization to quickly revoke access for a user who leaves the company, across 20 different clouds when each uses a separate account.

◆ Where requirements necessitate multi-factor authentication, this can quickly become impossible.

◆ Separate accounts likely need separate security questions for recovery purposes, which means many sites have access to information that a user likely uses across systems, introducing security risks.

What about extending the AD identity to the cloud? This only works with certain services if they support a concept called *federation*. A federation must be established between the organization and each cloud service, which requires certificate exchanges and configuration of token contents and claims that will be used, and these must be maintained. Additionally, the organization must maintain a federation infrastructure, which requires multiple proxy servers that are public-facing behind a load balancer and which talk to a farm of actual federation servers. This all requires management.

The point is, identity is everything in the cloud. When leveraging the cloud, it is the identity that is the key to accessing the service. There is no network boundary around the services you can control. To protect the application, you have to protect the identity. This means you need to have great visibility into the activities being performed by the identity in order to enable risk assessment and mitigation. You also need to be able to enforce levels of assurance during authentication and authorization that are appropriate for the systems and actions being performed—for example, require MFA when a user accesses a high-privilege system or a normal system but from a new location or machine that does not fit the user's normal behavior, as ascertained and identified through machine learning.

Strong authentication does not mean forcing MFA at every logon; users will get muscle memory from constantly being prompted and always accept without thinking (even when a bad guy triggered it). Strong authentication does not mean changing passwords every 30 days; users will just use the same strong password with a number added to the end of it each month. (Security experts have proven if they have a user's "secure" password from 6 months ago, they can get the current password in a few seconds.) Strong authentication is having a single identity that is well monitored, that utilizes protection mechanisms to learn normal behavior, that is compared against credentials found on the dark web, and that intelligently increases authentication strength based on risk assessment and other factors.

A Brief Refresher on Active Directory

Active Directory was introduced in Windows 2000 to replace the old domain technology in previous server versions. While the earlier domain implementation "worked," it had many limitations because it was built on the old SAM database used for local account management. These limitations included only a single writable domain controller, no delegation, no understanding of physical locations, no extensibility, and a 40 MB database size limit. As IT advanced and requirements increased, those limitations were impractical.

Active Directory is a true directory service for modern times:

◆ Is based on the IEEE X.500 Directory Services Implementation, providing a hierarchical structure

◆ Can be accessed via standard methods, such as LDAP

◆ Can store information about all aspects of a business, including applications and resources, not just users

◆ Can be modified to include custom attributes via an extensible schema (though care should be taken!)

◆ Is searchable

◆ Allows very granular delegation of duties

◆ Is highly scalable through a multi-master model

◆ Enables multiple domains to form hierarchies with transitive trusts via trees and forests

◆ Supports rich policy via Group Policy

◆ Uses Kerberos (in addition to NTLM) for authentication

These capabilities are enabled through a new database for the storage of directory data and the use of multiple domain controllers, which each hold a writable copy of the database for each domain. Active Directory also has constructs to describe the physical topology of an organization—for example, locations and links between them to optimize replication and client traffic.

One of the major benefits of domains continues with Active Directory: the ability to have a single credential that can be used across the entire organization. This is possible because every operating system has a secret that only it and the domain knows, and that secret can be used for various purposes, including the secure transmission of session tickets, which are the cornerstone of Kerberos. This requirement of a unique secret for each OS instance for the domain-based authentication is an important point.

Numerous services are at play in a domain—LDAP services, global catalogs for searching, Key Distribution Services, file shares, and more. These services are contacted over various ports, including RPC, which uses a huge range of random ports. Take a look at the following site for details about port requirements:

```
https://support.microsoft.com/en-us/help/832017/
service-overview-and-network-port-requirements-for-windows
```

To find these services, clients use DNS as the locator service for Active Directory. Various types of service location records are automatically registered that are queried by clients to find instances of the various services, primarily hosted on the domain controllers.

This means that in order for Active Directory to function, clients must be able to contact and use the DNS services that host the domain zones (typically on the domain controllers themselves) and then have a wide range of ports open between the client and the domain controllers (and, of course, ports also for the various types of service they wish to use on other member servers).

Using Cloud Services, Federation, and Cloud Authentication

As previously discussed, no organization is an island today. In the past, everything an employee used was on systems in the organization's network that could be part of a trusted domain. Today, pretty much every company in the world leverages SaaS applications outside of their network. This could be to book travel, manage customer relationships, utilize productivity applications, and much more. However, they:

◆   Don't exist on the customers network

◆   Are not joint to the customers domain

This means Kerberos can't be used. My network is really the useful boundary of my domain. In the early days, this meant every external application would have its own identity database and every user had a separate set of username/password for every application used, which was a nightmare for everyone involved. The user had to maintain a lot of sets of credentials; the user's local IT administrators have no visibility into these credentials, with limited ability to update or cancel if the user's position changed or was terminated, and the SaaS application provider had to maintain identity databases (which is a security risk) and provide services to constantly reset the inevitable requests when users forgot their passwords. Everyone loses.

Federation

Federation was the first solution to this. A solution that allowed services to utilize credentials managed by a separate identity provider, essentially extending your corporate identity out into the cloud—for example, your AD account. The most common implementation of federation is SAML (Security Assertion Markup Language); however, you will also see WS-Fed (WS-Federation), especially in the Microsoft world, which championed WS-Fed. They work in a very similar way. The sign-in protocols are different and the token types used are different versions, but the actual flow is the same. We will focus on SAML, but realize that WS-Fed is basically the same; it just speaks with a slightly different accent.

When we talk about federation, there are three actors in play (very similar to the three heads of the Kerberos protocol and a similar way in which the tokens are used):

◆   **User Agent**—The agent the user is utilizing for the interaction—most commonly, a web browser (passive profile where the agent is being redirected around without really knowing what is happening) but could also be an application on a device (enables active profile where the agent is proactively asking for tokens and sending to the target)

◆   **Service Provider (SP)**—The service the user agent is attempting to authenticate with and then utilize services—for example, Office 365 or Concur

◆ **Identity provider (IdP)**—The identity origin that will be creating tokens that will be utilized as part of the authentication (proving who I am) and authorization (what I can do). An example would be Active Directory Federation Services (AD FS), which is using Active Directory Domain Service (a domain) to actually provide the authentication.

Let's look at the flow to see exactly how this works. Figure 3.1 shows a basic SAML flow. (WS-Fed is basically the same.) In this example, both organizations are using AD FS for the SAML implementation, but SAML is a standard, and any federation software could be used.

FIGURE 3.1
SAML flow for
federation

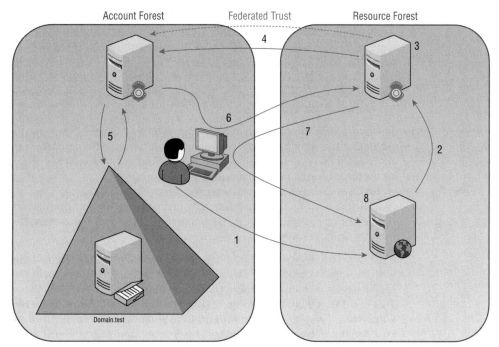

1. The user in the account forest tries to access a web server in another organization's forest that is connected to the account forest via a federated trust. The AD FS web agent on the web server checks for a security token for the user, which at this point will not exist.

2. Because the user has no security token, no access will be given, and the user will be redirected to the federation server in the resource forest.

3. The resource forest federation server will perform a "home realm discovery," during which the server will ascertain the home realm of the user. The federation server needs to send the user back to their home but doesn't know the user's home because it doesn't know who the user is. Home realms can be determined by prompting the user (via a web page, which by default displays all the forests that are trusted by the federation server in a drop-down list). As an alternative, the server can inspect a persistent cookie (if one exists) that is placed on the client by the resource federated server after the first communication. This saves future requests and prompts for a home realm. It may also ask the user for their email address (but not the password) to identify the home realm. Another common option is to have a realm hint as part of the accessing URL to a multi-tenant system. For example, instead of all the users from all the different companies accessing `<service>.com`, each unique tenant would have a different access URL—for example, `savilltech.<service>.com` for users of SavillTech, which would tell the receiving service where I am from.

4. Once the home realm of the requesting user has been identified, the resource federation server redirects the user to the user's local federation server to continue processing.

5. Authentication then takes place through the user's local federation service. The exact authentication protocol used may vary. It could be Kerberos, if integrated authentication is used; it could be forms-based; and so on. The local federation service, in turn, authenticates via Active Directory. Information pertinent to the token it will create is pulled from AD. Different information may be designated for the different resource forests that trust the account federation.

6. The local federation server then issues the client a token specifically for the resource forest and redirects the user back to the federation server in the resource forest. This token is XML-based and contains claims (attributes) about the user, which will vary depending on the target forest. The contents and format are agreed upon as part of creating the federation. The claims are in the assertion element of the SAML token, and you will often hear this referred to as the *assertion*. It is then signed with a certificate that has been shared with the resource forest and is therefore trusted and proves the token is really from the account forest and has not been modified.

7. The resource federation server checks the token and confirms that it is digitally signed with the correct certificate. After the certificate is confirmed, the resource federation server creates its own local token for use when communicating with the web application. This new token would have content based on the various claims in the received token, which would map to values and rights in the application's realm. The user is then redirected to the web application server. This may remind you of referral tickets in a multiple domain forest; it works in a similar fashion.

8. The web application then checks the token. The token is a SAML token (version 2.0 format, which is an industry standard format and allows maximum support from different web applications). The web application reads the SAML token and authorizes the use of the application and its content based on the access limitations specified in the token.

All this results in the user being able to use their normal, corporate identity on remote systems. Additionally, this would likely (but not always) be a single-sign on experience. Since the user is on a corporate machine in a corporate network, Kerberos could likely be used for the authentication to the IdP, which would be seamless to the user. Note that these tokens don't last forever—they have a certain lifetime. However, the token reissue commonly happens automatically after the initial connection, and the user's experience is not interrupted. You may wonder why bother limiting the lifetime of the token at all. It boils down to whether the user's position changes. Maybe they have a new role and should have different permissions, or maybe they have left the company. In these scenarios, the claims in the token would change or a new token would be denied. If nothing has changed, however, a new token would be issued, with the user being none the wiser.

In this example, the user's web browser is constantly being redirected. This is all very fast, and only if paying attention would the user see the URL flitter around as its bounced between the various services involved. This is the passive flow, as the browser has no idea what is happening and is just redirected around.

Federation is used in two ways: SP-initiated and IdP-initiated. SP-initiated, the most common, is what happens when the user tries to access the service and the flow previously described occurs. IdP-initiated, which is less common, would typically be seen if the IdP had a user portal where the user could click the cloud application they wish to use, which would then redirect them to the SP (and its federation service) with the pre-created token.

Notice the setup that is required for a federation. The two parties (IdP and SP) have to exchange a certificate (which will need to be updated periodically, as they have a finite life); there are metadata documents that have to be exchanged; and then the content of the assertion configured. Now multiply this by the number of cloud applications being used.

Also remember that while the federation service in the picture was drawn as a single server, that won't be the case. There are a number of components to maintain:

◆ Some kind of firewall since this is Internet-facing (a whole set of risks)

◆ Multiple proxy servers for the federation service that sit behind a load balancer

◆ Multiple federation servers in a farm to provide the actual federation services

Note that these are not simple services to architect, deploy, or maintain. Multiply this if the organization is multinational and needs deployments in multiple geographies. Don't forget how critical this service is. If federation is providing the ability to access all those cloud applications using the home identity, then if it's down or not performing well, that will impact every user's access to every application. Bottom line: a lot of work and responsibility!

Cloud Authentication and Authorization

While SAML and WS-Fed are still widely used, the behavior of cloud applications and the requirements have changed. It is very common today for a user to have data and services in a cloud service, and another service or application wants to do work on that data and/or service on behalf of the user—that is, some other party is authorized to perform certain actions on a certain scope of your property. A common example of this in the social space would be an application that wants to post on your behalf to Twitter and Facebook. In this case, Twitter and Facebook are *resource servers*, while you are the *resource owner*. You don't want to give this application (a client) the passwords for both services and trust it only posts specific things you say and does do other actions. Instead, you want to authorize this application to perform these actions for you—but only those actions. This authorization happens through consent, where you tell the service that you agreed to giving the set of actions to the set of data that the application is requesting. You've likely seen the message on your mobile device before: "Application X is requesting access to Y and Z." When you click Yes, you give it delegated authorization. Note that this delegation can be to an application, a site, a service, or an API—there are slightly different flows depending on what you are delegating to. Also note that often we talk about cloud authentication, but often what we are actually doing is cloud authorization completely separately from the actual authentication. Once you give the delegation approval, the client is given a number of tokens it can use to pass to the resource server that outline the specific scope (what the application can) that the client can do on behalf of the user.

OAUTH 2.0 is the protocol of choice today for this delegation of authorization. A bolt-on called OpenID Connect sits on top of OAUTH 2.0 to provide authentication proof when required. OAUTH 2.0 normally uses JSON Web Tokens (JWT, pronounced "jot") for the various flows involved. Technically, however, OAUTH 2.0 does not mandate a specific token content (although OpenID Connect does specify JWT). Figure 3.2 shows a simplified flow in which a user (resource owner) is using a local application (client) that wants to access the user's Office 365 (resource server) contacts. Office 365 uses Azure AD for its authorization, so Azure AD is the authorization server that can generate tokens that give delegated access for specific user-consented scopes. As you can see, the application wants to access data; however, first the resource owner (the user) must consent to the authorization server that specific permissions are given. Note this communication is direct between the resource owner and the Authorization Server—for example, a separate web page pop-up outside of the client's (the app's) control. With consent given, the authorization server gives a token to the client, which it can then present to the resource server, that says that application has specific scope for the resource owner—i.e., read that user's contacts.

FIGURE 3.2
Simple token flow

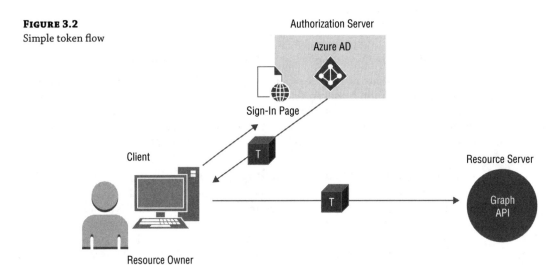

There are variations on the flow. In some scenarios, the client is actually a web service or a type of application that has its own secure areas and can have secrets with the authorization server, allowing the tokens to be redeemed via a more secure backend channel in exchange for an authorization code that was given via a frontend channel (e.g., a web browser). Other times, it may be a single-page application (SPA) that does not have a secure area, so it directly receives the token. The following website outlines the key types of token flows for the different types of applications:

https://docs.microsoft.com/en-us/azure/active-directory/develop/v2-app-types

As with SAML, the token used to access the resource server, the access token, is short-lived, which enables for permissions to be revoked or changed. To avoid the user from constantly having to re-authenticate to the authorization server so that new tokens can be fetched, however, a refresh token is also given to the client. This token lasts much longer and typically has a sliding window lifetime. Therefore, as new access tokens are requested via the refresh token, an updated refresh token is also returned with an extended expiry time. Figure 3.3 shows a more complex token flow where at the point the first access token's (AT) lifetime expires, the client automatically requests a new one using the refresh token. Additionally, the refresh token can be used to request other access tokens for other services, if consent has been given—for example, the client application has been consented to access two separate APIs on behalf of the user.

FIGURE 3.3
More advanced token
flow

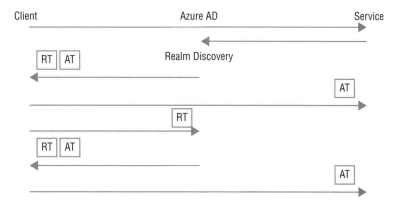

Note that this is all about authorization to access data and perform actions on behalf of a user; it is *not* authentication. Many times clients will use this as authentication by the very nature that if via the tokens given the client can access information such as the user's profile information, then it can make an assumption that the user is authenticated. OAUTH 2 is frowned on if authentication is the primary goal because an API server should not be involved as part of the authentication. The IdP should give a token that the client can use as proof of authentication. This is where OpenID Connect (OIDC) comes into play and provides an ID Token that provides authentication proof in addition to basic profile information to the client.

There is much more detail, and I have multiple courses on PluralSight related to this. For our purposes, however, understanding the various types of federation and authorization should be enough for the rest of the chapter.

Azure Active Directory Fundamentals

When first hearing the name "Azure Active Directory," or Azure AD as it is commonly referred to, you could be forgiven for assuming this was just an Azure-hosted instance of the Active Directory Domain Services that you know and use on premises. However, you would be wrong. While on-premises AD is focused on a hierarchical structure based on X.500, offering interaction via LDAP and authentication using primarily Kerberos, that is not at all what Azure AD is nor would we want it to be. Remember, AD works great on premises, where all the machines are part of my organizational island, with secrets shared and unlimited ports available for communication. When dealing with the cloud, however, that is not the case. We are communicating across the Internet, which means communication will mostly be limited to HTTPS (port 443). We are also potentially dealing with thousands of systems, where secrets may not be possible. The goal is for an identity solution that enables a single identity that can be used in the cloud while giving the control and security needed. This means it needs to talk to cloud protocols such as SAML, OAUTH 2, and OpenID Connect—something AD can't do even with AD FS by its side. Even if AD FS did have the capability, remember the work involved in creating the federated relationships, maintaining the relationships, and maintaining the AD FS infrastructure itself—especially the complexities for a multinational organization. This is the goal of Azure AD: to provide a cloud-enabled identity provider that can be used across all cloud applications.

Look around you right now. Consider a 5' radius. How many different devices are around you? Your phone? That's one. Laptop or desktop computer? That's two. Maybe a table? That's three. And so on. When I speak at conferences, I ask people to raise their arms and keep them up while I go from one upward regarding the number of devices people have on them. The average is between two and three and has gone as high as six. (That guy was sitting by himself.) The point is that in this day and age, we are accustomed to using many different devices. We expect to be able to use all these devices from anywhere to perform both personal and work-related tasks. Often, users are leveraging not just services within their organization but also services hosted externally. Users access Office 365, Salesforce, Twitter, Amazon—the list goes on. As discussed, we need a single identity that can be used, secured, and have the right policy applied that is seamless for the user and ideally does not require a huge team to maintain.

Azure AD, though having some aspects of a directory service, is really an identity solution. It allows users and groups to be created, but in a flat structure without OUs or GPOs (although, as you will see, there is a capability to have Azure AD act like AD for some services). You cannot join a machine to Azure AD in the traditional sense. There is no Kerberos authentication. You cannot query it via LDAP. This is fine, as those things do not make sense on premises, where all types of communication are possible. Azure AD is focused on identity throughout the Internet, where the types of communication are typically limited to HTTP (port 80) and HTTPS (port 443). Azure AD can be used by all types of devices, not just corporate assets. Authentication is done through a number of protocols, such as SAML, WS-Federation, and OAuth. It is possible to query Azure AD, but instead of using LDAP, you use a REST API called Microsoft Graph API, which replaces the older Azure AD Graph API. These all work over HTTP and HTTPS. This is a key point: Azure AD works using Internet protocols.

Additionally, Azure AD already has thousands of the most common SaaS applications federated. This means that if your organization uses Azure AD, you can easily make those SaaS applications available for your users. You don't have to run a federation environment, and you don't have to maintain federation relationships. One of the greatest benefits Azure AD brings is acting as a federation broker. If you have a SaaS application that is not already built-in, then you can still add it to Azure AD for your tenant using SAML and OAUTH 2. Figure 3.4 shows the main entry point for adding enterprise applications for your Azure AD tenant (your organization's instance of Azure AD). Notice that there are more than 3,000 applications federated via Azure AD. You can add applications you are developing, applications from on premises (published out with pre-authentication via Azure AD), and add your own that are missing from those that are built-in. Notice some of the names in the featured list—for example, Box, G Suite, and Salesforce. These applications compete with Microsoft's offerings but are very much front and center. Azure AD has many capabilities and benefits, but this federation broker is one of the biggest for many organizations.

FIGURE 3.4
Viewing some
of the built-in
federated
applications

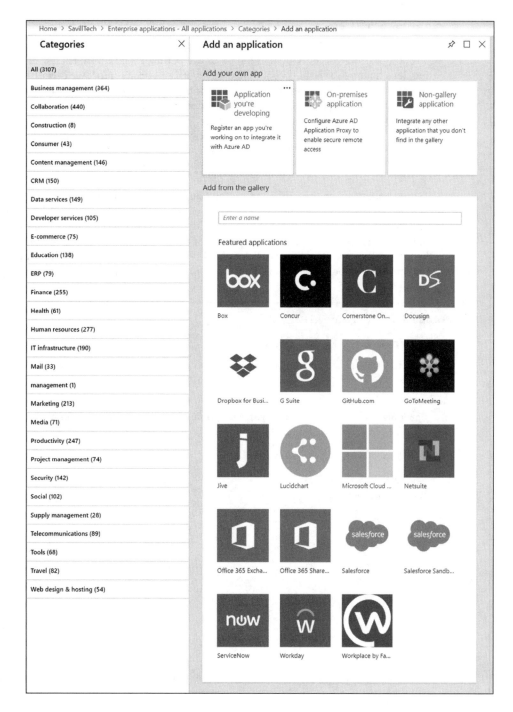

Azure AD SKUs

The easiest way to start to get an understanding of the breadth of Azure AD's capability is to look at its various SKUs. Note that the SKUs are per user per month. Each user in an organization does not have to be at the same license level. It is common to have certain groups of users at different Azure AD SKU levels based on their requirements and role. Also note that while you can purchase Azure AD SKUs directly, it is more common to purchase them as part of a larger suite, such as the Enterprise Mobility Suite or Microsoft 365.

Table 3.1 is a subset of that found at the following site, which has explicit detail on the functionality, and I recommend that you review it:

```
https://azure.microsoft.com/en-us/pricing/details/active-directory/
```

I am not including the functionality for Azure AD when you have Office 365, which is included in that link. You should note that the Azure AD functionality via Office 365 applies only to the Office 365 applications. Also note that the Azure AD tenant becomes whatever the highest license present is, even if only one. For example, if there is one Premium P2 license in the tenant, then that tenant is an Azure AD Premium P2 tenant, and all the applicable configuration options will be available. (You still need to license per-user for the required capabilities!)

TABLE 3.1:   Azure AD SKUs

FEATURE	FREE	BASIC	PREMIUM P1	PREMIUM P2
Directory Objects	500,000	No limit	No limit	No limit
User/Group Management	Yes	Yes	Yes	Yes
Single Sign-On	10 apps per user (limited apps supported)	10 apps per user	No limit	No limit
B2B Collaboration	Yes	Yes	Yes	Yes
Self-Service Password Change for Cloud Users	Yes	Yes	Yes	Yes
Security/Usage Reports	Basic	Basic	Advanced	Advanced
Group-based management		Yes	Yes	Yes
Self-Service Password Reset for cloud users		Yes	Yes	Yes
Company Branding		Yes	Yes	Yes
Application Proxy		Yes	Yes	Yes
SLA		Yes	Yes	Yes
Advanced Group features			Yes	Yes
Self-Service Password Rest/Change/Unlock with on-premises writeback			Yes	Yes

TABLE 3.1: Azure AD SKUs *(CONTINUED)*

FEATURE	FREE	BASIC	PREMIUM P1	PREMIUM P2
MFA and third-party MFA integration			Yes	Yes
Connect Health			Yes	Yes
Password rollover for group accounts			Yes	Yes
Conditional Access			Yes	Yes
Terms of Use			Yes	Yes
Microsoft Cloud App Security			Yes	Yes
Identity Protection				Yes
Privileged Identity Management				Yes
Access Reviews				Yes

`https://azure.microsoft.com/en-us/pricing/details/active-directory/`

I will touch on many of these areas throughout the rest of this chapter, but I want to quickly generalize some of the major differences and how to think about which populations will need which SKUs. For most organizations, a typical worker will start at the Premium P1 level, as this provides integration with the on premises (i.e., the Active Directory) account. The free and basic SKUs only allow for password and management for cloud users—that is, they were created directly in the cloud and were not replicated from an Active Directory account. If your organization has certain populations that need only a very basic cloud identity and access to a small number of cloud SaaS applications, then the Basic SKU may work well. Some organizations can even use the free SKU (although it has no SLA or password reset capability).

It will be no surprise that for most organizations the Premium SKUs will typically be leveraged. At Premium, the following key features are available:

◆ Support for cloud management of AD-originated accounts with writeback to on premises. What this means is the user's AD account is replicated to Azure AD and then via the Azure AD account the user can change their password and even self-service reset. The password would be written back to on-premises AD as well. This provides a great experience for the end user and a huge benefit for the organization.

◆ Multi-factor authentication, which is primarily focused on the user's mobile device via call, text, or application. This MFA is integrated with conditional access.

◆ Conditional access, which enables policies to be defined that are based on various conditions and the requirements for connecting to services. This can include the acceptance of Terms of Use.

- Unlimited number of SaaS applications that can be assigned based on group memberships, including dynamic groups.

- Cloud App Security, which provides insight and control at the edge via network appliances and various APIs to cloud applicaton usage.

The Premium P2 adds to this with three core capabilities:

- **Identity Protection**—Insight and control based on the risk of the user and logon. This includes integration with the Microsoft Intelligent Security Graph that exposes risks found on the dark web. This risk can also be integrated with conditional access as part of requirements for connectivity.

- **Privileged Identity Protection**—Just-in-time and just-enough-administration, allowing users to be granted the right to elevate up to certain Azure AD and Azure Resource Manager roles, as required and for a limited amount of time after potentially performing MFA. This is critical for many organizations.

- **Access Reviews**—The ability to review via administrators, delegated people, or self-review for continued application, role, and or group access

When you consider the importance of security today, the Premium P2 version is very attractive to organizations. Look at the recent guidance from NIST around account security (800-63-3):

- Remove periodic password change requirements and arbitrary password complexity, and instead require change based on compromise evidence. Research has shown making users frequently change the password means they just use the same password but with an incremental number at the end. By knowing someone's 6-month-old password, you can quickly ascertain the current password. Instead of complex passwords (which normally just switch characters for numbers or symbols, such as Pa55word), think of longer passphrases. Azure AD Identity Protection provides the leaked credential intelligence by scanning the dark web and comparing credentials found to those in your tenant.

- Use MFA intelligently based on risk. Azure AD Identity Protection provides the risk assessment and can integrate with conditional access and its own policies to require MFA in elevated risk scenarios.

- Screen passwords against a list of commonly used passwords. Azure AD provides this capability.

The Identity Protection component alone is a big driver for many organizations; and the Privileged Identity Management is very applicable to organizations that need elevated rights, for example, your Global Administrators of Azure AD (like Domain Administrators of regular AD), but also for other roles across Azure AD and Azure.

Take some time to look at the requirements of your organization—for example, for MFA, security, policy, enterprise application access, reporting, end-user self-service, etc. Identify the right SKUs for the various populations of your organization, and then think about other needs. Most likely, needs will align across SKUs, including the right Azure AD SKU, such as EMS/Microsoft 365.

Populating Azure AD

Azure AD needs objects to be useful—at minimum, users, although there also will be groups, devices, applications, licenses, and more. This requires an Azure AD instance and a means to populate it with required objects.

Getting Your Own Azure AD

It's highly likely you already have Azure AD. Many Microsoft services use Azure AD for identity management, including services such as Microsoft Azure, Dynamics 365 CRM, and Office 365. If you logged on to Azure with a Microsoft Account (MSA), behind the scenes an Azure AD instance is created, and the MSA added as a guest to it. Azure AD itself is free. An Azure AD instance is known as a *tenant*, and an organization commonly will have a single production tenant that will contain all it's users. (There may be a separate development tenant for testing capabilities.)

Azure AD instances do not live within a subscription; instead, they are part of their own service, and Azure subscriptions are then connected to an Azure AD instance as their identity provider for authentication and authorization. Creating an Azure AD instance is simple. An unused name is required, and then a location is selected, as shown in Figure 3.5. The organization name is a friendly name for the instance, whereas the initial domain name must be unique across all of Azure and will have `onmicrosoft.com` appended. You also select a country or region for your Azure AD instance, which can be very important for data residency considerations.

FIGURE 3.5
Creating a new Azure
AD instance

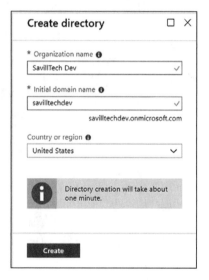

This does not mean every country has their own set of servers hosting and replicating Azure AD instances. At the time of writing there are three actual replication boundaries of Azure AD:

- **North America**—Any country selected that falls within this boundary

- **EMEA**—Any country selected that falls within this boundary

- **Worldwide**—Any other country not in North America or EMEA

For each of those boundaries the data is replicated across multiple regions within that boundary, ensuring that the service is resilient and highly performant while staying within that residency boundary. Additionally, the sovereign clouds host their own Azure AD replication boundaries—i.e., China, Germany, and, the U.S. Government. Note that the sovereign clouds have their own separate sign-up experiences.

Note that even though Azure AD instances run on a shared infrastructure, each tenant is its own partition and is completely isolated from any other tenant. You cannot browse or interact with the content of another Azure AD tenant, nor resources tied to a tenant, without explicit permissions.

Let's take a quick look at the Azure AD architecture to better understand how interactions with Azure AD work. Note that Figure 3.6 is not exhaustive—there are many other services—but it shows some of the core services with respect to the focus areas for this chapter. Many features—such as Privileged Identity Management, Access Reviews, Dynamic Groups, Conditional Access Engine, and so forth—are actually separate backend services. For our purposes, however, we don't need to show them. Just realize that Azure AD has many more services than Figure 3.6 shows!

FIGURE 3.6 Some architectural elements of Azure AD

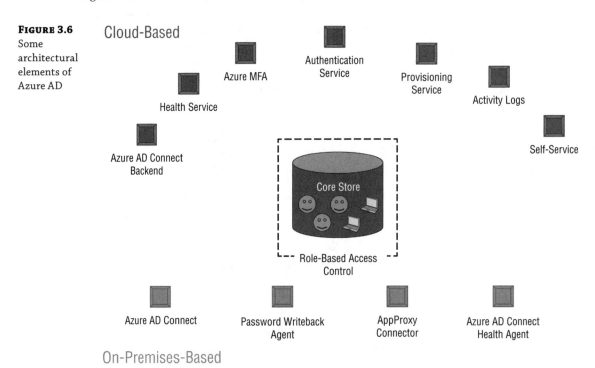

For now, focus on two parts of this picture. The first area of focus is the Core Store, which holds all the stateful data: the users, groups, devices, etc. This is hosted on that shared, replicated infrastructure previously discussed. with each tenant fully isolated from any other. The other area of focus is the Authentication Service, which, along with the Core Store, enables the most basic functionality of an identity provider: authenticating to actually be able to do something! The Authentication Service's frontend has no state. Its job is to receive authentication requests from a client (via a geo-aware gateway service that sends the requests to the geographically closest instance of the Authentication Service). This means a user travelling will still talk to an Authentication Service instance close to them initially. The Authentication Service will then communicate to the Core Store hosting the actual database (again via the gateway) for the actual authentication of the identity. This optimizes the end-user experience regardless of where they are and where the Azure AD is regionally hosted.

REPLICATING FROM AD DS TO AZURE AD

If your company is brand new, with no existing infrastructure, then maybe you don't need an Active Directory instance—i.e., an on-premises AD (although on premises is not accurate, as you can [and most likely will] run your AD in Azure infrastructure services in addition to on premises). For that brand new, cloud-first organization, your users may be created directly into Azure AD. That's great, but it's not the norm. Most organizations already have an identity investment in Active Directory and want to extend those existing user identities into the cloud, both for use with Microsoft cloud services like Azure and Office 365 but also for other cloud services.

It is not possible for Azure to just "use" Active Directory as its IdP; it must use Azure AD to store its identities (although there are various authentication options, which we will cover for those identities). The architecture used is to replicate the AD objects into Azure AD with the same UPN and password and enable seamless sign-on. To the end user, it seems like they just have the single account. In reality, however, they have two accounts; they are just kept synchronized, and the Azure AD account has a link to the AD account to tie them together.

ANCHORS AWAY!

One of the attributes of an Azure AD user is called `ImmutableID`, which is also referred to as the source anchor attribute. This contains the reference to the AD source account. The default value is that of the AD user's `mS-DS-ConsistencyGuid`, which is populated by the sync engine (Azure AD Connect) the first time the user is replicated. The value of `mS-DS-ConsistencyGUID` is copied from the user's `objectGUID` when initially populated. The reason `objectGUID` is not used directly to link the accounts (anymore, it was originally) is to keep the link between the Azure AD account and the AD account even if the user is migrated between forests, which will cause the `objectGUID` to change, although the value of `mS-DS-ConsistencyGUID` would replicate to the new forest, thus keeping the link between the Azure AD account and the AD account. Additionally, if you deleted a user and re-created them, the `objectGUID` would change in certain scenarios.

Notice that as I view my AD account, the `ObjectGUID` matches the `mS-DS-ConsistencyGUID` (since the account has never been cross-forest migrated):

```
PS C:\ > get-aduser john -Properties samaccountname, mail, userprincipalname,
objectguid, 'mS-DS-ConsistencyGuid' |
    select samaccountname, mail, objectguid, @{name='ms-ds-
consistencyguid';expression={[guid]$_.'ms-ds-consistencyguid'}}

samaccountname mail                          objectguid                          ms-ds-
consistencyguid
-------------- ----                          ----------                          ---------------
------
john           john@savilltech.net 480ef113-a973-4051-92ab-9109e49a11b6
480ef113-a973-
4051-92ab-9109e49a11b6
```

Now if I look at my Azure AD account, I see a perfect match on `immutableID`:

```
PS C:\ > Get-AzureADUser -ObjectId 'john@savilltech.net' |
```

```
Select-Object -Property userprincipalname, immutableid

UserPrincipalName    ImmutableId
-----------------    -----------
John@savilltech.net  E/EOSHOpUUCSq5EJ5JoRtg==
```

Well, nearly. The values are stored in different formats. (The `immutableID` is a base-64 version of the source anchor. Azure Identity Converter, found at the following website, has a nice utility to convert between the value formats:

```
https://gallery.technet.microsoft.com/scriptcenter/
Azure-GUID-to-ImmutableID-d27c5b12
```

As you can see in Figure 3.7, the values are the same.

FIGURE 3.7
Matching ImmutableID to ObjectGUID

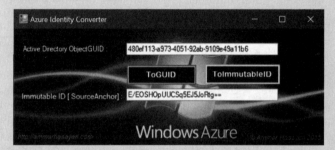

Note that there is another type of match. What I described previously is a hard match, since the match is based on the immutableID. However, there is also a soft type match. Imagine that you are setting up synchronization to Azure AD; however, you already created some accounts directly in Azure AD and now want to replicate from AD DS and have the AD DS account match on the existing account. This soft match is possible, provided that the accounts have the same SMTP address or UPN (if SMTP is not possible). To use UPN matching, follow the process at:

```
https://support.microsoft.com/en-in/help/3164442/
how-to-use-upn-matching-for-identity-synchronization-in-office-365-azu
```

The synchronization is performed by an on-premises component named Azure AD Connect (AAD Connect), although many organizations run this on Azure IaaS, as I will touch on later. This free download from Microsoft installs to a Windows Server operating system instance. You can have only one active AAD Connect instance, although it is possible to also install additional instances in a staging mode that can become active if the primary instance is lost. AAD Connect is built on the Microsoft Identity Management (MIM) solution, and some of the management tools will look familiar, especially when diving into some of the internals. The MIM foundation enables AAD Connect to perform joins from multiple objects to a single target via the connector spaces and the MIM metaverse, which provides the consolidated knowledge from all the systems connected. Remember, the replication of objects from AD to Azure AD does not require any paid Azure AD SKU; this is available for any user. When it comes to synchronization, the paid SKUs really come into play replicating passwords from Azure AD.

There are some third-party solutions that replicate to Azure AD. I don't recommend these. AAD Connect uses a private API to replicate to Azure AD and updates as capabilities change and covers the full breadth of supported attributes. Third-party solutions use public rest APIs that will not be as performant nor support the full set of capabilities.

Microsoft maintains a comprehensive document that walks through all the supported Azure AD Connect supported topologies at:

```
https://docs.microsoft.com/en-us/azure/active-directory/hybrid/
plan-connect-topologies
```

I recommend that you review the entire document, but I want to cover some of the most important points:

◆ An AAD Connect instance synchronizes with a single Azure AD instance.

◆ An Azure AD instance can synchronize only with a single AAD Connect instance (plus staging server)—that is, there is a 1:1 relationship between Azure AD and Azure AD Connect.

◆ AAD Connect can synchronize from multiple forests and domains (and even join together where a user has multiple accounts using various options).

◆ It is possible to connect multiple AAD Connect instances to the same domain, provided that each instance is not replicating the same objects. For example, you may replicate the content of different OUs to different Azure AD instances via separate AAD Connect instances, as shown in Figure 3.8. This could be if production and development accounts need to go to separate AAD instances or perhaps different business units.

◆ A user can only sync to a single Azure AD.

FIGURE 3.8
Replicating objects to different AAD instances

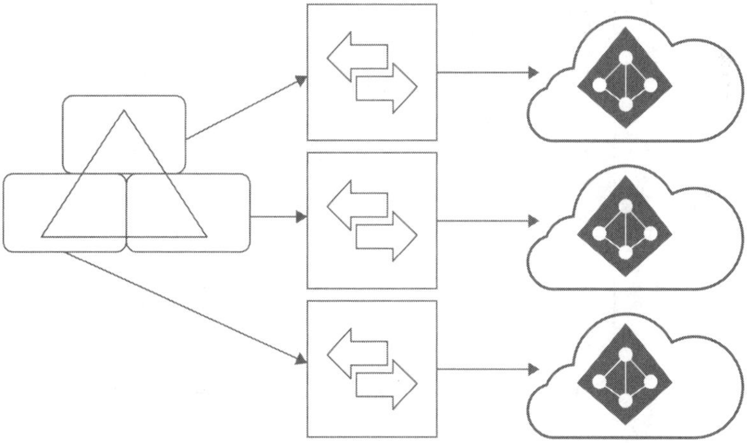

Note that customizations can be made to AAD Connect because it's built on MIM. Just because something is possible, however, does not mean your organization should do it if it means the environment is now unsupported. With identity being the key to all services, you don't want that identity to be in an unsupported state!

Azure AD Connect can do more than just synchronize. It can also handle federation configurations and maintenance (such as updating certificates). They are express installs and then custom installations, but don't worry—even if you do an express install, you can modify settings and change configurations post deployment.

I previously talked about Azure AD instances having a name (`<custom name>.onmicrosoft.com`), but this is just the initial name. You will add custom domains—often the domains you use in your domain and email, if different. This should be done before starting replication. Adding domains is simple and requires only a simple verification that you own the domain by creating a record in the DNS zone, as directed by the AAD custom domain addition process. Once the custom domain has been added and verified, you can change the Azure AD to use that custom domain as its primary domain name, as shown in Figure 3.9. When you are thinking about Azure AD usage, the end-user experience and usability is critical. The preferred configuration is for the user's on-premises user principal name (UPN, e.g., `john@savilltech.net`) to match that of the account in Azure AD. If the UPN from AD is configured to populate the UPN in Azure AD for AAD Connect and the domain in the UPN has not been verified in Azure AD, then the UPN in AAD will use the `<custom>.onmicrosoft.com` name which, you don't want. (But don't worry—it can be changed.) In an ideal world, the UPN would also be the same as the primary SMTP address for the user. What if the UPN were not the same as a user's email address and the user really only understood their email address as a logon name? The email address (along with other attributes) could be used as an alternate id, if required, to populate the Azure AD UPN. This could also be required if you used a non-routable domain in AD—for example, `savilltech.local`. This really would be only if it can't be fixed, though, especially if Office 365 were involved. Remember, the AD UPN, the SMTP address, and the Azure AD UPN should all be the same!

FIGURE 3.9
A custom domain as the primary domain for my Azure AD instance

Care needs to be taken in any decisions and evaluations of the end-user experience; as when different names are used, it can cause loss of productivity and even non-functioning applications. You have to consider your user base. If they are non-technical people, then even a single authentication pop-up, which is often not very descriptive, will likely grind them to a halt.

To actually deploy AAD Connect, you will need accounts in your Active Directory and Azure AD. These accounts are not used in the normal operation of AAD Connect; instead, these accounts help with the initial connections and the setup of accounts with required permissions for the ongoing synchronization. You will need the following accounts when setting up AAD Connect:

- Azure AD Global Admin account (used to configure Azure AD and create the Azure AD account used for synchronization)

- AD Enterprise Admin account (used to configure AD and create the AD account used for synchronization). Note that this can be customized and the account pre-configured and then specified during the installation, if automatic account creation is not desired.

- Account that is local administrator on the OS where you are installing Azure AD Connect

- If you are using SQL Server instead of the built-in SQL Express, an SA account on the SQL instance will also be required.

Once installation is complete, the following accounts will be created:

- A local virtual account on the AAD Connect OS that is used to run the Microsoft Azure AD Sync service (NT SERVICE\ADSync). Since this is a virtual account, it is auto-managed.

- The Azure AD Connector account that will have a user name of `Sync_<name of AAD Connect OS>_<GUID>@<AAD name>.onmicrosoft.com`. It has a regular name of "On-Premises Directory Synchronization Service Account" to make it easy to spot. It is automatically assigned the Directory synchronization account's role. Make sure that you don't have any blanket rules that require MFA, as this will break the replication, as there is no way to interact with MFA requirements for this account. If you have MFA policies, make sure this account is added as an exception! The same would apply to any blanket terms of use that have to be accepted!

- The AD account that will have a name of MSOL_<identifier> used for synchronization with AD (Note that this account will not replicate to Azure AD, as it's explicitly filtered out by default AAD Connect rules.)

For details on the exact permissions given, review:

```
https://docs.microsoft.com/en-us/azure/active-directory/hybrid/
reference-connect-accounts-permissions
```

Additionally, you should review all the official documents for the prerequisites and installation process. (That may change over time.) A good place to start is:

```
https://docs.microsoft.com/en-us/azure/active-directory/hybrid/
how-to-connect-install-prerequisites
```

Note that if you reinstall AAD Connect, a new AAD synchronization account will be created each time, so you may end up with multiple accounts. Interestingly, the Microsoft 365 admin portal shows the exact name of the account currently being used at:

```
https://portal.office.com/AdminPortal/Home#/dirsyncmanagement
```

Knowing the used account would allow you to delete the old accounts, as shown in Figure 3.10. You can also see the accounts used via the Synchronization Service Manager (which is installed as part of Azure AD Connect and is the same tool used with MIM) via the

Connectors tab then looking at the Azure AD connector connectivity, as shown in Figure 3.11. This is the same tool that would allow you to update the AD connector account's password if you had requirements to change it. This is also the same tool where you can see all the details of the flow of identities and even customize the flow, if required.

FIGURE 3.10
The Microsoft 365 admin center shows details on directory sync

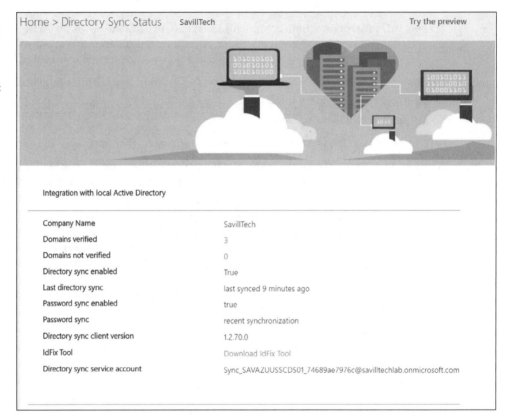

FIGURE 3.11
The connector accounts used by Azure AD Connect

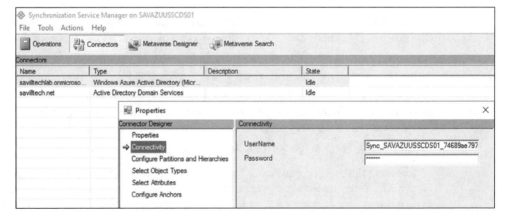

When installing Azure AD Connect, there are various configurations to select. You can rerun the Azure AD Connect setup process at any time to modify the initial options chosen during installation, including features such as password writeback, the use of seamless SSO, and even which objects to synchronize. When you rerun the setup, you will be prompted for your Azure AD credential. This is just used to connect to Azure AD for configuration and is not using that account for the ongoing synchronization. (It already has that account it generated.) You will notice during the installation the option to select filtering. There was an option to filter by group membership; however, this was only designed to be used for limited testing and does not scale well. If you need to filter objects, you should filter them based on OU structure, as shown in Figure 3.12. I recommend the following key settings:

- Password hash synchronization (It's a hash of the hash, and I'll cover more on this soon but it brings additional security.)

- Password writeback (requires premium SKUs)

- The seamless sign-on configuration (when not using AD FS). Note that AAD Connect can even help with the configuration of AD FS

FIGURE 3.12
Filtering the objects that will replicate to Azure AD

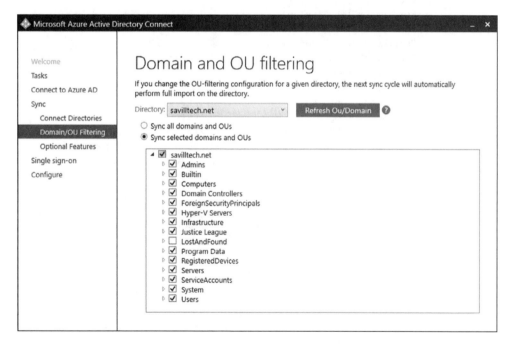

Azure AD Connect has frequent updates. By default, however, it will auto-update, which means you don't need to manually check for a new version, download it, and then upgrade. To check if the auto-update is enabled, use PowerShell. (Note that if it's suspended, it may be you are currently making configuration changes.)

```
PS C:\> Get-ADSyncAutoUpgrade
Enabled
```

Once Azure AD Connect is deployed, it will start synchronizing. There are two synchronization schedules:

- Regular synchronization, which is every 30 minutes but can be modified and manually initiated, if required, via the run profiles in Synchronization Service Manager or from PowerShell by running:

```
Start-ADSyncSyncCycle -PolicyType DELTA
```

- Password hash synchronization, which is every 2 minutes and runs outside of the regular AAD Connect operations.

The interval of the regular synchronization can be changed, if required, using PowerShell. In the following example, I change the interval to every 10 minutes:

```
PS C:\> Get-ADSyncScheduler

AllowedSyncCycleInterval          : 00:30:00
CurrentlyEffectiveSyncCycleInterval : 00:30:00
CustomizedSyncCycleInterval       :
NextSyncCyclePolicyType           : Delta
NextSyncCycleStartTimeInUTC       : 3/3/2019 4:52:27 PM
PurgeRunHistoryInterval           : 7.00:00:00
SyncCycleEnabled                  : True
MaintenanceEnabled                : True
StagingModeEnabled                : False
SchedulerSuspended                : False
SyncCycleInProgress               : False
PS C:\> Set-ADSyncScheduler -CustomizedSyncCycleInterval 00:10:00 -Force
WARNING: The sync interval you provided will only become effective after a sync
cycle. You can choose to wait for the automatic sync cycle to happen
in next 30.00 minutes, or you can manually start a sync cyle by running Start-
ADSyncSyncCycle cmdlet.
```

Once Azure AD Connect is running, you can view basic information on its status in the portal via Azure AD ➤ Azure AD Connect, as shown in Figure 3.13. You can see that the last synchronization was within the last hour, so you know the overall health is okay, but you don't have details.

FIGURE 3.13
Viewing basic Azure AD
Connect status

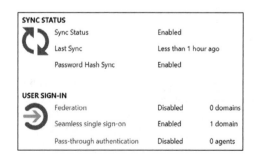

What if you have other identity sources on premises that you want to leverage? As part of Azure AD Premium, you also get license rights for Microsoft Identity Management (MIM), which is the technology that powers Azure AD Connect. With MIM, you can connect other identity sources and data sources together. The idea is to enable synchronization between identity sources and AD DS on premises and then AD DS to Azure AD via Azure AD Connect. MIM can also be used to enable the various joiner/mover/leaver (JML) scenarios organizations have when integrating with on premises or even cloud-based Human Resource Management (HRM) tools. As I will touch on later in this chapter, however, there are opportunities for direct Azure AD integration.

Note that Azure AD Connect should be deployed close to domain controllers (multiple controllers, for resiliency). If you have domain controllers in Azure IaaS, it is common to also move Azure AD Connect to Azure IaaS VMs, as this removes any reliance on connectivity to on-premises networks for the synchronization to continue. Note that if the link to on premises is down, it means AD multi-master replication is no longer running, so changes originating from on premises will not replicate to DCs in Azure, which means Azure AD Connect won't see them to synchronize to Azure AD.

BREAK GLASS ACCOUNTS

Azure AD Connect can replicate accounts from on premises to Azure AD. Therefore, administrators in AD typically will be the same people who administer Azure AD, and the replicated accounts will be given permissions. This means a problem on premises could potentially lock out the account in Azure AD, leaving you unable to manage Azure AD. A best practice is to create "break glass" accounts—i.e., accounts to use in an emergency. These are cloud accounts natively created in Azure AD. As part of best practices, the accounts will often be excluded from conditional access and, to maximize their security, may not allow the use of phone-based MFA. One account may not have MFA enabled, to protect if the MFA service is having problems. "Break glass" accounts should definitely be used. For exact guidance on "break glass" accounts, please read:

```
https://docs.microsoft.com/en-us/azure/active-directory/users-groups-roles/
directory-emergency-access
```

USING AZURE AD CONNECT HEALTH

In addition to the installation of Azure AD Connect, a health agent is also installed on the server. The agent, Azure AD Connect Health, reports far more detailed information to an Azure service about the state of the directory health. Despite its name, Azure AD Connect Health provides health information on more than just Azure AD Connect. It provides health information on the hybrid identity health—specifically, Azure AD Connect, Active Directory Domain Services, and Active Directory Federation Services (if used). An agent needs to be installed on your AD DS and AD FS servers to feed AAD Connect Health with the required information. The agents for Azure AD Connect Health can be configured to automatically update, removing maintenance work.

Figure 3.14 shows some of the detail available for Azure AD Connect, and Figure 3.15 shows some of the detail available for Active Directory itself, including information on the domain controllers and their health, along with details on authentication and any problems with replication between the domain controllers, which is critical. If the AD DS replication is unhealthy, then the data replicated to Azure AD will not be reliable, even if AAD Connect itself is healthy. (Think garbage in garbage. In this case, if the DC being replicated from has old data, then that old data will be replicated to Azure AD.) This helps to emphasize the importance of holistic monitoring and health insight when you are thinking about identity, and is why Azure AD Connect Health enables the monitoring and insight into all the key elements related to identity: Azure AD, AD DS, and AD FS (but hopefully AD FS is being used less and less).

FIGURE 3.14
Azure AD
Connect
Health
information
for Azure AD
Connect

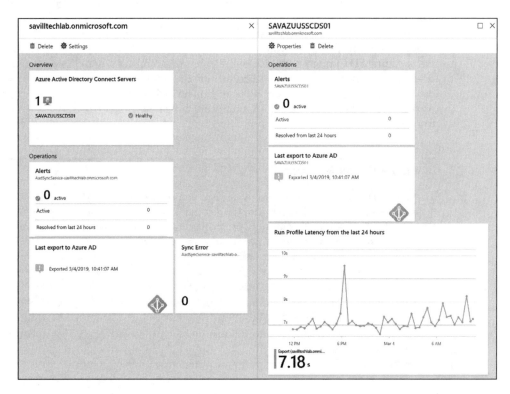

Notice that both sets of information (and AD FS is the same) have an Operations section, which includes alerts. While these alerts surface in the portal, it is also possible to configure notifications, which can include all global administrators in addition to specific email addresses specified. When configured, emails are also sent when the alert condition has been resolved.

There is a caveat. Azure AD Connect Health is a premium feature. To meet the licensing requirements, the following must be adhered to:

◆ 1 license for the first agent (typically, an AAD Connect sync agent)

◆ 25 licenses per monitored server role

Therefore, if you have an environment with an AAD Connect server and 4 domain controllers, you should have 101 user licenses with Azure AD Premium. Note, there is no enforcement of this from a licensing perspective; however, if you don't meet these numbers, then technically you are out of compliance.

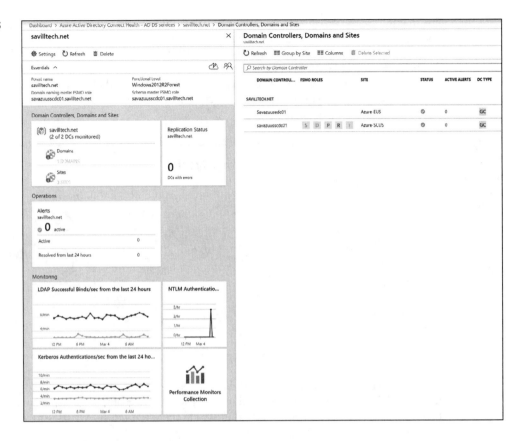

PROVISIONING TO AZURE AD FROM THIRD PARTIES

Up to this point, accounts in Azure AD have come from one of two places: directly in Azure AD as a cloud account or synchronized from AD DS via Azure AD Connect. There is a third option: from a Human Resource Management (HRM) system, as I touched on earlier. These systems are often the start of the HR chain and are where new employees have records created, updated, and, ultimately, retired/terminated. This is also referred to as the joiner/mover/leaver (JML) flow. In an ideal world, the HRM solution would automatically interact with the IdP for the account-related actions, including creating accounts and disabling accounts.

Figure 3.6 showed some of the services around the Azure AD core store, one of which was the provisioning service. In reality, however, there are multiple types of provisioning services, including first-party provisions and third-party provisions—i.e., an inbound provisioning. At the time of writing, there is one example of HRM inbound provisioning; however, this will expand. Workday is an example of this inbound provisioning and is documented at:

```
https://docs.microsoft.com/en-us/azure/active-directory/saas-apps/
workday-inbound-tutorial
```

Workday's architecture is interesting; it still adheres to the idea that AD DS is the source of objects. Remember, most organizations will have a hybrid identity environment, and just creating the user in Azure AD would not be helpful. The provisioning must populate AD DS and Azure AD, and Azure AD Connect cannot replicate users from Azure AD to AD. Instead, as Figure 3.16 shows, the flow is actually from the HRM to Azure AD, which works with an extra component, the Azure AD Connect Provisioning Agent (which can have multiple instances deployed as a lightweight agent to provide scale and resiliency that establish outbound connections to Azure AD). The provisioning agent creates the user in AD DS, which then replicates to Azure AD via the normal path.

FIGURE 3.16
Third-party
inbound
provisioning to
Azure AD

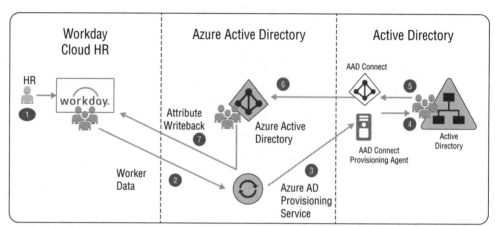

If you have an on-premises HRM system (for example, SAP), you likely already have integration with AD. This could be using MIM (which you have licensing for if users have Azure AD Premium). Once the objects are in AD, they would then replicate to Azure AD via Azure AD Connect.

Azure AD B2B

Accounts for people within an organization have been the focus for Azure AD. However, most organizations collaborate with people outside their organization: partners, suppliers, contractors, and customers. This collaboration is common in other SaaS applications, such as SharePoint Online. A traditional approach for handling this collaboration would be to create an account for the collaborator in the local identity store. However, this hits all the same problems as having multiple accounts across cloud applications, as mentioned at the start of this chapter: pain for the local organization to manage, pain for the user now having another account to remember, etc. These collaborators likely already have their own business or even personal accounts, and even if they don't, they likely have an email address. (And if they don't have an email address, you probably don't want to collaborate with them anyway.)

OVERVIEW

Azure AD B2B (business-to-business) provides a solution that works best for everyone and addresses the challenges previously mentioned for all parties. As shown in Figure 3.17, it basically enables an external account to become known to your local Azure AD. The account can then be granted rights to resources that trust that Azure AD, such as Office 365 and Azure. The Azure AD tenant inviting the user holds the resources to which you want to grant access, so it is often referred to as the *resource tenant*, and the tenant where the users account lives is the *home tenant*. The B2B account is not a regular account in Azure AD, but rather more a stub object that references the external identity where the actual authentication will take place. That is, there is no local password in your Azure AD to manage; the user is utilizing their existing identity, which, at the time of writing, can be another Azure AD account, a Microsoft account (MSA), or a Google account—or a one-time password (OTP) can be used. Work is also underway to integrate with other identity providers, including via SAML/WS-Fed, which would enable integration with technologies like AD FS, for example integration with GSuite (and not the consumer Google email) would be via this direct federation. This means there is no account password management for the resource (inviting) tenant, and the user's self-service password reset would be that of their native identity—e.g., an Azure AD self-service password reset, a Microsoft account reset, or a Google account reset. Remember, with B2B, if the source account (such as the user's company account) were disabled or deleted, then they would no longer be able to authenticate to their home IdP and would not be able to access resources assigned in your environment, even though the B2B guest would still be present.

FIGURE 3.17
Overview of Azure AD B2B

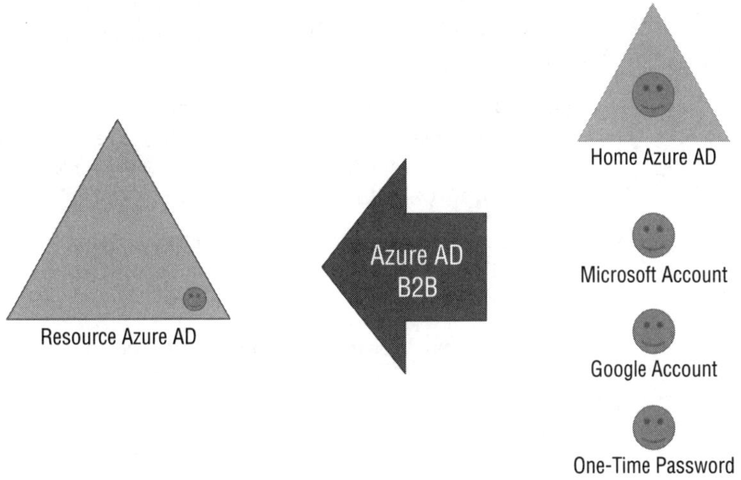

Once users are added via B2B, they can be assigned normal roles in Azure AD, with Azure enabling full partner interaction and collaboration. For example, I have a number of automation scripts that add users between tenants, add them to groups, and even grant roles in certain scenarios. The following is a simple example that adds a list of users via B2B and adds them to a group and also grants the helpdesk administrator role:

```
$HelpGroup = Get-AzureADGroup -SearchString "HelpdeskGroup"
$HelpRole = Get-AzureADDirectoryRole |
    Where-Object {$_.displayName -eq 'Helpdesk Administrator'}

foreach($user in $users)
{
    $AADB2BAdd = New-AzureADMSInvitation `
```

```
        -InvitedUserEmailAddress "$($UserDifference.InputObject)" `
        -SendInvitationMessage $false `
        -InviteRedirectUrl "http://myapps.microsoft.com"
    Add-AzureADGroupMember -ObjectId $HelpGroup.ObjectId `
        -RefObjectId $AADB2BAdd.InvitedUser.Id
    Add-AzureADDirectoryRoleMember -ObjectId $HelpRole.ObjectId `
        -RefObjectId $AADB2BAdd.InvitedUser.Id
}
```

I have done more advanced scripts that synchronize users based on group memberships between tenants, but they follow the same type of code as that shown. This enables a type of "friending" between tenants, and I would expect to see this part of B2B natively at some point in the future.

ADDING USERS

Inviting partners using B2B can be accomplished through a number of methods:

- Via the Azure portal (which will also send them a redemption email)

- Via PowerShell, which can suppress the redemption email as well as specify whether the user should be the default guest or added as type Member (More on this later.) For example:

```
$AADB2BAdd = New-AzureADMSInvitation `
        -InvitedUserEmailAddress "john@external.something" `
        -InviteRedirectUrl "http://myapps.microsoft.com" `
        -SendInvitationMessage $false
```

- Automatically by another process. For example, sharing content with an external partner in SharePoint Online will behind the scenes utilize Azure AD B2B to invite the partner and then grant access.

- By enabling partners to self-signup using a portal available in GitHub at:

```
https://github.com/Azure/active-directory-dotnet-graphapi-b2bportal-web
```

For all of these methods, the partner's account type will be accessed via a home realm discovery and the appropriate type of external account utilized, i.e. Azure AD, MSA, or Google (via OAuth 2.0) or, if none of those, OTP. If an email was sent to the user, they can click a link to redeem the invite and consent to allowing the inviting Azure AD to read certain information. Alternatively, the redemption email does not have to be used; instead, the consent will be performed the first time the B2B user attempts to access a resource tied to the inviting Azure AD. This is known as *just-in-time-redemption*. Once this consent occurs, additional information will be added to the inviting Azure AD user object—for example, the user's real name. The following (abbreviated) example output shows a Microsoft account added via B2B:

```
PS C:\ > get-azureaduser -Filter "displayname eq 'savtech007'" | fl

ExtensionProperty              : {[odata.type,
```

```
Microsoft.DirectoryServices.User], [createdDateTime, 8/29/2018 5:36:42 PM], [employeeId, ],
                            [onPremisesDistinguishedName, ]...}
DeletionTimestamp                   :
ObjectId                            : 1126f0a6-0076-4e8c-9574-7c718e7f0517
ObjectType                          : User
AccountEnabled                      : True
CreationType                        : Invitation
Department                          :
DirSyncEnabled                      :
DisplayName                         : savtech007
Mail                                : savtech007@gmail.com
MailNickName                        : savtech007_gmail.com#EXT#
Mobile                              :
OnPremisesSecurityIdentifier        :
OtherMails                          : {savtech007@gmail.com}
PasswordPolicies                    :
PasswordProfile                     :
ProxyAddresses                      : {SMTP:savtech007@gmail.com}
RefreshTokensValidFromDateTime      : 8/29/2018 5:36:41 PM
ShowInAddressList                   : False
SignInNames                         : {}
UserPrincipalName                   :
savtech007_gmail.com#EXT#@savilltechlab.onmicrosoft.com
UserState                           : Accepted
UserStateChangedOn                  : 2018-10-15T18:38:14Z
UserType                            : Guest
```

There is also a hidden attribute, `altsecid`, the alternate security identifier, which references the source identity of the user object. This is how Azure AD currently keeps the link to the originating identity, but this is subject to change and not something that is exposed directly.

Notice in the output that the user type (last line) is of type Guest, compared to a type of Member for a regular Azure AD user who is local to the Azure AD tenant. This is typically what you want, since users added via B2B are normally guests to the tenant. This user type is used for various purposes in Azure AD. For example, you may create a dynamic group that checks the user's type to create groups that contain guests; Access Reviews can target guest users, as can conditional access. There may be scenarios where B2B users are not considered guests— for example, you are a very large company with multiple tenants, or perhaps you purchase another company. In these cases, you can add the users as members by adding `-InvitedUserType 'Member'` to the `New-AzureADMSInvitation` command. You can also change existing users via PowerShell—for example:

```
PS C:\> get-azureaduser -Filter "displayname eq 'savtech007'" |
```

```
Set-AzureADUser -UserType 'Member'

PS C:\> get-azureaduser -Filter "displayname eq 'savtech007'"

ObjectId                            DisplayName UserPrincipalName
UserType
--------                            ----------- -----------------
--------
1126f0a6-0076-4e8c-9574-7c718e7f0517 savtech007
savtech007_gmail.com#EXT#@savilltechlab.onmicrosoft.com Member
```

The guidance is to only set people to Member who are legally part of your organization. Consider that while Azure AD does not differentiate for licensing based on the UserType, other solutions, such as Office 365, do. Setting the UserType manually can also be useful if you added users to Azure AD a long time ago, in which case the UserType may be null—and by a long time ago, I mean prior to August 2014!

USING ONE-TIME PASSCODES

Before one-time passcodes (OTPs), if an external user who was not Azure AD, MSA, or Google were added, then an Azure AD tenant would be automatically created for the user's domain, an account would be created, and the user would be prompted to create a password (for the Azure AD account created in this new Azure AD tenant). This Azure AD tenant—known as a *viral tenant*, an *unmanaged tenant*, or a *just-in-time tenant*—was basically an Azure AD tenant that had no standard administrators, and the only password reset was a self-reset by the user. There were also take-over scenarios when that company actually wanted a real Azure AD instance. Not a great solution for anyone.

With OTPs, viral tenants are no longer required. Instead, if an email does not match a federated provider (Azure AD, MSA, or Google, at the time of writing), then each time the user logs on, a passcode will be emailed to their email address, and the fact the user can access the message proves they have possession of the mailbox. Figure 3.18 shows the basic flow. This is also good for organizations that are either not in Azure AD yet or are partially replicated. The user's access is still tied to their corporate email address, which means if they leave the company and lose access to their mailbox, they can no longer use the B2B connections, since they cannot read the emailed codes.

At the time of writing, OTPs must be enabled, which you can do via Azure AD ➤ Organizational Relationships ➤ Settings, as shown in Figure 3.19. Note that Organizational Relationships is also where you add support for B2B with identity providers such as Google, which is not supported out of the box, and you must follow a process to enable. If you don't enable OTPs, then the old viral Azure AD tenants will still be utilized when required. Also notice in Figure 3.19 the ability to control whether guests have limited experiences (for example, cannot enumerate users) and other options.

Note that these are one-time passcodes, not one-time usages! Sometimes there are confusions. This is still a full guest user who will receive a new code via email for each logon. The codes last for 30 minutes and are 8 digits. At any one time, a user can have 10 valid codes, and a session can last up to 24 hours.

FIGURE 3.18
OTP usage flow

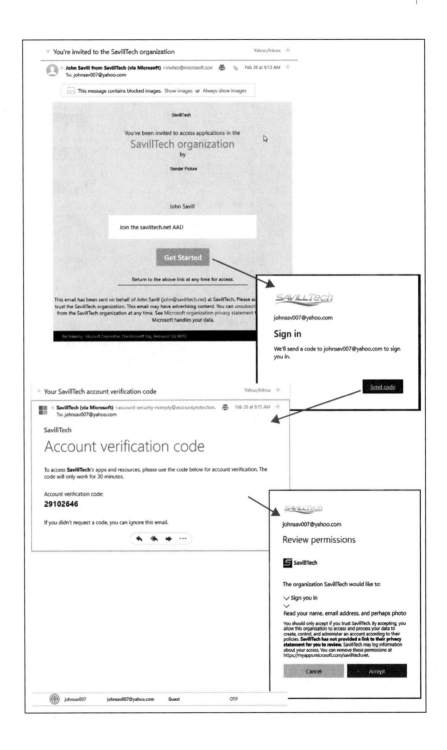

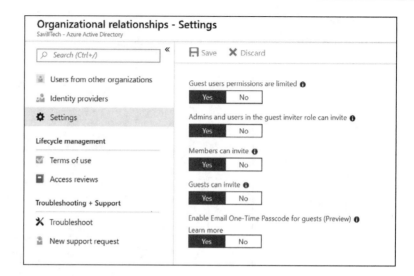

LICENSING AZURE AD B2B

Azure AD B2B is free; however, you might want to use certain features of Azure AD Premium, such as MFA and conditional access, for B2B users. Licensing of Premium features of Azure AD B2B users is via the license state of regular users. For every 1 person in the tenant licensed with Azure AD Premium, 5 B2B users can utilize those features. For example, if a company has 1,000 Azure AD Premium P1 licenses, then 5,000 B2B users can leverage P1 features. If that company has 100 Azure AD Premium P2 licenses, then 500 B2B users can leverage P2 features.

This is important. B2B users are not "lesser" users in terms of many functionalities. B2B users can still use MFA, and they can still be targeted as part of conditional access. Note that some Premium Features do not apply to B2B users—specifically:

◆ Identity Protection Sign-in Risk

◆ Any device management status would be on devices local to the resource tenant, as no data from the home tenant of the user about devices is known to the resource tenant.

◆ Self-Service Password Reset (as there is no password local to the resource tenant)

Access Reviews can be very useful for guest management. It enables checks of if guests should still be guests in the resource tenant either via delegated checks or by having users self-recertify.

Azure AD Authentication Options

Azure AD provides the identity that can be used throughout the cloud. but the first step to using that identity is authentication, which may be manual or through single/seamless sign-on. The exact manner of that authentication can vary based on existing identity architecture investments and requirements, but it really falls into two buckets: cloud authentication and hybrid authentication.

CLOUD AUTHENTICATION

Cloud authentication is the preferred authentication method to use with Azure AD, as the entire authentication is performed in Azure AD without any on-premises component part of the critical authentication path. Yes, account creations and changes may still happen against on-premises domain controllers that need to find their way to Azure AD. However, for provisioned accounts synchronized to Azure AD, if the link to on premises is not available, it has no impact on the ability to authenticate. The use of cloud authentication is not only preferred for on-premises network unavailable scenarios; consider a globally distributed organization. Azure AD is globally distributed, so as users travel around the world, there are close authentication points to Azure AD. However, if it relies on some on-premises component that's in a single location, then performance and scale will be impacted.

To utilize cloud authentication, both the user object and their password hash must be present in Azure AD. This means the password hash option must be enabled in the Azure AD Connect configuration. Having the password hash not only enables cloud authentication, but, as previously mentioned, it enables higher security, as all the resources available to Microsoft, in the form of its cyber security teams and digital crimes units, can compare that hash to any leaked credentials found on the dark web. It also enables actions to protect that identity from breach replay attacks—i.e., require MFA and change the password. The password hash is also required for some other Azure capabilities.

I have spoken to many organizations that have heartburn over this. "You are replicating our password to Azure AD." No, we are not replicating the password. "You want to replicate the password hash to Azure AD." No, we are not even replicating the password hash stored in AD. Instead, what actually replicates to Azure AD is a hash of the hash that cannot be reversed to even find the original AD has. The exact specifics of the hash generation and its synchronization are documented at:

```
https://docs.microsoft.com/en-us/azure/active-directory/hybrid/
how-to-connect-password-hash-synchronization
```

Many organizations' security teams will want to read this to get some degree of comfort, but I can tell you large financial institutions, medical institutions, and government entities send this information.

The basic journey of the hash goes something like this:

1. AAD Connect pulls the AD hash using standard MS-DRSR replication of the Unicode password. This MD4 hash is sent encrypted from the DC.

2. AAD Connect then performs some conversions on the MD4 hash and adds a per-user salt.

3. A 1000 PBDKF2 (Password-Based Key Derivation Function, `https://www.ietf.org/rfc/rfc2898.txt`) iterations using HMAC-SHA256 keyed hashing algorithm are then used with the hash and the salt to generate a new 32-byte hash.

4. This is then sent, along with the user salt and number of iterations (which would allow the number of iterations to possibly change in the future), to Azure AD over SSL.

5. This hash is then stored in an encrypted format in the Azure AD core store.

In summary, a very different hash is sent to Azure AD—one that is actually more secure than the hash stored in AD. Additionally, even if the Azure AD salt was compromised:

- You cannot reverse it to obtain the on-premises hash for accounts.

- Nothing in Azure AD actually enables you to send it a hash as part of authentication, so even if you know the Azure AD hash, it's useless.

I'm spending time on this because it's really important to have the true story of what sending the hash really is and how it's not a real security risk. Even if you choose to use one of the hybrid authentication approaches I will discuss, you should still send the hash of the hash for the security benefits previously mentioned but also as a "break glass" option if your hybrid authentication has a problem. For example, I know of organizations that had their on-premises infrastructure completely wiped out by WannaCry, which, because on-premises components are part of the critical path of hybrid authentication, meant cloud resources could not be accessed. Well, those companies that sent the hash of the hash to Azure AD flipped Azure AD to cloud authentication, enabling users to at least still be able to use cloud services (which was a large portion of the services).

The reason it is cloud authentication is that the authentication is taking place in Azure AD. The user enters their username and password via the Azure AD authentication service. The password runs through the same MD4 plus salt, then 1000 PBKDF2 iterations using SHA256, and is then compared to the hash stored in Azure AD. If they match, the authentication is successful.

If a user's password is changed in AD, it can take up to two minutes for that change to replicate to Azure AD. Additionally, if a user is locked out or has restricted hours in AD, that lockout or restriction does not replicate to Azure AD. If the user's password has expired, that will not impact the ability to continue to use it in Azure AD without having to change it. This can initially seem jarring, but remember, we are talking about cloud authentication and protocols that use access and refresh tokens. There is nothing you can do to impact that access token until it expires (which by default is an hour but can be longer). For the refresh token, it is long lived but is revoked if the user's password changes or is explicitly revoked—for example, by using the `Revoke-AzureADUserAllRefreshToken` cmdlet. The point is, once authenticated, processes work differently in the cloud; therefore, having changes to security principals instantly replicate doesn't have the impact you think it will. Additionally, these items are likely to be remediated at some point in the future.

HYBRID AUTHENTICATION

There are two flavors of hybrid authentication, both of which require interaction with other identity sources as part of the critical authentication flow—for example, communication with AD DS domain controllers (which could be on premises or in the cloud within IaaS VMs). That the source of the identity is part of the authentication flow means state such as account lockout, restricted hours, or password expired will all be enforced as part of an Azure AD authentication.

Remember when authentication actually takes place with cloud protocols. At the start of the day, a user begins a new session and has to authenticate to Azure AD, which goes through the authentication process. This gets them an access token (that is short-lived) for the service they are trying to access and a refresh token to renew that access token, but can also request access tokens for other services—and this is a key point. With the refresh token, the user does not have to re-authenticate for each service accessed. This means that even when upi are using hybrid authentication, the source IdP won't be contacted as each new application is accessed, which is critical when considering *why* you want hybrid authentication, as it can't be used to apply policy for each application access, for example. That will need to happen in Azure AD as part of the authorization that takes place for each application access and access token request.

Pass-Through Authentication

In the past, I would refer to pass-through authentication (PTA) as cloud authentication. However, it is more precise to call it hybrid authentication, because that is the authentication flow: a mix of Azure AD and another IdP—in this case, AD DS.

Pass-through authentication uses a number of pass-through authentication agents that are deployed near your AD DS domain controllers. As part of the deployment, a unique public/ private key is established between the agent and Azure AD. These agents establish an outbound connection to Azure AD over port 443 (which means no inbound firewall exceptions need to be enabled) and wait for authentication requests. When a user authenticates to Azure AD, the password is encrypted using the unique key for each authentication agent, and then placed on a service bus queue, along with the username for the authentication agent instance. The agent retrieves the username and password from the queue, decrypts it using its private key, and then validates against AD using the standard logon API. The authentication result is then sent to Azure AD and utilized by the Azure AD Secure Token Service (STS) to continue the authentication flow. Figure 3.20 shows the process. Note that AAD Connect is still required to synchronize the actual identities; it is just not shown in this picture. AAD Connect is also still required for federation. The synchronization and the authentication are separate. Synchronization will always be AAD Connect, whereas authentication can vary.

FIGURE 3.20
High-level flow of pass-through authentication

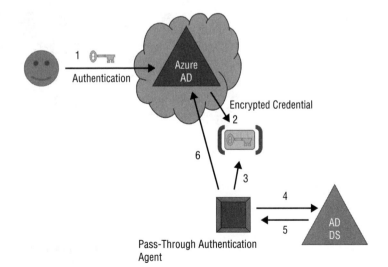

All of this really means that the actual validation of the user credentials takes place against your domain controllers. Sending the password hashes to Azure AD is therefore not required, although still highly recommended for the reasons previously discussed. While we often think of this as on premises, the domain controllers and pass-through authentication agents can all be running in the cloud on IaaS, just like any on-premises component.

Organizations may have concerns about the flow of the password from Azure AD to the authentication agents. To help to remedy those concerns, Microsoft has a very detailed security document about all the aspects of pass-through authentication from adding agents, the establishment of connections, and the actual credential flow. You can find the document at:

```
https://docs.microsoft.com/en-us/azure/active-directory/hybrid/
how-to-connect-pta-security-deep-dive
```

Federated Authentication

Federated authentication builds on the same type of SAML authentication flow I previously talked about in this chapter, except this time, Azure AD is federating with another IdP for the authentication of the Azure AD users. This IdP could be AD FS; it could be Okta; many solutions are available. Federation was very common in the early days of Azure AD because it was the only way to get single sign-on for users to Azure AD trusted resources. That is, a user on a corporate machine on the corporate network would be able to use applications federated with Azure AD without being prompted for credentials. Today, this end-user experience is also available using cloud authentication (password hash) or pass-through authentication via seamless sign-on, as I will discuss later. Figure 3.21 shows the basic flow of federated authentication, which will look very familiar to the previous discussion of SAML.

FIGURE 3.21
High-level flow of federated authentication

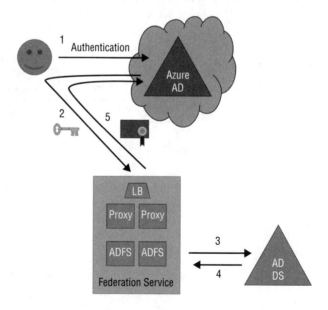

A big difference here is that the password never goes to Azure AD. The authentication is redirected to the federation service (in this example), which facilitates the authentication and then returns the assertions in the SAML token, which is then utilized by Azure AD. Also notice that with federation, you have a lot of infrastructure to architect, deploy, and maintain. You have to have multiple Internet-facing boxes behind a load balancer (and firewall), and then a whole farm of actual federation servers.

Many organizations already have a federation infrastructure because of on-premises applications and the utilization of cloud services, and don't want the account pains previously talked about at the start of this chapter, and there wasn't a better option. With Azure AD, all those federations can actually be migrated to Azure AD (and Microsoft has a whole set of help and scripts to assist at `https://aka.ms/migrateapps`), and the on-premises federation infrastructure retired. That's a North Star and will take time, but certainly the recommendation is to not use federation for Azure AD authentication.

At the time of writing, there are actually a few scenarios where you have to use federation. One scenario is when you want to use an on-premises MFA solution. For example, at the time of writing, Azure AD MFA is not FIPS-certified, which means if FIPS MFA is a requirement, the use of an on-premises solution may be required. Another scenario is when you want to use certificate-based authentication. Federation is still required, but that requirement is becoming less common, as cloud MFA solutions and other authentication options, including technologies like Windows Hello for Business, become more prevalent.

Another reason I hear is that the customer wants policy at the federation server. Remember, this is not valid. Given the way authentication and tokens work in the cloud, the federation server would only be used on the first application access of the day; after that, the refresh token would be used. For policy, you need that at the authorization point—i.e., conditional access, Microsoft Cloud App Security, etc. This is shown in Figure 3.22.

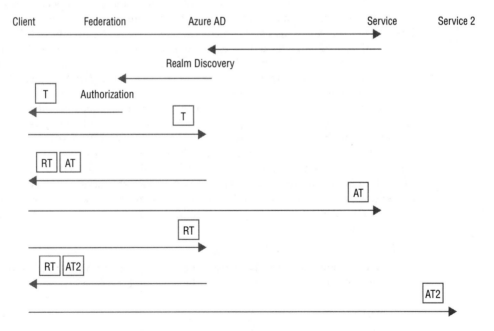

FIGURE 3.22 Modified token flow with federation in the picture

Another reason is simply because people search for guidance online and find old guidance or utilize partners that are simply more familiar with federation. Remember, it is not that it will not work but that you are adding complex components to an authentication flow that benefits from being as minimal as possible in terms of resiliency, scale, and manageability.

How to Pick an Authentication Configuration

The way I always approach this with customers is I see a very clear preference: Use cloud authentication. From here, the discussion should be why you can't use cloud authentication which would drive the use of passthrough authentication or federation. This does not mean if you are using federation, you made a mistake. Many companies are using federation, as a couple of years ago this was the only way to achieve SSO. However, if you are still using it for that reason and still maintaining the whole federation infrastructure and associated risk and work, then now may be the time to change. Cloud authentication is the only cloud-scale authentication option that removes any hybrid component as part of the critical authentication flow.

We can look at some of reasons to use an alternative, as if you can't use cloud authentication (password hash), then the order of preference is as follows:

- ◆ Passthrough authentication (because this is the minimal footprint and maintenance and establishes an outbound connection to Azure, avoiding opening up Internet-facing services)

- ◆ Federation

"I don't want password hashes in the cloud." If this is the prime reason to not use cloud authentication. I would encourage you to reread the benefits and real risk position of having the non-reversable hash of the hash stored in Azure AD, and try to challenge this position and consider the benefits of a cloud-scale authentication solution. If this position cannot be changed, then using passthrough authentication would solve this requirement while minimizing overhead. Federation would also meet this requirement but at a far greater IT price.

"I need to ensure that locked users cannot authenticate in the cloud and/or that logon hour restrictions are enforced." Remember, the point about tokens and how they live for a period of time. However, if this is a real requirement, then, once again, passthrough authentication (or federation) can meet this requirement.

"I want to use on-premises MFA and/or smartcard/certificate authentication." This is where federation uniquely meets the requirements. It becomes a less often requested requirement, but if it's there, this is the only way to meet it. Another reason for federation may be that it's required for other applications that either can't or don't want to migrate to Azure AD, so why not use it for Azure AD. I would stress even if something is required for one thing, it does not mean it should be enforced where it's not needed. Gain the more resilient and scalable cloud authentication if you can and use the federation where you have to, with a goal to migrate as much as you can off it, removing it from the critical flow.

Single/Seamless Sign-On

Users have accounts in Active Directory and get a separate account in Azure AD. In an ideal world, however, the fact that this second, cloud account exists should be transparent to the end user. This transparency should not just be that it's the same username and password but that they should never even have to authenticate with it when accessing cloud resources, in the same way that once a user logs on to their machine in the office, they don't have to authenticate again each time they access a file share, a printer, or other service that is part of the domain. They have a single sign-on experience, and this should be extended to the cloud.

If you refer back to Figure 3.21, something was missing from the picture. When the user is redirected to the federation service, they must authenticate. Yes, AD FS talks directly to AD, but this is only to get attributes about the user to populate the SAML assertion. The actual authentication of the user to the AD FS servers is via the normal Kerberos authentication. This means if the user is on a domain-joined machine in the corporate network, then the authentication to AD FS is transparent (as a ticket for the AD FS server can be obtained from a domain controller using the Ticket Granting Ticket obtained at initial logon), which means the overall authentication to Azure AD—and therefore the app—is also transparent. This SSO experience is the ultimate goal because it provides such as a great user experience, and initially federation was the only way to achieve this.

Seamless sign-on provides the exact same user experience when using cloud authentication (password hash) or passthrough authentication. It can be set up easily as part of Azure AD Connect along with a small Group Policy change. At the time of writing, the conditions for seamless sign-on to work are the same as for federation. The user must be on a domain-joined device in the corporate network, but the goal is for this to work anywhere.

Behind the scenes, seamless sign-on works by creating a computer account, as shown in Figure 3.23, in the Active Directory that represents Azure AD. When a user is authenticating to Azure AD, a 401 response is sent, challenging for a Kerberos ticket as that computer account. A ticket is returned, which is then sent to Azure AD, where it is decrypted and mapped to the Azure AD user, and the authentication and authorization flow continues, basically utilizing Kerberos to Azure AD. Because of this Kerberos interaction, the user interaction is seamless, just like with federation.

FIGURE 3.23
Computer account in AD representing Azure AD

The following website walks through the process in detail:

```
https://docs.microsoft.com/en-us/azure/active-directory/hybrid/
how-to-connect-sso-how-it-works
```

Do not skip the step to create a Group Policy object that adds `https://autologon` `.microsoftazuread-sso.com` to the Intranet zone and configuring the Allow updates to status bar via script setting, as shown in Figure 3.24. Without these policies applied, the seamless sign-on will not work.

FIGURE 3.24
Required
configuration
for Seamless
Sign-on

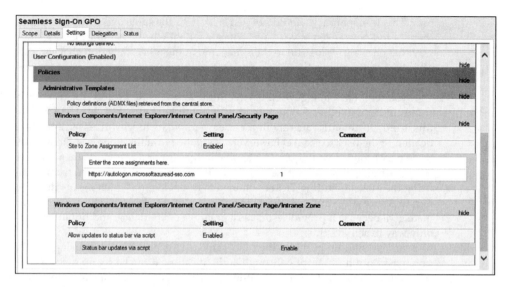

The only other requirement is to roll the key for the computer account every 30 days in order to provide protection if the decryption key were compromised. This is covered in the Microsoft documentation, but I simply run a basic piece of script to roll the key:

```
#Roll password
cd "$env:ProgramFiles\Microsoft Azure Active Directory Connect"
Import-Module .\AzureADSSO.psd1
New-AzureADSSOAuthenticationContext
Get-AzureADSSOStatus
$creds = Get-Credential
Update-AzureADSSOForest -OnPremCredentials $creds
```

AZURE AD–JOINED MACHINES

The previous SSO solutions were based on a user accessing resources from their AD-joined machine. However, many organizations are transforming to cloud first with users mobile, and having a reliance on connectivity to domain controllers is not logical. Another option is to focus identity on Azure AD as part of a modern desktop architecture.

Workplace join was introduced to enable devices such as Windows, Android, and iOS to become known devices to Azure AD, to enable that knowledge of the device to be utilized as part of decisions around application access. With Windows 10, this has been enhanced to Azure AD Join and enables Windows 10 machines to actually join Azure AD in the same way devices could join regular AD. Now you can log on to the device directly as the Azure AD user account. In addition, the device can automatically be enrolled in a Mobile Device Management (MDM) solution (e.g., Microsoft Intune) for the assignment of configurations and policies, the deployment of applications, and more. Intune maps to much of the functionality that previously would have been achieved with Group Policy and System Center Configuration Manager.

When you Azure AD join a machine, the user gets completely seamless access to cloud services because they are logged on with a cloud identity and behind the scenes have something called a Primary Refresh Token (which you also get when using the Microsoft Authenticator application on a mobile device) that is used to obtain tokens for services without prompting the user for credentials each time. Additionally, it is easy to roam the user's environment between machines without having to manually set up roaming profiles or other user experience virtualization technologies. The user's environment seamlessly gets stored in Azure, provided that the Enterprise State Roaming feature has been enabled, as shown in Figure 3.25. The data is stored in the same region as the region of the Azure AD instance.

FIGURE 3.25
Enabling
Enterprise
State Roaming

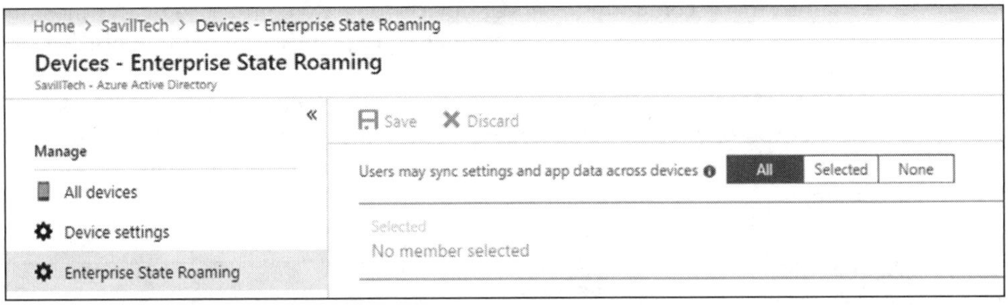

It is also possible to add an Azure AD account as a work account to an AD-joined machine that will also enable cloud SSO through applications and browsers.

Back to Azure AD join, though. What about when that Azure AD–joined machine does go to the corporate office and tries to access a resource that is in the AD domain? SSO, the other way, can be enabled! This is facilitated by Azure AD Connect writing some attributes to Azure AD that help Azure AD know about the AD instance, such as its DNS name, NetBIOS name, and the SAM account name of the user. With this configuration in place, when the user logs on within the corporate network, not only do they receive a PRT for Azure AD, but they will also communicate to AD and receive a Kerberos Ticket Granting Ticket (TGT), which can be used to request tickets for accessing AD–joined resources. This is documented in detail at:

https://docs.microsoft.com/en-us/azure/active-directory/devices/azuread-join-sso

Azure AD Groups

While the focus is often on users, most actions performed and entitlements granted will be to groups. Trying to assign roles and access to individual users is very difficult and typically will result in users being left with permissions when no longer required; for example when a person changes roles they will have new entitlements. But will the old ones be removed? Often not, as the work to check if entitlements are still required is too cumbersome. Eventually, a user ends up with access to everything, which defeats a directive of just-enough-access. By adding users to groups for specific tasks at an organization and then assigning the group entitlements, it is much simpler to add, remove, and audit access.

You likely have groups in AD, and Azure AD Connect can synchronize those groups to AD. Once again, however, the flow is from AD to Azure AD. You cannot change the membership of the groups in AAD and have that membership flow back to AD. When viewing the group in AAD, it will show as a synced membership type, which means you cannot change it in AAD. You can still use the group as part of entitlements—for example, to assign licenses or grant access.

Groups can also be created in Azure AD. There are various types with different methods of assigning membership. For Azure purposes, you will leverage the Security group type, as the Office 365 group type, as the name suggests, can only be used within Office 365 for email, etc. (but can replicate back to AD as a distribution group if the Exchange schema has been applied to AD). The security group can be assigned to roles and access control, which is commonly how it will be used, though it also is used for various types of entitlements, which I will cover in the next section.

The membership of a security group can be set manually by assigning users, or it can be dynamically set containing users or devices. The dynamic group is the most interesting, as queries can be created that are evaluated frequently (but not in real-time when the group is used).

Dynamic rules can be simple or advanced. A simple rule is created by selecting an attribute from a drop-down and then selecting conditions and values, as shown in Figure 3.26, which populates the group with anyone with a job title starting with Hero (useful for a super hero group).

FIGURE 3.26

A simple dynamic group rule

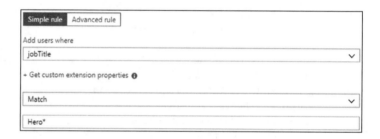

If the simple rule is not enough. you can start with the simple rule and then switch to the advanced rule. This will take the simple rule and express it as an advanced rule, which you can then modify as required. For example, the actual query that matches the shown simple rule would be as follows:

```
(user.jobTitle -match "Hero*")
```

Alternatively, you may want to match on multiple titles:

```
(user.jobTitle -eq "Technical Architect") -or (user.jobTitle -eq "Chief
Technical Architect")-or (user.jobTitle -eq "National Technical Director")
```

The following website walks through all the different options and the syntax to craft your own advanced rules:

```
https://go.microsoft.com/fwlink/?linkid=2014390
```

Azure AD Entitlements and Application Publishing

This section examines how various experiences and resources can be made available to users and groups.

OVERVIEW

I mentioned entitlements when talking about groups, but what exactly is an entitlement? Think of an entitlement as something a user has rights to, either implicitly or explicitly. Examples include the following:

◆ An application or site

◆ A resource

◆ A role

◆ A license

These entitlements often are provided via group membership, as managing entitlements at a per-user level can be very cumbersome. Figure 3.27 shows the management properties of a user compared to a group. As you can see, both have the same configurations around applications, licenses, and resources. The ability to drive assignments through groups becomes even more powerful when dynamic groups are utilized whose membership dynamically changes based on the matches to the rules that define the membership.

FIGURE 3.27
User vs. Group Management Properties

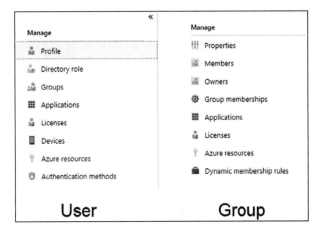

Focus on assigning licenses and application access to groups. If groups that have assigned or synced membership meet the requirements, then you should use them, as it's best to try and minimize the number of groups and maximize the utilization of the groups you have. If you have a mapping to an application, license, or resource that cannot be met by a current group, then a new one can be created. When creating a new group for entitlements, consider how else it may be used and decide whether the membership should be dynamic in Azure AD or assigned in Azure AD, or if it could also be used in AD, in which case, create the group in AD and allow it to synchronize to Azure AD. Avoid having multiple groups serving the same purpose, as it will cause confusion, and ultimately, something tends to break.

APPLICATIONS

Azure AD has many applications already federated—at the time of writing, over 3000 in the gallery. The exact nature of the federation varies according to the cloud application. There are "levels" of federation available, but the primary goal is to provide an SSO experience for the user who will be consuming the application, removing the need for a separate credential or ideally even a prompt for a credential. (This can be achieved through a domain hint as part of the connection—for example, `savilltech.sharepoint.com`.) Remember that while federation may enable SSO, the service may still require its own local object as part of its service, and Azure AD's ability to create objects on the resource provider's service will vary based on the APIs they provide. Most commonly, this connector uses SCIM (System for Cross-Domain Identity Management), which is an industry standard for identity provisioning and is where Microsoft is focusing when adding new connectors.

Let's walk through the key levels of federation, from best to worst:

- True SSO using SAML/WS-Fed/OAUTH2 and a connector to enable object management on the resource provider

- True SSO using SAML/WS-Fed/OAUTH2 but without a connector, which means there may be some actions required on the resource provider. As next steps, unstructions often are provided as part of the application provisioning in Azure AD.

- Credential stuffing, semi-emulating SSO. Here, the resource provider does not support federation; however, credentials can be sent. In this case, either the administrator can set the credentials for an application and assign to users (via groups), who can then leverage it, or the administrator can add the application and assign to users, and then the users will be prompted for credentials the first time, which are then stored for future access. The administrator setting the credential can be useful for a corporate resource—for example, a corporate Twitter account that is shared between all of marketing. A nice feature of Azure AD Premium is that for certain applications, Azure AD can automatically roll the password periodically—e.g., every 30 days, it could change the Twitter account password. A user setting the credential is useful when it's a per-user account.

- A link in the user's portal with no SSO. This is more common when you are adding custom applications to Azure AD that don't support federation.

Administrators of Azure AD can add applications to their tenant and then assign them to groups (or users). Depending on the application, different roles may be available, which will also be specified as part of assignment. For applications that use SAML/WS-Fed, it is possible to customize the assertions to ensure that the claims have the required content based on specific requirements.

There may be applications that are not in the gallery. In these scenarios, you can add a non-gallery application using SAML/WS-Fed (or just a link to a site). Figure 3.28 shows adding applications. As you can see, these applications could be from the gallery; they could be applications you are developing as an organization; they could be on-premises applications that Azure AD is publishing via Azure AD Application Proxy; or, as previously mentioned, they could be non-gallery applications. If you were able to add the application previously using an on-premises federation tool using SAML, then there is a strong chance you can add it to Azure AD.

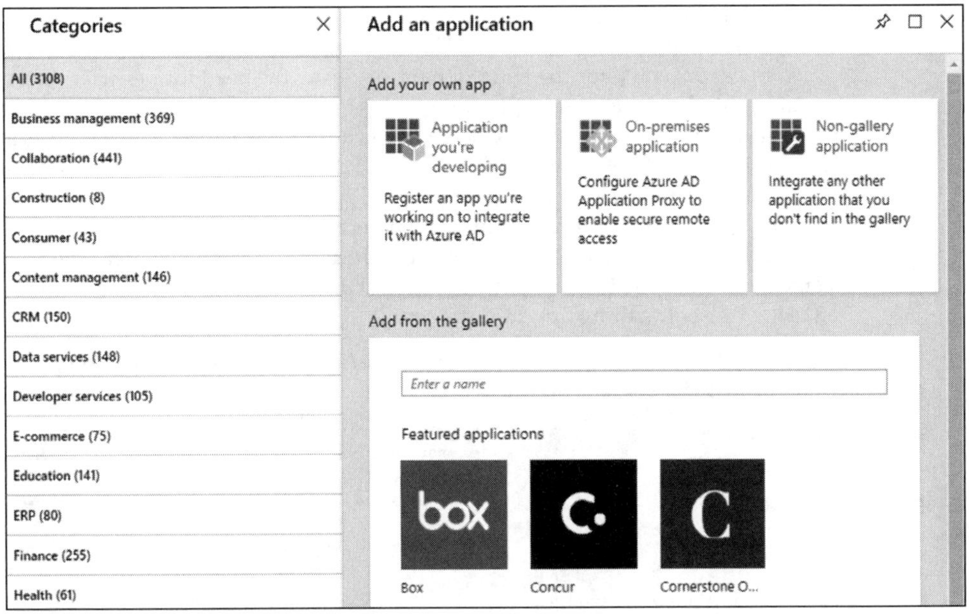

FIGURE 3.28 Adding an application to Azure AD tenant

You may wonder where OAUTH2 is in the list of custom applications. After all, that is the future of cloud authorization. Generally, because OAUTH2 is consent-based, you don't have to add the application or assign it to users. When the user accesses the application for the first time, they will consent to the application and it will be made available to them and added to the Azure AD tenant, unless as an administrator you have blocked this ability by setting the user consent option to No from the default of Yes, as shown in Figure 3.29. It is not recommended to block this option, since if you block the users, they most likely will use a different identity that you no longer control the security of or have insight to. It is better to know that the users are leveraging the service and be able to control use of the applications via conditional access, as required. Notice also in these settings is the ability to enable users to add applications that have not been added by the administrator.

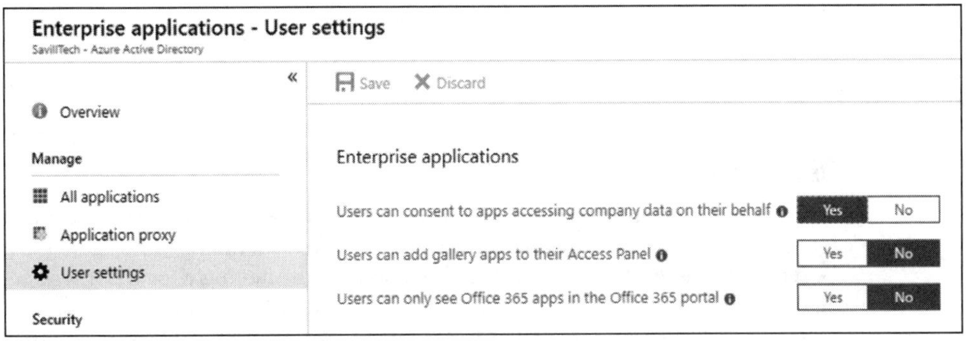

FIGURE 3.29 User settings related to enterprise application

Additionally, users can only consent to "user consent" scopes (aka delegated permission), which is access to their specific data. There is also an "admin consent," which enables an application to be consented for the entire tenant, avoiding the need for per-user consent, and which can also give the requesting application access to data that a user cannot consent to. For example, reading all user data can only be given via admin consent and is known as an *application permission*. The difference scopes of content are displayed when you register an application and must define the scopes required, as shown in Figure 3.30 for the Microsoft Graph (which is only showing a small selection of the application permissions and delegated permissions). Notice that the application permissions always require admin consent, whereas the delegated permissions depend on whether that data is user-specific or organization-wide. For more information on using consent within applications, see:

```
https://docs.microsoft.com/en-us/azure/active-directory/develop/
v2-permissions-and-consent
```

FIGURE 3.30
User vs. admin consent scopes

APPLICATION PERMISSIONS	REQUIRES ADMIN
Read and write all chat messages	✓ Yes
Read and write all risk detection information	✓ Yes
Read and write all risky user information	✓ Yes
Read files in all site collections	✓ Yes
Read all identity risk event information	✓ Yes
Read a limited subset of the organization's roster	✓ Yes
Read the organization's roster	✓ Yes
Read and write the organization's roster	✓ Yes
DELEGATED PERMISSIONS	**REQUIRES ADMIN**
Read user chat messages	⊖ No
Read and write user chat messages	⊖ No
Read and write your organization's trust framework policies	✓ Yes
Read trust framework key sets	✓ Yes
Read and write trust framework key sets	✓ Yes
Read and write risk event information	✓ Yes

USER EXPERIENCE

A primary goal around identity is to provide a seamless user experience while ensuring the integrity and security of that identity. Having a single identity for the user helps with both a better user experience and to enable better security by having a focal point on reporting, risk analysis, and adaptive controls. With the SSO features, the user has their corporate credential that extends to the cloud via Azure AD. In many instances, the access to resources will be seamless. However, on the first use of some cloud services that do not utilize a domain hint (an indicator of the user's home realm and IdP source), a home realm discovery will be required by that service, which will typically take the form of prompting the user for their email address. After this home realm discovery, the necessary redirects and tokens will be applied in addition to a cookie to identify the home realm on subsequent access to that specific cloud application. These steps are all performed if the user goes directly to the cloud application.

Another option is to provide a starting point for users that contains all the applications they are entitled to. For Azure AD, this is known as the *access panel* or the *MyApps portal* and is available at `https://myapps.microsoft.com`. In addition to displaying icons for applications that will redirect to the cloud application in a seamless manner (well, as seamless as possible based on the target), as shown in Figure 3.31, the access panel provides the ability for users to manage groups, Access Reviews, and their profile, which includes security settings such as MFA and password reset methods. I will cover aspects of the security settings in the next chapter.

FIGURE 3.31
Example
MyApps portal
experience

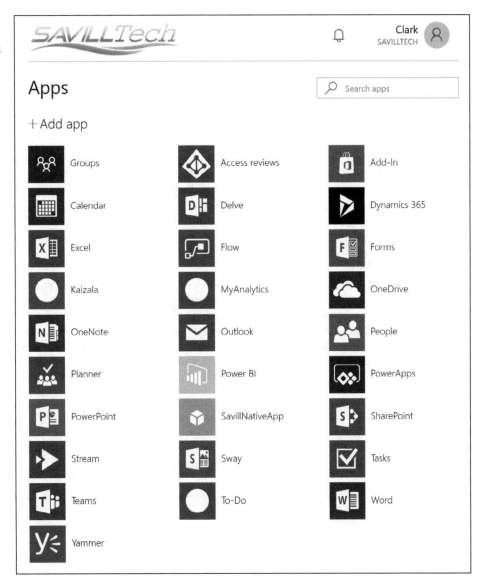

There is also a My Apps Secure Sign-in extension for Chrome, Firefox, and Microsoft Edge. The extension not only provides some additional easy access features, such as access to most commonly used applications, and searchable applications, as shown in Figure 3.32, but will also enable SSO when the user directly types in the URL of the target application, avoiding the home realm discovery.

FIGURE 3.32
MyApps browser exten-
sion providing easy
access to applications

Finally, for mobile devices, there is a My Apps application. This provides a similar experience to the portal, offering an entry point, and facilitates the SSO to the application.

A great article to review for all things user experience is available at:

```
https://docs.microsoft.com/en-us/azure/active-directory/user-help/
active-directory-saas-access-panel-introduction
```

USER ROLES

Users can be assigned various roles that have certain privileges. Aim to grant users the mini-mal level of role that enables them to perform their duties. For example, don't grant a user the Global Admin role when they only need to perform helpdesk actions. By default, when a role is assigned, it applies to the entire tenant; however, administrative units can also be used. Administrative units are created, and users added into the administrative units. Roles can then be assigned and scoped at the administrative unit, instead of the whole tenant. This enables the granular delegation of roles to a subset of the objects in Azure AD.

Chapter 4

Identity Security and Extended Identity Services

With the foundation of Azure AD understood, the next step is to dive into some of the more advanced capabilities and richer sets of functionalities. If identity becomes the new security perimeter instead of the network, then great focus must be given to that identity.

Azure AD Security

This section will explore key considerations around Azure AD security, with a focus on the user. As with any type of security, you can be secure and out of business—that is, an organization can implement great security that renders the business unable to function. The key is to provide security while not significantly impacting the ability of business to function.

Multi-Factor Authentication

You can barely read any identity security article today without seeing the words "the password is dead." I don't think this is actually true yet, but the industry is definitely heading in that direction. Passwords are unpopular for a number of reasons, but the primary reason is that they are a network secret. If I know a password, I can use it from anywhere on anything. That is very different from a PIN, which only works on a specific device. A challenge with passwords is making them complex enough so they are not prone to brute force attacks while not so complex that users can't easily remember or use them. As previously mentioned, the days of password changes every 30 days are gone. NIST no longer recommends it, as users will just add an incremental number to the same complex password and use it for years! It is better to have longer password phrases. It is even better to use multi-factor authentication, or MFA, *but* in the right way.

MFA is based on using more than one factor to authenticate—i.e., at least two of the following:

- Something you know (a password or PIN)
- Something you have (a token or device, such as a PC or phone)
- Something you are (a retina scan or fingerprint)

It is important, however, to use MFA the right way. If you constantly prompt users for MFA for everything they do, they will just get muscle memory to always accept the request (even if they didn't do something to need MFA and it's actually a bad actor attacking). It is better to use MFA based on risk analysis—for example, the user is doing something out of normal behavior, such as logging on with a strange device or at a strange hour, or is doing something requiring elevated permissions. This will typically be driven by Conditional Access (Azure AD P1), Identity Protection (Azure AD P2), and Privileged Identity Management (Azure AD P2), which assess what the user is doing, their risk, and elevation tasks, respectively.

Azure AD MFA

Azure AD provides a native MFA capability that can use a variety of authentication methods in addition the user's password. These are largely focused around a user's phone—for example:

- A phone call
- A code messaged (SMS) to the device
- The Microsoft Authenticator application via notifications or codes
- Other authenticator application for codes

Additionally, an OATH token (specifically, OATH-TOTP SHA-1) can be used. This is a hardware token that displays a code that changes at a set time interval—for example, every 30 seconds. Figure 4.1 shows the Yubico Authenticator application displaying the code generated by my YubiKey 5, which is registered to my Azure AD user. Only when the key is inserted into my machine is a code displayed, although there are other hardware tokens that display the code directly on the key. The use of OATH tokens is very useful for customers in situations when their employees may not have mobile devices or are in locations that prohibit mobile devices. The exact options are configured by the administrator via the MFA service settings for cloud-based MFA, which allow the selection of methods that a user may utilize.

FIGURE 4.1
Using an OATH
token

Using the Microsoft Authenticator application is typically the best experience for the user, as it not only enables notifications that an MFA is required and which can be accepted on the device, but it also acts as a token broker for all the applications on the device, which means users don't have to authenticate on each application that uses Azure AD. Instead, Microsoft Authenticator has a primary refresh token that can be used to access other applications on the device. When users register for MFA and select the Microsoft Authenticator application, a QR code will be shown, as well as a link, to make installing the application simple.

To use Azure AD MFA, a user typically will have an Azure AD Premium license, which gives rights to the cloud MFA service and the on-premises MFA Server (which is not receiving further investment; on-premises integration with MFA is utilized via Azure AD MFA extensions for Network Policy Server). Additionally, a subset of capabilities of MFA is available for Office 365 licensed users—i.e., it can be used around Office 365 services. Global Administrators in Azure AD also can use Azure AD MFA for admin-specific activities.

While you can enforce MFA on the user account, it is not recommended, as the user will constantly have to perform MFA and will lead them to just always accept MFA requests. Instead, you should use technologies such as conditional access to require MFA when logical.

Azure AD MFA Registration

The registration process is constantly evolving, so I will not dive into the specifics, as I think this process will constantly evolve based on new capabilities and customer feedback. However, I do want to cover the fundamentals. There is another piece of functionality that historically users had to register for, self-service password reset (SSPR), which is utilized if a user forgets their password and wants to reset it. The MFA and SSPR were completely different registration processes, even though many of the data points were common. The new experience combines MFA and SSPR to a combined security registration process, which is available via https://aka.ms/mysecurityinfo or via MyApps ➤ Profile ➤ Edit Security Info, as shown in Figure 4.2. You'll notice that I have both Microsoft Authenticator and an authenticator app (my OATH token). A user can have up to five Microsoft Authenticator application instances and five other authenticator applications. Note that OATH tokens are uploaded and assigned by administrators.

FIGURE 4.2
User Security Info interface

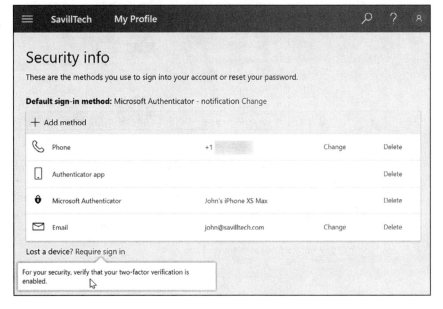

On initial registration, the user will be guided through a wizard-based experience encouraging the use of the Microsoft Authenticator application, aiding in its installation, and then requesting other data, such as phone number (and confirming during registration) and challenge questions (for SSPR). The specifics will depend on the MFA and SSPR methods enabled for the tenant. After the initial registration, methods can be changed using the aforementioned URL.

A challenge for many organizations is to get users to actually register. Often a user is not motivated to register until they actually need the functionality, which, for SSPR, would be too late. Communications can be used to encourage the registration, but there are also methods to force registration and interrupt a user's normal logon experience until they have registered:

♦ Identity Protection (Azure AD Premium P2) has specific MFA registration functionality that can be assigned to groups and require them to register. Even though this is MFA, with the combined security, the SSPR questions and options will also be required as configured.

♦ Use Conditional Access with a policy that requires MFA and target a resource that users will access. On access, if the user has not registered for MFA, then they will be interrupted and made to complete the combined security registration. Note that they will continue to have to use MFA when accessing that resource once registered, which, while getting the users registered, may lead to a non-optimal user experience.

♦ Use the Password Reset Registration functionality, as shown in Figure 4.3, which requires users to be registered for SSPR, which, once again, via the converged experience, will provide the MFA registration as well.

FIGURE 4.3
Using password reset registration requirements

Make sure only one registration enforcement option is chosen; otherwise, depending on speed of synchronization on the backend, users may be forced to register twice, which should be avoided. Also note that I believe the options around registration will evolve based on this new converged process, so be aware of changes related to forcing registration.

For help deploying MFA, view the deployment plan at:

`http://aka.ms/deploymentplans`

To see a list of methods supported for MFA and SSPR, see:

```
https://docs.microsoft.com/en-us/azure/active-directory/authentication/
concept-authentication-methods
```

THIRD-PARTY MFA INTEGRATION

If an organization owns Azure AD Premium, they own Azure AD MFA, which is typically what will be used, as it integrates well with Azure AD federations but is also the only MFA that integrates with capabilities such as Privileged Identity Management, Windows Hello for Business, and baseline administrative policies. It is possible to integrate with third-party MFA providers. One option is via ADFS. However, most organizations are moving away from ADFS; therefore, using it just for MFA should be avoided if there is another way.

Third-party MFA cloud-based providers can integrate with Conditional Access, which is typically how MFA is required. A third-party MFA provider is added as a custom control, which then becomes available as a grant access control on the policy along with the built-in conditional access grant controls. As mentioned, this integration via a custom control does not integrate with scenarios that require trusted MFA—i.e., PIM, Hello for Business, etc.

WINDOWS HELLO FOR BUSINESS

Windows Hello for Business replaces the user's password with a credential that is tied to the device (something you have and, ideally, using the TPM in the device) and utilized via a PIN (something you know) or biometric (something you are—commonly, but not limited to, facial recognition). From the previous sentence, you can see this uses two factors of authentication and is therefore providing MFA for Azure AD.

Windows Hello for Business can be deployed in a cloud-only architecture, requiring the device to be Azure AD joined and running Windows 10, and the user needs Azure AD MFA. It can also be deployed in a hybrid deployment using keys or certificates and, while still requiring Windows 10, the MFA can be integrated with a third party. There is also an on-premises-only deployment but with a focus on AD that is not useful for us.

The key point is that Hello for Business drives a great user experience. It is more secure (as the authentication is not based on a password), and it satisfies MFA requirements (as the tokens will show the authentication used MFA). So, users won't be further prompted for MFA when it would normally be required.

Password Policies

As much as we want to move away from passwords, they will still be with us for some time. As such, policies are required to help ensure levels of security related to their usage. The actual password policy that applies depends on whether the account is a cloud account or is synchronized from AD. If the account is synchronized from AD, then the password policy (including fine-grained password policies) is used. If the account is a cloud account, then the Azure AD password policy is used, as documented at:

```
https://docs.microsoft.com/en-us/azure/active-directory/authentication/
concept-sspr-policy#password-policies-that-only-apply-to-cloud-user-accounts
```

In summary, passwords:

◆ Must be between 8 and 16 characters

◆ Must use three out of lowercase, uppercase, numbers, and symbols

◆ Must be changed every 90 days (but this value can be changed)

◆ Accounts are locked out after 10 unsuccessful sign-in attempts for a minute and then increasing lengths of time after more failures.

Additionally, Azure AD has a password protection feature (Azure AD Premium required) that not only blocks commonly attacked passwords and variations—for example, P@ssw0rd— but also enables a custom banned list of passwords that automatically have common character substitutions also blocked. Common banned passwords may be your city's football team name, your company's name, etc. I'm fairly certain Microsoft blocks the name "Seahawks" as part of their policies. Take some time to think about passwords that are likely to be used and easily guessed, and add them to the list. Once again, you don't have to add generically common passwords; these are blocked automatically. The password protection feature can also integrate with Active Directory through agent password filters deployed to the domain controllers and which enforce or audit the use of banned passwords that have been configured in the Azure AD tenant via a deployed proxy service.

The password protection also has a smart lockout functionality, which is aimed at ensuring the Azure AD account is locked out before the AD account is locked out, which would leave an organization susceptible to a denial-of-service attack. For each lockout, the duration of the lockout is increased. Make sure the Azure AD lockout threshold is less than the threshold for AD (making sure Azure AD locks out first) and the duration of the lockout in Azure AD is longer than the AD reset counter. (And pay attention to the units: AAD is seconds; AD is minutes!)

Azure AD Conditional Access

Conditional access (CA) is one of the most powerful features of Azure AD, allowing access controls to be applied based on conditions. For example, you can create a policy that applies to a certain group of users of the Office 365 cloud applications (such as Exchange Online and SharePoint Online) and that requires either the device be compliant (managed by Microsoft Intune) or that an approved client application be used (such as the Microsoft Outlook client, which itself can have application management policies enforced when connected to corporate resources). Another policy could apply that requires the use of MFA if the device is not hybrid Azure AD joined when accessing certain applications. As the name makes very clear, you can give access based on conditions.

There are additional components that can be used as part of conditional access policies:

◆ **Named Locations**—These can either be locations you specify based on public-facing IP addresses that are Internet-facing. For example, you could add your corporate office by adding the IP address(es) that NAT your Internet traffic from that office, or locations can be countries. The countries are ascertained by mapping IP addresses to countries using various services.

◆ **Terms of Use**—These are PDF documents you upload that will be presented and (optionally) forced to be expanded and accepted by the user before access is given. Users can always review access policies they have accepted from their profile in MyApps.

◆ **Custom Controls**—This is where services like third-party MFA providers could be integrated.

At a broad level, the assignments (conditions) are broken down as follows:

◆ **User/Group/Role**—Commonly, groups or roles will be used, and remember that the exceptions can be just as useful, especially when testing to exempt administrators and also a bypass group. Once testing is completed, though, remember to ensure key users (such as administrators) are included, unless it's the break-glass account.

◆ **The Application**—This can be an application from the gallery, an application you have added, an application you have created, or an application published via AAD App Proxy. Multiple applications can be selected.

◆ **Conditions**—This can include sign-in risk, the device platform (once again, exclude can be useful here), location, the application (such as browser, modern authentication, active sync, and other [legacy]), and the device state, which is really driven by the exclude configuration, which can be based on the device being compliant and/or hybrid Azure AD joined.

The controls are then really focused on either blocking access or granting access, provided that one or all controls selected are met, which includes checks such as MFA (which will be prompted for if the token does not already show MFA has been used), device marked as compliant, hybrid Azure AD joined, an approved client app (such as, but not limited to, the Microsoft Office), and then terms of use, if created, and any custom controls, such as third-party MFA. Figure 4.4 shows one of the elements of a conditional access policy expanded, the sign-in risk. Note that to use the sign-in risk part of a conditional access policy, the user must have an Azure AD Premium P2 license, as this feature uses the Azure AD Identity Protection feature. Normal use of conditional access requires an Azure AD Premium P1 license. Note that in this example, I am not using this specific condition, which is why its configuration is set to No, and that is available for all the various conditions throughout conditional access.

FIGURE 4.4
The building blocks of conditional access

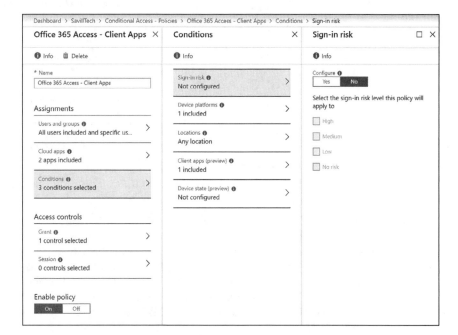

STAYING COMPLIANT!

Many features of Azure AD are part of different license SKUs; however, often this is not enforced. It is your responsibility to ensure that you are not targeting features to users that don't have the required license. While it will work, you would be out of license compliance.

Be careful when applying conditional access. Start off targeting a restricted group of users, in case the policy behaves in a way you don't expect and locks people out of the system. You don't want a scenario where you are locked out and can't get back in to fix it. (This is why we have break-glass accounts but really don't want to use them.) Test on a group of users, ensure that it behaves the way you expect, and then broaden its usage. I also like to add an empty exception group to policies. This gives the ability to "bypass" conditional access for users, if required. For example, imagine you have policies that require MFA, but your CEO is out somewhere and has lost their phone but has to get to a document. Yes, it's risky, but it may be an acceptable risk, so you could add their account to the exception group for a short period of time, let them access, and then remove them. Ideally, this exception group usage would be part of some workflow, to ensure that users are not left in the exception group. Think of it as a time-limited, one-time bypass capability. If the user had a new phone, you could instead make them re-register for MFA via the authentication methods of their Azure AD profile, as shown in Figure 4.5.

FIGURE 4.5
Forcing re-registration of MFA

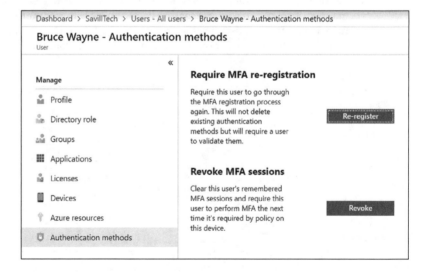

Conditional access should power many of your MFA requirements—ideally, in conjunction with the sign-in risk control. Take time to identify any controls you may need around groups of users, applications, locations, and so forth, and then identify what should be required to grant access. Take some time to review Microsoft's documentation on the controls and grants that are available. Walk through the portal, and take note of the grants where you can select if one of them is required or all, as utilizing the "require one of the selected controls" can be very powerful when handling various scenarios such as MFA if not at a corporate location or if not a hybrid joined device.

Azure AD Identity Protection

Identity is the new security perimeter as services move to the cloud, and Azure AD Identity Protection is the most powerful tool to have visibility into risks associated to users and individual sign-ins. Azure AD Identity Protection uses numerous technologies and resources, including machine learning and the Intelligent Security Graph, to provide insight into the health of your identities.

Identity Protection has a number of interfaces to identify users flagged for risk, risk events, and vulnerabilities, along with the ability to send alerts based on the severity of risks and weekly digests that summarize the state of the Azure AD tenant. These are very useful to enable response and knowledge to the identity health. Where there are risk events or users flagged for risk, you can drill down into the detail, provided that the users have Azure AD Premium P2 licenses.

As previously mentioned, Identity Protection sign-in risk assessment can be used as part of conditional access, but Identity Protection also has policies of its own: user risk and sign-in risk. At the time of writing, there are a number of different types of risk events, and these will likely expand over time. Some of these risk events can be detected in real time and are used as part of the sign-in risk and user overall risk. Others take more time to process, which would slow down sign-ins, and so are only parts of the user's overall risk. The following types of risk are currently identified:

Users with Leaked Credentials (high risk, offline detection)   This requires the password hash to be replicated to Azure AD and is alerting if a credential is found on the Internet/dark web that matches that username and password. It is critical to at minimum have user policy at high risk and require password change (post MFA).

Sign-Ins from Anonymous IP Addresses (medium risk, real-time detection)   Very little good things happen from an anonymized IP address/TOR browser.

Impossible Travel to Atypical Locations (medium risk, offline detection)   When first enabled, the machine learning of identity protection will look at locations used and even those connections that would normally be impossible—for example, connecting from London and then two minutes later from Dallas. However, when machine learning sees this, it will learn that's normal for that tenant and would be because of VPN, etc. After the learning phase, anomalies would be flagged that would indicate the credential has been compromised and is being used elsewhere.

Sign-In from Unfamiliar Location (medium risk, real-time detection)   Once again, the machine learning identifies normal patterns for each user and then will flag when a logon is outside of that behavior.

Sign-Ins from Infected Devices (low risk, offline detection)   This is flagging that the IP address that the request is coming from was part of some previous malware. These IP addresses are known as Microsoft works with agencies to take down large botnet servers providing access to this information.

Sign-Ins from IP Addresses with Suspicious Activity (medium risk, offline detection)   Behavior has been detected from the IP address that has been marked as suspicious. Remember, Microsoft has visibility across Azure AD tenants and its other properties, so it can see suspicious activity across services.

Note that even with machine learning there will still be false positives. This is to be expected, and the administrator should mark these as false positives, which will help train the machine learning to not alert on these in the future.

While the sign-in risk can be used as part of conditional access, the user risk cannot, which is where Identity Protection's user risk policy can be used. Based on a certain user risk level (for example, high), you can activate a control, which could be block access or, more commonly, require a password change (which would only be possible after they perform MFA to prove it's really them).

I previously mentioned that Identity Protection is an Azure AD Premium P2 feature, and in order to use the user risk component of conditional access, you should ensure that users have Azure AD Premium P2 licenses, although even non-P2 users get certain information.

- If a user has Azure AD Premium P2, they have visible risk levels, all at risk users' visibility and their individual risk levels and all risk event detail. This could be summarized as "tell me risky users, how risky, and why."

- If a user has Azure AD Premium P1, then users are flagged as "at risk" but with no risk level or complete detail about the risk. This could be summarized as "tell me the risky users." For P1 users, some detail is shown in a risk report, but some detections are not given detail and shown as "Sign-ins with additional risk detected."

- For non-premium users, if a risk is medium or high, the user is flagged as risky, but no risk level or detail is provided. This could be summarized as "tell me the medium and high risky users."

Risk reports are available via the Azure AD blade. Under the Security section, you will see "Users Flagged for Risk" and "Risk Events." This information is also directly available in Azure AD Identity Protection, in the Investigate section.

Azure AD Log Inspection

Insight into any system is critical—and even more so for identity. Two types of logs are available in Azure AD (in addition to the risk information previously discussed):

- **Sign-In Logs**—A record of any type of sign-in (successful or failure) and the details, such as MFA, app accessed

- **Audit Logs**—A record of all activity taking place in the tenant, such as creating a user, group changes, password resets, application usage

These logs power various types of reports, which are available via the Azure AD - Monitoring section. Both the sign-in logs and audit log reports have filtering available, although in many instances you will want to interface in a richer manner to these logs using different analytics. In addition to the native reports, you can also stream the Azure AD logs to another target via Azure Monitor, in common with most other types of log in Azure. The target for the logs is controlled by the Azure AD - Monitoring - Diagnostic settings, which enable either or both of the log types to be sent to any combination of the following (as shown in Figure 4.6):

- **Archive to a storage account**—The logs are just saved to the storage account specified. Another tool could then read the logs from the storage account and perform diagnostics, or you may just want to keep the logs as cheaply as possible, in case they are needed in the future.

◆ **Stream to an event hub**—An event hub is a publish/subscribe vehicle commonly used to integrate with an external SIEM system. In this configuration, the logs are published to the event hub, and then the SIEM system subscribes and receives the logs.

◆ **Send to Log Analytics**—This is the Azure native log storage capability. It also has powerful analytics capabilities that power Azure Monitor. Dashboards and solutions can be built on the native Kusto query language, offering very intuitive insight. This can also be used to keep data for a longer duration than the default 30 days.

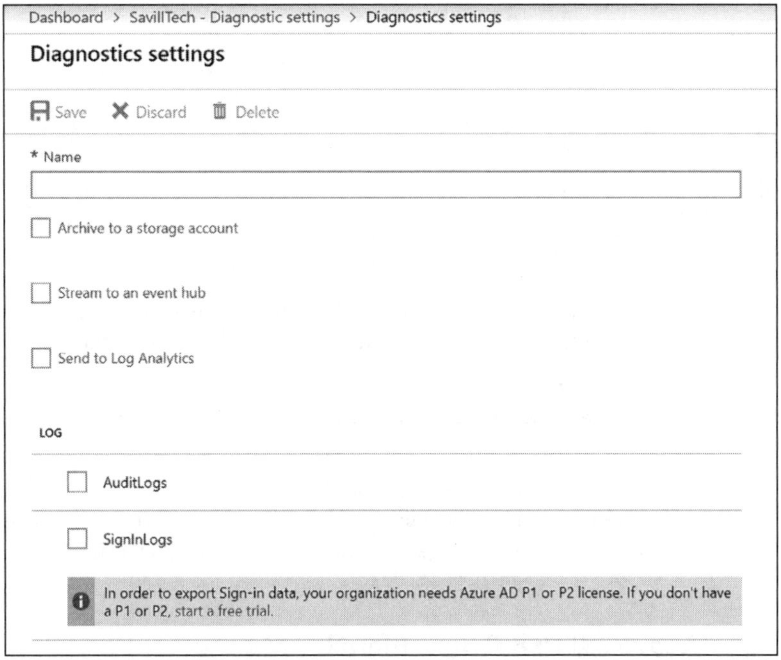

FIGURE 4.6
Diagnostic settings for Azure AD

Dashboard > SavillTech - Diagnostic settings > Diagnostics settings

Diagnostics settings

💾 Save   ✖ Discard   🗑 Delete

* Name

☐ Archive to a storage account

☐ Stream to an event hub

☐ Send to Log Analytics

LOG

☐ AuditLogs

☐ SignInLogs

ℹ In order to export Sign-in data, your organization needs Azure AD P1 or P2 license. If you don't have a P1 or P2, start a free trial.

Tools like Azure Sentinel (Azure's native SIEM solution), which can connect to Azure AD, are actually powered by this export to a Log Analytics workspace and then provide insights and AI-powered analysis, including the views I'm about to talk about. You can also manually import some views into Log Analytics once you stream logs to Log Analytics, to gain insight into activities and sign-ins. Full instructions are available at:

```
https://docs.microsoft.com/en-us/azure/active-directory/reports-monitoring/
howto-install-use-log-analytics-views
```

The instructions boil down to downloading two views from GitHub and importing them into the workspace. Figure 4.7 shows a small amount of the available detail; these lenses can all be drilled down into further for more investigation. Information about legacy authentication sign-ins, blocked sign-ins because of conditional access, MFA required sign-ins, and more is displayed.

FIGURE 4.7
Some of the
information
available via Log
Analytics views

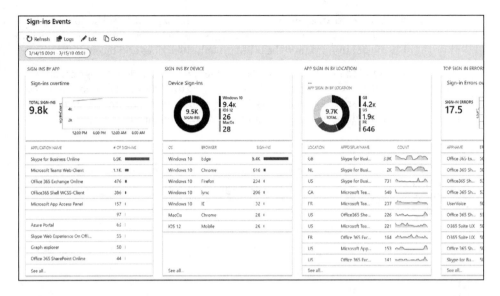

You can also author your own views using the Kusto language or just run queries. Following are two of my favorites. Try them out and work out what they are doing!

```
SigninLogs
| where TimeGenerated >= ago(1d)
```

```
SigninLogs
| where TimeGenerated >= ago(1d)
| summarize signInCount = count() by AppDisplayName, UserPrincipalName,
tostring(LocationDetails.state), tostring(LocationDetails.city)
| sort by signInCount desc
```

Azure AD Privileged Identity Management

Just-enough-administration (JEA)—giving someone only the rights they need to get the job done—is a core tenant of security. Often people will need privileges for specific duties, and the rest of the time, all they need are regular permissions. For example, sometimes you may need to be a Global Administrator or SharePoint Administrator, but you don't need that when you're just checking email or writing a document. In an ideal world, you would not always have these permissions, as it leaves your account open to compromise either directly or if you get some malware that then acts as you from your machine. Historically, this would be countered by having a privileged account and a normal user account (but this is painful), or the administrator would always have to perform strong authentication, such as always using MFA, which is not a good experience either.

Windows Vista introduced an extremely popular solution (I'm kidding, everyone hated it, although that was based on how it was implemented, not the actual technology): User Access Control (UAC). With UAC, when you logged on, you actually got two tokens: a privileged token (with all your heightened privileges) and a basic user token (which is what you actually ran with). If you wanted to perform an action that needed additional privileges, you would have to elevate by confirming you really wanted to do this action, entering a PIN, or doing whatever had been configured. (It was the fact Vista prompted you every 42 seconds to elevate that made UAC so unpopular, though this got much better in later versions.) The point was, the account was safer, and a user's consent had to be given to perform elevated tasks, helping protect the environment. Azure AD Privileged Identity Management (PIM) is very similar to this.

With PIM, users can be granted a certain Azure AD role, ARM role, or group membership that is not activated by default. Instead, the user can request to elevate to an assigned right either immediately or at a specific time in the future after entering a brief justification as to why they are elevating. The PIM administrator has a number of configuration options around the roles, such as:

◆ If MFA is required (This is hard required for more privileged roles and cannot be disabled.)

◆ If an email is sent to administrators when activated

◆ If a ticket number is required (to help track activities)

◆ If approval is required before activation

◆ The maximum duration of the activation (which the user can deactivate in advance of if the work is completed before the normal expiry)

Users can be assigned multiple roles and choose which they elevate as the task they are performing requires. Full audit logs are available for any elevations performed.

The Azure AD roles are tenant-wide when applied, and the users can do anything that the role assignment specifies. For the ARM roles, the assignment can be at a management group, subscription, resource group, or resource level, as shown in Figure 4.8. Change the filter to match the level at which you wish to apply the role, select the object, and then grant the required PIM role. For groups, users are added as eligible members, and then elevate up to be part of the group, as required, and will inherit any rights associated with that group for the duration of the group membership.

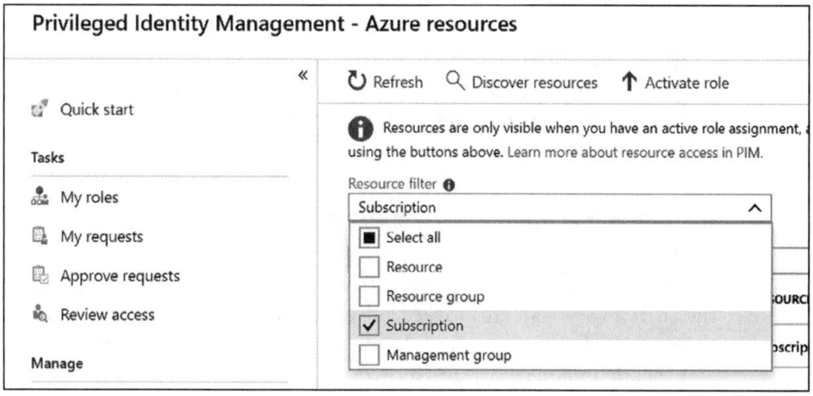

FIGURE 4.8
Change the resource filter to apply ARM roles at different resource levels.

Privileged Identity Management - Azure resources

«   ↻ Refresh   🔍 Discover resources   ↑ Activate role

🔲 Quick start

ℹ️ Resources are only visible when you have an active role assignment, using the buttons above. Learn more about resource access in PIM.

Tasks

Resource filter ℹ️

👥 My roles

Subscription   ∧

📋 My requests

■ Select all

📋 Approve requests

☐ Resource

🔍 Review access

☐ Resource group

Manage

✓ Subscription

☐ Management group

PIM is an Azure AD Premium P2 feature and is highly recommended for users who require privileged access to Azure AD, ARM, or even groups. This helps to protect both the user and the organization, as there are not elevated standing privileges. Instead, an explicit action and commonly stronger authentication are required to elevate rights, which are limited to the duration of the requiring activity. Remember that users can have different license levels, so the entire organization does not have to have Azure AD Premium P2 (although Identity Protection and Access Reviews, also P2 features, have value for most users). You could focus the P2 license on more critical employees who may have higher privileges and therefore are greater targets.

A common concern I hear from customers is whether PIM will extend to on-premises AD and resources. Remember, PIM is granting rights for Azure AD trusting resources. Most on-premises resources trust AD and not Azure AD. For on-premises equivalent functionality, a similar technology, called Privileged Access Management, can be deployed.

Azure Advanced Threat Protection

Most of what has been discussed to this point has been around the cloud identity—its security, assigning permissions, monitoring it, etc. For most organizations, the source of the identity will come from Active Directory on premises, which means that although securing the cloud identity is critical, if there were an undetected intrusion on premises against AD, then the synchronized cloud Azure AD identity would be put at additional risk.

Azure Advanced Threat Protection (ATP) is a cloud deployment of the earlier Azure Advanced Threat Analytics (ATA) solution. Azure ATA was an on-premises deployment that worked by sending a mirror of traffic to/from domain controllers to an intelligence service, which would analyze the traffic and identify various types of attack and alert accordingly—for example, identifying pass-the-hash, golden ticket, and other attacks. Azure ATP takes the on-premises service and moves it to a cloud service, removing the need for on-premises deployments and adding in cloud-scale and analytics capabilities. Azure ATP can also forward alerts to a SIEM solution.

While ATA primarily worked via port mirroring of domain controllers, this is not possible to the cloud, nor would sending all traffic be efficient. Instead, an Azure ATP sensor (similar to the ATA lightweight gateway and which is automatically updated) is deployed to all domain controllers which send relevant traffic to the cloud Azure ATP service, where analysis is performed. Azure ATP can also integrate with Defender ATP for additional analysis. Management and operational tasks are performed through the Azure ATP portal. Figure 4.9 shows some examples of attacks that were detected in my environment. Various alerting options are available.

Azure ATP is relatively lightweight in terms of the resources it consumes, and there is detailed sizing documentation and a calculation to plan in advance. Azure ATP is part of EMS E5 (which also includes Azure AD Premium P2).

Azure AD Application Proxy

Staying on the idea of on-premises services is Azure AD Application Proxy. Often an organization has applications on premises that are accessed via web protocols—i.e., HTTP/HTTPS. With the shift away from employees being on the internal network or having to VPN to the corporate network, it is often appealing to make on-premises applications available to the Internet. This is typically enabled through a reverse proxy solution that makes an internal resource available externally, such as Windows Web Application Proxy.

FIGURE 4.9
An example
timeline of activi-
ties detected by
Azure ATP

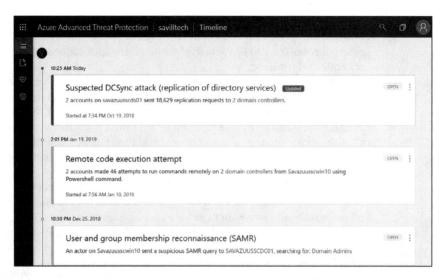

FIGURE 4.9
An example
timeline of activi-
ties detected by
Azure ATP

An alternative to hosting a reverse proxy solution is to use Azure AD Application Proxy. Azure AD Application Proxy is a cloud-hosted solution that acts as the endpoint for the service and then communicates to the hosting service via an Application Proxy Connector that is deployed on premises and establishes an outbound connection over HTTPS to Azure AD (avoiding the need to open up any firewall ports). This basic flow is shown in Figure 4.10.

FIGURE 4.10
Basic Azure
AD Application
Proxy flow

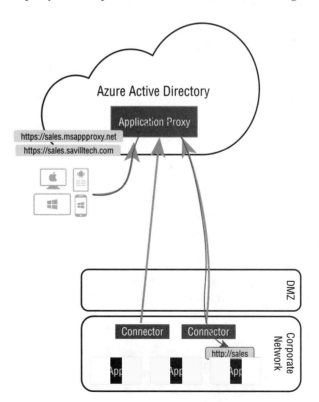

The Application Proxy Connectors deployed can be linked across multiple backend applications that are specifically assigned. These are known as *connector groups*. This allows certain groups of connectors to be exclusively utilized for applications where required to ensure necessary scale and resiliency.

Applications published through Azure AD Application Proxy are not only treated like any other Azure AD enterprise application, such as entitlements to users and integration with conditional access, but even though typically the backend application does not utilize Azure AD, but rather uses forms-based or integrated authentication with AD, Azure AD can still pre-authenticate the user at the endpoint and then enable a seamless authenticate to the backend using Kerberos Constrained Delegation (KCD), or pass-through authentication can be configured.

As part of the publication, the header URL can be translated between internal and external, and additional URLs in the body can also be translated. However, this will increase CPU load and potentially add some latency to the end-user experience.

Application Proxy works with a number of different types of applications, including web applications (using integrated Windows authentication, forms-based or header-based access), web APIs, applications accessed via Remote Desktop Gateway, and even rich client applications that integrate with Active Directory Authentication Library (ADAP). For details on the SSO experience across these, see:

```
https://docs.microsoft.com/en-us/azure/active-directory/manage-apps/
what-is-single-sign-on#choosing-a-single-sign-on-method
```

Azure AD Application Proxy is part of Azure AD Premium and Azure AD Basic, making it widely available. It just cannot be used by users of the free version of Azure AD.

Azure AD B2C

A year ago, my wife and I decided to lose some weight and made it interesting by having a little competition as to who could lose the most weight in 3 months. One day when I came home from work, my wife had purchased edible cookie dough and placed it in the fridge—a delight I didn't even know existed, and it was glorious. Obviously, this was an act of sabotage, but I didn't care. I ate it all and then rushed to my computer to find the website to buy more. The website had several account options:

◆ Sign in with Facebook.

◆ Sign in with Google.

◆ Sign in with an Amazon account.

◆ Sign in with a Microsoft account.

◆ Create a new account.

If you think back to Azure AD B2B, it was designed to enable users from other organizations to collaborate with your organization, to avoid them from having to maintain a separate account. In the consumer world, my cookie dough experience is very common. Consumers don't want to create separate accounts for every website or service they consume; instead, they want to use a single consumer identity that allows them not have to remember 50 accounts and that often they strengthen through MFA. It also minimizes the account effort the company must support.

A company offering a consumer service doesn't want to have customer accounts, such as AD or Azure AD, in its corporate identity store; instead, a separate identity store that can be used for customers is desirable. By having a separate identity store for customers, if a company has multiple applications, customers can use the same store across applications. As you have likely guessed, Azure AD B2C (Business to Consumer) is the Azure solution for consumer directories. An Azure AD B2C instance is created, and then the company's applications utilize that B2C instance (using the standard Microsoft Authentication Library, MSAL) for the identity requirements. To be clear, Azure AD B2C is a completely different Azure AD type and instance from the corporate Azure AD, which is different from Azure AD B2B, which integrates with the corporation's existing Azure AD tenant. This is because the goals are very different.

◆ **Azure AD B2B**—I want to collaborate with you as my partner and grant access to resources like Office, Teams, and SharePoint.

◆ **Azure AD B2C**—You are my customer, and I want to make certain web or mobile applications created by my organization are available to you.

The goal of Azure AD B2C is for organizations to be able to select which consumer identities they want to support for their customers while also offering them the ability to create a local account if they don't have an existing consumer account or don't want to use it. Where local accounts are created, B2C provides the ability for password resets, and for all types of accounts, you can add MFA based on policies you create. Figure 4.11 shows the interface to add a social identity provider to your B2C instance. (This list continues to expand.) You can customize the structure of the local usernames and attributes stored, which are utilized by the applications you write to utilize the B2C instance.

The B2C instance will be used by your customers, so you don't want to see Microsoft branding on any element of the user experience. A core tenant of B2C is "customize every pixel." You can customize all the dialog boxes, the flows, everything around B2C, to create an experience that matches your organization's look and feel. For a fun little example of some of that customization, see http://Aka.ms/aadb2cdemo.

While pricing is not something I will typically cover in this book, I want to touch on the pricing for B2C, since it is fairly unique and designed to handle all the different ways it will be used by different types of organizations. Billing is based on the following three pivots:

◆ Number of users

◆ Number of authentications

◆ Number of MFAs

FIGURE 4.11
Adding identity
providers for a
B2C instance

These different billing pivots enable different scenarios to be covered. You could be a company with a small number of users, but those users authenticate many times a day. Or you could be a company (or country) with millions of users but only use the service once a year. This flexible billing enables organizations to optimize their spend. Note that there is a 50,000 user, 50,000 authentication free tier, which means for a lot of developers, B2C is free.

By the way, my wife won the competition!

Active Directory in the Cloud

Many customers will use the Azure IaaS services, which are fundamentally virtual machines. The reasons for having a domain on premises (central authentication, policy, directory services) likely still apply to the operating systems deployed in Azure IaaS, which means often the AD services from on premises need to be extended to Azure.

As mentioned at the start of this chapter, two things are required for Active Directory to be leveraged by computers, users, and services:

◆ The ability to locate a domain controller or specific service, which for Active Directory means DNS name resolution for DNS servers hosting the domain DNS partitions

◆ The ability to communicate with the located domain controller using a variety of protocols, such as Lightweight Directory Access Protocol (LDAP), Kerberos, RPC, or Netlogon

A complete list of protocols is available here:

`http://technet.microsoft.com/en-us/library/dd772723(v=ws.10).aspx`

The key point is that communication is required over a wide range of TCP and UDP ports.

Fortunately, both DNS name resolution and the ability to communicate are easy to accomplish once you have connectivity between Azure and on premises established using either the site-to-site VPN connectivity or ExpressRoute. Connectivity to domain controllers (initially on premises) will already be in place via Layer 3 routing. If there are specific firewalls between on premises and Azure that restrict traffic flow or if you are using network security groups (NSGs) in Azure, it's important to make sure the required traffic can flow on the required ports.

Once IP connectivity is established, the next step is to configure the Azure resources to use your on-premises DNS servers to enable name resolution for domain services. (DNS services most likely are provided by your domain controllers, but that is not necessarily the case.) Ascertain the IP addresses and names for your on-premises DNS servers by talking to your AD and networking teams. Although you could examine your machines' network configuration to ascertain the DNS servers (for example, `ipconfig /all` shows the DNS servers configured), this would show the DNS servers your machine in your location is configured to use. Based on the point of connection to Azure, other DNS servers in your organization may be preferred—or even required—if network traffic is controlled between Azure and on premises. Working with the AD and networking teams will ensure the correct configuration. These DNS servers will be configured as the DNS servers to be used on the Azure virtual networks, which will enable the required name resolution.

Active Directory Site Configuration

Active Directory is a location-aware service that uses a multi-master model wherein all domain controllers can make changes. Through multi-master replication, the directory is kept synchronized between all the domain controllers. The replication topology is automatically generated by the Inter-Site Topology Generator (ISTG), which creates different models of replication depending on whether domain controllers are in the same physical site (a ring of replication) or in different sites (a least-cost-spanning tree). This enables efficient replication. You provide the site information to Active Directory by defining AD sites (which are IP address spaces) and then defining IP site links. Those links tell the ISTG which sites have direct communication and the connection speed to enable the replication topology to be generated.

In addition to being used for the replication of Active Directory data, the sites are used by AD clients and other services that want to use services in their local site or as close to their local site as possible. For example, a user logs on to a machine. That machine has an IP address that will be part of a subnet. The subnet is associated with an AD site. The site enables clients to locate domain controllers and other services. If no domain controller or service is found in the local site, services in the closest site can be used. Closeness is determined based on the site links and their speed (or cost) between sites.

As you can see, an accurate site and site link topology are critical for the health of AD replication, the efficient utilization of AD, and any service that is site aware. When extending your infrastructure to Azure, it's critical that Azure also become part of your site and site link definition, even if you don't place DCs in Azure—but especially if you *do* place DCs in Azure.

The Azure virtual networks are an IP space you have allocated, which corresponds perfectly to an Active Directory site. Your Azure virtual network will become a new site in Active Directory. You likely have an existing naming scheme for your Active Directory. Follow your existing scheme for your Azure site(s), but try to incorporate the fact that the site is in Azure and some information about the corresponding virtual network when you name the Azure site. An AD site name can be up to 63 characters in length, and since site names are used as part of DNS names, they cannot contain characters not allowed in DNS. The details on site names can be found in the Site Names section at `http://support.microsoft.com/kb/909264`.

Azure-based sites can be named Azure-<*Region*>-<*virtual network name*>—for example, Azure-EastUS-VNet113—or whatever scheme you prefer. Once the Azure virtual network is defined as a site, the next critical step is to define the site link that represents the connection between on premises and the Azure virtual network. Remember that the site links are used by the ISTG to decide how data should be replicated and which domain controllers should replicate with each other. Most likely, one of your on-premises locations has a link to Azure using either site-to-site virtual private networking or through ExpressRoute. The on-premises site should have an IP site link to the Azure site. Do not just add all sites to the default-first-site-link. Instead, create specific site links between locations that are connected. Remember to configure the interval desired for replication and follow your organization's existing cost scheme to accurately represent the speed of connection between your on-premises location(s) and Azure. If you have multiple on-premises sites connected to your virtual network, add multiple site links representing that connectivity. Defining the sites and site links before creating services in Azure ensures optimal AD integration and avoids erroneous traffic and suboptimal AD functionality.

Placing a Domain Controller in Azure

Just reading the title of this section will leave many AD administrators in a panicked state. AD contains information about every object in your organization. It controls who can access what. Domain controllers have the sacred duty of storing and servicing the directory content. The idea of placing one of these sacred objects outside of your own datacenter, where you can no longer nurture and protect it, seems sacrilegious. However, it's important to dismiss your initial emotional responses and take a look at the reality of the situation.

A big part of this is a concern about the security of services running in Azure. Spoiler alert: These concerns are not based on the realities of Azure. The datacenters that host Azure services are some of the most secure and resilient datacenters you will ever see. The physical security can stop a tank. Azure has been audited and certified for almost every major standard there is, which speaks to how secure and well processed the services are. Azure datacenters are used by governments, financial institutions, and the largest organizations in the world. They are secure.

However, *you* are responsible for ensuring that your services are secure. If you place a domain controller in Azure with the default RDP port open for logon, that is a bad (but easily avoided) thing. I will talk later in this chapter about some best practices for hosting domain controllers in Azure to maximize security. Do you host domain controllers in branch offices today? How secure are they? Remember that Azure will likely be a substitute for branch offices, for disaster recovery, or even other datacenters. You need to afford Azure domain controllers the same services that would accompany those on-premises facilities to be able to properly meet requirements.

This is not to say you should always place a domain controller in Azure, but you should consider it, depending on how integrated with Active Directory your Azure resources are. If services running in Azure are highly dependent on Active Directory to function, consider what will happen if the link to on premises is unavailable. How would the services continue to function? Even while the link to on premises is available, how much traffic will be sent from resources in Azure to domain controllers on premises? Remember that you pay for egress traffic. Consider also how sensitive your traffic is to latency if you are using the site-to-site VPN gateway. On the flip side, if you place one or more domain controllers in Azure, you must take into account the replication traffic between the domain controllers on premises and those in Azure. If the majority of change is sourced on premises, then most replication traffic will be ingress to Azure—and therefore free of charge. For most organizations, the replication traffic will not be a significant consideration. The more important factor will be having domain controllers close to the resources using Active Directory in Azure and ensuring availability even if the link to on premises is unavailable. If you are treating Azure as another datacenter and you would normally place domain controllers in a datacenter, then you should place them in Azure!

Some organizations will consider creating a separate domain (or even a separate forest) in Azure, which then has trusts to on premises. The key to success here is in determining which domain services need to be part of the trusted domain and then leveraging those services and trusted domains. If creating a separate domain or forest makes it difficult to manage services, then I would argue it would be detrimental to your organization's chances of being successful in a hybrid environment. Remember, Azure is an extension of your datacenter.

Domain Controller in Azure Considerations

Assuming you make the decision to create a domain controller in Azure, there are some special factors and operational practices for running a domain controller in Azure to consider. Prior to Windows Server 2012, virtualizing a domain controller was supported, but there were problems in organizations that used checkpoint functionality. Checkpoint functionality creates a point-in-time saved state of a VM and then reverts a VM back to a previous point in time when a checkpoint is applied. This is a huge problem for any kind of directory service, including Active Directory, that generally expects time to move forward. These services would be unaware that they had been reverted to a previous point in time. Problems arise when a reverted domain controller tries to replicate with a DC that has already received newer updates. This is cumbersome to fix.

Windows Server 2012 solved this by adding Active Directory virtualization safeguards through the use of a new attribute named VM-GenerationID. VM-GenerationID provides a unique ID that stays consistent, provided that nothing changes with the VM's view of time. For example, the application of a checkpoint would result in a VM-GenerationID change. The Active Directory service would detect the change to VM-GenerationID and go into a "panic" mode to protect Active Directory from any risk of corruption or bubbles of replication. The service would reset its invocation ID, dump its Relative ID (RID) pool, and set SYSVOL as nonauthoritative.

Although this protects Active Directory, it causes a lot of additional replication and work on other domain controllers to correct that state.

VM-GenerationID support was added as part of the Windows Server 2012 Hyper-V server release, and since Azure runs on Hyper-V, Azure also supports VM-GenerationID. This is both good and potentially bad. It should be noted, though, that Windows Server 2008 R2 Active Directory does not support this functionality, which means that you should think carefully before running Windows Server 2008 R2 domain controllers in Azure.

On the good side, if an unplanned failure occurs and the VM that contains Active Directory running in Azure has to be healed by the Azure fabric and is shunted back in time slightly, there will not be any corruption. On the bad side, if the VM running Active Directory was deprovisioned (removed from the Azure fabric) and then reprovisioned, the VM would get a new VM-GenerationID and cause Active Directory to go into the panic mode. You don't want this to happen frequently. Although you can shut down VMs running Active Directory in Azure, you should not deprovision them. Shut them down from within the OS so that they stay provisioned on the Azure fabric. Do not shut them down from the portal. This does mean that you will need to continue paying for the shutdown VMs.

There are two other considerations for domain controllers running in Azure that relate to storage and networking. First, remember that Active Directory has a database, and this database should not be stored on storage that uses caching. You cannot place it on the Azure VM OS drive. Domain controllers assert Forced Unit Access (FUA) and expect the I/O subsystem to honor the request, thus ensuring that sensitive writes are persisted to durable media. Instead, ensure that a data disk is added to the Azure VM and configured for no caching. When running the DC promotion process, ensure the Active Directory database, logs, and SYSVOL are placed on the data disk rather than the C: drive.

Second, all VMs in Azure have their IP configuration assigned by DHCP. As a result, when running the promotion process for the domain controller, a warning will be generated, as you will probably make the domain controller a DNS server, and DNS servers should not have their IP configuration assigned via DHCP. What the promotion process does not know is that, using PowerShell, your domain controller Azure VMs will be reserved in an IP address.

These points are very important. To summarize the factors you must consider for domain controllers running in Azure:

◆ Use Windows Server 2012 and later DCs—ideally, the latest OS.

◆ Do not shut down and deallocate DCs in the Azure management portal. (Instead, shut down or restart the VM within the guest OS.)

◆ Store the Active Directory database, logs, and SYSVOL on a data disk with no caching.

◆ Assign a reserved IP address.

Microsoft has an official page with guidelines for domain controllers in Azure. Take time to read it. The page features any updated guidance:

```
http://msdn.microsoft.com/library/azure/jj156090.aspx
```

READ-ONLY DOMAIN CONTROLLER AZURE CONSIDERATIONS

The baby step that many IT teams consider when they realize they need a domain controller in Azure is to deploy a read-only domain controller (RODC) instead of a writable domain controller. RODCs were introduced in Windows Server 2008 primarily as a solution for branch offices where hardware could not be physically secured but the site required a local domain controller. RODCs had a number of key features that made them attractive for locations that could not physically secure hardware:

Read-Only Database   The read-only copy of the database prevents any changes from replicating to the rest of the domain if the server is compromised.

Filtered Attributes   A filtered attribute set prevents certain attributes in AD from being replicated to the RODC. For example, attributes containing very sensitive data could not be replicated.

Limited Password Caching   The only passwords that are cached on an RODC are for accounts specified, such as those used at the location. If the server were compromised, any password attack would only expose limited accounts. Deleting the RODC object from AD management tools gives the option of resetting any passwords that were cached on the RODC.

Limited Administrator Rights   An individual can be made an administrator of an RODC without being made a domain administrator.

For organizations that are unsure about the security of Azure, placing an RODC in Azure instead of a typical read-write DC (RWDC) provides a level of comfort. However, Azure is not a branch office. In a branch office, users log on, and some basic directory interaction is performed. In Azure, there are likely services running that interact with Active Directory, and many applications do not support RODCs—they expect to be able to write to the DC and do not understand the referral to an RWDC that the RODC returns if a write is attempted. Therefore, the decision to use RODCs in Azure will depend on whether the services running in Azure will work with an RODC. Even if they do, you should consider how much write activity they perform and what the impact on their functionality will be if every write has to travel back to on premises, especially on the high-latency site-to-site VPN connection. Ultimately, is Azure a physically insecure branch office? No. But it will take some time to gain that trust.

If you decide to go that route, see the following articles for more guidance on RODC deployments:

```
http://technet.microsoft.com/library/dd728028(WS.10).aspx
```

```
http://technet.microsoft.com/en-us/library/dd734758(WS.10).aspx
```

Azure AD Domain Services

I lied a little earlier in this chapter when I said that Azure AD does not speak legacy authentication. It can, kind of, if you really need it to. As the previous section emphasized, you can extend regular AD into virtual networks in Azure, which will likely be required if services are running in those VMs that need to use legacy authentication, such as Kerberos or NTLM, or need to bind using LDAP or perhaps native AD communication, such as ADSI. Extending AD to Azure virtual networks is the right solution if you already have AD and can extend it to Azure virtual networks, but there are also organizations that may be cloud-first and don't have an AD, or there are restrictions (real or perceived) that don't allow AD to be extended to the cloud but may still have Kerberos, NTLM, and/or LDAP requirements. Azure AD Domain Services is a feature directly aimed at this requirement—the need to support Kerberos, NTLM, and LDAP for Azure virtual network-based resources against Azure AD.

Azure AD Domain Services provides AD services to the Azure virtual network it is deployed to. Additionally, any other networks that are connected to that AAD DS deployed virtual network could also take advantage of the AAD DS deployment, provided that their DNS points to the AAD DS DNS services or at least has conditional forwarders for its zone. Remember, in order for AD to function, it requires name resolution and connectivity. AAD DS deploys not only domain controllers (two, at the time of writing) but DNS services, which must be utilized to locate and resolve the AAD DS services. At the time of writing, AAD DS can be deployed only to a single virtual network (which itself exists in a single region), and additional managed DCs cannot be added in other networks.

So what is AAD DS? AAD DS is a managed AD deployment deployed to a specific virtual network. Accounts are replicated from Azure AD to the managed AD instance. It is a fully managed AD. You have no access to these domain controllers; they are automatically patched, monitored, and everything else. You don't have domain administrator privileges, but there are various levels of administrative access, and you can still apply Group Policy. It is also possible to create users into the AAD DS instance. However, these users will *not* replicate to Azure AD; they will exist only in the AAD DS environment, which means in most instances, accounts should be those replicated from Azure AD. It is also not possible to move AAD DS to a different network. You would have to delete AAD DS and then redeploy, so take time and ensure that you deploy to the most appropriate network.

ADDITIONAL PASSWORD HASHES REQUIRED

Previously, I wrote that a hash of the hash is sent to Azure AD, which is not reversible, which means it is of no use to AAD DS. When you are deploying AAD DS, the password hashes from AD must be replicated to Azure AD to enable password hashes to be available in the AAD AD instance to support Kerberos and NTLM. These are in addition to the normal hash of the hash replication via AAD Connect.

Microsoft has a huge amount of great documentation about AAD DS. My focus here is to ensure that you realize it's available, but I want to point out a few key points:

◆ When creating an AAD DS deployment, you need to give a domain name. I recommend adding aadds. to the start of the name. For example, if my domain were savilltech.net, my AAD DS domain name would be aadds.savilltech.net. The NetBIOS name is the prefix (i.e., the part up to the first dot—in this case, aadds). Adding aadds removes any risk of conflict with the actual domain, including DNS.

◆ For password policies, if the account is sourced from AD DS, then the on-premises AD password policy would apply. If a cloud user, the Azure AD password policy would apply. You never change passwords in AAD DS (unless it's a local AAD DS user who does not sync back to AAD, and those accounts are managed by domain policies of AAD DS that support FGPP).

◆ Account lockout policies impact all users in AAD DS, but this lockout does not replicate back to AAD. (FGPP can be used to change an account lockout policy, as the domain policy cannot be changed, since only the domain admin can change the domain policy, which is not delegated with AAD DS.)

◆ If you wish to use secure LDAP/LDAPS, then the domain name you picked will dictate if this is possible, since only one certificate can be uploaded. Provided that you picked a domain name you own, you will be able to upload a public certificate for the name.

◆ If you don't currently have AD available in Azure and are trying to decide between AD and AAD DS, Microsoft has a whole comparison at:

```
https://docs.microsoft.com/en-us/azure/active-directory-domain-services/
active-directory-ds-comparison
```

Typically, however, the decision will boil down to whether privileges like domain admin are required or whether the schema needs to be extended, which is not possible with AAD DS.

◆ AAD DS supports joining the domain via REST APIs, which is something you can't do with regular AD but which is very useful in the cloud!

Chapter 5

Networking

Networking is a critical element for any architecture, and in the cloud there are many considerations. This chapter will explore the core networking capabilities and how they should be used in your Azure architecture. Networking is typically broken into four key pillars, which will drive much of this chapter (although I will cover some of the technologies in slightly different orders):

♦ **Connectivity**—Virtual networks, Azure Virtual WAN, ExpressRoute/VPN, and Azure DNS

♦ **Protection**—NSGs, Azure Firewall, web application firewalls, DDoS protection, and virtual network service endpoints

♦ **Delivery**—Azure Load Balancer, Azure Application Gateway, Azure Traffic Manager and Azure Front Door

♦ **Monitoring**—Azure Network Watcher, ExpressRoute Monitor, Azure Monitor, and Azure Virtual Network TAP

Connectivity

When thinking about connectivity, there are two major elements: something to place resources on (i.e., a network) and how to enable communication to that network. In this section, I will explore all the key elements related to connectivity in Azure.

Virtual Networks

Much like a network in a physical location, a virtual network is utilized in Azure as a means to group and provide connectivity between services connected to the network. Virtual networks are broken up into one or more virtual subnets to which the resources are actually connected. A virtual network is bound by both subscription and region and cannot cross those boundaries—i.e., a single virtual network cannot span regions or subscriptions. If you have multiple subscriptions using multiple regions, you must have a virtual network per region, per subscription. (However, you can connect those networks, as I will discuss later.)

The IP space chosen for the virtual network should not overlap any IP space used on premises or in any other service used by your organization. For example, if your organization uses the 10.0.0.0/8 IP range on premises, you would likely choose the 172.16.0.0/12 range in Azure to avoid any risk of overlap. Always consider that, even if you don't want to connect Azure to your on-premises network today, you may want to connect in the future. While often IP ranges from RFC 1918 are used in virtual networks, just like on premises, this is not a limitation, and other ranges can be utilized, including shared address space defined in RFC 6598. As a quick reminder, RFC 1918:

◆ 10.0.0.0–10.255.255.255 (10/8 prefix)

◆ 172.16.0.0–172.31.255.255 (172.16/12 prefix)

◆ 192.168.0.0–192.168.255.255 (192.168/16 prefix)

If you plan to use non-RFC 1918 IP addresses in Azure, it is obviously important that you use only non-RFC 1918 addresses for IP spaces you own in your organization. For most organizations, the use of RFC 1918 ranges is still the best option; non-RFC 1918 use would be on an exception basis. A virtual network can have multiple IP ranges assigned to it—for example, you could have some 10.*x.x.x* scope and some 172.16.*x.x*, etc.

UNDERSTANDING CIDR NOTATION

When defining virtual networks, CIDR notation is used. CIDR notation combines the IP network address and the associated mask that defines which part of the IP address represents the network. It is presented in the format of *xxx.xxx.xxx.xxx/n*, where *xxx.xxx.xxx.xxx* is the IP network and *n* represents the number of bits used for the subnet mask.

An *n* value of 24 indicates a subnet mask of 255.255.255.0. Since each part of the address is 8 bits, 24 bits means the first three parts are all 1s and therefore 255.

192.168.1.0/24 equates to an IP range of 192.168.1.0–192.168.1.255.

Once you decide the IP address range you want to use for the Azure network, you can then divide that address range into subnets for use by different types of service. I like to create different subnets for my Azure infrastructure servers, such as domain controllers, and another for my Azure application services, such as SQL servers. The Azure gateway requires its own IP subnet for VPN/ExpressRoute, as do many other services.

Subnets can be as large as /8 and as small as /29 (using CIDR subnet definitions). Remember, Classless Interdomain Routing (CIDR) subnet definitions show the number of bits in the IP address that defines the network. An /8 provides a subnet mask of 255.0.0.0. (I doubt you would ever have a subnet anywhere close to this size.) Gateway functionality between subnets in a virtual network is provided automatically by the virtual network. However, you cannot ping the gateway for each subnet, nor will tracer type utilities work. Also, the subnets you define cannot have overlapping address spaces.

Within a virtual network subnet, the protocol reserves the first and last IP addresses of a subnet: A host ID of all 0s is used for the network address, and a host ID of all 1s is used for broadcast. In addition, Azure reserves the first three IP addresses in each subnet (binary 01, 10, and 11 in the host ID portion of the IP address) for internal purposes. Figure 5.1 shows an example of a virtual network with a number of subnets. Note that in this example the first two subnets use /24, but the remaining networks use different sizes, all the way down to a /29 network, which should normally allow six usable IP addresses (192.168.4.1 to 192.168.4.6). But, as shown in Figure 5.1, notice that the address space shows only three IP addresses are usable (.4 to .6). This is because Azure has reserved the first three usable addresses (.1 to .3) for its own purposes.

FIGURE 5.1
Viewing the
address space
for virtual
subnets

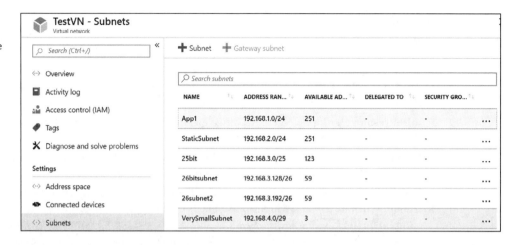

Once you define subnets and add virtual machines (and other types of services) to those subnets, you must allocate an IP address for each VM. The address will be allocated from the subnet IP address range as an infinite lease. This means that even though Dynamic Host Configuration Protocol (DHCP) is used to assign the IP address to the virtual machine, the actual IP address will never change as long as the virtual machine is provisioned, which means you are paying for it. It is also possible to configure machines to always receive the same IP address, as we will explore further later in this chapter, and even have multiple IP configurations for a single network interface. This IP address is known as the NIC's private IP address since it is only contactable on the virtual network and any connected networks.

Within a virtual network, most IP-based protocols, such as TCP, UDP, and ICMP, will work, although you should be aware that multicast, broadcast, IP-in-IP encapsulated packets, and Generic Routing Encapsulation (GRE) packets are blocked. The GRE blocking is very logical when you consider that, behind the scenes, Azure leverages Hyper-V Network Virtualization, which itself uses GRE. This could change in the future. Multiple virtual networks can be connected via on-premises connectivity or through the Azure fabric.

This is really all a virtual network is: an IP address space you define and then divide into subnets, and virtual machines are then assigned to a subnet when the virtual machine, or specifically the network interface card (NIC), is created. Although I am talking exclusively about IaaS virtual machines, other services, like containers and other PaaS services, also integrate with virtual networks.

WARNING Once VMs are created, it's difficult to move them into a virtual network. It is critical that, before any real workloads are created in Azure, you work with your on-premises network team, identify the IP space for use in Azure, create your Azure virtual network, enable connectivity between networks, and then start using the virtual network with services. Note that you can move vNICs and therefore workloads (e.g., VMs) between subnets but not easily between virtual networks.

Like nearly every resource in Azure, a virtual network can be created via the portal, Azure CLI, or PowerShell. Ideally, however, you should leverage a JSON template.

Adding a VM to a Virtual Network

Once the virtual network is created, the next step is to add virtual machines. Here are some key rules:

Regions matter... VMs can only be part of virtual networks in the same region as the cloud service. If a cloud service is in the East US region, the virtual network must be in the East US region.

...but resource groups don't. Resource groups do not affect virtual network affiliation. A VM can be in a different resource group from the virtual network.

Plan well. You cannot (easily) move VMs between virtual networks post-creation. Carefully plan virtual networks and VM architecture before deployment.

NICs are objects too. While often we talk about adding VMs to networks, the actual resource structure in ARM is that a NIC is its own object that is connected to a virtual network. Then the NIC is attached to a VM, thereby giving the VM connectivity via the NIC.

Subnets NICs are added to virtual subnets, which are part of a virtual network.

MOVING A VM BETWEEN VIRTUAL NETWORKS OR INTO A VIRTUAL NETWORK

Once a VM is created, there is no way to move it between virtual networks. The only solution is to delete the virtual machine and re-create it. This is not as bad as it seems. What is a virtual machine? A virtual machine is primarily virtual hard disks (VHDs) that contain the OS, data, and most of its state. The rest of the VM in Azure—the VM size, location, cloud service membership, and so forth—is likely the part you want to change. Therefore, a good way to "move" a VM is to delete the VM but retain its VHDs. Then, create a new VM in the target virtual network and attach it to the VHD files of the old VM. This essentially moves the VM. It's similar in concept to taking the hard drive out of one computer and putting it in a new computer.

NIC IP Configurations

A virtual machine can have one or more NICs attached to it. The exact number depends on the type and size of the VM. The following website provides a reference for the detail as to the number of NICs along with the (expected) aggregated network bandwidth—for example, a D4_v3 supports up to two NICS for a total of 2,000 Mbps:

```
https://docs.microsoft.com/en-us/azure/virtual-machines/windows/sizes
```

A VM must have a minimum of one NIC, and all NICs must be connected to the same virtual network (but can be connected to different virtual subnets). It is the requirement of always having one NIC that stops you from being able to move a VM between networks by simply removing all the NICs and adding to a network, as does the restriction that the NICs must be connected to the same virtual network. NICs can be added and removed from VMs, but the VM must be deprovisioning from the fabric–i.e., stopped. Note that one of the NICs is the primary, and this is the only NIC that is assigned a default gateway. If other NICs need to be able to communicate outside of the local subnet using their private IP, then within the guest OS, add a default route to the first IP of the subnet (e.g., .1).

For each NIC, there are one or more IP configurations. This is very similar to a physical NIC on your desktop computer. If you look at the NIC properties, there is a default IP configuration, but you can add additional IP addresses on the adapter. This is the same for IP configurations on the NIC in Azure. For each IP configuration, there can be two IP addresses:

◆ **The Private IP**—This is mandatory and for the first IP configuration can be dynamic or static. For subsequent IP configurations on a NIC, it must be static, as DHCP cannot assign multiple IP addresses to a single NIC. Additionally, when using multiple IP addresses per NIC, the IP addresses will need to be configured manually inside the guest OS; therefore, typically even the first private IP will also be configured statically.

◆ **An optional Public IP Address**—A public IP address enables connectivity from the Internet directly to the VM. The guest OS is not aware of the public IP address directly; rather, the fabric directs traffic to the public IP into the VM via its private IP. Ordinarily, regular VMs should not have a public IP, and instead a load balancer is used to front any published services to the Internet to provide distribution and additional security. There are two SKUs of public IP: Basic and Standard. Standard is a newer SKU that is always static and is typically paired with a standard load balancer but can also be assigned to other types of resource including a NIC. A standard public IP is zone redundant and zonal (can be guaranteed within a specific availability zone) and by default blocks inbound traffic.

There are limits both on the number of private IP addresses and public IP addresses per NIC. Review the Azure limits documentation for current values at:

```
https://docs.microsoft.com/en-us/azure/
azure-subscription-service-limits?toc=%2fazure%2fvirtual-network%2ftoc
.json#azure-resource-manager-virtual-networking-limits
```

Even at the time of writing, however, these limits are very high—for example, 25 private IPs per NIC—so these are unlikely to have a real impact on your planning.

Typically, a VM created for normal purposes will have a single NIC with a single IP configuration. The use of multiple NICs and IP configurations is typically leveraged by various types of virtual appliances—for example, a virtual firewall or virtual load-balancing device provided by a third party via the Azure marketplace. Multiple IP configurations can be useful for hosting multiple websites that need separate SSL certificates, as an example.

TALKING TO THE INTERNET FROM THE PRIVATE IP

Even though a private IP is contactable only on the virtual network, Azure automatically provides SNAT (source NAT) services, enabling outbound connectivity to the Internet with a stateful firewall that enables the responses to be returned to the VM. You don't need a public IP to talk to the Internet or perform any special actions. When a private IP talks to a public IP address, a mapping is automatically performed to a public IP, but which public IP?

◆ If the VM has a public IP address, then the SNAT uses that public IP.

◆ If the VM is part of a set behind a public load balancer (and has no public IP of itself), then the public IP of the load balancer is leveraged with SNAT and port masquerading (PAT).

◆ If the VM has no public IP and is not part of a load balancer with a public IP, then a public IP address is automatically designated and used via SNAT and PAT.

Note there are some special considerations when using standard load balancers and standard public IP addresses. Manual steps are required to enable outbound connectivity to the Internet. For full details, review:

```
https://docs.microsoft.com/en-us/azure/load-balancer/
load-balancer-outbound-connections
```

Additionally, NAT can be provided through other services, such as Azure Firewall, which provides SNAT (and DNAT for inbound). At the time of writing, there are discussions around other types of dedicated NAT services. Some of the benefits of Azure Firewall and assigned public IPs are predictability of the IP address that traffic from the VMs to the Internet will be coming from, which can be important when configuring firewall rules in other services based on source IP—i.e., coming from Azure IaaS VMs.

If you *don't* want Internet connectivity, then Network Security Groups can be utilized to block traffic to the Internet service tag along with other types of first- and third-party virtual appliances.

Reserved IPs for VM

VMs inside a virtual network receive their IP address from the Azure fabric using DHCP based on the IP range of the virtual subnet that the NIC is connected to. This IP address is chosen by the fabric based on the addresses available in the subnet and is known as a *dynamic IP* since it could potentially change. Remember that each IP address lease is an infinite lease. Apart from service healing operations, an IP address will never change as long as the VM is provisioned in Azure.

Regardless of whether your VM is on premises or in Azure, you should avoid reliance on the IP address of a VM wherever possible. Ideally, you will leverage DNS to communicate with OS instances. Then, if the IP address does change, the DNS record would automatically update via dynamic DNS, and clients could continue communication even after an IP change. However, there are circumstances where you need to ensure that the IP address of a VM never changes, even if it is deprovisioned or healed. In some instances, you need to use the IP address for a specific VM. For example, for DNS services in Azure, the IP addresses for domain controllers are specified directly in the virtual network configuration.

You can reserve specific IP addresses, known as a *static IP*, through the various Azure management interfaces from the portal, through PowerShell, Azure CLI to JSON templates. You can only configure an IP address that is available in the virtual subnet and that is within the range of the virtual subnet. If you try to configure other addresses, you will receive an error. I typically have separate subnets for my dynamically and statically assigned IP addresses to make it easier to track.

Note that at no time was the networking configuration inside the VM modified. The VM is always configured to use DHCP and never a static IP address within the OS (except when using multiple IP configurations per NIC). The IP reservation is through the Azure network fabric, which ensures that the VM always gets the same IP address.

Public IP addresses, which are their own resource, can also be configured as dynamic or static. Public IP addresses also have an optional DNS name that can be used to utilize the address, which is region-specific. For example, Figure 5.2 shows a public IP address created in East US. Note the DNS suffix and the fact the IP address is actually blank. This is because it's a dynamic public IP address and not currently being used. Public IP addresses cannot be moved between regions.

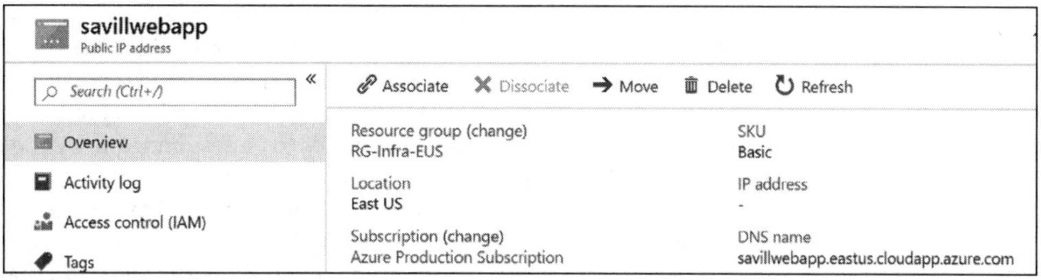

FIGURE 5.2
A public IP
address in East
US

Accelerated Networking

Latency is a major performance consideration for networking and typically the flow of network data from a VM outbound is via the software-based virtual switch that runs on each compute node. This vSwitch is the Hyper-V virtual switch and has a number of layers, including the virtual filtering platform that enables numerous networking capabilities. While the vSwitch delivers great functionality, it also introduces some latency.

Accelerated networking leverages the SR-IOV technology that has been present in Hyper-V for a number of versions and enables the VM to talk directly to the NIC via "virtual" NICs (the correct term is a virtual function) that the physical NIC provides, which are then mapped 1:1 with a NIC of the VM. Accelerated networking is available on most SKUs, including D/DSv2, D/DSv3, E/ESv3, F/FS, FSv2, and Ms/Mms; the Microsoft documentation confirms exactly which. It also works on Windows and most Linux distributions. Note, you may wonder if the vSwitch is bypassed, how do all the wonderful Azure networking capabilities still function that rely on the vSwitch? Behind the scenes, Microsoft research works closely with the Azure team and has been heavily investing in hardware offloading via programmable hardware. One of the outputs of those efforts is that large parts of the software vSwitch now run on the NICs in the hosts, offering many benefits, and, in this case, the networking functionality normally enabled via the software vSwitch is provided by the programmable hardware, providing faster services with less compute required.

There is no cost to enabling accelerated networking, and my guidance is to always enable if it's available. You gain reduced latency, more packets per second, less jitter, and fewer compute cycles. Only good things!

Azure DNS Services and Configuration Options

VMs in Azure always get their IP configuration via DHCP. By default, for VMs in a virtual network, the Azure-provided name resolution is utilized and will provide name resolution via the fully qualified domain name (FQDN) or hostname for workloads in the same virtual network. There are, however, many limitations, such as you cannot change the DNS domain name and you cannot add additional, custom records. These limitations are documented at:

```
https://docs.microsoft.com/en-us/azure/virtual-network/
virtual-networks-name-resolution-for-vms-and-role-instances#azure-provided-name-
resolution
```

In most environments, leveraging virtual networks using a custom DNS server configuration is desirable. For example, you can use domain controllers in your organization to offer consistent name resolution across different services and different locations. You can set the DNS servers through the virtual network configuration.

The Azure dedicated DNS service, Azure DNS, offers both public and private zone services. Like regular DNS, it is focused around a DNS zone, which for a public zone needs to be registered and delegated to Azure DNS. For both public and private zone services, the record management can be done through the normal Azure management options. Azure DNS is a globally distributed service that uses anycast to enable queries to be responded to by the closest instance of Azure DNS to the requesting client.

The Azure DNS private zone option addresses the many limitations of the Azure-provided name resolution that is used by default for a virtual network. With an Azure DNS private zone, name resolution is possible across different virtual networks, with full record management available. For Azure DNS private zones, there are two types of interactions from virtual networks:

- **Resolution Networks**—These are networks that are allowed to resolve records from the zone.

- **Registration Networks**—These are networks that register records into the zone for resources added/modified/removed from the network—for example, a VM created. A registration network, by default, is also a resolution network—i.e., it can resolve records from the zone.

Each Azure DNS private zone can have one registration virtual network and up to 10 resolution virtual networks. Likewise, a virtual network can be configured as a registration virtual network for only one Azure DNS private zone and linked as a resolution virtual network to up to 10 Azure DNS private zones.

Connecting Virtual Networks

A virtual network is by default an isolation boundary. Within a virtual network, all resources can communicate by default (although this can be controlled, as you will see later in the chapter), but there is no communication between different virtual networks other than publicly exposed endpoints available via the Internet.

For infrastructure architects, the goal often is to limit the number of virtual networks for exactly this isolation reason (and to minimize management overhead) to avoid having a lot of islands of connectivity, but remember the boundaries of a virtual network: region and subscription. If you have deployments in multiple regions, you will need at least one virtual network per region. If you have multiple subscriptions, then you will need virtual networks in each region for each subscription. With just two subscriptions and deployments to two regions in each, that would be four virtual networks.

While sometimes isolation between virtual networks is required (for example, perhaps there is a production and development network that requires complete isolation), there are often times isolation is not desired and is only present because of the boundaries of virtual networks (i.e., region and subscription), and the preferred approach would be one large network that spanned regions and potentially subscriptions.

A QUICK NOTE ON SEGMENTATION

Often on premises there is a single physical network that is then segmented, often through the use of VLANs, which offer separate broadcast domains and restrictions on traffic flow. While virtual networks by default provide isolation, this isolation may not be at the right level—i.e., more granular isolation is required not based on subscription or region but on some other criteria. Later in this chapter, I cover other types of segmentation that enable micro-segmentation in addition to more general subnet-based isolations that are common when using VLANs. As will be explored, there are numerous capabilities to segment, from IP/tag-based rules, through first- and third-party network virtual appliances, to NIC-level tagging for true micro-segmentation.

It is important to know these additional segmentation options are available when planning out virtual networks and the connectivity between them. Just because virtual networks are connected, it does not mean you cannot control traffic flows within the connected networks, and this includes other networks, such as those on premises.

There are numerous methods to connect virtual networks to enable connectivity between resources in separate virtual networks. From the early days of networking, there were primarily two methods utilized:

◆ Connect virtual networks using a site-to-site VPN. This provided connectivity, but all traffic was sent through the single VPN gateway per virtual network, which meant using up the limited total bandwidth available and throttling the flow of traffic.

◆ Connect virtual networks to the same ExpressRoute circuit. This provided potentially higher bandwidth since ExpressRoute gateways offer higher bandwidth options; however, the traffic must flow via the peering point—i.e., the external provider providing the "meet me" that connects the customers network to the Microsoft network. This would increase the latency because of this hair-pinning (the traffic is turned around) at the peering location, which potentially could be 10s or 100s of miles from the Azure datacenters.

Both options limited the traffic flow and increased latency. Network peering solves this problem by allowing virtual networks to be connected together via the Azure backbone without the use of gateways, enabling resources to operate and flow traffic at their native capabilities. This is both an ingress and egress cost for network peering, which should be factored into the cost planning.

VIRTUAL NETWORK PEERING

Virtual networks can be peered within a region (VNet peering), across regions (Global VNet peering), across subscriptions, and even across Azure AD tenants. Adding peers is a simple process. There is a limit on the total number of peerings possible per virtual network, which currently stands at 500 but could change, so always check the Azure limits' website for current values. When using peering, the connectivity is between virtual networks and via the Azure backbone, providing the lowest possible latency and without any bandwidth throttling or bottlenecks. Resources will all communicate at their native capabilities.

The network peering relationship is not transitive. As shown in Figure 5.3, even if two virtual networks are peered to a shared hub virtual network, the two virtual networks cannot directly communicate. If communication between the two spoke virtual networks is required, a network peering relationship would need to be established between the spokes. As you can imagine, as the number of virtual networks increases, a large mesh of network peering relationships may be required if complete connectivity is required (although often spoke-to-spoke communication is not a requirement, only spoke-to-hub).

FIGURE 5.3
The non-transitive
nature of network
peering

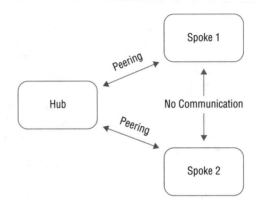

There are alternatives to adding peering relationships between all the spokes and even potentially between multiple hubs, if you have a larger spine-hub-spoke architecture where the spine network could be the corporate network or connectivity point, such as ExpressRoute.

The first alternative to adding peering relationships between all the spoke virtual networks is to add a default route or summary route encompassing the region's virtual network address space from the peering location (the "meet me" point) for ExpressRoute to the hub (which would then send to the spokes). If Spoke 1 tries to talk to Spoke 2, the traffic would go via the peering point, hairpin, and be sent to Spoke 2 via the hub, essentially bouncing the traffic via the peering location. This will increase latency; however, you will not have to pay peering charges since the source/target of the traffic is not between the virtual networks. No changes are required on the spoke routes.

The second alternative is to use a firewall in the hub. This could be Azure Firewall or a third-party NVA. A user-defined route (the ability to change the next hop of traffic) can be added in Spoke 1 for the Spoke 2 address space, which says to route via the firewall and the reverse for the Spoke 2 network. This requires the use of the Allow Forwarded Traffic option as part of the peering relationship.

Also note that if you connect multiple hub networks to the same ExpressRoute circuit, then spokes connected to different hubs will be able to talk automatically, as essentially the first alternative approach for spoke-to-spoke is happening. Note that spokes on the same hub still won't be able to directly communicate without one of the preceding configuration options.

GATEWAY TRANSIT ROUTING

Another capability can be used along with VNet peering (including global). Consider the hub and spoke configuration. The hub network may have other connectivity (such as to an ExpressRoute circuit) that you don't have on the spokes. Gateway transit enables the use of a remote gateway in the spokes—i.e., the hub has a gateway, such as S2S VPN or ExpressRoute, to another network (e.g., on premises). With gateway transit enabled and configured, the spokes would have the address spaces forwarded to them from the hub via BGP and could use the hub's connectivity to get to those address spaces. The end result: Spokes can talk to everything the hub can!

The configuration for gateway transit is simply additional checkboxes during the peering configuration. On the hub networks, the option to enable Gateway Transit is selected, and on the spoke networks, the Remote Gateway option is selected. This facilitates the flow of routes and communication.

Connectivity to Azure

With the connectivity for Azure virtual networks established, the next logical step is to establish private connectivity from on premises to Azure. While access can be facilitated through Internet-facing endpoints, such as a public IP, it is neither efficient nor secure to open up RDP on a public IP for every server in a virtual network. Instead, the Azure virtual network should become an extension of the on-premises network connectivity and connections should be seamless. There are a number of options to provide this connectivity, depending on the organizational requirements. Note that when dealing with connectivity in and out of Azure, there are no ingress charges—i.e., data going into a region. There are egress charges—i.e., data leaving a region either via Internet paths or via private paths, such as VPN/ExpressRoute.

Site-to-Site VPN

The most basic and most accessible solution for securely linking Azure virtual networks to on-premises resources is the site-to-site (S2S) VPN. Note that the emphasis here is on linking Azure virtual networks to on-premises resources rather than linking VMs to on-premises resources. All mechanisms for connecting Azure to on-premises resources rely on the VMs being part of a virtual network. There are no options for connecting on-premises resources to VMs that are not part of a virtual network other than through the cloud service VIP or an instance-level public IP. One easy way to think about this is that the virtual network in Azure acts as a branch office to the main network on premises.

The S2S VPN uses IPsec to provide an encrypted connection between Azure and your on-premises network via the Internet. This means even though the connection is over the Internet, it is secure. Two types of gateways are supported by Azure: static and dynamic.

Static Routing Gateways   A static routing VPN, also known as a *policy-based VPN*, routes traffic based on a customer-defined policy. Typically, traffic is allowed based on an access list of entries that are manually added to a routing table. (That quickly becomes impractical in a large network.) A static routing VPN must connect to a static routing gateway. Internet Key Exchange version 1 (IKEv1) is used for the initial security association configuration. Static routing is the most simple to configure, but there are numerous limitations. Static gateways do not support coexistence with point-to-site VPNs, cannot be used to link to virtual networks, and permit only a single VPN connection to on premises.

Dynamic Routing Gateways   A dynamic routing VPN, also known as a *route-based VPN*, uses a tunnel interface for forwarding packets. Protocols are used to locate networks and automatically update routing tables, which makes it more suitable for larger networks. BGP is supported, which enables tighter integration with on-premises networking infrastructure. A dynamic routing VPN requires a dynamic routing gateway device, such as a Windows Server Routing and Remote Access Service, and employs IKEv2. Dynamic routing enables additional capabilities, such as linking separate virtual networks and connecting to multiple on-premises locations, and it can coexist with point-to-site VPNs.

A number of different encryption algorithms are available for use with traffic sent via IPsec—specifically, AES256, AES192, AES128, DES, and DES3. The particular algorithms supported depend on whether the gateway is static or dynamic. For details on the cryptographic options available, view:

```
https://docs.microsoft.com/en-us/azure/vpn-gateway/vpn-gateway-about-compliance-crypto
```

The encryption algorithm used not only impacts the security of the data sent over the Internet, but it also affects the speed possible from on premises to Azure: The higher the encryption, the more computation required, which reduces the available bandwidth. This will make more sense when I walk you through some of the Azure gateway internals later in this chapter. The algorithm used is negotiated upon gateway connection.

An S2S VPN supports private peering—i.e., connecting IP networks together. Full Layer 3 communication is enabled between on premises and the connected Azure virtual network for supported traffic IPv4 traffic: TCP, UDP, and ICMP. You cannot access other Azure services, such as Azure SQL Database or Azure Storage, over this connection.

An S2S VPN is enabled by deploying a gateway to the virtual network. The gateway is deployed to its own subnet, which typically will be at minimum a /27, to provide support for both S2S and ExpressRoute gateway coexistence. This subnet will be exclusively used for the gateways, and no other workloads should be placed in it.

There are various gateway SKUs, which are covered later in this section, but two of the primary attributes of the gateways is the maximum speed and number of connections. The speed is shared across the connections, which means if a gateway has a 1 Gbps maximum speed and you connect it to 10 networks, each of those connections could run at 100 Mbps if all saturated; however, if not saturated, it would be possible for a single link to run at the full maximum speed—i.e., 1 Gbps.

The ability to have multiple connections to a gateway enables multiple networks to connect via the gateway to the virtual network. Additionally, before VNet peering, using the S2S VPN capability was common to link different virtual networks in Azure; however, VNet peering is a better option for virtual network to virtual network connectivity.

The latency of the connectivity via an S2S VPN, however, will be variable, since the traffic is traversing the Internet and potentially bouncing via many hops. This means there is no consistent latency that can be counted on for the connection, and typically it will be quite high, given the paths taken between the customer and the Azure region. This, along with the private-only peering nature of an S2S VPN, is a major pain point for many customers, along with potentially the speed limitations and the fact the traffic travels via the Internet.

POINT-TO-SITE VPN

Point-to-site VPN capability is available and gives specific machines connectivity to Azure that leverages a special client downloaded from the Azure management portal. The clients receive an IP address from a pool defined as part of the Azure point-to-site VPN configuration. If you need this kind of VPN, it is available as an option. For most virtualization-type communications in the datacenter, you will want to use the S2S VPN options, so I'm not going to cover point-to-site VPNs in detail.

The point-to-site option is useful in scenarios where you have individual machines that need to connect to a particular virtual network in Azure instead of an entire location. Consider the case of a consultant working from home or an offshore developer who needs communication with VMs running in Azure.

The same gateway used for your S2S VPN connections can be used for point-to-site connections, provided that it is a dynamic routing gateway.

EXPRESSROUTE

The benefit of establishing an S2S VPN between your on-premises locations and Azure virtual networks should be clear. Azure is an extension of your datacenter with full Layer 3 routing between them. IPv4 TCP and UDP communication is enabled. Additionally, multiple locations can be connected to a virtual network. There are, however, limitations to using the S2S VPN, which for some scenarios and organizations may make it nonoptimal or even unfeasible:

Data Security   The connection is over the public Internet, and even though the connection is encrypted, this can be a showstopper for some organizations.

Latencies   Because the connection is over the Internet, the path taken by packets can vary, which also makes the speed and latency variable. The larger and unpredictable latencies may block certain hybrid scenarios that need lower and consistent latencies.

Transmission Speed   The maximum speed is limited based on the gateway but, at the time of writing, is around 1 Gbps.

Connection Limits   There is a limit to the number of locations and the number of virtual networks that can be connected via the S2S gateway (although gateway transit routing with VNet peering helps to address this).

Private Peering Only   Only virtual network-based resources are accessible, as the connection is to one or more virtual networks. Other Azure services are not available.

Cost   Egress traffic results in charges. For scenarios where there is significant egress traffic, these costs could become a factor.

ExpressRoute Fundamentals

To address the previously listed limitations, Microsoft introduced ExpressRoute. ExpressRoute provides direct Layer 2 or Layer 3 connectivity between your on-premises network and your services running in Azure. Notice that I said *services running in Azure* rather than your virtual networks. VMs must still reside in virtual networks to be connected via on premises, but the ExpressRoute connection can be used for other types of communication between on premises and Azure, such as Azure data services and PaaS services.

ExpressRoute does not leverage the public Internet. Instead, it uses dedicated connectivity through a service provider that provides high security and isolation. Additionally, because a dedicated connection is used, a predictable, fast path gives fast connection speeds (up to 10 Gbps for regular ExpressRoute connections) and very low latencies. Because a dedicated path is used, there is no need for cryptography on the wire. (Encryption typically uses large amounts of CPU, introduces latency, and can reduce overall speed.) Latencies experienced with ExpressRoute are typically much lower than via the Internet since it is a direct path with minimal hops. The exact latency depends on the distances between the customer, the peering point, and the Azure services being accessed.

The fast speeds, and especially the low latencies, make it possible for the new hybrid scenarios and services in Azure to be leveraged by on-premises resources. Scenarios such as using storage in Azure from on premises, backup and recovery, big data, media services, and hybrid applications with tiers mixed between Azure and running on premises are now plausible.

It is critical to understand what the ExpressRoute connectivity provides: a connection to the Microsoft network. It is not a connection to a specific region. Figure 5.4 shows this connectivity via an exchange provider, but a key point is that connectivity is available to any region in the connected geopolitical region (and to the world, when using ExpressRoute Premium). The peering point provides the cross connect between the customer's local edge routers and the Microsoft Enterprise Edge (MSEE) routers, thus connecting the customer and Microsoft networks. Often customers will place firewalls between the local edge routers and their internal network for extra security.

FIGURE 5.4
ExpressRoute
high-level view

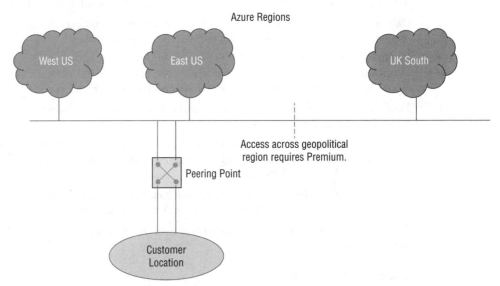

The peering locations are provided via a large number of partners, which are listed at:

```
https://docs.microsoft.com/en-us/azure/expressroute/
expressroute-locations-providers
```

This also shows the locations that the partners provide the peering locations at. To optimize latency, a peering location will be selected close to the customer's location.

Note in the figure there are two lines from the Microsoft network and the customer network. Two ports across two routers are leveraged to maximize resiliency. This enables a primary and secondary link to be provided for the establishment of active/active connections to provide resiliency in the case of both failures but also during maintenance activities where one router may need to be taken offline. The lines from the Microsoft network dictate the availability of the peering locations. Microsoft must invest and deploy the redundant fiber connections from its network to the peering locations to enable the cross connections at the peering location to customer networks. Microsoft extends its global network, its backbone, to those peering locations. This is not a trivial investment or endeavor, although if you view the list of locations, there are a large number available. Note that Microsoft does not operate the "last mile." The connectivity from the peering location to the customer is provided by the service provider. Note that there may be instances where the customer only has a single physical connection to the peering location; however, there must be an active/active redundant pair of BGP sessions in place to receive the ExpressRoute availability SLA, and ideally a redundant pair of network paths. As a customer, ensuring connectivity on both the primary and secondary connections is critical to ensure high availability.

There are two types of ExpressRoute service providers: network service providers and exchange providers. The version you use will depend on your requirements, physical location, and existing network connectivity. The overall capabilities are the same; it is really just the nature of the connection.

Exchange Provider   An exchange provider leverages an Ethernet Exchange Point (EXP), which provides a cross-connect via a peering point (also known as a "meet me" location) between the customer's network and the Microsoft network. This is a Layer 2 connection—i.e., VLAN. This can also be leveraged if the customer has their hardware hosted at a co-location facility that acts as a cloud exchange. When using an exchange provider, the customer is responsible for the routers on their side and the BGP/ASN configurations to establish the redundant BGP sessions and redundant paths.

Network Service Provider   A network service provider enables integration from your WAN, typically an MPLS VPN (any-to-any IP VPN), to the Microsoft network. This is a Layer 2.5 connection offering Layer 3 service (IP routing) and makes the Microsoft network look like another node on the MPLS network providing seamless access. This is typically the easiest option to set up for the customer since additional hardware and connections are not required and the routing is performed by the service provider, avoiding any customer BGP or router setup.

An ExpressRoute connection utilizes a circuit, and this circuit can be connected to multiple ExpressRoute gateways, enabling multiple virtual networks to be connected to from a single circuit back to the customer's network. The exact number depends on the type of the ExpressRoute circuit. At the time of writing, 10 is the limit for Standard, while the number for Premium varies depending on the size (speed) of the connection, ranging from 20 at 50 Mbps up to 100 at 10 Gbps. Details can be found at:

```
https://docs.microsoft.com/en-us/azure/expressroute/
expressroute-faqs#expressroute-premium
```

Connecting virtual networks to the same circuit also provides connectivity between those virtual networks; however, the traffic flows via the peering location, which introduces latency. This means once again VNet peering is the best option to connect virtual networks together, but remember the gateway transit routing. With ExpressRoute connected to a hub virtual network, all the spoke virtual networks connected to the hub virtual network can also leverage the connectivity to the ExpressRoute connected network—i.e., on premises.

In my experience, many customers will start out with a site-to-site VPN as they experiment with Azure but quickly move to ExpressRoute for production utilization and a service that offers an end-to-end SLA. With the wide range of ExpressRoute sizes available, a circuit can be purchased to meet your requirements. Note when purchasing ExpressRoute there are a number of cost elements:

- The ExpressRoute Azure service
- The connectivity provider (e.g., Equinix or AT&T)
- Egress charges (unless you choose the unlimited—unmetered—ExpressRoute option)
- ExpressRoute gateway (when connecting to virtual networks)

Review the following site for the details on sizes available, the pricing and egress charges, along with various add-on options, such as Premium:

```
https://azure.microsoft.com/en-us/pricing/details/expressroute/
```

Using Multiple ExpressRoute Circuits

Many organizations will deploy multiple ExpressRoute circuits, as this is highly recommended. This is both for resiliency but also if an organization has geographically distributed datacenters, having an ExpressRoute circuit at a peering location close to the datacenter provides the lowest latency to the Microsoft network from all customer locations.

There are additional considerations when using multiple ExpressRoute circuits and Azure services across multiple regions. If you imagine a scenario where as a company I have data-centers in East and West US and am using Azure services in East and West US regions, I would want data flows between the East office and the East region to flow via the East ExpressRoute circuit, not via the organization's local network to the West datacenter, over the West ExpressRoute circuit via the West US-based peering point and then over to the East region via the Microsoft network. This would add a lot of unnecessary latency. This path would be used if the East ExpressRoute circuit had a failure as the resiliency path but not under normal circumstances.

The reason the non-optimal East ≻ West ≻ West Peering Point ≻ East Region (and then back again) could potentially happen is the use of BGP. BGP is used to advertise and propagate the address spaces available via the connections—in this case, the East US Azure region and West US Azure region address prefixes over both ExpressRoute circuits. Without any other information, there is no way of knowing which address space belongs to which region, and so the routing decides to go via West, and misery for the East-based services ensues.

To ensure optimal routing, there are a number of configurations to consider. First, Microsoft leverages BGP Communities. These are values that are unique to each region and sent as part of the BGP exchange routing information. This enables the identification of which address prefixes belong to which Azure region. The BGP Community values can be looked up at:

```
https://docs.microsoft.com/en-us/azure/expressroute/expressroute-routing#bgp
```

With the address prefix identifiable by region, thanks to the BGP community, it is now possible at the customer side to use BGP local preferences to prioritize the use of the appropriate ExpressRoute circuit for the region while still having the alternate path available, should the preferred circuit be unavailable—thus keeping the resiliency. This ensures optimal path selection from on premises to Azure.

There are the same considerations for traffic from Microsoft to the customer if the connection is initiated from the Microsoft side. Once again, on the Microsoft side, it would see the same address spaces, the on premises, advertised via both ExpressRoute circuits and would not know which to use for which portion of the address space. While one option would be to only adver-tise the local part of each address space (i.e., a datacenter) on each circuit, this removes any resiliency if a connection were down. A better solution is to use AS path prepending. This enables the AS path to be lengthened for part of the address space when advertised, making that length-ened AS Path less preferred to be utilized. In this case, on the East US side, the AS Path for the West US datacenter would be lengthened, and the reverse performed on the West US side. This keeps both paths available but ensures on the Microsoft side the most optimal path is taken.

WHAT IS AS AND ASN?

You will often hear AS and ASN talked about along with BGP. While BGP is likely understood as the way routes are shared across networks, this sharing of prefixes (IP address spaces) is linked with the network that operates those IP spaces—i.e., the autonomous system (AS). An AS can be thought of as a particular network operated by a specific organization or ISP. The AS would be made up of its own mesh of routers sharing information for the IP space it manages. The AS must be identifiable, and this is the autonomous system number (ASN). The ASN is centrally managed and distributed in the same manner as the public IP space (and like the IP space, there are also private ASN ranges that do not require registration). Large networks operating on the Internet must register for an ASN, and this ASN is used with the IP prefixes as part of the BGP routing.

As part of the prefix (network) exchange between BGP peers, the ASN is added to the start of the prefix for paths the source peer is exchanging to its neighbor peer. This provides a route and is what BGP's fundamental goal is: the exchanging of routes. A route is the destination (the prefix) and how you get there (the AS path). This means as the path propagates out via BGP, all the ASNs of the AS that the path comprises (the collections of routers that must be traversed to reach the prefix) are appended, enabling the full route to be known. This is the AS path. You can think of peers as routers. Essentially, BGP sessions are established between BGP peers (routers on different AS) to enable the exchange of prefixes. Figure 5.5 shows a basic example of this with a prefix being exchanged along a series of AS and the AS path being created. Notice the network 1.10.10.0/24 (prefix) is managed by ASN 64500, which exchanges this route to its peer (step 1, adding its own ASN to the AS path). That AS then exchanges the route it has learned to its peer (step 2), adding its ASN to the AS path, which continues to another AS (step 3). Each AS will update its routing table, which is shown (step 4) for AS 64508, where the prefix has the complete AS path to be reached.

FIGURE 5.5
Route exchange
with BGP

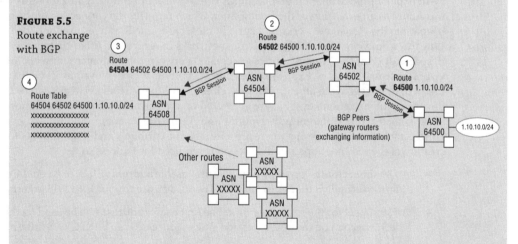

It is the list of ASNs on a path that enables the best route to be selected where multiple paths exist to the same IP prefix. The path with the smallest number of ASNs (hops) will be chosen (distance vector protocol) and is why using the ASN prepending (adding an additional ASN) makes a path less desirable since it is longer.

If multiple ExpressRoute circuits are connected to the same ExpressRoute gateway, giving a virtual network connectivity via multiple ExpressRoute circuits, the connections can be weighted to set a preference for which should be used where the same address space is available via multiple paths.

Peering Options, BGP Sessions, and Route Filters

An ExpressRoute circuit provides connectivity between on-premises networks and the Microsoft global network via a service provider; however, initially no traffic will actually flow. The services that should use the ExpressRoute link rather than the Internet must be configured. These fall into two buckets:

◆ **Private Peering**—Connecting to virtual networks in Azure

◆ **Microsoft Peering**—Connecting to PaaS and SaaS services in Azure—for example, Azure Storage and Azure SQL Database. This includes the services that were previously part of the separate public peering, which is no longer available.

The ExpressRoute circuit is established through the use of the ExpressRoute circuits service key (a GUID), which is generated once the circuit is created on the Azure side and acts as the common information shared among Microsoft, you, and the connectivity provider. Once established, one or both of the peering types is enabled on the circuit, and it is the peering enablement that utilizes the configuration of BGP when utilizing a Layer 2 provider. If you use a Layer 3 provider, i.e., MPLS, this routing is done for you. In the peering discussion, I will be focusing on Layer 2.

PRIVATE PEERING

I will explore private peering first, as this is often the first used by organizations as they initially use Azure as an extension of their datacenter, which requires the connection of the on-premises IP space to the virtual networks in Azure. In most cases, the IP ranges used will be from RFC 1918 and would overlap with other virtual networks in Azure and other customer on-premise IP spaces. It is for this reason tunnels are created between the customer's network and the target virtual network(s) via the ExpressRoute gateway that must be deployed to all virtual networks that will be connected to an ExpressRoute circuit. Multiple virtual networks can be created via the use of authorization keys that are generated on the private peering configuration. These can be redeemed across different subscriptions and Azure AD tenants.

To establish private peering, there are a number of attributes and requirements to enable the creation of the redundant pair of BGP sessions required for ExpressRoute:

◆ A /30 subnet for the primary link. The first usable address will be used on the customer side, the second on the Microsoft side. These addresses can be RFC 1918 (internal) or public.

◆ A /30 subnet for the secondary link. The first usable address will be used on the customer side, the second on the Microsoft side. These addresses can be RFC 1918 (internal) or public.

◆ The VLAN ID on the customer side that the peering will be established on. This must be different from any other VLAN ID being used for peering.

◆ The AS number. Both private and public ASN is supported.

Once private peering is established, connections are added to ExpressRoute gateways on virtual networks to provide the actual connectivity between the on-premises and virtual network IP spaces (up to 10 on Standard and between 20 and 100 on Premium, depending on the circuit size, as previously mentioned). The prefixes will be exchanged via BGP, enabling full connectivity. This is also why virtual networks connected to the same ExpressRoute circuit can communicate with each other.

MICROSOFT PEERING

Private peering is very logical. You are connecting IP spaces together: IP spaces on premises to IP spaces defined in virtual networks. Microsoft peering is also dealing with routing to IP spaces, but they are IP spaces you don't manage and are IP spaces normally advertised and routed via the Internet. The goal of Microsoft peering is to instead advertise the routes via the ExpressRoute connection, which will cause the traffic to flow via ExpressRoute instead of via the Internet. This not only provides the benefit of likely a faster and lower latency connection, but the source IP address will be more predictable.

Microsoft has a huge range of services, and previously they were split into two categories: public peering, for the Azure PaaS services (for example storage, database, etc.), and Microsoft peering, for the other Microsoft cloud services (for example, Office 365 and Dynamics 365). These are now combined into Microsoft peering. These services are offered over a range of IP addresses per service per region and are advertised to the Internet. Microsoft is working to group each service into a block of IP addresses to make it easier to advertise specific services per region, but we'll get to that in a second.

To establish Microsoft peering, the information is very similar to private peering, except that now instead of talking to resources in virtual networks, which are isolated, private IP spaces, the connection is now to services operating on public IP addresses, which means they need to talk to valid public IPs, which your internal network will not have (most likely). This requires the use of NAT, and NAT that must be performed on the customer side (which is different from the old public peering that performed NAT on the Microsoft side, making it hard to lock down services by source IP). This means the IP subnets used for the BGP peers must be valid public IP ranges, but also an additional public IP subnet is required that represents the NAT gateways on the customer side that will actually be communicating with Microsoft services on behalf of their internal network.

- A /30 subnet for the primary link. The first usable address will be used on the customer side, the second on the Microsoft side. These addresses must be public IP addresses owned by the customer/connectivity provider.

- A /30 subnet for the secondary link. The first usable address will be used on the customer side, the second on the Microsoft side. These addresses must be public IP addresses owned by the customer/connectivity provider.

- IP prefixes to be advertised—i.e., those being used for NAT gateways (unless your internal network uses valid public IP addresses). Do *not* also advertise these to the Internet. The recommendation is a separate set of NAT IP addresses be used for ExpressRoute than for the Internet. If the same IP addresses are advertised to ExpressRoute and the Internet, you risk asymmetric routing. This is where the data goes out via one path but comes back by another, which is a big problem where there are stateful firewalls that will receive return traffic that it never requested and thus block it. If you must advertise the same prefixes, ensure the advertisement to ExpressRoute is for a more specific range, which will ensure it will take preference over the Internet route (as more specific is preferred).

- The VLAN ID on the customer side that the peering will be established on. This must be different from any other VLAN ID being used for peering.

- The AS number. While both private and public ASN are supported, it is recommended to use public ASN, as the ASN path prepending cannot be performed with private ASN.

- Routing registry name where the ASN and prefixes are registered (since this will be validated).

Once the Microsoft peering is established, nothing will happen—very anti-climatic. No traffic will flow. You need to tell Azure which routes to advertise via BGP over the ExpressRoute to cause those services to be accessed via ExpressRoute instead of the Internet. This is accomplished by the creation of a route filter, which is then attached to the ExpressRoute circuit on which the Microsoft peering connection is established.

The public IP addresses on the Microsoft side are grouped into BGP communities (which are sent along with the route) to help map IP address to actual service, and it is these BGP communities that form the route filters. At the time of writing, there are no BGP communities per Azure service per region; instead, they are broken down by region and then the global Microsoft services, such as Exchange, SharePoint, Azure AD, etc. Over time, I would expect this to get more granular, with BGP communities per service per region enabling more control about which services are advertised over ExpressRoute and thus which use the ExpressRoute connection. Figure 5.6 shows a route filter as currently exists. Note the presence of Microsoft cloud services and then Azure regions.

FIGURE 5.6
Example route filter

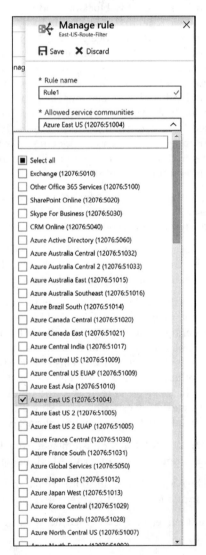

Once the route filter is connected to the circuit, the BGP routes will be exchanges and traffic will start flowing via ExpressRoute. Firewalls on Azure services can be locked down to only traffic coming via ExpressRoute by specifying the IP addresses of the customer NAT gateways. It is generally not recommended to send Office traffic via ExpressRoute, as this is specifically designed to travel via the Internet.

Note that if you are an existing customer using public peering, the recommendation is to move to Microsoft peering as quickly as possible.

ExpressRoute Direct

In the preceding sections, I talked about ExpressRoute operating at Layer 2 or Layer 3 in conjunction with a service provider that takes care of the actual Layer 1 (physical) connectivity, and these are the best options for most customers. There is also an offering that does not leverage a service provider that may be applicable to specific organizations that require massive connections, up to 100 Gbps (and remember, there are actually two connections in an active/active configuration for ExpressRoute, which means up to 200 Gbps) that do not leverage a service provider (although a provider will likely still be involved in the actual delivery of fiber lines). This means complete physical isolation from any other customer, which may be required for some customers that have strict regulatory requirements related to isolation. On the ExpressRoute Direct connection, a number of virtual circuits can be created, which include 40 Gbps and 100 Gbps options.

With ExpressRoute Direct, a letter of authorization is provided by Microsoft to the customer that allows their network to be connected to ports on the MSEE routers. This also means the customer is now responsible for Layer 1 activities, such as light level checking, ensuring they have redundancy in dark fiber runs and can hand off with the correct types of optics. This is not the case for most organizations, but for those that require this control, isolation, and massive data pipes, it is a great offering.

ExpressRoute Direct also exposes two other capabilities:

◆ **ExpressRoute Local**—This enables a virtual circuit to be established between the Azure region only that is local to the ExpressRoute site—i.e., for East US region access, you would have to use a peering location in Washington DC only. The benefit is there are no egress charges.

◆ **ExpressRoute Direct FastPath**—This enables connectivity to a virtual network without the use of a gateway, meaning potentially the full 100 Gbps to a virtual network providing very high single TCP flow throughput, packets per second, and connections per second. This will also provide a lower and more predictable latency, as a gateway is skipped.

GATEWAYS AND COEXISTENCE

When connecting virtual networks to other networks either via an S2S VPN, a P2S VPN, or ExpressRoute, a gateway is required on the virtual network which is hosted in a dedicated subnet. The minimum recommended size is a /28, as this provides support for both S2S and ExpressRoute gateway coexistence, even if not initially planned.

A number of different SKUs are available for both S2S VPN gateways and ExpressRoute gateways. These change over time and vary based on a number of attributes:

◆ Megabits per second (1.25 Gbps max for an S2S VPN and 10 Gbps max for ExpressRoute)

◆ S2S VPN and ExpressRoute coexistence

◆ Support of BGP and number of tunnels/connections for an S2S VPN

◆ Zone-redundancy for ExpressRoute gateways that distribute the gateway instances across a number of zones, increasing resiliency

For complete details on the SKUs, refer to the Microsoft documentation:

◆ S2S VPN

```
https://docs.microsoft.com/en-us/azure/vpn-gateway/
vpn-gateway-about-vpngateways#gwsku
```

◆ ExpressRoute

```
https://docs.microsoft.com/en-us/azure/expressroute/
expressroute-about-virtual-network-gateways#gwsku
```

As alluded to, ExpressRoute gateways and S2S/P2S VPN gateways can be deployed to the same virtual network, provided that the gateway is a /28 or larger and a route-based VPN gateway is utilized. There used to be a creation sequence requirement for coexistence; however, this has been removed, and the S2S and ExpressRoute gateway creation order is no longer important, enabling simpler coexistence deployment. When both S2S VPN and ExpressRoute gateways are present, the ExpressRoute gateway will be used, with the S2S VPN gateway acting as a fallback.

Do not configure a default route (0.0.0.0/0) in the UDR on the ExpressRoute gateway subnet nor deny Internet via an NSG on the ExpressRoute gateway, as the ExpressRoute gateway is a software-defined router that requires connectivity for the correct distribution of routes, which will appear as external to the virtual network address space—i.e., the Internet.

USER-DEFINED ROUTING AND FORCED TUNNELING

BGP enables the flow of routes between networks and other paths, such as default routes out to the Internet. It is also possible to add additional routes that are used on a network using user-defined routing, where a target IP network is specified along with its next hop. Note that the next hop does not have to be an IP address on the same subnet as the source traffic, which would be the case on a normal physical network. This is possible due to the software-defined networking used in Azure and the way the routing is implemented at the NIC level rather than an edge device on the subnet.

The static routes you define using user-defined routing are combined with routes advertised via BGP and system routes. The most specific prefix will take preference when multiple matches are present. If the prefix is the same, then the preference is user-defined ≻ BGP ≻ system. User-defined routes are typically leveraged to direct traffic to appliances such as Azure Firewall or a third-party NVA.

UDRs can also be used with forced tunneling, where all traffic is sent to a specific target—for example, instead of traffic using the Internet, it is redirected to the customer's network. This is achieved by adding a quad-zero route, 0.0.0.0/0 (i.e., default route) to an IP address that will then route to the desired network. Care should be taken with forced tunneling, as there are many services that need to reach other services within Azure, which this may break. Also remember to never set this on the gateway subnet. Refer to the following site for more information on using UDR:

```
https://docs.microsoft.com/en-us/azure/virtual-network/
virtual-networks-udr-overview
```

The following site walks through some of the exceptions required to a default route to ensure continued functioning of the API management:

```
https://docs.microsoft.com/en-us/azure/api-management/
api-management-using-with-vnet#-common-network-configuration-issues
```

Azure Virtual WANs and ExpressRoute Global Reach

As discussed in the previous section, most organizations are hybrid with many on-premises networks in addition to those in Azure. While technologies such as site-to-site VPN and ExpressRoute connect on-premises networks to resources in Azure, it is very common for organizations to face challenges for their own connectivity between datacenters. A challenge could be establishing a backup path to an existing connectivity solution between datacenters, or it could be enabling new connectivity between branch offices and a datacenter and/or Azure virtual networks. Microsoft has one of the biggest networks in the world, and Microsoft has two different services to help provide connectivity, each focused on a specific scenario:

◆ **ExpressRoute Global Reach**—Connects two or more datacenters with ExpressRoute to each other over the Microsoft backbone. Normally, ExpressRoute connections only connect a datacenter to Azure. Global Reach provides a path for transit between datacenters.

◆ **Azure Virtual WAN**—Provides connectivity between branch offices/datacenters and Azure resources via a hub virtual network in Azure

Firstly we can look at ExpressRoute Global Reach. This is a solution that provides connectivity between an organization's on-premises datacenters via their separate ExpressRoute circuits. Typically, an organization would already have connectivity between datacenters via an MPLS service provider. However, organizations may want a backup connectivity option or need to connect to a datacenter where their current service provider does not offer service. Using ExpressRoute Global Reach, it is possible to add the connectivity between the datacenters where an ExpressRoute circuit can be established via the Microsoft network backbone. This could be the primary communication path or as a backup to an existing communication path. Consider an organization with multiple datacenters in the US that are connected via MPLS provider and that adds a new datacenter in Europe where the MPLS provider does not operate. ExpressRoute Global Reach could provide this connectivity.

Azure Virtual WAN is aimed at a different use case. Primarily there are branch offices and potentially datacenters that want to be able to communicate to each other and also to Azure resources based in virtual networks, PaaS services, and even the Internet via the Azure backbone. Azure Virtual WAN supports all three of the primary private connectivity options to a virtual network; S2S VPN, P2S VPN, and ExpressRoute with the transit capability between VPN and ExpressRoute.

A virtual hub, which is a managed virtual network, is created in Azure. This acts as the communications hub for all connectivity. P2S, S2S, and ExpressRoute connections are established to the virtual hub in addition to other virtual networks in Azure, peered using VNet peering. This complete set of connectivity comprises the Azure Virtual WAN. Figure 5.7 shows an example configuration comprising a datacenter, a number of branch offices, and remote users. All are using different types of connectivity to the virtual hub but can now communicate with each other via that hub in addition to the various peered Azure resources and Internet resources.

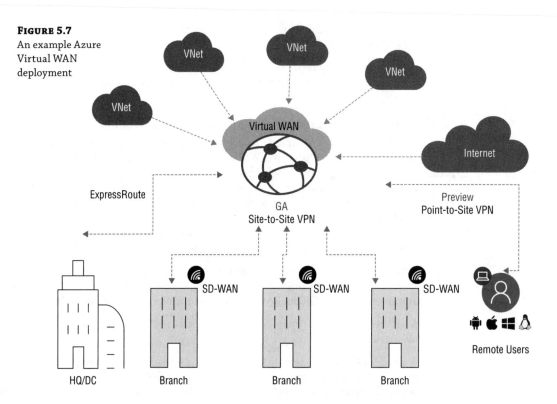

FIGURE 5.7
An example Azure Virtual WAN deployment

For the S2S VPN connectivity options, Azure has partnered with a number of companies to provide appliances to simplify the onboarding of branch offices to Azure Virtual WAN. For details on the partners and their offerings, refer to:

```
https://docs.microsoft.com/en-us/azure/virtual-wan/virtual-wan-locations-partners
```

PaaS VNet Integration

Although this book is focused on infrastructure services, most organizations will also use many PaaS services, which can be both custom applications using services like App Service Plans, data services like Azure Storage, Azure SQL Database, and Azure Cosmos DB, and others, such as Azure Key Vault for secrets and keys. There are typically two types of integration: controlling access to PaaS services from resources in virtual networks and enabling PaaS services to access resources in virtual networks.

The Azure PaaS services are public-facing—i.e., you access them via publicly accessible IP addresses. There are many architectures where the access should only be from services running in virtual networks. PaaS services have ACL and firewall capabilities to lock down access; however, it was very hard to lock down traffic to only traffic from a specific virtual network, since the access is still to the public IP address, which means the traffic from the virtual network goes through NAT, which typically would have a variable public IP (unless you architected specific NAT resources and public IPs), which historically meant you could only lock down resources from "Azure," which, given that Azure is a multi-tenant service and a bad guy could be running resources in Azure, trying to access your PaaS service is not very useful.

Service endpoints solve this problem. Service endpoints enable specific subnets in virtual networks to become known to PaaS services. This allows those subnets to be specified as part of the firewall rules, enabling PaaS services to be locked down so that even though they have a public IP address, they are only accessible to the subnets specified and the data stays on the Azure backbone network. Adding service endpoints is a two-step process (although for most services they can be combined).

1. On the virtual network, create the service endpoints required—for example, Azure Storage on the required subnets.

2. On the service (e.g., the Azure Storage account), navigate to its firewall's and virtual network's configuration and enable access only for the desired subnets. Note that for some services, the virtual network must be in the same region as that of the service.

Controlling access to PaaS resources, especially App Services (i.e., those typically hosted in an App Service Plan like a web or mobile app) can be partly solved through service endpoints. However, a deeper IP integration with PaaS services is often required, as the application in the app service may want to communicate with resources in a virtual network or maybe even to a network connected to the virtual network (e.g., on premises via ExpressRoute). This requires the opposite flow—the app service reaching into the virtual network. There are a number of solutions, which have different capabilities. Note there are IP restrictions on app services to block/allow access based on the source IP address in addition to being able to give an app service an assigned IP address instead of it using a shared IP address with other services. You may wonder about the value of a dedicated IP address for the app service. Consider an organization that restricts the outbound IP addresses that can be communicated to from on premises. (No more Facebook during the working day.) By giving the app service an assigned, known IP address, it can be enabled for access from the on-premises network.

The long-standing solution that has been available for many years is integration via a gateway in the virtual network. The app service establishes a point-to-site VPN connection into the virtual network, which enables it to communicate with resources that are connected to the virtual network. It cannot access resources in other connected networks, such as those connected via ExpressRoute, nor can service endpoints be applied to this traffic—i.e., you wanted to restrict access to Azure SQL Database from this PaaS service.

There is also a hybrid connection feature. This utilizes a hybrid connection manager that is deployed into a target network that is hosting resources that the app service wants to access. This means the target resources can be anywhere, including on premises or even other clouds. Behind the scenes, the hybrid connection manager uses a service bus relay through which it can communicate with the app service. This also means a single app service can communicate with resources served by different hybrid connection managers—i.e., on different networks. Additionally, because the hybrid connection manager runs within the network and establishes an outbound connection, there is no requirement to open firewall exceptions on the target networks.

The newer option removes the requirement for a gateway in the virtual network and instead multi-homes the PaaS service, giving it a network connection (in a dedicated subnet) directly into the virtual network. Because the PaaS service now has a presence in the virtual network, it can also access resources in connected networks (such as ExpressRoute) and can use service endpoints configured on the virtual network to other PaaS services. Note that you must have the virtual network be in the same region as the App Service Plan hosting the PaaS services.

Another solution for app services to integrate with a virtual network is the App Service Environment (ASE). Normally, app services are deployed to an App Service Plan that has a number of shared components between tenants, which is why there are limitations on its levels of isolation. Some customers require complete isolation and may also not want public IP addresses at all (even though they can be locked down). An ASE is a single-tenant deployment of the app service environment deployed into the customer's own virtual network. It does not have to have a public IP at all and has full access to any resource in the virtual network and connected to the virtual network (in addition to being subject to any service endpoints).

A number of these technologies are not just connectivity but also fall into the protection pillar of networking, which brings us to…

Protection

This section explores several technologies that help provide isolation and protection. There are often multiple options, and the right option varies based on existing knowledge and requirements.

Network Security Groups and Application Security Groups

A virtual network can be thought of as a trust boundary. Each virtual network is completely isolated from other virtual networks, unless you choose to connect them. Within the virtual network, each virtual subnet is automatically connected to every other virtual subnet through Azure-provided gateway functionality. This is represented as the first usable IP address in each subnet.

In some scenarios, virtual subnets should be isolated from one another and potentially even within subnets for micro-segmentation. Consider your datacenter. You likely have a separate network that connects to the Internet, your DMZ. There will be another network for your datacenter, another network for high-impact servers, and so on. Between these different networks are firewalls, which primarily are tasked with ensuring that only specific traffic for specific hosts is allowed to traverse the network boundaries. This same functionality can be enabled between virtual subnets in an Azure virtual network using network security groups (NSGs). NSGs provide segmentations within a virtual network by defining rules between virtual subnets and even for specific VMs. They can also be used to control Internet-bound traffic based on the virtual subnet. These groups can control connectivity to on-premises networks, such as through gateways.

Figure 5.8 shows an example use case with three virtual subnets: a frontend that receives traffic from the Internet, a mid-tier subnet that receives communication from the frontend and the backend networks, and then the backend network. Note that the mid-tier and backend networks cannot communicate directly to the Internet, nor can the frontend and backend networks directly communicate.

There are two primary steps to using NSGs. First create one or more rules, and then apply the rules to a virtual subnet or VM. Note that rules can be applied to both a VM and the virtual subnet that the VM resides in. The rules assigned to the virtual subnet are applied first, and then the rules are applied to the VM. This configuration effectively gives the VM two layers of protection.

FIGURE 5.8
Traffic control
can be achieved
using network
security groups.

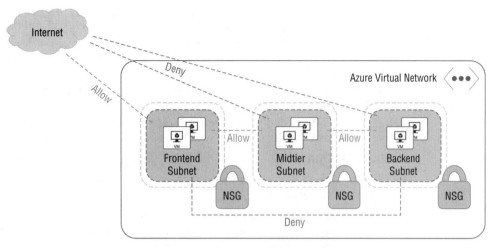

NSG rules use the following five tuples:

◆ Source IP

◆ Source port

◆ Destination IP

◆ Destination port

◆ Protocol—TCP, UDP, or Any (which includes ICMP)

The source and destination IPs can be presented as ranges in CIDR format. Protocols are specified as TCP or UDP, or by using the wildcard character (*). Additionally, the following attributes are used:

◆ Name (identifier for the rule)

◆ Direction (inbound/outbound)

◆ Access action (Allow/Deny)

◆ Priority between 100 and 4096

The priority attribute allows multiple rules to be applied, and in the event of a conflict, the rule with the highest priority (lowest number) wins.

A number of default rules are defined and accomplish the following:

◆ Allow full inbound/outbound communication between NSGs within the virtual network address space.

◆ Allow inbound communication from the Azure Load Balancer.

◆ Allow outbound traffic to the Internet.

◆ All other inbound and outbound traffic is denied.

These default rules have very low priorities (65000 and above—i.e., 65001), which means you can override the defaults with your own rules.

When discussing the rules, I said these were IP addresses; however, that is just one of the options: using a CIDR format block of IP addresses. There are two other options: service tags and application security groups (ASGs).

In the early days of NSGs, there were three system-provided service tags, which are identifiers for certain special types of traffic:

VIRTUAL_NETWORK   Identifies traffic within the virtual network address space and for connected networks, such as another virtual network or on-premises network

AZURE_LOADBALANCER   Identifies traffic from the Azure infrastructure load balancer

INTERNET   Identifies traffic from an IP address space external to the virtual network that is reachable from the Internet

Over time, it became clear that being able to identify other types of Azure service as part of NSGs would be useful to enable control on the utilization of those services, but given the wide range of IP addresses used by the various Azure services that frequently changes, this was almost impossible to accomplish using IP ranges. Therefore, additional service tags were added representing IP ranges used by other ARM resources that were managed by Microsoft, such as AzureCloud (IP address space used for all Azure datacenter public IP addresses), Storage, SQL, and many more. The full list is documented at:

```
https://docs.microsoft.com/en-us/azure/virtual-network/
security-overview#service-tags
```

Additionally, for the service tags where the resources are deployed to specific regions, it is possible to specify regional-level instances for some services by adding the region—for example, Storage.EastUS or Sql.EastUS. These service tags can be used instead of IP ranges within NSG rules.

Application security groups can also be used in place of IP address ranges. While using IP ranges may meet many requirements for isolation, there may be instances where services are not neatly arranged in IP blocks. Maybe you have database instances across many subnets but need special rules for communication to any database server—i.e., micro-segmentation. Application security groups (ASGs) are monikers you create and then assign to NICs in Azure—for example, SQLVM and WebApp1VM. At the time of writing, each IP configuration per NIC can have up to 20 ASGs applied. The NSG rules can utilize the ASG monikers instead of IP addresses to ensure application no matter which subnet the workloads are placed in.

ASGs and the ability to apply multiples of them to a single NIC can be utilized to implement a fast quarantine option. Imagine you suspect a machine that may be unhealthy. In the past, you would have to try and move the NIC to another network and control access. With ASGs, you could have a high-priority rule defined in the NSG for ASG quarantine that restricts all access except for maybe RDP from a management subnet. As soon as you add that quarantine moniker to the NIC of a VM, all other access is cut off.

NSGs can be applied to both subnets and NICs. My recommendation is to apply at subnet levels, as trying to manage at a NIC level can get very messy. However, if you do choose to deploy to NICs, try to avoid having any single machine having NSGs from the subnet and the

NIC, as strange behavior can be seen. Also be careful when restricting traffic that you don't block required paths for Azure resources to function—for example, blocking basic infrastructure services like DHCP, DNS, and activation. A list of some key considerations to be aware of can be found at:

```
https://docs.microsoft.com/en-us/azure/virtual-network/
security-overview#azure-platform-considerations
```

Firewall Virtual Appliances

Network security groups provide a virtual firewall, restricting traffic within the virtual filtering platform as it passes to and from the NIC, but it is not an actual edge device sitting at the subnet boundary. There are certain functionalities it does not support, such as deep packet inspection, and it may not integrate with an organization's existing management tools. Using firewall virtual appliances, which are VMs pre-configured with a firewall solution, is sometimes a better option. Azure has both first-party and third-party firewall network virtual appliances (NVAs).

AZURE FIREWALL

Azure Firewall is Microsoft's first-party firewall NVA, which is provided as a managed service. It is deployed using virtual machine scale set (VMSS) technology, which means it dynamically scales to meet any throughput requirement while providing a highly available service through automatically managed load-balancer integration.

Azure Firewall is deployed to its own subnet in the virtual network, which must be at least a /26. User-defined routes are then used to make the Azure Firewall the next hop for traffic from other subnets or connected virtual networks. (Remember, in Azure, the next hop does not have to be an address on the same subnet.) Additional virtual networks can be peered to the network of the Azure Firewall to use its functionality—i.e., spokes to the hub network containing Azure Firewall.

Network rules are created in the Azure Firewall instance to control traffic flow. These rules work in a manner very similar to NSGs, except they are enforced within the Azure Firewall service, since all traffic now flows via the service because of the UDRs, as opposed to assigning NSGs to each subnet where the rules are enforced at the NIC level. The central nature of the Azure Firewall also makes it easier to configure and view the rules in the system.

Azure Firewall can also have interfaces externally, enabling for inbound and outbound traffic flows to be managed, which include integration with Microsoft Threat Intelligence, which will flag (and block) communication with malicious IPs or FQDNs. For outbound traffic, FQDN custom filtering rules can be enforced, enabling outbound traffic to be restricted to only allowed FQDNs or specific FQDNs blocked. FQDN tags are provided for common services (for example, Windows Update), and, like NSGs, service tags are also supported as part of rules.

SNAT is another capability for outbound traffic, making it easier to configure filters on other Internet-based services to restrict traffic only to the Azure Firewall external IP address (which would represent the virtual networks it is providing NAT service for). Inbound DNAT (Destination NAT) is also supported, enabling services with a private IP to be made available via the Azure Firewall's public IP.

NETWORK VIRTUAL APPLIANCES (AND UNDERSTAND AZURE LOAD BALANCER INTERNALS!)

Network virtual appliances (NVAs) are widely available in the Azure marketplace, covering a range of network capabilities, including firewalls (and load balancers and traffic inspection devices and much more). Remember that an NVA is a virtual machine preconfigured with a certain workload—in this case, a firewall software product. A single VM solution is very dangerous, as during maintenance or if there were a failure, it would be unavailable. A single instance would also limit the scale of the solution. Therefore, the common pattern for using NVAs is that at least two (normally three) are deployed. However, they cannot share an IP address; that is not allowed in Azure. Instead, a load balancer is placed in front of the NVAs (which themselves will use availability sets or availability zones for resiliency) and the load balancer, which is an Azure managed service and highly resilient, comprising many instances distributed over racks and potentially availability zones, hosting the entry IP address for the NVA. The load balancer is typically a standard SKU that supports wide port ranges and resiliency across zones (as opposed to the basic SKU). When having multiple instances of the NVA providing a service, they may operate in an active-passive or active-active manner with or without NAT.

While an internal detail, the presence of the load balancer introduces its own set of considerations to the NVA solution. Most ordinary load balancers receive the traffic, send it to the destination, receive the response, and then send to the originator. However, this means a lot of unnecessary traffic flows via the load balancer, increasing its work since the return flow really has no reason to output via the load balancer other than fixing the IP addresses, and most of the traffic is the outbound flow anyway (the response). The Azure load balancer utilizes a multiplexer (mux) to receive and distribute the requests but is bypassed for the return traffic, with the vSwitch performing any IP address manipulation for the return packets. This is important when looking at multi-deployment NVAs that sit behind the Azure load balancer.

Consider if NAT is not desirable by the end services, which means the IP address of the source must remain through the entire flow. See Figure 5.9 to understand this. This scenario is focused where the traffic originates from the Internet. This works fine on the inbound flow, which will go via the load balancer (step 1), to the firewall NVA (step 2), and then to the back-end service—for example, a website (step 3). The problem is that the return traffic will see the source IP (since there was no NAT) and try to send functionality directly back via the normal Azure default gateway (fabric router), which means the firewall is bypassed, which is a problem for a stateful device. The return traffic needs to flow via the firewall. The only way to make this happen would be to set a default route (using user-defined routes) from the web server's subnet to the firewall service (via an internal load balancer since you need to utilize either one, step 4). When operating in an active-passive mode, this will work since only one NVA is running and therefore the load balancer probes will only send to the running instance, which is the one that would have received the traffic since it's the only one running (step 5). The firewall then sends the traffic to the source. This works, but it means you can only have two NVAs, with only one ever active to ensure the return flows via the same instance that received the traffic. (The load balancer probe would detect the running NVA.) To scale, you have to make the instances bigger; there is no scale out. It's not possible to have active-active with no NAT, as there is no realistic way to ensure the return traffic goes to the same instance of the NVA that received it.

FIGURE 5.9
Possible NVA deployment with load balancers

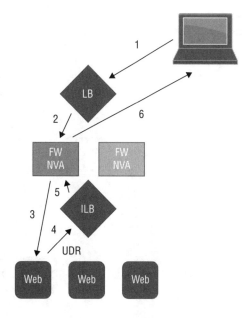

Note that if the requirement is between internal networks, then no NAT with active-active is possible, since the internal load balancer can be set as the hop in a UDR (an external load balancer *cannot* be set as the next hop in a UDR), and since it uses a hash-based distribution, the response would be sent to the same instance in the backend pool (the firewall NVAs) for data flowing in either direction, meaning the stateful firewall will see the incoming and outgoing traffic flow.

If you can have NAT, then the situation completely changes, as now the source IP can be rewritten as it flows through the same components, as shown in Figure 5.9. When the packet hits the firewall NVA, the source is rewritten to be the IP address of the firewall NVA, which means the backend resource will send the response back to the instance of the firewall NVA that sent it the traffic—all without any custom routing. This means you can have active-active with as many instances as you want (or could run in active-passive, if you wanted). This is shown in Figure 5.10.

In most cases, there are ways to solve any IP challenges introduced with NAT through other means. Header injection is a common solution, where the original source can be added into the header and read by the target application. This is typically populated in the X-Forwarded-For HTTP header field and avoids the requirement to keep the source IP in the actual packets.

Obviously, I spent more time on load balancers in this section than the NVAs themselves, but from an architecture perspective, the behavior of the networking is the most critical piece. The actual functionality of the NVAs will vary by vendor. I typically recommend trying to meet requirements using NSG first, then Azure Firewall, and then an NVA. This optimizes cost and complexity.

FIGURE 5.10
Traffic flow with NAT

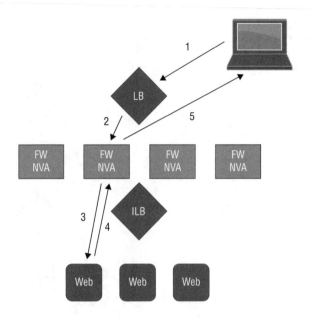

Distributed Denial-of-Service Protection

Distributed denial-of-service (DDoS) attacks are prevalent on the Internet today. There are even websites dedicated to allowing anyone with money to purchase an attack on a target of their choosing. These attacks typically cause large-scale service interruption for the targets, costing them money and reputation.

Azure has two levels of DDoS protection. The first level, DDoS Protection Basic, is enabled by default for every public resource in Azure. It is designed to redirect large-scale DDoS attacks away from the target, minimizing the impact of the attack; however, the key word is "large-scale" attacks. If a service is operated by a couple of instances, then the amount of DDoS required to cripple that service is fairly small and would not be mitigated by Azure DDoS Protection Basic. This is where the paid Standard offering can be used.

The DDoS Protection Standard offering is enabled on a virtual network and applies to any public IP resource offered from that network. DDoS Protection Standard uses machine learning to identify normal types of traffic and quickly responds to DDoS attacks, minimizing the downtime on attacked services, responding in a matter of seconds. User-definable policies can also be leveraged to tune required behavior. Additionally, the Standard offering provides insight into whether an attack is in progress and detailed metrics of the attack. There are also post-attack reports and access to DDoS experts to help during and after the attack. It is priced based on a monthly fee and then the actual usage.

Delivery

Making a service available from a single resource has a number of problems. You can only scale up—i.e., make the resource bigger (which has limits). If that resource fails or needs maintenance, the entire service is unavailable. The preferred approach is to scale out, having multiple instances, although this introduces its own set of challenges. These challenges are expanded when you want to offer the service over multiple locations, with each location having its own resilient instance. You cannot give customers of a service five different URLs and tell them to try in order, they need a single-entry point that distributes requests to a number of backend resources. There are two levels of this load balancing: within a region and between regions.

Intra-Region Load Balancing

There are two Microsoft-provided load-balancing solutions for load balancing within a region. They operate at different layers, giving each of them specific scenarios where they are the right solution.

AZURE LOAD BALANCER

Load balancing enables a number of resources that offer services, known as the backend set to have traffic distributed to them from a client-facing endpoint, known as the frontend. Azure Load Balancer provides this capability. For example, you can have a backend pool of web servers, all offering the same content, and an Azure Load Balancer instance with a frontend IP address that clients (via a DNS name) request from, and Azure Load Balancer will distribute those requests to the resources in the backend pool. As explained in the NVA section previously, the return traffic does not flow via the load balancer, as there is no need; the virtual switch in Azure takes care of any IP rewriting that is required, and the response is sent back to the requestor, bypassing the load balancer. This is known as Direct Server Return (DSR), although the exact exposure of functionality does vary with a specific DSR configuration available to utilize a floating IP on the backend pools with Azure Load Balancer.

Azure Load Balancer is a Layer 4 load balancer, which means it understands protocols such as TCP and UDP but has no knowledge of higher-level components, such as the application and SSL. (There is a different solution for that.) By default, it uses a 5-tuple load-balancing algorithm along with its distribution rules, which specifically uses the following:

♦ The source IP address

♦ The destination IP address

♦ The protocol type (TCP or UDP)

♦ The source port

♦ The destination port (For the standard load balancer, HA ports are also supported, which are all flows TCP and UDP, regardless of port, which is very useful for NVAs.)

Using a 5-tuple algorithm ensures a good distribution of traffic. It also ensures that all traffic from a specific session will be sent to the same specific member of the load-balanced set. Note that the way the hashing algorithm works to distribute traffic will result in the same target, regardless of direction—i.e., if the source and destination IPs are switched.

There are times when 5-tuple causes problems. If a client closes a connection and then reconnects, they will likely use a new local port. That new local port would not match the 5-tuple, and therefore the traffic would be directed to a different set member. Likewise, if a communication uses multiple ports or protocols, the 5-tuple mode would distribute the connections to different members, which likely would break the communication. Two additional distribution modes that help enable additional stickiness can be configured: 2-tuple and 3-tuple.

For a 2-tuple distribution mode, only the source and destination IP are used to map traffic to target members. This means any traffic from a specific IP will always go to the same member of the load-balanced set, no matter which port or protocol is used. The 3-tuple distribution mode uses protocol in addition to the source and destination IP addresses.

When using distribution, a health probe is leveraged to check the availability of the backend pool members to ensure traffic is only sent to healthy members. A number of health probe configurations are possible, including the path to check for health on (this helps to ensure the actual application is responding rather than just the OS), the number of probes that can be missed, and the interval.

In addition to the distribution options, it is also possible to configure port forwarding where a specific port on the frontend IP is forwarded to a specific backend instance.

As alluded to at the start of this section, there are two types of Azure Load Balancer: Basic Load Balancer and Standard Load Balancer. The Standard Load Balancer offers a number of enhancements over the Basic Load Balancer, as detailed at:

https://docs.microsoft.com/en-us/azure/load-balancer/
load-balancer-standard-overview

Following are some of the key features:

◆ Offers support for 1,000 backend instances (instead of 100 for basic)

◆ Offers support for a larger variety of backend instances across sets and standalone VMs

◆ Offers support for availability zones

◆ Offers HA ports for internal load balancer

◆ Is secure by default where inbound flows must be whitelisted

◆ Defines specific outbound NAT for different pools behind the load balancer, as opposed to a random frontend IP utilized with the Basic Load Balancer

◆ Includes 99.99 percent SLA

While the backend resources for Azure Load Balancer must reside on the virtual network the load balancer is deployed to, there are a number of deployment options. Multiple backend pools can be created behind a single load balancer, along with multiple frontend IPs. Azure Load Balancer's rules provide the mapping of the frontends to the backend pools.

For the frontend IPs, both internal and external (public) IPs can be configured, enabling a load balancer to be used for both internal load balancing and external load balancing. However, both types are not supported on a single instance—i.e., a load balancer is either internal or external. It is very common to require internal load balancers—for example, to front services between different tiers of an application and also in front of NVAs that also provide intra-network features. Note that the external load balancer is just providing distribution of traffic; it is not providing additional firewall capabilities. This means when publishing sites to the Internet, you typically would want some additional protection, such as Azure Firewall, an NVA, or a load-balancing service targeted for publishing web content that has firewall functionality as an option. Azure has such as service.

Azure Application Gateway

While Azure Load Balancer operates at Layer 4, meaning anything TCP or UDP will work, the lack of knowledge about the Application layer limits its functionality. Azure Application Gateway is a Layer 7 load balancer, which means it operates at the application and is specifically aimed at HTTP/HTTPS/HTTP/2 and WebSocket workloads. The knowledge of the application allows distribution of traffic based on data within the URL—i.e., different paths can be directed to different backend pools. In addition, SSL termination (with the option to re-encrypt to the backend) can be performed on the application gateway, reducing computation requirements on the backend resources, and cookie-based session affinity can be leveraged. The frontend configuration can be a public and/or private IP address, allowing Azure Application Gateway to be used for external or internal applications. The backend pool members can be resources on the virtual network, such as VMs, but also Azure App Service resources and even public IP addresses.

A single Application Gateway instance can support multiple sites (up to 100 sites, at the time of writing), with each website directed to separate backend pools. HTTP to HTTPS redirection can also be performed in addition to URL rewriting if required. There are a number of SKUs available for Application Gateway that drive the amount of data it can process.

There are a number of steps and components to using Application Gateway, as shown in Figure 5.11.

FIGURE 5.11
Components used with Application Gateway

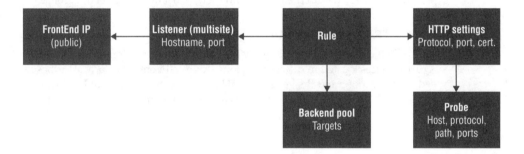

At the following site, I walk through creating a multi-site configuration to publish a number of onsite SharePoint and Office applications:

```
https://savilltech.com/2018/03/17/
using-azure-application-gateway-to-publish-applications/
```

This demonstrates some of the more advanced configurations available, but I will walk through the basic relationship here.

Notice the relationships between components, as this drives the order of creation in more advanced scenarios. (For simple configurations, the portal-driven experience drives this, although hopefully we are deploying through a JSON template.)

◆ Frontend IP is the address incoming requests will be received on.

◆ Listener defines the port that is being listened on, the protocol, the certificate to use with SSL, and the frontend IP to use.

◆ Backend pools are the resources requests will be sent to.

◆ Probes enable the checks to see if targets are healthy. These can be customized to specific paths and also expected results.

◆ HTTP settings control some of the encryption and affinity options, and bind to the probe.

◆ The rule connects everything together and drives how the traffic received is routed.

Additionally, an optional web application firewall (WAF) can be enabled on the Application Gateway instance that protects from some of the most common types of threats based on the Core Rule Set (CRS) 3.0 or 2.2.9, which provides protections from threats like SQL-injection and cross-site scripting, in addition to many more. Most customers will deploy a WAF with Application Gateway unless a separate firewall solution is leveraged.

Inter-Region Load Balancing

Azure Load Balancer and Azure Application Gateway provide great load-balancing solutions within a region, enabling highly available and scalable services to be offered at Layer 4 and Layer 7, respectively. However, the recommendation for customers to maximize availability is to deploy to multiple regions. Balancing traffic between regions requires a separate set of technologies, and once again, Azure offers two solutions: Azure Traffic Manager, which uses DNS to balance traffic, and Azure Front Door, which leverages IP anycast and is focused on HTTP/HTTPS, only operating at Layer 7. Both solutions are typically paired with an intra-region solution to provide resiliency within the region, and then distribution between regions.

AZURE TRAFFIC MANAGER

Azure Traffic Manager provides globally aware DNS resolution to Azure services and non-Azure services located in different regions. An intelligent set of processes based on specified configurations and the geographical location of the user's local DNS server (LDNS) are employed. It's easiest to understand this by looking at an example, such as the one shown in Figure 5.12.

FIGURE 5.12
Example Traffic Manager usage scenario

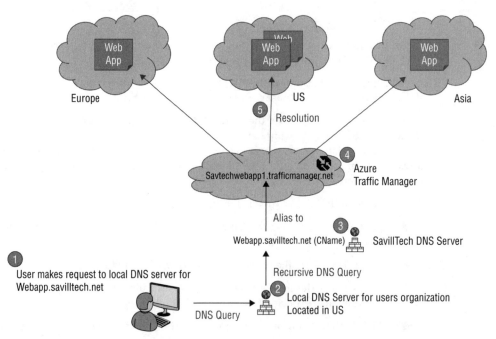

In this example, a Traffic Manager profile (a specific set of configurations for an address) was created for `savtechwebapp1.trafficmanager.net`. The site is configured with three endpoints that are separate deployments of the application hosted in Europe, the United States, and Asia Azure regions. An endpoint is a possible target that traffic can be directed to.

The Traffic Manager profile name always has `trafficmanager.net` as the DNS suffix, but you set the prefix part of the name. That prefix must be unique within the Traffic Manager service. However, this prefix will not actually be seen by end users.

The organization's actual DNS server has a CName (alias) record created for the public DNS name in the organization's own DNS zone. (That DNS zone is known as a *vanity domain* in this case; it's the public name used to make it look nice for end users.) The alias record points to the Traffic Manager profile name record. Here, `webapp.savilltech.net` is an alias that resolves to `savtechwebapp1.trafficmanager.net`.

There are several load-balancing options for Traffic Manager profiles. These control how requests are distributed. The most common is Performance, which attempts to resolve requests to the Azure service that's closest to the requesting user's local DNS server. Here's how it works:

1. A user in the requesting organization enters `webapp.savilltech.net` in a web browser.

2. The user's local computer has a DNS configuration, which connects to their organization's DNS server, which in turn sends the DNS request for `webapp.savilltech.net`. The local DNS server performs a recursive lookup to resolve the name.

3. The authoritative DNS servers for the target DNS domain (`savilltech.net`) have an alias record that was created for webapp. That record points to the Traffic Manager profile named `savtechwebapp1.trafficmanager.net`.

4. The local DNS server now resolves the record returned by Traffic Manager. This resolves via the Traffic Manager service. Traffic Manager attempts to ascertain the geographically closest Azure service based on a network ICMP latency map between DNS servers and Azure regions. The closest endpoint that is available is returned to the client.

Note the ICMP latency; whichever Azure region is considered closest is always based on the user's local DNS server, not where the users are physically located. This means if users are located in Asia but are using a DNS server located in the United States, then those users would be directed to services in the United States—even if there is a service physically located in Asia. Users who use global DNS servers will not be redirected to the closest Azure service with a high degree of confidence. Also, the network latency maps are generated based on ICMP echo requests (pings) to DNS servers. This means if the local DNS server blocks ICMP, then the latency information is not ascertainable. (This isn't common since this ICMP approach is an industry standard.)

I previously mentioned different types of load-balancing options. What follows is a description of the options:

Performance   Requests are directed to the Azure service that is closest to the local DNS server and is online.

Weighted   Requests are directed in a round-robin fashion between all endpoints that are online. It is possible to set weights that enable certain endpoints to receive more traffic than others.

Priority All requests are directed to the first endpoint. If that endpoint is not available, the requests go to the next endpoint. This is completely independent of the local DNS server's physical location.

Geography Specific endpoints are returned based on the geographies selected, which can be high level, such as continent, and then down to more detailed, such as state.

Multivalue Only IP addresses can be configured as endpoints, and all healthy endpoints are returned.

Subnet Sets of end-user IP address ranges are mapped to specific endpoints.

To ascertain if an endpoint is online, every 30 seconds the Traffic Manager service performs a request using HTTP or HTTPS. The request can use a custom port to a specific URL—for example, the URL of a specific application on the web service. Specifying a path (as opposed to the base DNS name) is useful to ensure that the service is responding rather than just the base web hosting infrastructure. If four requests go unanswered or if it takes longer than 10 seconds for each request, then the endpoint is considered unavailable and requests will not be directed there. The requests will continue every 30 seconds, and when the endpoint responds again, it will be considered online and requests will once again be directed to the endpoint as appropriate.

Note that a TTL (the time-to-live of the record in the DNS cache) can be configured as part of the profile. TTL is set to 5 minutes by default. The smaller the TTL, the faster clients will be directed to another endpoint if an endpoint is not available. You should be aware that lowering the TTL setting increases the number of requests to Traffic Manager, which might increase your cost.

Traffic Manager endpoints can be Azure endpoints—i.e., a VM with a public IP, an App Service, and other public-facing services. (It must be public-facing.) Traffic Manager endpoints can also be a non-Azure resource, such as a website hosted with another service provider or even on premises, and can be IPv4/IPv6. You can also nest Traffic Manager profiles for more complex scenarios.

There are a large number of scenarios where this functionality is very useful. Consider an organization that has operations all over the world. Services could be deployed in each major geographical region and then Traffic Manager used in the Performance load-balancing mode as the initial point of entry. Clients then would be redirected to the service closest to them, offering them the lowest latency and best experience. Imagine a customer who wants to use his on premises for normal hosting of his web applications but uses Azure for disaster recovery. With Traffic Manager in Failover mode, clients would only be directed to the Azure hosting if the on-premises web presence were unavailable.

Note that this relies on DNS and DNS TTL. If a client caches a DNS record for a long time, then even if the resolution changes on Traffic Manager, the client would continue to go to the old value. This can potentially cause a significant delay.

AZURE FRONT DOOR

Azure Traffic Manager provides distribution over multiple backends by pointing clients to a target. However, it relies on DNS, which can be slow to update and does nothing else to improve the end-user experience. The end user still talks directly to the backend over the Internet wherever that may be and over whatever path is used. For HTTP(S) and HTTP/2 workloads that go through a number of handshakes for each connection, this Internet-based, potentially far communication can impact the performance, and often the same content is served to multiple parties. Enter Azure Front Door.

Azure Front Door was available as a service in Azure in 2019 but was actually in use for many years before that by various Microsoft services, such as Bing, Xbox Live, Outlook, etc. It provides similar balancing options as Traffic Manager but works at an IP level instead of DNS and also provides numerous accelerations and optimizations. Figure 5.13 shows the basic Azure Front Door architecture, which highlights one of its biggest assets, the use of globally distributed point-of-presence (POP) locations to act as the initial contact points, which are close to clients.

FIGURE 5.13 High-level Azure Front Door architecture

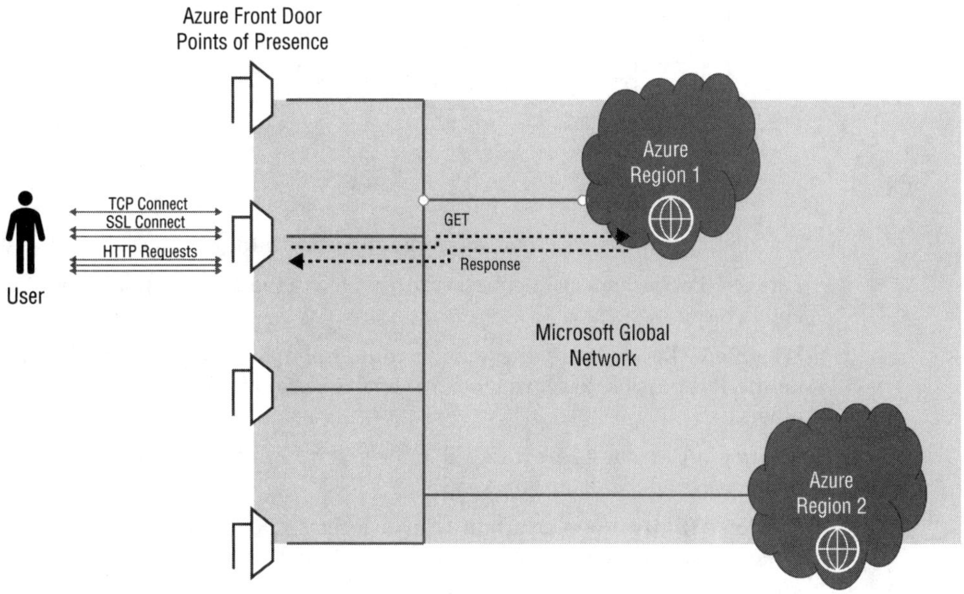

Azure Front Door, like Traffic Manager, enables multiple backends to be defined in a backend pool for a front door instance, which can be services in Azure regions (Figure 5.13 shows a web service running in two regions), such as Web Apps, Kubernetes, Storage, and any public IP or publicly resolvable DNS name. Health probes are used to ensure the backends are available using the same TCP ports used for the client requests.

As shown in Figure 5.13 the client initially talks to a front door POP, which is available in many locations around the world. Anycast is used to enable a user to talk to the closest POP. It is at these POPs that much of the communication takes place, such as the TCP and SSL session negotiation, and then the actual bytes of data sent and acknowledged. The POP goes to the actual backend via the Azure global backbone (which will be faster and more direct than any normal path over the Internet) to get chunks of data to the server to the requesting client. All of this conversation locally to the POP reduces latency and speeds up the experience. This is known as *split TCP*, where the user connection is terminated close to the user and a separate connection is used to actually get the data. Figure 5.14 shows this in more detail. Additionally, data is cached to expedite further future requests for the same data.

FIGURE 5.14
Split TCP detail

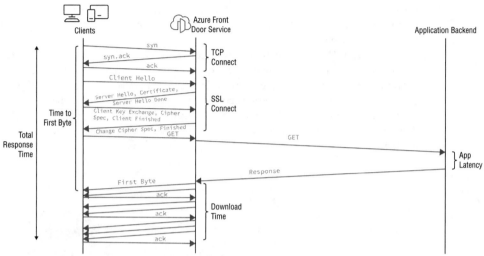

The routing options for Front Door are similar to Traffic Manager:

Latency (Performance)   Requests are directed to the backend that is the closest online backend in terms of latency.

Weighted   Requests are directed in a round-robin fashion between all backends that are online. It is possible to set weights that enable certain backends to receive more traffic than others.

Priority   All requests are directed to the first backend, and if that backend is not available, the requests go to the next backend.

Session Affinity   Session affinity can be leveraged to ensure user requests are sent to the same backend service.

Azure Front Door also provides DDoS and WAF protection, including the ability to author custom rules for additional protection. Rate limiting can also be leveraged, if required.

What this means is the end-user experience will be greatly accelerated compared to them going over the Internet to the backend resource because of the close session establishment and the actual content acquisition going over the Microsoft backbone network. This contrasts to Azure Traffic Manager, which would direct the user to the closest backend, but the actual communication would still be between the user and the backend server. If your workload is HTTP-based, use Azure Front Door; if not, use Azure Traffic Manager.

Monitoring

Chapter 10 covers monitoring in more detail. However, since this is one of the core pillars, I wanted to quickly touch on it here as part of architectural decisions. As architects the exact operation of services will typically fall outside of the scope; however, an organization may have requirements for insight into network traffic and/or accompanying logs. Additionally, the ability to check the health and flow of traffic may be required.

Like nearly all Azure resources, the diagnostics logs associated to networking can be sent to Log Analytics, a storage account, and/or an event hub (where the logs can be consumed by a SIEM solution). Network Watcher provides a number of capabilities around network health, including diagnosing connection and routing issues, troubleshooting VPN and ExpressRoute, and providing easy insight into NSGs deployed and in effect in an environment. It also has capabilities to capture packets via an extension in the VM, which is separate from the virtual network TAP feature that streams VM traffic to a network packet collector.

Additional insight can be gained when using network security groups and enabling the NSG flow logs, which log details of the flows both successful and unsuccessful. If the NSG flow logs are sent to Log Analytics, Traffic Analytics can be used. Traffic Analytics not only provides graphical insight into traffic flows but can also be used to spot threats.

Where the native capabilities of Azure do not meet packet insight requirements, organizations will typically deploy NVAs and route the traffic to them. Remember that this means the traffic flows via the NVAs, which may introduce bottlenecks if not scaled appropriately.

Chapter 6

Storage

This chapter focuses on the storage capabilities in Azure related to infrastructure services. This starts with the services provided by Azure Storage, which can be used by both infrastructure and other services, and then proceeds to VM-specific storage architectural elements. The chapter will close by looking at database services.

In this chapter, you will learn to:

◆ Use key Azure services.

◆ Leverage Azure managed disks.

◆ Integrate with Azure database services.

Azure Storage Services

An in-depth knowledge of the internals of Azure Storage is not a requirement for leveraging the services. The whole point of cloud services is that, as the consumer of the service, you do not need to know or care how your services are being delivered. As long as the capabilities and performance that you signed up for are available and any SLAs are met, as the customer, you should be happy.

I do believe, however, that it can be useful to understand how services are provided. That knowledge can enable a better understanding of why things behave the way they do and are used the way they are. This section provides a basic overview of the Azure Storage architecture. If you want a detailed explanation, I recommend you download and read the white paper from this site:

http://sigops.org/sosp/sosp11/current/2011-Cascais/11-calder-online.pdf

This white paper was written by the Azure Storage team to document their architecture.

Azure Storage Architecture

In most enterprise datacenters, you will find one or more storage area networks (SANs). These are very large, multirack systems that consist of hundreds, if not thousands, of enterprise disks. They are typically a mix of HDDs and SSDs. The SAN has a number of controllers, which are essentially scaled-down operating systems, that enable access to the storage services and management. The SANs then connect to hosts that leverage the storage through various media, typically Fiber Channel and iSCSI. This requires the hosts consuming the storage to have a specific type of host bus adapter (HBA)/network card in addition to the often expensive switching equipment in the datacenter.

SANs offer many benefits, including redundant connectivity, power, controllers and everything else, high levels of performance and functionality, and centralized shared storage. These benefits come at great financial cost. You will not find a SAN in an Azure datacenter. SANs are not economically viable at the mega-scale of any enterprise public cloud service. Instead, Azure leverages its own distributed, software-defined storage solution, which enables the use of more commodity hardware. By using software-based solutions, the level of customization and ability to respond to the needs of services is much higher.

In Chapter 1, I discussed Azure clusters and stamps. There are compute clusters, which are racks of compute nodes that run the actual VMs. Similarly, there are Azure Storage clusters, which consist of nodes of a lot of disks that together offer the Azure Storage services.

Azure Storage is provided using a three-tier architecture, as shown in Figure 6.1. On the compute side, each host has some local disks. They are used as part of the local cache and for the temporary drive. The persistent storage of items such as the OS and data is serviced via the VHD driver, which in turn accesses the Azure Storage service.

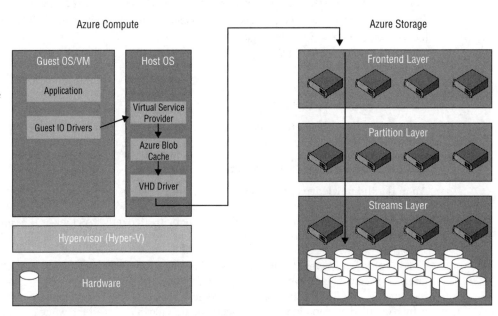

FIGURE 6.1
Azure Storage architecture and its interaction with Azure compute services

The frontend layer is a stateless system that provides REST authentication and interfaces, accepts requests, performs actions such as throttling performance, and then routes the requests to the partition layer. The partition layer understands higher-level data abstractions, such as Blobs, tables, queues, and files, and provides the scalable namespace. Finally, the stream layer contains the disks, manages writing the actual bits to disk, and ensures data durability by taking responsibility for the distribution and replication of the data across servers in the stamp. Within the stream layer are file streams, which are ordered lists of large storage chunks (also called *extents*). These units of replication are themselves made up of blocks. If you are interested in more detail on these internals, refer to the white paper mentioned earlier.

There are two types of replication for Azure Storage, both of which are critical to providing the various resiliency levels offered:

Intra-Stamp Replication (Stream Layer)   Intra-stamp replication provides synchronous replication. This keeps data durable within the stamps through replication across nodes in different fault domains.

Inter-Stamp Replication (Partition Layer)   When inter-stamp replication is employed, asynchronous replication of data is provided across stamps.

DNS is used for the Azure Storage namespace, which is why when talking about Azure Storage accounts and services, you will see the following format:

```
http(s)://<account>.<service>.core.windows.net/<partition>/object
```

Using Storage Accounts and Types of Replication

I've already referred to storage accounts, so it's important to understand what a storage account is, how Azure limits storage accounts, and how to choose your storage account design. All data stored in Azure Storage is stored in a storage account. It should be noted that when dealing with VMs, you typically don't deal with storage accounts. You used to, as the VHD files for VMs were stored in page blobs, which were stored in storage accounts, which required tracking of the number of VHDs per storage account to ensure limits of the storage account did not impact performance and also had challenges when you wanted to change the performance tier. All this was solved with managed disks (covered later), which abstracted away the storage account (it's still there but basically hidden from you) and made disks a first-class Azure resource. It is still useful to understand storage accounts because even when you are dealing with infrastructure, the capabilities of storage accounts may be useful.

A storage account has a number of attributes:

◆ Each account must have a name that is unique across all of Azure Storage namespace. Azure Storage can be accessed using URLs, and the name you specify is a component of the URL.

◆ Each account must belong to a subscription.

◆ Each account must be created in a particular region. For best performance, you try to keep the location of the storage account in the same region as the service using it.

◆ Each account must specify the replication to be used for the content.

◆ Each account has a performance type—for example, standard (HDD-based) or premium (SSD-based).

◆ A default access tier is specified, hot or cool (this impacts costs related to storage and transactions), but can also be set per object for most account types.

◆ Storage accounts have a type, such as general-purpose v1, v2, blob storage, or file storage.

◆ Each account has a maximum number of IOPS. The Azure storage limits page should be checked for exact, current values, as they do change.

◆ Each account also has size, ingress, and egress limits.

◆ Each account has a set of URL endpoints that are used to access the storage. The URL includes the name specified during creation. A different URL is used for each of the four types of storage services available: Blobs, tables, queues, and files. The URLs use the following format:

```
https://<storage account name>.<storage service>.core.windows.net
```

For example, `https://savillstorage.blob.core.windows.net/` would be my BLOB end-point. You can add custom URLs to access storage accounts. Custom URLs are documented at:

`https://docs.microsoft.com/en-us/azure/storage/blobs/storage-custom-domain-name`

◆ Each account has storage keys, which are used to securely access storage accounts, in addition to shared access signatures for more granular controls.

◆ There are other controls, such as secure transfer requirements, service endpoints (i.e., integration with virtual networks), and types of data protection. When using secure transfer, it means REST API interactions must be via HTTPS, and Azure Files interaction must use SMB 3 (which requires port 445).

Many of these elements can be seen in Figure 6.2, which shows the Basics tab from the portal when you are creating a storage account.

FIGURE 6.2
An example Azure Storage account showing many of the key attributes

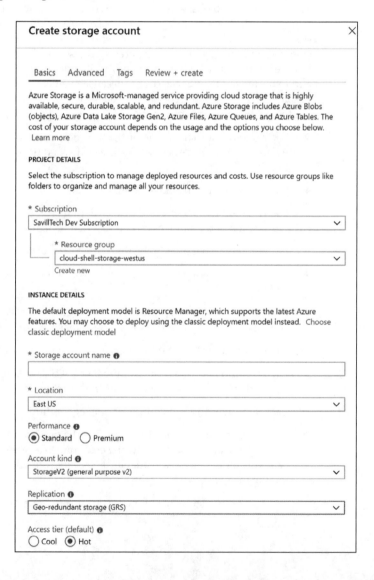

The storage account replication choice is a major decision and one that should be carefully considered, because you cannot always change the replication type of a storage account post-creation. It is possible to change the replication type between all types of replication except the zone-redundant storage (ZRS). ZRS organizes the copies of data differently and typically would require a manual migration of the data. The types of replication available are as follows:

Locally Redundant Storage   With locally redundant storage (LRS), the data is stored within a single Azure facility in a region. More specifically, all data is replicated three times within an Azure Storage stamp. Each copy of the data resides on a different disk, node, and rack. This offers the highest resiliency possible for the data. All copies of the data are written synchronously; therefore, any risk of data loss in the event of a failure of a disk, node, or rack is removed.

Zone-Redundant Storage (ZRS)   When you create an Azure Storage account, you select a region for your storage. However, many regions today offer availability zones, separate datacenters with independent power, communications, etc. ZRS distributes the three copies of data over three AZs within the region. At the time of writing, ZRS is available for general-purpose v2 account types and supports block blobs, non-disk page blobs, files, tables, and queues.

Geo-Redundant Storage (GRS)   Geo-redundant storage (GRS) takes LRS, asynchronously replicates the data to the paired region (which is hundreds of miles away), and then stores the data in that paired region three times. Under GRS, a total of six copies of your data are stored. If there is a failure in the primary region, the Azure Storage account is failed over to the secondary region. Because the replication between regions is asynchronous, there is a risk of data loss in the event of a disaster. There is no specific SLA outlining any timing related to the asynchronous replication. However, the documentation states a target RPO (Recovery Point Objective—i.e., how old the data will be) of 15 minutes, meaning in the event of a failover, you could lose up to 15 minutes of data. If this does not meet your requirements, you should look at other options to replicate data. For example, application-level replication could be AlwaysOn in a SQL Server scenario.

Read-Access Geo-Redundant Storage   Read-access geo-redundant storage (RA-GRS) is much the same as GRS, except that the replica copy of the data is available only for read via a secondary endpoint. The secondary endpoint has -secondary appended to the storage account name—for example, savillstorage-secondary.<service>.core.windows.net.

Geo-Redundant Zone-Redundant Storage   Geo-redundant zone-redundant storage (GZRS) combines ZRS at the primary location and then replicates to the paired region, where it is stored at LRS. This provides the best resiliency within the primary region while still providing asynchronous replication to the paired region.

NEVER LESS THAN THREE COPIES OF DATA!

You should note that in all the preceding replication options, there is never less than three copies of the data spread over three racks. The data is highly durable, and Azure states they have never lost customer data due to any kind of disk failure. When you are considering the total cost of solutions, this should be factored in, as it means there is no need to implement features like RAID inside VMs that have multiple disks and therefore no paying for extra disks just to meet durability requirements. You don't need mirroring or parity because each disk is already highly durable. If you use multiple disks and want to join them, then use simple striping. There is no need to lose capacity. This may differ from other cloud providers, where RAID is required for durability, requiring more storage than you can actually use.

When choosing the type of replication, you should consider whether application-level replication is available. If so, you can natively replicate data instead of relying on the storage subsystem. Think about your RPO and the costs for different types of replication. The higher the level of durability, the greater the cost. In terms of durability, GZRS is the best, then GRS, then ZRS, and, lastly, LRS:

GZRS > GRS/GRS-RA > ZRS > LRS

The same applies to the cost. A storage account is required in each region where services will use the storage. Remember the IOPS limit for each storage account. You will likely need multiple storage accounts spread over the various Azure regions. You also may need multiple storage accounts within each region, since different workloads need different replication options. If you are using application replication, then you don't need GRS at the storage account level; instead, use LRS at each region for the local copy of the data, which would cost the same as one GRS.

Note that when thinking about the paired regions, it is possible for customers to perform a forced failover. In this circumstance, the timestamp of the replication state will be shown to the customer, who can then decide to perform the failover, which will result in any data post that time being lost.

When creating your storage accounts, use a naming convention that makes obvious the purpose, region, and replication type of the storage account. For example, you might use a naming scheme with the following format:

```
<purpose/business area><region><replication type>
Project1EastUSGRS
```

The maximum length for the storage account name is 24 characters and can only contain lowercase letters and numbers. Use some kind of descriptive naming scheme so that when you look at reports, it will be easy to identify basic details about the account.

Storage accounts are encrypted completely transparently using 256-bit AES encryption, which cannot be disabled. For Blobs and Files, customer-managed keys can be used through integration with Azure Key Vault. If the account is using replicated storage, the replicas have the same replication level as the primary copy of the storage.

Storage Account Keys

More Azure Storage services (such as Azure Files and Blob) are starting to integrate with Azure AD. However, there are also Azure Storage account-specific keys that can be leveraged. Each storage account has two access keys: a primary and a secondary. These keys must be kept secure because, as the name suggests, they are the keys for entry to your storage account. Armed with the URL for the storage service and one of the keys, anyone has full access to the data. Two keys are displayed, because, over time, you may wish to regenerate a key. Having two keys makes it possible to regenerate one key while allowing access to continue with the second key, thus avoiding any interruption to storage access and service. As Figure 6.3 shows, regenerating the keys is a simple process. Just click the Regenerate button. The new key can be placed into the tool or script that leverages the key. The clipboard icon next to the key makes it easy to paste the key into the script that needs to use it. (I regenerated the keys immediately after taking this screenshot.)

FIGURE 6.3
Displaying the access keys for a storage account

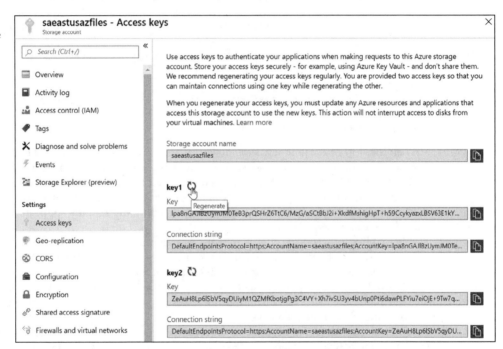

Keys are commonly used when performing storage actions using PowerShell or third-party tools. When creating a handle to an Azure Storage account, a context, a key must be passed along with the storage account name. For example, as shown here, I can connect to my storage account and then examine the basic information about it. Note that rather than typing in a key, I fetch the key using an Az PowerShell command, since the account I have authenticated with has permissions to fetch the key. You could also hardcode a key, but definitely do not place this in a script. You would store the key in something like Azure Key Vault as a secret.

```
$AzStorAccName = 'savtestazurefileswestus' #Storage account name
$AzResGroup = 'RG-SavWestUS' #resource group name
$AzStrAct = Get-AzStorageAccount -Name $AzStorAccName `
-ResourceGroupName $AzResGroup
$AzStrKey = Get-AzStorageAccountKey -Name $AzStorAccName `
-ResourceGroupName $AzResGroup
$AzStrCtx = New-AzStorageContext $AzStorAccName `
-StorageAccountKey $AzStrKey[0].Value
$AzStrCtx

StorageAccountName : savtestazurefileswestus
BlobEndPoint       : https://savtestazurefileswestus.blob.core.windows.net/
TableEndPoint      : https://savtestazurefileswestus.table.core.windows.net/
QueueEndPoint      : https://savtestazurefileswestus.queue.core.windows.net/
FileEndPoint       : https://savtestazurefileswestus.file.core.windows.net/
Context            : Microsoft.WindowsAzure.Commands.Storage.AzureStorageContext
Name               :
StorageAccount     :
BlobEndpoint=https://savtestazurefileswestus.blob.core.windows.net/;QueueEndpoi
nt=https://
ExtendedProperties : {}
```

When the storage account key is too powerful and you can't use Azure AD integration (at the time of writing available for Blobs, queues, and aspects of files), there are also shared access signatures. Shared access signatures (SAS) enable an ad-hoc or policy-based signature to be generated that has granular scope (i.e., objects it applies to) and permissions in addition to an expiration time (and a start time, if required). These are commonly used by applications for access to Azure Storage services.

Note that like an access key, the shared access signature is self-contained, and possession of it enables its use, which means they should be kept secure. I've heard people say that because they are sent as part of the URL, they can easily be read, but that really confuses how HTTPS works. In reality, only the IP and port are sent unencrypted; the actual rest of the URL is sent as part of the HTTP request, which is sent over the already established SSL connection; therefore, any keys that are in the URL cannot be viewed.

A SAS can be a service or account type. A service type is applicable to only one type of service (for example, Blob or Queue), whereas an account type is applicable to whichever services you specify, potentially all of them. A SAS can also be ad hoc—i.e., you specify all the properties at the time of SAS creation and the only way to revoke would be to change the access key that signs the SAS. A SAS can also be based on a stored access policy—i.e., the policy that contains the settings is then used by the created SAS. When you are using a SAS with a stored access policy, changes to the policy will reflect on the SAS. Figure 6.4 shows an example screen of the portal-based SAS creation.

FIGURE 6.4
Portal screen for creating a SAS

Azure Storage Services

Within the storage accounts, various types of objects are created, such as containers for BLOBs, tables for entities, and queues for messages and file services. Other Azure services, such as an Azure SQL Database, use the storage differently.

AZURE BLOB STORAGE

As infrastructure architects in a world of managed disks, we rarely utilize blob storage for VMs. However, there are still many other services that leverage blob storage, such as SQL Server and Azure Data Lake Storage Gen2. Three types of Blob storage are available, all of which are focused around the storage of unstructured data—for example, images, videos, CAD files, executables (pretty much anything you want). There are numerous ways to interact with all storage services, and Blob is no exception, making it a good option for applications that need to interact with unstructured data via APIs. A special type of storage account just for blobs introduced the concept of tiering. However, that functionality was rolled into the v2 version of the general-purpose storage account, which would be the preferred choice.

Storage accounts have limits on the size of individual blobs (which vary by type) and the total storage capacity for the storage account (2 PB for US and Europe at the time of writing). The limits per blob are driven by the nature of blobs in that they are made up of blocks or pages and each block/page has a maximum size and a blob can be made up of a finite number of blocks. Blobs are placed into containers, and a storage account can have multiple containers. You may use different containers for organizational purposes or for security.

Block Blobs and Premium Block Blobs

Block blobs are composed of blocks that are programmatically inserted, replaced, or deleted, and then committed to create a new version of a blob. Block blobs are aimed at many types of unstructured data but very commonly for streaming and storage purposes for media, backups, documents, and more. If an application just needs to store some unstructured object, a block blob is commonly used. Based on a maximum number of blocks of 50,000 and a maximum size of a block of 100 MB, the maximum size of block blob (at the time of writing) is around 4.75 TB. Note that it's also common to see very small block blobs. Windows Clustering uses a 0-byte block blob as a cloud witness resource to be locked if required, and because you pay for the storage used, this amounts to a 0 cost lockable object. There are also premium block blobs, which have different limits and leverage different account types but are used in the same way.

Block blobs are commonly leveraged using the Blob REST API when applications need to work with unstructured object data. Note that the same common blob storage can also be accessed via the ADLS Gen2 API—i.e., Azure Data Lake Storage Gen 2. Data Lake provides a Hadoop filesystem file-based interaction with files and a folder hierarchy. There are granular POSIX-compliant ACLs with atomic file transactions. This is just another API on top of a blob. Note that while blobs have some published limits (which are really focused around ensuring workloads don't interfere with other customers), Azure Data Lake does not have limits, other than single maximum file sizes. The goal of Azure Data Lake is to provide an infinite, secure store that can be used for analytics workloads. ADLS Gen2 has full integration with Azure Databricks, HDInsight, Data Factory, SQL Data Warehouse, and Power BI—i.e., all the key analytics and data services.

Another feature currently in preview is the ability to interact with a blob using NFSv3. This provides three application interface options to interact with a blob.

Page Blobs

Before managed disks, a page blob was heavily used for VMs, as a page blob housed the VHD file used for the disks attached to a VM. I should be very clear: A page blob is still used to house the VHD with managed disks, but the page blob and storage account are abstracted from you and managed automatically, leaving only a disk object to interact with. It is still possible to directly use page blobs and VHDs via unmanaged disks, although this is not advised. Using unmanaged disks removes a lot of functionality and control, and there is only one benefit when using non-premium storage and that is because with unmanaged standard storage, you pay for the data written to the VHD (i.e., the page blob), rather than the size of the VHD, commonly known as *thin provisioning* or *sparse storage*. This means that if you create a 1 TB unmanaged standard VHD and only write 100 MB of data, then you pay for 100 MB of storage. For managed disks (and premium unmanaged), you pay for the size of the disk, not the amount of data written. Overall, the negatives outweigh this one positive. And remember, this is only for standard storage, which won't be used in production environments (as we will explore when looking at disk types for managed disks).

Page blobs are optimized for random reads and writes. They are made up of 512-byte pages. At the time of writing, the maximum size for a page blob is 8 TB.

Append Blobs

Append blobs are similar to block blobs; however, they are optimized for append operations—i.e., adding blocks to the end of a blob is the only supported operation. Updating or deleting blocks in an append blob is not supported. These are useful for logging purposes and can comprise up to 50,000 variable-sized blocks that can be up to 4 MB in size, giving a maximum append blob size of 195 GB.

Azure Blob Storage Capabilities

With the wide range of usage of blobs, there are a number of key capabilities related to blobs that I want to briefly cover.

The first set of capabilities relates to the protection of blob data. Soft delete is enabled at a storage account level. When enabled, a retention time is set between 1 and 365 days and any blocks deleted (which also includes entire blobs) or overwritten are saved for that retention and tracked as part of a soft deleted snapshot. Because these blocks are saved, there is additional storage costs associated with their storage. Note that this does not protect the blobs if the container or account is deleted. To protect against those actions, use resource locks. While soft deletion helps protect against deletion, there are often requirements to ensure that data is not deleted or altered that can be proven via a policy. This can include legal hold scenarios and regulator compliance. Immutable storage for Azure blobs enables policies to be configured that can set how long data must be stored immutably—i.e., read-only. The policy is set at a container level, enabling different policies to be applied within a single storage account. A tag can also be configured to enable tracking. For example, the tag could be a case ID related to the hold. Only blob and general v2 storage accounts support the immutable policies.

Blob snapshots can be utilized to hold point-in-time views of blob storage. Only the deltas are stored which means the additional cost is proportional to the changes made from the point the snapshot is taken. Multiple snapshots can exist per blob. A snapshot is read-only; however, a snapshot can be copied to a regular blob and then used per any other blob and can also be copied over its parent, replacing the parent with the snapshot content. Note that snapshots are associated with the parent. If the parent blob is deleted, the snapshots are also deleted (although in normal operations, you must delete the snapshots before deleting the parent blob).

It is possible to allow anonymous access to blobs, which can make them available directly via their URI to the Internet. However, it is also possible to show static websites directly from blob, which includes specifying a default file and custom 404 page. This capability is only available in general-purpose v2 storage accounts and is part of the storage account configuration (even though it's actually a blob service feature). When the feature is enabled, only a default document and error document name are specified. A new container, $web, is created, which is where all the content related to the static website must be copied to.

There are numerous tools for interacting with Azure Storage (including blobs), a primary one being Azure Storage Explorer, which has a portal-based version as part of the storage account and a desktop version available for download at:

```
https://azure.microsoft.com/en-us/features/storage-explorer/
```

AzCopy, which is a free download, is another powerful tool to upload and download content to blob storage. Linux even has a virtual filesystem driver, Blobfuse, that enables storage accounts as a filesystem.

Consider if you want to copy data between storage accounts. Ordinarily, a file copy operation results in the data bouncing via the client issuing the command. That is, if you are copying a 1 TB blob between two accounts in East US (or any other combination of regions), the data will bounce via your machine at wherever you are sitting. This is very inefficient. A better option is to leverage an asynchronous, server-side copy. This means you submit a request to Azure to copy/move blobs, which it then performs directly in Azure, without the data bouncing via your client. It runs as a job separate from your session, but you can query that job to check on the status. AzCopy does this automatically when the source and targets are storage accounts; no other actions are required. This can also be done via PowerShell and CLI. For example, in PowerShell, you would use the `Start-AzStorageBlobCopy` command to perform a server-side copy.

At the time of writing, Blob does not integrate with Azure Backup. There are other options that can be utilized to create backups of Blob storage, such as snapshots and AzCopy. A full flow is outlined at:

```
https://azure.microsoft.com/en-us/blog/microsoft-azure-block-blob-storage-backup/
```

Tiering and Lifecycle Management

A storage account has a type, standard or premium, which relates primarily to the performance of the storage in terms of IOPS, throughput, and latency. At the time of writing, standard performance accounts that are blob or general-purpose v2 (notice there are rarely features for general-purpose v1; if you have a v1, convert it to a v2!) also support access tiering, of which there are three levels: hot, cool, and archive. A default access tier of hot or cool can be set for the storage account, but tiers can also be configured at a per-blob level for block blobs. You can think of the order as follows (from best to worst in terms of performance but also from most expensive to least expensive in terms of data storage):

♦ Premium storage

♦ Standard storage hot

♦ Standard storage cool

♦ Standard storage archive

The primary goal of tiering is to provide the service required for the blob at the optimal cost. As an organization, I may have data that is frequently used but also data that I must keep for 7 years but rarely, if ever, need to access, and if access is required, a delay in availability is acceptable. As an organization, I would prefer to pay less money for the data I don't access than the data I intend to access all the time. There are two dimensions to costs for blob storage: the amount of data stored and the transactions (i.e., operations such as read and write) against it. Figure 6.5 shows a screenshot of two parts of the pricing at the time of writing. Note that these frequently change, but I just want to show the difference.

FIGURE 6.5
Blob storage
pricing

	PREMIUM	HOT	COOL	ARCHIVE
First 50 terabyte (TB) / month	$0.15 per GB	$0.0184 per GB	$0.01 per GB	$0.002 per GB
Write Operations (per 10,000)[1]	$0.0175	$0.05	$0.10	$0.10

Note that as you move from hot through cool to archive, the cost of the storage gets cheaper. Also note that the transaction costs for cool are twice as much as for hot (i.e., you pay less to store it), although the idea is that you access it less but when you do, it will cost more. Let's expand on the three access tiers:

Hot   Higher storage costs but lower access costs. 99.9% availability SLA with millisecond latency

Cool   Lower storage costs but higher access costs. 99% availability SLA with millisecond latency

Archive   Very low storage cost, but data is not available live; instead, it must be moved back to cool or high before it can be accessed. The time taken may be measured in hours.

Note that when we talk about tiering, because premium is a separate storage account than the tiers in standard, it is not easy to move data between premium and standard and access it through a unified endpoint. This should be considered when planning storage accounts. Many people wonder about the goal of the premium blob offering, which is SSD-based. Consider an application that wants high-performance object interactions using a RESTful API. While Azure Files has a RESTful interface, it is not commonly used by applications today, whereas blob is widely used via REST. By having the Premium blob offering, it is possible to have a high-performance object store that can be accessed via REST APIs.

Figure 6.6 shows an example of a storage account where each blob is in a different access tier. The blobs in hot and cool can be accessed, but the blob in archive cannot. You would have to move the blob in archive to cool or hot before it could be read.

FIGURE 6.6
Blobs in different access
tiers

NAME	MODIFIED	ACCESS TIER	BLOB TYPE	SIZE
Image1.jpg	9/14/2017, 9:36:43 AM	Hot	Block blob	1.58 N
Image2.jpg	9/14/2017, 9:36:18 AM	Cool	Block blob	6.4 Mi
Image3.jpg	9/14/2017, 9:36:35 AM	Archive	Block blob	7.65 N
images.html	9/14/2017, 9:48:22 AM	Hot (Inferred)	Block blob	131 B

Many organizations may write scripts to automatically move data between tiers (and these processes could also move blobs using the server-side copy between a premium and standard storage account, although you would have to consider the fact that the URI to the blob would change, so any application would have to handle data being spread over two separate storage accounts), but there is also a built-in lifecycle management feature. Lifecycle management is configured at a storage account level and enables rules to be defined using JSON that can move data between tiers—for example, if a blob is not accessed for 7 days, move from hot to cool, or if not accessed in cool for 30 days, move to archive. Following is an example policy that does exactly this but also deletes data after 7 years and only applies this policy to blobs that start with cad in the blobcontainer1 container:

```
{
  "rules": [
    {
      "name": "ruleTier",
      "enabled": true,
      "type": "Lifecycle",
      "definition": {
        "filters": {
          "blobTypes": [ "blockBlob" ],
          "prefixMatch": [ "blobcontainer1/cad" ]
        },
        "actions": {
          "baseBlob": {
            "tierToCool": { "daysAfterModificationGreaterThan": 7 },
            "tierToArchive": { "daysAfterModificationGreaterThan": 30 },
            "delete": { "daysAfterModificationGreaterThan": 2555 }
          },
          "snapshot": {
            "delete": { "daysAfterCreationGreaterThan": 90 }
          }
        }
      }
    }
  ]
}
```

Azure Tables

Azure Tables provides a key-attribute store where each key-attribute pair is an entity that resides in a table instance. There is no fixed schema in tables, which means that each entity can have its own structure—i.e., a NoSQL implementation. While an entity may be a single key-attribute pair, an entity can actually consist of up to 252 attributes, and the key is actually made up of a row-partition pair to provide a unique key value. A timestamp attribute is also automatically added.

A common use case is to store documents in XML or JSON format in attributes that can be parsed, but this is not required. Figure 6.7 shows a very simple Azure Table. You can see that the combination of PartitionKey and RowKey must be unique. For example, I could not add another Dog-Krypto entry. The attributes are values that were set for each entry. When adding a new entity, I can add values for attributes that have been previously used or create entirely new ones. Again, there is no fixed schema, so nothing is required other than the unique key made up of the partition and row keys.

FIGURE 6.7
An example
Azure table

🔲 Query	＋ Add	✏ Edit	▣ ˅ Select All	▦ Column Options	✕ Delete	⋯ More			

PARTITIONKEY ^	ROWKEY	TIMESTAMP	ALIAS	COLOR	AGE	CAR	CHILDREN	HOBBY
Dog	BruceWayne	2019-04-10T20:15:23.4660363Z	test	null	null	null	null	null
Dog	Krypto	2017-06-27T15:19:42.0859522Z	Superdog	White	null	null	null	null
User	BarryAllen	2018-07-09T23:15:33.563743Z	Flash	null	24	null	null	null
User	BruceWayne	2018-01-16T14:17:40.5780169Z	Batman	null	null	Batmobile	null	null
User	ClarkKent	2017-06-27T15:18:11.3348184Z	Superman	null	null	null	1	null
User	JohnSavill	2017-06-27T15:17:28.3254703Z	null	null	null	null	3	Ironman

AZURE QUEUES

Azure Queues are very useful for decoupling components and provide a reliable queuing solution for asynchronous communications using first-in, first-out (FIFO), which means messages are read in the order they are written. Messages are written to queues where each message can be up to 64 KB in size. The 64 KB size may seem very small. However, the goal is not to store entire artifacts in a queue; rather, it could be to reference another location, such as blob storage, that actually has the data to be operated upon. There is no concept of priority. If you need higher priority messages, then either use multiple queues or look at other messaging services that do have priority capabilities, such as Azure Service Bus.

Queues can contain millions of messages, and expiry times can be configured where messages past that expiry time are removed. In the post 2017-07-29 API version, it is possible to have messages that can live longer than seven days. By setting a message time-to-live (TTL) of -1, the message will never expire.

AZURE FILES

Azure Files provides SMB shares in the cloud, enabling utilization of skills that have been learned over the years from on-premises administration. Mapping to these shares is very simple, with instructions given directly in the portal. REST APIs are also available for modern, built-for the cloud applications.

As an infrastructure architect, Azure Files may be the most interesting storage service in Azure Storage accounts in a world where managed disks (we are getting close to those, I promise) have removed interactions with storage accounts for most VM storage. It is critical to note, though, how useful blob, queues, and tables are for applications. Don't overlook how powerful they can be. When thinking about architecting solutions for an organization, an infrastructure architect should understand what services can do and how they can be leveraged. That said, Azure Files is very interesting to infrastructure architects, as it provides a direct, file-based service using SMB (and REST, which enables application interaction, whereas SMB is not desired or available)—specifically, SMB 2.1 or 3 at the time of writing, although expect SMB versions to increase over time.

The SMB access for Azure Files is very useful where you have workloads that want a shared storage area that does not require the use of special code, with SMB you can just mount and utilize. If you are connecting via SMB 2.1, the Azure Files share is only available within the region of the storage account. If you are using SMB 3 (or above), the Azure Files share can be accessed from other regions and on premises. This is because SMB 3 supports encryption. The SMB version is negotiated when the session is established, with the highest common version utilized. Provided that the client is Windows 8 or Windows Server 2012 or above, SMB 3 will be used.

Note that Linux and MacOS also support SMB and can utilize Azure Files. There are big differences between SMB 2.1 and SMB 3 beyond just the availability of native encryption, as shown in Table 6.1. Note that for non-Windows systems, the SMB support varies by the OS distribution and version.

TABLE 6.1:   SMB versions

SMB 2.1	SMB 3
Primarily used for document storage	Used by enterprise applications with features such as active-active, transparent failover, multi-channel and more. SQL Server can store database files on SMB 3 shares.
No encryption	Encryption supported
Windows 7 and Windows 2008 R2 and above	Windows 8 and Windows Server 2012 and above

I see Azure Files used for a number of reasons instead of just hosting a file server in an IaaS VM:

◆ Managed service with SLA

◆ Shared, scalable service that is not limited by VM or disk limits

◆ Provides a hierarchical namespace

◆ Worldwide footprint

◆ Redundancy and disaster recovery capabilities

◆ REST API interactions

◆ Fully managed backups in the cloud

◆ Additional performance with premium files

For scenarios that can take advantage of Azure Files there is a wide range from simple lift and shift, hybrid solutions, and born-in-the-cloud applications that need a shared storage area; storage for cross-platform solutions are really any workload that needs a file service via SMB.

Like a regular file server, to use Azure Files, a share is created in the storage account, and then content is copied to it. Each share has a name and an optional quota, with multiple shares possible within a single storage account.

Note there is also an Azure NetApp Files solution. This is not built on Azure Storage but rather uses Microsoft deployed and managed NetApp solutions deployed in Azure datacenters. At the time of writing, this solution is focused around NFS access and is aimed where customers need NFS support and are used to NetApp and Data ONTAP services. NetApp Files is consumed by created Azure NetApp accounts in a specific region, creating capacity pools of a certain performance type, and then creating volumes within that capacity pool. At the time of writing, NetApp Files has an Ultra performance tier that is not present in Azure Files, which along with ONTAP format compatibility and NFS would be a reason to use NetApp Files over Azure Files.

Performance

There are both standard and premium performance accounts for Azure Files, with a special Files type of storage account required to use premium Azure Files. I suspect at some point in the future this will merge into a general-purpose v3 type account, but that's just speculation on my part. However, that precedent has been set around blob capabilities that were initially in a special blob storage account type, which then merged into a new general-purpose version! Capacity and performance differ between standard and premium, and the exact numbers will change over time, so checking the Azure limits page is the best option:

```
https://docs.microsoft.com/azure/azure-subscription-service-limits#storage-limits
```

At the time of writing, a standard file share has a maximum capacity of 100 TB. For performance, standard has a flat number of IOPS and throughput. Premium performance increases linearly with capacity. The larger the provisioned storage (you pay for provisioned size, not data written), the higher the IOPS and throughput. Therefore, for premium, the capacity provisioned will not be only driven by the amount of data to store; you will need to identify required IOPS and throughput (remember throughput is the number of IO operations and the size of those operations, which could be small or large, depending on workload) and provision size that meets all requirements.

Security

The storage account key is often used for connections to an Azure Files share. By default, if you look at the connect option for a file share, it will show the PowerShell and command-line option to connect with the storage account name as the username and the storage account key as the password. For example:

```
net use Z: \\saeastusazfiles.file.core.windows.net\data ↵
/u:AZURE\saeastusazfiles lpa8nGE1kYNBMw==
```

Remember that to make this connection outside of the region, you must use SMB 3.0, which requires port 445. To test if port 445 is open, use the Test-NetConnection PowerShell cmdlet (or Telnet). For example:

```
Test-NetConnection -ComputerName savtestazurefileswestus.file.core.windows.net
-Port 445
ComputerName      : savtestazurefileswestus.file.core.windows.net
RemoteAddress     : 52.239.153.8
RemotePort        : 445
InterfaceAlias    : Primary NIC
SourceAddress     : 10.7.30.108
TcpTestSucceeded  : True
```

If this fails, then port 445 is not available and the connection will not work. Remember the use of port 445 is because encrypted SMB is utilized, which is critical when traveling over the Internet or outside the native region. By setting secure transfer on the storage account, encryption will be required even for intra-region communications. Remember, as a PaaS service, storage accounts also support features like service endpoints, enabling access only for specific subnets, IP addresses, and even having a private IP directly on the VNet. A secure VPN tunnel can also be leveraged to access if port 445 is blocked by adding a route to the IP of the storage account.

If connecting to the Azure Files share using the REST APIs (which include things like PowerShell), then the communication goes over the regular RESTful endpoint (i.e., port 443, which is open in most environments). In addition to using the storage account key, the RESTful interface can also use shared access signatures for more granular security—for example, granting access only to specific shares and files in addition to limiting the timespan for the access. Following is an example of interacting with Azure Files using the REST API via PowerShell (i.e., over port 443). Remember, if Azure File Sync is used, then port 445 is not leveraged.

```
$s = New-AzureStorageShare images -Context $StrContext
New-AzureStorageDirectory -Share $s -Path jpg
Set-AzureStorageFileContent -Share $s -Source <file> -Path jpg
Get-AzureStorageFile -Share $s -Path jpg | Get-AzureStorageFile
```

If instead the share were simply mounted, the same actions could be performed, but now it would be via SMB as normal filesystem operations.

Another option for security around Azure Files shares and the contents is through integration with Azure AD. At the time of writing, this is the first release of this interaction, so there are several limitations, which I suspect will be removed in the future. The integration works through Azure AD Domain Services, which is the managed AD DS instance that can be deployed to a virtual network, and through the managed instance, which supports Kerberos, NTLM, LDAP, and other AD DS capabilities. The current requirements are as follows:

◆ The connection to the Azure Files share must be joined to the AAD DS domain and be on the virtual network that AAD DS is deployed to (not a peered or connected network).

◆ The storage account must have been created post September 24, 2018.

◆ The file share cannot be part of a sync group. (I'll cover these soon.)

◆ The ACLs on the file share must be copied via Robocopy (with /copy:s to keep ACLs) or set via icacls, *not* via the GUI.

◆ The client OS must be Windows OS, and access is via a mapped drive.

To summarize the current implementation means today the Azure AD integration only works for machines deployed to a specific virtual network and joined to the AAD DS managed domain, and the ACLs must be set in a very specific way. I think these requirements will change quickly for integration with regular AD DS instances and across networks, making this applicable to a wider range of scenarios. The reason for the AAD DS integration first is that AAD DS provides a RESTful way to join the domain, avoiding some security challenges joining a domain from an Internet-based resource. However, there are solutions, such as offline domain join, to solve this. The storage account has to have an account in the domain to enable the interaction for authentication and authorization. Figure 6.8 shows this account in the managed AAD DS instance. I would also expect to see the limitations around setting the ACLs and not being part of a sync group to be removed, but, once again, that is speculation. As you read this, these requirements may be removed and the AAD integration could be seamless!

FIGURE 6.8

The computer account for the storage account in my managed AAD DS instance

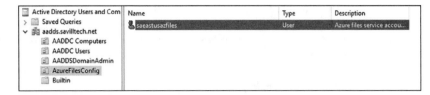

Remember that there are two levels of interaction for file shares: permissions on the file share itself and then the file and folder objects. To set the share permissions, a custom role is created. In the following example, it is a change permissions role (which is normal; restrictions typically are enforced at the filesystem and not the share):

```
{
  "Name": "StorageShareChange",
  "Id": null,
  "IsCustom": true,
  "Description": "Allows for read, write and delete access to Azure File Share
over SMB",
  "Actions": [
        "*"
],
  "NotActions": [
        "Microsoft.Authorization/*/Delete",
"Microsoft.Authorization/*/Write",
        "Microsoft.Authorization/elevateAccess/Action"
  ],
  "DataActions": [
        "*"
],
  "AssignableScopes": [
        "/subscriptions/<subscription ID>"
]
}
```

The role is created and then assigned. For example:

```
New-AzRoleDefinition -InputFile azurefilesharechangerole.json

#Assign to admin, bruce and clark
#Get the name of the custom role
$FileShareContributorRole = Get-AzRoleDefinition "StorageShareChange"

#Constrain the scope to the target file share
$scope = "/subscriptions/<sub
ID>/resourceGroups/RGEastUS/providers/Microsoft.Storage/storageAccounts/saeastu
sazfiles/fileServices/default/fileshare/data"

#Assign the custom role to the target identity with the specified scope.
New-AzRoleAssignment -SignInName admin@savilltech.net `
-RoleDefinitionName $FileShareContributorRole.Name -Scope $scope
New-AzRoleAssignment -SignInName bruce@savilltech.net `
-RoleDefinitionName $FileShareContributorRole.Name -Scope $scope
```

Once the share permissions are set, the files and folders can be populated and ACL'd either via Robocopy or by setting through tools such as icacls (at the time of writing). Note that for superuser type ACL operations, you need to connect as the storage account key, not as an AAD user.

Snapshots and Backup

Snapshots enable a point-in-time delta copy of a file share to be taken. The delta nature means only the changes are stored, rather than a complete copy, which impacts storage charges. Snapshots are read-only and can be interacted with through various means, including the native Windows Explorer's previous versions. To restore small amounts of data, the best option is to mount the snapshot and just copy the data. If it's a large amount of data, then leverage the portal or API, which has a more optimal large data copy capability. At the time of writing, 200 snapshots are supported per file share. If you delete the file share, then all snapshots are also deleted (since they are only deltas).

Azure Files can also interact with Azure Backup. This provides separate storage of the content into a recovery vault, with the backup managed by Azure Backup. Like a snapshot, it is possible to restore individual files or folders in addition to the entire share. Data can be restored to the original location or to an alternate location, as shown in Figure 6.9.

FIGURE 6.9
Restore options for a file restore

Azure File Sync

The Azure Files solution provides an SMB service in the cloud, which, as we have seen, can be accessed from remote regions and other locations using SMB 3. However, many organizations already have SMB deployments running on Windows file servers on premises and are looking to address challenges today around replication of data and providing a copy of the data off premises for disaster recovery purposes. Azure File Sync meets this need by providing a service to store a copy of the data in the cloud and synchronize the content between replicas running on

Windows file servers. The Windows file servers can offer the content replicated via SMB, which is the norm for a Windows file share, but could also offer the content using other protocols, such as NFS or even FTP.

An agent is deployed to the Windows file server. By default, the agent can auto-update via Microsoft Update but can also be updated manually via a special Azure File Sync updater tool, via a patch, or by installing the latest version. A Storage Sync Service instance is created in Azure, and the Windows server agents are registered to the Storage Sync Service instance. One or more sync groups are created within the Storage Sync Service instance. A sync group consists of the following:

◆ An Azure Files share in the same region as the Storage Sync Service instance (only one Azure file share), known as the *cloud endpoint*.

◆ One or more registered server locations (folders), known as *server endpoints*. At the time of writing, up to 50 server endpoints can be in a single sync group.

Additionally, as part of the endpoint configuration, cloud tiering can be configured. This enables infrequently accessed files to be removed from the local storage of the endpoint and instead a thumbprint remains that represents the now cloud-tiered file. This is transparent for users accessing the share. If a user tries to access a cloud-tiered file on the local file server, the data is automatically fetched and stored locally again. The tiering is based on a specified free space percentage for the server and optionally only keeping files accessed or modified within a certain number of days. When the free space drops below this target, the less recently accessed data is tiered to the cloud, along with files not accessed or modified based on the number of days if that is configured, as shown in Figure 6.10. Note that the cloud tiering option is configured per endpoint, not at the registered server level. A single registered server can contain endpoints for multiple sync groups.

FIGURE 6.10
Endpoint cloud tiering options

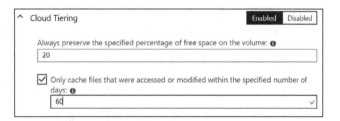

The replication of data is via the Azure Files share instance, not server-to-server. As data is created on a file server, it replicates to the Azure Files share and then replicates to the other server endpoints, as shown in Figure 6.11. Data can also be created directly on the Azure Files share, which then replicates to the endpoints. However, you will notice a delay in replication if you do this, as while change notifications exist for on-premises file servers, enabling replication quickly, this does not exist for Azure Files shares; instead, a scheduled job detects direct changes on Azure Files shares. Note that connectivity is over port 443, which means special firewall exceptions should not be required.

FIGURE 6.11
Replication of
data in a sync
group

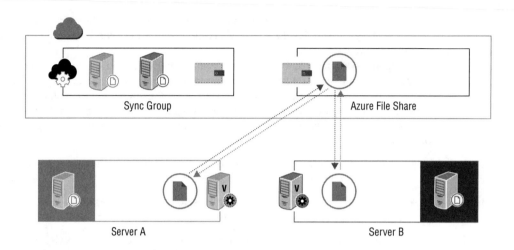

When you are planning for replication bandwidth consumption, there are two primary methods outside of the networking stack. If the file server is running in a VM, you can utilize hypervisor QoS to control bandwidth, but that would be all network traffic and not targeted at the sync traffic. The better way is to use the storage sync agent's QoS capabilities, which enable an amount of bandwidth at specific times to be defined for the sync traffic. For example, to limit the traffic to 20 Mbps during working hours, use the following:

```
New-StorageSyncNetworkLimit -Day Monday, Tuesday, Wednesday, Thursday, Friday `
    -StartHour 7 -EndHour 18 -LimitKbps 20000
```

NTFS ACLs are replicated from Windows file servers and are maintained on the Azure Files share as metadata, and are then synchronized to the other file servers that are part of the sync group. Note that the ACLs are not currently enforced on the Azure Files share. As previously mentioned, the Azure AD integration today only works for machines joined to Azure AD Domain Services, not for files synchronized via Azure File Sync. This means that if you want to use Azure for disaster recovery of the content to make it usable with ACLs enforced, you would create a Windows VM, create a file server on that VM that is joined to the sync group, and have users access that file server. When the requirement for an AAD DS join is removed and ACLs from Azure File Sync are supported, then access directly to the Azure File share would be possible.

There are some considerations when leveraging Azure File Sync, especially when using tiering, which is based on data being accessed. Avoid actions that would cause data to be pulled down from the cloud unnecessarily—for example, running a full antivirus scan on the server of from end-user connections (although work is being done with antivirus vendors to not cause recall, so check with your vendor for compatibility with tiering) or performing a backup from on premises. Be careful when attempting to combine Azure File Sync with other data replication technologies, such as DFS-R, as unforeseen results may be seen. If tiering is used, the full copy of data will only be in the Azure file share and not on premises. Remember to leverage Azure Backup to protect the cloud endpoint—i.e., the Azure Files share.

Storage with Azure VMs

This section will explore how storage can be leveraged with Azure IaaS virtual machines, which also applies to VM-based services, such as virtual machine scale sets and more. Only storage services directly related to VMs are covered in this section, but remember that other types of storage service can be utilized by workloads running inside the VM, like any other application service.

VM Storage Basics

When talking about virtual machines, it's often useful to take a step back and think about what a virtual machine is in Azure. I think about it as two parts:

- Metadata about the VM, which describes its size, name, and other resources it may use, such as NICs, extensions, and disks. When the VM is running, there are compute resources utilized on the node the VM is provisioned on.

- The disks of the VM, which include its operating system disk and any data disks. The durable storage of the VM is stored in Azure Storage on storage stamps separate from the compute stamps. There is also an amount of temporary storage, which again is housed on the node the VM is provisioned on.

The OS disk and the data disks are really the most important parts of a VM. As long as you have the storage of the VM, you can re-create it quite easily. There is nothing that unique about the metadata. When we think of the direct storage for a VM, it is the durable disks stored in Azure Storage and its temporary storage that are local to the node the VM is running on. This is shown in Figure 6.12. The C: drive is the OS disk, and the D: drive is the temporary drive, which by default is D: (but can be changed), while additional data drives can surface as drive letters or mounted folders. Note that I am talking about drives on a Windows guest OS. For Linux, the various disks would surface as mount points.

FIGURE 6.12
The storage of an Azure VM

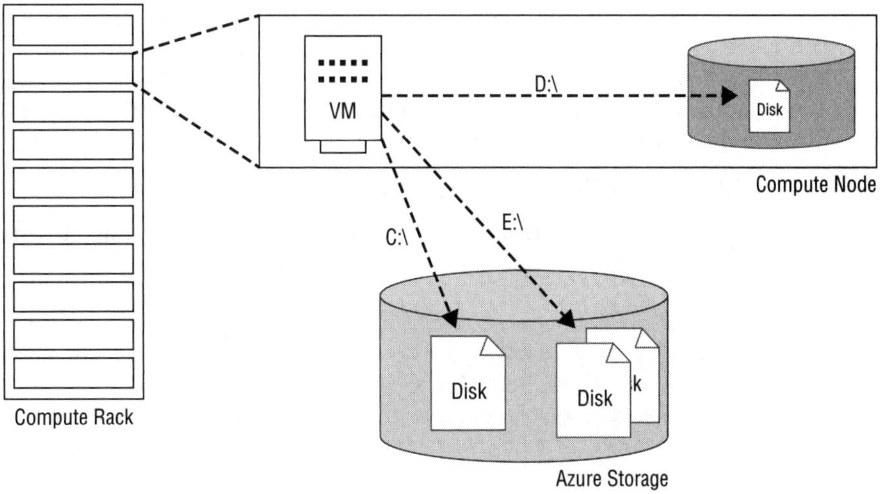

Compute Rack

Compute Node

Azure Storage

Different caching options can be configured on a per-disk basis, as many different workloads have different sensitivity and compatibility with caching. Remember, you should never place data on the OS disk. Always add data disks to the VM and store data on those data disks. The caching options per-disk are as follows:

- **Read & Write Caching**—This is the default for OS disks but can be changed to read-only if desired.

- **Read Caching**—This is a common setting for database disks.

- **No Caching**—All read and write operations are pass-through with no caching.

You should research the guidelines for your workloads when configuring the desired caching option. Enabling caching will result in much lower latencies for operations compared to operations being serviced by Azure Storage.

When you are architecting storage for VMs, note that there are metrics at the fabric level and within the guest OS. This enables throughput to be seen, queue depths, latencies, and much more. Metrics are critical when planning and right sizing workloads, so take some time to look at those available via Azure and then within the guest OS.

Temporary Storage

As Figure 6.12 shows, each VM has a certain amount of temporary storage that is provisioned from storage local to the host where the VM is running. Because this storage is local to the host, its content could be lost at any time and is considered non-durable. If you resize the VM, deprovision the VM (shut down from the portal/API), or if there is some kind of host problem, the content of the temporary drive will be lost. For Windows VMs, this temporary drive is D:\ by default and contains the pagefile. There is also a data loss warning file written to the root of the drive, DATALOSS_WARNING_README.txt, to try and raise awareness to users of the temporary nature of the storage. For Linux VMs, the temporary drive typically is available as /dev/sdb1.

That the storage is not durable does not mean you shouldn't use it. It just means don't store data on it that you can't afford to lose, but it can be very useful for temporary data or as a cache, populated from a durable storage location. For example, it's very common to use the temporary drive for database purposes, such as storing TempDB, and even for buffer pool extensions. Note that some steps may be required at startup to create the required folder structures on the temporary drive, since it may have been re-created. I've seen startup jobs that:

1. Check if the folders are present.

2. If the folders are not present, create them and ensure that the correct ACLs are in place.

3. Start the services, such as SQL Server. (The services are set to manual as opposed to automatic.)

The temporary drive's capacity and performance vary, depending on the SKU and size of the virtual machine. Like all VM services, the resources available vary depending on the SKU and size. The bigger the VM, typically the more resources in terms of CPU, memory, network, and temporary drive.

Two types of temporary storage are available, which are based on the SKU of the VM:

◆ **HDD** - Regular spinning disks. This is used for A (v1 only) series VMs.

◆ **SSD** - Lower latency and higher performing solid-state disks. All SKUs apart from the A (v1) series

Additionally, the Lsv2 series VMs also have a number of NVMe drives directly mapped to them to provide very low latency storage with very high IOPS and throughput. The largest Lsv2 has 10 1.92 TB NVMe disks available, providing 3.8 million read IOPS with 20,000 MBps of throughput. Like the temporary storage, this is ephemeral and will be lost if the VM is deallocated, resized, etc. This storage is in addition to the normal temporary storage.

Realistically, I don't think many people are using Av1 VMs anymore, which means the temporary storage is SSD-based, and because it is local to the host, the latency is very low. The exact available IOPS and throughput vary based on the SKU and size. Those details are all listed on the VM types and sizes page at:

```
https://docs.microsoft.com/en-us/azure/virtual-machines/windows/sizes
```

Note that the amount of temporary storage for the -s variants of VMs (for example, DS) is lower than the non-s variants, since a portion of that temporary storage is used for caching purposes. For example, the D2_v3 has 50 GB of temporary storage, whereas the DS2_v2 has 7 GB of temporary storage. The other 43 GB are used for caching related to the premium storage that is supported.

Managed Disks

As mentioned previously, it is possible to create unmanaged storage, which is a VHD in a page blob in a customer managed storage account. While this option is available, it really is not recommended, as it has no real benefit compared to managed disks. Therefore, as you plan your deployments, you should leverage managed disks, which provide a first-class Azure resource that is fully managed, RBAC, better availability in conjunction with availability sets, and more. Managed disks will therefore be the focus for VM storage. Managed disks still leverage storage accounts, but these are automatically managed and hidden from the customer. Remember, however, that these disks are still running on separate storage clusters from the compute clusters that run the actual VMs.

MANAGED DISK SKUs

Four types of managed disks are available and come in various sizes related to capacity, IOPS, and throughput. The main types are as follows:

◆ **Standard HDD**—Aimed for non-critical and non-production data with latency common to HDD drives. IOPS numbers are maximums, not guaranteed.

◆ **Standard SSD**—Lightly used enterprise applications. IOPS numbers are maximums, not guaranteed. Lower latency than Standard HDD, typically in single millisecond ranges

◆ **Premium SSD**—Aimed for production and performance workloads. IOPS numbers are provisioned and guaranteed.

◆ **Ultra SSD**—Highest levels of performance with capacity. IOPS numbers and throughput are separate dials. For example, once you hit 1 TB in size, it is possible to configure 160,000 IOPS and 2,000 Mbps, or you can continue to scale up capacity up to 64 TB in size.

For all the managed disks, the capacity, IOPS, and throughput typically scale lineally—i.e., as capacity increases, so do the IOPS and throughput. The exception is Ultra SSD, which allows each attribute to be dynamically adjusted independently. For details on the disks, review the following:

```
https://docs.microsoft.com/en-us/azure/virtual-machines/windows/
disk-scalability-targets
```

```
https://docs.microsoft.com/en-us/azure/virtual-machines/windows/disks-types
```

The links talk about the SKUs available and the capacity, IOPS, and throughput available. At the time of writing, all SKUs (apart from Ultra SSD, which scales up to 64 TB) max out at 32 TB. Remember that for managed disks, you pay for the disk SKU, not for the amount of data written.

A single VM can have a mix of disk types, including the OS and data disks. Note that to use a premium disk, the VM must be an s variant—e.g., DS, ES, etc. A premium disk is Premium SSD or Ultra SSD. Both Standard HDD and Standard SSD do not require the s variant.

PERFORMANCE CONSIDERATIONS

I want to look at a little more detail to get an idea of how the scalability changes. Note that these numbers could change, so always check the Azure documentation, but the current numbers help you to understand how the offerings work. The smallest Premium SSD is the P4, which is 32 GB in size, 120 IOPS, and up to 25 Mbps. The largest Premium SSD is the P80, which is 32 TB in size, 20,000 IOPS, and 900 Mbps. As you can see, a wide range of offerings is available, and the SKU you pick will be driven by your storage requirements, which will be a combination of IOPS, throughput, and capacity. You need to ensure that the disk you purchase meets all your requirements. For example, you may only need 2 TB of storage but require 16,000 IOPS. This would require you to purchase the P60, which is actually 8 TB in capacity.

If a single disk cannot meet your requirements, then you can add multiple disks to the VM and then aggregate capacity and performance across them. You do not need to leverage RAID or other resiliency technologies. Typically, we use mirroring or parity because we have a number of separate disks that could fail, and then we would lose all the data. The managed disks are on Azure Storage, which has three copies of the blocks. Therefore, we don't need to worry about disk failure, which means no resiliency within the guest. Use simple striping via Storage Spaces (for Windows VMs) or native logical volumes in Linux. The resulting volume will have the aggregated capacity and performance of the separate managed disks. Another option is to use an application's native ability to leverage multiple disks. For example, SQL Server can use separate disks and split the database across them. Data disks can be hot added and removed from Azure IaaS VMs—i.e., we don't need to shut down the VM to add or remove data disks. The exact number of data disks that can be added to a VM varies based on the SKU and size along with the number of IOPS and throughput supported by the VM, which brings us to an important point when thinking about storage performance from an IaaS VM.

Up to this point, the focus has been on the disk—the capacity of the disk, the IOPS of the disk, and the throughput of the disk (with the throughput being the IOPS x IO size). Like everything else, the VM has its own limits around storage performance, which means just adding storage to a VM may not yield the desired performance, as the VM's own limits may be the bottleneck, not the storage. Just like a disk, the VM also has capacity, IOPS, and throughput limits, which are documents in the VM sizes site. This means when determining the resource requirements, you not only need to consider the SKU, size, and number of managed disks but also the right VM SKU and size to connect them to, since you need the VM to not have lower limits than the storage attached.

As an example, the DS3_v2 was chosen, as it meets the CPU and memory requirements of the workload: 4 vCPUs and 14 GB of memory. It also supports 16 data drives with 12,800 IOPS and 192 MBps throughput. (There are separate cached and temporary storage numbers to consider if caching can be enabled.) The customer plans to add two P60 disks to the VM. Each P60 supports 16,000 IOPS and 500 MBps. As you can see, even one of these disks exceeds the capability of the VM; instead, the DS4_v2 may better meet needs that support 25,600 IOPS or another SKU entirely that is more storage-focused. The key point is to remember that when it comes to planning storage, you must consider both the disk's and the VM's capabilities.

One of the great features of a managed disk is that you can change its SKU. For example, it can be moved from Standard HDD to Premium SSD, and only a reboot of the VM is required to complete the change. Before managed disks, trying to change the performance of a disk would require a copy of the page blob between storage accounts and multiple operations on the VM. It is also possible to convert unmanaged disks to managed disks with minimal downtime. Remember, if you are changing from standard to premium, the VM must be of an SKU that supports premium storage (i.e., the s variant—for example, DS, ES, etc.).

AVAILABILITY SET AND AVAILABILITY ZONE RESILIENCY

Availability sets provide resiliency for VM-based services by spreading the VMs over three fault domains, which can be thought of as racks in a datacenter. (This will be covered in detail in the next chapter.) The distribution of the compute provides protection from a node or rack failure; however, until managed disks, there was no way to know the actual storage of the VMs were spread out over separate storage clusters, as if all the storage were on one storage cluster that had an issue, then all of the VMs would be unavailable. No storage means no VM. With managed disks, an aligned mode is utilized for the availability set. This means for each fault domain, a separate storage cluster is utilized for the disks associated with the VMs, as shown in Figure 6.13. This provides the optimal resiliency within a datacenter. Note that for some regions, only two fault domains are available, instead of the normal three when using aligned mode. This is documented at:

https://docs.microsoft.com/en-us/azure/virtual-machines/windows/manage-availability

Another approach is to use availability zones for workloads. The disks should be placed in the same datacenter as the VMs to optimize latency and match the resiliency target of the VM, providing resiliency at a datacenter level instead of at a rack level. Managed disks are one of the services, along with VMs, that support availability zones and are zonal, which means they can be deployed to a specific zone.

FIGURE 6.13
Availability sets with aligned managed disks

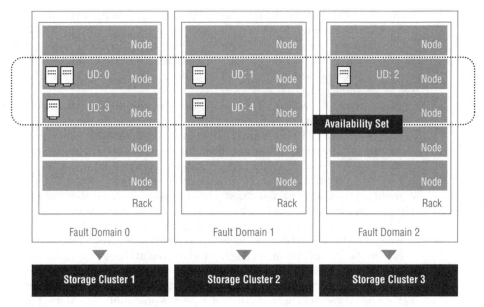

WRITE ACCELERATION

Write Accelerator, at the time of writing, is a feature available for M-series virtual machines that use premium managed disks. The goal is to improve latency of write operations for premium managed disks through the utilization of a three-way replicated, durable write buffer. To use write acceleration, the disk must not have write caching enabled and the I/O size must be less than 512 KB. There are also limits on the number of disks that can be write accelerated, which are documented at:

```
https://docs.microsoft.com/en-us/azure/virtual-machines/windows/
how-to-enable-write-accelerator
```

This should be used for applications that are latency-rather than throughput-bound. Workloads such as databases that use a write log or journal that need to wait for the IO to complete before completing the transaction can be a good fit providing they do not parallelize the IO (which means they would be throughput-rather than latency-bound). Database products such as SAP HANA, MongoDB, and MySQL tend to be latency-bound, as they support less parallel IO compared to databases like Microsoft SQL Server that tend to be throughput-bound because it supports parallel log writes. This means the first set of databases would be a good fit for write acceleration, whereas Microsoft SQL Server would not benefit as much (but may still benefit, depending on other factors, such as throughput). Because of the way write acceleration works, it has a throughput limit, which will be a key factor in deciding if write acceleration will help (or potentially hurt) the workload.

In summary, use write acceleration if:

◆ Low write latency is necessary to support low application response time or high application throughput.

◆ Application write throughput (IOPS) will not exceed the write acceleration throughput limit.

MANAGED DISK SNAPSHOTS

One feature missing from unmanaged storage was the ability to have snapshots, point-in-time read-only copies of a disk. There were some workarounds using blob snapshots; however, they were cumbersome to use. With managed disks, there is native snapshot capability available that provides a read-only copy of a managed disk, which is stored as a standard managed disk regardless of the source disk type, to optimize cost. (There is no reason to have a high-performance snapshot.)

Managed disk snapshots are independent of the source disk, which means the source disk can be deleted without impacting the snapshots. Unlike regular managed disks, with managed disk snapshots, you only pay for the data written, not the size of the disk. Note that a snapshot creation does not trigger any kind of VSS within the VM. This means the snapshot is crash-consistent, not application-consistent. Also note that a snapshot is of a disk. If a VM has multiple disks, each snapshot would be its own separate entity, with no relationship to each other. New VMs can be created from a snapshot, or disks from the source VM can be switched with a snapshot using the OS disk swap capability.

MANAGED IMAGES

In many cases, images from the marketplace will be used as the foundation for VMs that are created. These images are curated and maintained, which includes having the latest updates applied to them. Environment-specific configurations, such as application deployments, can be layered on at deployment time through various methods—for example, using declarative technologies such as PowerShell DSC, Chef, or Puppet. There may also be circumstances where custom images are required with certain configurations pre-applied. Where possible, try to avoid these, as it means maintaining the image, such as keeping it patched, although there may be instances where it's required. A managed image can be created that consists of the disks of the VM (stored on standard storage to minimize cost) along with the VM configuration. The disks of the image must contain the OS disk and can optionally contain the data disks. When creating an image, if it is of a Windows VM, the source must be generalized (using SYSPREP) prior to the capture of the image. Once the image is created, it will be available as the source for new VMs to be created from.

Notice the difference between images and snapshots. Snapshots are point-in-time copies of a single disk. Images contain the VM configuration and all disks (if requested) in a generalized format. Creating a VM from a snapshot would be that single disk; creating a VM from an image contains the VM configuration in addition to all associated disks.

If you have an environment with multiple subscriptions or use many regions, the management of images can be complex, as you want the images you create available in different regions and also across subscriptions. Under normal circumstances, you would have to copy the images across regions and subscriptions. A shared image gallery capability is available, providing storage of VM images (OS, configuration, and optionally data disks), or just OS images, which can be shared across subscriptions. The concept of versions is added to the images, enabling multiple versions to be available. In addition to being able to configure replication to other regions of the images, it is also possible to specify a number of replicas within a region. This is useful if you have an image that will form the source for a large number of new VMs to be created where trying to duplicate 100s of new copies from one source may delay processing. By scaling to multiple replicas of the image, higher concurrent deployments can be achieved. ACLs are supported on the image repository, enabling granular access as required.

Bulk Data Options

Azure has numerous ways to access the storage services. This access can be by using the public endpoints over the Internet or ExpressRoute via Microsoft peering. Additionally exposing services to virtual networks enables access to storage from the resources on the virtual network or connected to the virtual network. There may also be times when the amount of data to be imported (or exported) is not practical through any online mechanism due to the volume of data. While very large throughput solutions are available, such as 10 Gbps for regular ExpressRoute or 100 Gbps for ExpressRoute Direct, if a data transfer is a one-time requirement or very infrequent, the establishment of higher throughput communications may not make sense.

Azure Import/Export and Azure Data Box Disk

Azure Import/Export is the original offline service for importing and exporting Azure data. The service enables customer-owned disks to be prepared for the data transfer process (encryption via BitLocker) and then data copied to the disks, which are then sent to a specified Azure datacenter where the data is imported into Azure Blob or Azure Files storage (after which the disks are returned). Data can also be copied from Azure Blob (but not Azure Files) to disks for export purposes. If a customer wants to use Microsoft-provided disks, then Azure Data Box Disk can be leveraged which are solid-state disks provided by Microsoft that are shipped to the customer. The customer copies the data (once again BitLocker encrypted) and the data imported into blob storage. Azure Data Box Disk is only available for import purposes.

There are limits on the size of disks, the number of disks per job, and the number of jobs per customer. These change over time, so refer to the Microsoft documentation to confirm the current limitations.

Azure Data Box

If copying data to individual disks is not practical due to the amount of data, another option is to use Azure Data Box or Azure Data Box Heavy. These are devices shipped to the customer with very large capacities. At the time of writing, Azure Data Box supports up to 100 TB, while the Data Box Heavy SKU supports up to 1 PB. Customers place an order, and the unit ships to their location, where data is copied to the device (which is encrypted using AES 256-bit encryption), which is then shipped back to the datacenter where the data is uploaded. Like the Import/Export option, data can be imported into Blob or Files, and like Azure Data Box Disk, these are only for import purposes.

The appliance is connected to the customer's network via RJ 45 (an Ethernet connection) or SFP+ (QSFP+ for the Heavy version) for fiber optic connectivity. The minimum recommended connectivity speed on premises to the device is 10 Gbps to optimize data transfer. Once the appliance is connected and configured, data can be copied via SMB or NFS to the device.

Once the data has been imported, any data is securely erased in accordance with NIST 800-88r1 standards.

Azure Data Box Gateway and Data Box Edge

These are appliances that act as storage gateways (and more) that sit inside the customers' networks and transfer data to storage services in Azure. This still requires network connectivity; however, the data experience can be improved via caching and/or data preparation to potentially reduce the data that is sent over the network.

Azure Data Box Gateway is a virtual appliance deployed to a hypervisor on premises. It acts as a storage gateway, providing easy access to Azure storage services through the gateway using SMB or NFS. The device then transfers data to an Azure block blob, an Azure page blob, or Azure Files storage. A local cache on the gateway enables high ingestion rates, and the data is then sent to Azure as the available network capacity allows or the allowed capacity allows. (Throttling is configurable to avoid the gateway interfering with other workloads on the network.) Data is also cached on the device (to a certain threshold), providing improved read performance of that cached data. The Data Box Gateway can be used for a single large data ingestion to Azure or as part of a continuous data-ingestion requirement. Shares are created on the device, with each share enabling the configuration of how data is stored in Azure—i.e., block blob vs. page blob vs. files.

Azure Data Box Edge has the same storage capabilities as Azure Data Box Gateway but also includes edge compute capabilities. Azure Data Box Edge is a 1U appliance that is deployed on premises. It is part of a service billed to your Azure subscription. The goal of the Edge device is to provide data pre-processing, optimizing data before being sent to the cloud, but it also has machine learning inferencing available. Inside the device is the Brainwave FPGA, which is used for accelerating machine learning and enables a number of key Azure edge services to be available locally—for example, vision cognitive services (and more).

The Azure Data Box Edge uses IoT Edge to enable it to run containers where actual workloads will run. Like the Azure Data Box Gateway, it supports SMB and NFS interactions, where data is then transferred to the cloud; however, its local capabilities make it a very useful edge compute solution. This will commonly result in modification to the data or even reducing down the set of data that needs to be stored in the cloud.

Note that in some scenarios, the Edge may be used simply as a cloud-managed compute device without any data interactions with the cloud, other than the management and deployment of updated containers. Because of its hardware capabilities, including the Brainwave FPGA, it can meet a number of local scenarios where compute is required, including machine learning integration.

Azure Database Offerings

An in-depth examination of database offerings in Azure is outside the scope of this book, but I want to touch on two key database services in Azure: Azure SQL Database and Cosmos DB. Note that there are other offerings for databases such as PostgreSQL, MySQL, and MariaDB, which are offered as fully managed, enterprise-ready community versions of Database as a Service in Azure. There are more, but I am going to focus on what I consider the two main offerings that many organizations leverage.

Azure SQL Database

Microsoft SQL Server is a relational database offering where data is stored in tables that are made up of rows and columns based on a strict schema. Rows represent items, whereas columns represent attributes. Each table has a primary key, which must be unique within the table and can be used to quickly locate data, along with other indexed values that are often used for referencing or searching. Microsoft SQL Server is available in various SKUs and utilizes the Structured Query Language (SQL) to query and maintain the database. Many features are available, including replication, analytics, encryption, and security.

Microsoft SQL Server can be installed in an IaaS VM, and there are images in the marketplace that have Microsoft SQL Server pre-configured with options to bring your own license or lease the license from Azure. When deploying Microsoft SQL Server in an IaaS VM, you should always use Premium storage for the database and logs. The SSD temporary drive of all the series except the A is commonly used for TempDB and buffer pool extension. While deploying to an IaaS VM makes SQL Server available in the cloud, you are still responsible for all the management and tuning of SQL Server. You still need to patch, upgrade, tune, worry about IOPS, configure replication, enable backups, etc. You also have full access to all SQL functionality and configuration options.

Azure SQL Database is a managed PaaS offering based on Microsoft SQL Server. This provides an evergreen SQL environment running the latest SQL branch with a number of database compatibility levels available where specific functionality versions are required.

A number of different tiers and sizes are available, although the features are largely the same across tiers. The tiers and sizes impact the number of databases supported, the maximum size, and the performance. Azure SQL Database can be purchased in three models:

Managed Instance   This is a dedicated, managed instance of SQL Server deployed into your virtual network that provides the best compatibility for on-premises SQL workloads migrated to the cloud in addition to the broadest set of capabilities. Multiple database instances can be created within the managed instance and use the assigned resources. This has some features, such as SQL agent and cross-database queries, that are not available in the other models.

Single Database   A single database that can utilize the assigned resources. This works for workloads that have a predictable resource requirement, enabling the correct resources to be purchased.

Elastic Pool   Utilizes a shared resource model, enabling multiple databases to share the resources assigned to the elastic pool. This enables better overall utilization for databases with variable requirements.

Both the single database and elastic pool offerings are hosted in a multi-tenant environment separate from a customer's virtual networks; however, as covered in the networking chapter, there are numerous options for securing and integrating with virtual networks.

All the models enable features such as transparent data encryption and can be accessed like a regular SQL instance. For example, SQL Server Management Studio can be used to connect and create tables and to perform queries, and applications can use regular SQL interfaces. Authentication can be via SQL authentication or integration with Azure AD.

Once the model is selected, the actual resource is available in two options, vCore-based and DTU-based, where the managed instance only supports the vCore-based model. DTU was the original purchasing scheme for Azure SQL Database and utilizes a blend of the compute (CPU and memory), storage, and IO resources, which are expressed as a Database Transaction Unit (DTU). This means the compute and storage scale proportionally. These are known as *elastic DTU* (eDTU) when using elastic pool. The vCore model separates the compute and storage, enabling the independent scale of the resources. While the DTU model is simpler, if you have workloads that are more compute- or more storage-centric, you will end up paying more with the DTU model than separately paying for the resources via vCore model. Another benefit of the vCore model is that Hybrid Use Benefit can be used—i.e., you can utilize the Microsoft SQL Server licenses you already own to reduce costs. For details about all the options, review the pricing page at:

`https://azure.microsoft.com/en-us/pricing/details/sql-database/managed/`

There are some calculators to help assist in estimating DTU requirements at:

`http://dtucalculator.azurewebsites.net/`

Azure SQL Database provides 5-minute increment recovery points through a combination of database and log backups as a built-in capability. For basic SKUs, these are available for 7 days; for other SKUs, they are available for 35 days, with a customizable duration available for the vCore pricing model. There is also a long-term backup retention option for the single database and elastic pool (but not for a managed instance at the time of writing), which enables backups to be stored in Azure Blob storage for up to 10 years based on a retention policy you configure. Data can also be exported and imported via bacpac/dacpac. (bacpac contains schema and data, whereas dacpac is schema only).

Local HA within the region is automatically provided with sub 10-second failover for the basic, standard, and general-purpose tiers, and even faster through the use of SQL clusters with in-region replicas for premium/business critical tiers.

For resiliency between regions, it is possible to add up to four read-only asynchronous secondary replicas where in the event of a primary region failure, a replica can be promoted to the master and be writable. Note that it is possible to deploy read-only replicas to the same region as the primary. This may be done to improve read-scale at the region. It is also possible to layer on top of the replication failover groups, which provide capabilities such as automatic failover and read-write and read-only listeners for use by applications accessing the database.

The single-primary nature of Azure SQL database can prove restrictive for some modern applications that want to be deployed in multiple regions, because the database can only be written to at the primary region. There are various solutions, depending on the application's interaction with the database and tolerance for latency:

◆ The application can be deployed in multiple regions but all database interactions go to the primary instance across the network. Obviously, this may not be acceptable from a latency perspective for some workloads. There would be asynchronous replicas, which could be used in the event of a DR.

◆ The application can be enlightened to understand there is a writable copy of the database (read-write listener) and a read-only copy of the database (read-only listener). The application would have to be written that any read-after-writes always go to the primary (or risk getting stale data), while read-only transactions could be satisfied from the read-only replica. This may satisfy more applications where the writes are far less of the transactions compared to reads.

If you have applications that need extensive writes to local copies of the database, then Azure SQL Database is not going to be a good fit. But there is another option, if some re-architecture of the application is possible.

Azure Cosmos DB

Azure Cosmos DB was written from the ground up to be a cloud-scale database. It is not a relational database but rather a schema-agnostic, horizontally scalable data store with a comprehensive set of SLAs that covers performance (which is unique to Cosmos DB) and 99.999 percent high availability. Azure Cosmos DB is designed to be a globally distributed database with single-digit latency at the 99th percentile anywhere in the world and automatic homing. Replicas that can accept writes can be created in any Azure region with no limit on their number (other than the number of available regions in Azure).

I want to quickly cover something called the CAP theorem. This may seem strange, but when talking about geographically distributed data, it's very important. I think of it like asking for a job to get done:

◆   You can have it done fast.

◆   You can have it done well.

◆   You can have it done cheap.

Pick any two—i.e., you can't have all three. You can't have a job done fast and well and cheap. You can have it done fast and well, but it won't be cheap. You can have it done fast and cheap, but it won't be done very well. This applies to data and databases. For databases, the choices are as follows:

Consistency   Reads receive the most recent write from any node.

Availability   Every request receives a non-error response.

Partition Tolerance   The system continues to operate despite network interruption between nodes.

You can't have all three in a globally distributed database. You can't support breaks in the network (which is a must-have), always receive the latest data (which would require synchronous replication), and always get that response. Physics just do not allow this. You have to pick between either always getting data that may not be the latest *or* ensuring data integrity but with the risk of unavailability in case of a network partition. Traditional SQL Server focused on consistency and availability in a local network and could leverage synchronous replication since the nodes are close enough together for synchronous replication. This can't work over longer distances. SQL Server Always On (and therefore Azure SQL Database) sacrifices consistency, since the replicas may have older data. Azure Cosmos DB lets you choose the consistency level that best fits your business requirements.

The CAP theorem is fairly easy to understand, but there is another one named PACELC that builds on CAP and introduces the concept of choices between consistency and latency when there are not any network partitions—i.e., everything is running normally. The Azure Cosmos DB consistency levels let you pick how you want a database to handle consistency over a range, spanning from strong consistency to eventual consistency (with three other levels in between). The application developer can pick what is required from the database to enable the right access, as shown in Figure 6.14.

Strong – Linearizability   Once the operation is complete, it is guaranteed to be available to replicas. This only makes sense to use if you have a single write deployment. If you have multiple write deployments, you would use that model to enable lower latency writes which would mean waiting for replication to all instances would not be logical.

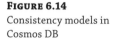

FIGURE 6.14
Consistency models in
Cosmos DB

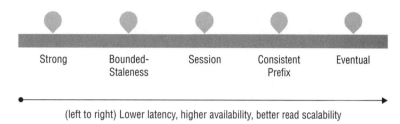

| Strong | Bounded-Staleness | Session | Consistent Prefix | Eventual |

(left to right) Lower latency, higher availability, better read scalability

Then you relax consistency to increase performance (lower latency) and increase availability.

Bounded Staleness   Replication will be in order; if have update 3, you are guaranteed to have 2 and 1. A staleness window based on a time and number of operations is configured. This option gives low latency with still fairly strong consistency.

Session   Provides strong consistency within a session, which means within your session you see consistency. A very popular option providing good throughput. This is based on a session token, which can be extracted from a session and given to other clients to have consistency from multiple clients.

Consistent Prefix   The only consistency guarantee is no out-of-order writes (no gaps).

Eventual   The only guarantee is replicas will eventually converge. Lowest possible latency

Remember that Cosmos DB is not a relational database. It supports a number of different data models, each of which leverage their own query mechanisms best suited for that model. Note that within the data itself, other formats are supported. For example, it's very common to store JSON in values of elements, which may be parsed to enable interactions with the values within the JSON. Following are the models supported by Cosmos DB, which would be something the application developers would investigate and pick based on their requirements. The APIs supported vary by the data model but include many common ones, such as MongoDB, Cassandra, Gremlin, Azure Tables, and more.

◆   Document

◆   Key-value

◆   Column

◆   Graph

If you have an existing application using a relational database like SQL Server, it will not be able to just switch to Cosmos DB without modification; however, the effort may be worthwhile if you want to enable the application to take advantage of the infinite scalability and geo-distributed nature of Cosmos DB.

Chapter 7

Azure Compute

This chapter focuses on infrastructure compute services—VMs, primarily, but also some of the other key compute services—to ensure that you are aware of the options available. While the IaaS functionality in Azure is very rich, it should not be considered "first choice" in many scenarios; instead, PaaS should be examined as a possible compute solution. By having knowledge of the possible options, you can make the right architectural decisions, although the focus of this chapter will be around the IaaS solutions.

In this chapter, you will learn to:

◆ Architect the right VM-based solution.

◆ Understand the role of containers and container services.

◆ Explain other types of PaaS solutions available in Azure.

Virtual Machines

As an infrastructure architect, you will think about the cloud as a virtual machine. While this is not wrong, there are many other solutions, which should be well understood to enable an architecture to be created that meets requirements in the most optimal way in terms of management overhead, cost, interoperability, and more. The majority of this chapter will focus on virtual machines; however, I would urge everyone to continue reading about the other services so that you're aware of all the possible options. Through these capabilities many richer services can be deployed—for example, high-performance computing and very large enterprise applications, such as SAP.

Fundamentals of IaaS

One reason IaaS is so popular as an initial cloud service to consume by customers is that it's easy to understand and relate to. Organizations have been using virtualization for years and understand the idea about taking a piece of hardware and dividing that hardware up into virtual machines that have a subset of the available resources assigned, primary CPU, memory, and storage, but there are other types of resources, such as network bandwidth. Virtual machines bring a number of benefits to organizations, with some of the primary ones being better utilization of hardware and faster provisioning of environments (since for each OS instance, a physical box no longer has to be racked). Largely, however, virtualization does not improve the operations of datacenters, as the OS instances still have to be patched, backed up, monitored, secured, etc. Remember those tasks as if we think of IaaS as a VM in the cloud—those responsibilities still apply (but I'm getting ahead of myself). Additionally, virtualization on its own still leaves islands of resources, which means unutilized resources, limited control and scale, and administrators still creating resources. The next step is a private cloud, where management services enable pooling of all resources with quota controls, show and charge back to business units, and even self-service. In my experience, very few companies actually moved from virtualization to a private cloud. Even if they say they have a private cloud, often it's just virtualization.

Think back to the layers of service and the responsibilities for IaaS, as shown in Figure 7.1. With IaaS VMs, the customer is responsible for everything within the guest, while Azure is responsible for providing the VM and the supporting fabric and hypervisor. I've had numerous customers ask me which hypervisor Azure uses, and I always respond, "Why do you care?" It's Infrastructure as a Service; the physical fabric (compute, storage, and network) and the hypervisor are the responsibility of Azure. As the customer, you get services that are enabled through those elements and the management layer. You get a VM of certain performance and capability. You get storage from the available storage services. You get networks from the network services. What is underneath is transparent to the customer. You're not responsible for those things, and you shouldn't want to know or care about them. IaaS frees you from those responsibilities. As a customer, all you really care about is that the service provides what you are paying for in terms of capability and SLA.

FIGURE 7.1
The layers for IaaS

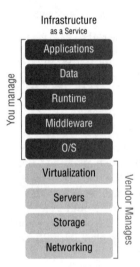

A common discussion point from customers I work with that I want to address up front is why use the cloud for VMs if they have hypervisors on premises. First, remember those responsibilities. By using the cloud, you remove a lot of responsibility around the fabric and hypervisor. You can focus on the OS and application, but there is a lot more than that.

Cost is often a major talking point, at least for now. Typically, the decision pivots on the fact that with the public cloud, you pay only for the service you consume. This is key in many scenarios, including the following:

◆ A service is needed only for a short term.

◆ The amount of service varies over time.

◆ It's not clear what the service need will be.

Although the public cloud is uniquely positioned for many of these fluctuating resource requirement scenarios, it may also be the case that the public cloud can deliver any service less expensively than you can offer it in your own datacenter. This can be a sobering thought for many datacenter administrators—who almost certainly will push back. "How can a company possibly offer a service cheaper than I can and still make a profit?" is a common response. But that argument does not consider the economies of scale achieved by mega-cloud providers like Microsoft and Amazon. I always think back to industrialization. Originally, factories generated their own power, but utilities were quickly established that could produce a better quality and cheaper power source. Computing will go the same way (and is there already compared to many organizations). You also must consider the various ways to provide service and resiliency. As I discussed previously in this book, on-premises' high availability of services is accomplished through expensive storage arrays and clusters of servers. Instead, through software, Azure ensures that all data is replicated within the datacenter and to another datacenter hundreds of miles away through various replication and synchronization options.

What constitutes the right mix of public cloud and on premises will differ for every organization. Some won't want to be in the business of running datacenters at all; they want to move everything to the cloud. Others, like the computer company that used Azure for Black Friday sales' web hosting, will focus on hybrid scenarios and supplement their on-premises resources with the public cloud when required. (That organization, in total, paid only a few hundred dollars for services to handle the entire day's sales traffic.) Still other organizations will use the public cloud in regions where they have no local datacenter but want to offer low latency services. Some will use Azure to enable disaster recovery for services.

When considering the costs of hosting on premises compared to in the public cloud, it can help to think about how some of the key costs can vary. Figure 7.2 is a small picture that I originally created on a whiteboard while talking to a customer who was convinced they could host anything less expensively than was possible in Azure. I wanted to be sure they were thinking about all the various aspects.

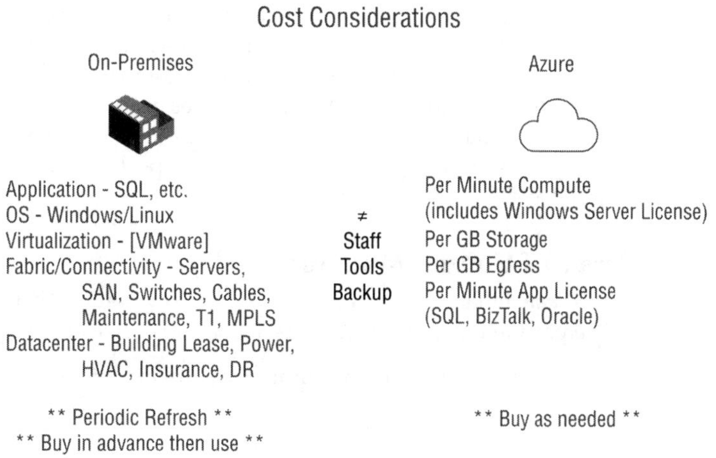

FIGURE 7.2
Key cost considerations for on premises and Azure

Cost Considerations

On-Premises

Azure

Application - SQL, etc.
OS - Windows/Linux
Virtualization - [VMware]
Fabric/Connectivity - Servers,
SAN, Switches, Cables,
Maintenance, T1, MPLS
Datacenter - Building Lease, Power,
HVAC, Insurance, DR

$\neq$
Staff
Tools
Backup

Per Minute Compute
(includes Windows Server License)
Per GB Storage
Per GB Egress
Per Minute App License
(SQL, BizTalk, Oracle)

** Periodic Refresh **
** Buy in advance then use **

** Buy as needed **

Ultimately, you should use the right solution for your organization. That could be on premises, hybrid, or the public cloud. Of course, price is not necessarily the deciding factor. Maybe you can host a service on premises less expensively, but will you have the same disaster recovery capabilities as available in Azure? Maybe you can host in the public cloud less expensively, but can Azure meet the regulatory requirement challenges you face? I'm not going to go into detail of the on-premises costs but rather think about Azure IaaS. In an Azure IaaS solution, there are no separate costs for the datacenter, power, HVAC, insurance, servers, network equipment, storage services, cables, virtualization software, or the management fabric needed to keep everything running. As a customer, you see various menu items for the services you wish to use, such as:

- Per-minute compute resources based on the size of the VM

- Per-minute Windows Server license (included in the price of Windows VMs in Azure with options to bring your own)

- Per GB of data storage used (Different tiers of storage and different types of storage are available.)

- Per GB of egress data (Data sent from Azure—there is no cost for ingress data to Azure.)

- Per-minute application license when applications such as SQL Server, BizTalk, or Oracle are used

The key point is that you pay only for the services you need. None of the physical plant or fabric costs associated with providing the services are exposed to you. They are baked into the costs for the services you buy. Remember that with an Azure IaaS solution, you are purchasing a VM and, optionally, certain applications. For the majority of instances, you will need to bring your own license for the applications you want to run on those VMs. You may also need to bring licenses for any Linux distributions you want to run in Azure. Finally, you will need to bring licenses for the software you want to use to manage the OS or other software running inside the Azure VMs.

Cost is not the only consideration. I find that the speed in which new services can be created in Azure is very appealing to customers, as are the huge number of regions available for the provisioning of services, in addition to all the security services natively available. Azure has a vast number of regulatory and compliance offerings, and I'll discuss where to find out more information on these in Chapter 12. In reality, most companies realize the benefits of the cloud and if they are not using it now, they are looking at what makes sense for them.

Remember that Azure VMs are a type of resource, and, like all Azure resources, they live within a resource group. An Azure VM relies on other Azure resources, such as NICs, which connect to virtual networks, and managed disks, for storage, among other things. When architecting your VMs, remember to consider all aspects of the solution, including connectivity (internal and public) and storage.

Types of Virtual Machines

I previously talked about what a VM is. The key point is that it's a collection of resources that can be used in place of a physical box. Some of the key resources are:

- CPU (type of processor, number of cores, use of hyperthreading)

- Memory

- Supported types and amount of storage plus non-durable temporary storage

- Number of NICs and throughput

- More advanced resources, including GPUs, enhanced networking, and more

VM Series

In Azure, there are various types and sizes of VMs, which are grouped into categories. With access to the hypervisor, you create a VM on premises to meet your needs in terms of numbers of cores, amount of memory, etc. You can't create a custom VM in Azure; instead, however, there are many different types to meet different requirements. For example, there are general-purpose VMs, with a typical core-to memory-ratio; compute-optimized VMs, with a higher core-to-memory ratio; memory-optimized VMs, with even higher memory-to core-ratios; storage-optimized VMs; GPU-optimized VMs; high-performance VMs—and the list goes on. Details on all the types of sizes available can be found at:

https://docs.microsoft.com/en-us/azure/virtual-machines/windows/sizes

I recommend going to the site and taking a look. You will notice that as the size gets bigger, the resources scale proportionally, which makes sense if you think about the physical resources. In Azure, there are datacenters full of servers. Those servers have certain amounts of resources and need to proportionally use those resources to avoid having wasted resources. That is why certain server clusters have larger amounts of CPUs, some larger amounts of memory, and so on, to support the different resource-optimized types of VMs.

The exact types (also known as *series*) of VMs change over time, but I wanted to briefly cover the key ones available at the time of writing and discuss any unique points about them. These are listed in Table 7.1.

TABLE 7.1:   Azure VM Series

TYPES	DESCRIPTION
A	General-purpose VMs with HDD temporary drive
B	Burstable VMs
D	SSD temporary drives with faster processors than A
E	Memory-optimized series with 8 GB of RAM and 16 GB of SSD per core
F	Compute-optimized series with 2 GB of RAM and 16 GB of SSD per core
G	Performance-compute series with massive scale and SSD temporary drives
H	High-performance VMs
Ls	Storage-optimized series with high throughput and IO
M	Largest VMs available in terms of CPU and memory
N	GPU capabilities for various types of workloads, including computational, visual, and deep learning

Source: https://docs.microsoft.com/en-us/azure/virtual-machines/windows/sizes

The A series was the original Azure VM offering, and the v1 is the only series that uses HDD for its temporary storage. This is no longer available, however, but has actually been split over the new Av2 and the H series. Previously, some of the A series (8–11) had RDMA network adapters offering very high-performance networking between instances and high numbers of CPUs for high-performance computing purposes. These are now offered within the H series.

Along with the Av2, the D, E, and F series offer various different types of optimized VMs to meet different requirements. As mentioned, the H series offers RDMA network adapters. The G and M series provide the largest VMs available in Azure.

There are also some variants that are constrained vCPUs, which may seem like a strange concept. These are found in the memory-optimized category. The reason for these constrained vCPU variants is that some workloads require very large amounts of memory with relatively low CPU requirements. The memory-optimized types already provide large amounts of memory, compared to the number of virtual CPUs. For example, the M8ms has eight vCPUs and 218.75 GB of memory. Ordinarily, it would be acceptable to simply not use all of the vCPUs available; however, there are many products that are licensed by vCPU count, which means they have eight vCPUs present that would require eight vCPUs of potentially very expensive licensing—for example, Oracle database. The vCPU-constrained variants cost the same but disable vCPUs at a hypervisor level from the OS. For example, the M8-2ms exposes only two vCPUs to the OS, instead of the normal eight, which means you're required to license only two vCPUs.

Then there are more specialized types, such as the N and Ls. The N series utilizes NVIDIA GPUs by attaching one or more cards to the VM. These are commonly used by CUDA- and OpenCL-based workloads. Variants of the N series— the NC, ND, and NV versions—are focused on compute, deep learning, and visualization. Different types of GPUs are utilized across the different variants that are best suited to the type of processing. The Ls series is optimized around storage, with directly mapped NVMe storage along with AMD EPYC processors. This NVMe storage is designed to be used for very high-performance local storage processing.

There is also the DC series, which is focused on confidential compute. This utilizes hardware to help protect the security of the workload—specifically, the Intel SGX, which enables enclaves (partitions) to be used to isolate code from other parts of the operating system. The DC is also UEFI-based (Generation 2 Hyper-V VM) instead of BIOS-based (Generation 1 Hyper-V VM).

Remember that VMs can have their size changed. While you should attempt to create VMs of the right series and size at creation time and, if migrating workloads, perform a right-sizing first based on performance data gathered, you can always tweak the size post creation. Azure Advisor is a free feature in Azure that will monitor resources and recommend actions to optimize spend. For example, if it sees a VM with more resources than it's using, it will recommend a resize.

VM PROCESSOR PROVISIONING

In an on-premises hypervisor environment, it is common to overprovision CPU resources. This means a host may have 2 physical processors with 8 cores each, which provides 16 cores. If these cores supported hyperthreading, that would result in 32 logical processors. On that host, 20 VMs may be created with 4 vCPUs each, resulting in a total logical processor commitment of 80, far exceeding the resources of the host. This is okay, as the hypervisor can time-slice the physical resources among the various workloads and, provided that all the vCPUs don't try and run at 100 percent at the same time, the normal distribution of processor workload should see all VMs receiving enough CPU. There are limits, of course, and part of planning on premises is ascertaining resource requirements and planning accordingly.

HYPERTHREADING ≠ DOUBLE PERFORMANCE

Hyperthreading does not double performance. Aspects of the processor are duplicated to enhance performance by enabling two sets of logical state per core. Typically, during a thread of execution, the core is not fully utilized for various reasons, such as a particular instruction stream only uses specific types of ALUs, leaving others unused, and more commonly, a cache miss, which causes the thread execution to stall while data is fetched. With hyperthreading and the two sets of logical state, if one thread is stalled because of a cache miss, the chances are good the other thread can execute. This therefore keeps the core better utilized and improves the overall performance. Notice that both threads are equal; there is not a big thread and a little thread. Which thread does more work just depends on how busy they are kept, the type of computations, the frequency of cache misses, etc. Thirty percent is a commonly accepted performance gain through the use of hyperthreading, though exact mileage will vary.

In Azure, processor resources are not overprovisioned. Your virtual machine has a certain amount of processor resource (I'll cover this soon), and that amount is reserved for your VM. Whether you are running at 100 percent CPU or 1 percent CPU, you pay the same. There is an exception to this paying for the whole allotment of CPU all the time: the B series, or burstable VM. The B series works a lot like rollover minutes on your cell phone plan. On my cell phone, I have a base number of minutes—let's say 100 minutes per month. If I use less than 100 minutes, I can rollover the unused minutes to the next month. Let's pretend I can continue rolling them over for a year. If I spoke for only 50 minutes each month, by the end of the year, I would have an extra 600 minutes available, and on that last month, I could burst up and talk for 700 minutes. Maybe it's Christmas, so I can save the minutes for when I really need them: for all the Christmas best wishes phone calls to friends and family. The B series is the same idea. Sizes are available with different numbers of vCPUs; however, the base CPU performance is a percentage of that—for example, 10 percent. If I use less than that amount, I bank the delta as credit, with a maximum amount of credit allowed. For example, the B1s is a single vCPU with 10 percent base performance, allowing 72 credits to be banked. Each credit is 100 percent of a vCPU for 1 minute. This means for a VM that has a base of 10 percent, if it runs an average of 5 percent, then each minute I bank 0.05 of a credit, or 3 credits an hour. If I then have a burst of CPU, I can use those credits as required to exceed my normal 10 percent. There are B series sizes with multiple CPUs—for example, there is one with 8 CPUs. The math works the same. For the 8 vCPU size, the base performance is 135 percent (i.e., 135 percent of one vCPU), since there are actually 8 available to the VM, or just under 17 percent for each vCPU, but can burst to 800 percent (i.e., 100 percent on all 8 of the vCPUs).

Note that if you stop a B series VM (i.e., deprovision it from Azure and stop paying), your credits are lost. Figure 7.3 shows metrics for a B series, including the CPU credits being consumed and the CPU usage. In this example, the VM has two CPUs, which is why the credit doubles the CPU usage; four percent of two vCPUs is .08 credits. The graph is Figure 7.4 shows the credits consumed (the line at the bottom) and the credits banked (remaining). Notice that it has maxed out, since this VM uses far less than its allowed .4 credits per minute.

FIGURE 7.3
B series credits
consumed

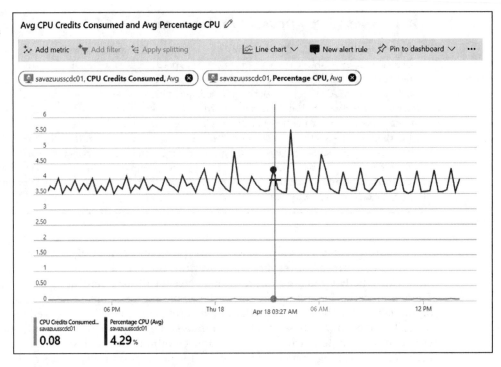

FIGURE 7.4
B series credits
remaining

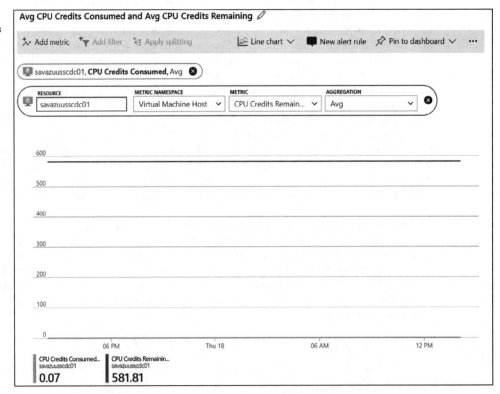

This burstable series is very useful. Many workloads typically have low CPU requirements but may have peaks. Think of domain controllers and logon storms, file servers, etc. As you would expect, they are cheaper than VMs, where you always have 100 percent of the vCPU reserved for you.

VM Series Variants and Processor Specifics

When looking at specific VM sizes, you often will see letters or numbers—for example, Dsv3. What exactly does that mean? The D is the series, but what about the sv3? There are a number of variants, as follows:

◆ s—Premium storage

◆ i—Isolated

◆ m—High-memory

◆ r—RDMA

◆ t—Tiny

In this case, the *s* in *Dsv3* means that it can use premium storage. There are many other variants that help identify properties of the VM, such as the presence of RDMA, a high-memory version, etc. The *v* denotes a version—in this case, version 3. Azure has huge numbers of servers, which, over time, need to be replaced with newer hardware. However, new offerings that take advantage of advancements in hardware are made available. As new hardware is deployed, that often means numerous new components, including newer processors. Important requirements for customers are predictability and consistency.

Imagine a customer deployed three D series virtual machines in the early days—and therefore on older hardware. Then the customer needed to add two more VMs to the farm, but the new two VMs happened to deploy to brand new servers and thus performed faster. There would be an inconsistency depending on where workloads ran, which makes planning difficult. The use of the versions enables the customer to choose specific versions rather than see inconsistent performance.

Number of cores and hyperthreading is just two dimensions of processors. You also need to consider the performance of the cores and possibly supported instruction sets, which vary by processor, model, and generation. You may have noticed ACU mentioned when viewing the various types and sizes available. Processor performance in Azure is measured in Azure Compute Units (ACUs). Each series and version has a particular ACU score, which is documented at:

https://docs.microsoft.com/en-us/azure/virtual-machines/windows/acu

Even if your VM is deployed to newer hardware, hypervisor limits will be used to ensure the VM only operates at the appropriate processor performance, as specified by the ACU.

To better understand the ACU, let's look at an example—the D series:

◆ D - 160 - 250

◆ Dv2 - 210 - 250

◆ Dv3 - 160 - 190

These numbers are based on the A1, which has a score of 100. The range is because Intel Turbo technology is utilized to increase CPU frequency, and this varies. As you can see, there was an improvement between the D and Dv2, as newer processors were used. Then it dropped from the Dv2 to the Dv3, which initially is surprising, considering once again newer processors were deployed, until you look at the other column in the ACU chart, which lists vCPU-to-core mapping. The D and Dv2 is a 1:1 mapping. The Dv3 is a 2:1 mapping—i.e., hyperthreading is enabled, meaning two vCPUs to one physical core. Until recently, hyperthreading was not used in Azure; however, many customers requested it to be available due to the gains available that are not present in a number of series, such as Dv3, Ev3, Fv2, and the M series. In addition to supporting hyperthreading, these series also support nested virtualization (i.e., running a hypervisor such as Hyper-V within an Azure VM, which is possible because the processor virtualization extensions are exposed to the VM). This was first added to Hyper-V in Windows Server 2016, as it was needed for kernel mode isolated containers. Because Azure uses Hyper-V, this capability is now enabled for certain series. This does not mean you should run hypervisors to run other VMs in Azure. You then lose all the benefit of the processes, agents, extensions, management framework, and more of Azure. However, it may be useful for certain other technologies that leverage hypervisor components for types of isolation of processes—for example, kernel mode isolated containers!

Take a look at the graveyard of VM generations to see how older versions are retired and replaced by generally a newer version:

```
https://docs.microsoft.com/en-us/azure/virtual-machines/windows/
sizes-previous-gen
```

If you have these older VMs created, they will still work—there is just no new capacity added for them. When possible, switch to the newer version.

The type of a VM can be changed easily. It simply requires a reboot of the VM. Note that not all VM series and sizes are available at all regions, which means you would need to check if the desired series and size is available. Additionally, if you are using availability sets, then the VMs are deployed to a specific cluster, which will dictate the VMs that are supported. Use Get-AzVMSize with the -AvailabilitySetName parameter to check which VM series and sizes are available for a deployed availability set. One trick can be to ensure that the first VM you deploy in an availability set is of a higher performing VM series and size. This will ensure that it is deployed to a newer cluster, maximizing the VM types available.

Azure VM Agent and Extensions

As previously mentioned, you are responsible for what is inside the VM (i.e., the guest OS), such as backup, antivirus, firewall, configuration, etc. While the responsibility is yours (the customer), there are numerous Azure services to help you fulfill it. Many of the services are enabled through extensions that work through the Microsoft Azure Virtual Machine Agent (VM Agent).

The Azure VM Agent is automatically installed on the Windows and Linux marketplace images and is automatically updated as new versions are released. If you create custom images that are not based on marketplace images (for example, you create a VM in Hyper-V on premises and then upload), then you should download and install the VM Agent prior to upload.

The VM Agent comprises two parts: the Provisioning Agent (PA) and the Windows Guest Agent (WinGA). The PA is required in order for the VM to boot, whereas the WinGA, while highly recommended, does not have to be present, although any interactions via extensions and other services will not function.

The VM Agent enables certain interactions with the VM, such as gathering information within the guest, and sending commands. However, the real benefit is through the extensions that the VM Agent facilitates. These extensions may be provided by Microsoft or by third parties, and each provides a specific type of functionality. A nice capability is utilizing a pluggable authentication module (PAM), which, at the time of writing, enables Linux VMs to authenticate directly to Azure AD. I want to quickly touch on a number of the key extensions and functionality areas:

Antivirus   There are a number of extensions for antimalware. This includes Microsoft's own Defender antimalware but also numerous third-party solutions that also provide integration with cloud management.

Monitoring   Integration with Azure Monitor logs (Log Analytics) and other integrations are via the Microsoft Monitoring Agent, which is available as an extension and is automatically added to VMs when they are enabled for a Log Analytics workspace integration. There are also monitoring extensions for other monitoring solutions.

Configuration   Commonly used today is declarative configuration, which enables a desired end-state to be specified and the solution "makes it so." Extensions for Microsoft's native declarative configuration PowerShell DSC are available, in addition to others, such as Chef and Puppet.

Security   A number of security solutions that require interaction with the guest OS surface via an agent. These solutions include file security capabilities. Azure Disk Encryption, which leverages guest OS encryption (BitLocker for Windows and DM-crypt for Linux), is applied as an extension.

Backup   While Azure Backup integration does not require an extension but instead leverages the VM Agent, there are third-party backup integrations that leverage an extension.

Note that this is not an exhaustive list. However, what do you do if an extension is not available for the functionality or set of actions you require? Perhaps the most useful extension is the Custom Script Extension (CSE). As the name suggests, it enables a PowerShell script to be executed inside the guest via the extension. (Note that this is separate from the Run command capabilities available on-demand for a VM, as shown in Figure 7.5, which use a similar, but different extension—the Run command extension.)

FIGURE 7.5
Quick Run command options for a VM

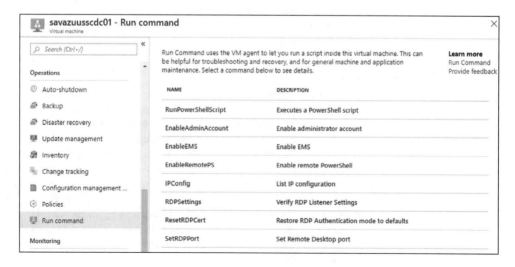

Scripts that execute via the CSE run as System. Keep this in mind if your scripts need to interact with network resources. Remember, you can always store credentials in Azure Key Vault and utilize secrets in the vault from scripts with authentication to the Key Vault using managed service identities (which are identities managed by Azure and unique to each Azure resource—e.g., a VM). Through the execution of scripts via CSE, there is really no limit to what can be accomplished, from installing software to performing complex sequences of actions. If you are deploying a script via CSE as part of a VM deployment, remember that the script will execute after provisioning, which means you may be able to connect to the VM and use it while the script is still being executed.

The Custom Script Extension can run any PowerShell script that it can access. For example, it could be stored in blob storage, in GitHub, and you can even pass commands directly instead of using a script. I recommend reviewing the following site, which describes a number of key tips and tricks when using the extension, in addition to some internals about where scripts are cached during execution that can help when troubleshooting:

```
https://docs.microsoft.com/en-us/azure/virtual-machines/extensions/
custom-script-windows
```

Following are some critical considerations when using the CSE:

◆ Ensure that no user input is required, that there is no way to interact.

◆ Test your script running as System; check for any network access.

◆ Only one instance of the CSE can be added to a VM. If you want to trigger a second CSE, then remove the first. Ideally, however, if you have sequences of actions, build them into the flow, potentially by using scheduled tasks within the guest OS.

Remember, this is IaaS. If you have existing solutions you wish to leverage for consistency between on premises and Azure, you can. Already use an operations manager for monitoring? Use it in Azure VMs. Have a preferred antivirus? Great! Use it in Azure. There are exceptions due to logistics and data flow. You likely will want to modify backup to use the cloud rather than send backup data to on-premises-based solutions, as you would have to pay for the data egress from Azure to on premises. Furthermore, Azure is likely a better place to resiliently store the backup and would be where you would want to restore to, as opposed to having to restore from an on-premises copy, which could be slow.

Boot Diagnostics

One of the biggest challenges customers in the cloud face is when a VM is not responsive and appears to not be booting correctly. On premises, it is easy to connect to the console of the VM via the hypervisor and examine the current state and interact. In the cloud, however, access to the hypervisor is blocked, so different approaches are required.

Many types of problems can be solved through the various Run command options I previously mentioned. For example, often people accidently disable RDP or turn off required firewall extensions, both of which can be fixed via the Run command. The ability to run a PowerShell script for Windows or a shell script for Linux through the Run command enables almost any OS configuration problem to be solved; it just requires knowledge of the CLI. However, without seeing the console or seeing elements of the boot process, it can be hard to identify the problem, and sometimes the problem is actually during the boot of the OS, which means running commands in the OS is not possible.

Boot diagnostics help provide insight into the VM state during and post boot. A storage account must be specified where data is stored relating to the boot process. A container is created for each VM that uses the storage account for boot diagnostics where an image of the console output is stored (and updated) and the serial console output (which is especially useful for Linux VMs). This information can be queried via the storage account, but also the portal provides an easy view of the screenshot and the log, as shown in Figure 7.6.

FIGURE 7.6
Boot diagnostics console screenshot

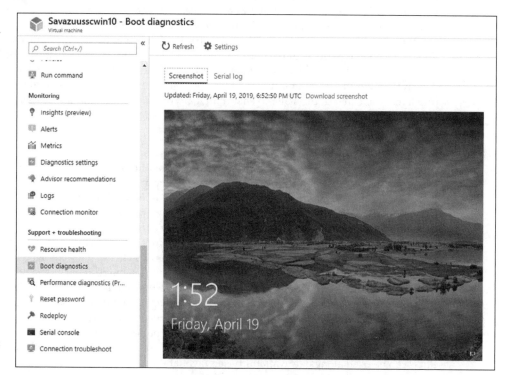

When you enable boot diagnostics from the portal, you will also notice an option to enable OS guest diagnostics. When enabled, this sends certain performance counter values from inside the guest via the Azure Diagnostics Agent extension (which is automatically installed) to be viewable via the Guest metric namespace, and exposes guest performance data, such as memory, processor, logical disk, and system.

Ephemeral OS Disks

The previous chapter examined the storage available for virtual machines. At minimum, this consisted of an ephemeral temporary drive that was stored locally on the host and an OS drive that was stored in Azure Storage and that was highly durable. The durable storage of the OS drive is important when you consider that the actual state of a VM is really via its disk content and, therefore, cannot be lost. There are circumstances where this is not the case.

There is a move from pets to cattle. Let me explain. Traditionally, our OS instances have been pets. They have unique names; we care for them by patching them; we fix them when they're sick. In modern environments, OS instances become cattle. There is nothing unique or special about them, and they can easily be replaced. If it's sick, we shoot it and stand up one in its place. Microservices embrace this. (I will explore this later in the chapter when talking about containers.) However, the idea of non-persistent OS state is not unique to microservices. There are many circumstances where there are a number of VMs offering a service that have no durable state requirements and can be re-created as needed. These could be regular VMs or VMs created as part of a scale set (VMs created from a gold image, which I'll cover shortly). OS disks (i.e., as managed disks) have a certain cost and performance when hosted in Azure Storage.

Ephemeral OS disks enable the OS disk to be created on local storage on the host (like the temporary drive) from an image in the marketplace. This saves money on storage for the OS disk and also will perform at the performance and latency of the local storage in the host. This only works for managed disks and is set at VM creation time. Note that this means you cannot deprovision the VM without losing the OS disk state. Remember, however, that if there are any problems, you can lose the state, so ensure that anything you care about is stored elsewhere—for example, on a SQL database backend or some persistent service/storage.

Proximity Placement Groups

As mentioned in Chapter 1, availability sets and availability zones are about resiliency by spreading resources over multiple blast zones—i.e., the area impacted by an incident such as hardware failure. There are different racks (i.e., Fault domains) for availability sets and different datacenters for availability zones. It is important to always use one of these resiliency features for workloads within a region to maximize availability.

Availability sets and zones have a side effect: proximity. In an availability set, the resources are in the same cluster (although the exact dimensions of a cluster have changed and continue to change. In an availability zone, the resources are in the same resilient datacenter or group of datacenters; however, there will be instances where the goal is proximity, and relying on the way other constructs work is not acceptable. A challenge of availability sets is the range of VM series and sizes available, since they all run on the same Azure cluster.

Proximity placement groups (PPGs) are focused around the placement of workloads. By placing workloads in the same PPG, you ensure that they are placed in the same physical datacenter. PPGs can be used alongside availability sets/availability zones. The use of PPGs helps ensure the proximity of workloads that can span different clusters (and therefore a wider range of VM series and sizes is available), thereby reducing latencies for VM-to-VM communication that are in the same PPG. The ability to span different Azure clusters is important when you consider some workloads, such as the use of M-series VMs for solutions such as SAP HANA that you want to frontend with compute-optimized VMs, such as the D and F series. By placing the VMs in the same PPG, you can achieve this.

PPGs only have a name and region defined. When the first workload is placed into a PPG, the PPG is pinned to a specific datacenter. When all workloads are removed from the PPG, it floats again until a workload added.

PPGs can be used to achieve a "hack" of Azure. You cannot combine availability zones and availability sets. That is, you can't pick an availability zone when creating an availability set—one is chosen. However, consider the following sequence, which enables an availability set to be created in a specific availability zone through the use of a PPG:

1. A PPG is created.

2. Add a VM that is in the PPG and a specific availability zone. The PPG is now pinned to this availability zone.

3. Create an availability set and add to the PPG. The availability set is now also tied to the availability zone!

4. You can now delete the original VM that was used to pin the PPG to the availability zone.

You could now repeat these steps for the other two zones in the region, if required.

Virtual Machine Scale Sets

As mentioned multiple times in this book, workloads in Azure should ideally have at least two instances to enable them to be distributed over Fault domains or datacenters in a region. A step further would be also to have at least two instances in another region as well, to provide region-level resiliency in addition to rack/datacenter resiliency. The use of multiple instances not only provides resiliency but enables scaling, Because multiple instances are running, it should be possible to add additional instances when existing instances are busy and stop instances when the existing instances are quieter, thus optimizing cost, as you pay compute charges only for services running. That these multiple instances are offering the same service means they must (or should) be exactly the same, with nothing unique about them. This means there are three requirements:

♦ Some master image or configuration to use when creating the instances

♦ A load balancer to front the services

♦ Some method to perform the scaling as required

Using a JSON template or scripting, it would be possible—and even quite easy—to create multiple machines. It would also be possible to use action groups with metrics around utilization to trigger scripts to start/stop VMs. This is a fair amount of custom work and does not consider requirements around updating instances from new base images, etc. Virtual machine (VM) scale sets address this by enabling a gold image to be specified along with a VM configuration, and then scale conditions to be configured based on metrics or schedules—for example:

♦ If average CPU is > 70 percent, add two instances.

♦ If average CPU is < 30 percent, remove two instances.

♦ If queue depth is > 100, add two instances.

♦ If time is Friday 5 p.m., add four instances.

You get the idea. You will notice in my examples that it was not adding one at a time. This is because you want to make a meaningful scale action, and time must be given to the action to have impact before checking again, which means checks may be made every 15 minutes. Additionally, load balancing membership is automatically handled. The only real work is the maintenance of the gold image; everything else is a basic configuration.

VM scale sets enable the set to easily be updated in a number of ways, including a rolling update (with only a subset updated at a time, ensuring the ongoing availability of the service) or an automatic update (which could take down the whole service) or a manual update. VM scale sets work using the update domains of an availability set or availability zone to which they are deployed.

When you are thinking about your golden image, I recommend reviewing the following article, which talks through some key concepts about making VMs provision and boot faster:

```
https://github.com/Azure/Avere/blob/master/docs/
azure_vm_provision_best_practices.md
```

Low-Priority VMs

There are certain types of workloads that are flexible with the resources assigned to them. Consider a stateless service whose numbers can vary, as there is nothing unique about any one instance—for example, a VM scale set or a workload without stringent infrastructure requirements like batch processing that needs to be completed but is not time critical and simply needs to be done as cheaply as possible. Azure consists of datacenters full of servers where the capacity is mostly consumed by on-demand workloads, such as regular VMs and other services. This means there is also spare capacity that at any moment is not required by a full-paying service.

The low-priority VM offering takes advantage of this spare capacity by offering the spare capacity at a significant discount. This discount will vary by region and by VM series and size, and based on the current spare capacity of that series and size. The more spare capacity of a certain size, the cheaper it may be to encourage its use. However, the amount spare will change, so there are considerations to the low-priority use:

◆   There is no SLA for low priority. If you make a request for low priority and there is not sufficient spare capacity, the request will fail.

◆   If the capacity is needed back for full-paying on-demand workloads, the low-priority capacity is evicted with 30 seconds of notice (which can be subscribed to for notification).

Those two considerations are why the use of low-priority VMs is really aimed at flexible, stateless workloads or non-time-critical. At the time of writing, VM scale sets and regular VMs can use low-priority VMs. When dealing with VM scale sets, you can get the best of both worlds. Create a VM scale set using on demand, which has SLAs for service availability for a number of instances that meets core requirements, and then a second VM scale set that uses low priority for increased scale. Both VM scale sets can be part of the same load balancer, provided that the scale sets are of type Standard (as opposed to Basic) or the same application gateway. This means requests will be sent to available instances in both scale sets.

Azure Dedicated Host

Azure is a multi-tenant service, which means customers' services are hosted on shared infrastructure. There is complete isolation between workloads at the hypervisor, network, and storage levels. Details on some of the technologies leveraged can be found at:

```
https://docs.microsoft.com/en-us/azure/security/azure-isolation
```

An item to note in that article is that certain very large VMs will be the only VMs on a particular host (since they consume the entire host), thereby giving host-level isolation.

There is also the option to have dedicated hosts for other VM series and sizes. Customers pay for the entire host and can then run whichever VMs can fit on the hosts. OS licenses are still billed separately. This is not necessary for most customers, given the isolation provided, but for very sensitive customers who have high risk workloads and want to eliminate the chance of side attacks (when workloads run on the same hardware/hypervisor) from other tenants.

Hosts are placed into host groups, which are created in a specific availability zone. Additionally, hosts are placed in a Fault domain (rack), with three Fault domains exposed per host group. Note that Fault domains are specific to a host group only. If you have multiple host groups, there is no correlation between Fault domains between the different host groups in a similar way that there is no correlation between availability zones in different Azure subscriptions.

Hosts are purchased for a specific SKU (for example, DSv3 or ESv3), which then supports VMs of that series running on the host up to the host limit.

Windows Virtual Desktop

Hosting desktops and applications for remote use is a common requirement for many organizations. Hosting those environments in the cloud starts to be a logical decision when users are distributed and/or the backend services the desktops/applications are accessing are hosted in the cloud.

There are a number of solutions for hosting desktops—from manually created solutions using Windows Remote Desktop services to marketplace offerings such as those from partners such as Citrix. Azure has its own native offering, Windows Virtual Desktop, that offers both desktop and application publishing through a very simple deployment experience that supports automatic scaling based on utilization. Following are some of the key points about the offering:

- Supports Windows 10 and Windows Server–based environments

- Fully managed Remote Desktop Services–based solution managed through Azure management interfaces

- Publishes full desktops or applications through host pools. A host pool supports either desktops or applications (RemoteApp) and can be pooled or personal (persistent). Multiple host pools can be created and offered to individuals. This means a single user can see many offerings.

- A unique capability is to have multiple sessions to a Windows 10 instance—something normally only possible with a server OS.

- Full support for Office 365 licenses via existing Office licensing

- Pooled and persistent desktops. For most users, a pooled desktop is preferred, which is reset after logoff to minimize maintenance. However, a persistent desktop can be used for power users who need to maintain OS state between sessions.

- Integrates with Azure AD, including MFA for authentication, and also requires AD DS for desktop joining

If you require virtual desktops or application publishing, I would recommend starting with the Windows Virtual Desktop offering to see if it meets your requirements. If it does not, then investigate partner offerings that integrate tightly with Azure.

VMware in Azure?

This may seem very strange, but I wanted to touch on this. I mentioned at the start of this chapter that customers should not care about the hypervisor, as the service is IaaS. However, sometimes this isn't true, as sometimes customers are really after hosting and not IaaS. With hosting, the requirement is some hardware to host their workloads, which means managing the same way. Customers may run VMware's hypervisor ESX on premises and want to get to the cloud but are not yet ready to change processes but are in a hurry to get out of their datacenter, which means staying on VMware and then moving to cloud services. If customers had more time, they could use technologies like Azure Site Recovery to migrate from ESX VMs to Azure IaaS. Customers may also want VMware in Azure for capacity expansion or for disaster recovery purposes.

Azure runs Hyper-V, the hypervisor in Windows Server, not VMware's ESX. Even if it were running on ESX (which it isn't), normal tools would not work, since it is IaaS, in the same way Hyper-V management tools can't interact with Azure fabric. To help customers who need to initially get out of their datacenter with the smallest changes possible, there is a limited Azure offering.

In partnership with VMware and through VMware's VCPP partner program, Microsoft has partnered with CloudSimple, where a VMware environment can be provisioned in Azure that is supported and certified by VMware. It is a VMware as a Service experience, with each customer running on their own dedicated, isolated, and hosted private cloud in Azure that can be managed and integrated with existing VMware assets and tools. The networking is automatically configured to enable integration with other Azure services and can connect to on premises via ExpressRoute or S2S VPN. The networking also supports deploying an L2 stretch between on premises and the Azure deployment.

Clusters of ESXi hosts (3 to 16 nodes) can be provisioned by the customer through the Azure portal and this includes ultra-fast vSAN-based storage which aggregates local host storage into a highly available shared storage subsystem which is similar to Storage Spaces Direct in Windows Server. NSX-T is leveraged for the network overlay in addition to a custom underlay and Azure SDN.

To move workloads, you can use technologies such as VMware vMotion or Hybrid Cloud Extension (HCX), or you can use third-party tools. For new deployments, you can leverage ARM templates or Terraform to provision both Azure and VMware VMs in customers' environments.

Platform as a Service Offerings

While IaaS solutions are extremely powerful, they generally should not be the first choice. Virtual machines require a lot of maintenance, such as patching, protection, resiliency planning, and a lot more. For custom applications, organizations should first look at the Platform as a Service (PaaS) offerings, as these enable the focus to be the application and not maintaining all the OS components that you really don't care about as an organization. Azure's initial offering was PaaS, and IaaS was added later. While the focus of this book is IaaS, I want to cover the basics around the key PaaS services available.

Note that I am not covering all services. There are many, including Azure Batch, which is a massive scale job scheduling service, and then messaging building blocks such as Event Hub, Event Grid, and Service Bus. I am going to focus on what I see as some of the core PaaS compute services that are the focus for many architectures today.

Containers

There are many "in" technologies today. You hear about Dev/Ops, microservices, and more, but one of the biggest is containers. Containers provide virtualization of the operating system, whereas virtual machines virtualize the hardware.

THE NEED FOR CONTAINERS

Organizations today have numerous challenges with traditional application deployment. Let's explore some of those challenges through a simple example of a common custom application deployment.

Say that an application developer has completed work on a masterpiece that has taken six months to write. The application now needs to be deployed to production. The developer uploads the compiled application to a folder, along with vague instructions that the application needs Windows Server 2016, Internet Information Services (IIS), and some other components. The IT administrator gets the request and needs to find the spare resources to create a new Windows Server 2016 instance. After those resources are found, the creation of the VM is undertaken, which takes about 30 minutes, as the IT shop has a pretty good provisioning system utilizing a well-maintained gold Windows Server image. A few hours later, the administrator checks back, logs on to the OS instance, and reviews the email from the developer about the requirements for the app. After meeting the requirements by adding the various roles, features, and extra software (and a few reboots), the administrator installs the custom application and tries to start it. The application does not start. After rechecking the vague instructions from the developer, the administrator still cannot make the application start. The administrator contacts the developer for help. The developer logs on to the server, installs some of the organization's troubleshooting tools, and gets the application to start. The application had requirements on items that were installed on the developer's machine, but these were not understood as requirements and therefore not previously installed.

This common scenario highlights some of the key challenges of deploying custom applications and even commercial software. To summarize, here are the common causes of failed application deployment:

♦ Difficulty modeling application deployments and dependencies

♦ Inconsistent library and sharing for custom and commercial applications

♦ Lack of portability of applications

♦ Low density, as each application runs in its own OS instance to achieve basic levels of isolation

♦ Slow provisioning of environments

While virtualization helps with many aspects of IT operations, it does not solve this set of challenges. Instead, another technology that belongs to the virtualization family saves the day: containers.

CONTAINER FUNDAMENTALS

Consider the challenges highlighted at the start of this chapter: the amount of time for provisioning environments, wasted resources (as every application has its own OS instance in order to attain a basic level of isolation from other applications), and the problems associated with the deployment of applications and their dependencies. Containers solve these challenges by enabling multiple applications to share a single OS instance while providing isolation between them. Furthermore, containers utilize a model that enables applications to be encapsulated and dependencies to other containers containing various libraries and binaries to be documented as part of the container metadata.

For any readers who may have dabbled in the desktop space, some of these features may sound like App-V. This technology enabled desktop applications to run in their own bubbles, with their own virtual view of the filesystem completely isolated from other App-V virtualized applications. As you will see, similarities exist between containers and App-V, especially related to the isolation capabilities, but containers go a lot further.

Containers can be thought of as another type of virtualization, because they enable any application running inside the container to perceive that it has its own isolated operating system view that is separate from any other application that happens to be running in a different container on the same OS instance, known as a *sandbox*. This isolation is at a user-mode level. Each container has its own isolated namespace, which provides the following to the application:

- Its own view of the filesystem, which consists of its own virtual filesystem content that is unioned with the underlying pristine OS filesystem content and any container filesystem content upon which it is dependent. This requires updates to NTFS.

  - For example, I may have a web application in a container that depends on another container that contains IIS, which depends on the Nano Server image that contains the OS image. Inside the container instance, I would see the union of my application container filesystem, the IIS container filesystem (containing the IIS binaries), and the underlying container OS image (containing the OS), enabling the application to function.

    - Any writes from the application are made to its virtual filesystem overlay (the sandbox), avoiding any cross-pollination to other containers, and any other images in the dependency chain are read-only.

- Its own view of the Registry. And just like the filesystem, the Registry layers are unioned through a new VREG capability.

- Its own view of processes, hiding processes from other containers

- Its own networking configuration that leverages virtual switches on the container host (the OS instance that hosts the container instances)

Figure 7.7 shows a graphical, high-level representation of containers compared to traditional virtualization. Notice that with traditional OS virtualization, each application runs in its own VM with its own OS instance and all the associated overhead. However, the application enjoys total isolation from other applications, and the resources available can be controlled through configuration of the virtual CPU, memory, and network resources assigned to the VM. With containers, each application runs in its own container, which is isolated at a user-mode level and can have dependencies on other containers that may contain libraries that are then dependent on a host OS image (which needs to match the container host OS). Notice that different containerized applications can be dependent on the same containers or different containers. This is useful, as some applications may require the same version of libraries, while other applications may need different versions of libraries—something that is difficult to achieve traditionally on a shared OS. Control groups (known as *job objects* in Windows) enable the grouping of processes. The access to resources they are allowed to have is a key point of the isolation. Containers provide state separation between applications and allow multiple versions of an application to be maintained.

FIGURE 7.7
Traditional
virtualization-
hosting appli-
cations vs.
applications
running in
containers

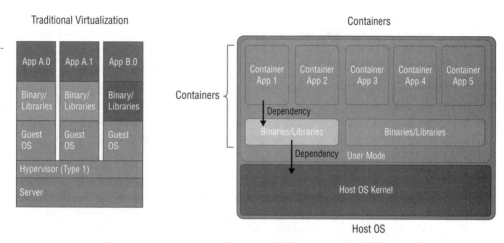

The dependencies between containers are prescribed by the application developer at the time of the application creation, and the container technology is leveraged throughout the application's lifecycle. This is achieved by creating a *composition file* that specifies the images used and any actions required. (In Docker, this is called a *Dockerfile*, and it is different from a Docker Compose file, as explained at https://docs.docker.com/compose/compose-file/.) The container images are stored in a central repository, and when you combine a composition file by using a shared set of images, the result is immutable. It will always provision and perform the same, ensuring consistency as it is deployed between environments. This is not the case when developers normally install "stuff" on their machines, write the code, and then try to describe the same "stuff" to be installed in QA, then live, and so on. But as an application developer writes an application to be run in a container, the developer presses F5 to debug; the container is created, the application is instantiated into it, and testing is performed. Once development is complete, the application developer publishes the containerized application to either a public or private repository, which includes the dependency information related to other containers. The IT operations team performs a pull from the repository for the application, which also pulls down any containers on which the applications container depends, and deploys the application to a container host. No complicated deployment instructions are required, as the deployment is essentially self-contained. This is a completely immutable operation that ensures that the containerized application will always run the same way. The operations team then monitors the application and provides feedback to the developers in the form of insights and metrics that may lead to updated versions of the application, and the entire lifecycle begins again. The containerization of the application also helps if a rollback of an application update is required. If version 2.5 has a problem, for instance, version 2.4 of the container can be quickly pulled and deployed. The composition files and images provide immutability; a deployment is guaranteed to always be the same and helps embrace a Dev/Ops mentality.

The deployment is also fast. There is no creation of a new OS instance and no finding of resources. The container is deployed to an existing container host, which could be physical or virtual, and it happens quickly, potentially in a subsecond, which opens up new ways to run applications.

In the new "cloud era," we see more microservices; an application is broken into its component processes, and each process runs as its own microservice. Containers embrace the microservice philosophy and enable it, which is best understood with an example. Consider a stock application. The stock application's web frontend runs in a container, and a request is made for information about five stocks. A container instance is created for each request, thus five containers, and the application in the container performs the research into its delegated stock and responds with the required information, and then the container is deleted. This approach not only is efficient with resources but also scales the application, with the only limit being the resources available in the farm of container hosts.

Because each container shares a common container host instance, a greater density of workloads is realized when compared to traditional machine virtualization, in which every virtual machine requires its own complete OS instance.

Using a separate virtual machine for each application provides another benefit beyond isolation: control of resource consumption. Containers provide resource controls (for example, quality of service, or QoS) to ensure that one container does not consume more than its fair share of resources, which would negatively impact other containers on the same container host—the "noisy neighbor" problem. The container QoS allows each container to have specific amounts of resources—such as processor, memory, and network bandwidth—to be assigned. This ensures that a container does not consume more than its allotted amount of resources.

Containers rely on container images, which are analogous to a VHD with Hyper-V. A container image is read-only (although layers can be added on top of images to create new images, as you will explore later in this chapter). A container image is utilized by container instances, and it is the container image that depends on other container images. A container image consists of its metadata, which includes items such as its name, commands to execute when using it to start a container instance, its dependencies, and its payload, which comprises the files and folders that make up its virtual filesystem layer. Multiple container instances created from the same container image are guaranteed to start and behave in the same way.

Containers originally started life in Linux and were also added to Windows in Windows Server 2016. Windows Server and Linux containers provide user-mode isolation for applications in different container instances. All the container instances on the same container host share common host operating system instances and a common kernel. In a trusted environment such as within a private cloud, or when the applications being deployed are from a well-managed and audited library, user-mode-only isolation may meet the required levels of security. In a public cloud, the environment utilized by different tenants sharing a common kernel may not be desirable, as each application may not be trusted and a tenant running a container on the same container host could possibly try to use the shared kernel to attack other containers.

Another challenge of regular containers is the dependency on the container host OS version, which is specified as part of the dependency chain from the application, through its binary and library containers, and through to the host OS specified in those dependent libraries. If the OS changes on the container host, it may break the containers running on it.

To address these concerns, Windows Server 2016 has an additional type of container: Hyper-V isolation. As the name suggests, a Hyper-V isolation instance leverages the Hyper-V role of Windows Server 2016 and above to automatically create and manage (and eventually delete) a virtual machine into which the containerized application is instantiated, along with the other containers upon which it depends and its own base OS image. This approach gives the Hyper-V isolation container standard user-mode isolation but also kernel-mode isolation. This is shown in Figure 7.8, where both types of containers are running on a single container host.

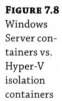

FIGURE 7.8
Windows
Server con-
tainers vs.
Hyper-V
isolation
containers

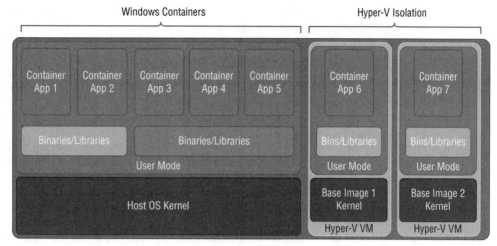

The virtual machine created for a Hyper-V container is automatically managed and is not visible in standard Hyper-V management tools, such as Hyper-V Manager. However, if the list of processes for a container host is examined, a VM worker process (vmwp.exe) will be present for each Hyper-V container. This is a special type of Hyper-V VM specifically created just to launch a container: a utility VM. Because a Hyper-V container requires a VM to be created and a separate OS instance to be built, it will provision slower than a regular Windows container, which typically deploys fast because the container instance is created on an existing container host. Additionally, having a separate base image for a Hyper-V container will make it "heavier" from a resource perspective, since it needs its own instance-specific OS disk storage along with additional memory and processor resources to run a complete Windows Server instance. However, Hyper-V containers use the Nano Server deployment mode for Hyper-V containers, which provides the lightest possible Windows Server deployment along with fast provisioning times that enable even Hyper-V containers to be provisioned in seconds. Additionally, because this Hyper-V VM is being used for a known reason (that is, to run containers), special steps are taken to accelerate the provisioning of the Hyper-V container VMs. This includes creating a single VM, making it read-only, and then cloning it for future containers, greatly accelerating the provisioning times. If a regular container deploys sub-second, a Hyper-V container based on Nano Server will deploy in around 5 seconds (and even less once the cloning is utilized), which demonstrates that these are still fast deployments.

Note that virtual machines are not going anywhere. There are still instances where virtual machines are the right choice. Containers are an additional option. Often this will be driven by the developers. Over time, I would expect to see more applications deploying to containers instead of an entire separate OS instance—i.e., a VM.

DOCKER

A container solution has various requirements, such as the isolation technology itself to enable containerized applications to run in their own isolated namespace, which is known as the *container runtime* and is provided by Windows Server. Another requirement is the ability to communicate over the network, which is enabled through virtual switches. You also need an entire toolset to develop and manage containers. Initially, during the technical preview stages of Windows Server 2016, Microsoft had two management approaches: its own native PowerShell-based management fabric and Docker. This scenario, however, was complicated for users, as it led to two container implementations with no real cross-management set interaction or visibility. Thus, Microsoft removed the native PowerShell management version of containers and instead embraced the Docker management fabric.

Docker is the de facto industry standard for container development and management in the Linux world. Microsoft worked closely with Docker and the open-source community to bring Docker to Windows in order to enable a consistent toolset and management fabric across Windows and Linux. If a container host installation is performed you will see that Docker is a required component for containers to exist on Windows. In fact, I believe that it's the first time an in-box feature has required external software to function.

At the foundation of Docker is the Docker Engine, a lightweight runtime and set of tools for building and executing Docker containers. It has been updated to enable execution on both Windows and Linux. Several components run on top of the Docker Engine, including the following:

Docker Client Performs actions against the Docker Engine

Docker PowerShell Executes against the REST API provided by the Docker Engine

Docker Compose Enables the definition and running of multi-container applications

Docker Registry Enables the storage and distribution of Docker images

Docker Swarm Provides clustering capabilities to groups of Docker hosts, enabling a single virtual Docker host that provides greater scale and resiliency

Docker Universal Control Plane (UCP) Enables a single management pane of glass to manage thousands of nodes (container hosts managed by Docker) as if they were one

Figure 7.9 provides a high-level overview of the way the various components fit together to provide a complete container solution.

FIGURE 7.9
Container architecture with Docker

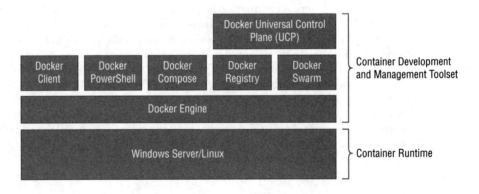

Other technologies, such as Mesosphere and Kubernetes, offer management solutions that run on top of the Docker Engine and other components. (I'll be talking more about Kubernetes!) Through these various components, Docker enables the complete lifecycle of services, from

the initial build using the Docker client and Docker Compose, the shipping of containers with Docker Hub (a cloud-hosted public and private container image repository), and the Docker Trusted Registry (an on-premises image storage solution), through to the actual execution using Docker Cloud (which hooks into Azure) and the Docker UCP. It's also possible to create and run containers directly on premises without any external service connectivity, as you will explore in this chapter. It's important to realize, however, that higher levels of service are available for more enterprise scenarios.

For more information on Docker, I recommend the following resources (as this chapter focuses more on the Windows container functionality and its primitives rather than on the full set of Docker functionality):

◆ www.docker.com/what-docker

◆ https://docs.docker.com/

◆ https://blog.docker.com/

KUBERNETES

Containers provide a lot of value, but on their own they don't provide all the answers, in the same way that virtual machines without management are only part of the solution. There are many operational aspects that still need to be considered with containers—for example:

Scheduling   Deciding where containers should run and if instances should be near (affinity) or far (anti-affinity) from others

Scaling   Increasing/decreasing the number of individual containers or groups of containers

Failover   Detecting failed container hosts and rescheduling containers on the failed hosts to healthy hosts

Lifecycle and Health   Keeping containers running despite failures, and monitoring for problems and resolving them

Identity and Authorization   Controlling access to containers

Storage Volumes   Providing data access to containers

Load Balancing   Distributing traffic across containers at scale

Naming and Discovery   Enabling how containers or groups find one another even when moving between hosts

Logging and Monitoring   Keeping track of what containers are doing

Debugging and Introspection   Getting inside running containers

Host Management   Managing the containers' hosts

Networking   Differentiating container networks from host networks at scale and providing network overlay capabilities

Application Upgrade   Enabling the ability to update a service in a rolling manner without taking down the entire service and rollback if required

All these requirements are grouped under orchestration solutions, which is a key element of any container deployment. Although there are a number of container orchestrators, such as Docker Swarm and Apache DC/OS, one solution really has become the standard: Google Kubernetes. Kubernetes provides all the capabilities to meet the requirements previously mentioned and is provided as an open-source project. Note that while Kubernetes normally orchestrates Docker management, it can also work with others. Kubernetes clusters consist of masters and workers. Workers are the container hosts (also known as *minions*, but that seems harsh) that run a component, the kubelet that enables the management of the workers by the Kubernetes orchestration masters (the hosts running the actual Kubernetes orchestration solution). The workers run a pod, which is an instance of an application, and that pod is made up of one or more containers based on the application's scale and resiliency requirements. It is the orchestration solution–i.e., Kubernetes to create and remove container instances within the pods and even the pods themselves.

Solutions such as Azure OpenShift build on Docker and Kubernetes to bring a complete application platform to enterprises that aids in application development, deployment, scaling, and overall lifecycle management. Azure OpenShift is a fully managed offering based on OpenShift and hosted in Azure.

CONTAINER SERVICES IN AZURE

I've spent a lot of time walking through what containers are, why we care about them, and the core management and orchestration solutions. Containers are everywhere in Azure. They power many services and even aspects of the portal. For example, when you open the cloud shell in the portal, that's running in a container instance. There are also services specifically around containers.

At the most basic level, you can create IaaS VMs running Linux or Windows Server 2016+ and run containers within those VMs. Remember, I spoke about some of the VM series that support nested virtualization. With those, you could even run the Hyper-V isolated container instances that utilized the hardware-assisted virtualization from the processor. The downsides are all the management that comes with VMs and the cost of the VMs. While containers often will be created as part of application deployments, you may have existing OS instances that you would like to convert the applications running inside the OS to a container. This can also be useful when you have applications running on legacy OS instances that are no longer supported. Image2Docker is a tool that will scan an OS instance, both Windows and Linux, find middleware and runtimes installed, find a suitably based container image, and then create a composition file that can be used to create a new container, migrating the application from OS to container.

Azure Container Instances (ACI) provides Container as a Service. An image is specified that then runs on the Azure fabric with per-second billing. With ACI, you still must manage the image on which the container instance is based; however, that is minimal, since a base OS image is utilized that is separately provided/updated along with other layers for runtime/middleware, and there will always be some aspect of image management, although that can be automated through various Dev/Ops and repository solutions. Windows and Linux containers are supported with ACI, and deployments are isolated from each other at a kernel level, which is important in a multi-tenant environment. ACIs start in seconds, and each instance has a public IP and fully qualified domain name (FQDN) that can be custom along with virtual network integration options. ACIs are available in custom CPU and memory sizes and can utilize Azure Files for persistent storage.

Azure Kubernetes Service (AKS) is a managed Kubernetes deployment. With a single command, an entire Kubernetes cluster can be created consisting of both the masters and the workers. A few minimal maintenance tasks are required, such as rebooting nodes post upgrade, but, for the most part, AKS is fully managed. AKS can automatically scale pods and nodes within a deployment. By default, a deployment consists of three nodes, but this can be modified to meet specific requirements. Additionally, you can integrate with ACI through use of a virtual kubelet, which makes the ACI fabric appear as an infinite scale node to AKS. Note that, as the customer, you cannot see the master nodes; they operate on a different subnet and are hidden. Once AKS is deployed, its interactions are the same as any other Kubernetes deployment—e.g., kubectl, helm, etc. Containers are deployed from private or public repositories, including Azure's own private Docker repository service, Azure Container Registry.

Before AKS, there was ACS (Azure Container Service). ACS deployed one of three orchestration solutions, which then had to be managed by the customer—essentially, ACS just created the deployment. ACS was retired in favor of the managed AKS service. However, ACS lives on as ACS-Engine, which can still create deployment files for the three orchestration solutions in Azure and which is available on GitHub at `https://github.com/Azure/acs-engine`. However, this has also evolved to AKS-engine, with a focus on Kubernetes only, and is available at `https://github.com/Azure/aks-engine`. This is used for the creation of AKS deployments in Azure but can also be used by customers to create their own Kubernetes clusters in Azure. Azure Service Fabric can also be used as an orchestrator for containers, in addition to its own native application model.

Azure Application Services

The Azure Application (App) Services is where Azure initially started providing PaaS services, which Microsoft believed was what customers would want in the cloud. This is true, but customers also wanted VMs in the cloud, which is why IaaS was added, in addition to many more PaaS and other services. Still, App Service is one of the most used services in Azure.

App Service Plans

An App Service plan is the container for the various types of application services. An App Service plan has a number of attributes:

Region   This is where the service will run. This should be close to the users of the service, to minimize latency. For resiliency, there should be App Service plans in two separate regions running the same workloads with inter-region balancing using Azure Front Door or Azure Traffic Manager. Ideally, these will run active-active; however, based on database utilization, it may only be possible to run active in one location.

Type   There are different types of plans available that have different characteristics and features. Some core differences relate to the maximum number of instances, deployment slot availability, virtual network integration, SSL, auto-scale, and Traffic Manager integration. The following site details the various plan types:

`https://azure.microsoft.com/en-us/pricing/details/app-service/plans/`

There are others, but those are some of the big ones.

Size   Once a type is selected, a number of instances that run the actual applications are added. These instances come in different sizes with different numbers of cores, memory, and local storage. The actual type of VM used for the instances also varies. For example, the premium sizes use the new D series VM types.

Scale   This is the number of instances in the plan. Note that with auto-scale, this can change based on defined triggers.

The size and scale attributes of the plan reveal the VM-based nature of the plan. These nodes are shared by all the deployment slots and applications deployed to the plan. These nodes are also unique to a single tenant. (As previously mentioned, other components are shared between tenants, but isolation is still in effect.) However, there are two exceptions to this: the Free plan and the Shared plan. Here, the worker nodes are shared between tenants with quotas in-place to limit the amount of CPU time, RAM, and storage that can be utilized. The Free and Shared plans are not for enterprise production use, where you will want the scale and capabilities of the other types of plans available.

It is possible to deprovision a regular virtual machine from the fabric such that the storage state is kept but the compute cost stops. This is not possible with an App Service plan; it cannot be deprovisioned. Instead, either the plan can be scaled to reduce/increase the number of nodes via manual or automatic means, or the plan can be deleted and then re-created via templates as needed. This may sound extreme, but remember that many applications are stateless, with the stateful data stored in database tiers that are separate. Creating an App Service plan via a template and then populating it with applications through automation is simple and fast. Remember, you are paying for the number of instances, not how busy they are!

Deployment Slots and Multiple App Service Plans

The Standard and Premium plans (along with isolated and Linux App Service [that uses containers!]) support deployment slots, which are a great feature when dealing with application rollout. By default, an application has a single production deployment slot. This is where the application runs. However, for the plans that support it, additional deployment slots can be created, each with its own name and configuration. For example, a staging slot could be used to deploy and test a newer version of the application. Once the application has been tested, the staging and production slots could be switched, essentially promoting staging to production and making that content live. If there was a problem, the slots could be switched again (since staging now contains what was production), which would roll back the content to the original content. There are also auto-swap capabilities that can be utilized with DevOps scenarios in which code is deployed to staging and then automatically promoted to production once the code deployment is completed and warmed up—i.e., ready to use.

Remember that you specify a number of nodes and the capacity of those nodes. All the applications that you deploy into a single App Service plan share that resource. When you create deployment slots, they run on the same shared capacity; therefore, ensure that the plan has sufficient resources for the workloads added to it. Figure 7.10 shows this. As you can see, this plan has three nodes with two applications deployed to it. Application 1 has two deployment slots. All the deployed applications and slots share the same resources.

FIGURE 7.10
Applications
and deploy-
ment slots in
an App Service
plan

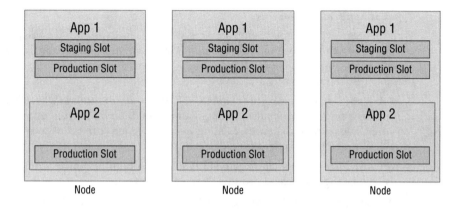

Any scaling of a plan impacts all applications and all deployment slots. Scaling typically is done on a schedule where known usage patterns exist but also have auto-scaling based on metrics to cater for unexpected traffic loads. While scaling out increases the number of instances and is the best way to optimize cost and increase resiliency, you may still need larger instances if you have large applications deployed that are resource hungry or simply have many applications/deployment slots. Multiple Fault domains are used for the multiple instances in a plan to help protect against rack-level failures. Normally, in Azure, if you change the size of a resource (i.e., scale up instead of out—for example, with a VM), there is some downtime. If you have multiple instances, the overall service stays available, but there is some dip in scale, as each instance is resized one at a time. This is not the case in an App Service plan. If you resize an instance, new instances of the desired size are created and then the application is moved over. There is no dip in scale or resiliency. You should still focus scaling horizontally (i.e., in and out) for the most responsive scale actions. However, you may want to scale up and down to really optimize cost. For example, if you have really quiet times, you want to not only reduce the number of nodes but also make them smaller.

By nature of the resource sharing for all applications deployed to the same plan, there will be times when you should use separate App Service plans. While there are a number of reasons, I see three key ones:

◆ An application needs to scale differently from others—for example, a different number of instances or different size instances.

◆ A deployment to a new region is required. (Remember that a plan is deployed to a specific region.)

◆ An application may use a large amount of resources, which would negatively impact others deployed in the same plan. In this scenario, separate plans help to stop the "noisy neighbor" problem and one application from impacting others.

It is possible to move applications between plans, provided that the target is in the same region and resource group. Most likely, however, you would simply redeploy the application to a new plan.

Types of Application Services

Three primary types of application services are available in an App Service plan (with the additional option to also run Azure Functions in a plan, to take advantage of resources you are already paying for). If you look under the hood, these three types are really web applications—they just respond differently and have different capabilities.

Web App   This listens on port 80/443 TCP only and can respond with HTML over HTTP (with web socket support also). A huge number of different languages and runtimes are supported, and, in most instances, existing web applications can be taken and run in a web app with minimal to zero changes.

API App   This listens on port 80/443 TCP but responds primarily with JSON over HTTP. It also has configurations related to API management.

Mobile App   This listens on port 80/443 and responds via HTTP but has a simplified API that is preconfigured to support mobile applications. There are a number of built-in libraries to enable simplified projects related to mobile devices. It also includes support for cross-platform apps written with Xamarin and Cordova with native SDKs.

APP SERVICE ENVIRONMENTS

As previously mentioned, while App Service plans have dedicated nodes, the workers, where the applications run that are used only by a specific client unless using the Free or Shared plans, there are still shared components that are part of the complete solution. It is because of these shared components that there are some limits around integration with virtual networks (although this is changing even as a I write this chapter). An App Service Environment (ASE) is an isolated deployment where the components that are normally shared also have dedicated instances deployed, which means the entire solution is dedicated to a customer. Because all components are dedicated, they are deployed to a customer's virtual network, which not only enables integration with resources on the virtual network (or connected to the virtual network), but traffic can also be redirected to/from the ASE—for example, to a network virtual appliance for inspection. It is also possible to not have a public endpoint.

In addition to the complete isolation and virtual network integration, ASE has greater scalability than a regular App Service plan. It is important to note that ASE costs more than a regular App Service plan, because you also need to pay for the additional components that are normally shared.

Azure Serverless Compute Services

While with the application services previously mentioned there is no maintenance of operating system environments running in VMs, that is still how you pay. You purchase a number of nodes that make up your App Service plan of certain size, and then your applications run on those nodes. You pay for the number of nodes currently deployed based on various auto-scale capabilities. (The cost for shared components—such as load balancers, frontends, file shares, and so forth—is baked into the node price.) As with an IaaS VM, you pay the same if those nodes are running at 100 percent or at 1 percent.

The Azure serverless compute offerings do not work this way. There are still VMs running things behind the scenes, but they are invisible to you. You don't specify a number of nodes or size. You have code, and you pay for the resources consumed during its execution.

This optimizes your cost and gives infinite scale, if needed. Serverless offerings have bindings to inputs and outputs, where the inputs can be a trigger such as a message to Twitter, a blob created, a RESTFUL call, or even a schedule. There are numerous options.

AZURE FUNCTIONS

Azure Functions are fairly simple. As their name suggests, they consist of a block of code that can be written in a number of languages, which is constantly expanding. The language commonly is C# or JavaScript, but it can also be others, including Python, Bash, and PowerShell, which opens up using Azure Functions as an engine to run PowerShell automation activities instead of solutions like Azure Automation!

Azure Functions have a trigger defined, such as a data write, a webhook/API, or a schedule. The code, which can have additional inputs, executes and then binds to output services. There are many use cases for Functions, some common examples of which include performing an action based on some file activity, performing an action based on a schedule, or performing an action based on a call from another service.

Azure Functions can also operate with an App Service plan or App Service Environment. You may choose to use this if you have an existing plan or ASE that has spare capacity and you wish to avoid additional consumption costs based on the Azure Function executions.

AZURE LOGIC APPS

Logic Apps are very different from Functions. While still serverless, a Logic App is built around workflows, which are created through a graphical designer, and is focused on integrating various services. A large number of connectors are available that can easily be added to a workflow to enable a workflow to be created in which some service initiates the workflow and then the data moves through the flow to other services, with transformations possible along the workflow. Logic apps are used in other Microsoft offerings—for example, Microsoft Flow, which is used heavily behind the scenes with Office 365. A large number of "getting started" flows are provided. For example, based on a tweet, a Logic Apps is triggered, which then interfaces to various services (such as sentiment analysis services), and then writes a message to SharePoint or another service. Another example is uploading a video into blob storage, which triggers a job that compresses the video into multiple formats. Take a look at `https://flow.microsoft .com/en-us/`, which has some nice visual templates available, to get an idea of Microsoft Flow's capability.

Chapter 8

Azure Stack

This chapter focuses on Azure Stack, which helps to provide a consistent set of functionality and experience for organizations that need Azure but on premises. The reality is that many organizations will be hybrid for a long time, potentially forever, and removing the distinction related to supported applications and services between on premises and the cloud provides huge benefit.

In this chapter, you will learn to:

◆ Choose the right target for Azure services.

◆ Understand capabilities and tasks associated with Azure Stack.

◆ Use Azure Stack and Azure Stack HCI.

Azure Stack Foundation

It is important to understand what exactly Azure Stack is and, for many organizations, when it should be used. Additionally, the exact capabilities that are supported are critical as part of planning.

Azure Stack 101

Azure Stack is purchased as a turn-key appliance, which means you purchase Azure Stack, connect it to power and the network, turn it on, and it's ready to go. You don't install an operating system on the hardware. (In fact, as with many hardware appliances, you have no direct access to the operating system on the bare-metal hardware.) You don't configure a hypervisor. You don't install "Azure." You don't manually patch the underlying operating systems or management layers. Instead, the Azure Stack is delivered by the vendor you purchase it from, who will then complete the deployment on-site, and it's ready to go. This does not mean there is no management. Updates are provided, but these are a single step that encompasses all aspects of the maintenance, including OS, management layers, hardware drivers, firmware, and everything related to Azure Stack. There are also management tasks related to enabling usage of Azure Stack by your organization. These will be covered later in this chapter.

During the initial setup, a number of settings must be defined, and walking through these will help you to explore some of the relationships between Azure Stack and the public cloud. These settings are configured via a deployment worksheet (a Windows Forms application), which is used to generate the actual configuration files used during the deployment:

Method of Authentication Typically, this will be Azure AD. However, if you have a disconnected scenario where the Internet is not available, or if you simply don't want to use Azure

AD, then federation can also be used via ADFS. The linking for authentication is where Azure Stack is "deployed" to. For Azure AD, this requires a global admin in the target tenant, and several applications will be registered to the Azure AD instance to provide service principals, which are used for aspects of the Azure Stack operations to enable interactions with Azure AD and the Graph API. Figure 8.1 shows some of these for my Azure Stack. An account is also configured as the service administrator that will own the default subscription on the Azure Stack, which is the conduit for all management. Note that if your organization uses least privilege (which is a great idea), then a custom role can be created that provides only the privileges needed for the registration. A walk-through of creating this role is provided at:

```
https://docs.microsoft.com/en-us/azure-stack/operator/
azure-stack-registration-role
```

I actually like to create a separate Azure AD for the Azure Stack deployment. This is because of all the registered applications and to keep things clean. This does not mean I use separate users for Azure Stack. Instead, I add users from my corporate Azure AD using B2B, making them guests in the Azure Stack's specific Azure AD instance, which still enables them to have all the same roles that may be required.

Subscription Used to Establish the Billing Relationship   This is the Azure Stack's registration. Think about it as Azure Stack is deployed to an Azure AD and registered to an Azure subscription. This is where charges related to service consumption of Azure Stack will go. Yes, you buy the Azure Stack appliance, which provides the capacity (e.g., compute, storage, and connectivity), but you still pay for the services that run on top of Azure Stack, such as IaaS VMs, storage services, PaaS, and so on. I'll cover this more later.

Customization   Customization related to VM and physical node prefixes in addition to private and external domain names used by Azure Stack can be configured. These configurations will be utilized as part of the URLs to leverage Azure Stack.

Internal AD   Azure Stack creates its own internal AD for aspects of its management, which includes internal DNS servers for its zones. Your corporate DNS servers will need to have conditional forwarders added for the Azure Stack DNS servers to enable name resolution. Additionally, you need to configure Azure Stack with the DNS servers it should use for DNS forwarding to enable it to resolve Internet names. It also needs time servers to be specified. DNS zones must also be configured for private (internal) and public (external) access by Azure Stack.

Region Name   A region name for your Azure Stack deployment that will surface to many management tasks in the same way as public cloud Azure regions (although your Azure Stack will be in its own cloud) is configured. This region name will also surface in the Azure Stack DNS names. For example, `https://portal.dallas.cloud.savilltech.net` would become the end-user URL if the region were Dallas and I configured the Azure Stack DNS zone to be `cloud.savilltech.net`.

Certificates   Certificates are required for Azure Stack management and user integrations. These could be from an organizationally trusted certificate authority or Internet trusted. There is also a Certificate Checker tool to help ensure the certificates meet requirements and help remediate problems.

FIGURE 8.1
Registered applications during the Azure Stack deployment to Azure AD

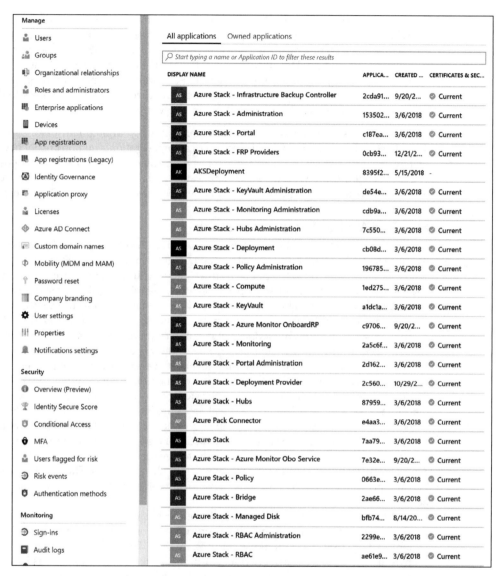

CloudAdmin Account   A CloudAdmin account is created in Azure Stack's internal AD. This is used when interacting to privileged endpoints. This account will be AZURESTACK\ CloudAdmin. (Take a guess as to the NetBIOS AD name that Azure Stack uses.) A password must be configured (and kept safely). During setup, this account is the AzureStackAdmin, but it becomes CloudAdmin once the internal domain is created.

Network IP   Network IP ranges must also be assigned to the stack for private use (within Azure Stack for storage and private VIPs), public use (access external to Azure Stack), infrastructure use (internal Azure Stack use), switch infrastructure use (used for routing and switch interfaces) along with integration access with the company's network infrastructure. Integrations with other infrastructure are based on BGP (an ASN number must be specified) or static routing. The networking architecture is a major design element, as the goal is a hybrid environment. For example, you will likely want to connect Azure Stack to Azure via ExpressRoute if you have an ExpressRoute circuit. If you don't have ExpressRoute, then various types of NAT and site-to-site VPNs can be leveraged.

Azure Stack is designed to be an extension of Azure to your on premises (or perhaps a partnered hosting provider). In an ideal scenario as an organization, you don't really have to differentiate how you architect solutions or even deploy. Azure Stack would act as another possible region you could deploy to. You like the Azure application and data model. You write applications and services for Azure and can just as easily run them on premises on Azure Stack if needed.

Services Available on Azure Stack

In order for Azure Stack to be an extension of Azure, it needs to operate in a consistent manner. By consistent, I mean that if you create a deployment template using JSON, then that template should be able to deploy to the public Azure cloud or your private Azure Stack cloud. If you write an application to run in an App Service Plan, then that application should run in public cloud Azure or on Azure Stack. If your application interacts with Azure Storage REST APIs, it should work against storage accounts in public cloud Azure or Azure Stack. You get the idea.

This consistency is key, but it does not mean that Azure Stack is equal to Azure, nor does it mean it works the same way. Consistency means the various exposed APIs will be consistent across Azure and Azure Stack. Under the covers, however, the actual implementations may be very different, although that has no impact on the usage. For example, think about Azure Storage accounts. In public cloud Azure, the storage accounts sit on top of a three-tiered custom storage solution, which is not practical on Azure Stack, which instead uses Storage Spaces Direct. However, that is an internal detail of how data is stored. The data plane implementation does not impact the exposed endpoint interactions. Against either service I can use the same RESTful API calls to create and interact with storage services. It is important to remember that Azure Stack does lag behind the public cloud, including the APIs. This means the consistency may not match the latest API versions in Azure but rather may be an older version, so this will need to be taken into account.

Additionally, the API is consistent for the services offered on Azure Stack, which are not *all* services available in Azure. Forget about Azure Stack for a second. Azure is made up of many regions that offer services, and those services are provided by a number of resource providers, such as the Compute Resource Provider (CRP) that provides features such as VMs and managed disks. As services are rolled out to Azure, they do not appear in all regions at the same time; instead, new services are initially offered to a limited number of regions in a preview state before moving to General Availability (GA), where they may roll out to all regions or may be limited to certain regions. To see the availability of certain IaaS VM SKUs, visit:

```
https://azure.microsoft.com/en-us/global-infrastructure/
services/?products=virtual-machines
```

Even something as fundamental as VMs has differences by region. This is because of the hardware required to offer some of these special SKUs, which may not make sense to be available everywhere.

Now add Azure Stack back in and remember that the underlying components of Azure are very different from those in Azure Stack. Depending on the service, significant work may be required to enable the service to work on Azure Stack, and some services that leverage special hardware or massive scale may not be practical. This means that services on Azure Stack will always lag behind those available in Azure (it also means you won't see services on Azure Stack that are *not* available in Azure), and not every service in Azure will be available on Azure Stack. Azure Stack offers a subset of the Azure services, but the services it does offer are provided in as a consistent manner as in Azure. New services will first appear in public cloud Azure, then on Azure Stack in a preview mode, and then move to GA. To check on services supported on Azure Stack, view:

```
https://azure.microsoft.com/en-us/overview/azure-stack/keyfeatures/
```

Additionally, many items in the marketplace will also work in Azure Stack which can be available through marketplace syndication (which I will cover in the management section). At the time of writing, core services such as the following are available:

◆ VMs

◆ Managed Disks

◆ App Services

◆ Functions

◆ Storage Accounts

◆ Key Vault

◆ SQL

◆ Others are in development or coming soon, such as AKS, IoT Hub, and Event Hubs.

Note that you can absolutely use Azure Stack to just run VMs, and there is a benefit there, including consistency of deployment and management. Where I really think Azure Stack's value shines in a unique way is when you move into the higher-level services, such as the App Services, Functions, Key Vault, etc. An IaaS VM on Azure Stack is not that different from a VM running on Hyper-V—but a C# Azure Function? I can't do that on Hyper-V!

It is important to not put Azure and Azure Stack as islands. Remember to think of Azure Stack as an extension of Azure. You may run services on Azure Stack but use Azure for backup, for resiliency, for scale, and so on. The maximum benefit will be gained by using them together. The idea is a consistent hybrid cloud across identity, management, data, development, and services.

How to Buy Azure Stack

Azure Stack is an appliance (also known as an integrated system) and is purchased in blocks of nodes that can be thought of as a scale unit. At the time of writing, Azure Stack can be purchased as 4 to 16 node systems. If 16 nodes are not enough to meet capacity requirements, then you can deploy multiple Azure Stack systems as separate clusters. (Think of clusters as nodes that are managed by a common controller, also known as a scale unit.)

A growing number of hardware vendors sell Azure Stack. Although a hardware provider (for example, Dell), provides the physical hardware (to Microsoft's very specific Azure Stack specification) and Microsoft provides the OS and software, there is a single support contact. You will not find yourself being passed between hardware and software vendors in the event of a problem; you just call Microsoft or the OEM, and tickets will be routed accordingly on the back-end. One throat to choke, so to speak, which is very important for organizations.

While Microsoft has a very specific specification that the vendors must adhere to in terms of architecture, connectivity, etc., this does not mean every Azure Stack is the same. Vendors can choose to provide models with different amounts of memory, performance, storage, and net-working, so time should be taken to understand the exact characteristics and relative benefits of the various offerings.

DON'T FORGET THE AZURE IN AZURE STACK

The Azure services in Azure Stack are provided by software running on the hardware. This may seem obvious, but it's critical to remember this when planning the capacity of Azure Stack. The underlying components that make Azure Stack tick (including management, network controllers, SLBs, DCs, etc.) are provided by about 30 VMs, which are deployed across the nodes to ensure resil-iency. These VMs consume about 230 GB of memory, 140 virtual cores, and about 3.5 TB of storage. Remember, also, that Azure Stack has to consider that a node can fail, so it performs a host reserve on each node to ensure that these internal service VMs can always run. If you buy the minimum size Azure Stack, where each node has 256 GB of memory and consists of 4 nodes, then when you consider the host reserve and OS reserve (around 15 percent), around 70 percent of the total Azure Stack's memory is reserved, leaving you with 30 percent of the memory for your workloads. New services like IoT Hub will not install on this. It is critical to ensure that you consider this in your capacity planning. For any real-world deployment, I would recommend nothing less than 512 GB per node. Use the Azure Stack Capacity Planner at https://aka.ms/azstackcapacityplanner to ensure that you pick the right sizes!

At this point, you have purchased the hardware that provides the capacity. Now you buy the services (i.e., Azure) that provide functionality on that capacity. Typically, a pay-as-you-go bill-ing is utilized where, like the public cloud Azure, you are billed for the Azure services used. The pricing is available at:

https://azure.microsoft.com/en-us/overview/azure-stack/how-to-buy/

At the time of writing, a base VM is $6 per vCPU per month, while a Windows Server VM is $34 per vCPU per month (since this includes the licensing for Windows Server). Note there is no charge related to its memory, etc., since this is capacity on your hardware. An App Service is $41 per vCPU per month. Here, more of the value is provided by the Azure services—hence, more consumption charge (compared to a VM where the Azure technology is providing less addi-tional value beyond the hypervisor, but still some value when you think about the management, extensions, and so forth). It is also possible to use capacity-based billing, which is available in a number of SKUs and lets the customer "buy out" the capacity of the Azure Stack appliance and deploy whatever they want within the services of the SKU with no consumption charge. In the capacity model, each core of Azure Stack is covered for either IaaS services or IaaS and PaaS services. (IaaS and PaaS SKUs logically cost more than the IaaS-only SKU due to their increased available services.) Both offerings include the Azure Storage capabilities.

In addition to the nodes you purchase for capacity, a smaller Hardware Lifecycle Host (HLH) may be provided (although not every vendor includes it). This is used for various low-level interactions with Azure Stack and also hosts the initial Deployment VM (DVM) that is used to initially deploy Azure Stack software onto the hardware. (This DVM is removed after the deployment is completed.)

Note that customers will purchase the complete Azure Stack solution in one of two ways: as self-managed (i.e., you buy it and manage it on premises yourself) or via a managed service provider (which will host, manage, and provide the first-line support). Azure Stack is the same—it's just the hosting and support that changes.

Also note that this is not a cheap endeavor. What if you just want to experiment with Azure Stack as a developer or IT architect? While you can't deploy your own Azure Stack on clusters of your own hardware, there is a single-node self-deploy option that provides non-production testing, the Azure Stack Development Kit (ASDK).

The ASDK is a free download available from:

```
https://azure.microsoft.com/en-us/overview/azure-stack/development-kit/
```

The exact hardware requirements may change over time, but at the time of writing, you need a box with a minimum of 192 GB of RAM (256 preferred), 4×240 GB (400 preferred) of storage to create a Storage Space, and two processors (16 cores minimum, 20 preferred). It is possible to deploy this into an Azure VM, provided that the VM supports nested virtualization, enabling the hardware-assisted virtualization of the processor to be made available to the guest—for example, the Dv3, Ev3, or M-series. Once installed, it behaves very similarly to normal Azure Stack, except that it has no high availability and there is no ability to customize DNS or region names. Additionally, since it is a development environment, there is no support for it.

When to Use Azure Stack

There is what I would call some "hero" scenarios for Azure Stack, but certainly usage would not be limited to these. Different organizations have different requirements, different goals, and different politics. With my customers, I always position Azure first. Wherever possible, use the public cloud Azure service. It provides the truest form of consumption billing with no physical assets to manage and host. It gets the services first; it gets the enhancements first; and there will be features only available in Azure. It has infinite scale. It has global availability and often built-in high availability and disaster recovery. It has less to manage. (I'll get to this in the next major section.) So when would I use Azure Stack? Following are some key reasons I have seen, from most obvious to "gray area":

Disconnected Scenarios   You may work where there are locations without Internet connectivity or at least not Internet connectivity good enough to support services operating across. Think about a cruise ship. There are many systems that keep these floating cities operating, and being able to run application services on each ship provides the best option. There are many other types of industries where there are disconnected environments.

Azure Regions That Are Not Available or Not Usable   Azure has regions throughout the world, but perhaps there is not a region where you need services made available. You can create your own region with Azure Stack. There could be regulatory requirements that prohibit the storing of data off premises. The reality is that Azure has many certifications related to types of compliance. Azure has regions specific to certain countries to meet data sovereignty requirements—for example, Germany and the Black Forest cloud. However, if there are regulations or simply your company "isn't there yet" in terms of trusting the cloud, then Azure Stack provides the Azure services on premises. For example, the organization wants to adopt the cloud model with serverless compute.

An Anchor That Needs Services Close to It   This was a fairly new concept to me, until I had two customers in a month tell me about their anchor. An anchor is some system that cannot be moved to the cloud—for example, a mainframe. If the need is to have Azure services interact with the anchor, then hosting those services in the public cloud may not work even with ExpressRoute, as, depending on the types of communication, the latency may be too high. If that is the case, then running those services in an Azure Stack sitting next to the anchor in the datacenter will provide the optimal latency. And who knows—if one day you can get rid of the anchor or move it to the cloud, it will be easy to transport the Azure services to public cloud Azure.

The Appeal of Black Box Appliances   I have seen companies that like the black box appliance model over buying hardware, installing the OS, setting up the hypervisor, setting up the management, etc. While I don't feel it's getting the full benefit of Azure Stack, there is certainly a case for using Azure Stack as a low-maintenance VM appliance.

Managing Azure Stack

In this section, I walk through the unique management aspects of Azure Stack. For services and many interactions, the management is consistent with Azure, which is the whole point of a consistent, hybrid-cloud solution. However, there are some additional management considerations for Azure Stack, which I will cover here. I am not going to cover the details of actually registering Azure Stack, etc., as these are well documented and will be walked through with you as part of the Azure Stack provisioning.

How to Interact with Azure Stack

As previously mentioned, each Azure Stack integrated system becomes its own region. These Azure Stack–hosted regions are in a separate cloud from the commercial cloud that hosts the majority of the publicly accessible Azure regions. You saw this in Chapter 1 when we looked at the available Azure environments. If you remember, in that output, you saw an additional environment, AzureStackDallas, which was the environment I had configured to enable interaction with my Dallas-based Azure Stack. But how do we get this and how do we use it?

As part of the configuration, a DNS suffix and a region name were specified. This makes up the core part of the various URIs that will be used. If my region were Dallas and the DNS suffix provided were cloud.savilltech.net, my base URI would be dallas.cloud.savilltech.net. From this, there are four very important URIs that will be used frequently (well, some more frequently than others), as shown in Table 8.1.

TABLE 8.1:   Core Azure Stack URIs

PURPOSE	FORMAT	EXAMPLE
Admin portal	`https://adminportal.<region>` `.<external DNS name>`	`https://adminportal.dallas` `.cloud.savilltech.net`
User portal	`https://portal.<region>.<external` `DNS name>`	`https://portal.dallas.cloud` `.savilltech.net`
Admin ARM endpoint	`https://adminmanagement.<region>` `.<external DNS name>`	`https://adminmanagement` `.dallas.cloud.savilltech.net`
User ARM endpoint	`https://management.<region>` `.<external DNS name>`	`https://management.dallas` `.cloud.savilltech.net`

If you are using the Azure Stack Development Kit, the region is always local and the external DNS name is always `azurestack.external`, which means, for example, the admin portal would always be `https://adminportal.local.azurestack.external`.

Once these URIs are known, they can be leveraged. For the portals, they can simply be navigated to, provided that you have enabled the conditional forwarding from your corporate DNS infrastructure to the DNS servers of Azure Stack. The IPs are part of the generated `AzureStackStampInformation.json` file as the ExternameDNSIPAddress01 and 02 values (along with many other useful bits of information, so keep this file safe) that should be used as part of the forwarding of DNS from corporate DNS. The `AzureStackStampInformation.json` file that is created as part of the deployment contains a lot of very useful information related to the deployed solution. However, at this point, only the cloud administrator will actually have any rights to do anything on the default subscription, and no other subscriptions will exist—but we'll get to that. The end-user portal looks and behaves the same as the public cloud Azure portal, while the admin portal contains elements unique to Azure Stack.

For PowerShell management and interaction, there are two sets of resources:

◆ PowerShell module for Azure Stack, which is a special API-compatible version of the regular Azure PowerShell and which is available at:

`https://docs.microsoft.com/en-us/azure-stack/operator/`
`azure-stack-powershell-install`

◆ The Azure Stack tools, which are available on GitHub at:

`https://github.com/Azure/AzureStack-Tools`

Once you have the PowerShell module and the Azure Stack tools, you need to create a new environment that represents access to Azure Stack. If you are just a user, then only the user endpoint is required. If you need to perform management, such as marketplace management, plans, offers, subscriptions, etc., then you need the admin endpoint. Following is some example PowerShell to set them both up. You need to authenticate. This could be with the cloud admin, although you should be adding additional users with rights, especially on the user side, and with their own subscriptions.

```
#First setup some variables
$StackTenantName = "dalstack.onmicrosoft.com"
$StackTenantID = "<AAD Tenant ID>"
$AdminArmEndpoint = "https://adminmanagement.dallas.dallasmtc.com/"
$UserArmEndpoint = "https://management.dallas.dallasmtc.com/"

#Setup endpoints for Admin and User
Add-AzureRMEnvironment -Name "AzureStackAdmin" `
    -ArmEndpoint "$AdminArmEndpoint" -ErrorAction Stop
Add-AzureRmEnvironment -Name "AzureStackUser" -ARMEndpoint "$UserArmEndpoint" `
    -ErrorAction Stop

#Connect to the admin environment
Login-AzureRmAccount -Environment "AzureStackAdmin" -TenantId $StackTenantID
#Select the default provider subscription
Select-AzureRmSubscription -Subscription (Get-AzureRmSubscription `
        -SubscriptionName "Default Provider Subscription").Id

#Do admin stuff
<commands>

#Login to user endpoint to perform user items
Login-AzureRmAccount -Environment AzureStackUser -TenantId $StackTenantID

#Do user stuff
<commands>
```

Notice that each time I log on, I specify the tenant ID of the Azure AD for Azure Stack. This is because, in my case, Azure Stack has its own Azure AD instance separate from the main corporate Azure AD. The users I am logging on with are guests (B2B) to the stack tenant, which means I need to specify it. The same applies when accessing the various portals. To use an account from a guest, you need to add the AAD name of the stack (dalstack.onmicrosoft.com) to ensure proper access. For example, if I were connecting as a guest account to my admin portal, I would use the following:

```
https://adminportal.dallas.savilltech.net/dalstack.onmicrosoft.com
```

If I were connecting a guest account to the user portal, I would use the following:

```
https://portal.dallas.savilltech.net/dalstack.onmicrosoft.com
```

There is nothing special about Azure Stack related to passing the AAD instance as part of the URL. You use this in many other aspects of Microsoft cloud services when using guest accounts.

At this point, you can use consistent interaction with PowerShell in addition to JSON templates for deployment and other types of integrations.

Marketplace Syndication

Before giving users access to Azure Stack, you need to populate it with base assets, such as VM templates, extensions, etc. In the public cloud, there is a rich marketplace populated by

Microsoft and partners. One of the reasons that Azure Stack must be registered with an Azure subscription is not just for billing purposes but because it also allows marketplace syndication—i.e., the downloading of assets to Azure Stack.

The downloading of assets can be done through the portal using Marketplace Management, as shown in Figure 8.2. Items already downloaded are shown, and you can add additional items. I recommend also reviewing the Azure marketplace syndication content at:

```
https://docs.microsoft.com/en-us/azure-stack/operator/
azure-stack-download-azure-marketplace-item
```

FIGURE 8.2
Using the
Admin portal
Marketplace
management

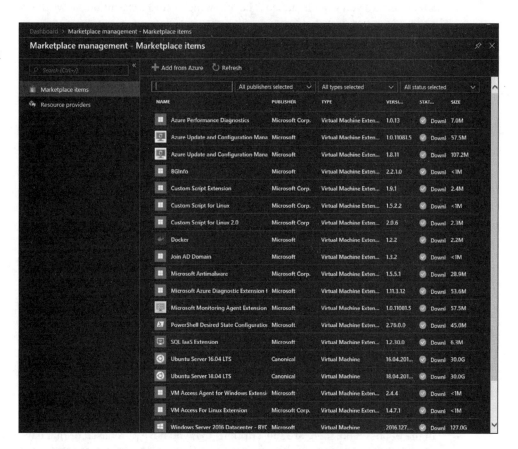

While the portal works fine, the challenge will quickly become keeping the content up-to-date, especially if you have a lot of downloads. Fortunately, you can also use PowerShell to syndicate content. I wrote a script that does the following:

◆ Connects to the admin endpoint

◆ Searches the Azure marketplace for all extensions

◆ Downloads any extensions not currently installed

◆ Allows an array of desired images to be specified

◆ Downloads the latest version of each image

◆ Deletes old versions of extensions or images

The script can be found at:

`https://github.com/johnthebrit/AzureStack/blob/master/azurestackmarketplace.ps1`

You should update the script with your Azure Stack and AAD details. Additionally, replace which images you want installed. The following example execution shows the various checks and updates performed:

```
Checking for microsoft.azuremonitor-1.0.11081.4
** Didn't find microsoft.azuremonitor-1.0.11081.4 in your gallery. Downloading
from the Azure Stack Marketplace **
Checking for microsoft.antimalware-windows-arm-1.5.5.1
Checking for microsoft.custom-script-linux-arm-1.5.2.2
Checking for microsoft.vmaccessagent-2.4.4
Checking for microsoft.dsc-arm-2.76.0.0
Checking for microsoft.customscriptextension-arm-1.9.1
Checking for microsoft.custom-script2-linux-arm-2.0.6
Checking for microsoft.azuremonitor-dependencyagent-windows-9.7.4
** Didn't find microsoft.azuremonitor-dependencyagent-windows-9.7.4 in your
gallery. Downloading from the Azure Stack Marketplace **
Checking for microsoft.bginfo-2.2.1.0
Checking for microsoft.iaasdiagnostics-1.11.3.12
Checking for microsoft.azuremonitor-dependencyagent-linux-9.7.4
** Didn't find microsoft.azuremonitor-dependencyagent-linux-9.7.4 in your
gallery. Downloading from the Azure Stack Marketplace **
Checking for microsoft.azureperformancediagnostics-arm-1.0.13
Checking for microsoft.sqliaasextension-1.2.30.0
Checking for microsoft.jsonaddomainextension-1.3.2
Checking for microsoft.vmaccessforlinux-1.4.7.1
Checking for microsoft.azuremonitorforlinux-1.8.11
** Didn't find microsoft.azuremonitorforlinux-1.8.11 in your gallery.
Downloading from the Azure Stack Marketplace **
```

Plans, Offers, and Subscriptions

In the public cloud. there are subscriptions that you have purchased or that have been created as part of an enterprise enrollment. For Azure Stack, plans are created that consist of certain quotas for specific enabled services, and then an offer built from one or more plans is created. Add-on plans can also be added, which are not enabled by default but can be added to the subscription post creation if required—for example, to add more quota. Subscriptions can then be created by administrators from an offer and assigned, or an offer can be made public and users can request a subscription from the public offer.

There is also a default subscription. This default subscription contains all the core resources and is what enables access to administrative functions. Someone who has the contributor role on the default subscription can perform full management. Someone who has the read role on the default subscription can view all aspects of the admin portal but cannot make any changes.

The administrative portal can be used or PowerShell can be leveraged. In the following example, I create a plan (a non-public offer) and then create a subscription to which I grant an AAD group access. Notice that I create a separate resource group to store the plans and offers. Additionally, in order to grant permissions to the subscription, I have to switch to the user endpoint instead of the admin endpoint used for the rest of the actions. I include the code to make the offer public, but it is commented out.

```
Login-AzureRmAccount -Environment "AzureStackAdmin" -TenantId $StackTenantID

#Create a plan
$OfferName = "remote-user-offer"
$PlanName = "remote-user-plan"
$RGName = "RG-PlansandOffers"
$RGLocation = (get-azurermlocation).location

$APPGroup = get-azureadgroup -SearchString "APPUsers"

#Create Compute Quota
$ComputeQuota=New-AzsComputeQuota -Name RemoteUserComputeQuota -CoresLimit 50 `
        -AvailabilitySetCount 10 -VmScaleSetCount 10 -VirtualMachineCount 25 `
        -StandardManagedDiskAndSnapshotSize 2048 `
        -PremiumManagedDiskAndSnapshotSize 2048

#Create Network Quota
$NetworkQuota=New-AzsNetworkQuota -Name RemoteUserNetworkQuota `
        -MaxNicsPerSubscription 50 -MaxPublicIpsPerSubscription 10 `
        -MaxVirtualNetworkGatewaysPerSubscription 1 `
        -MaxVirtualNetworkGatewayConnectionsPerSubscription 2 `
        -MaxVnetsPerSubscription 50 -MaxSecurityGroupsPerSubscription 50 `
        -MaxLoadBalancersPerSubscription 25

#Create Storage Quota
$StorageQuota=New-AzsStorageQuota -Name RemoteUserStorageQuota `
        -CapacityInGb 4096 -NumberOfStorageAccounts 40

#Get KeyVault Quota
$KeyVaultQuota=Get-AzsKeyVaultQuota

#Create new Plan & Assign Quotas
$quota=($ComputeQuota.id,$NetworkQuota.id,$StorageQuota.Id,$KeyVaultQuota.Id)
$ResoureGroup=New-AzureRmResourceGroup -Name $RGName -Location $RGLocation
$Plan=New-AzsPlan -Name $PlanName `
        -ResourceGroupName $ResoureGroup.ResourceGroupName `
```

```
        -DisplayName "Remote User Plan" -QuotaIds $quota

#Create Offer
$Offer=New-AzsOffer -Name $OfferName -DisplayName "Remote User Offer" `
        -ResoureGroupName $ResoureGroup.ResourceGroupName `
        -BasePlanIds $plan.Id
#$Offer=Get-AzsManagedOffer -Name $OfferName `
        -ResourceGroupName $RGName #private offer

#Make Offer Public - Don't want to here
#Set-AzsOffer -Name $offer.Name -State public `
        -ResourceGroupName $ResoureGroup.ResourceGroupName

#Create Subcriptions
$Sub = New-AzsUserSubscription -OfferId $Offer.Id -Owner $subOwner `
        -DisplayName "App Team Tenant Subscription"

#Move to user endpoint
Login-AzureRmAccount -Environment AzureStackUser -TenantId $StackTenantID

#Register all the providers for each sub
Select-AzureRmSubscription -SubscriptionId $sub.SubscriptionId | Out-Null
Write-Progress $($sub.SubscriptionId + " : " + $sub.SubscriptionName)
Get-AzureRmResourceProvider -ListAvailable | Register-AzureRmResourceProvider

New-AzureRmRoleAssignment -ObjectId $APPGroup.ObjectId `
        -RoleDefinitionName "Contributor" `
        -Scope "/subscriptions/$($Sub.SubscriptionId)"
```

Updating Azure Stack

A few months prior to writing this section, I would have talked about checking a website, downloading files to a special storage account, and then triggering an update. (These steps are still required in disconnected scenarios.) Now, however, updating is very simple for connected systems, like updating a Windows machine. Updates show as available, and you click Update! These updates include every aspect of Azure Stack, from hardware firmware and drivers to the Azure Stack software and resource providers.

Figure 8.3 shows the Update screen. In this case, only a minor update is available, which can be installed simply by selecting and clicking Update Now. You will be prompted to run the Test-AzureStack cmdlet prior to updating to ensure the overall health of the stack. Larger updates may be multiple gigabytes in size and take considerably longer (i.e., multiple hours). It is important to ensure that you keep your Azure Stack updated. If you have multiple environments, there is integration possible with Log Analytics to provide a centralized view of the patch status of all your Azure Stack deployments. This can be found at:

https://github.com/Azure-Samples/AzureStack-AdminPowerShell-OMSIntegration/blob/master/docs/setup.md

At the time of writing, this requires a special VM to be created and maintained. Over time, however, as the integration becomes a core feature, I expect this requirement to be removed.

FIGURE 8.3
Azure Stack's
update
experience

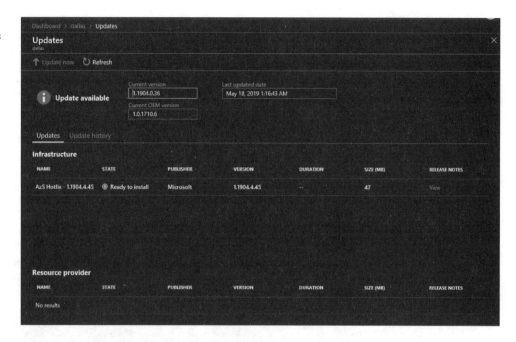

Privileged Endpoint and Support Session Tokens

For most administrative operations, you will use the portal or PowerShell (maybe even the REST API). However, there are some things that need a little bit more power. For these circumstances, there is the Privileged EndPoint (PEP), which is hosted by special VM, and the IP addresses are detailed in the `AzureStackStampInformation.json` file as the `EmergencyConsoleIPAddresses` values. To connect to the endpoint, there are a number of steps to make it a trusted host, since you will be using the IP address, and therefore no mutual authentication is possible. The cloud admin account must be used to connect (i.e., AZURESTACK\CloudAdmin). Even with the cloud admin account, the access is still limited, and the connection is to a special JEA (just-enough-administration) endpoint that exposes about 30 cmdlets, which provide more information but still prevent you accessing everything or doing anything damaging. Everything that occurs is logged via the PEP. Following is an example connection establishment:

```
$CloudAdminCred = Get-Credential -UserName "AZURESTACK\CloudAdmin" `
    -Message "Enter the cloud domain credentials to access the privileged endpoint."
Enter-PSSession -ComputerName 10.1.50.224 -Credential $CloudAdminCred `
    -ConfigurationName "PrivilegedEndpoint"

#Do stuff, e.g
Get-AzureStackStampInformation
```

This endpoint can be unlocked by support if required. During a support call, they may ask you to run a command `Get-SupportSessionToken` and then `Unlock-SupportSession`, to which the support representative will provide a response token to enable unlocking. Once the endpoint is unlocked, other commands are possible for deeper troubleshooting and resolution, but only perform the actions given by support.

Understanding Azure Stack HCI

I want to quickly touch on Azure Stack HCI, as there seems to be some confusion about what it is. Azure and Azure Stack are well understood. Azure Stack is a hyper-converged system (meaning the compute and storage are provided on the same nodes), with software providing most of the core storage and network capabilities. The Azure capabilities are enabled on top of this hyper-converged platform.

Azure Stack HCI is an evolution of the Windows Server Storage-Defined program, which was a set of hardware designed and certified to support Storage Spaces Direct (S2D). Storage Spaces Direct is the solution Azure Stack utilizes for its highly available storage that is enabled by duplicating data between disks on different nodes and sufficing it as aggregated, shared storage. Azure Stack HCI uses this same S2D technology for its software-defined storage and overall hyper-converged solution—hence, the "Azure Stack" in "Azure Stack HCI." They share the same hyper-converged architecture; however, Azure Stack HCI does not provide any Azure-consistent services. Instead, it is focused on providing a virtualization platform via Hyper-V and built on Windows Server 2019 and the Windows Admin Center solution.

Azure Stack HCI does consume a number of Azure services to enhance capability, such as backup, disaster recovery, Azure File Sync, update management, monitoring, and more. Figure 8.4 shows the Azure Stack HCI stack.

FIGURE 8.4
The Azure Stack HCI stack

You can buy an Azure Stack HCI solution from a number of partners, but you can also build your own very similar solution, as the Windows Admin Center is a free download from Microsoft and the Azure services exposed today are not exclusive to Azure Stack HCI. Azure Stack HCI solutions, which can range from 2 to 16 nodes, are not based on a consumption model; instead, you pay up front for Windows Server 2019. The Azure Stack HCI solutions are available for browsing at:

```
https://www.microsoft.com/en-us/cloud-platform/azure-stack-hci-catalog
```

Also, don't forget about Azure Data Box Edge, which was covered in Chapter 6, "Storage." In addition to providing storage services, Azure Data Box Edge provides near-compute services that are built on IoT Edge in addition to a number of cognitive services via its built-in Project Brainwave FPGA card. Another on-premises member of the Azure family!

Chapter 9

Backup, High Availability, Disaster Recovery, and Migration

This chapter focuses on a lot of different topics, but it really boils down to the availability of services and their resiliency. There are multiple dimensions to achieving the right levels of availability and resiliency, which will be explored in this chapter.

In this chapter, you will learn to:

◆ Understand the requirements and dependencies of applications to help design the right availability and resiliency solutions.

◆ Use the right high availability solution within a region.

◆ Use Recovery Vaults to provide backup and disaster recovery.

◆ Use geo-balancing for multi-region deployments.

◆ Plan migrations.

Availability 101

There are many aspects to availability and it's important to understand how the aspects fit together to architect the right solution for your organization.

Distinguishing High Availability vs. Disaster Recovery vs. Backup

Before examining solutions for availability, it's important to understand which type of availability we need and the architectural decisions and technologies that will be leveraged. Note that we often don't pick; we often need all three of the types of resiliency I am going to cover. You will hear about RPO and RTO when discussing backups, high availability, and disaster recovery, which relate to:

Recovery Point Objective (RPO)   The recovery point in the event of an incident—i.e., how much data can be lost, e.g., 30 minutes (for unplanned incidents; planned incidents ideally would suffer no data loss)

Recovery Time Objective (RTO)   The amount of time it takes to activate the resiliency and be up and running—that is, how long the system can be unavailable (e.g., 5 minutes)

Backups are most likely the easiest to understand. This provides a point-in-time copy of a workload saved to storage (for example, a copy of a VM at 1 a.m. every day), or a backup of a database with optional transaction log storage, or saving file share content every 4 hours. The idea is to save a copy of some source to separate storage at a certain interval. We back up for a number of reasons, including:

◆ To restore to the most recent backup if the source is lost.

◆ To restore to a previous point in time if some logical corruption or deletion occurs (although often undelete is used before backup restoration, where possible). This could also be because of a malicious event, such as an attack or virus that deletes/encrypts data.

◆ To restore to an alternate location if the primary location is lost. (This is really now part of disaster recovery and requires the backup content to be replicated to another region.)

◆ To keep a certain amount of historical data for company and/or regulatory requirements. Using retention policies can be useful to optimize storage, such as keeping a daily backup for 2 weeks, a weekly backup for 2 months, a monthly backup for 12 months, and then an annual backup for 7 years.

Backups often enable us to recover from some kind of human act, such as a deletion of data, corruption, or even attack. This is different from disaster recovery, which is often required in the event of an "act of god," such as a flood or earthquake.

It's important that backup data is stored both close to the source, for optimal restoration, but also far from the source, so that an event at the primary location does not impact both the source and only copy of the backup data. This is achieved by replication of the backup stores. Backup data needs to be as protected as the source data in terms of people that can access the data and encryption. In an ideal world, we hope to never have to use backups, but it's critical they be routinely tested to ensure they could be restored if needed. I remember in my early days (where backup was to tape) seeing banks, having a disaster, then realizing the failover location never updated their tape drive and couldn't read the backups. They were not good days. Additionally, ensure that backups are isolated from the primary data if possible—i.e., some bad actor cannot corrupt the primary data and then go delete/corrupt the backups!

No matter what else you have, you should always have backups for anything that has state you care about—i.e., data. Nothing replaces the need for backups of data. If you have deployments that have no meaningful state, you might not care about backups. If you are an IIS frontend in a VM or PaaS instance, you likely don't care if it's destroyed. Note that you may care about this sometimes. Imagine that you have a DNS resource and configuration on that PaaS resource. Redeploying from the source would not restore those types of resource configurations, but those are exceptions. You typically can re-create faster than restoring, provided that you have a good process in place to build, such as a DevOps pipeline that pulls the configuration from a repository, builds, and releases.

High availability (HA) is about making a service available within a location—for example, within a specific Azure region. This provides protection against some isolated failure, such as a compute instance or physical node failure. HA is typically achieved through multiple instances of a compute service distributed over Fault Domains/racks (availability sets) or datacenters (availability zones) that are balanced using a load balancer or client mechanism. We use availability sets or availability zones to protect the multiple compute instances from a common physical failure. For storage services, the availability would be provided by synchronous replication of data, which is possible since the copies are within a region and therefore low latencies (at most 2 ms). If a service supports only a single instance, then high availability is not really possible, and there will be downtimes for certain types of incidents and even planned maintenance. This is an important point: High availability provides protection from incidents but also maintenance, such as patching of guest operating systems (if a VM), updating the application or Azure maintenance. Multiple instances using availability sets or availability zones ensure that any planned maintenance impacts only a portion of the deployed instances (update domain) at any one time, meaning the service stays available, albeit with a slightly reduced scale. We don't expect to lose data for intra-region problems, nor would we expect any downtime.

Disaster recovery is about keeping business running for a region-level event—i.e., we have lost the primary location. Disaster recovery (DR) is very different from high availability. We hope to never use DR outside of routine testing, as it means something very bad has happened. When activating DR, this may be planned or unplanned. A planned event is when we know some outage is coming and can take steps ahead of the actual impact and should not have any unplanned data loss. For an unplanned event (e.g., where did the datacenter go?), we would expect to have some data loss, but it should be within our expected SLAs. This is where things like RPO and RTO really come into play and will be driven by the business. For the business-critical app, we may have an RTO of 15 minutes (we have to be up and running in 15 minutes) and an RPO of 2 minutes (we can lose only 2 minutes of data). Depending on the requirements of RPO and RTO, it will drive how we implement DR, which will consist of services in a second location that can be started in the event of a disaster and some asynchronous replication of data. We also then need a way to redirect clients of the services to the new instances, such as a geo-balancing solution like Azure Front Door or Azure Traffic Manager, if the service is publicly facing. There are many different ways to architect DR solutions, with different balances of RPO, RTO, and, of course, cost! We can often say we want the lowest RPO and RTO possible, which will cost a million dollars, or an RPO of 5 minutes and RTO of 15 minutes, for five thousand dollars, for something that we hope never happens and would be a major issue. We need to weigh the business impact, reputation, trust, and cost versus the cost to protect. We often find a middle ground.

In the cloud, we may be able to change architecture to simply have multiple active sites spread over multiple regions, instead of an active site and a passive site. This gives resiliency from a region failure while also putting services closer to clients through distribution of services, but it does require certain application architecture considerations around services and data access (which I will cover). The nature of our distributed deployment provides inherent DR. We simply would need a scale action in the event of a region outage, as now we would have lost a significant chunk of capacity, so we just increase the remaining deployment's capacity.

In short, we typically need all three. We always need backups—at least for any important state/data. We always want high availability, and we typically want DR, either as a separate solution, if we can't run active-active across locations, or just as part of a geo-distributed deployment.

I am going to cover all of these in more detail throughout this chapter.

Understanding Application Structure and Requirements

Before it is possible to start implementing any type of availability solution, it is critical to understand what you are trying to protect and its requirements. As you will see throughout this chapter, there are numerous technologies and options to provide resiliency and no single "right" answer; rather, there are pros and cons, which weigh differently based on what is trying to be protected and what the resiliency requirements are.

Many applications today have multiple tiers. For example, even the most basic application today tends to at minimum have a frontend tier where requests are made and handled and then a backend tier that stores data—for example, a database such as SQL Server, as shown in Figure 9.1. Some also have a middle-tier that acts as the interface between the requests and the backend database, providing business logic or validation, and some even more than this. Additionally, they may interact with various other services for processing or temporary storage—for example, dumping data initially to a blob. Services may have dependencies on other services. This could be Active Directory, Azure AD, Azure AD B2C instances, load balancers, firewall appliances, and so on. You must understand the components of the application and all of its dependencies (and follow the chain so that you understand any dependencies of the dependencies). It's no good to protect the application and then during an incident realize you hadn't protected a dependency, rendering the overall service unavailable. Whatever your agreed-upon RPO and RTOs for the service, any dependency tree has to meet or exceed those as well. (We have a similar concept when thinking of security that any dependency must be at least as secure as that required for the service.)

FIGURE 9.1
A very simple applica-
tion architecture

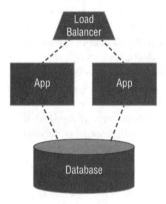

There are tools to assist with determining dependencies. One solution, which is part of Log Analytics, works by detecting network communications between machines. This is called Service Map. Additionally, Application Insights has an Application Map capability that per-forms a similar functionality, but instead of triggering from network traffic, it works by tracking the function calls in .NET—although this obviously only works for your custom applications. Ideally, these would simply be sanity checks on a pre-existing understanding of the relationship between applications and services.

Once the basic structure of the application is known, you need to understand the appli-cation. Look again at Figure 9.1. Notice in this instance that there are two instances of the application behind a load balancer talking to "database." This means the application supports multi-instances of itself. This is huge and is required to really have any kind of high availabil-ity within a region. If an application supports only a single instance, we are very limited with regards to the type of availability that can be offered, so this must be well understood. Having multiple instances behind a load balancer also infers the applications don't have any "state" stored locally (i.e., data that is only stored in the application), but rather the data is persisted to the database. There may be some transient state (maybe basic session data), but typically this would not be important. You need to validate this, as it would impact the protection of data aspect.

What is the access pattern of the application to the database? Is it mainly reads? Mainly writes? Is it tolerant to latency, etc? This becomes important when we start thinking about disaster recovery and potential access across distances, especially when we use single-master data solutions like SQL Server.

How are people accessing the application? Is it via IP address? Is it via DNS? Is it via a browser or hard coded inside a client application? Is the access from the Internet or from an internal network connected via a site-to-site VPN or ExpressRoute. All of these items need to be well understood before any kind of resiliency plans can be formulated. As you can see, there is a lot to do, and the business owners of the application will need to be involved in order to ascertain all the information.

Architecting for Multi-Region Application Deployments

Before looking at specific aspects of availability, I want to drill down into some more detail about considerations for having an application active in multiple regions. I'm going to focus around a typical scenario with a stateless frontend that talks to a database. I will examine the considerations for making it work in an active fashion in multiple regions.

The first step is to ensure that multiple instances of the frontend are supported. This is really a prerequisite even for high availability within a region. These instances would sit behind a load balancer, such as the Azure Load Balancer, Azure Application Gateway, or a virtual appliance from the marketplace. If the frontends are PaaS, they will automatically use availability sets/availability zones. If the frontends are VMs, however, make sure you have used availability sets or availability zones as part of the deployment. Then the instances talk to a backend database. For now, we'll assume it's a SQL database instance. In my example, it's the Azure SQL database PaaS service; however, even if it's SQL Server in a VM, the considerations would be the same. At this point, our service is highly available, as we have multiple frontends balanced behind a load balancer, and the database hosted by Azure SQL Database is highly available as part of the service. If you were running SQL Server in VMs, you would need to ensure that you had at least two SQL Servers that were part of a SQL Always On Availability Group and those VMs were part of an availability set or availability zone (to protect against rack/datacenter failure). This is our Figure 9.1 that we used earlier in the chapter.

Now we want to run the service in two regions. Once we create an architecture for two regions, the hard work is done. Adding a third or forth region would not really add any additional complexity until we hit replica limits of SQL Server. (Four secondary database instances currently are supported.)

The first part is the frontends. Since we already support multiple instances of the frontend within a region, spreading those instances over multiple regions does not introduce much additional complexity. The architecture would have multiple frontend deployments, each with their own load balancer, although at this point each instance has a different endpoint, which is likely not desired. I don't want to direct users to different endpoints and tell them to use a different endpoint if one is not available, and also don't want users to have to think about "where am I right now or which endpoint is closest to me?" We need to place an additional traffic-balancing solution on top of the regional load balancers that acts as a single endpoint, which then balances the traffic among the possible targets. Ideally, a performance traffic distribution algorithm is used, which will direct clients to the target closest to them from a latency perspective.

Both Azure Traffic Manager and Azure Front Door support this and are the key geo-balancing technologies offered by Azure. As discussed in the networking chapter, if the service is HTTP/HTTPS-based, use Azure Front Door; if not, use Azure Traffic Manager, which works for any type of service. Figure 9.2 shows our deployment with multiple frontend farms spread over two regions.

FIGURE 9.2
Architecture extended to have the frontend in two regions

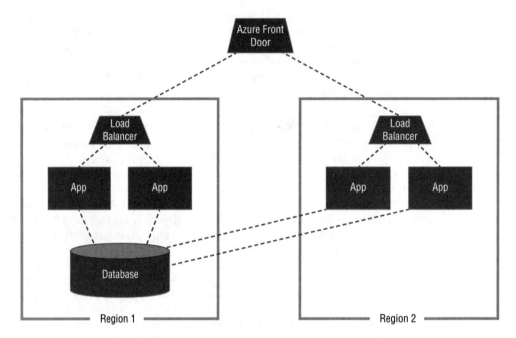

A big benefit here is that now we have DR for our frontend and all without a lot of extra compute spend. We have distributed our scale over regions, which means instead of four instances in Region 1, we can have two instances in each. Only the additional load balancer in Region 2 and the geo-balancer are additional costs. In the event of a regional outage, we may need to increase the number of instances to ensure that we can meet capacity, but that would be simple with auto-scale capabilities based on CPU/queue metrics, and so forth—i.e., if Region 2 were down and the instances in Region 1 were now getting more traffic, then additional instances could automatically be added to Region 1 to meet demand.

Figure 9.2 may be exposing an obvious challenge straightaway with our current state. Yes, the frontend is now available in multiple regions, balanced from a single global endpoint; however, the database only exists in a single region. This has the following two problems:

♦ The region with the database is a single point of failure. If Region 1 fails, then even through the frontend is still available in Region 2, it won't work without the database.

♦ The database access from Region 2 is travelling across potentially large distances, meaning large latencies, which will likely negatively impact the performance of the application. This was something we needed to understand as part of our discovery—how the application interacts with the database, tolerance to latency, etc.

How we proceed next really depends on how the application interacts with the database and our appetite for possible change. As previously mentioned, Azure SQL Database supports secondary replicas. This means to solve the first problem, the single point of failure, the solution would be to add a replica in Region 2. Now, if Region 1 failed, the secondary could be promoted to primary and be used by the instances. (This can all be automated.) This would look like Figure 9.3. Note that the applications in Region 2 are still talking to the instance in Region 1 for the database. The replica in Region 2 is for failover only. The applications would only be using the SQL read-write listener. This is not likely to be acceptable for most applications. One option is the applications in Region 2 are not used unless there is an actual failover (i.e., keep the applications and the database failover together), as this keeps the applications close to the database—but hopefully we can avoid this, as it is not an active-active solution.

FIGURE 9.3
Architecture
with a replica
in Region 2 of
the database
for DR
purposes only

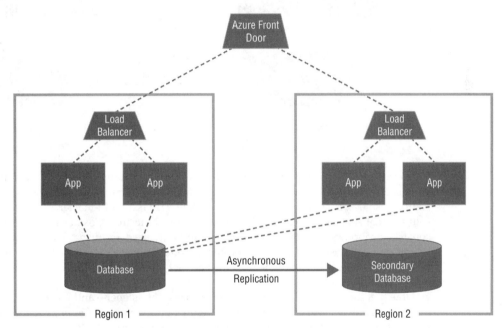

We can enable the secondaries for read-access. This would enable the application instances to perform read operations from the secondary replica, while write operations would still go to the primary replica in the remote region via the read-write listener. For many applications, the bulk of interactions are read operations, which means the additional latency for the relatively infrequent write operations may be acceptable. This would now give a solution as shown in Figure 9.4, which is really as far as we can go with a single-master database like SQL Server. This requires the application to differentiate between read operations and write operations and the target they should use (database server endpoint for read-only access versus the read-write listener for read-write access). Also remember that the replication is asynchronous, so the reads from the replica may potentially be from data that is a little stale. The application may need to understand to read operations from the primary replica (i.e., the read-write listener) if it's trying to read based on data it just wrote.

FIGURE 9.4
Architecture using
the replica for read
operations

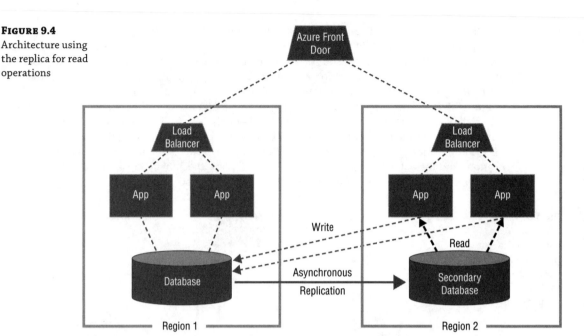

If write operations are required locally at the locations of the applications' instances, then you need to move away from a single-master database to a multi-master database—for example, Azure Cosmos DB, as shown in Figure 9.5. Cosmos DB is a multi-master, global-scale database solution that enables replicas in every Azure region, if desired. Cosmos DB supports various consistency models. Session consistency is commonly used, ensuring that read-writes are consistent across processes that need consistency (commonly at a regional level), but allows replication asynchronously between the regions. Each set of applications has full read-write to their local instance of the Cosmos DB database.

Note that the move to Cosmos DB is not a change of listener—and you're done. Cosmos DB has various models (but commonly uses documents) and is a NoSQL implementation. Items are typically JSON, and there are different design considerations. Also, the application will interact with the database using different APIs and data structures. This means there is work involved in a move from SQL Server to Cosmos DB, which may be significant.

Different applications have different requirements. It may be that the SQL Server secondary replicas with read-only access locally work for the application, providing active-active availability and giving customers access to services close to them while providing HA and DR for the application. In the event of a regional failure, the failover would be fast and have minimal impact. If the latency for write operations is not tolerable, then either the application only runs in one region and fails over to another region with the database or a move to something like Cosmos DB is required.

FIGURE 9.5
Architecture
using
Cosmos DB

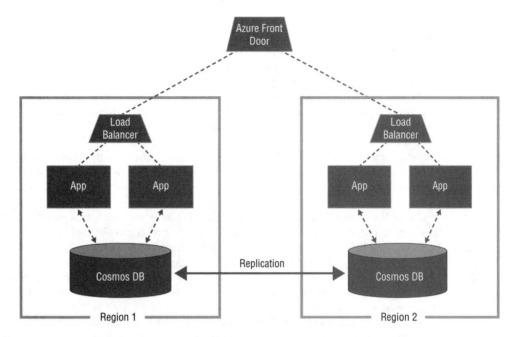

Backups in Azure

While many replication and DR technologies are available today, these often won't remove the need to back up. Careful planning is required to understand the right way to achieve the restoration, which is the end goal for any backup planning.

Thinking About Backups

When planning for backups, always flip it round and instead ask what you want to be able to restore. This will guide what and how you actually back up. Think through what the workload is and what you care about. While the first instinct may be just to "back up the VM," that's not thinking about it in terms of what you want to be able to restore—or, maybe more precisely, the granularity of the restore you want. Consider a VM that has SQL Server running inside. The most likely scenario of restore would be a database restore, which would not be easily performed by backing up the VM, since the backup would have no concept of the application running inside the VM. Instead, you would only be able to restore the entire VM or files from the VM. Alternatively, if a backup agent were deployed inside the VM that was application-aware, the backup data would be in terms of the application workload (i.e., databases and tables), which would be the restoration granularity.

When thinking about what you want to restore, you should also consider what would be the best way to restore, which is slightly different. For example, consider an IIS web server that is part of a farm. If something happened, you would want to restore the web server instance so that it could resume its work. However, it was originally created via an OS template from the marketplace, and then a declarative configuration was applied using PowerShell DSC (or Chef, Puppet, a custom script extension, or really anything else) that came from a repository or storage account. There is nothing stateful in the VM, so why would you restore it? It would likely be faster to just spin up a new VM in its place and not bother backing it up. The same thinking can apply to many types of workloads. Imagine you have 10 domain controllers. You definitely want at least one backup of a domain controller, but do all 10 need to be backed up? Not likely. Like many workloads, domain controllers are "tin soldiers." If one falls down, you simply stand up another in its place. The state the domain controller is between all domain controllers using multi-master replication. Any backup would be relatively stale compared to the information that could be restored from the peers. This means if a domain controller failed, you wouldn't restore it; you would just create a new one (using your ARM template), and it would replicate the Active Directory database from its closest peer. Note that you do want one of them (from each domain) to be backed up, just in case something really bad happens!

You apply this thinking to all workloads. What do I want to restore? What is the most logical way to restore what I want to restore? Once you have this identified, you'll know whether you actually need to back up the workload and, if so, whether the backup can be taken at the Azure fabric level (i.e., backing up the entire VM) or can be taken from within the VM (i.e., an agent that is application-aware).

Always remember to think about any dependent systems and data your workload requires—for example, maybe the application uses a database service with other workloads. You may need to work with the database administrators to ensure that they have the ability to restore that meets your requirements.

When you move outside of Infrastructure as a Service (i.e., VMs), the backups often become part of the service, with minimal configuration required. For example, Azure SQL Database and Cosmos DB have backups built-in with point-in-time restore capabilities. Others may use snapshots or copies of data to other instances. Also be careful with snapshots as the only mechanism of protection, as they live with the source data. This means that while snapshots provide restore capabilities to certain points in time, if the source data becomes completely unavailable, so too will the snapshots become unavailable. While snapshots are useful as part of a backup solution (for example, fast execution and fast restore for more recent backups), the data should then be copied somewhere else (i.e., another storage cluster or recovery vault) for the most resilient protection.

Thinking about the storage of the backup data and building on the snapshot thinking is where are the backups stored? I remember my first job as a VAX/VMS systems administrator (which was a grand title for changing backup tapes, among other glamorous duties). The backup tapes would be shipped off-site each morning in a two-weekly rotation, and that night's backup tape would arrive. The thinking was to ensure the backups were physically separated from the source systems, as having the backup tapes sitting in a cupboard next to the server would not be useful if the entire facility were unavailable, such as in a fire. This same thinking should be applied when thinking of backup storage in Azure. The primary storage of the backup target will be the same region as the source. This optimizes the speed of backup and restore; however, you also need to think worse case. What if the region is unavailable? The restoration may need to be to another region, which means the backup data needs to be replicated to another region as well, *with* the ability to restore from the backup replica.

The other consideration is retention. For some data, the only goal for the backup is to be able to restore to the most recent backup, which means the retention is only a couple of days. For other types of data that may be pruned on the source system (i.e., older data is deleted), there may be the potential that older data may be required at some point in the future—for example, during a legal litigation or financial investigation. In this case, data may need to be kept for much longer—potentially, many years. (Seven years is fairly common in many times of regulatory requirement.) Multiple backups are often stored very efficiently, only the delta (i.e., the data changed) between backups is actually stored and charged (similar but even better than incremental backups, in that sub-file changes only are stored, but when restoring, it looks like a complete backup). However, even with this delta storage, saving a daily backup for many years would likely get expensive but also cumbersome to navigate. Instead, retention settings are often used. For example:

- A daily backup for 4 weeks

- A weekly backup for 6 months

- A monthly backup for 2 years

- An annual backup for 10 years

Once you fully understand all the data, location, and retention requirements, you can design the overall backup solution. Remember, it likely won't be one size fits all.

Using Azure Backup

Azure Backup is the primary backup, restore, and protection service in Azure. It is built on recovery vaults, which are pools for storage that can be replicated to other regions on which various protection services are layered to meet the various requirements of customers. In addition to providing protection for workloads in Azure, it can also be used to provide protection for workloads outside of Azure—for example, on-premises workloads. Remember how I used to send those backup tapes off-site each day? If I use Azure Backup, those backups are already off-site and away from the primary data. A nice benefit of Azure Backup is no egress charges. Typically, data into Azure is free (i.e., backing up data from on-premises workloads to Azure would be free of any data transfer costs), but ordinarily there are charges for data egress (i.e., when you perform a restore). With Azure Backup, the egress charges are waived, which means no additional data transfer costs if you need to restore data.

Azure Backup is essentially unlimited scale. There are some limits per recovery vault, as outlined in the Azure limits page, but at the time of writing, a single on-premises source could be around 50 TB (larger for Azure VMs), and you can have hundreds of vaults in a region. Retention is top of mind, with granular retention policies authorable to meet exact requirements, as shown in Figure 9.6, with the daily, weekly, monthly, and annual options in addition to when you should perform the actual backups. Note that up to 9,999 recovery points are supported per protected instance, and while the maximum age used to be 99 years, the age limit has been removed. Obviously, no one has even tested 99 years yet.

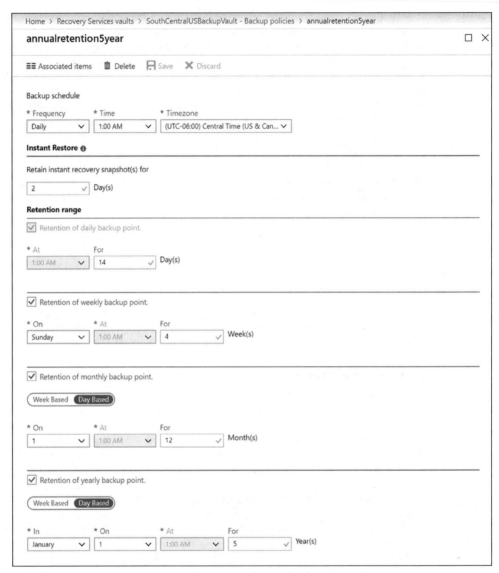

Also notice the Retain Instance Recovery Snapshot(s) For option, which by default is set to 2 days but can be anywhere from 1 to 5 days. In the early days of Azure Backup, the backup was considered complete only once the data had been copied to the Recovery Services Vault, which may have delayed other operational tasks. Now the backup works by taking a snapshot that is almost instant, allowing the workload to then continue normal operation. The data from the snapshot is then copied to the Recovery Vault in the background. With this Retain Instance Recovery Snapshot option, the snapshot that is used as part of the backup is kept for the configured number of days. This is useful for many recovery operations that typically would want the most recent backup. By keeping this snapshot, the restore would take minutes instead of potentially hours if the data were restored from the vault, but data is also stored in the vault for longer-term retention and off-region storage (via replication when the vault is configured for geo-redundant storage [GRS]). There is a slight incremental cost based on the changed pages from the point the snapshot is taken, but this is typically minor; most workloads see a churn of between 2 and 7 percent.

Azure Backup can be used with a number of workloads, from Azure IaaS VMs to workloads running on premises. Depending on the workload location and the restoration granularity, different approaches are used.

The simplest option is protecting a VM in Azure where the entire VM or files from the VM will need to be restored. In this scenario, the backup is completely backup agentless. The Azure VM agent (which is in all Azure VMs) is used as part of the backup orchestration, as although the backup is being taken outside of the guest OS, the backup components inside the guest OS for a Windows VM still need to be involved to ensure the backup is application-consistent. (This is different from application-aware.) This is achieved by the Azure VM agent talking to the Volume Shadow Copy Service (VSS) of the guest and acts as a requestor telling VSS a backup is going to be taken. VSS then works with the VSS writers (which are installed as part of the OS and by certain applications like SQL Server) to enable data to be flushed to disk and changes quiesced (paused) to disk while a snapshot is taken. Because the VSS writers are written by the OS components (in-box writers) and application's authors, they know what to flush to disk and how to stop writing during the backup to ensure the data is consistent. The snapshot creation is very fast, and the pause is typically seconds. For Linux, the backup is filesystem-consistent (i.e., the disk is frozen via `fsfreeze`) while the snapshot is taken, but the workloads inside the OS are not aware, so there is no guarantee everything is flushed neatly to disk, and so the restored state would be just like if you just had previously shut down the OS. You can make Linux backups application-consistent if you use the process described at:

```
https://azure.microsoft.com/en-in/blog/
application-consistent-backup-for-linux-vms-using-azure-backup-is-generally-available/
```

This is a long way of saying that even though the backup is taken at the Azure level, where possible, the guest OS is still aware, making the backup taken as consistent and therefore usable as possible. For Azure IaaS VMs, a single backup per day is supported. This type of backup is very simple to deploy. You simply create the backup policy and then apply it to the VM. This could be done via the portal, through templates, or even policy.

This type of backup, however, is not application-aware. It has no idea of what is running inside the VM, such as SQL Server, SharePoint, Exchange, etc. This means you cannot restore items in terms of the application workload, such as a database, SharePoint item, or mailbox.

SQL SERVER—THE EXCEPTION TO THE RULE

Actually, this is not strictly true for SQL Server. An extension is available for SQL Server that enhances the agentless backup to understand SQL Server and enable database-level backup and restore, but that is the exception to the rule. You can read about this at:

```
https://docs.microsoft.com/en-us/azure/backup/backup-azure-sql-database
```

To achieve application-aware backup and restoration capabilities or even more granular file/folder protection, an agent is required inside the guest operating system. You may have an existing backup solution that you use on premises and may be able to extend this to the cloud. Ideally, this should be able to run in Azure and leverage Azure Backup for the longer-term retention in addition to its local storage leverages as part of the initial backup. Alternatively, Azure Backup Server is a free backup server that is deployed to Azure IaaS VMs (or it can run on premises to protect on-premises workloads) with a certain amount of storage to support the backups but quickly offloads the backup data to the backup vault. Azure Backup Server is essentially System Center Data Protection Manager, the Microsoft enterprise backup solution, albeit a slightly cut down version. In fact, instead of using Azure Backup Server, you could leverage System Center Data Protection Manager; they are pretty much interchangeable for Azure purposes.

Both Azure Backup Server (ABS) and System Center Data Protection Manager (DPM) leverage an agent deployed into the guest operating system. This guest provides the insight into deployed applications and enables application-aware backup and subsequent restore. While both ABS and DPM initially use locally attached storage to store the data sent from the agents, the data is quickly copied and offloaded to the recovery vault for longer retention, with typically only a few days kept on the server storage. When using ABS or DPM, two backups per day are supported to the Recovery Services Vault, while data can be sent to ABS/DPM from the agent hourly or even in 15-minute increments for SQL Server. The same approach would apply to protect most workloads on premises to Azure. Use ABS or DPM for the initial backup target, which would then send the data up to Azure and the vault, providing higher resiliency storage and off-site.

There is another option if you just want to protect an OS instance or specific files/folders but don't need application-aware backups. If the Microsoft Azure Recovery Services (MARS) agent (which is different from the ABS/DPM agent) is installed in a guest OS, then both the entire OS or specific files/folders can be protected. This applies both to on-premises workloads and Azure VMs. (For Azure VMs, this would be used only if you didn't want to protect the entire VM but instead wanted only certain files or folders.) Using the MARS agent, up to three backups per day are supported. For SQL Server and SAP HANA, there are zero-infrastructure solutions that don't require any agent installations within the guest VM.

Very relevant to infrastructure is Azure Files and Azure Files Sync. Azure Backup can also protect content stored here.

As you use other recovery services, you will quickly see they can share a common recovery services vault. It is at the vault you configure if the vault storage in locally redundant or geo-redundant. Geo-redundant costs more money but has the obvious benefit of having a copy of your backups at another Azure region hundreds of miles away. You can also restore directly from the replica. You may opt to only use the locally redundant option if you want the ability to quickly restore a region-specific instance of the service but already have other instances in other regions and some application-level replication is already copying any important state. For example, you may have a SQL deployment spread over two regions that uses Always On availability groups to asynchronously replicate the databases between regions. You may want to be able to restore a server due to a failure (which would then catch up from the other server) within the region; however, if the entire region were down, you wouldn't care about it since you already have instances in other regions with the data and offering service.

High Availability in Azure

I covered a lot of the key concepts at the start of this chapter when it comes to thinking about high availability (HA). Typically, HA is thinking about keeping a service available and resilient within a region. For many services, such as storage, this is built-in. For example, Azure Storage (with its three synchronous copies), Azure SQL Database, and Cosmos DB also have resiliency built-in. For the Platform as a Service options, HA is native, and all that is required is to have at least two instances.

For IaaS VMs, you need to be able to have at least two instances. This is a minimum; three is preferred, as you have to consider there are times when there is planned maintenance, rendering a certain percentage unavailable, or a failure. If you only have two instances, then you are down to one, meaning you cannot tolerate any other problem. Having three instances enables something to happen and you still have a level of resiliency left. Since the VMs will likely be identical, by virtue of the fact they are all running together in a farm offering a single service, where possible, use VM scale sets (VMSS) to deploy. Using VMSS will make it very easy to change scale, and turn on auto-scale to provide the most optimal spend (possible with VMs).

When deploying multiple instances, remember to split them out over either availability sets (multiple Fault Domains/racks within a datacenter) or availability zones (multiple isolated facilities within a Region). Availability zones provides greater isolation from possible failures, but the instances will be further separated than if in an availability set, meaning slightly high latency but still within the 2 ms latency envelope that defines a region. When using availability sets, remember to use the aligned mode with managed disks, which ensures each Fault Domain uses a separate storage cluster, which ensures a storage cluster-level issue would not impact VMs on separate Fault Domains.

For availability sets, in addition to Fault Domains, there are update domains. These update domains are used as part of Azure maintenance. The number of update domains can range between 5 and 20 based on your configuration. Only one update domain has maintenance at any instance in time, which means this helps you plan for the scale impact during maintenance. If you leverage 5 update domains, then 20 percent of your instances will be unavailable at any one time. If you have 10 update domains, then 10 percent would be unavailable at any one time. You get the idea. Also remember to never, ever, under any circumstance mix workloads in a single availability set. Azure has no idea what is running inside your VM and is blindly round-robining the VMs between three Fault Domains. If you mix workloads, through sheer bad luck one workload may end up all on the same Fault Domain, rendering it susceptible to a rack-level failure. There is no cost of availability sets, so don't be stingy with them. Use one availability set for each unique workload—that is, one for IIS App 1; one for IIS App 2; one for SQL Cluster 1; one for SQL Cluster 2; one for your domain controllers; and so on.

Depending on the service running inside the VMs, you may also need load balancing, which enables a single endpoint that is then balanced between the instances available. Azure has a number of load balancer solutions operating at Layer 4 (Azure Load Balancer) and Layer 7 (Azure Application Gateway). Both of these can be external (virtual IP that is Internet-facing) or internal (virtual IP that is internally-facing on a virtual network). Remember that if you are leveraging availability zones, you must use the standard SKU of the Azure Load Balancer, not the free basic SKU. For Azure Application Gateway with availability zones, you must use the v2 or above SKU.

Disaster Recovery in Azure

Disaster recovery (DR) is a very interesting topic when it comes to Azure. Let me start off by answering a common question. *Yes, you need DR in Azure!* If you take one thing from this chapter, it is this. I often hear companies say the VM (note the singular here so they also don't even have high availability configured) is deployed in the cloud, so it already has DR. This is not correct. If they deploy two VMs and remember to use availability sets or availability zones, they have HA but still don't have DR. They may learn this fact in a very painful way if there is a rare region-level incident and their service goes dark and a lot of uncomfortable discussions commence.

This is important to understand, and it applies to both IaaS and PaaS. Your deployments are to a region. Very rarely, even for PaaS, are deployments across regions. This does not mean there are not technologies to help deploy to multiple regions, to balance between them, or to set up some kind of replication and failover plan—but it's not there as a default, nor should it be. There is additional cost to these solutions, understanding is required to be able to use them and there are many options for DR, with the right one depending on requirements and cost appetite, which means the DR approach needs to be architected with discovery and careful planning across the entire organization. Once the architecture is defined, *then* the numerous technologies available in Azure can easily be leveraged to enable the DR architecture to be made real. Only SaaS solutions like Office 365 have DR built-in, since the service is responsible for the application and data, enabling them to architect the right DR solution.

Take a second to pause and look at your workloads. As part of planning for DR, there may be another approach. Can you move the service to a SaaS solution and not worry about DR of that service? For example, many organizations are moving from Exchange and SharePoint to Office 365. This removes hosting and maintenance of the systems while lighting up new capabilities and an improved, fully managed service. Also, given the criticality of communications during a disaster, having that communications service already running will help other DR-related activities. The same thought process can be made to many systems. Can it be moved to SaaS? Can it be moved to PaaS and reduce the DR process? There will still be planning, but the overall DR process will be simpler, as responsibilities shift from the customer to the provider—i.e., Azure. Definitely something to consider!

At the start of this chapter, I walked through discovery and thinking about if DR is required. There may be workloads with no state that are created from a template and a declarative configuration. In those cases, you don't need to replicate anything other than the declarative configuration, but you would need to ensure that any changes to that configuration are reflected in the DR region's copy (ideally by using a geo-replicated repository). You also need to ensure that their creation is part of the failover plan.

I want to spend time focusing on VMs we have decided to require DR—i.e., their state needs to be replicated to another region with the ability to failover. We likely have options, but before thinking about that, I want to take a step back and consider about how we may think about DR on premises, then we'll think about DR from on premises to Azure, before circling back to DR for Azure to Azure.

For all of these options, if the service is Internet-facing and is going to move between locations, we often will use a technology like Azure Traffic Manager (if it is not HTTP/HTTPS based) or Azure Front Door (if it is HTTP/HTTPS-based) to point to the possible targets. Both services support backend members that are hosted in Azure and outside of Azure, (i.e., some public-facing service hosted on premises). Another option would be a DNS name that is updated, but this can face challenges due to time-to-live configurations.

On-Premises Disaster Recovery

Figure 9.7 shows how we typically think about DR on premises. We have two locations and have workloads running in the primary location. I can replicate at a number of different levels, starting from the bottom up.

FIGURE 9.7
Disaster recovery
on premises

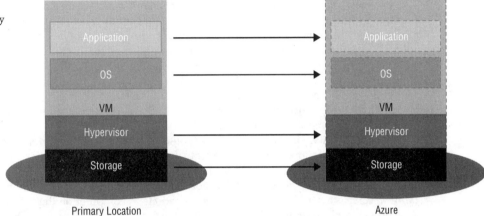

Storing   Organizations typically use some kind of storage area network (SAN) that has asynchronous replication options, enabling replication to a SAN at another location. This is completely agnostic to the workload and simply copies the blocks over as they change. If an organization has moved to a hyper-converged solution, such as Storage Spaces Direct, this approach is still possible by combining Storage Spaces Direct with Storage Replica (if using a Windows Server–based hyper-converged solution). While this will work for any solution, there is minimal control and, in the case of a SAN, requires expensive solutions.

Hypervisor   Hypervisors like Hyper-V and ESX have hypervisor replication capabilities. For Hyper-V (on which Azure is built), a feature called Hyper-V Replica enables the initial configuration of a VM to be replicated to a target Hyper-V replica server, and then changes to the virtual hard disks of the VM to be replicated to the replica at a configured interval. This often also allows some integration with the guest OS, enabling an application-consistent recovery point (a periodic "stamp" of the replication) to be generated.

Operating System   Solutions exist that run inside the guest operating system. Typically, these will sit between the filesystem and volume manager of the operating system, capture changes as they pass through, and send them to a target. This removes any dependency on specific physical hardware or even hypervisors.

Application   If the application has a native DR solution, this will typically provide the best experience in terms of RPO and RTO—i.e., the failover will be faster and less data will be lost in unplanned failovers. Examples include SQL Always On availability groups and Active Directory multi-master replication.

In my experience, many on premises often leverage storage replication for nearly everything, and then use application-level replication for very important databases. This checks the box of saying DR is enabled for everything, with only thought given to the most critical work-loads. There are pros and cons. Obviously, the storage level is very easy in terms of one tech-nology that enables a DR for everything. It is the lowest common denominator. Additionally, the DR site is there; it is already being paid for. Aside from the bandwidth for the replica-tion traffic between facilities, there is no real downside in just enabling the replication for everything.

As you move up the layers, the deployment gets more workload-specific, which means additional technologies and configuration but also potentially more steps during an actual failover—something that is important to remember. We don't deploy DR because we want to deploy DR. We deploy DR in case we ever need to failover to another site, so that failover pro-cess must be part of the thought process when designing and deploying. An overly complex failover process is likely to failover. Remember, in a real failover, there may be other things happening—for example, severe weather, a natural disaster, or some terrorist event. There will be human beings enacting the DR plan who likely will not feel the failover of a computer system is the most important thing compared to if their loved ones are okay, or perhaps they can't get to the facility. The failover process should be as simple and as automated as possible once the decision to failover has been made. In an ideal world, we could click a big red button (feel free to use a different color) and the failover would commence, *but* we want that big red button rather than a fully automated decision *to* failover. Issues can occur that may not warrant a failover, such as a network impact between locations. A computer on the DR side would see the primary workload unavailable and may decide to failover. That would be bad. Therefore, while we want to automate the failover process, the initiation of that failover should be made by humans.

This does not mean use the lowest common denominator. The solution needs to meet requirements. This means you should build automation into the failover so that even if differ-ent technologies were used or if certain steps had to be performed in sequence, some failover engine would do that for you. This is how the Azure DR service, Hyper-V Recovery Manager (HRM), started. HRM was a cloud-based orchestrator for on-premises Hyper-V to Hyper-V failovers. The modern version, Azure Site Recovery (ASR), can still act in that capacity and also supports ESX on-premises replication.

On Premises to Azure Disaster Recovery

Organizations don't like disaster recovery. It costs a lot of money to maintain a second location filled with hardware for something they hope to never use. This is why most organizations don't have any DR plan or have one that they are pretty sure wouldn't work. Using the cloud and its consumption-based costing makes it ideal for DR. The costs are proportionally low to replicate to the cloud, with the majority of costs only really hitting during an actual failover (or a test failover) where compute services are spun up and start accruing cost.

When performing DR to the cloud, more care will be taken in the design than when per-forming DR on premises. On premises, you have the DR site; you have the equipment; and you often just replicate everything. In the cloud, there will be some per-instance cost associ-ated, and the failover RPO and RTO will be different, depending on the type of replication used. Figure 9.8 shows a slightly different view when thinking about replication to the cloud. Remember as discussed early in the chapter. consider that there may be workloads on premises that need no replication; they can be re-created in the event of a disaster.

FIGURE 9.8
Disaster recovery on premises to Azure

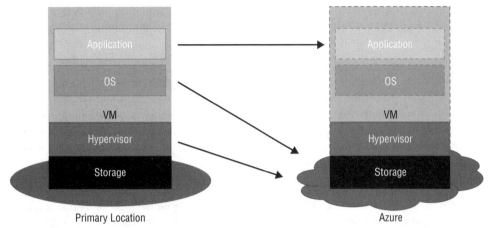

The replication at the storage subsystem is gone. This does not mean there are no storage-level replication options. Some SANs have partnered with ExpressRoute partners to enable SANs to be placed as close to the Azure network as possible, which would make data available to Azure-based services with minimal latencies, but it would not be possible to run VMs off this storage. For practical purposes, the replication starts at the hypervisor and moves up.

For organizations using Hyper-V, the Hyper-V Replica feature can be utilized to replicate VMs from on premises to Azure. While Hyper-V Replica normally works to a Hyper-V server, this is not the case to Azure. Instead, the replication is to "Azure," which then writes the changes to VHDs stored in Azure. There is not a direct connection to a specific Hyper-V server in Azure. The Hyper-V–based replication can be enabled with or without System Center Virtual Machine Manager. The replication to Azure is on a 5- or 15-minute interval.

For organizations using ESX or hosting bare metal OS instances (i.e., not running on a hypervisor), an in-guest agent is used. This agent, the Mobility Service, operates as a disk driver that sits under the filesystem but above the volume manager. As writes percolate down from the application to the filesystem on their way down to the disk, the writes are fractured, enabling a copy of the write to be sent to an on-premises target, the process server, while still allowing the write to continue down the normal disk path. Organizations need to deploy a virtual appliance on premises to provide the process server instance for the local replication. The process server bundles up the writes and sends them to a master target service hosted in Azure that performs the writes to disks in Azure. The replication is not on an interval but rather is as quickly as possible.

I want to answer an obvious question. If you failover to Azure using either the Hyper-V replica or in-guest technology, you can failback. This is not a cunning plan by Microsoft to enable migrations to Azure. Once the workload is failed over, if using the in-guest technology, you can reverse the replication back to an ESX server (but you cannot failback to physical hardware—the failover would need to be to an ESX VM). If you were using Hyper-V Replica, the replication would be reversed at the time of failback.

Both the Hyper-V–based replication and the in-guest replication to Azure use an Azure Site Recovery (ASR) license. This is a per-protected instance, per month-based license. In addition, the cost of the storage in Azure would be part of the pricing. ASR is free for the first 31 days. This is to enable the technology to be used as part of migrations from on premises to Azure, but I'll cover that later.

As part of the replication, application-consistent snapshots are supported. Additionally, if you have multiple VMs that need to replicate together, then a replication group can be created that includes the VMs that require consistency for ESX- (and Azure-) based VMs, but not at this time from Hyper-V.

Normally, replication traffic to Azure Site Recovery is sent via the Internet (encrypted using SSL). If you have ExpressRoute, you can enable Microsoft peering, which will enable the ASR traffic to also travel via the ExpressRoute connection, providing a lower latency and potentially faster pipe for the traffic.

While thinking about the overall solution, don't forget about networking and the communication to the services if you failover to Azure. As part of a normal failover, one or more virtual networks will exist in Azure. These virtual networks will use a different IP space than on premises to avoid conflicts. To ensure the smoothest failover, access to machines should be via DNS, which will automatically be updated via dynamic DNS when the workload starts on Azure, gets a new IP, and updates its DNS registration. Note that DNS records do have a time-to-live (TTL). This is the amount of time a record can be cached on a client to avoid constant DNS lookups. The longer the TTL, the less utilization of the DNS server, but it will also mean it will take longer for the client to notice the IP address has changed on the record. This is a balancing act between too lower of a value and hammering the DNS server with constant queries and too larger of a value rendering stale resolution. If the service is publicly facing and not internal, you can leverage Azure Front Door or Azure Traffic Manager, as mentioned at the start of the chapter. Both use probes and would only direct clients to the live instance of a service.

If you have services that talk to an IP address, this will be a painful exercise. Ideally, start moving them to use DNS or start working on some automation to update the IP configuration during a failover. If you absolutely cannot change the IP address and the Azure virtual network is only going to be used during a failover and the primary site is gone, then you could take a portion of the on-premises IP space and use it in the virtual network. This is possible since the routing uses BGP, which allows a configurable number of bits for the network. Technically, you could even use /32 mask to only move a single IP address. The following link has details on retaining IPs when moving services to Azure:

```
https://docs.microsoft.com/en-us/azure/site-recovery/
site-recovery-retain-ip-azure-vm-failover
```

Replication at the OS or hypervisor level is not the only option. It is also possible to replicate at the application level—for example, SQL replication or Active Directory multi-master replication. This will give the best RPO and RTO; however, this will be at the expense of, well, expense. For the OS/hypervisor-level replication, there is no compute running in Azure. You pay for the ASR licenses and the storage consumed for the replicated disk, but you don't pay for a VM, unless you failover. If you use application replication, then an application instance must be running in Azure to participate in the application replication—i.e., a compute instance must be running and costing money. There are ways to minimize the cost, such as using a small instance size and incurring a small downtime to resize it during an actual failover. Even then, however, the cost will be higher than using ASR, although for a critical workload, this may be worth the extra cost and the right thing to do. Each organization will have different cost appetites and SLAs to meet, which will drive the technologies used. At the opposite end of the scale, some may not want to replicate and instead would be willing to just restore a backup in the event of a DR for certain workloads. It could be a nice-to-have system that could wait a number of hours before being available. Remember, this is a disaster recovery scenario that hopefully won't be used, so optimizing cost and using the right option per service is critical. You don't want to pick one that meets the lowest or highest common denominator.

As mentioned previously, using different technologies for different systems will mean a more complex failover process. I stressed the idea of wanting to make this a simple process which means we need to automate. In addition to replication, Azure Site Recovery includes recovery plans, and these are critical. Recovery plans bring everything together because, up to this point, we have really been having a replication conversation. Now we need to use that replicated content. A recovery plan allows the complete failover to be mapped out. In a recovery plan, we can do the following:

♦ Group VMs and select the order in which groups failover. This is important where VMs are dependent on VMs to be present first. For example, failover the domain controllers, then the SQL cluster, and then the applications.

♦ Run pre- and post- scripts for each VM group—for example, PowerShell via Azure Automation. This enables actions to be performed that may not directly be VMs. Maybe some DNS entry has to be updated or some other application interacted with. This could be deploying a template. (Remember those resources we didn't replicate but that would need to be created.)

♦ Perform SQL failovers. This provides integration with the SQL Always On Availability Group to enable orchestration as part of a wider recovery plan.

♦ Wait for manual actions. Maybe someone has to pull a great big lever before the rest of the plan can continue.

Once the plan is created, it can then be executed to perform the failover in an automated fashion. It can also be run in a test mode, where the failover will be isolated from the production environment to enable testing of the failover over resources without impacting live operation or ongoing replication.

Azure to Azure

Remember, just because services are deployed to the cloud, we still have to think about disaster recovery if something happens to the Azure region we are deployed to. The thought process is basically the same as on premises to Azure. Figure 9.9 shows our new options. There is still storage and a hypervisor, but at this point they are invisible to us. We have visibility into the VM, the OS, and the application.

Our options are to replicate the VM using ASR (which uses the in-guest component used by ESX and physical replication), which can be enabled with a few clicks to any region in the geopolitical boundary, or replication at the application level. Of course, we also have the same option of does it need replicating or could we just create the service when needed during a failover.

FIGURE 9.9
Disaster recovery
for Azure to Azure

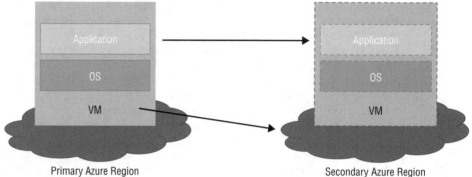

Just like on premises to Azure, there is a cost difference. Using the ASR replication means ASR license and storage; using the application replication means the application must be running in the replica region to participate. The decision will be made based on the RPO, RTO, and cost appetite (assuming the application replication is even an option, since many applications do not have replication capabilities).

One interesting consideration for Azure is to which region should we replicate. There are very different viewpoints on this. For some services (for example, Azure Storage), there are hard regional pairings. When using geo-redundant storage, the replica pairings are defined by Microsoft, as documented at:

```
https://docs.microsoft.com/en-us/azure/best-practices-availability-paired-regions
```

If GRS Azure Storage were part of your service, then that would dictate the failover region, as you would not want storage replicating to one region and compute services to another. There are benefits to following the Microsoft pairings. Microsoft ensures that updates are not rolled out to paired regions at the same time. This protects both regions in a pair from possibly being impacted by a problem introduced by an update. This is a good thing. On the flip side, in the event of a failover, you would be failing over to that same paired region, along with every other company in that failed primary region. Failing over to a region other than the paired region would face less congestion and resource contention but would block being able to use services that have hard coded pairings, and also leave you at risk if the outage were caused by some update that also was rolled out to your chosen region.

Also don't forget about whether you could use active-active instead of failover. This will depend heavily on the application, as discussed in detail at the start of this chapter. If possible, however, that is the optimal plan for resiliency, as not only does it provide region-level impact protection but also will improve the experience for customers of the service.

Migrating Workloads to Azure

You may wonder why migration is part of the resiliency chapter as opposed to the management chapter. The reason is simple: A rehosting migration is essentially the same process as implementing disaster recovery from on premises to Azure. You need to perform discovery, identity dependencies between workloads, understand resource requirements to size correctly in Azure, enable replication, and then failover. The difference is that for a migration, we don't ever failback. It is also for this reason that Azure Site Recovery is free for the first 31 days for a workload. It enables the technology to be used for free as part of migrations. But I'm getting ahead of myself.

Migration Benefits

At the start of this book, we looked at benefits of the cloud. Some of the biggest benefits include its consumption-based nature (i.e., you pay for what you use), its agility and scalability, the availability of a broad range of services, including cutting-edge technologies like AI, regions throughout the globe, and much more. New workloads will often find themselves in the cloud. Once an organization has decided to use the cloud, there are very few reasons why hosting on premises would be a better decision than hosting in the cloud. For workloads that already are running on premises, the decision to migrate those to the cloud can be for a variety of reasons. The following are some of the main reasons:

Datacenter Contracts or Hardware/Software Contracts Expiring Organizations often lease datacenter space. As these contracts expire, the organizations may decide that this is the time to get out of the datacenter business and have a hard deadline that they must be out of the datacenter by. It may also be that expensive licenses need to be renewed (for example, hypervisors), or perhaps servers need refreshing. This can be the push to get to the cloud, and again there will be a hard deadline to avoid having to renew contracts.

Integration of Acquisitions If a company is purchased, then there may be an urgent need to move their systems, especially if only part of a company is being purchased and it needs to move its IT out of the former company's facilities.

Capacity Needs Maybe the company is doing well and cannot keep up with demand. A move to the cloud may be the only way to meet new scale requirements without significant on-premises investment. Note that if the capacity requirement is temporary, that may not be a migration; instead, the additional capacity would be used in the cloud as burst, but normal running would continue on premises.

Security and/or Compliance Azure has a huge number of compliance certifications in addition to industry-leading security. Some organizations want to move to the cloud to take advantage of this and to help meet their own or regulatory requirements.

Software End of Support This may seem like a strange one, but there are some operating systems and products that have extended support when hosted in Azure. This is possible, as Microsoft can run the applications on hardware and hypervisors they can control, thus limiting potential testing and vulnerabilities. Additionally, this may include initial moves to services like Azure SQL Managed Instance, which provides strong compatibility with SQL in a VM but is fully managed and is evergreen—i.e., it will be kept updated and patched from that point on.

Application Innovation This is a huge one for companies focused more on benefits—i.e., a carrot instead of a stick. The range of services and options in the cloud help organizations really innovate.

Cloud First Many organizations now have a cloud-first mentality, and any new service is deployed to the cloud if possible. As systems are updated, they deploy to the cloud, and as services have dependencies on other systems, often they will bring on-premises services to the cloud as part of a complete solution. Once a certain critical mass hits the cloud, the organization looks to get everything else moved to the cloud so that the on-premises facilities can be retired.

Note that items like disaster recovery and needing services in additional regions are not necessarily migrations. Instead, the cloud is being used in addition to on premises, but obviously moving the on premises to the cloud could also be part of the plan to standardize operations and architecture.

I'm sure there are other reasons as well, but these are some of the most common reasons I see. Depending on the driver, the timeline will be vastly different, which may restrict the migration approach.

Migration Approaches

There are several approaches to migrate workloads to Azure. We often talk about the four R's:

Rehost A lift-and-shift that takes existing workloads from on premises and moves them to VMs. There may be some service optimizations, such as moving SQL Server clusters from IaaS to managed instances, but for the most part there are no changes.

Refactor Also thought of as repackaging. The goal here is to avoid having to change the codebase but potentially running it in a different way. As an example, a web application could move from running on a VM to running as a web application in an App Service Plan. Another approach would be moving the application to containers.

Rearchitect Modifications are made to the application to enable greater benefit from cloud technologies. Applications move to micro-services with containers. Databases move to Azure SQL Database or Cosmos DB. DevOps practices will also be embraced as part of this shift.

Rebuild Applications will be rearchitected from scratch as cloud-native apps. Server-less technologies, such as Azure Functions and LogicApps, will be used for the application tier, while Azure SQL Database and Cosmos DB will be used for the data tier. Other services, such as blockchain, AI, and Internet of Things (IoT) may be introduced into the solution.

Which one we pick really depends on the timeline for the migration and the type of workload. As we move down the list, we gain enhanced value from the cloud. The customer has fewer responsibilities while having access to new types of technology, but there will be a greater time investment with potentially greater changes required to the workloads. It may be that a faster approach is initially used, but, over time, once the workload is in the cloud and the initial time pressure removed, additional work can be performed, enabling greater optimization and greater adoption of cloud technologies, and improving the overall service, while reducing customer responsibility. For example, a rehost may initially be used, but once in the cloud, some refactoring may take place, and then, over time, rearchitecting and even rebuilding.

Customers facing an aggressive timeline will often rehost, with maybe some minimal refactoring. Organizations with a longer timeline and that are following a cloud direction may not rehost existing workloads but rather adopt the cloud as applications are refreshed, taking a rearchitect/rebuild approach. Every organization has different drivers and compelling events in addition to different budgets.

Migration Phases

Before embarking on a migration, make sure you have the necessary scaffolding (i.e., governance) in place. You don't want to start moving services and then realize you lack the proper controls. Instead, take some time up front to understand requirements around policy, tagging, naming, cost management, and all the items I talked about at the start of this book. Once the governance is in place, you can start migrating with confidence.

ASSESSMENT

The first phase of migration is assessment. You need to understand the workloads you have, their resource requirements, their compatibility with cloud capabilities, and the dependencies between them.

Azure Migrate is a free solution from Microsoft that does this for you, and more. Azure Migrate is a cloud service but uses an on-premises collector as part of its server assessment capability to discover and provide information about the workloads. The collector is available as a virtual appliance for VMware or Hyper-V to discover resources on the respective hypervisors. It runs completely agentless, and it utilizes WMI to gather information. At the time of writing, the latest version supports up to 10,000 VMs on VMware or 5,000 VMs on Hyper-V for a single collector instance. If you need to discover more than 10,000/5,000 VMs, you would deploy multiple collectors.

The collector initially feeds information about the VMs—such as the resources, the OS, disk, and boot partition, and format information—in addition to the application configuration. It can also be configured to gather performance data over a certain period. On-premises workloads often are heavily over provisioned, which is not something we want to carry over to the cloud, where the cost is based on the resources consumed. By using the performance data, the assessment can recommend a size in Azure based on the resources used, known as *performance-based sizing* (aka *right sizing*), instead of just duplicating resources currently configured on premises. A comfort factor can be configured, which is a multiplier of the resources recommended based on the CPU, memory, and disk resource utilization observed during the time-limited window (not network, at the time of writing, but that is on the plan). For example, a common factor is 1.3, which would give some breathing room if a resource utilization peak were missed during the observation period. You can also configure a percentile utilization number (for example, 95%), which is the resource peak you will size to, as opposed to setting a size potentially on a very rare spike. The longer the resource observation period, the better the sizing recommendations will be. Remember, it's very easy to change sizes both up and down in Azure, which means the sizing exercise here is just one opportunity to adjust, but we have plenty of others.

The assessment will show the estimated cost for the resources when migrated to Azure. This cost assessment can be configured with a number of settings including specific regions, if hybrid benefit is used, various levels of Reserved Instance purchasing, and the expected uptime of the workloads.

If you fully understand the relationships between workloads, you can create groups of VMs that will migrate together, as it is important to move workloads together. If you migrated the web frontend but left the database on premises, the performance would likely be terrible, so having a well-understood mapping of dependencies between workloads is critical to a successful migration. If you do not believe you have a good knowledge of the dependencies, then Service Map can be used. This requires an agent to be deployed to each VM, as it utilizes network mapping technologies that must be run on the OS. Service Map will ascertain dependencies between instances based on TCP communications and display a graphical view of the type of relationship—for example, VMs using a database on another VM. This Service Map can then be used to identify and create the groups of VMs that should be migrated together.

Note that there are also third-party tools. If you are running Hyper-V or VMware, the Azure Migrate tool is the obvious choice. It's free and does a great job. However, if you want to access physical OS instances in addition to virtualized, want agentless dependency mapping, or want more advanced cost modeling, there are various other offerings. Two I've used first hand are Cloudamize and Movere, but there are certainly others.

The key point is that you need to assess thoroughly before any migration. Ideally, you will include right-sizing before migrating to the cloud, but this right-sizing can be done post migration through Azure Advisor. What is critical is to be sure the configuration is supported in Azure and that you move VMs in groups based on their relationship to each other.

Migration

With the groups of VMs to be migrated understood, the migration must be performed. Azure Migrate orchestrates this and guides you through the entire process. For the migration of VMs, the ASR technology is used and can handle a number of scenarios that ordinarily would be a challenge to run in Azure, including the following:

- Physical servers using UEFI
- Linux configurations with system directories on multiple disks
- GPT support
- LVM-managed OS and data disks

ASR takes care of any conversions that are required to ensure the workload runs as expected on Azure. Remember, though, that we may decide to not just rehost but potentially to refactor.

For SQL Server instances running in VMs, the Azure Database Migration Service will perform an assessment of the SQL configuration inside a VM, understand the features and sizing being utilized, and then recommend if the database could be hosted in Azure SQL Database managed instance or in Azure SQL Database. If suitable, it will perform the actual database migration in addition to enabling a migration simply to SQL Server running in an Azure IaaS VM.

For web-based applications, it is very common that the application could run as a web app in an App Service Plan. Head over to `https://appmigration.microsoft.com/` and enter the website you want to check for compatibility. The website will be scanned for compatibility, including the various components it uses. If suitable, it can even be packaged up and a template generated that would enable its fast deployment to Azure.

What about if you have a large amount of data to move to Azure? If the data is running in VMs, the data would migrate as part of the VM migration. However, for other data (and potentially even for that data), an offline approach may be required because of the data volume or storage. Here, some of the other Azure storage offerings could be used, such as Azure Import and Azure Data Box, both of which offer large amounts of offline data transfer.

Optimize

This is not migration-specific but still very important, especially if you created resources based on the size on premises without any performance-based right sizing. Once the workloads have been running for a period of time, take some time to review the recommendations from Azure Advisor. These recommendations may include changing the size of VMs or purchasing reserved instances to reduce monthly spend. These are not one-time actions. Workloads change over time, and new VM sizes and capabilities are released. Reviewing Azure Advisor should be a recurring activity, and it goes beyond just Azure VMs in terms of cost but also gives great information around security, availability, and performance.

Once workloads are in the cloud, remember the earlier sections of this chapter. The workloads need to be highly available, need DR, and need to be backed up. As part of the migration planning, make sure that these items are considered or left as "day-two" activities. Placement of services in availability groups/zones, having backup policies applied, and having a DR plan needs to be implemented straightaway.

Chapter 10

Monitoring and Security

This chapter focuses on the monitoring capabilities and responsibilities for resources and services in Azure. Monitoring leads into and is part of the overall security considerations for Azure. A number of the Azure monitoring and security solutions can also expand beyond Azure to bring benefit to on premises and even other clouds. I want to stress that this book is focused on architecture, not operations; therefore, my priority is to walk through what is available and how you can use it in a complete solution, as opposed to the specifics of using a technology, although I'll still show that for critical functionalities.

In this chapter, you will learn to:

◆ Use native Azure monitoring capabilities and evaluate to trigger actions.

◆ Architect security processes for resources in Azure.

Azure Monitoring

This is a good time to be writing about monitoring in Azure. Even a year ago, this would have been a very different content, as monitoring was scattered all over Azure, with different capabilities and usage almost service by service. Azure Monitor has changed this and become the central hub for *nearly* all things monitoring in Azure. Some technologies have even been rebranded and assimilated into Azure Monitor to further cement Azure Monitor's place as the definitive monitoring entry point.

Why Monitor?

There are a large number of reasons to monitor anything, not just Azure, not just computer systems. We monitor our cars. We check the fuel gauge to know when we need to add more fuel; cars have alerts to let us know when the fuel is critically low in case we are not paying attention. We look at the oil temperature to ensure it's not over heating. We monitor our speed to ensure we are operating within the allowed speed for the roads we are on. We look at miles per gallon. We look to ensure we have locked the doors when we park the car. We are monitoring to ensure the car is healthy; we are monitoring to ensure the care is performing as expected; and we are monitoring to ensure it is secure. We monitor our children for the same reasons. We monitor ourselves; we monitor our houses; we monitor our computers; and we monitor our services in Azure.

Every organization has different drivers that will impact the exact goals for monitoring and the monitoring implemented, but there are some general categories that are widely adopted. The key point is that monitoring is required and, like many things, just because the cloud is utilized does not mean the customer has no responsibility related to monitoring. The exact responsibilities, however, will vary depending on the type of service. Where the customer is responsible for the monitoring, there are capabilities in Azure to assist and gain meaning from the data gathered in addition to alerting as required. Some of the key monitoring drivers include the following:

Performance   Metrics provide insight into the performance of a system which could be resource consumption, availability, SLA adherence, and more. Performance monitoring is also important to establish a baseline of expected, normal performance. It is important to be able to quantify current performance compared to that normal baseline in times where there are complaints that the system is "slow." This baseline will evolve over time as workloads and resources change. Machine learning often can be used to track this baseline and alert when performance deviates from this by a significant amount. Performance data can also provide insight into where services are being used, and this may then drive how we provision services in the future. For example, maybe we are seeing a lot of use from a country we don't currently have services deployed to. This can help us in our planning—another reason for monitoring!

Health   Some health can be determined via performance monitoring—i.e., sudden low memory could indicate that a process is sick and leaking memory, or high latency on storage could be a hardware fault or perhaps an error in an application. Other types of health status are found by viewing log files, which may indicate error codes or service health notifications. Logs may also indicate maintenance activities that are going to be performed to help plan. The health can also show if the service is available from different locations around the world.

Security   Bad actors are constantly attacking organizations. Monitoring provides insight into those attacks, such as brute force attacks via logons, traffic on network edge devices, malware on machines through integration with antivirus, and advanced threat-protection services. Logs on their own often are not enough for security. Keeping logs helps in forensic analysis after a security incident takes place, but to actually detect and respond to an attack requires analysis of multiple signals that together indicate an attack is in process or has succeeded. Monitoring also gives us insight into whether the service is configured in a secure manner and some misconfiguration is not exposing our service to additional vulnerabilities.

Compliance   Organizations have standards both internal and mandated by regulations. Monitoring helps to ensure adherence to those configuration requirements.

Capacity and Cost   Monitoring enables us to see how much of our capacity we have used and where that usage is trending. For example, maybe we need to buy more, maybe we need to enable auto-scaling. This information can also help us understand our costs, which may lead to other activities, such as automating actions at certain thresholds of budgets.

Dependencies   Monitoring communications between services can help show the dependency between services, such as an application being dependent on a database server. This is useful when planning for availability, migration, and normal runtime operations.

Types of Telemetry in Azure

Before talking about features of monitoring, it is important to first understand the types of logs and metrics available in Azure that we may want to monitor and even be alerted and perform actions upon. Some sources are for an entire Azure AD tenant, some for an entire subscription, and others per resource instance. Some types of resources will have additional telemetry coming from services inside the Azure resource—for example, a VM has a guest operating system with applications deployed. These can all generate telemetry we may want. A HDInsight cluster runs an open-source framework that has its own metric and alerting. We likely will want this. Even an application service plan running our customer application may generate information with its runtime, such as .NET or J2E, that we want. And as the architects, we want to design a monitoring solution that has as fewer panes of glass (i.e., different views) as possible and can consolidate our alerting and automation across them.

I'm going to start with a fairly terrifying picture. Figure 10.1 shows the various relationships between resources and solutions in Azure (and beyond). Don't panic—I will build on this throughout the chapter, but I want to get this out there up front so that you have a vision of the end goal. Note that this figure is not complete. Other Microsoft services feed into various services but follow one of the other shown relationship patterns. For example, Microsoft's Cloud App Security service can feed alerts into Log Analytics. Network security groups produce flow logs that can (and should) be fed into Log Analytics, which then feeds into a Traffic Analytics solution that is part of Network Watcher that is built on Log Analytics. I also should point out another name for Log Analytics. Its proper name now is Azure Monitor Logs; however, as we will see, Log Analytics workspaces are still utilized behind the scenes.

FIGURE 10.1
Monitoring relationships in Azure

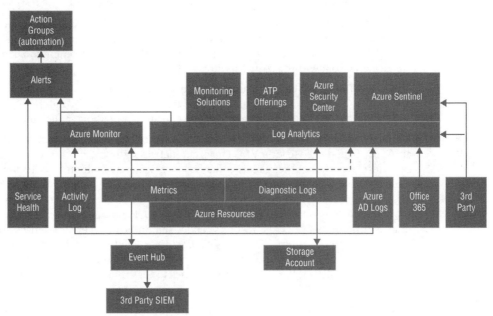

We can work our way from most far-reaching sources of telemetry to the most specific. Like most things, we think about layers of the solution. There is higher-level information about identity and the fabric, which then drills down into resource specifics and then, in some cases, data from applications/services/frameworks running inside a resource.

Azure AD Azure AD has a number of types of logs available and these logs are tenant-wide. Most companies have a single Azure AD tenant that represents the entire company.

The two basic ones are sign-ins, which provide details on sign-in activities for the tenant, both successful and failed (for Azure AD Premium users), and the audit log, which details activities performed on the tenant. There are also security reports that provide information on users who are flagged for risk and risk sign-ins. The security reports have varying levels of detail depending on the Azure AD licenses assigned to users. Azure AD P2 shows all the detail possibly available, while free and basic show only if a user is flagged for risk and risky sign-ins, but no detail. Data can be sent to Log Analytics or storage/event hubs. Data is kept for different durations based on the data types and license of the user. Details are available at:

```
https://docs.microsoft.com/en-us/azure/active-directory/reports-monitoring/
reference-reports-data-retention
```

Activity Log   The activity log provides detail on all activities for a subscription that are performed via the Azure APIs (for example, creating and modifying resources) but also actions initiated via the Azure API on a resource (for example, resetting a storage account key). Data includes the operation performed, the time and the user or service performing the operation—i.e., who, what, and when. This can be thought of as control plane log information. The activity log data is kept for 90 days, per the following:

```
https://docs.microsoft.com/en-us/azure/azure-monitor/learn/tutorial-archive-data
```

However, as Figure 10.1 shows, the data can also be sent to Log Analytics for additional processing and longer-term storage. It can also be exported to storage accounts and/or event hubs. The activity log is directly accessible from within Azure Monitor and can be used to create alerts from within Azure Monitor.

NSG Flow Logs   When using network security groups, the data flow logs can be configured to be sent to a storage account and Log Analytics through Traffic Analytics. This log data is important to gain insight into traffic patterns, including possible malicious access.

Resource Metrics   These are specific to an instance of a resource, such as a storage account, an Azure SQL database, or a VM. The exact metrics will vary but are some type of numerical information about the resource that has a very fast data pipeline, which means near real-time visibility into the resource. These metrics are very useful for a number of monitoring purposes, including performance and health evaluation. Metrics are commonly used to trigger various actions via alerts—for example, CPU usage is over a certain threshold or a certain number of HTTP response codes that indicate an error. Metrics are kept for 93 days but can be sent to a variety of other storage solutions, including Log Analytics. Metrics are visible within Azure Monitor (and also from the resource monitoring, which will automatically set the scope of the metrics to the current resource) and can be the source of alerts.

Resource Diagnostic Logs   The diagnostic logs provide log information from within the resource—i.e., the data plane. These will vary greatly depending on the specific resource. For example, Azure SQL Database has a lot of different logs available. These logs are not natively available in Azure Monitor; instead they can be directed through the diagnostic settings of the resource you are interested in to an admin-defined combination of Azure Monitor Logs

(Log Analytics), storage account, or event hub. Additionally, the same diagnostic settings can be used to direct the resource's metrics to the same combination of targets. Depending on where you send the diagnostic logs, different approaches will be used to interrogate and act on the data. For analysis, you typically will leverage Log Analytics, as from there its rich analytics built on Azure Data Explorer can be leveraged.

Application Insights   Application Insights provides insight into your custom business applications that use .NET, Node.js, or J2E. The integration can be at compile or runtime. The information enables insight into performance, causes of performance degradation, availability and latency from points around the world, and even advanced testing using synthetic transactions. The data gathered is stored in Log Analytics. The data gathered can also feed Application Map, which provides dependency mapping based on code base monitoring—i.e., function calls between services (which differs from Service Map, which works by mapping network communications at the IP level). Application Insights not only gathers the data but also has a solution that sits on Log Analytics to provide various dashboards and insights based on the gathered data.

VMs   While there are various metrics available from the Azure fabric about VMs, there is also rich metric and log information within the guest operating system. This includes OS performance counters and OS logs. These can be gathered and sent to Log Analytics via the Microsoft Monitoring Agent (MMA). The exact data to capture is configured via Log Analytics. Note that this works for Windows and Linux in addition to OS instances not in Azure; only the MMA agent is required. VMs also have a diagnostic settings, which via the optional diagnostics agent, enables metrics/logs to be sent to storage or an event hub. (This same extension is used to gather information from some other Azure services.) In my experience, if an organization is leveraging Log Analytics, then they will use the MMA-based in-guest monitoring rather than the diagnostics extension. There is also a separate dependency agent that builds on MMA for the IP port-based mapping.

Apps/Services/Frameworks   There may be additional information from services like IIS, an application, or even a deployed framework. The exact nature of the information collection may vary. For example, IIS logs can be gathered as part of the in-guest MMA agent-collection configuration. For HDInsight clusters, the diagnostic setting directs additional collection, which triggers deployment of MMA to the cluster nodes with data sent to Log Analytics. The key point is, if there is additional metric or log data available, there is typically some way to extract it, normally to Log Analytics.

Azure Monitor Fundamentals

Azure Monitor is the central hub for all things monitoring-related. It provides a single pane of glass to interact with almost any monitoring data, including data in a Log Analytics workspace through Azure Monitor Logs (which replaces the previously separate advanced analytics interface). Additionally, most Azure resources use Azure Monitor for their scoped monitoring interfaces; it just automatically sets the scope of the output to the resource you are investigating. For example, in Figure 10.2, I select metrics for a VM. This is the exact same view as Azure Monitor; it just automatically sets the Azure Monitor metric view to the VM.

FIGURE 10.2
Viewing metrics for a VM

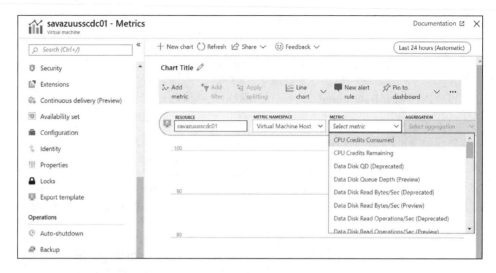

Azure Monitor places the most common monitoring data at the forefront. In the navigation pane, the first block of monitoring provides access to the activity log scoped to the current subscription but can be changed to a management group or multiple subscriptions. Additionally, the time range and event severity can be changed, with optional filters configurable. For example, a filter could be applied to only show events related to a certain resource group, a certain type of resource, or details around the event. Metrics are available that can have multiple resources displayed with any metrics available for the selected resources available—once again, with a configurable time frame and view options. If you create a chart you like, you can pin it to a dashboard for easy access, and, over time, you can build a custom dashboard with the information you care about. I'm not covering this in detail, but this is amazing functionality. Take some time to examine the options. For some metrics, once you add a metric, the Add Filter option will become available. This allows a more granular display of data. For example, if you add a metric from storage account availability, the Filter option becomes available, enabling you to filter based on a geo type, authentication type, or API name.

Service health is also displayed, providing information about any service issues, planned maintenance, and health advisories, as shown in Figure 10.3. (This is the same information available by directly accessing Service Health from the portal.) In this example, you can see there is currently a service issue and full details are available. You can scope to specific subscriptions, services, and regions to only show the status that you care about—and once again, the configured output can be pinned to a dashboard.

Also in Azure Monitor are various types of insights that you should take a look at. These continue to evolve, but solution-specific insights are geared towards intelligent information about specific resources. Insights for containers provide a lot of information about AKS clusters in an environment with an emphasis on plural, i.e. a single view across multiple clusters. Application Insights brings the information for any custom business applications that are being monitored.

FIGURE 10.3
Service Health
information in
Azure Monitor

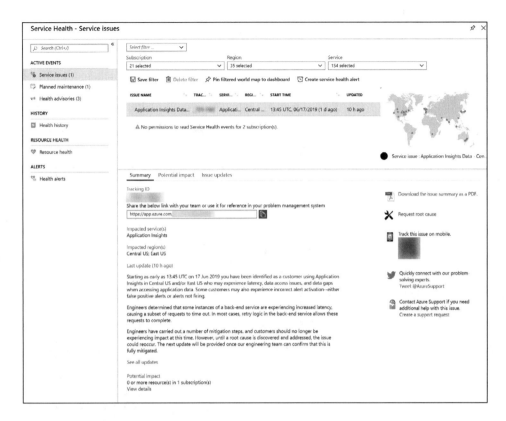

Then you see diagnostic settings, and this is huge. If you look at almost any resource in Azure, it also has a diagnostic setting option. The Azure Monitor diagnostics setting shows all resources, with the ability to centrally configure diagnostic settings across resources instead of configuring via the properties of each individual resource—but the actual configuration process is exactly the same. Multiple diagnostic setting configurations can be created on a single resource; however, there are restrictions on using the same output (sink) in multiple configurations for the same category of data. (But why would you want to? You would be sending the same data to the same place.) Each configuration can have a combination of possible sinks (outputs for the data). For some resources, you may have one output; for others, two; and for others, all three. It depends on your goals for the logs and retention requirements. Each of the possible sinks has specific use cases, as shown in Figure 10.4 for an Azure SQL database instance (as this shows the more common diagnostic setting layout compared to a VM, which has a specialized configuration). The exact logs available will vary greatly by resource type, but the three sink options will be the same.

FIGURE 10.4
Diagnostic setting
configuration

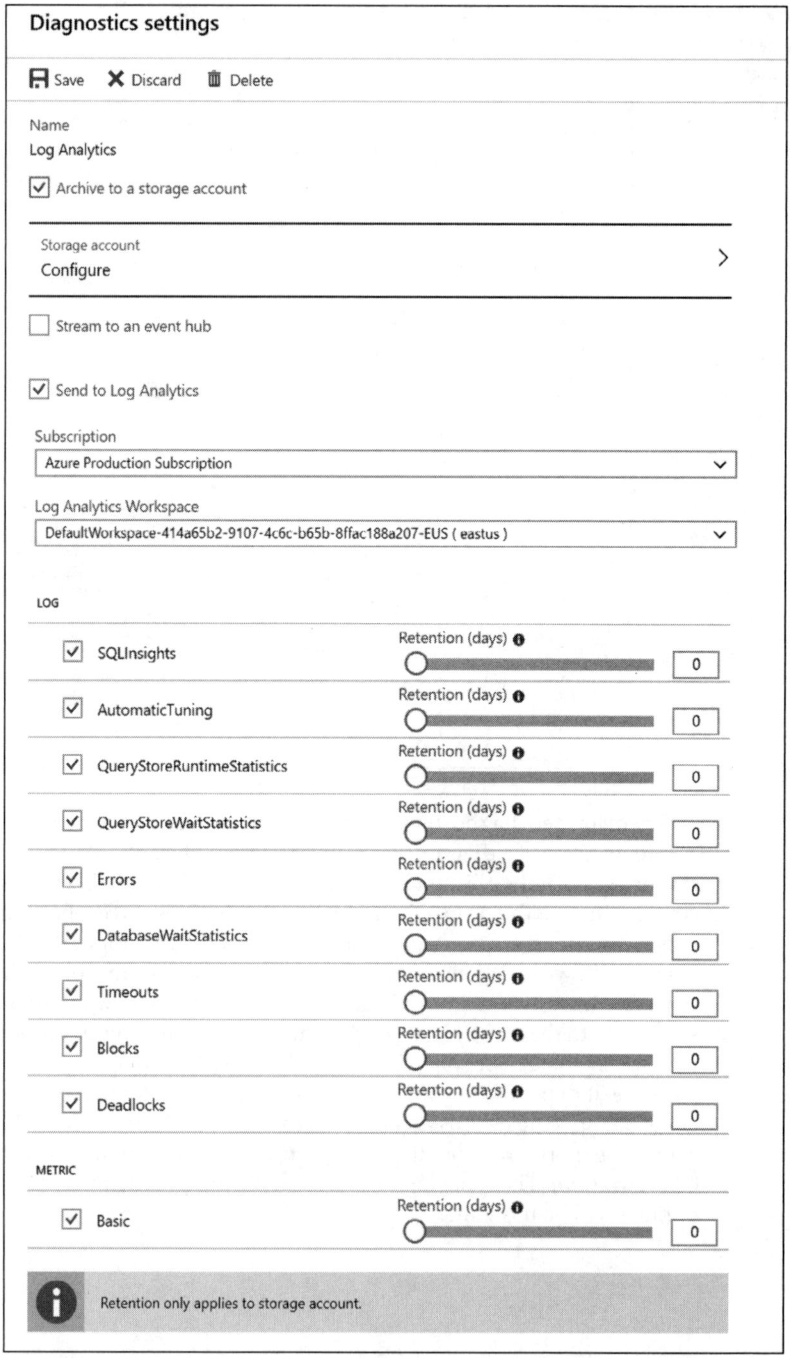

Diagnostics settings

🖫 Save   ✕ Discard   🗑 Delete

Name
Log Analytics

☑ Archive to a storage account

Storage account
Configure   〉

☐ Stream to an event hub

☑ Send to Log Analytics

Subscription
| Azure Production Subscription   ⌄ |

Log Analytics Workspace
| DefaultWorkspace-414a65b2-9107-4c6c-b65b-8ffac188a207-EUS (eastus)   ⌄ |

LOG

☑ SQLInsights   Retention (days) ❶ | 0 |

☑ AutomaticTuning   Retention (days) ❶ | 0 |

☑ QueryStoreRuntimeStatistics   Retention (days) ❶ | 0 |

☑ QueryStoreWaitStatistics   Retention (days) ❶ | 0 |

☑ Errors   Retention (days) ❶ | 0 |

☑ DatabaseWaitStatistics   Retention (days) ❶ | 0 |

☑ Timeouts   Retention (days) ❶ | 0 |

☑ Blocks   Retention (days) ❶ | 0 |

☑ Deadlocks   Retention (days) ❶ | 0 |

METRIC

☑ Basic   Retention (days) ❶ | 0 |

ⓘ   Retention only applies to storage account.

Storage Account   Selected logs and/or metrics are written to blob storage. This is useful for a very cheap archive of data, which may also then be read by other systems for ingestion, but is hard to directly query and use in a real-time manner. If storage account is configured, the time slider that is shown in Figure 10.4 is enabled; otherwise, if a storage sink is not enabled, the time slider will not be shown. A value of 0 means data is kept forever; otherwise, a value between 1 and 365 days can be specified, where data older than this setting is automatically deleted. This retention is only used for storage and does not apply to the other types of sinks. Data is organized in a container, with a "folder structure" implemented via the naming of the blobs. (Blob storage is not hierarchical and therefore has no real folders, unless you enable Data Lake; however, if you use forward slash (/) in the blob name, many tools will visualize this as folders.) The schema for the naming is long and discussed in detail in the Microsoft documentation, but the format is as follows:

```
insights-logs-{log category name}/resourceId=/SUBSCRIPTIONS/
{subscription ID}/RESOURCEGROUPS/{resource group name}/PROVIDERS/
{resource provider name}/{resource type}/{resource name}
/y={four-digit numeric year}/m={two-digit numeric month}/
d={two-digit numeric day}/h={two-digit 24-hour clock hour}/m=00/PT1H.json
```

Figure 10.5 shows an example of the blob created for an Azure SQL Database metric. Note the very long location! The logs are per hour, so the minute is always 00.

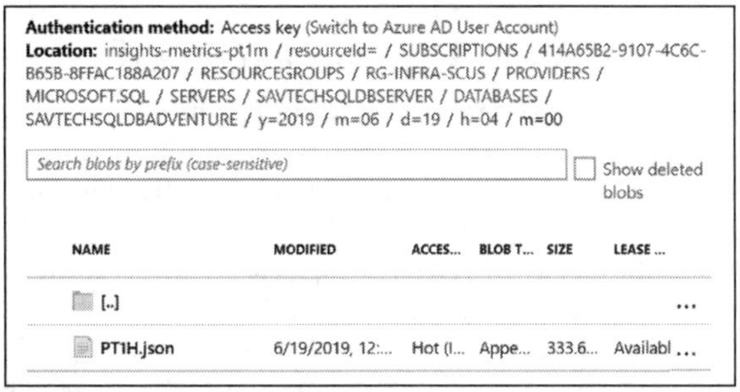

FIGURE 10.5
Example blob created as part of diagnostic setting sink to storage

Event Hub   Azure Event Hub is a publish/subscribe solution. It allows a service to publish data to an event hub instance in a namespace, which is then consumed by event receivers that have subscribed to the hub via a consumer group that provides an independent view of the data. This stream of data from the publisher (in this case, the Azure resource) and the subscribers is in real time. This option is commonly used to feed data to another system. For example, if you have an external SIEM (Security Information and Event Management) solution, this would be the method of choice to get data to it from resources in Azure. While the primary reason to use this is to send data to a third-party SIEM solution, you may also want to use this for a fast data pipeline to services like Power BI or another customer solution.

Log Analytics   I've saved the best for last. In the Azure, nay the Microsoft world of monitoring and analytics, this is the 900-pound gorilla and the foundation on which nearly all other monitoring and security solutions are built. Log Analytics will be covered in detail in the next section. However, one of its features is as a sink for massive amounts of variable format log data. In this case, the diagnostics data can be sent to Log Analytics for storage purposes. Once it is stored, rich analytics can be executed against that storage. For the many security and monitoring solutions in Azure, the diagnostic data must be sent to Log Analytics. The only configuration is to specify the workspace—i.e., an instance—of the Log Analytics service to receive the data.

To summarize, when thinking about which targets you want for diagnostic settings, follow these basic rules. For integration with Microsoft solutions or deeper analysis, you send to Log Analytics. To send to a third-party SIEM, you send to Event Hub and to keep for archival purposes very cheaply, send to storage.

Note that while you can set these on each service, you can also set them via the CLI/PowerShell or, even better, as part of the JSON ARM template during deployment. Azure Policy could also be used. A large number of policies to configure are built into Azure, with more available in GitHub. For example, the following configures Azure SQL Database to use Log Analytics, if not already configured:

```
https://github.com/Azure/azure-policy/tree/master/samples/Monitoring/
apply-diagnostic-setting-azsql-loganalytics
```

If you are using services built on Log Analytics for compliance and/or security purposes, it's important that services are not missed in the configuration, which is where using Azure Policy is so useful.

Azure Monitor Logs Fundamentals

Azure Monitor Logs is the new name for Log Analytics. Behind the scenes, there are still Log Analytics workspaces, and the functionally remains the same. Log Analytics provides storage for massive amounts of log data, from pretty much any type of system that is written to tables in the workspace. Using Azure Data Explorer, powerful analytics can be executed against the data using the Kusto Query Language (KQL) in the form of log queries. The query environment provides IntelliSense, making it intuitive to craft queries, in addition to a large number of sample queries available in the portal. The results from queries can be visualized in a number of ways, and many pre-created monitoring solutions are available from the gallery to provide insight across many services.

DATA IN A WORKSPACE

Data can come from a large number of sources. Nearly all Azure services can send their logs and metrics to a workspace. The Microsoft Management Agent (MMA) can be deployed to Azure and non-Azure workloads to provide logs from other workloads into the workspace. The agent is available for Windows and Linux, and each workspace has its own ID and a primary and secondary key. The deployment can be done for Azure resources via an extension or through any other deployment method into the OS, such as a declarative configuration or a group policy, etc. The exact data gathered is configured via the Advanced Settings of the workspace. This includes information such as performance counters, event logs, service logs—(such as IIS), syslog, and custom fields and logs (for example, text file-based data). Figure 10.6 shows the data configuration screen. In this example, I have added a number of performance counters. (A recommended set is available.) It is easy to add a large amount of data to be gathered, but remember that the more data you collect, the more storage is required and the more cost.

FIGURE 10.6
Configuring data
to collect via
connected sources

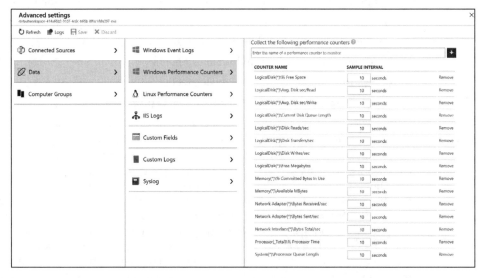

There are also APIs that can be used to ingest data into Log Analytics—for example, the HTTP-based API collector enabling RESTFUL pushes, as documented at:

https://docs.microsoft.com/en-us/azure/azure-monitor/platform/data-collector-api

Once data is flowing into a workspace, you do need to understand cost implications. Thirty-one days' of data up to 5 GB per month is free, as documented at:

https://azure.microsoft.com/en-us/pricing/details/monitor/

More data and/or longer retention incur costs. Therefore, you need to consider how long you need the data in the workspace and the amount of data you are ingesting. It may be that only a month of hot data is required in Log Analytics, after which the results of analysis are stored in other services.

The retention for data in a Log Analytics workspace is configured on a per-instance level using the usage and estimated costs blade. Here, the current pricing is displayed based on data ingestion volume and configured retention. The data retention can also be configured from the default 30 days up to 730 days.

By default, to use data in a workspace, you need permissions on the workspace that gives access to all data. If you need more granular control, you can change the access mode for the workspace to resource-centric. In the resource-centric access mode, you can only view logs that are associated with resources you have access to. Note that this does not work with all types of resource, as it requires the records to have the _ResourceId property correctly populated with the resource ID of the source, which can then be checked for the user's RBAC.

QUERYING A WORKSPACE

Data is organized into various tables within the workspace, which can be queried using Kusto. There are a number of standard tables, with custom tables creatable by workloads if required. Some of the key tables you will likely want to leverage include the following:

Perf Data sent from metric feeds

Heartbeat Data generated by deployed agents

Event Information from Windows event feeds

Syslog Information from Linux syslog feeds

SecurityEvents Details about security events from solutions

As previously mentioned, the KQL leverages IntelliSense, which provides an intuitive experience when querying the data. Additionally, you can explore the data in the workspace. Figure 10.7 shows the main interface for a workspace. The left of the display shows the schema of the workspace instance—i.e., the structure of the tables, views, and other artifacts. As shown, if you hover over a table, an eye icon is displayed, which, if clicked, will show the top 50 rows in the table. Note in the top-right query window, it populated a query to fetch the data. The results are shown in the lower-right area of the screen. As can be seen, I can drill into the details—in this case, I am looking at alerts. Notice there are various options to change the display to chart views, and in the query area there are options to change the time, in addition to saving the query, pinning the query, exporting the results, and even creating an alert. By default, when you open a workspace, it will show a history tab, providing easy access to previous queries in addition to a number of common queries, which can be great starting points.

FIGURE 10.7
Viewing the schema of a workspace

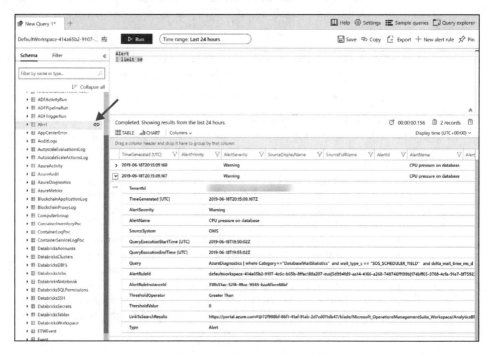

Queries will generally start with a data source (in this example, Alert), and then that data is piped to the next part, which limits the output to only 50 results. I recommend reviewing some of the sample queries but wanted to quickly walk through a few others. Note that Kusto is case sensitive. The case of a single letter being wrong will render the query unusable.

```
Perf
| where CounterName == "% Processor Time"
| summarize avg(CounterValue) by Computer, bin(TimeGenerated, 15m)
```

In this example, we look at the performance data and only look at records that related to the % Processor Time counter. Those records then continue down the pipeline to summarize the records (group together) by computer, with an average of the vaults at 15-minute intervals:

```
Perf
| where TimeGenerated > ago(1h)
| where (CounterName == "% Processor Time" and InstanceName == "_Total")
| project TimeGenerated, Computer, CounterName, CounterValue
| summarize avg(CounterValue) by Computer, CounterName, bin(TimeGenerated, 1m)
| render timechart
```

This example is similar to the previous one, except this time it generates a time chart at 1-minute intervals. There really is very little you cannot accomplish with the Kusto Query Language. By studying the examples and the schema, you can quickly learn how to extract the insight you need. These queries can also power various alerting options, as we will see later in this chapter. However, there is an even easier way to find useful queries.

MONITORING SOLUTIONS

While it is possible to manually create all queries you care about, to create your own visualizations, and to create dashboards focused around different technologies, this is often far harder than it seems. What is the right data to inspect? Which metrics and logs are important? How are separate data items combined to form insight? For many key solutions, monitoring solutions are available from the Azure marketplace. These monitoring solutions are combinations of queries, visualizations, and dashboards that bring the level of insight required based on the expertise of typically the same product group that build the solution you are monitoring. For example, there is an Azure SQL Database monitoring solution; there are numerous HDInsight monitoring solutions for the different types of clusters; there are Azure AD monitoring solutions; and so on. These are easily installed and provide easy access to things you likely care about. These do sit on Log Analytics, which means it's important that the resources have their diagnostic settings configured to send data to the Log Analytics workspace to which the monitoring solution is deployed. Monitoring solutions may instruct agents to gather additional data that can be used as part of the insight generation. The monitoring solutions have no magic. They are built on queries, and you can dive down into the displayed information to find the queries used behind the scenes, and many even have lists of additional queries you can use to get more information.

In the workspace, there is an overview pane. If you click Add, all of the monitoring solutions from the marketplace will be shown (see Figure 10.8). These can be added to the workspace and then used.

FIGURE 10.8
Searching available monitoring solutions

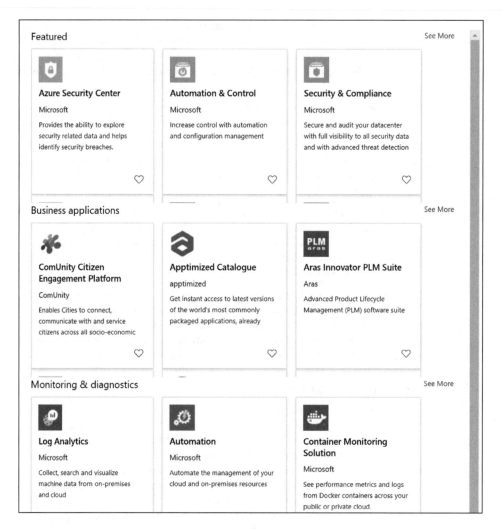

NETWORK WATCHER

Azure Network Watcher is not directly part of Log Analytics. However, it provides data to Log Analytics that is then utilized by a solution that is part of Network Watcher (circular logic, I know). Network Watcher has a large number of capabilities but is aimed at providing insight into all things networking in Azure, including connectivity troubleshooting, connectivity monitoring, and metrics. These capabilities are for virtual networks and for connectivity technologies, such as ExpressRoute. The solution is built on a Network Watcher instance, which needs to be deployed at a regional level. There is no cost for turning on Network Watcher, so I recommend turning it on for all regions where you have resources. Some key capabilities include the following:

◆ A topology viewer, which shows resources in a selected virtual network and their virtual subnet membership. This topology can also be downloaded to an SVG file, which can be useful for documenting the deployed network configuration.

♦ IP flow verify enables the ascertainment of communication allowance between resources. It utilizes investigation of network security groups and route tables to establish whether communication would be allowed, as opposed to actually performing a communication test between resources. It does not use any communication between the nodes but instead relies completely on the configuration defined. The next hop is also shown between resources.

♦ Connection monitor utilizes a configurable set of rules to probe resources and provide visibility to connectivity to the resource.

♦ Connection troubleshoot provides a similar output to IP flow verify, except it requires an agent on the VM, as it performs actual connectivity tests to establish the state of connectivity. Because of this agent availability, additional information is returned, including the state of any internal firewalls that may be impacting connectivity. This is very useful if you know there is a problem and want to identify what the cause of the problem is.

♦ Packet capture is provided using an agent installed into the VM.

♦ Security group view shows an aggregated rule set for a resource—i.e., the combination of NIC-level and subnet-level network security group rules. This is a great way to view the effective rules for a resource.

♦ NSG flow logs is very powerful, as it provides insight into the actual traffic flowing across resources. The flow logs are configured to be sent to a storage account with the option to also send to Log Analytics (by turning on Traffic Analytics). Enabling NSG flow logs is required to use Traffic Analytics.

♦ Traffic Analytics provides analysis of traffic passing through cloud resources. It is built on Network Watcher, which means Network Watcher must be enabled, and it also uses the data from NSG flow logs, which means those logs must be enabled and be set to send to Traffic Analytics—i.e., Log Analytics. It provides a lot of information, including:

  ♦ Who is talking to whom

  ♦ On which ports that communication is taking place

  ♦ Who the top talkers are

  ♦ Which ports are open

  ♦ Which sessions are open for long periods of time

This information helps in a number of ways. For security, I can quickly see ports that are open that should not be and can also see if bad actors are talking to my resources. It helps to identify the performance of my environment and also helps with capacity planning.

APPLICATION INSIGHTS

We often think about rings of maturity when it comes to monitoring. Azure Monitor can be thought of as ring 0. It's where everyone starts and gives comprehensive but fairly basic information. This does not mean it's bad—quite the opposite. Having comprehensive, basic information enables everyone to use that information and will suffice for most requirements related to visibility to resource state and alerting. Now consider an application's custom line of business application. The metrics and logs available from Azure services suddenly are not enough, as they don't provide any insight into the inner workings of the application (unless the application happens to write its logs to something like the IIS log, which we can capture). When dealing with a custom application, we need the ability to extend our monitoring to information within the application. Now we move into the next ring of monitoring maturity—ring 1.

Application Insights enables you to gather information from inside a custom application either by attaching the Application Insights components into the customer application at compile time or by attaching at runtime either through an Azure extension for a website or through a status monitor for your own VMs that utilize IIS or J2EE. The level of insight is the same. When you are using the runtime option, the various SDKs are added to the appropriate folder and the configuration is modified so that the SDKs are consumed into the code base at next start. This enables insight into custom applications without developers having to write their own solutions. For a full list of what is supported with Application Insights, see:

```
https://docs.microsoft.com/en-us/azure/azure-monitor/app/platforms
```

Application Insights feeds information to Log Analytics and uses that for much of its functionality. This use of Log Analytics also means you can create your own Kusto queries to inspect information about your application.

Application Insights has a number of benefits, but there are three primary ones I commonly talk to my customers about. First, and probably most importantly, is monitoring of the application in terms of its performance and any problems. This information can be monitored from the Azure portal and also from tools like Visual Studio. Baselines are automatically established for the application's normal performance. If that baseline is breached, then configurable notifications will fire, enabling you to know before any end user is impacted. The level of detail would include information related to the function that is impacted, the call that is calling the problem, and to what resource. For example, it may tell you that within a certain function, a call to a certain database with a specific statement is taking 50 ms, whereas historically it takes 20 ms. This would enable detailed investigation to quickly be performed and is more useful than a user shouting at the application developer that their "application is slow." Now the developer can quickly shout at the database administrator that their "database is slow."

But on a serious side, the developer can give the DBAs the exact statement being run, which will aid the DBA to identify potentially missing or fragmented indexes as a possible example.

The next useful functionality is around the availability of services. This goes beyond simple probes. The availability monitoring can monitor any service and can contact your site from around the world and report on availability and time taken, but that's just the basics. The availability monitoring can also be configured to perform synthetic transactions, provided that the developer of the application supports synthetic transactions. For example, if it were a sales website, a synthetic transaction could simulate a person logging in, buying something, and checking out, ensuring not only that all the steps worked but how long they took, providing insight into the end-customer experience.

Finally, Application Insights has Application Map. This is similar to the Service Map functionality of Log Analytics, except instead of working from TCP monitoring, Application Map works by monitoring the code base. For example, Application Map would see a certain call in .NET calling an HTTP/HTTPS service (which means some kind of dependency) and capture the details of that call. Since calls are prebuilt in .NET, the meaning of the call is known, and correlation IDs can be captured, which then hook into server-side components like Azure SQL Database or Cosmos DB, providing complete information. This is focused on finding the base set of resources an application is talking to.

If you have custom applications, then Application Insight is a no-brainer. It requires almost no work to start using and only minimal efforts to maximize its value.

Alerting

Having access to view data in its raw form or visualized is very useful for a number of scenarios. In many cases, however, we want some proactive communication when certain circumstances occur and don't want to wait for someone to see it on a dashboard. To meet this requirement, alerting is leveraged.

WHO AND HOW DO WE NEED TO ALERT?

Before diving into technologies related to alerting, it is first important to understand who we want to alert and how we want to alert. Different types of incidents require different severities of alerting. A major system outage that has brought down the business may warrant phoning or texting someone; a warning about a system may warrant an email or an alert in the Azure application. It is also important to notify the right people.

To identify the right people, many organizations will leverage a RACI matrix. This identifies people or groups of people that are:

Responsible   The team or person responsible for getting the work done

Accountable   The team accountable for the completion of the task. This is commonly a single person who is the sponsor for the project.

Consulted   The team communicated with for information/input. These are likely subject matter experts.

Informed   People who need to be aware. These might be people using a solution or a team that just needs to know the outcome.

Most organizations will have defined teams for many aspects of IT systems, such as networking, storage, compute, identity, and more. These systems are used by business applications that have their own teams. When looking at the cloud services, you need to understand the team responsible, as they will often be the ones to be alerted for system issues. You also need to understand the teams responsible for business applications that rely on those services, as they will also need to be alerted and then need to be informed. Depending on the severity, those accountable may need to be informed.

Now the options for how to communicate and potentially other types of actions outside of communication need to be evaluated. Sometimes an alert may not require any communication. There may be certain alerts that are known and have a solution that can be automated to resolve the issue.

Automation   Some kind of script or mechanism that performs a set of actions against resources.

Notification   An email, SMS, phone call, or application notification.

Ticket Generation   Many organizations have some kind of service management system. These systems utilize tickets to track incidents and those tickets assigned to groups to resolve. In the event of an alert a ticket can be raised through the service management system. That ticket would be assigned to a group who likely would be notified.

As mentioned at the start of this section, you must pick notification mechanisms that are appropriate for the level of event. If you notify too often, it becomes noise and its purpose is invalidated.

ACTION GROUPS

Action groups enable the centralized management of sets of defined actions, which can then be used across the Azure subscription by alerts. The goal is to avoid having to reconfigure the same sets of actions across multiple alerts. By using the action groups, common sets of actions can be defined—for example, email a certain group and trigger an automation that could be used across all alerts that required that action to be performed. An action group consists of one or more actions across a number of action types, as shown in Figure 10.9.

FIGURE 10.9
Action options in
an action group

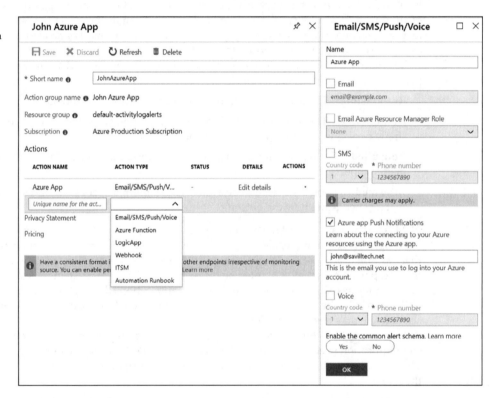

The following action types are available:

Email/SMS/Push/Voice This detail is shown in Figure 10.9 and, as the type name suggests, a combination of emails (either direct email or email anyone in a certain Azure role), an SMS text message, a push to the Azure mobile application, and/or voice can be selected. The option to use the common alert schema standardizes the alert notification content to be the same across metric, activity log- and diagnostic log-sourced alerts, which historically had been different and therefore difficult to automate the handling of because of differing formats. This is available across action types. Note that there are rate limits that will limit how many of specific types of notifications can be performed in a certain time window. At the time of writing, a single SMS and voice can be sent every 5 minutes and no more than 100 emails in an hour, per:

```
https://docs.microsoft.com/en-us/azure/azure-monitor/platform/alerts-rate-limiting
```

Other types of notification are not limited. This is to avoid inundating a recipient with too many unmanageable notifications.

Azure Function   Enables an Azure Function to be triggered, which, along with the other compute type actions, is useful to perform actions in response to an alert where responses can be automated

LogicApp   Allows an Azure LogicApp to be triggered

Webhook   Allows a webhook to be called. This is useful to interact with any RESTful endpoint via an HTTP call, which can then perform some kind of processing or custom action.

ITSM   Enables interaction with an IT Service Management solution. This commonly will be creating a service ticket, which would then be assigned to a certain group. To utilize this, an ITSM connection solution must first be installed—for example, to enable communication to ServiceNow (among others).

Automation Runbook   Trigger a runbook in an automation account. This will commonly be PowerShell, but other languages are also available. This enables almost any custom action to be performed. I see this commonly used for a common alert that can be remediated through a set of tasks—for example, stop and start a process, which is simple via PowerShell.

Create action groups for the most common actions you need to take across alerts. It is likely you will have certain severities of alerts where you want to email a certain set of people—some where you may want to text people and others where some kind of automation can be leveraged. Whatever the combinations, pre-create those action groups, enabling them to be used across many types of alert sources for the subscription.

SOURCE FOR ALERTS

There are a number of places where alerts can trigger, as shown in Figure 10.10. While we often think of Azure Monitor with metrics and the activity log, it is also possible to trigger alerts from Azure Monitor Logs (Log Analytics, which receives feeds of information from almost anywhere means alerts can be generated from signals from almost anywhere) and from Service Health. There are even others that use action groups. The budget thresholds in cost management also leverage action groups, and I'm sure there are others. Notice that I show a dotted line from metrics and the activity log to Azure Monitor Logs. While alerts can be generated directly from Azure Monitor, for metrics and the activity log, that telemetry can also be sent to Log Analytics, which means alerts could also be triggered from there (which has the benefit of a richer set of criteria to trigger the alert above the built-in Azure Monitor alerting). At the time of writing, Service Health alerts can only be triggered from Service Health, but I expect this to change soon.

FIGURE 10.10
Sources of alerts in Azure

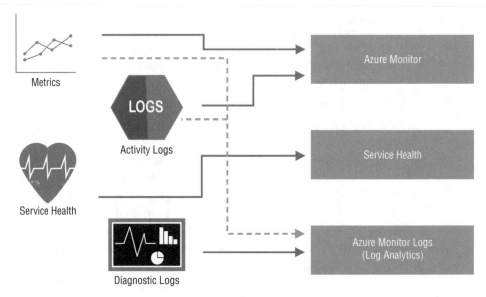

CREATING ALERTS

Details on the operational configuration of alerts is covered in detail in the Azure documentation and is outside the scope of an architecture book. However, I want to touch on some of the key points, starting with alerts created in Azure Monitor (which is a different experience from Azure Monitor Logs, aka Log Analytics, which I know is a little confusing). The following online course also covers alerting in a lot of detail:

> https://www.pluralsight.com/courses/microsoft-azure-alert-playbook-configuration

This course is available (along with a lot of others) with a free Pluralsight account, which you can get at:

> https://www.pluralsight.com/partners/microsoft/azure

When creating an alert in Azure Monitor (via the Alerts node and creating a new alert rule), the first option is the resource you wish to monitor. While you can select a specific resource, such as virtual machine or a SQL database instance, you can also set the scope to be a subscription or resource group. When the scope is not a specific resource but rather one of these higher container constructs, you are creating an alert for anything within the contained scope. For example, if you create an alert rule for a resource group, the alert would apply to anything within that resource group. Note that the types of signals will vary depending on the scope. If you select a subscription or resource group, then the only signals you can create an alert rule from would be the activity log. If you select a specific resource, then the available signals would also include metrics, as shown in Figure 10.11. This is because metrics vary based on resource type.

Once the resource is selected, the conditions are selected, which commonly will be from metrics and the activity log (of which there may be different types). Once a signal is selected, a graph will show historical data, which can help you consider what the right logic should be in your alert, as you don't want to alert too frequently. We always want to avoid generating noise, which will be ignored! For metrics, you can select a static threshold (for example, alert when the CPU is over a certain percentage), or you can use a dynamic threshold, which will use machine learning to identify the normal pattern and then alert you based on a certain sensitivity when the metric is outside that pattern, as shown in Figure 10.12. You can also configure the type of aggregation (for example, the average) and the period for which that aggregation is calculated (by default, 5 minutes). The frequency of evaluation can also be tuned, which is also 5 minutes by default. There are advanced settings that enable a number of violations (threshold exceeds events) over a certain time period. This is useful if a single occurrence does not warrant an alert but rather a continued state is what is important.

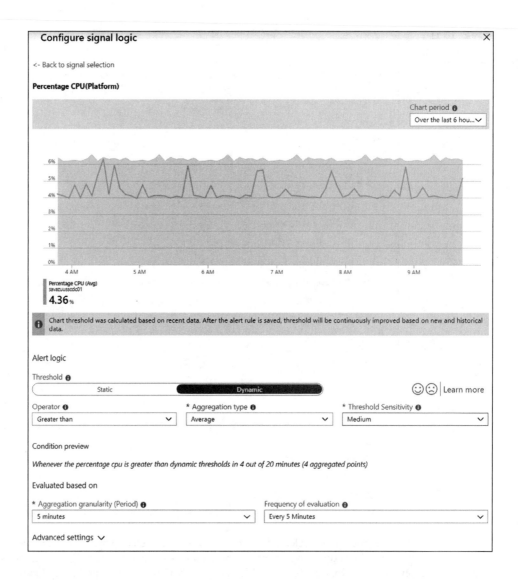

Actions can be configured for the alert rule—i.e., selecting one or more action group (or creating a new one)—but do not have to be. You are not required to have actions. You may simply want the alert to fire and be visible in the list of alerts, or you may want to centrally configure action rules, which we will shortly cover, which enable actions to be defined at a certain scope for any alerts within that scope rather than configuring action groups per alert.

A name for the new alert rule with an optional description, along with the severity of the alert rule, is defined. The severity is important, as this will be surfaced in the alert interface and can also govern how action rules fire if defined at the scope. By default, the rule will be enabled as soon as it is created, but this can be changed if required via the Enable toggle.

Alerts can also be created from Azure Monitor Logs (Log Analytics). The process is to work out your query that returns the data you care about. In my case, for example, I care about CPU pressure on my SQL database instance. I cannot monitor actual CPU percentage on the hardware, as that is meaningless in Azure. Remember that my resources in Azure are created of a certain SKU that has an assigned quota of resource. The actual underlying hardware has far more capacity, and our quotas will limit our resources way beyond any actual hardware capacity. Therefore, for a SQL database I care about database wait statistics and specifically the SOS_SCHEDULER_YIELD and since this will happen as part of normal operation, I only want to know if the time is greater than 100 milliseconds. Therefore, I use the following query:

```
AzureDiagnostics
| where Category=="DatabaseWaitStatistics"
and wait_type_s == "SOS_SCHEDULER_YIELD"
and delta_wait_time_ms_d >= 100
```

Once I have my query correct, I click the New Alert Rule button. This is now using the alert rules from Azure Monitor. The only thing different is that the condition is using Log Analytics (in fact, all alert rules are shown in Azure Monitor and it shows the source of the logs, as shown in Figure 10.13, where you can see I have alerts sourced from metrics, the activity log, and Log Analytics). While the alert rule is populated with the query, the threshold will need to be configured. You typically will want the alert to fire if the query returns a certain number of results. For example, if you want to be alerted if there are any results over a time period, you would select Greater Than 0, as shown in Figure 10.14. A Log Analytics alert can also directly include a customization of the email subject (if you have that as an action within action groups that are triggered), along with customizing the JSON payload if you use webhooks. You can also choose to suppress alerts for a period of time once the alert fires, to stop a constant alerting.

FIGURE 10.13
Alert rules generated across possible sources

NAME	CONDITION	STATUS	TARGET RESOURCE	TARGET RESOURCE TYPE	SIGNAL TYPE
DirSync over 50 percent CPU	Percentage CPU GreaterThan 50	⊘ Enabled	savazuusscds01	Virtual machines	Metrics
Savazuusscdc01 CPU credit less than …	CPU Credits Remaining LessThan 200	⊘ Enabled	savazuusscdc01	Virtual machines	Metrics
CPU pressure on database	AzureDiagnostics | where Category= ="DatabaseWaitStatistic…	⊘ Enabled	defaultworkspace-414…	Log Analytics workspaces	Log Search
Multiple resources created	AzureActivity | where OperationName contains "create" | wh…	⊘ Enabled	defaultworkspace-414…	Log Analytics workspaces	Log Search
Storage Key Regeneration	category equals Administrative and resourceId equals /subsc…	⊘ Enabled	sainfrastroragescus	Storage accounts	Service notificatio…

Displaying 1 - 5 rules out of total 5 rules

Search alert rules based on rule name and condition…

Alert rules based
on Log Analytics
queries

Note that there are price differences between standard alerts created in Azure Monitor and those created in Azure Monitor Logs (which use Log Analytics queries). Review the alert rule pricing at:

`https://azure.microsoft.com/en-us/pricing/details/monitor/`

Note the difference between metrics and log (which means Log Analytics). At the time of writing, regular metric alerts are 10 cents per month, while the log-based queries (not the activity log-based alerts within Azure Monitor, which are free) are 50 cents every 15 minute or greater interval per month. If you set a 5-minute interval, this would be three of these. which means $1.50 per month.

USING ACTION RULES

Action groups enable groups of actions to be defined, which are then used with an alert rule. This provides centralized management of the actions, but the action rules still have to be configured on every alert rule. If you had hundreds of alert rules that all required the same actions to be performed, this is cumbersome and very problematic if you wanted to change the action rule used. Action rules enable the separation of the alerts and the actions performed in response to an alert. Remember that an alert does not have to call an action group; it can simply fire and be visible in the alerts node of Azure Monitor. It is very common that the same actions are required for all resources in a certain resource group, since the same people always want to be notified for incidents for any resource in that resource group.

The idea is that you create your various alert rules, which will commonly target a specific resource but may also be scoped to resource groups or even subscriptions. These alert rules have the conditions of when alerts fire, but you don't set actions within these alert rules (but you can if you want).

You create action rules separately. An action rule can be scoped at a subscription, one or more resource groups, and/or one or more resources. The action rule can have filters applied—for example, a severity (this is why it's important to set an appropriate severity in the alert rules), as shown in Figure 10.15, but other filters are also available. Next, the goal for the action rule is selected, which can be Suppression or Action Groups. As the name suggests, if you select Suppression, it will actually suppress any action groups from firing that may have been configured directly in alert rules or by action rules. When defining suppression, you can select a time frame for the suppression of the actions or a recurrence. Maybe you want to suppress on a national holiday or during the weekend. Alternatively, you select action groups, which will call the action group set for any alerts to fire within the scope of the action rule that meets any defined filters configured.

FIGURE 10.15
Action rule filters

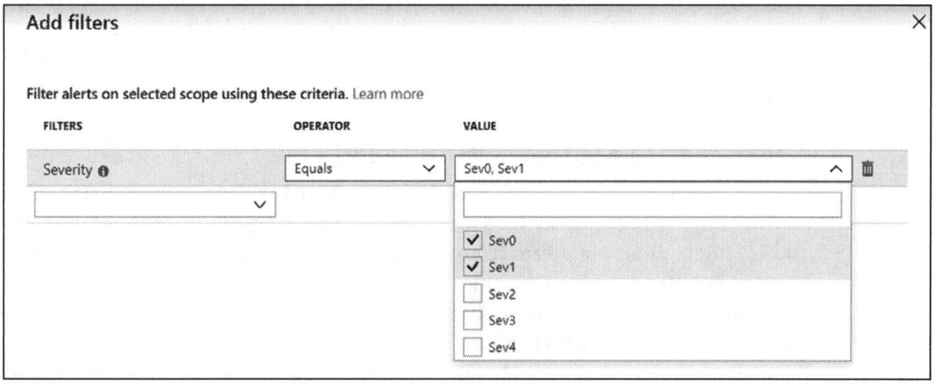

ALERT SMART GROUPS

By default, any alerts will surface in the alert's main view; however, you may get many instances of the same alert. Smart groups use machine learning algorithms to gather together alerts to reduce clutter and to enable the groups of alerts to be collectively managed—for example, closing them all, as shown in Figure 10.16, where I have selected all the alerts in this smart group and can now change the alert state of all three separate alerts by clicking the arrowed button.

I can also change the smart groups' state, which is separate from the individual states of the alerts. You can choose to ignore the smart groups, although there is no cost to them and they do help to keep a cleaner view of the alerts and provide simpler state management.

FIGURE 10.16
Viewing alerts with smart groups

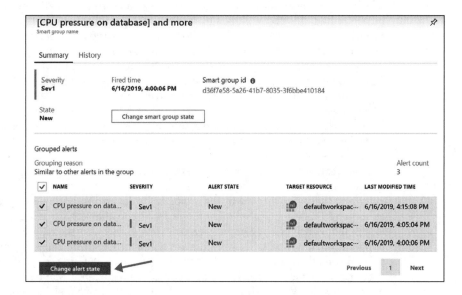

Security in Azure

Security is a core part of everything, not just in Azure. Throughout the book, I have talked about security aspects of the technologies and services covered. However, I want to spend a little more time on a few key topics and ways of thinking about certain aspects of cloud usage that are broad across any specific technology.

Advanced Threat Protection (ATP)

This follows very closely from looking at monitoring available in Azure. When I talked about storing various signals, such as logs and metrics, I pointed out that simply looking at signals and trying to generate alerts from a single piece of telemetry for security purposes is typically impractical. Keeping logs and metrics is useful for forensic purposes after an attack, but trying to detect an attack from manually created rules based on metric values or log content is likely to fail. To detect threats, we typically need to not only look at combinations of signals but also apply intelligence. This is where the various advanced threat-protection solutions available across the Microsoft cloud come into play. The goal for the ATP solutions is specifically to take the telemetry from services and apply intelligence to detect and protect against threats. The ATP family consists of a number of solutions, which is constantly growing. I already touched on some of them—for example, Azure ATP, which provides cloud-based protection for Active Directory by ingesting and analyzing network traffic from domain controllers.

There are also ATP solutions such as Defender ATP, which builds on the known threats, such as malware covered by Windows Defender (i.e., antivirus), and adds threat detection and protection for threats not yet known (i.e., zero-day protections). Defender ATP does this by gathering information from across server and desktop operating systems, feeding this data into the cloud, and is then analyzed by machine algorithms and security researchers to look for behavior that indicates an attack, and then quickly notifies and works to mitigate and protect. Defender ATP provides a blackbox recording, enabling detailed forensic analysis if there is an attack. For example, consider an employee who opens a bad document from an email on their PC. This bad document starts a bad process on the machine; that process starts talking to a malicious website; the process tries to gather credentials and then reach out to other machines on the network. All of this would be centrally logged and available for forensic analysis.

Office 365 has its own ATP solution to provide protection across the Office 365 solutions, such as detonation chambers for attachments, to ensure they are safe by opening them in an isolated environment in the cloud before being deemed safe and available for users—i.e., safe attachments. There are also services like safe links, anti-phishing, automated responses, and user training components, just to scratch the service.

When it comes to Azure services, the threat protection focuses on the data services. The two key services today are Azure Storage ATP and Azure SQL ATP. Both services are built on Log Analytics and analyze the telemetry sent to the workspace and add machine learning to detect threats to services.

For Azure Storage, details can be found at:

```
https://docs.microsoft.com/en-us/azure/storage/common/
storage-advanced-threat-protection
```

At the time of writing, however, only the Blob data service is protected and is priced based on the number of transactions to the storage account, which is where the service is enabled. Storage ATP, like all the services, can also be enabled via templates and through Azure Policy. Using Azure Policy is a good option for this type of critical service, to ensure services are not missed by forgetting to enable the protection.

SQL Database ATP is part of the Advanced Data Security feature, which is purchased on a per-database server level. That's right. Per server, which means I can have many databases on the server and still only pay the $15 per month (at the time of writing) ATP protection cost. Advanced Data Security has three capabilities: data discovery and classification (which scans the metadata of your databases and looks for types of data you may want to classify, such as personally identifiable information and credit cards, and suggests classifications), vulnerability assessment (which scans for common security misconfigurations and recommends remediations), and advanced threat protection (finally). I'm a huge fan of the SQL ATP. They have done an amazing job. In Figure 10.17, you can see my alerts which are surfaced via Azure Security Center (which I will cover next). As you can see, I had a pretty bad day on 6/21, where pretty much every type of attack was performed on my database. (Don't worry—I did it!). As you can see, it detected threats such as brute force attacks, SQL injection, logon from an unfamiliar principal, logons from unusual Azure datacenters, attempted logon from a potentially harmful application, and more. The full list of protections can be found at:

```
https://docs.microsoft.com/en-us/azure/sql-database/
sql-database-threat-detection-overview
```

FIGURE 10.17
Viewing threats
for Azure SQL
database

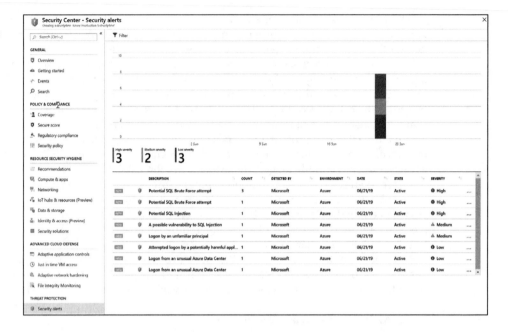

Because these solutions are built on Log Analytics, they are also visible directly within Log Analytics. As shown in Figure 10.18, I can see them by looking at SecurityAlert, which means I could create a custom alert from them to do anything I want beyond the simple email, which is configurable from SQL ATP directly.

FIGURE 10.18
Viewing threats
through a query
in Log Analytics

▷ Run	Time range: **Last 3 days**		🖫 Save ⊙ Copy ⤴ Export

```
SecurityAlert
| limit 50
```

Completed. Showing results from the last 3 days.   ⏱ 00:00:00

▤ TABLE   ᴫ∥ CHART   Columns ⌄

Drag a column header and drop it here to group by that column

	TimeGenerated [UTC] ▽	DisplayName ▽	AlertName
>	2019-06-21T13:04:12.000	Potential SQL Injection	Potential SQL Injection
>	2019-06-21T13:31:09.000	Logon by an unfamiliar principal	Logon by an unfamiliar principal
>	2019-06-21T13:31:09.000	Attempted logon by a potentially harmful application	Attempted logon by a potentially harmful
>	2019-06-21T13:31:09.000	Logon from an unusual Azure Data Center	Logon from an unusual Azure Data Center
>	2019-06-21T13:31:09.000	Potential SQL Brute Force attempt	Potential SQL Brute Force attempt
>	2019-06-21T13:31:10.000	Logon from an unusual Azure Data Center	Logon from an unusual Azure Data Center
>	2019-06-21T19:33:46.000	A possible vulnerability to SQL Injection	A possible vulnerability to SQL Injection

Azure Security Center (ASC)

In the same way that Azure Monitor is the central hub for all things monitoring-related, Azure Security Center is the central hub for all things security-related. I touched on this in the previous section, where the alerts from ATP are surfaced as part of the threat protection component of ASC. ASC extensively uses the Microsoft Monitoring Agent (MMA) for most of its functionality and will automatically deploy the agent to VMs (with this being configurable through the settings of ASC). ASC also extensively uses Log Analytics and by default creates its own workspace to use, but this also can be customized.

ASC is available as a free and standard offering. Even the free offering provides a lot of functionality that provides insight into the security health of many resources through the deployment of a number of security policies that evaluate configuration of deployed resources and then provide recommendations. The standard offering adds additional services that use machine learning, such as threat protection, and services like just-in-time VM access. The standard offering is purchased on a per-node, per-month basis and can be used for Azure, on premises, and other cloud-based resources.

The first part of ASC helps to provide insight into the overall compliance of your environment based on policies you have applied and the regulatory compliance assessments that are built into ASC. It starts with a secure score that gives you a number based on the resources in your subscription and the reasoning behind that score. This is a useful place to start, as you can quickly see some actionable steps to improve your score and, more importantly, improve the security of your environment. Figure 10.19 shows the state of my subscription. The number of points is what is available. If you click an item, it will show you how many points you have attained. The more red that is in the bar, the less you are getting; and the higher the number of points, the more important. This helps prioritize any actions you will take. A standard set of Azure policies is deployed via an initiative, which can be viewed through Azure Policy. This is what powers the evaluation shown in ASC. If you look in Azure Policy, you will see an assignment of an ASC Default initiative that has over 80 policies in it that is scoped to your subscription. The ASC navigation enables you to quickly view the security assessment across the different types of resources.

The second part of ASC focuses on advanced cloud defense. A very popular technology is just-in-time VM access. Access to your VMs should be via your private network connection. Your on-premises locations have either a site-to-site VPN configuration or an ExpressRoute linking the IP ranges from on premises to those in Azure, making Azure an extension of your network and enabling direct access to resources on virtual networks in Azure using their private IP addresses. Alternatively, you can use point-to-site to connect a single machine to a virtual network using a tunnel and use the private IP addresses. If this is not possible and resources must have public IP addresses, you should *never* enable RDP or SSH on them, as they will be attacked and they will be hacked. If you require RDP or SSH and have no other choice (noting Azure Bastion Host is now available and is covered in the next chapter), then you can use just-in-time (JIT) VM access. JIT uses network security group (NSG) rules to enable access from a specific IP address or range for a limited amount of time when access is requested, and that access request is logged. The maximum amount of time the access is enabled for is configurable on a per-VM basis, as are the allowed ports that can be requested. Figure 10.20 shows an example request. Note that it detects my public-facing IP address and will enable only that IP address for the direction specified (noting I can change the time to an amount lower than the maximum) by manipulating the NSGs at the VM and/or subnet level to provide access, and then modifies the rules again to block access once the time has expired. If you are enabling this from a location, then it is that location's public IP that is enabled—i.e., your entire office or anyone at Starbucks. Someone else at Starbucks is unlikely to be trying to hack your VM, but it would be possible.

FIGURE 10.19
The overall secu-
rity state for my
subscription
and actionable
recommendations

FIGURE 10.20
Enabling access
via JIT for my
machine

Other capabilities include adaptive application controls, which help to restrict malware by only allowing known applications to execute, which are determined through machine learning to update whitelisting rules. Because the whitelist must be generated, there is a period of two weeks when first enabled for the solution to whitelist what should be considered a normal and therefore whitelisted application. You can run this solution in an audit or enforce mode. Typically, you will start in audit mode to avoid blocking applications that may be required, which is what happens with enforce mode. File integrity monitoring enables the tracking of files and the Registry (for Windows) across environments. Both the application controls and file integrity monitoring are available for Windows and Linux for resources in and outside of Azure. The other capability is adaptive network hardening, which looks at the actual traffic flowing across the network and modifies applied NSGs to make them more restrictive to better match the actual traffic patterns, removing any unnecessary gaps.

ASC provides integration with the threat protection, providing views into the alerts. Playbooks can also be created. These are logic apps that can be triggered in response to alerts. Of course, you can do this any way with Azure Monitor Log-based alerts, which then call action groups, which actually have more functionality. I tend to ignore this feature and instead focus on using the Log Analytics queries for alerts with action groups, if I need to automate triggering actions in response to ATP alerts.

Azure Sentinel

I struggled with where to talk about Azure Sentinel. It is very much a security solution, but it's built on Log Analytics, so I wondered if I should have covered it there with monitoring solutions. However, because of its security focus, I wanted to save it for here and ensure it gets the focus it deserves.

Log Analytics provides an amazing capability of ingesting data from almost any source, and the Kusto-based queries enable deep analysis of that information and are taken advantage of by the many monitoring solutions available in Azure. However, Log Analytics has never been considered a SIEM (Security Information and Event Management) solution, as it lacked the focus on analyzing the data from a security perspective in real time. Nor was it considered a SOAR (Security Orchestration, Automation and Response) since without the security analysis, while it has the ability to create alert rules which can trigger action rules that can automate responses, it couldn't do this as a result of security incidents.

Azure Sentinel uses Log Analytics extensively but is more than just a set of log queries and dashboards. Azure Sentinel provides both a SIEM and SOAR solution through the use of not only artificial intelligence to detect and respond to threats but also a large number of connectors to enable data to be ingested from systems previously unsupported by Log Analytics. Azure Sentinel provides a single interface to configure all aspects, including connection to services, creation of threat alert rules, playbooks (logic apps), and the underlying workspace.

Once the various connectors are established, data will flow into Azure Sentinel that can then be analyzed and threats watched for. Any threats detected trigger a case to be created that contains all the data that relates to that specific incident. Figure 10.21 shows the example case screen. Note that at the time of writing, Azure Sentinel is in early preview days, so functionality is subject to change. Cases are assigned a severity based on the calculated risk level, and any case can be investigated with a single click that will show a graphical picture of the entities involved in the case, such as security principals and computers, along with a timeline of the activities. The investigation is interactive, with any entity available for more detailed insight, such as other alerts, other access, and more.

FIGURE 10.21
Security cases in
Azure Sentinel

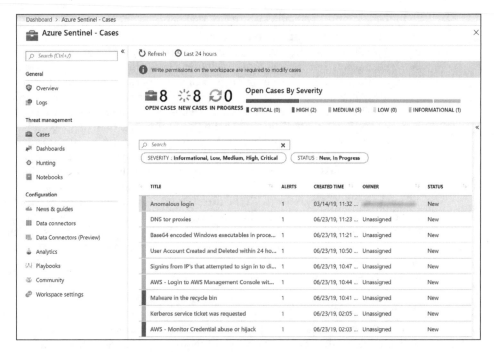

Dashboards provide specific insight into certain aspects of the environment. For example, there are dashboards focused on Azure AD sign-ins, Azure Firewall, AWS Network Activities (yep, it monitors across different cloud vendors, critical for a SIEM solution), Exchange Online, Insecure Protocols, and more.

You can also perform hunting by running queries against the data in the workspace. A number of queries are included, covering many common types of hunts you may want to perform. For example, there is query to find masquerading files commonly used by malware to make malicious processes blend in with legitimate ones.

```
SecurityEvent
| where NewProcessName endswith "\\svchost.exe"
| where SubjectUserSid !in ("S-1-5-18", "S-1-5-19", "S-1-5-20")
| where NewProcessName !contains ":\\Windows\\System32"
| where NewProcessName !contains ":\\Windows\\Syswow64"
| summarize minTimeGenerated=min(TimeGenerated),
maxTimeGenerated=max(TimeGenerated), count() by Computer, SubjectUserName
, NewProcessName, CommandLine
| project minTimeGenerated , maxTimeGenerated , count_ , Computer ,
  SubjectUserName , NewProcessName , CommandLine
```

Notebooks are also available, which are Jupyter notebooks that enable many types of asset to be combined—such as text, executable code, graphics, and more—into a sharable canvas. These can be used as the single point to work on cases and collaborate with other security team members.

The best way to start with Sentinel is to deploy it. With security being so important today, it's great to see this service available as a focal point for anything security-related in Azure and beyond.

Keeping Secrets with Azure Key Vault and Managed Identities

I've mentioned Azure Key Vault a number of times throughout this book as an HSM-based service for storing secrets and keys. I want to talk about it here as part of thinking about the security of secrets you have in your organization. I also created a video to go with this, available at https://youtu.be/PbrKmX-jryQ, to really try to ensure this is clear, as this is so important.

Every organization has secrets that need to be used by IT systems. The secret could be a password, an access key, or a token. These secrets may be needed from applications, from services, orfrom automation scripts. Often the temptation is to take these secrets and put them where they are needed—i.e., we put the password in our automation script; we place the key in our service configuration file. The problem is in today's world of repositories and source control, we end up placing those secrets in places we may not have locked down as well as we should have. If you go search GitHub, you will find a lot of secrets that developers and administrators forget were in there just available to the public. We need to not do this.

But first, can we remove the secret completely? We often use secrets as we have some compute service that needs to access some resource (for example, an application running in a VM) or an Azure Function needs to access something in Azure Storage or Azure Cosmos DB or Azure SQL Database. That means either a security identity is required or some access key (depending on the service being accessed). Let's start with the security identity. We have to store the password since our application has to authenticate to the target resource, right? If the compute resource is running, the answer is no. Azure has a feature called *managed identities.*

A system-assigned managed identity, when enabled for a supported Azure resource, provides a security principal in Azure AD for that resource that can only be used by that specific resource. That resource simply calls an endpoint that will return a token for that managed identity. That identity can be assigned access to resources, such as an Azure SQL Database or blob, using standard Azure role-based access control. Without any separate security principal, the service can access the resource using its own managed identity. The system-assigned managed identity is simple to enable and is unique per resource. A user-assigned managed identity is also configurable, which, as the name suggests, is created and assigned manually. This enables multiple resources to be able to use the same managed identity, but, once again, only resources that have been assigned it can request (this time, as part of the request, it needs to specify which identity it is requesting a token for) and use it—once again, completely transparently. They make a call to the endpoint and get the token. No secrets need to be maintained. The following website lists the resources that can use a managed identity:

```
https://docs.microsoft.com/en-us/azure/active-directory/
managed-identities-azure-resources/overview
```

If the service does not support Azure AD integration but instead requires some kind of key, such as certain storage services in Azure Storage or Azure Cosmos DB, we need a different approach. This time, we may need to store a secret. However, before embarking down that path, can the key be requested via an API? Most likely, it can. A common pattern emerging for many services is to grant a security principal the right to request the key and then use the key. This is very common with Azure Cosmos DB, which, while it supports scoped resource tokens with restricted permissions, they are not used very much. Instead, one of the read-write or read-only keys are used. This means the managed identity of a service could be given the right via RBAC to read the key, allowing the application to read the key from the service at startup via its managed identity, and then use it. Once again, no secret needed. If we really must use a token, then we now need to store it—and for that storage, we should use Azure Key Vault. As you may have guessed, we will give the managed identity of the services that need access to it the rights to access the secret, once again removing the need to actually store a secret in any code and avoiding the chicken-and-egg problem of how can the application get access to the secret in Key Vault without a security principal. This pattern of gaining the secret from Key Vault and using it is shown in Figure 10.22, but remember, this is our last choice. Ideally, we would directly use the managed identity and avoid any secret (which then has to be managed, rotated, and so forth).

FIGURE 10.22
An application using its managed identity to gain access to a secret, which is used for resource access

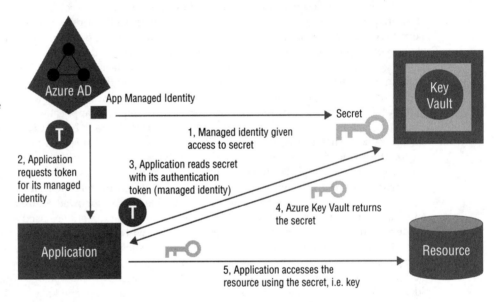

Note that Key Vault should always be where any secrets or keys are stored. When I create JSON templates, if I need a secret in them (for example, a password), I store the password in a secret and then reference the secret in the JSON template (making sure ARM template deployment use is enabled in the Key Vault's advanced access policy). If you ever find yourself having to put any kind of secret directly in any script or configuration file, stop and find another way!

Chapter 11

Managing Azure

This chapter focuses on a few management aspects of Azure. This is an architecture book, so the goal is not to go into operational details but rather to focus on aspects of management that are important to the overall governance, security, and effectiveness of the environment. The primary focus will be on the best way to deploy resources, command-line interactions, and automation.

In this chapter, you will learn to:

♦ Perform management using PowerShell and the CLI.

♦ Deploy resources with ARM JSON templates.

♦ Use technologies such as Azure Bastion Host and the Windows Admin Center.

Command Line, Scripting, and Automation with Azure

Interactions with Azure will be for different purposes, and the different options have relative advantages and disadvantages, depending on the type of interaction you are performing. Consider the primary methods of interaction available to us for Azure:

The Azure Portal   The Azure portal is very useful for quickly browsing the resources deployed and interacting with dashboards. However, the portal is very slow and prone to user error for provisioning.

The PowerShell and CLI   These can expose anything the portal can but require more skill to ascertain the right command. However, they are invaluable for performing management actions, especially if you want to automate/script them—something that can't be done with the portal.

JSON Templates   These are used to provision resources and provide the best experience for provisioning, as they are idempotent, declarative, and easy to integrate with change control systems.

There are others. You can call the Azure REST API directly, there is the Azure resource graph that enables powerful querying of data within subscriptions, third-party declarative deployment and special tools, but the PowerShell/CLI and JSON templates are the primary ones I am going to focus on in this chapter, with a sprinkling of a few other technologies.

Using PowerShell with Azure

In the world of Windows command-line interfaces and scripting, PowerShell is the primary technology. Because it was open sourced with PowerShell Core, it can also be leveraged on Linux and MacOS. As a Microsoft technology specialist, I have a heavy bias towards PowerShell over Bash and the accompanying Azure CLI. In this chapter, I will focus more on the PowerShell side, although much of what I talk about here is also possible with the CLI. You can use the CLI for interactive command-line usage and for scripting purposes; however, it does not have the same automation integration options with technologies like Azure Automation runbooks and Azure Functions, which is another reason I tend to lean more towards PowerShell.

GETTING READY FOR AZURE POWERSHELL

PowerShell functionality for technologies is primarily provided through modules. There are modules for Azure (actually, a number of them), but before getting to that, I want to quickly touch on the right PowerShell to use. As previously mentioned, PowerShell was recently open sourced. This created PowerShell Core, which is distinct from Windows PowerShell that ships as part of Windows and is updated with new versions of Windows. PowerShell Core is built on .NET Core instead of the full .NET on which Windows PowerShell is built. PowerShell Core is a separate download and install and updates more frequently than the OS-based Windows PowerShell. There are also functionality differences because of the different .NET foundations. PowerShell Core does not support all the same capabilities or modules of Windows PowerShell, although that gap is closing, and Microsoft is actually working to bring them back together for PowerShell 7. That's right—Core is being dropped from the name, as they have found it's confusing people and stifling its adoption. It will still be Core behind the scenes, but publicly it will be known as PowerShell 7 and will be built on .NET Core 3.0, which adds a lot of functionality that PowerShell 7 will be able to take advantage of.

All that background is really just so that I can encourage you to adopt PowerShell Core. It is the future and is what you will be using if you use the Cloud Shell (which I'll cover later) and will also enable you to leverage PowerShell across different platforms. Adopting PowerShell Core will also mean adopting Visual Studio (VS) Code as the built-in scripting environment for PowerShell. The PowerShell Integrated Scripting Environment (ISE) does not work with PowerShell Core, but it's inferior to VS Code anyway, and ISE is not seeing further development investment. So, before doing anything else, download PowerShell Core (from https://github.com/PowerShell/PowerShell) and VS Code (from https://code .visualstudio.com/Download), and then configure VS Code to use PowerShell Core instead of Windows PowerShell. This is simple to do:

1. In VS Code, open the command palette (Ctrl+Shift+P).

2. Type **JSON** and select the Preferences: Open Settings (JSON) option, as shown in Figure 11.1

FIGURE 11.1
Opening the JSON settings file

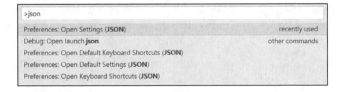

```
>json

Preferences: Open Settings (JSON)                                    recently used
Debug: Open launch.json                                            other commands
Preferences: Open Default Keyboard Shortcuts (JSON)
Preferences: Open Default Settings (JSON)
Preferences: Open Keyboard Shortcuts (JSON)
```

3. In the file, enter the following between the curly brackets:

```
"powershell.powerShellExePath": "c:\\Program Files\\PowerShell\\6\\pwsh.exe"
```

Note that this is for version 6 of PowerShell. If you have a later version, such as PowerShell 7, change the version and confirm the path is correct.

4. I also turn on autocomplete and make PowerShell the default language by adding additional lines to the file. Make sure you add a comma to all lines except the last line, as follows:

```
"editor.tabCompletion": "on",
"files.defaultLanguage": "powershell"
```

5. Save your settings.

There are a lot of other extensions for VS Code I recommend, such as the PowerShell extension, the Azure Account extension, and more. Also, if you are working with repositories for your code, you'll want to install Git and integrate it with VS Code by telling the code where the install Git executable is. For example:

```
"git.path": "C:\\Program Files\\Git\\bin\\git.exe"
```

There are two global settings that you should also configure for Git—your name and email address:

```
Git config --global user.name "John Savill"
Git config --global user.email "john@savilltech.com
Git config --global --list
```

I walk through all of this in my free YouTube-based PowerShell course—specifically, the Getting Ready for DevOps with PowerShell and VS Code module. You can watch these at https://youtu.be/yavDKHV-OOI.

The final step, once you have all that set up, is to get the Azure modules. We will use the newest Az modules. To install them, ensure that you have an elevated PowerShell Core window. (It's very important this is the PowerShell Core window you install from if you are going to use PowerShell Core, as PowerShell Core and Windows PowerShell use different module paths.) You select Run as Administrator from its context menu, and then run the following:

```
PS C:\Users\john> install-module az
Untrusted repository
You are installing the modules from an untrusted repository. If you trust this
repository, change its InstallationPolicy value by running
the Set-PSRepository cmdlet. Are you sure you want to install the modules from
'PSGallery'?
[Y] Yes  [A] Yes to All  [N] No  [L] No to All  [S] Suspend  [?] Help (default
is "N"): y
```

Note that after the initial command, you have to enter **y** to accept the fact that you are installing from an untrusted repository. If you were using Windows PowerShell, you would also be prompted to pull down NuGet to enable the actual download. Once the installation has finished, you will now have all the Az modules installed. Run the command Get-Module -ListAvailable to see them all. There are a lot of them, but thanks to the autoload capability of Azure, the required module will automatically load as needed. If you want to update to the latest version from an elevated PowerShell session, you need to install again, as opposed to using Update-Module. This is because Az is a meta-module—i.e., it comprises separate modules. To update and not have the old version left behind, you could remove the Az modules then install again. Microsoft has a script at

```
https://docs.microsoft.com/en-us/powershell/azure/uninstall-az-ps?view=azps-2.3.2
```

that performs the complete uninstall. You could also delete the modules from the filesystem. (The location is shown from the Get-Module -ListAvailable command.)

If you want to check which version is available and which one you have, use the following:

```
PS C:\> find-module az

Version              Name         Repository           Description
-------              ----         ----------           -----------
2.3.2                Az           PSGallery            Microsoft Az...

PS C:\> Get-Module Az -ListAvailable | select-object -Property Name, Version,
Path
Name Version Path
---- ------- ----
Az   2.3.2   C:\Users\john\OneDrive\Documents\PowerShell\Modules\Az\2.3.2\Az.psd1
```

CONNECTING TO AZURE

The first step is to connect to Azure. There are different ways to authenticate to Azure. The default interactive method uses a device token that is enabled by a web-based code input. This avoids having to enter credentials interactively to PowerShell and enables support for any type of MFA you may have, as the authentication is via a browser instead of the PowerShell window. The Azure CLI uses the same process.

To log on to Azure, you add an account (also known as a *context*) to your session. If you enter Connect-AzAccount with no other parameters, the interactive logon will be used, and you will be directed to open a web browser. Enter the displayed code, as shown in Figure 11.2, and then select the account to authenticate with. A confirmation will be displayed, confirming PowerShell has been signed into on the device you executed Connect-AzAccount from. (Note that this could be a different device completely.) This is known as the *device code flow.* You are now ready to run PowerShell commands as that authenticated account, with whichever rights that account is authorized to perform via the Azure role-based access control. This is an important point. You can't do anything with PowerShell that you don't have rights to do via the portal. PowerShell is not a back door, in the same way that PowerShell is not a back door for a normal operating system. It's always funny to me when organizations block PowerShell, when the users could perform the same things with other applications. Note that you can also use Add-AzAccount, which is a PowerShell alias to Connect-AzAccount. If you look in your user profile, there is a .Azure folder that contains all the various tokens. (This same folder is used by PowerShell and the CLI, although they use different formats at the time of writing.)

```
PS C:\Users\john> Connect-AzAccount
WARNING: To sign in, use a web browser to open the page
https://microsoft.com/devicelogin
and enter the code FX4V8T4BF to authenticate.
```

FIGURE 11.2
Performing an interactive logon via a browser

There are other methods to authenticate, which are covered in detail at:

`https://docs.microsoft.com/powershell/azure/authenticate-azureps?view=azps-2.3.2`

These will be required if you want to authenticate as part of an automation, where an interactive logon would not work. Note, if you want to use other methods, it's important those accounts do *not* require MFA. For automation, a service principal will commonly be used, which is a non-interactive type account that uses a secret (password) or a certificate for authentication. It is also possible to use a managed identity or even an OAuth token directly. If you are connecting and want to access resources that are linked to another Azure AD tenant (i.e., your account is a guest in that tenant), then you need to pass the tenant ID (-TenantId) for the resources you want to access—i.e., the Azure AD tenant ID or fully qualified domain name that you are a guest in.

Before going any further, I want to talk about contexts, as they are very useful if you have access to multiple environments where different credentials are used. One of the benefits of the device-based token that is used by the Az module is that it persists beyond the current PowerShell session. This means you don't have to do the browser-based code validation every time you open a new PowerShell window. Behind the scenes, your device has a refresh token that is used to acquire access tokens (this is OAuth 2.0 at work) to enable authorization to the resources in Azure. Provided that you continue to use the device routinely, you will stay logged on indefinitely if you continue to use the environment. These are the same OAuth 2.0 tokens used by many aspects of Azure AD. Table 11.1 shows a few more specifics about the use of the tokens and their lifetime, and also shows that by default you must use the context at least once every 90 days; otherwise, the refresh token will expire and you'll have to re-authenticate.

TABLE 11.1:   Configurable token lifetime properties

PROPERTY	POLICY PROPERTY STRING	AFFECTS	DEFAULT	MINIMUM	MAXIMUM
Access Token Lifetime	AccessTokenLifetime	Access tokens, ID tokens, SAML2 tokens	1 hour	10 minutes	1 day
Refresh Token Max Inactive Time	MaxInactiveTime	Refresh tokens	90 days	10 minutes	90 days
Single-Factor Refresh Token Max Age	MaxAgeSingleFactor	Refresh tokens (for any users)	Until revoked	10 minutes	Until revoked
Multi-Factor Refresh Token Max Age	MaxAgeMultiFactor	Refresh tokens (for any users)	Until revoked	10 minutes	Until revoked

Source: `https://github.com/MicrosoftDocs/azure-docs/blob/master/articles/`
`active-directory/develop/active-directory-configurable-token-lifetimes.md`

Think of a context as a collection of information that directs the Azure cmdlets. This includes the account, credentials, subscription, tenant, and cloud environment. You can have multiple contexts and switch between them to quickly change which account, subscription, etc. you are acting as and on.

By default, the context has an awkward name that consists of the subscription name you are accessing and its GUID. When we come to switch contexts later, this is hard to work with; fortunately, however, they can be renamed easily, as shown below, where I save my current context to a variable and then rename it. I only use a variable to avoid having to type in the very long current name with the GUID in it.

```
PS C:\Users\john> $context = Get-AzContext
PS C:\Users\john> $context

Name                                       Account       Subscription Environment
TenantId
                                                         nName

----                                       -------       ----------- ----------- -
-------
SavillTech Dev Subscription (466c1a5d-e... John@savill... SavillTech... AzureCloud
ba211445-c...

PS C:\Users\john> Rename-AzContext $context.Name 'SavillTech Dev'
PS C:\Users\john> Get-AzContext

Name                                       Account       Subscription Environment
```

```
TenantId
                                                      nName
----                                        -------   ----------- ----------- -
-------
SavillTech Dev                              John@savill... SavillTech... AzureCloud
ba211445-c...
```

If your credential has access to multiple subscriptions under your home realm Azure AD tenant, additional contexts will be available for those subscriptions. Once again, I like to rename them. Here, I output all the contexts to an array and change the ones that I have not already modified (remembering the first element of an array is 0, not 1).

```
PS C:\Users\john> $contexts = Get-AzContext -ListAvailable
PS C:\Users\john> $contexts

Name                                     Account       Subscription Environment
TenantId
                                                       nName
----                                        -------   ----------- ----------- -
-------
Azure Production Subscription (414a65b2... John@savill... Azure Prod... AzureCloud
72f988bf-8...
SavillTech Dev                              John@savill... SavillTech... AzureCloud
ba211445-c...
SavillTech Lab Subscription (5a7b82eb-b... John@savill... SavillTech... AzureCloud
ba211445-c...
PS C:\Users\john> Rename-AzContext $contexts[0].Name 'SavillTech Prod'
PS C:\Users\john> Rename-AzContext $contexts[2].Name 'SavillTech Lab'
PS C:\Users\john> Get-AzContext -ListAvailable

Name            Account       Subscription Environment TenantId
                              nName
----            -------   ----------- ----------- --------
SavillTech Lab   John@savill... SavillTech... AzureCloud  ba211445-c...
SavillTech Dev   John@savill... SavillTech... AzureCloud  ba211445-c...
SavillTech Prod  John@savill... Azure Prod... AzureCloud  72f988bf-8...
```

I can now easily switch using Select-AzContext '<*name of context*>' (e.g., Switch-AzContext 'SavillTech Lab'). You can also add contexts for different accounts. First, you connect to the new account (which requires authentication) and then, once again, you rename the context. In this example, I then look at any other subscriptions I may have access to via Get-AzSubscription and then directly add a new context for one of those subscriptions, giving it a friendly name. In this case, environments I use for work in the MTC are configured.

```
PS C:\Users\john> Connect-AzAccount
WARNING: To sign in, use a web browser to open the page
https://microsoft.com/devicelogin
```

and enter the code FESVNAUHB to authenticate.

```
Account           SubscriptionName TenantId      Environment
-------           ---------------- --------      -----------
johnsav@onemtc.net EXP Prod        <ID>          AzureCloud

PS C:\Users\john> Get-AzContext

Name                          Account        Subscription Environment TenantId
                                             nName
----                          -------        ----------- ----------- --------
EXP Prod (595a74d5--979ba... johnsav@one... EXP Prod    AzureCloud  32dc2feb-7...

PS C:\Users\john> $context = Get-AzContext
PS C:\Users\john> Rename-AzContext $context.Name 'EXP Prod'
PS C:\Users\john> Get-AzContext -ListAvailable

Name                          Account        Subscription Environment TenantId
                                                          nName
----                          -------        ----------- ----------- --------
SavillTech Lab                John@savill... SavillTech... AzureCloud  ba211445-c...
SavillTech Dev                John@savill... SavillTech... AzureCloud  ba211445-c...
SavillTech Prod               John@savill... Azure Prod... AzureCloud  72f988bf-8...
EXP Prod                      johnsav@one... EXP Prod    AzureCloud  32dc2feb-7...

PS C:\Users\john> Get-AzSubscription
<LIST SHOWN HERE THAT I HAVE ACCESS TO AS THIS NEW ACCOUNT>
PS C:\Users\john> Set-AzContext -Name 'OneMTC Prod' -Subscription
'<subscription ID value>'

Name                          Account        Subscription Environment TenantId
                                             nName
----                          -------        ----------- ----------- --------
OneMTC Prod                   johnsav@one... OneMTCInfr... AzureCloud  32dc2feb-7...

PS C:\Users\john> get-azcontext

Name                          Account        Subscription Environment TenantId
                                             nName
----                          -------        ----------- ----------- --------
OneMTC Prod                   johnsav@one... OneMTCInfr... AzureCloud  32dc2feb-7...

PS C:\Users\john> get-azcontext -ListAvailable

Name                          Account        Subscription Environment TenantId
                                             nName
----                          -------        ----------- ----------- --------
SavillTech Lab                John@savill... SavillTech... AzureCloud  ba211445-c...
SavillTech Dev                John@savill... SavillTech... AzureCloud  ba211445-c...
SavillTech Prod               John@savill... Azure Prod... AzureCloud  72f988bf-8...
OneMTC Prod                   johnsav@one... OneMTCInfr... AzureCloud  32dc2feb-7...
EXP Prod                      johnsav@one... EXP Prod    AzureCloud  32dc2feb-7...
```

The ability to quickly switch between environments and accounts via the contexts without ever having to authenticate after the initial authentication (provided that each credential is used at least once every 90 days) makes it seamless to work across many environments. In my normal environment, I have nine different contexts covering the four different credentials and many different environments I interact with—all of them using a consistent naming so that I can easily switch.

These contexts are automatically saved per the default configuration. If you want to stop the saving of contexts between sessions (meaning you would have to re-authenticate every new PowerShell session), then you could use `Disable-AzContextAutosave`—but obviously I wouldn't recommend this. If you execute `Get-AzContextAutosaveSetting`, it will show the current status and where it is saving the cache data.

DOING THINGS IN AZURE WITH POWERSHELL

Now that you have connectivity to Azure subscriptions in Azure clouds, you can now start to perform various tasks. Going into the various cmdlets available is impossible, so my recommendation is to view the various Microsoft resources that relate to using PowerShell for Azure management (and the same applies for the CLI with Azure). Instead, I'm going to focus on a few examples outside of those normally seen in the documentation that I've personally found useful over the years. Also, you can look around at the various cmdlets available, which are fairly self-explanatory thanks to PowerShell's consistent verb-noun naming of cmdlets (e.g., `Get-AzVM`). What do you think that does? If you said get the VMs, you are correct! I've also used PowerShell examples throughout this entire book.

The first piece of code I want to explore is around creating a custom role in Azure and applying it to a group of users. I needed the ability for all architects to register providers in the subscription, which by default they could not, as it's a subscription-level right and the architects only had rights on their specific resource groups. This custom role only enabled the registration of providers. It works by fetching an existing role, removing all its rights, changing its name, and then setting its scope to be the target subscription (since I don't have permission to create a new role at the Azure global cloud level, strangely enough).

Finally, I get a reference to the group I want to assign the role to and assign it to the group.

```
#Create new role
$sub = "/subscriptions/<subscription ID in here>"
$role = Get-AzRoleDefinition -Name "Virtual Machine Contributor"
$role.Id = $null
$role.Name = "Resource Provider Register"
$role.Description = "Can register Resource Providers."
$role.Actions.RemoveRange(0,$role.Actions.Count)
$role.Actions.Add("*/register/action")
$role.AssignableScopes.Clear()
$role.AssignableScopes.Add($sub)
New-AzRoleDefinition -Role $role

#Assign to the Architects
$group = Get-AzADGroup -SearchString "Architects"
New-AzRoleAssignment -ObjectId $group.Id `
-RoleDefinitionName $role.Name -Scope $sub
```

If you are writing secrets and need to have some secrets in your code, such as passwords or keys (and you can't use managed identities), then interacting with Key Vault is critically important. It's very easy to interact with Key Vault. If there is a secret in Key Vault you want to access the value of, you can just use:

```
(Get-AzKeyVaultSecret -VaultName 'SavillVault' `
    -Name JohnPassword).SecretValueText
```

If you first need to write the value into the secret in Key Vault, the plaintext value must be converted to secure text, and then it can be written:

```
#Create a new secret
$secretvalue = ConvertTo-SecureString 'Pa55wordT0p' -AsPlainText -Force

#Store the secret in Azure Key Vault
$secret = Set-AzKeyVaultSecret -VaultName 'SavillVault' `
    -Name 'JohnPassword' -SecretValue $secretvalue
```

What if you are using managed disks and want to copy those managed disks to another subscription? Ordinarily, you could use a server-side asynchronous copy from one storage account to another, even across subscriptions, since you can connect to storage contexts using account keys. But where is the storage account for a managed disk? You don't know. Fortunately, for a finite time, you can obtain a grant to the underlying storage, which allows you to interact with the underlying page blob that powers the managed disk. In the following example, I copy a managed disk from one subscription to a storage account in another subscription. Note that for the target, I directly have a key specified. If your account had access to both, you could obtain the key directly, as follows:

```
$storageAccountKey = Get-AzStorageAccountKey `
    -ResourceGroupName $DestinationRG -Name $DestinationStorageAccount
```

And then you would access as `$storageAccountKey.Value[0]`, which is the first of the two storage keys available for each storage account. Because this is a server-side operation, it runs in the background once you submit. You can check on the status of the copy, which I do here in the last line:

```
$SourceRG = '<resource group containing the managed disk>'
$SourceSubscrpitionId = '<subscription id hosting the managed disk>'
$SourceTenantId = '<tenant id of the source subscription>'
$ManagedDiskName = 'disk.vhd'
$DestinationRG = '<target RG of the target storage account>'
$DestinationStorageAccount = '<target storage account name>'
$DestinationStorageKey = '<key>'
$containerName = 'vhds'
$vhdName = $ManagedDiskName + '.vhd'

#Managed disk source
Select-AzSubscription -Subscription $SourceSubscrpitionId `
    -Tenant $SourceTenantId
#Obtain a grant to the underlying storage of the managed disk
$grant = Grant-AzDiskAccess -ResourceGroupName $SourceRG `
```

```
        -DiskName $ManagedDiskName -Access Read -DurationInSecond 10800

#Destination storage account
$storageContext = New-AzStorageContext `
        -StorageAccountName $DestinationStorageAccount `
        -StorageAccountKey $DestinationStorageKey

$container = Get-AzStorageContainer $containerName `
-Context $storageContext -ErrorAction Ignore

$CopyToBlob = Start-AzStorageBlobCopy -AbsoluteUri $grant.AccessSAS `
        -DestContainer $containerName -DestBlob $vhdName `
        -DestContext $storageContext


$CopyToBlob | Get-AzStorageBlobCopyState
```

I'm not going to cover creating a VM in PowerShell in any detail. I don't want you to create resources with PowerShell (as we'll see in the JSON section), but if you really wanted to, it's possible to perform a quick create with a single line. I've added some extra parameters in the following snippet, so it does not actually create the VM but rather shows you verbosely what it would do. As you can see, it assumes a lot of things but creates a small VM, creates a network, and enables access:

```
PS C:\> New-AzVM -Name johnvm -Credential (Get-Credential) -Verbose -WhatIf
PowerShell credential request
Enter your credentials.
User: bob
Password for user bob: *****
VERBOSE: VMScaleSetName = "johnvm"
VERBOSE: Credential = System.Management.Automation.PSCredential
VERBOSE: ResourceGroupName = "johnvm"
VERBOSE: ImageName = "Win2016Datacenter"
VERBOSE: InstanceCount = 2
VERBOSE: VirtualNetworkName = "johnvm"
VERBOSE: SubnetName = "johnvm"
VERBOSE: PublicIpAddressName = "johnvm"
VERBOSE: DomainNameLabel = "johnvm-1688f1"
VERBOSE: SecurityGroupName = "johnvm"
VERBOSE: LoadBalancerName = "johnvm"
VERBOSE: BackendPort = 80
VERBOSE: Location = "eastus"
VERBOSE: VmSize = "Standard_DS1_v2"
VERBOSE: UpgradePolicyMode = Automatic
VERBOSE: AllocationMethod = "Static"
VERBOSE: VnetAddressPrefix = "192.168.0.0/16"
VERBOSE: SubnetAddressPrefix = "192.168.1.0/24"
VERBOSE: FrontendPoolName = "johnvm"
VERBOSE: BackendPoolName = "johnvm"
VERBOSE: SystemAssignedIdentity = False
VERBOSE: UserAssignedIdentity = $null
```

```
VERBOSE: EnableUltraSSD = False
VERBOSE: Zone = $null
VERBOSE: NatBackendPort = 3389,5985
VERBOSE: DataDiskSizeInGb = $null
What if: Performing the operation "New" on target "resourceGroups/johnvm".
What if: Performing the operation "New" on target "virtualNetworks/johnvm".
What if: Performing the operation "New" on target "publicIPAddresses/johnvm".
What if: Performing the operation "New" on target "loadBalancers/johnvm".
What if: Performing the operation "New" on target
"virtualMachineScaleSets/johnvm".
```

You could just as easily make the VM Linux by adding -Image UbuntuLTS to the command. Try both of them. The -whatif stops anything from actually being created. In reality, you would want to do a lot more customization, but again this is not the best way to create resources.

I have some interesting blog articles that go into detail about using various PowerShell capabilities. Note that some of these use the older AzureRM module; simply replace AzureRM with Az in the cmdlet names.

Creating Multiple Subnets https://savilltech.com/2018/03/25/ easily-create-multiple-subnets-in-an-azure-virtual-network/

Using Marketplace Images https://savilltech.com/2018/03/23/ use-an-application-image-from-the-azure-marketplace-using-powershell/

Deploying a VM (Yes, okay, I wrote one.)

https://savilltech.com/2018/03/17/deploying-an-azure-iaas-vm-using-powershell/

Checking Creation Times of VMs https://savilltech.com/2018/02/13/ checking-the-creation-time-of-an-azure-iaas-vm/

Using Custom Actions https://savilltech.com/2016/08/10/ automating-deployments-to-azure-iaas-with-custom-actions/

Using the CLI with Azure

The Azure CLI is very similar to PowerShell in terms of capability. Behind the scenes, both of them are built on the REST APIs Azure provides, but the CLI started out as cross-platform and still is, except now that cross-platform capability is not unique to the CLI since PowerShell and the Az module are also cross-platform. The CLI is available across platforms, including Windows, MacOS, and Linux (just like PowerShell Core and the Az module), and Microsoft has detailed installation instructions for the various options. You can even run it as a Docker container, which, as discussed in the "Leveraging Azure Cloud Shell" section, is something Azure itself leverages! The installation instructions and downloads are available from:

https://docs.microsoft.com/cli/azure/install-azure-cli

The sign-in options are the same, including service principal, managed identity, etc. However, at the time of writing, the CLI is a little more mature with the interactive sign-in experience and uses the authorization code flow for sign-in. This means if you are running on an environment with a desktop, it will automatically open the default browser and populate the code—all you have to do is select the account to sign in with. Only if there is not a desktop it will guide you to open the devicelogin site, type in the authorization code, and sign in. The following shows this enhanced experience:

```
C:\Users\josavi>az login
Note, we have launched a browser for you to login. For old experience with
device code, use "az login --use-device-code"
You have logged in. Now let us find all the subscriptions to which you have
access...
```

Like PowerShell, the tokens used are stored in the .Azure folder of your profile folder, except at the time of writing the CLI uses JSON files instead of the binary format used by PowerShell. This means you can actually go and look at your tokens—not that you should; since this is an implementation detail and transparent to you, you don't care about this.

Also, like PowerShell (I warned you they are basically the same), there is a concept of contexts, except these are subscriptions and are managed via the az account set of commands. For example, to view them, you can use:

```
az account list
```

To switch, you would use (note this automatically uses the profile for the selected subscription, including the credential):

```
az account set --s "subscription name"
```

To see the current profile, you can use:

```
az account show
```

You are now ready to start. Following are a few very simple commands to get you started. With the CLI, if you ever need help, add --? to a command—for example, az account --?
To view the available regions, you would use the following:

```
az account list-locations
```

To view the VM sizes available in a region (note the 2 dashes before location):

```
az vm list-sizes --location eastus2
```

To quickly create a VM with many default values:

```
az vm create -n MyVm -g MyResourceGroup --image UbuntuLTS
```

Leveraging Azure Cloud Shell

Browsers are everywhere, and that is one of the nice features of the Azure portal. If there is a web browser, you can get to your resources. For both the PowerShell Az module and the CLI, you need to install tools (and maybe even the environment) before you can leverage them. If you are at grandma's house using her machine or on a device where you can't install components, you're stuck—at least you used to be.

On the Azure portal, as shown in Figure 11.3, there is a command prompt icon. If you click this, it will open a window at the bottom of the screen that provides a command-line experience. This is the Azure Cloud Shell, a full command-line environment that provides either PowerShell or Bash-based CLI. You can also access just the Azure Cloud Shell by navigating to `https://shell.azure.com` (even from the Azure mobile application).

FIGURE 11.3
Accessing the Cloud Shell

The first time you access the Cloud Shell, you will be directed to select whether you want to use Bash or PowerShell (which can be changed at any time from the drop-down shell option) and also to select a subscription where the storage will be created for your cloud drive. If you click Advanced Settings, the storage account and region can be manually specified, as shown in Figure 11.4, instead of automatically generated values.

FIGURE 11.4
Setting up advanced cloud drive options

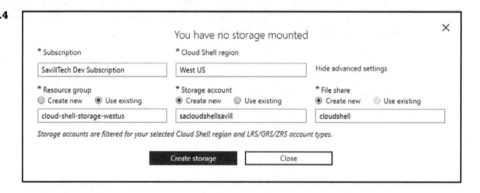

This storage is for your home drive where your profile and any persistent data you want (for example, scripts) will be stored. If you wish to change the settings post-creation, the easiest way is to dismount the cloud drive, which will prompt you to reconfigure next time it starts, where the settings can be reconfigured, including the advanced options:

```
PS Azure:\> Get-CloudDrive

FileShareName      : cloudshell
FileSharePath      : //sacloudshellsavill.file.core.windows.net/cloudshell
MountPoint         : /home/john/clouddrive
Name               : sacloudshellsavill
ResourceGroupName  : cloud-shell-storage-westus
StorageAccountName : sacloudshellsavill
```

```
SubscriptionId     : 466c1a5d-e93b-4138-91a5-670daf44b0f8


Azure:/
PS Azure:\> Dismount-CloudDrive

Do you want to continue
Dismounting clouddrive will terminate your current session. You will be
prompted to create and mount a new file share on your next session
[Y] Yes  [N] No  [S] Suspend  [?] Help (default is "Y"): y
```

Once the Azure Cloud Shell starts, you will already be authenticated with the same credential you are currently authenticated with to the Azure portal, and you can switch between PowerShell and Bash (CLI). Behind the scenes, this is powered by containers running Linux—yes, even for the PowerShell option. The container is created on demand and destroyed on close. This is why there is a brief delay when opening the Cloud Shell; it needs a few seconds to spin up the container. You can see this if you look at your PowerShell environment. For example, Figure 11.5 shows that I am running PowerShell Core (the PSEdition) and am running on Linux (OS).

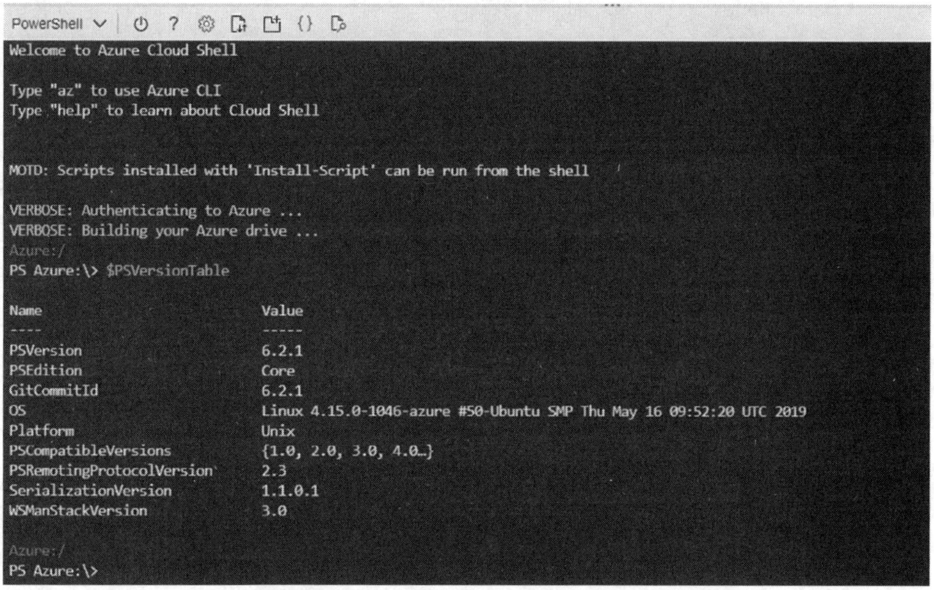

FIGURE 11.5
Viewing the $PSVersionTable information for a Cloud Shell instance

Within the Cloud Shell is the respective tool enabling full Az/CLI interaction with Azure, in addition to other components–for example, for Azure AD interaction. Whether you are using the PowerShell- or the Bash-based Cloud Shell, the only persistent storage available is that of your cloud drive. Anything stored anywhere else in the environment would be lost on restart of the shell.

Within the environments, you have access to most of the regular capabilities. This includes the ability to run any scripts you may have. Remember, however, that this is PowerShell Core if you are using PowerShell, so any scripts will need to be compatible with PowerShell Core. The idea is that the Cloud Shell provides fast, anywhere access to an Azure-capable PowerShell or Bash environment without having to install anything.

If you need to edit a script, you can type code in either environment to bring up an editor environment. This is based on the open-source Monaco Editor. If you need to import or export scripts to edit, there is an Import/Export button in the Cloud Shell menu bar, or you can directly interact with the Azure Files share that backs the Cloud Shell for your account.

There is also the Azure Drive available in PowerShell. This is different from the Cloud Drive, which is your private storage area. The Azure Drive is implemented as a PowerShell provider. PowerShell providers enable access to capabilities through a hierarchical namespace—i.e., you can navigate like a filesystem. For Azure, this is the Simple Hierarchy in PowerShell (SHiPS) provider and can be easily seen as shown in the following example. Note the last entry in the list. Also note that the default starting point for the PowerShell Cloud Shell is in this Azure drive. This means the resources in your subscription can be navigated as though they were a filesystem.

```
PS Azure:\> get-psprovider

Name          Capabilities                              Drives
----          ------------                              ------
Alias         ShouldProcess                             {Alias}
Environment   ShouldProcess                             {Env}
FileSystem    Filter, ShouldProcess, Credentials        {/}
Function      ShouldProcess                             {Function}
Variable      ShouldProcess                             {Variable}
SHiPS         Filter, ShouldProcess                     {Azure}
```

Note that this is not exclusive to the Azure Cloud Shell. The SHiPS provider can be used on premises as well. In the following example, I install, load, and use the provider, and then navigate through some resources. I have trimmed away some details to optimize space usage. Remember that in order to install the module, you must run the command from an elevated PowerShell instance.

```
PS C:\ > Install-Module AzurePSDrive
PS C:\ > Import-Module AzurePSDrive
PS C:\ > New-PSDrive -Name Azure -PSProvider SHiPS -root 'AzurePSDrive#Azure'

Name          Used (GB)      Free (GB) Provider       Root
CurrentLocation
----          ---------      --------- --------       ----
---------------
Azure                                  SHiPS          AzurePSDrive#Azure


PS C:\ > cd azure:
```

```
PS Azure:\> ls


    Directory: Azure:


Mode SubscriptionName              SubscriptionId   TenantId        State
---- ----------------              --------------   --------        -----
+    SavillTech Dev Subscription af44b0f8           ba211445-c143 Enabled
+    SavillTech Lab Subscription 3e15d6193          ba211445-cf43 Enabled

PS Azure:\> cd '.\SavillTech Dev Subscription'
PS Azure:\SavillTech Dev Subscription> ls


    Directory: Azure:\SavillTech Dev Subscription


Mode Name
---- ----
+    AllResources
+    ResourceGroups
+    StorageAccounts
+    VirtualMachines
+    WebApps


PS Azure:\SavillTech Dev Subscription> cd .\ResourceGroups
PS Azure:\SavillTech Dev Subscription\ResourceGroups> ls


    Directory: Azure:\SavillTech Dev Subscription\ResourceGroups


Mode ResourceGroupName           Location        ProvisioningState
---- -----------------           --------        -----------------
+    cloud-shell-storage-westus  westus          Succeeded
+    dashboards                  southcentralus  Succeeded
+    Default-ActivityLogAlerts   eastasia        Succeeded
ETC ETC


PS Azure:\SavillTech Dev Subscription\ResourceGroups> cd .\RG-SCUSA
PS Azure:\SavillTech Dev Subscription\ResourceGroups\RG-SCUSA> ls


    Directory: Azure:\SavillTech Dev Subscription\ResourceGroups\RG-SCUSA


Mode ProviderName
```

```
---- ------------
+    microsoft.insights
+    Microsoft.KeyVault
+    Microsoft.Network
+    Microsoft.Storage
+    Microsoft.Web


PS Azure:\SavillTech Dev Subscription\ResourceGroups\RG-SCUSA> cd
.\Microsoft.Storage
PS Azure:\SavillTech Dev Subscription\ResourceGroups\RG-
SCUSA\Microsoft.Storage> ls


    Directory: Azure:\SavillTech Dev Subscription\ResourceGroups\RG-
SCUSA\Microsoft.Storage


Mode ResourceTypeName
---- ----------------
+    storageAccounts


PS Azure:\SavillTech Dev Subscription\ResourceGroups\RG-
SCUSA\Microsoft.Storage> cd .\storageAccounts
PS Azure:\SavillTech Dev Subscription\ResourceGroups\RG-
SCUSA\Microsoft.Storage\storageAccounts> ls

PSChildName         : sascusadls
PSDrive             : Azure
PSProvider          : SHiPS\SHiPS
PSIsContainer       : False
Identity            :
Kind                : StorageV2
Location            : southcentralus
```

Automating with Azure Automation and Azure Functions

The PowerShell Az module and the CLI provide a great management experience for interacting with Azure live. However, you may also want to create automation tasks that run as part of a defined schedule or are triggered by certain activities. Azure has a number of capabilities that can be used to run these automations in the cloud. The two I am going to focus on are Azure Automation and Azure Functions, both of which are either focused around running PowerShell (Azure Automation) or can run PowerShell as one of its supported languages (Azure Functions) in the cloud. While it is possible to run Python in both Azure Automation and Azure Functions, which would enable calling the CLI, often from Python the native Azure REST APIs would be used. I am therefore going to focus on using the technologies to trigger PowerShell, but know that they can both run Python, so it would be possible to call the CLI if you wanted.

Additionally, think back to many of the alerting capabilities covered in this book, especially action groups, which are the universal groupings of activities leveraged by most alerting functionality. When configuring the actions to take, they include calling an Azure Automation runbook, calling an Azure Function, and calling a webhook (which can be enabled for runbooks and functions), among other things. Having knowledge of runbooks and functions will give you ways to automate in response to many types of triggers, which includes alerts.

There is not a "right" one to use. Automation accounts have many features beyond just running the code, which may make it the right solution. Also, automation accounts have the hybrid runbook workers, enabling them to interact with workloads on other networks. Azure Functions is focused on being triggered from something and then performing code, including bindings to many services which enable a function to easily integrate with many other services. I've started to lean more towards the Azure Functions, but take a look at them both and use the one that makes the most sense for you.

AZURE AUTOMATION

Azure Automation is the original PowerShell execution engine for Azure. It started life as only running PowerShell workflows (durable, resumable executions) but then added regular PowerShell support through its runbook capability, in addition to Python 2 support. Azure Automation also supports graphical PowerShell scripts and workflows. This enables commands to be dropped onto a canvas, with logic used to link them together. I have never been a fan of these graphical runbooks. They take a very long time to create, as you have to search for each command, then fill in the parameters in a window, and then create the links between them. It is much faster to just write PowerShell, which you still need to know even to use the graphical view. The one benefit of the graphical runbooks is that you can label each action on the canvas so that if you only wanted to ascertain what a runbook is doing, you could follow the flow and the labels to quickly understand—something not possible with regular PowerShell unless it is really well commented! You can create your own runbooks and you can import runbooks that perform many common types of activity from the very large gallery that is part of the automation experience. Figure 11.6 shows a runbook that is automatically created when a new Azure Automation account is created. You can see that for each item on the canvas (in this case, the Login to Azure), it is using a specific cmdlet (in this case, `Add-AzureRmAccount`— it's an old example), and then all the parameters must be configured.

This runbook is an example of using the automatically created Run As account (which is an option at account creation time), which is a service principal created for you that authenticates via a self-signed certificate and is given contributor rights on the Azure subscription. This account can be used in your runbooks to perform any actions in your subscription without you having to worry about accounts and permissions. You can view the service principal created by opening App registrations for your Azure AD tenant and selecting All Applications. An entry will be present for your automation account name with a long string after it. If you then look at your Azure subscription, you will see this account has the Contributor role, as shown in Figure 11.7, where you can see the two Run As accounts for my two automation accounts. You do not have to have these created nor use them; it is simply a convenience feature. You could also create your own service principals and manage them. In the past, I even wrote a runbook that did nothing except create a new random password, update the Azure AD account with that password, and then set that new password on a credential in the automation account. If you don't want to use the built-in Run As accounts, this is still a useful capability. The article can be found at:

```
https://www.itprotoday.com/iaaspaas/
handling-passwords-azure-automation-service-accounts
```

FIGURE 11.6
An included
example runbook

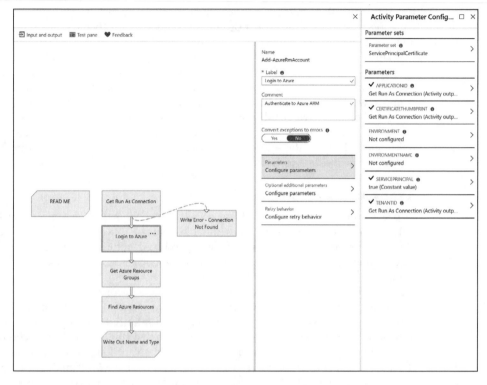

FIGURE 11.7
Permissions for
the created Run
As account

Note that it's an old article, so you would want to update it with the modern cmdlets.

Credentials lead into one of the nice features of automation accounts. The ability to run PowerShell and Python in the cloud on a robust execute engine is very useful, but other assets are required for scripts that can sometimes be cumbersome to work with, such as credentials. As I've talked about elsewhere in this book, you don't want them in your code; instead, if you must have a secret, you should store it in Azure Key Vault. Azure Automation accounts have a number of shared assets, one of them being credentials, which leverage Azure Key Vault behind the scenes. A credential is exactly what it would seem to be: a securely stored username and password that is never stored within your script. These shared assets are easily used in your runbooks. Simply drag the asset onto your script, and the required code is automatically populated to read the asset, as shown in Figure 11.8, where you can see the Get-AutomationPSCredential was added to my script when I added MyCred to the canvas.

FIGURE 11.8
Working with
credential
assets

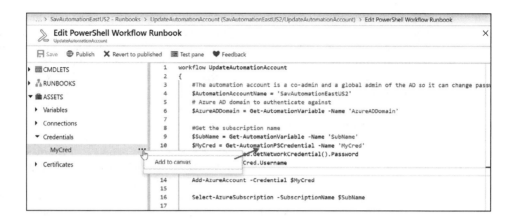

There are other types of shared assets, such as connections, which is how the built-in Run As accounts are surfaced and utilized in the example runbooks. For example:

```
$connectionName = "AzureRunAsConnection"
try
{
    # Get the connection "AzureRunAsConnection "
    $servicePrincipalConnection=Get-AutomationConnection -Name $connectionName
}
```

Variables are also very useful for storing data that you want to use across runbooks, such as subscription names and other information. Within the automation account, there are also modules and Python 2 packages, which can be uploaded to be used by the runbook engine as part of executing your automations. This extends the capabilities beyond the modules/packages that are built into Azure Automation.

When thinking about extending the reach of automations beyond just Azure, it is important to first remember that you can add additional modules/packages to add support for other technologies, but you have to be able to communicate to that endpoint. If the services you are interacting with have an Internet-facing endpoint, then it should just work but what if the resources are on a private network such as a virtual network in Azure, a network in AWS, or on your on-premises network. You are unlikely to want to expose remote connectivity to the Internet just to enable management via runbook automations. This is where another feature of automation accounts can be utilized: hybrid runbook workers.

Hybrid runbook workers consist of a small agent installed on either Windows Server or Linux machines on the local network where the resources are connected that you wish to interact with from your runbooks in Azure. These workers establish an outbound connection over port 443 to the automation account, which is typically allowed outbound on any network and means no inbound firewall exceptions are required on your network. Once connected, the workers establish a session and wait for commands from runbooks running in the account that need to be actioned against resources on the workers' connected network, which they then issue on behalf of the runbook. This provides full management capability for the automation runbooks without having to expose workloads to the Internet directly. Multiple workers can be deployed on a network to provide scale and resiliency, and workers can be grouped into groups. It is the group that is targeted (via the -RunOn parameter) when a runbook wants to perform actions against resources on other networks via the workers. Note that if you use certain solutions, the hybrid runbook worker may be automatically installed. For example, if you manage patching via the update management solution that leverages a Log Analytics workspace and Azure Automation, the hybrid runbook worker is automatically installed on all machines to enable them to run the required runbooks to install patches.

Once you have runbooks created that do what you require, you likely will want to trigger them in various ways. While it is possible to manually trigger them, there are many other options. As previously discussed, they can be called from many other Azure services, including alerts, as part of an action group. Schedules can be created to run automations on a recurring interval, such as every night at 6 p.m. (very useful for an automation that shuts down all VMs in a test environment). A webhook can also be added to runbooks that enables them to be triggered along with parameters by using that webhook. You can also integrate automations with Azure Event Grid that can trigger off almost any type of event. For example, if someone creates a new VM, an event grid could trigger from this event and call an Azure automation that performs some action on that newly created VM. (However, Azure Policy may be a better option, depending on what you are trying to achieve!)

Azure Automation accounts do far more than just executing runbooks. Through integration with a Log Analytics workspace, it is possible to not only inventory resources but also to enable change tracking across Windows and Linux and includes tracking of software, files, services and on Windows the Registry can also be tracked. The update management capability provides not just insight into the patch status of Windows and Linux workloads but can also orchestrate large-scale patch deployments (which is why the runbook worker has to be installed on the machines, to enable actions to be triggered—i.e., install these patches).

Finally, PowerShell Desired State Configuration (DSC) can not only be change-controlled within an automation account, but the automation account can also act as a pull server from which DSC clients can pull their configurations. There are a number of steps to leverage the DSC to provide state management of machines:

1. Create your declarative DSC configuration and save to file.

2. In the State configuration of the account, add a new configuration and select your created file.

3. Compile the configuration, which is a simple click of the Compile button. The created MOF files will automatically be made available via the built-in pull server.

4. Add nodes to the automation account. Select Azure-based VMs from the Nodes menu, and a configuration will be applied along with behavior settings, such as frequency of polling for configuration changes and the configuration mode. For non-Azure OS instances, there is a documented process to add the required metadata to the OS to enable them to pull from the automation account.

Finally, reporting is available to see the deployment status of configurations and compliance.

AZURE FUNCTIONS

Azure Functions are the poster child for serverless compute in Azure. While we normally think of Azure Functions as running some type of code, such as C#, Azure Functions also support

PowerShell. Because Azure Functions are serverless, they run from some type of trigger, which could be an HTTP call, a schedule, or some type of event. They also have inbound and outbound bindings with other services that can be used within the function—for example, some storage service or a cognitive function. If you enable experimental language support, as shown in Figure 11.9, you can create functions using PowerShell for a number of the core templates, including a trigger-based on HTTP, a timer (schedule), or messages on a queue.

FIGURE 11.9
Creating a new function with PowerShell as an option

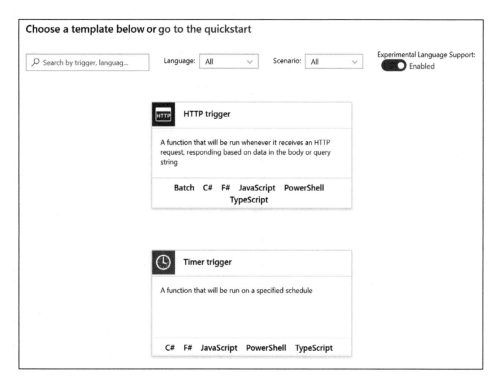

A skeleton PowerShell script will be created based on the template you select, which for the HTTP trigger just says Hello to whatever parameter you pass it. Following is the sample code it generates:

```
# POST method: $req
$requestBody = Get-Content $req -Raw | ConvertFrom-Json
$name = $requestBody.name

# GET method: each querystring parameter is its own variable
if ($req_query_name)
{
    $name = $req_query_name
}

Out-File -Encoding Ascii -FilePath $res -inputObject "Hello $name"
```

You don't have to do anything else. You can run it from within the portal via the Run button, and a new blade will pop out where you can type in the parameters in JSON format (needed for POST) and test, as shown in Figure 11.10.

FIGURE 11.10

Testing a function

If you click the Get Function URL, you will obtain the URL needed to call your new function via HTTP. The following is an example of me using this using a GET, but you could also use POST. You would replace the URL with your own function's URL.

```
PS C:\> $FunctionURL =
'https://testfunctionsavill.azurewebsites.net/api/HttpTriggerPSHello?code=9mWWJ
SkQ=='
PS C:\> Invoke-RestMethod -Method Get -Uri $FunctionURL
Hello

PS C:\> Invoke-RestMethod -Method Get -Uri "$($FunctionURL)&name=John"
Hello John
```

To POST, I could use:

```
$Body = @{name = 'John'} | ConvertTo-Json
Invoke-RestMethod -Method Post -Body $Body -Uri $YourURI
```

Remember to keep the URL safe. If someone has the code, they can call the function. The same goes for any webhooks you create, such as with Azure Automation. Also remember it's sent over HTTPS, so the code is encrypted when sent over the Internet. The SSL connection is established to Azure, and *then* the full URL is sent over the encrypted connection, i.e., the code. Functions can also be triggered from many other services—very similar to automation runbooks.

Remember that Azure Functions support managed identities (via the Platform Features menu on the top-level Azure Function plan to which the functions belong), which allows a function to be given access to resources via Azure RBAC, avoiding the need to deal with any kind of separate credential.

Deploying Resources with ARM JSON Templates

There are many ways to deploy resources: using the portal, PowerShell, the CLI, the REST API, third-party tools, Azure application—the list goes on. The challenge with nearly all these tools is that they are imperative—that is, you have to explicitly say how to create the resources. If you were creating a number of resources and there was a failure, you often would not be able to just restart the script, as some resources would already exist, and it would fail. Instead, you would have to check at every stage if a resource exists, use a reference to that existing resource if it's used elsewhere in the script, etc. What if you want to make a small change to the deployment that already exists or compare what is deployed to what you defined in the script? Using the portal or applications is prone to human error and unlikely to scale well. Yes, you can create one VM, but 100? Ouch.

Everything Is JSON

Behind the scenes, everything related to modern Azure (i.e., Azure Resource Manager [ARM] configuration and metadata) is stored as JSON. You may have noticed when you create resources in the portal that on the final confirmation screen is often text at the bottom next to the Create button, "Download a template for automation." If you click this button, a screen like Figure 11.11 appears. You should try this out. In the portal, create a new storage account (I'm using a storage account, as it's one of the most simple types of resource but you could do this with practically anything) and click the template link instead of actually creating the resource. You'll notice in the Template tab that you can see the details of what you are about to create, and then the Parameters tab has your actual values. The remaining tabs provide sample code to deploy the template from PowerShell, the CLI, .NET, and Ruby. View each of them. You will see they have a lot of validation code in them, but the actual deployment is very simple. For example, the PowerShell boils down to creating the resources defined in the template with a single command (assuming the target resource group already exists which the script checks and creates the resource group if required). Also notice you have options to add the template to an Azure-hosted library and also to deploy the template. Don't worry too much about any of this; I will be covering all of it in more detail.

```
New-AzureRmResourceGroupDeployment -ResourceGroupName $resourceGroupName `
        -Name $deploymentName -TemplateFile $templateFilePath `
        -TemplateParameterFile $parametersFilePath;
```

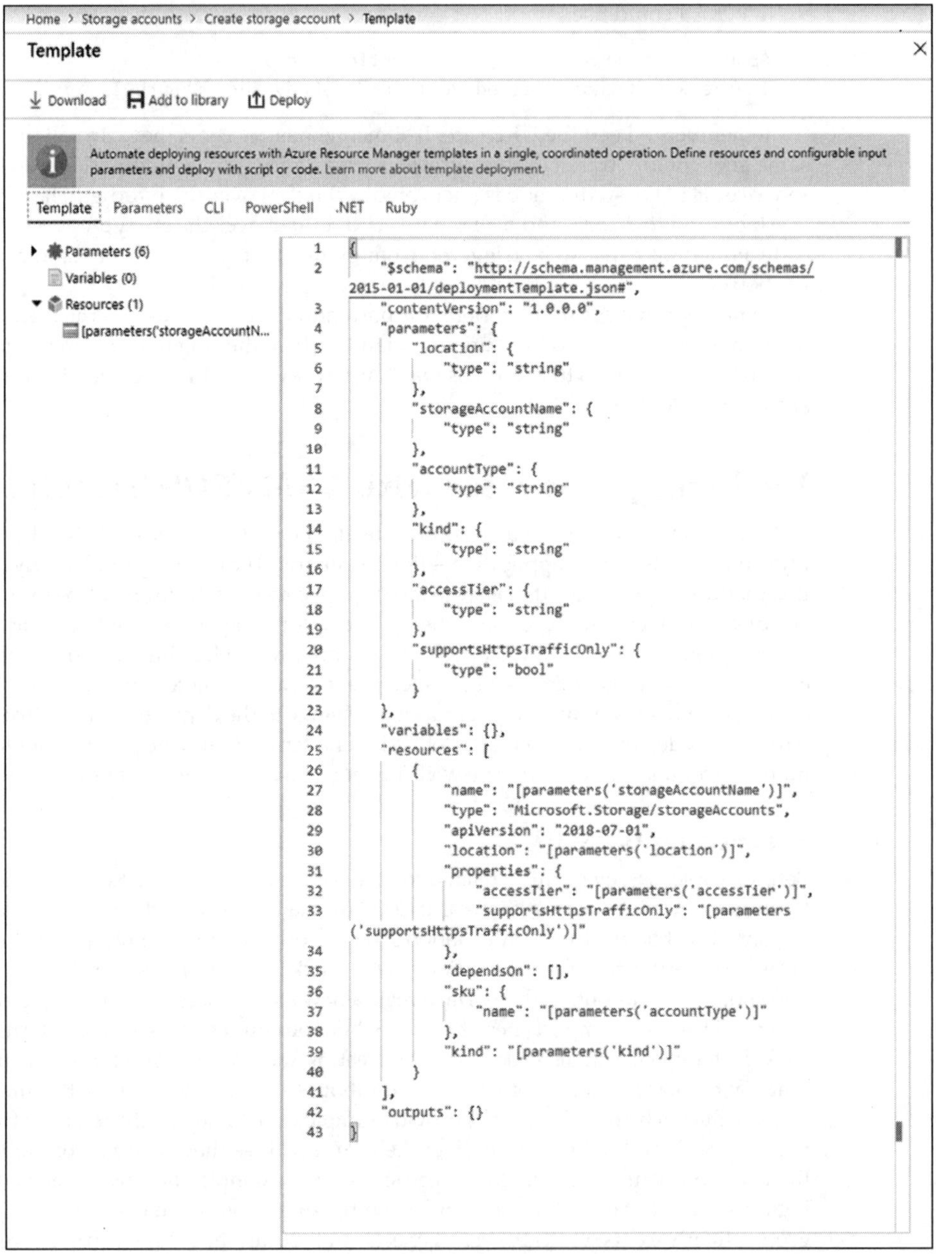

FIGURE 11.11
Viewing the
template that
will be used to
create resources
authored in the
portal

```
Home > Storage accounts > Create storage account > Template

Template                                                              ×

⬇ Download    🖫 Add to library    ⬆ Deploy

ⓘ   Automate deploying resources with Azure Resource Manager templates in a single, coordinated operation. Define resources and configurable input
    parameters and deploy with script or code. Learn more about template deployment.

Template   Parameters   CLI   PowerShell   .NET   Ruby

▶ 🔧 Parameters (6)            1   {
  📄 Variables (0)             2       "$schema": "http://schema.management.azure.com/schemas/
▼ 📦 Resources (1)                     2015-01-01/deploymentTemplate.json#",
    🗔 [parameters('storageAccountN...  3       "contentVersion": "1.0.0.0",
                                4       "parameters": {
                                5           "location": {
                                6               "type": "string"
                                7           },
                                8           "storageAccountName": {
                                9               "type": "string"
                               10           },
                               11           "accountType": {
                               12               "type": "string"
                               13           },
                               14           "kind": {
                               15               "type": "string"
                               16           },
                               17           "accessTier": {
                               18               "type": "string"
                               19           },
                               20           "supportsHttpsTrafficOnly": {
                               21               "type": "bool"
                               22           }
                               23       },
                               24       "variables": {},
                               25       "resources": [
                               26           {
                               27               "name": "[parameters('storageAccountName')]",
                               28               "type": "Microsoft.Storage/storageAccounts",
                               29               "apiVersion": "2018-07-01",
                               30               "location": "[parameters('location')]",
                               31               "properties": {
                               32                   "accessTier": "[parameters('accessTier')]",
                               33                   "supportsHttpsTrafficOnly": "[parameters
                                       ('supportsHttpsTrafficOnly')]"
                               34               },
                               35               "dependsOn": [],
                               36               "sku": {
                               37                   "name": "[parameters('accountType')]"
                               38               },
                               39               "kind": "[parameters('kind')]"
                               40           }
                               41       ],
                               42       "outputs": {}
                               43   }
```

The ability to view the template for resources about to be created is very useful when you are architecting your deployment templates. While there are other sources of templates, the ability to configure settings in the portal and then export them can be a useful way of ascertaining how to configure certain features, and it's a technique you will use. For example, I recently needed to deploy the SQL Server marketplace image, which had a huge amount of SQL-specific configurations that were required in the template. I just quickly went through the creation flow in the portal, viewed the template it would use, and then copied the relevant parts into my own template.

You can even view the JSON of the existing resources. If you go to an existing resource in the portal, you will notice an Export Template link under Settings. This will bring up the exact same experience as the previously discussed download template. If you want to explore the JSON of more than just a single resource, open `https://resources.azure.com`. From this site, you can explore all the subscriptions and resources that your security principal (i.e., who you are logged in as) has access to, and the full JSON will be shown.

Most of the time, how data is stored behind the scenes is not important. When it comes to provisioning resources, however, there are numerous benefits to using JSON templates to define what you want to deploy and using them for the actual provisioning:

◆ JSON templates are idempotent. You can run a JSON template multiple times. If a resource that matches the configuration already exists, nothing happens to it. If a resource is missing or does not match the configuration, it will be created/modified. If you deploy a template in Complete Mode, then any resources in the targeted resource group that are not in the template will get deleted. (This does not happen if you deploy in Incremental Mode, which will leave any resources that exist in the target resource group but which are not defined in the template alone.)

◆ JSON templates are declarative. You are not saying *how* to deploy the resources but rather what you want the end state to be. This also means that in addition to deploying a template, you can view the drift between what is deployed and what is defined in a template.

◆ JSON templates are prescriptive. Therefore, they can be tightly change-controlled, which enables you to track changes. They also become a core part of the organization's DevOps process, which enables you to deploy resources at the time of application deployment as part of a release pipeline, instead of having to provision them potentially weeks in advance, which wastes money. Using templates lights up Infrastructure as Code, a popular motion right now and one I explore in detail at `https://youtu.be/gDW6N2nvVzI`.

◆ New types of resources and capabilities will first be available via templates and the REST API and then find their way into PowerShell, the CLI, and the portal.

I can think of only two disadvantages to JSON templates. The first is that they are Azure-specific. If you need to deploy resources to Azure, to AWS, to ESX, and to other environments, the ARM JSON template is only useful for Azure, meaning you will need to use something else for the others. This is where a technology like Terraform from HashiCorp is useful, as its templates and providers work across a number of providers, enabling one template format to be used pretty much anywhere. The second disadvantage is not really a disadvantage but will cause concern initially for some people: When you first look at JSON, it is intimidating and complex. The reality is it's actually very simple; it is just very verbose, so it looks far worse than it is. Once you sit down and examine what it actually consists of, you will see it's actually very straightforward. Additionally, you are unlikely to ever create a JSON template from scratch. A huge library of starter templates is available at:

`https://github.com/Azure/azure-quickstart-templates`

You will use this to find a template close to what you want to achieve and then tweak it. You can also get template data from the portal if you are struggling with how to author a certain type of resource provisioning. Tools like Visual Studio can create templates from scratch, but it really is unnecessary. Most of the time, you will use VS Code with the Azure Resource Manager Tools extension, which adds support for ARM templates.

Anatomy of an ARM JSON Template

I'm going to look at a JSON template that creates a storage account. Rather than show the whole template, I'm going to show each of the three main sections. At the start of a JSON file, you will see the $schema attribute, which points to the file that describes the supported attributes and resources that can be used in the template. There is also a contentVersion attribute, which you can use to track the version of your template as you make changes to it. For example:

```
"$schema": "https://schema.management.azure.com/schemas/2015-01-
01/deploymentTemplate.json#",
    "contentVersion": "1.0.0.0",
```

The first major section is the parameters section. This defines the values that you want to pass to the template at time of deployment—i.e., the values that will change for each deployment. These could be names of services, IP addresses, SKUs leveraged—pretty much anything you want. In addition to accepting basic string values, you can also set a list of allowed values. In my parameters section, you can see I have two parameters: storageAccountType (i.e., the SKU, which has to be one of the allowed values, for which I set a default) and location (i.e., the region I want to deploy to):

```
"parameters": {
    "storageAccountType": {
      "type": "string",
      "defaultValue": "Standard_LRS",
      "allowedValues": [
        "Standard_LRS",
        "Standard_GRS",
        "Standard_ZRS",
        "Premium_LRS"
      ],
      "metadata": {
        "description": "Storage Account type"
      }
    },
    "location": {
      "type": "string",
      "defaultValue": "[resourceGroup().location]",
      "metadata": {
        "description": "Location for all resources."
      }
    }
},
```

Notice that the default value for the location parameter is in square brackets. This means it is running some piece of code, an expression, and the output will be set as the value. In this example, it is looking at the resource group that the template is being deployed to and using the region (location) of that resource group. The resource group is passed as a parameter to the template deployment and is not actually in any template.

The defined parameters can be passed with as values when calling the execution of the script. For example, I could pass the location by adding -location southcentralus when I call the deployment of the template. The challenge with passing the parameters as part of the call is that now I can't really source control those parameters in a good way. The better option is to leverage a separate JSON-based parameters file. Normally, this parameters file is named <original json file>.parameters.json. For example, if my main JSON file were called StorageAccount.json, I would name my parameters file StorageAccount.parameters.json. In the parameters file, I would define the values I want to pass, and then pass the parameters file as part of the execution using the -TemplateParameterFile parameter. In my example, my parameters file contains only the following (as the default location value of the resource group is fine for me, so I don't need to pass a value):

```
{
  "$schema": "https://schema.management.azure.com/schemas/2015-01-
01/deploymentParameters.json#",
  "contentVersion": "1.0.0.0",
  "parameters": {
    "storageAccountType": {
      "value": "Standard_GRS"
    }
  }
}
```

You may wonder why bother with the separate parameters file. Why not just update the values in the template? Consider that the goal is to change-control the template file. Have a version that is tested and then blessed as the template to be used across the environment. Consider that you have a template file that needs to first be deployed to testing, then user acceptance, and then production. There is an element of invalidating the testing if you modify the template each time. The better option is to have the template in a repository that is change-controlled. Then have different parameters files for the different environments and instances of deployments. This enables the template to stay pristine and a source of truth, while the parameters file has any instance- or environment-specific values.

The next section is variables. I feel "variables" is a very generous word here, as they are more like constants, in that I define a value in the variables section and then use it in the template. The idea is that any value that you define for the template (no matter where it is deployed, meaning this is not a parameter) is placed as a variable, so it is centrally defined in the template, not scattered over the template. Additionally, using functions to define values avoids having that code scattered around the resource definition, which complicates readability.

```
    "variables": {
      "storageAccountName": "[concat(uniquestring(resourceGroup().id),
  'standardsa')]"
    },
```

In my case, I have only one variable. Once again, you see that I use the square brackets to use an expression to output a name. In this case, I add together the resource group name and a static string 'standardsa' to create the storage account name I will use.

The final main section is the resources themselves—in my example, a single resource, which is a storage account that is defined in the Microsoft.Storage resource provider (hence, it's type is Microsoft.Storage/storageAccounts). Also notice how it uses variables and parameters by placing those expressions in the square brackets:

```
"resources": [
    {
        "type": "Microsoft.Storage/storageAccounts",
        "name": "[variables('storageAccountName')]",
        "location": "[parameters('location')]",
        "apiVersion": "2018-07-01",
        "sku": {
          "name": "[parameters('storageAccountType')]"
        },
        "kind": "StorageV2",
        "properties": {}
    }
],
```

Finally, there are outputs that return values from the deployment. Typically, these are used to return the name of something created in the deployment—in my case, the name of the storage account. These outputs can be retrieved as attributes of the deployment via the outputs attribute of the deployment object—in my example, Outputs.storageAccountName.value:

```
"outputs": {
  "storageAccountName": {
    "type": "string",
    "value": "[variables('storageAccountName')]"
  }
}
```

There are other optional sections, such as defining your own custom functions that can be used in the script. If you think about what all of the JSON did, it was very simple:

◆ Some parameters were passed into the template.

◆ Some variables that could be used in the template were defined.

◆ Resources were created, with some attributes populated with values from the parameters and variables.

◆ An optional output provides some value to what called the deployment.

Although the JSON template is big, it's really not complicated. It is just very spaced out and verbose, but it's actually very simple. You are now ready to look at a more-advanced template. Head over to the following templates repository and pick a template to review:

https://github.com/Azure/azure-quickstart-templates

The 101 templates are the simplest. They get more complicated as you move through the 201 and 301 templates. I recommend starting with the 101-vm-simple-windows template at:

https://github.com/Azure/azure-quickstart-templates/tree/master/
101-vm-simple-windows

Notice that it has all the same sections. It has more parameters, more variables, and more resources, but it uses exactly the same format. You will see some of the resources. For example, the network interface (`Microsoft.Network/networkInterfaces`) has a `dependsOn` section, which references some other resources. As the name suggests, this tells the Azure Resource Manager that this resource depends on those other resources, which means those resources will be created before attempting to create this resource.

When you are faced with creating a new template, I recommend finding the closest template (or potentially multiple templates) from the GitHub repository and modifying them to meet your needs. If you find you don't know how to create or customize the template as required, see if you can go through a provisioning flow in the portal, and then look at the template it would create. You can always test your deployment without actually creating the resources by using the `Test-AzResourceGroupDeployment` cmdlet.

I also recommend reading Microsoft's best practices around templates, available at:

```
https://docs.microsoft.com/en-us/azure/azure-resource-manager/
template-best-practices
```

Template Tips

In this section, I want to walk through a few tips I've picked up over the years that may help in your own template authoring. Although I've mentioned it already, I recommend editing templates in VS Code and ensuring that you have the Azure Resource Manager Tools extension. This combination will add IntelliSense to your template authoring, providing recommendations for values as you create your template. Figure 11.12 shows the possible values I could use for the `storageAccountType`. It will also do this for attributes that are available, providing a great JSON editing environment.

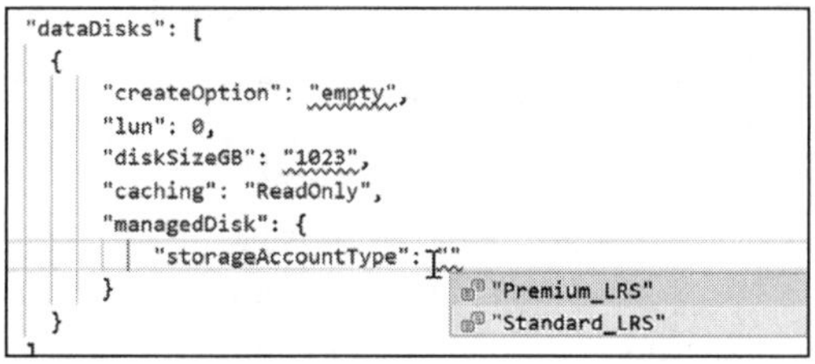

FIGURE 11.12
Azure ARM JSON template editing IntelliSense in action

```
"dataDisks": [
    {
        "createOption": "empty",
        "lun": 0,
        "diskSizeGB": "1023",
        "caching": "ReadOnly",
        "managedDisk": {
            "storageAccountType": ""
        }                        "Premium_LRS"
    }                            "Standard_LRS"
}
```

You do not have to author everything in a single template. It is possible to link a template from a template. This is known as an *external template*. It is also possible to define a template within a template. This is known as a *nested template*. Either one is defined as a `Microsoft.Resources/deployments` resource type and then has a deployment mode specified (complete or incremental). For external, a link to the template file and either a parameters file or list of passed parameters is specified; while for nested, you would then simply define the template as a template object. The following website walks through both types:

```
https://docs.microsoft.com/en-us/azure/azure-resource-manager/
resource-group-linked-templates
```

I like using linked external templates, as they enable me to define a certain set of resources, which can then be reused in other templates, instead of having to copy and paste the code into multiple templates, which is then a problem if I want to update it. Think about building up a library of templates focused on the deployment of specific sets of resources that can then be called from a parent template that composites them together to deploy a complete solution.

Continuing on the theme of referencing items outside the templates, I want to talk about secrets. We don't want them in the template, and sometimes we need a secret as part of the deployment. It could be a password that I want to set for the VM's local administrator; it could be a password for the account to join a VM to the domain; it could be a shared access signature to be used to connect to blob storage that contains content I want to install in the VM as part of a custom script extension. Those secrets should be stored in Azure Key Vault. We can easily reference those secrets in the parameters file as something we pass in. For example, in the following example, I reference a secret name (savadminpass) in a vault named SavKeyVault. (You would also need to put in your subscription ID and the resource group name the vault is created in.)

```
"domainAdminPassword": {
  "reference": {
    "keyVault": {
      "id": "/subscriptions/<subscription ID>/resourceGroups/<resource
group name>/providers/Microsoft.KeyVault/vaults/SavKeyVault"
    },
    "secretName": "savadminpass"
}
```

You need to ensure that the person deploying the template has access rights to the secret and that the vault is configured to allow the secrets to be used for template deployments. This is configured via the advanced access policy and ensures Enable access to Azure Resource Manager for template deployment is set, as shown in Figure 11.13.

FIGURE 11.13
Enabling the use of a key vault's contents for template deployments

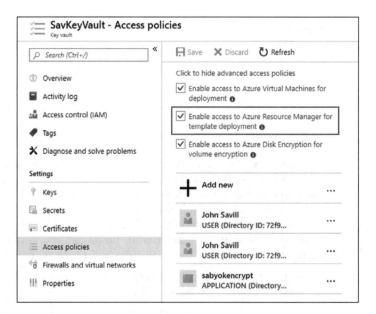

Also, you don't have to only use resources in a template that you create in the template. For example, I may be creating a resource, such as a network adapter (which will then be used by a VM), that needs to connect to a subnet on a virtual network. That virtual subnet can pre-exist and be in a different resource group. You would just create a variable that references the existing resource. For example, in the following example, I get the ID of a virtual network using the passed resource group and virtual network name parameters, and then get the subnet reference by adding the subnet name parameter to the generated virtual network ID:

```
"vnetID": "[resourceId(parameters('virtualNetworkResourceGroup'),
 'Microsoft.Network/virtualNetworks', parameters('virtualNetworkName'))]",
    "subnetRef": "[concat(variables('vnetID'),'/subnets/',
 parameters('subnetName'))]",
```

To store your templates, use a repository that is compatible with Git. This could be GitHub, Azure Repos (which is part of Azure DevOps), or something else. This provides not only a central repository, but with the Git compatibility, it is easy to integrate with many tools, including VS Code. This enables a local copy of the repository to be stored on your machine and then synchronized to the central repository when you make changes or need the latest versions. Version tracking is a core part of these solutions. As part of your release pipeline, if you leverage DevOps processes you can easily pull from these repositories and even automatically trigger pipelines when new versions of the templates are checked in (uploaded) to the repository. This is shown in Figure 11.14, where the continuous deployment trigger is enabled, which means any time the repository is updated, the release pipeline will run which will redeploy the template in the repository.

FIGURE 11.14
A very simple release pipeline that consists of a single task for the release: deploy the template

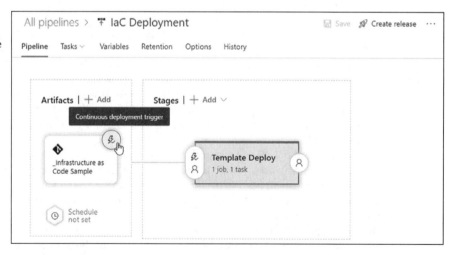

I previously referenced a video (https://youtu.be/gDW6N2nvVzI) in which I walk through using Infrastructure as Code. The idea for Infrastructure as Code is simply that the infrastructure resources we deploy are defined in a prescriptive format. We can change control and store the resources in repositories. We can then take those assets and deploy them through release pipelines and integrate them with build pipelines to compile/test custom code and more. Technologies like Azure Policy help to provide the deployment-time guardrails that are required when we move to DevOps, since there is no longer control by an IT administrator looking at a request before deployment (although review stages can be included in pipelines).

If you are new to DevOps and repos, you can create an Azure DevOps instance at `https://dev.azure.com/`. You may already be part of organizations, or you can create a new organization and then create projects within the organization. To start, you likely just want to version control and store files. Within a project, there is a section called Repos (which contains files, commits, etc.). You will see an option to Clone the Repo, which, when selected, will provide a URL you can use with the Git command to create a local clone of the remote repository. There is also a button to directly clone using VS Code (remember that I mentioned earlier to set up Git in your VS Code configuration), along with many other tools.

If you want to create the clone locally using the Git command line, you would perform the following:

```
D:\ >mkdir clone

D:\ >cd clone

D:\ \clone>git clone
https://account@dev.azure.com/account/project/_git/Infrastructure%20as%20Code%20Sample
Cloning into 'Infrastructure%20as%20Code%20Sample'...
remote: Azure Repos
remote: Found 57 objects to send. (109 ms)
Unpacking objects: 100% (57/57), done.
```

You now have a local copy that you can work with. VS Code has complete integration with Git, will know this folder is a clone, and will enable you to add files, perform commits to your local copy, and then push changes to your local repository that you make to the remote (source) repository to make the updates visible to other people working with the same repository.

Azure also has the concept of a template library available via the portal. You saw this option when you viewed the deployment template, and there was an option to send the template to the library. Templates in the library have their own RBAC, which means you can share with other people. Once a template is in the library, you can edit the JSON of the template and trigger deployments. This is a useful way to quickly use a library of templates if you don't have a separate repo and DevOps process.

Don't forget about the custom script extension for virtual machines, which can be fully utilized via JSON templates. While Azure has a lot of technologies and built-in extensions, there often will be tasks you need to perform that you can't with the native functionality and instead need to run some custom script. I recently worked on a project where we needed to pull down a set of installations and then trigger them for new VM deployments. This kept the image clean but still enabled customization. Note that another approach would have been to use a declarative configuration, such as PowerShell DSC or Chef, but the customer did not want to take that approach. This was easily accomplished using the Custom Script Extension, which can really call anything. In my case, however, I called a PowerShell script. If you are interested, I wrote up the complete solution at:

```
https://savilltech.com/2019/05/17/
deploying-agents-to-azure-iaas-vms-using-the-custom-script-extension/
```

Remember, you also may want to perform configuration inside the guest operating system.

Finally, there are other options. If you are trying to create templates to use across clouds or in the cloud and on premises and don't want a separate template format just for Azure, look at other solutions like Terraform and Ansible (and others). These have the benefit of supporting the Azure resources but also other non-Azure resources. Both the solutions mentioned work closely with the Azure product groups to keep their providers as current as possible to support the newest capabilities in Azure.

Additional Useful Technologies for Azure Management

There are numerous management technologies in Azure. As you saw in this chapter, Azure Automation alone has a large number of management capabilities. Log Analytics also has a lot of functionality around management, with its various monitoring solutions that tightly integrate with Azure Automation capabilities. Also don't forget about some of the mobile tools available. For example, the Azure application for mobile devices is very useful when you need to quickly perform management or check the state of services. With the Cloud Shell, you can even run PowerShell or the CLI from a mobile device which is part of the mobile Azure application! As shown in Figure 11.15, I'm unlikely to be typing too much on the phone keyboard; however, if I had scripts in my cloud drive (or if I was really good on a mobile keyboard, which I'm not), I could do some useful work.

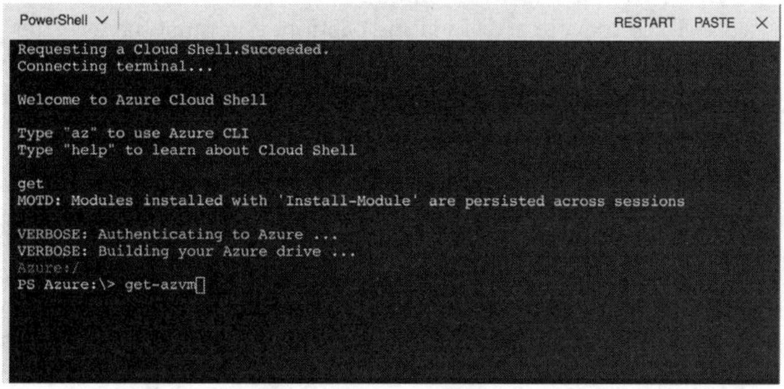

FIGURE 11.15
Using the Cloud Shell within the Azure application

There are a few technologies I have not really touched on elsewhere in this book that I want to quickly introduce.

Azure Bastion Host

When VMs are deployed to Azure, they are connected to a virtual network. The VM has a private IP address that is only usable by devices that have a communication path to that network—i.e., they are on the same virtual network or are connected to that virtual network, such as a peered virtual network or an on-premises network connected via a site-to-site VPN or ExpressRoute. If connectivity is needed to the console (i.e., RDP or SSH), then historically the solution is to either give the VM a public IP or create a NAT rule on a load balancer with a public

IP to the VM. Either solution now provides Internet-based RDP or SSH, which makes it a prime target for port scanning and hacking. There are technologies to help mitigate the attack surface. Network security groups can limit source machines that can communicate to IP addresses, and this can be further strengthened using just-in-time VM access, which manages the NSG rules to open up exceptions for a limited amount of time on a request basis and can even detect the requesting machine's public-facing IP and allow access only to that machine. The NSG flow logs can be sent to Azure Traffic Analytics so that you can further view the connectivity and possibly detect threats. However, there is another option.

Azure Bastion provides a per-network entry point accessible only via the Azure portal (today) that enables connectivity for RDP and SSH to only virtual machines in the same virtual network as the bastion deployment. (This is the case at the time of writing, although I expect this will change.) The service does not span virtual networks. You need a bastion deployment per virtual network you wish to use the bastion functionality on. An Azure Bastion host is provided as a fully managed PaaS service. The only configuration required is to have a special subnet named AzureBastionSubnet that is at least /27 in size. You also need to ensure any NSG rules to your VMs or subnets allow communication from the bastion subnet, which typically will be there by default, as default NSG rules allow unlimited communication within the known IP space of the virtual network and any connected networks.

The actual VMs you are connecting to have no public IP addresses; only the bastion service has a public IP, which not only protects access but blocks any kind of port scanning activity. The protection of the public IP address of the bastion host is Microsoft's responsibility and not something you have to worry about.

To connect to a VM via the bastion, you must have reader privileges on the VM, the VM NIC, and the bastion service. The pricing of the service is based on outbound data transfer, which means for light use (the first 5 GB per month of outbound data transfer), the cost may be free or very small. This is published at:

```
https://azure.microsoft.com/en-us/pricing/details/azure-bastion/
```

To use the bastion service, simply click the Connect button on the VM, select the Bastion tab, and then enter your credentials, as shown in Figure 11.16. A pop-up will open with a window to the VM. (Make sure you don't have popup blockers or add an exception for portal.azure.com.) That's it! You are now connected with no risk of public access. Note that at the time of writing, the bastion cannot be used as a remote desktop gateway (i.e., you cannot use a remote desktop regular client—for example, mstsc.exe) to connect to a VM via the bastion. You can only connect via the portal.

If you want to block certain VMs from being available via bastion, you could either block the bastion subnet using NSGs or use role-based access control if the restriction is focused on the user rather than the machine. If you remove Read access to the bastion service, the impacted users would not be able to connect via the bastion host.

FIGURE 11.16
Connecting to my
VM via the bas-
tion host service

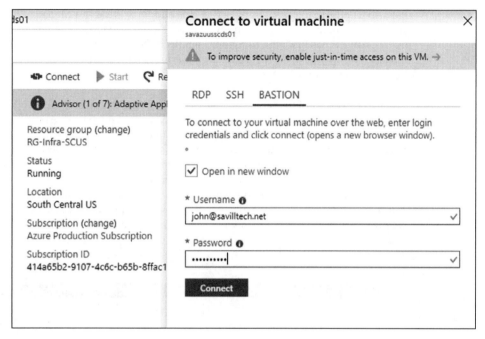

Windows Admin Center

Windows Server has gone through a number of evolutions of its management experience. The Microsoft Management Console (MMC) had technology-specific snap-ins to a common console interface, which evolved to Server Manager, which provided a task-focused set of views, bringing together the information you cared about for each type of technology, including the management tools, performance counters, events, service state, and so on. However, it was a local experience and only updated when the OS updated. Server Manager was available for desktop operating systems but had no web version, was not very extensible, and provided little in terms of using the cloud.

The Windows Admin Center, formally known as project Honolulu, is an entirely web-based experience that is a very thin install (less than 50 MB) running on Windows Server or a Windows desktop operating system. It can also be deployed to clusters in a highly available active-passive configuration. You can install it on your laptop and use it to manage your remote servers if you want. This is known as *desktop mode*, whereas when installed on a server and accessed remotely via browser, it is known as a *gateway mode installation*. There is no software or agent to install on the servers you wish to manage, nor is there a client tool to manage. You access the Windows Admin Center via the browser. It uses only the default-enabled WS-Management, which is core to all Windows Server management communication for the management between the Windows Admin Center installation and the servers it manages.

This also means it can manage any server that supports Windows Management Framework 5.1, which enables management of Windows Server all the way back to Windows Server 2008 R2 (provided that it has WMF 5.1 or higher installed). Different credentials can be used for different servers, enabling management across domains and workgroups. Azure AD and MFA can also be enabled to add additional security to the access, and RBAC can be configured when using a gateway model.

Machines you want to manage are added to the Windows Admin Center. These machines can be anywhere, provided that an IP connection can be established. Almost all elements of management are available, including (but not limited to) role management, users, updates, hardware, networking, virtual machines, processes, firewall, files, storage, Registry, services, and even a PowerShell prompt. If you are connecting to a hyper-converged cluster, you also can manage Storage Spaces Direct (S2D), as shown in Figure 11.17, where I am viewing the drives in my hyper-converged cluster. A really great ability is that because this is using PowerShell behind the scenes, you can actually click the View PowerShell Scripts icon on the title bar to see the PowerShell being used, which you can then use in your own scripts!

FIGURE 11.17
Managing S2D with Windows Admin Center from the browser

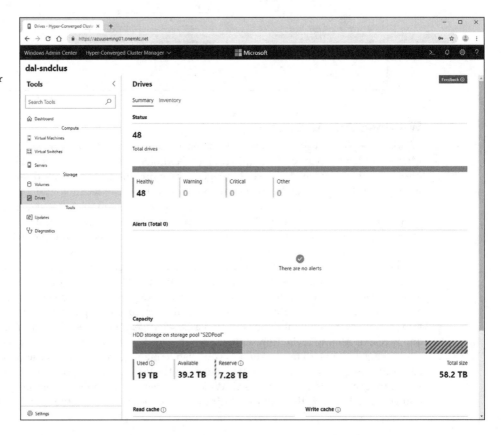

Because this is not part of the actual operating system, it is frequently updated, with new functionality constantly being added, in addition to a large number of extensions available from Microsoft and partners. Additionally, there are exceptions, which is why I'm talking about this feature in a book about Azure, as, yes, managing Windows Server operating systems is important, and this is a great, browser-based tool to manage the OS inside the VMs, although it integrates with Azure at a whole additional level.

Windows Admin Center deployments can be registered with Azure. With this registration, a number of Azure features are enabled for the VMs that are configured via the Admin Center, which performs any install on the OS and configuration to complete the configuration. At the time of writing, these integrations include the following:

Backup   Enables backup to Azure Backup using a defined policy

Replication   Enables replication to Azure using Azure Site Recovery

File Share Replication   Adds file shares to a synchronization group for Azure File Sync, enabling replication to a file share in Azure Storage

Updates   Enables patch management through the Azure Update Management feature that is part of Azure Automation accounts

Monitoring   Deploys the Microsoft Management Agent and registers the agent with a Log Analytics workspace. This enables insight using custom queries and the various monitoring solutions available.

Windows Admin Center is the future vision for Windows Server management, and I recommend downloading it and trying it out. To get started, you can install it on your local machine and connect to a few machines. Remember, there is no agent to install on the server; Windows Admin Center is just using WS-Management, meaning there is no risk to trying it out. Windows Admin Center is just a small install on your machine, and you can uninstall if you decide not to use it. Start at `http://aka.ms/windowsadmincenter`, which has links to the download and the documentation. Did I mention that it's free?

Remember also that Windows Admin Center is a core part of Azure Stack HCI, along with hardware, Storage Spaces Direct, and Azure services. Windows Admin Center provides the connection with Azure Stack HCI between the on-premises components and Azure, making it a truly hybrid solution.

Chapter 12

What to Do Next

The technical capabilities of Azure infrastructure services have been described in detail throughout this book, and the key point that Azure becomes an extension of your datacenter is hopefully clear. Those services in Azure can be used in many different ways: to offer complete solutions, to supplement on-premises environments, as test/development environments, and even for disaster recovery. Often the adoption of a public cloud technology such as Azure is not solely based on technical capability but also on learning to trust a solution and overcome barriers—both real and imagined. This chapter focuses on overcoming both types of barriers and starting your journey to Azure services.

In this chapter, you will learn to:

◆ Address the common concerns related to using the public cloud specific to Azure.

◆ Use encryption in Azure.

◆ Understand the first steps when adopting Azure.

Understanding and Addressing Azure Barriers

Most concerns related to the utilization of public cloud services, including Azure, relate to perceived security risks. For systems running in your own datacenter, you have full control. You can see the physical servers; you can see if someone enters the server room; you know the other administrators who have access; and you know all the various users of the infrastructure. You are the master of the environment and all things are known to you. It's similar to having kids. When the kids are at home, you know you have the doors locked, and you know who else is in the house. If friends of your kids visit, you know those friends and know they will not steal your kids' lunch money. Compare this to sending your kids to a summer camp. Do the people at the summer camp remember to lock the cabin doors? What if one of the counselors is a mass murderer? Some of the other kids on the bus looked mean and were looking very intently at the goodie bag you packed for your little Timmy. In reality, the kids are safe at camp, the counselors are probably better trained to handle a problem if there is one, and the kids have a great time. But there is a perceived risk because you don't have control. This is the same for the public cloud. The majority of the fear is because you must trust others rather than have direct control. The reality is that Microsoft operates some of the most secure datacenters in the world—probably more secure than yours. They operate with processes that adhere to the highest standards, but I will expand on this later in the chapter.

The one aspect that I do think is very real is access and awareness of access to your data. It has been the focus of a lot of media attention and legal actions. In your datacenter, if someone wants access to your data (outside of hacking), you are aware of it. If the government wants your data, you are handed a warrant, and you hand over the data. The data was acquired, but you are aware of the fact. If your data is in the public cloud, that vendor may be handed a warrant to hand over the data, but it could also say that any notification to the affected parties is prohibited, which means that you (the customer) are not aware your data was handed over. This is a big difference. You might not be aware of access or the focus of the ongoing legal proceedings between public cloud vendors, including Microsoft, and many government bodies. The solution to this, as you'll see later in this chapter, is for customers to encrypt their data in such a way that the public cloud vendor cannot decrypt it. Therefore, if asked for the data, all they can provide is encrypted data—which is of no use.

Building Trust

The ultimate barrier to adopting the public cloud is a lack of trust, so trust in your public cloud vendor—that is, Microsoft—needs to be established. Microsoft needs to earn that trust through actions, sharing information, and proving capability. This trust will come. Any change initially is resisted until the trust is established. Look at how many organizations are leveraging Office 365, a public cloud Software as a Service (SaaS) solution hosted by Microsoft that hosts several of a company's most critical assets: its email, its communication, and its document storage. The trust in this service was earned, and the same datacenters that host Office 365 host Azure. I heard a great analogy once about trust from David Chappell and Associates, which is roughly paraphrased in the following:

> If you would have told me 30 years ago most of our goods would be manufactured in communist China, I would have laughed at you. But here we are today; most items are manufactured in China. That trust in the goods has been built, and we accept it.

Of course, once trust is earned, it has to be maintained with constant investment in the technology and constant vigilance for security. Azure has some of the brightest minds in the industry focused on its security. Security expert Mark Russinovich, who is CTO of Microsoft Azure, is focused primarily on the core security of Azure. However, there is still a perception that the public cloud is less secure than on-premises solutions, which is what I will look at in detail next.

Understanding Risks for Azure

Of all concerns organizations have related to the public cloud, the number-one concern is security. The loss of control, compliance, and complexity are also big concerns. To a lesser degree, concerns such as maturity of technology, lack of expertise, and cost exist, but security is the big one. Every public cloud vendor knows this. A major security vulnerability in any of the major public cloud vendors could set back the public cloud many years. But why is security such a major concern? This is best answered by examining the various elements and potential vulnerabilities of Azure (or any public cloud service), as shown in Figure 12.1. You will notice many of the perceived possible vulnerabilities are the same ones that are concerns for your on-premises datacenters.

- Azure is a service offered in the public cloud.
- Azure runs on Hyper-V, which is a known hypervisor in the industry.
- Each customer has its own services.

- Customers also have their own datacenters.

- Azure customer resources are linked to their on-premises resources, using links such as S2S VPN or ExpressRoute.

- Services can also be accessed from the Internet using endpoints to compute services, which could be direct via an instance IP or via a load balancer resource. You may want these endpoints to offer services out to the Internet but want protection also.

- Microsoft people in various roles touch your data and/or services. Developers write the code, and DevOps people may need to connect to the fabric. Some people just do datacenter operations tasks on the servers but don't have access to service information; they have a separate private network to access the fabric via a private backbone.

- Then, you have the primary concerns. People accessing your information or services via the Internet who attempt attacks may be trying to steal data; they may be attempting to prevent access through denial of service, or DoS; or they may be trying to redirect your traffic.

- Someone in another tenant may try to attack you. Another enterprise or some guy in a basement could set up a tenant next to you. They could try to inject a virus into the Azure infrastructure/Hyper-V. They could attempt to hurt your performance by using more than a fair share of resources.

- Microsoft operations people could be bad or could be ordered to do something by someone more powerful, such as the government or in response to an issued warrant.

FIGURE 12.1
Elements and perceived possible vulnerabilities for a public cloud service

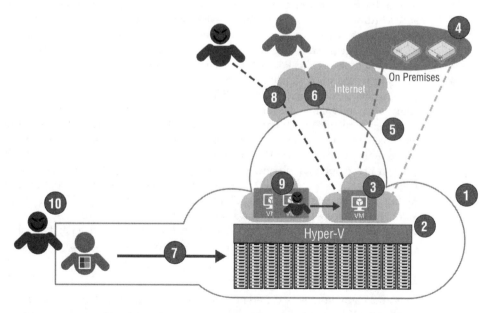

As it turns out, there are nine common concerns related to the public cloud. The Cloud Security Alliance calls them the Notorious Nine. Their report is available here:

```
https://cloudsecurityalliance.org/
download/the-notorious-nine-cloud-computing-top-threats-in-2013/
```

I will walk through each of these, in reverse order, and discuss specifically how they relate to Azure.

EXPOSED SOFTWARE

Azure has its own specification for fabric elements such as compute and storage. However, commodity components, such as off-the-shelf processors rather than some Azure-specific CPU, are used. This means that common CPU firmware is used. Azure also uses a common hypervisor, Hyper-V, the same way other major public cloud operators do. (Amazon Web Services [AWS] uses Xen, and Google uses Kernel-based Virtual Machine [KVM].) Common web components— for example, IIS in Azure—and common API support are used. If there is a vulnerability in one of these, it exposes the risk in a huge way when in the public cloud at the mega-scale of Azure where the resources are shared between organizations. If, and I'm stressing the *if* here, there was a hypervisor boundary exploit in Hyper-V (one VM could access resources in another VM through nonstandard means) within your company, it's not a huge pain point; all of the users of the Hyper-V servers are within your organization and trusted. In a public cloud, where your VM is next to some other entity that could have malicious intentions, it is a huge concern.

Cloud organizations have to constantly balance security and stability. You can be secure and out of business. As author Mark Minasi explains, you can be so super-secure that no one can get to your business, so you are out of business anyway. You have to assess the vulnerability and act accordingly. When a vulnerability exists within your company, you assume a certain level of trust for the tenants. There are consequences if someone acts irresponsibly or with malicious intent—they get fired. There is not a huge rush to patch vulnerabilities unless the vulnerability is exposed to the public. For example, if a vulnerability exists on your public Internet website, then you would want to patch quickly.

This balance of security and stability is more complex in public cloud environments, especially when international boundaries are involved and fewer consequences may be possible. (If someone outside the United States attacks American resources, it's likely difficult to pursue legal recourse.) The exposure for vulnerabilities may be greater. Consider the implications of a vulnerability that punctured the hypervisor to enable access to other tenants. This would be a disaster in the public cloud and is a great concern for all public clouds, so there is a huge engineering effort, and procedures are in place to protect against these types of attack. For Azure, Microsoft is constantly evaluating all possible attacks and vulnerabilities and then patching accordingly. Microsoft has a bug classification, Cloud Critical, that is specific to the impact of a bug on its public cloud services. If a Cloud Critical bug is found, a patch is rolled out as quickly as possible, since the bug represents a vulnerability to the cloud and the risk outweighs stability.

INSUFFICIENT DUE DILIGENCE

This area has a number of different concerns, but the principal one is *shadow IT*, or *bring your own IT (BYOIT)*. This occurs when a business group sidesteps the IT department and uses cloud services because the IT department does not offer the service they want or cannot respond with the speed required. I see this a lot in organizations. A certain business unit believes the IT department responds too slowly, so the business unit takes out a credit card and directly procures services in the public cloud. Now they are in control and can provision very quickly. In reality, the IT department with its private cloud infrastructure *can* be faster but may need to change how they offer services and the like. The big problem with business groups directly using services in the public cloud is that the IT, compliance, and security departments are not involved and may not even be aware that business units are directly using public cloud services. This represents a liability for the organization in a number of ways. If corporate intellectual property (IP) is being stored in the public cloud, is it properly secured? Does the service meet corporate policies and regulatory requirements in terms of the manner in which data is stored and the processes that are used? Is the data being backed up? These things are typically details that business units will not concern themselves with, but if something goes wrong, those same business groups will come to IT for a fix. IT will also get the blame if there is a data breach, which causes a "résumé generating event" for the IT department.

The solution is to make using services provided by the IT department, whether on premises or as part of an IT-managed public cloud, preferable and less painful for business users than directly purchasing their own public cloud services. This means the IT department needs to embrace the public cloud, embrace the private cloud, and enable use in a way that the corporate governance can be enforced, data secured, and all other requirements met. Really communicate to the business about the services available. To find out if, how, and by whom public cloud services are being used in your organization, Azure provides Azure AD Cloud App Discovery, which can track usage of cloud services and presents the data in an easily digestible portal. Additionally, the use of governance solutions like management groups can help detect and manage Azure subscriptions linked to corporate Azure AD.

ABUSE OF CLOUD SERVICES

Consider the scalability of the cloud and how relatively easy it is to set up infrastructure. (For IaaS, this means a VM in the cloud.) Obtain a stolen credit card, set up a cloud service, and then start attacking whomever you choose using bot masters, distributed DoS (DDoS) platforms, and so on—all hosted in a public cloud service. Because most companies trust the IP addresses of public cloud services such as Azure or AWS, use of public cloud services becomes even more appealing to parties with malicious intentions. If you look at the top ISPs hosting malware, the main cloud providers are high in that list. This is because it's so easy to spin up VMs in the public cloud and run pretty much anything you want. Think of storing bad data in the public cloud. Think about governments blocking access to services. Users can just set up a VM in Azure and access services from there.

It's not even users with malicious intentions that cause problems. Look at modern cryptocurrencies such as BitCoin. Want to mine BitCoins or more specifically cryptocurrency, which then converts to BitCoins? Set up some VMs in Azure and get mining. To give an idea of the scale of this problem, Azure shuts down tens of thousands of VMs a month that are performing illegal activities of some kind. Microsoft worked out that with an Azure trial account with $200 of free usage, you could mine about $40 worth of Quark cryptocurrency. You may wonder what is the harm in this type of activity—who is being hurt? These activities use large amounts of resources that then cannot be used by other parties. Although Azure has mechanisms in place to avoid "noisy neighbor" issues that allow these activities to steal your CPU or memory, they still use resources that aren't being paid for, increase the cost of Microsoft doing business, and affect

Microsoft's bottom line—thus affecting the price of Azure services. The impact is the same as credit card crime. Microsoft uses machine learning to try to detect the fraudulent use of Azure services and close them down quickly using various heuristics, such as the use of the same credit card or the same email address in addition to the actual resource usage characteristics of the VMs.

Note that this is not unique to the public cloud; it happens on premises as well. There was an interesting story about Harvard being hacked and someone using their supercomputer (that was supposed to be turned off) to mine cryptocurrency. The hack was discovered when the electric bill was received.

Malicious Insiders

The idea here is that a DevOps person puts something bad into code or processes that are deployed to the fabric or uploads something directly into the cloud service that does something bad. Maybe the datacenter operations personnel try to do something malicious, such as stealing information.

To mitigate this risk, Microsoft employs a number of processes and procedures. Most obviously, Microsoft performs background checks on all personnel who interact with the Azure service. The best way to stop people performing activities they shouldn't is to remove their ability to do so by minimizing their privileges. But then, how can people perform their jobs without privileges? The key is just-in-time (JIT) administration or, more specifically, JIT granular access—grant privileges only as the need requires. When some action in the Azure environment is required, a request is made through the service system in the form of a ticket. The ticket then interacts with a JIT access control system. Each ticket specifies the system that needs to be accessed and the permissions needed. After the ticket is reviewed and approved, granular permissions are assigned to the systems required for a limited amount of time. This enables the support person to perform the actions required. All of the actions performed are logged and reviewed, and once the actions are performed, the permissions are revoked. This ensures that people do not have any standing permissions and cannot perform actions that are not approved and reviewed. In addition, there is constant monitoring for any signs of unauthorized activity.

To help you have trust in their processes, Microsoft goes through a number of industry standard certifications and audits. These certifications are published and can be viewed here:

```
https://www.microsoft.com/en-us/TrustCenter/CloudServices/Azure
```

Also available through the Trust Center are compliance details, which are important. When people are new to the cloud, they tend to focus on security. Once the use of the cloud is better understood and the usage more mature, the main focus becomes compliance.

Denial of Service

This covers any scenario where your services are not available. On the malicious side, this could be parties attacking the Azure Internet endpoints of your specific services or generic Azure service endpoints with a DoS attack. Azure has DDoS appliances that are placed on datacenter routers and other applicable elements of the Azure infrastructure. If these appliances detect a DoS attack, the traffic is redirected to limit its effect. This is done for the Azure fabric and for customer endpoints, but note that this protects only against large-scale attacks, not small-scale attacks, although the standard DDoS SKU does enable customer customization and then can protect against smaller, more targeted attacks. It's important to practice defense-in-depth and have your own protection in the VMs. Remember, if you don't need a service on the Internet, remove the endpoints from the VM.

On the flip side, there could simply be an outage of an Azure service due to a hardware failure in a datacenter, a software bug, human error, and so on. One well-publicized example of this was reported here:

www.huffingtonpost.com/2011/08/08/amazon-microsoft-dublin-lightening_n_920875.html

This outage was basically the result of the electrical design of the datacenter. A brownout (a minor interruption of power to the servers) occurred, just for a second. That minor interruption caused the entire Azure fabric to reboot. Every server had to reboot; the outage lasted hours. Obviously, Microsoft learns from these types of events and rearchitects accordingly, and this was a long time ago, but it's good to see the types of impact that can happen. Efforts are also focused on additional levels of resiliency through hardware and software.

INSECURE INTERFACES AND APIS

Consider how quickly new services are being added to Azure. Those services typically involve new APIs and interfaces to enable interaction with the service. In other cases, an existing API or interface is being used in new ways. Perhaps it is just a matter of services offered in the public cloud instead of on premises. The concern in any of these scenarios is that a vulnerability may exist. Perhaps it's poor encryption or even simple mistakes made when implementing the service in production.

For those who have used Azure, the concept of features being released in a preview mode first enables customers to help test new features and validate all functionality. Additionally, Microsoft follows strict development practices, security lifecycle, and validations throughout the entire process to minimize risks associated with the concerns mentioned.

ACCOUNT OR SERVICE TRAFFIC HIJACKING

When someone gets unauthorized access to your account, it could be for a number of reasons:

◆ Weak passwords can be attacked through brute force. I read an interesting study from Deliotte that found that 10,000 passwords account for 98 percent of all the passwords that exist. In a matter of seconds, 98 percent of passwords can be found by brute force trying those 10,000 passwords.

◆ Passwords can be stolen through weaknesses in services that expose data, through malware, and even through social engineering attacks.

◆ Passwords are reused. When one service is compromised and people used the same password on multiple systems—Facebook, the "I love puppies" website, and their corporate network—all of those systems could be compromised.

This is where using multifactor authentication (MFA) is so important and the use of a single, federated credential that has rich identity protection enabled. The industry direction is to move away from passwords because they are inherently weak. It is far better to leverage something a person *is* (biometric data, like a fingerprint), something a person *has* (a secure ID device or even application on their phone), instead of just something a person *knows* (their password). MFA leverages two of these types to maximize security. I've seen some organizations attempt to solve this by setting very complex password requirements, such as 25-character minimum lengths. This can work if people focus on a passphrase, ImUsingAComplexPasswordWhichIsGreatAndIllRememberThisEasily, instead of a password, such as Qy684jfhy&4#thckp70dF. Unfortunately, setting very complex password requirements typically fails, as people either write them down or keep forgetting them. The resulting help desk calls cause lost productivity. Focus on leveraging MFA to mitigate risks related to passwords. Also avoid making people arbitrarily change passwords. Best practices no longer recommend changing passwords every x days, as it has been shown that people simply add some incremental numeric to their single complex password. Instead, make people change their password if identity protection shows elevated risk, such as credential compromise.

Note that this is not a cloud-specific risk, but potentially it can be more prominent in the cloud since the services are accessible through public interfaces. Microsoft also considers this; if a Microsoft person gets attacked and their access is used, that could expose services. However, remember that Azure uses JIT access with no standing permissions, so even if an account were compromised, that account would not be able to do anything without a ticket.

In addition to leveraging strong passwords and MFA, remember to minimize your attack surface. For example, delete unnecessary endpoints and ensure you use antimalware in your services. If you do require endpoints to the Internet, use network control lists where possible to control who can access those endpoints. Where possible, use private connections, such as S2S VPN or ExpressRoute, for communications between on premises and Azure.

Data Loss

Data loss is a concern that's simple to understand. People don't want to lose their data—this is really the most important asset of almost every organization today. This category covers data loss through the following:

◆ Customers accidentally deleting data

◆ Attackers intentionally deleting or encrypting data

◆ Microsoft deleting the data

◆ Datacenter blows up and the data is lost

The mitigation here is simple. If you care about data, you need to back it up. Microsoft does not back up IaaS disks in Azure storage. Also, remember that you should never store data on the nonpersistent temporary disk. Although Microsoft replicates all data in Azure storage three times at a minimum, if there is a deletion of data, that deletion would replicate three times. Multiple copies of the data protect from hardware failure and not from deletions. To provide some level of protection from data loss due to a Microsoft datacenter failure, use geo-redundant storage (GRS) or zone-redundant storage (ZRS).

There is one area where Microsoft can help with lost data. Microsoft tombstones accounts for 90 days when they are deleted, in case you delete an account by mistake. If you delete your Microsoft account and then realize you left important data in it, you can contact Microsoft support and they can help get you access to it again.

DATA BREACH

Nearly all these threats end up with this as the concern: Someone gets access to your all-important data. How could this happen?

I'm sure one of the most common concerns related to this in the public cloud—and Azure specifically—is some kind of physical attack on the media. Maybe a disk taken from the datacenter. Realistically, I don't consider this a very likely scenario for the following reasons:

- The Azure datacenters are highly secure. They employ huge amounts of security and have outer gates that can literally stop a tank.

- For an internal person to remove a disk, a work order must exist. Every disk has a bar code that must match the bar code on the work order, which is checked by a separate person prior to leaving the particular co-lo the disk was in. Additionally, any disk leaving a datacenter is destroyed by machines that reduce the disk to parts that render them impossible to read data from. Remember that Azure goes through many industry-standard audits and compliance exercises to ensure this happens.

- Even if someone got a disk, I doubt it would be useful. Remember that Azure distributes content across a storage stamp, which consists of thousands of disks. Any single file has parts spread over many disks. One disk would be of limited value, especially when you consider storage accounts are encrypted by default.

Note that even while data is encrypted by default, ideally the customer should also encrypt the data and hold the key. This way, Microsoft cannot access the data if they wanted to and have no ability to hand over your data to anyone. It is this ability for users to encrypt their own data that Microsoft is focused on. They have added, and continue to add, features to enable this. For example, Azure Disk Encryption (ADE) is an easy way to perform OS encryption for Windows and Linux. Also, remember that you can leverage application features such as SQL's various encryption capabilities.

Another form of data breach is a man-in-the-middle attack. In this scenario, your data is sniffed on the network. This attack has gained a lot of attention after the 2013 Edward Snowden document leaks that highlighted all the ways the National Security Agency (NSA) sniffs the data on the Internet and from public cloud providers. Note that the flip side of the Snowden case is that if the NSA practiced no standing privileges and JIT access, it may have been much harder for Snowden to take all those documents in the first place. Additionally, solutions such as Cloud App Security Broker can detect behavior such as bulk downloads by a user and trigger actions such as disabling! An interesting article on this topic is available here:

```
www.washingtonpost.com/world/national-security/
nsa-infiltrates-links-to-yahoo-google-data-centers-worldwide-snowden-documents-say/
2013/10/30/e51d661e-4166-11e3-8b74-d89d714ca4dd_story.html
```

One solution to this problem is to make sure data is encrypted as it travels between Azure and your computers. The Azure APIs support Transport Layer Security (TLS) for encryption using strong ciphers with Federal Information Processing Standard (FIPS) Publication 140-2 (FIPS PUB 140-2) support. The Azure S2S VPN uses Internet Protocol Security (IPsec) to encrypt all data sent over it. Do not use unencrypted communications to Azure over public connections—i.e., via the Internet.

Side attacks, where a VM on the same host as your VM can try to look at processor side effects to get keys, are yet another concern. Realistically, the chances of this happening are almost nil. To accomplish this kind of attack, even in the most controlled lab environment:

◆ You would need to know who to attack and find a way to co-locate on the same physical server; there is no way to do that in Azure.

◆ You would need to be using the same processor core, which does not happen for many types of Azure VMs and is even harder to make happen.

◆ You would need to know which key and cryptographic type are being used.

Another concern is access to the data via your account or a breach of Microsoft protection. I have already discussed these concerns and shown the mitigations in place. Although I would never say something is impossible, I consider the Azure fabric like Fort Knox. If someone gets access to your data, it would likely be because your credentials were compromised and used, rather than some weakness in Azure.

Skynet

Microsoft Azure CTO Mark Russinovich has jokingly expressed another concern: Azure becomes self-aware and tries to take over, like Skynet. If you look at some of the new capabilities, such as Azure machine learning, it's getting closer. The best course of action here is to adopt Azure early and use it well, so you will be a favored human pet when it does take over.

There are new risks in adopting the public cloud, but teams of very smart people are working on them, mitigating the concerns and taking steps to ensure that those concerns are not as bad as they initially seem. The end goal is for you to place your data in Azure and give Microsoft no way to access it.

Why You Should Use Azure and Getting Started

This is probably the most important part of the book. Now that the technical capabilities are understood, why should you choose to use Azure and how do you get started? There are many providers of public cloud services, and deciding which one is right for your organization can be challenging. Remember that there are many types of public cloud service (IaaS, PaaS, and SaaS), and providers offer one or more of those types. At the start, you likely will have on-premises services, so you need to consider not only the capabilities of the provider but how it can integrate with your on-premises services and management.

Understanding Azure's Place in the Market

A good place to start to understand the capabilities of providers and their positioning against their competition is to look at the Gartner quadrants. Gartner quadrants are maintained for many types of service, such as on-premises x86 virtualization, cloud IaaS, enterprise application PaaS, and more. Figure 12.2 shows the structure of Gartner quadrants. Notice that the quadrants focus on the ability to deliver the service and the completeness of what they deliver. You'd want a service that appears in the leader quadrant.

FIGURE 12.2
Gartner Methodologies
and Magic Quadrant
Source: www.gartnder.com/
technology/research/
methodologies/research_
mq.jsp

NOTE Gartner does not endorse any vendor, product, or service depicted in its research publications, and does not advise technology users to select only those vendors with the highest ratings or other designation. Gartner research publications consist of the opinions of Gartner's research organization and should not be construed as statements of fact. Gartner disclaims all warranties, expressed or implied, with respect to this research, including any warranties of merchantability or fitness for a particular purpose.

Microsoft Azure IaaS is one of only three (as of this writing) leaders in the Magic Quadrant for Cloud Infrastructure as a Service, published April 2018 by Lydia Leong et al. for Azure IaaS, its cloud IaaS solution. Microsoft is one of only two leaders in the Magic Quadrant for x86 virtualization (while it was maintained; it is not anymore) with Hyper-V. Azure PaaS is in the leader quadrant for the Magic Quadrant for Enterprise Application PaaS, as is Azure Storage for the Public Cloud Storage Services. Microsoft is the only company to have solutions in all those leader quadrants, which I believe shows their leading position in delivering true hybrid solutions. I should point out that there are many other Microsoft services in the Magic Quadrant for other services, but those mentioned here are the critical ones when thinking of leveraging Azure and integrating with on premises. Azure is one of the leaders in the public cloud.

But what about feature x provided by service y? That's a common concern for customers just starting to evaluate services. You may have heard that a certain service has a specific feature that Azure does not. Frequently, you will be prompted to ask about that feature while evaluating Azure or another vendor. Consider the rate that new features are being introduced to Azure; if Azure is missing a feature that a competitor has, it's a safe bet that that feature is being worked on and will be coming to Azure in time. Many times when a feature is missing, it is because there are other ways to meet your needs. I suggest that you focus on your requirements and see if those requirements can be met with the capabilities available from the vendor. The second evaluation tool is the Hype Cycle, as shown in Figure 12.3.

FIGURE 12.3
Gartner Methodologies
and Hype Cycle
Source: https://www
.gartner.com/en/research/
methodologies/
gartner-hype-cycle

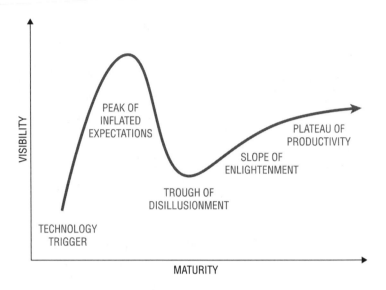

NOTE Gartner does not endorse any vendor, product, or service depicted in its research publications, and does not advise technology users to select only those vendors with the highest
ratings or other designation. Gartner research publications consist of the opinions of Gartner's
research organization and should not be construed as statements of fact. Gartner disclaims all
warranties, expressed or implied, with respect to this research, including any warranties of
merchantability or fitness for a particular purpose.

What is interesting about the Hype Cycle is that, although in this case I am using it specifically to address adopting public cloud services, it applies to anything, including non-IT acquisition scenarios.

Initially, you obtain a technology, the technology trigger, and as you research and use that
technology, you rapidly build excitement. It appears to solve all your problems. This is the peak
of inflated expectations. Once you pass the peak, you start to find things it cannot do. Maybe
it's slower than you thought. Maybe it only works with a subset of systems. Maybe a certain
feature costs more than you thought. The excitement drops until you hit a low, the trough of
disillusionment.

Once you have hit rock bottom, you grudgingly try to make the best of the technology and
gradually discover what the technology can offer (the slope of enlightenment) and that, though
it's not as great as those inflated expectations, it does provide benefits. You achieve the plateau
of productivity where you get real value from the technology.

The reason I use this squiggle with the customers who are fixated on feature x and feature
y is that, when a technology is initially being evaluated, the parties are in the "peak of inflated
expectations" phase. They are focused on features because, at this point, they don't understand
what technologies will work with other technologies, so they can only focus on individual
features. For example, they are focused purely on features in the public cloud, with no consideration of how it will integrate with other systems for a hybrid solution. The thinking is simply
"best-of-breed," without any thought to integration with the rest of your environment. Once
technologies reach the plateau of productivity, organizations care more about integration with
their other technologies and the holistic solution rather than specific features.

Don't get me wrong—I want features. But don't make a decision today based on *a* feature. That feature will come, and looking at the history of innovation in things like Azure and even Hyper-V, it will come very soon. Focus on how the solution will integrate with your environment and your management. Hybrid is a key consideration that sets Azure apart.

Azure is a safe horse to bet on. Realistically, it's one of the two main players that will be leaders in the IaaS public cloud. (The other is Amazon; yes, there is Google, but I barely ever see them.) There will be other providers of IaaS in the public cloud, but they will struggle to really compete against the big two, given the billions of dollars needed to be geographically available and commit to the scale required for hyperscale. Exact numbers are not known, but Microsoft invests billions every year in datacenter infrastructure. Other providers will likely carve out niche markets. Some major providers have already exited the public cloud IaaS market because they cannot compete.

Remember what I said earlier in this chapter. If Azure does become self-aware and takes over, by being an early adopter, you will be treated well.

First Steps with Azure IaaS

The first steps to start leveraging Azure will vary based on the needs of each organization: its existing environment, its goals, and its knowledge of the cloud. In this section, I want to call out some key considerations to think about as you start your Azure IaaS journey. These will help you to maximize efficiency and long-term manageability.

Plan how your organization will use Azure. Specific project details are not required, but you do need to think about what subscriptions you require, and if you have a Microsoft Enterprise Agreement (EA), you will need to decide who owns the agreement, who will be the enterprise administrator, and who will be account owners with the ability to create subscriptions. It's important to get this right; it can be difficult to reorganize services later on. Implement your Azure model early on, or business units may start to buy their own Azure subscriptions or use MSDN subscriptions, which will be harder to consolidate later on.

Governance is key, which is why it was discussed so early in this book. Think policies required, RBAC, management groups, cost management. Your on-premises datacenter likely has a naming standard, and your Azure resources should follow this naming standard, even if it means updating the standard to enable the correct identification of resources in Azure. Ideally, the naming standard should include location (which in Azure would be the region) along with a way to identify the project or business unit that owns the VM and use of the VM. If your Azure subscriptions are project- or business unit-specific, identifying the project in the name may not be required—although you should consider that including the project or business unit in the name does provide a benefit when running reports that may be broader than just a specific subscription and can help identify where VMs are used. Also remember to use tags. Yes, people like to include a lot of information in the name, but tags enable you to save whatever information you require.

Once you have an Azure subscription, the first thing you create should be a virtual network. Even if you have no plans to connect to your on-premises environment today—even if you will only have a single cloud service—create a virtual network and use an IP space that is unique and that does not overlap with your on-premises environment. Additional virtual subnets can be added to that virtual network in the future, should your needs change. The important point is to create the virtual network and create services on that virtual network. There is no harm in using the virtual network; it does not add any complexity. It safeguards your deployment if requirements change in the future. Consider whether you have a requirement to connect to on premises, communicate with services in different cloud services, need custom DNS configuration, or need static IP addresses. These require your services to be on a virtual network. There are so many benefits to using a virtual network, and few if any negatives, so you should always use one. Trying to move existing services to a virtual network post-creation is difficult and very time consuming.

Connect the virtual network to your on-premises environment using the site-to-site VPN gateway or ExpressRoute. This will make Azure an extension of your datacenter and is the first step to enabling the hybrid cloud. Once the site-to-Azure connectivity is in place, configure the virtual network to use on-premises DNS servers. This will enable Azure resources to resolve on-premises names and join the on-premises Active Directory (AD) environment.

Decide on the type of storage to use. Think managed disks! Remember to plan for backup and potentially replication as part of disaster recovery.

If Azure resources will integrate with the on-premises AD, consider deploying domain controllers (DCs) as VMs in Azure. Remember that Azure should be configured as a separate AD site, and be sure to define an AD site link between Azure and the location that has the connectivity to Azure. This will ensure efficient replication of AD content and also that AD clients will use the DC closest to them. DCs in Azure should use a reserved IP address, and once that is done, the DNS configuration of the virtual network is changed to point to the Azure DCs first, which ensures Azure clients will use Azure DCs for name resolution first.

Decide how VMs will be created in Azure for infrastructure purposes. Will Azure gallery images be used, or will your organization's customized image be uploaded to Azure for use? Ideally, you will not use the Azure portal for large-scale VM deployment. Instead, use a repeatable process, such as a provisioning engine, ARM JSON templates, or maybe just a PowerShell script. This is necessary not just to simplify the deployment of resources, but also so that the VMs can be re-created when necessary. For example, in the event of an Azure disaster, VMs must be re-created using the replicated storage.

Ensure that Azure is part of your change control, disaster recovery, and other processes. It's important that the same procedures and checks be performed for services deployed to Azure as would apply to on premises. Ensure that services deployed to Azure are managed. These services will require patching, backup, antimalware, and monitoring. The Azure fabric does not perform those actions on IaaS VMs by default, although there are capabilities in Azure to assist with that.

Once core infrastructure services are available in Azure, if end users will be deploying to Azure, you need to enable a controlled process through a deployment service/service catalog that your users can use. Ideally, the end-user experience for deploying services to Azure should be the same as the experience for deploying to on premises.

Take time to reevaluate how you deliver solutions. Initially, you will most likely move OS instances into Azure IaaS VMs, as this matches how the services were deployed on premises. Remember that there are other types of services in Azure—such as App Services, containers, Azure SQL Database, Cosmos DB, Azure Functions, and more—that require less maintenance than a traditional VM. Over time, as your knowledge and experience in Azure grows, look to re-architect how services are delivered and take advantage of the broader Azure service options. Move your websites from an Azure IaaS VM running IIS to Azure App Services, move the database from an Azure IaaS VM running SQL Server to Azure SQL Database—you get the idea.

Finally, stay current with the changes to Azure. New features are constantly being added, and it's important to be informed about them. Evaluate how you could use them in your organization and determine whether a re-architecture of a service is required to use the new capabilities. I recommend frequently reviewing the following resources to stay current:

◆ Azure blog:

   `http://azure.microsoft.com/blog/`

◆ Azure Networking blog:

   `https://azure.microsoft.com/blog/topics/networking/`

◆ Azure VM documentation:

   `https://docs.microsoft.com/azure/virtual-machines/`

◆ My blog (information about new videos I create and other resources):

   `https://savilltech.com`

I hope this book has put you on the right path to maximizing the benefits of Azure in your organization.

Index